ESSENTIAL TRUTHS FOR CHRISTIANS

A Commentary on the Anglican Thirty-Nine Articles and an Introduction to Systematic Theology

By

The Right Reverend

John H. Rodgers, Jr., Th.D.

Dean/President and Professor Emeritus of Trinity School for Ministry

Foreword

The Rev. Dr. J.I. Packer

Classical Anglican Press

An Imprint of
Episcopal Recorder
826 Second Avenue
Blue Bell PA, 19422
(610) 292-9852
episcopalrecorderinc@verizon.net

©2011 by John H. Rodgers, Jr.

All rights reserved. No part of this book may be reproduced without written permission from Classical Anglican Press.

Unless otherwise indicated, Scripture quotations are from The Holy Bible, English Standard Version® (ESV®), copyright © 2001 by Crossway, a publishing ministry of Good News Publishers. Used by permission. All rights reserved.

Cover Photograph of Trinity Cross and Sky ©Peter Frank

ISBN: 978-1-893-29359-5 (cloth: alk. paper)
      978-1-893-29353-3 (pbk.)

Printed in the United States of America

CONTENTS

FOREWORD by J.I. Packer — iv

ACKNOWLEDGMENTS — vii

PREFACE — viii

INTRODUCTION — 1

SECTION ONE OVERVIEW - The Apostolic Faith (Articles 1 to 5) — 10

Art. 1	*Of Faith in the Holy Trinity*	*13*
Art. 2	*Of the Word, or Son of God, Which Was Made Very Man*	*62*
Art. 3	*Of the Going Down of Christ into Hell*	*109*
Art. 4	*Of the Resurrection of Christ*	*115*
Art. 5	*Of the Holy Ghost*	*145*

SECTION TWO OVERVIEW – The Rule of Faith (Articles 6 to 8) — 165

Art. 6	*Of the Sufficiency of the Holy Scriptures for Salvation*	*167*
Art. 7	*Of the Old Testament*	*179*
Art. 8	*Of the Three Creeds*	*196*

SECTION THREE OVERVIEW – Salvation (Articles 9 to 18) — 215

Art. 9	*Of Original or Birth Sin*	*217*
Art. 10	*Of Free Will*	*234*

Art. 11	*Of the Justification of Man*	*254*
Art. 12	*Of Good Works*	*272*
Art. 13	*Of Works before Justification*	*287*
Art. 14	*Of Works of Supererogation*	*299*
Art. 15	*Of Christ Alone without Sin*	*306*
Art. 16	*Of Sin after Baptism*	*315*
Art. 17	*Of Predestination and Election*	*331*
Art. 18	*Of Obtaining Eternal Salvation Only by the Name of Christ*	*351*

SECTION FOUR OVERVIEW – The Church, Ministry, and Sacraments (Articles 19 to 36) — 365

Art. 19	*Of the Church*	*367*
Art. 20	*Of the Authority of the Church*	*386*
Art. 21	*Of the Authority of General Councils*	*408*
Art. 22	*Of Purgatory*	*419*
Art. 23	*Of Ministering in the Congregation*	*433*
Art. 24	*Of Speaking in the Congregation in such a Tongue as the People Understandeth*	*448*
Art. 25	*Of the Sacraments*	*456*
Art. 26	*Of the Unworthiness of the Ministers, which Hinders not the Effect of the Sacraments*	*475*
Art. 27	*Of Baptism*	*484*
Art. 28	*Of the Lord's Supper*	*506*
Art. 29	*Of the Wicked Which Do Not Eat the Body of Christ, in the Use of the Lord's Supper*	*535*
Art. 30	*Of Both Kinds*	*543*
Art. 31	*Of the One Oblation of Christ Finished upon the Cross*	*548*
Art. 32	*Of the Marriage of Priests*	*561*
Art. 33	*Of Excommunicate Persons, How They are to be Avoided*	*566*
Art. 34	*Of the Traditions of the Church*	*580*
Art. 35	*Of Homilies*	*598*
Art. 36	*Of Consecration of Bishops and Ministers*	*607*

SECTION FIVE OVERVIEW – Civic Rights and Duties
(Articles 37 – 39)   625

Art. 37   *Of the Civil Magistrates*   *626*
Art. 38   *Of Christian Men's Goods, Which Are Not Common*   *645*
Art. 39   *Of A Christian Man's Oath*   *664*

CONCLUDING REMARKS   676

SELECT BIBLIOGRAPHY   679

APPENDIX A   Reflections on the Arguments for the Existence of God   683

APPENDIX B   The Thirty-Nine Articles and Anglican Hermeneutics   687

APPENDIX C   Contemporary Anglican Views of the Ordained Ministry   692

GENERAL INDEX   703

SCRIPTURE INDEX   718

Foreword

When Christianity moved out from Jerusalem into the larger Greco-Roman world, the main intellectual task of its teachers and adherents changed from vindicating Christian belief against the various modes of Rabbinic Judaism to similarly countering the many philosophies, ideologies, cults and prejudices that bubbled together in the melting pot of Empire culture. Proclamation, catechesis and apologetics blended as the church fought to clear a confessional space for itself, from which it might reach out to the bewildered and bemused. Philosophical Gnosticism, corresponding in an almost spooky way to post-Tillichian liberalism, snapped constantly at the heels of the faithful, representing itself as the sophisticated and mature reality of which apostolic faith was actually a crude distortion. In face of all this, it is no wonder that the churches produced creeds as benchmark standards of true Christian faith.

These creeds grew out of what we know as the Apostles' Creed, which apparently began life as a syllabus for instruction in the catechumenate of the second century (late first century, perhaps), the institutional instruction of adult enquirers which congregations rightly regarded as an integral part of their mission of outreach to the watching, wondering world. Forms of the Apostles' Creed established themselves as church creeds, which were supplemented in due course by the conciliar creeds that made explicit what was implicit in the church creeds regarding the Trinity and the Incarnation, both of which topics became matters of dispute in the church itself as full clarity of thought about both came to be required. The Nicene-Constantinopolitan Creed (381), the Chalcedonian definition (451), and in the Western church the so-called Athanasian Creed (fifth, or perhaps fourth, century), are the landmark documents that supplemented the Apostles' Creed in this way.

With the coming of the Reformation, deep internal division on doctrine reappeared in the church – not now about Trinity and Incarnation, nor regarding the truth and trustworthiness of the Bible, on all of which the established consensus continued, but on the terms of the gospel, the plight of sinners, the place of the church in the economy of salvation, and the nature of saving faith. The outcome of debate on these matters was that the churches of the Reformation, Lutheran and Reformed, produced extensive church confessions while the counter-Reformation Council of Trent produced canons and decrees reaffirming familiar medieval positions across the board.

Both the Reformation and Tridentine statements were lengthy where the Conciliar formulations had been short, but they all had the same fivefold purpose.

They were definitional, formulating what was seen as truth against what was seen as error. This applies already to the Apostles' Creed, which was full on Jesus' birth, crucifixion, death, resurrection, present reign and future return just because denial or perversion of these facts by Gnostics, Jews and others during the late first and second centuries was so widespread.

They were declaratory, functioning as the theological identity card of those who professed them, making clear what these people stood for.

They were didactic, a syllabus for instruction on key points of doctrine. Thus, they were tools for discipling.

They were disciplinary, teachers could be required to subscribe them (as was done in the fourth century, and as Anglicans and Presbyterians still do), and could then be called to account if they spoke or taught against them.

Moreover, they were doxological, celebrating the mighty works of God's grace, which is why the patristic creeds are so widely recited in Christian worship.

Thomas Cranmer's 39 Articles, reduced from his original 42, drafted probably in 1552, were enacted as the Church of England's constitutional declaration of its faith and order in 1571. They take the form of a series of affirmations on key issues, grouped as follows:

Articles 1-5 reproduce the creedal doctrine of God the triune Savior, with a powerful statement on the atonement inserted into the Christological declaration in Article 2.

Articles 6-8 affirm the sufficiency and finality of canonical Scripture, the books of which are listed.

Articles 9-19 together state the doctrine of a sinner's personal salvation by grace only, through personal justification by faith only, with a cross-reference in Article 11 to Cranmer's own Homily on Justification (Salvation) in the 1547 Book of Homilies; a book commended in Article 35 as containing godly, wholesome and necessary doctrine.

Articles 19-31 cover a range of controverted specifics on the church and the sacraments.

And Articles 32-39 deal with particular questions of order and discipline within the newly-reformed Church of England.

In their own day, the Articles were understood as a Reformational, indeed a Reformed, declaration of faith, and, historically and theologically, there is really no other way to understand them. It has been argued that they were Articles of peace rather than of profession, declaring what must not be denied rather than what must be affirmed, but this is a hollow evasion. As all the Reformers knew, God's people are called to profess and live by God's revealed truth, and to fight for it in debate if necessary, and this is an obligation that may not be watered down.

Bishop John Rodgers grasps the spirit and substance of the Articles exceedingly well. As American Anglicanism agonizes today, struggling against the liberalism that has lodged in its vitals, this book will come into its own as a resource for the resistance-and-reform contenders. I commend it with gratitude and joy.

J.I. Packer, Regent College, Vancouver B.C.

Acknowledgments

There are far too many people who have contributed to the writing of this book for all of them to be listed and thanked publicly. There are some, however, that simply must be named and thanked.

I wish to thank the Rev. Dr. Jonathan Riches and the Classical Anglican Press for believing in this book. There are the students who taught me so much in my classes in systematic theology at the Trinity School for Ministry. They even urged the writing and completion of this book. One student, the Rev. John Heidengren, researched the scripture verses for Article 8. There are my faculty colleagues who have helped me think about the great matters of theology and encouraged me to complete this book. I must not fail to mention Mrs. Susanah Hanson, the Director of the Library at Trinity, who prepared the index for the book. Her contribution is particularly valuable due to the particular organization of the book around the various Articles. Mrs. Maxine Moore and the Rev. James Beavers helped us get materials ready for the classes on the Thirty-Nine Articles. Mrs. Peggy Noll did the final proofreading for this book. Finally, one stands apart for her sustained contribution, Mrs. Cynthia Macleay Campbell, who gave direct, hands-on attention to this book during its writing. She is an alumna of Trinity, and an educator in her own right. She has co-taught courses on the Thirty-Nine Articles with me. Chiefly, she served as the overseer of the manuscript, making certain that I was always working on the latest revision, that the formatting was in order and was unafraid to suggest improvements of all sorts as the book took shape. Her contributions were invaluable.

To all of these people and so many more, I wish to say thank you.

Preface

It is a privilege, and a great responsibility to write an exposition of the Anglican thought found in the Thirty-Nine Articles of Religion of the Church of England. These Articles serve as a formulary for a large portion of the wider Anglican Communion. I write this exposition because I am firmly convinced that the Anglican Reformers "got it right" that is, that they are profoundly biblical on these crucial matters of the Christian Faith and have a great deal of light to shed upon our path today.

I write it also because there is no small measure of ignorance of the teaching of the Articles among many Anglicans, not to mention an ignorance of Reformation doctrine among the other historic Churches. We in the "mainline" Churches in the West are increasingly victims of theological amnesia.

At present, there is a resurgence of evangelical Anglicanism in the Anglican Communion and this movement needs the depth and balance of the biblical truth that the Articles supply.

When looking for a book on the Thirty-Nine Articles to use in the pastorate or in teaching at an introductory level in seminary, I found that the books on the Articles were mostly out of print, and those that were in print were either too Victorian in style to be easily understood, or too scholarly in style for those I hope to serve, or too brief to offer a full introduction to their teaching. Some of the commentaries seemed to me to be inaccurate in what they supposed the Articles to teach. That being the case, I felt led to seek to supply the book that is needed. I hope that what I have written will serve the several purposes for which it has been written.

I pray that my excitement about the truth, the wisdom and richness of these Articles of Religion is communicated throughout this book and that in the end this enthusiasm will be shared by the reader.

Let me conclude by expressing my thankfulness to the Reverend Dr. J. I. Packer, the leading contemporary Anglican Evangelical theologian and a friend, for writing the foreword for this volume. His willingness to do so enhances the value of this book and honors my attempt to serve the Church in this way. Needless to say, he must not be held responsible for all of the views I set forth in this volume.

To God be the glory!

The Right Reverend John H. Rodgers Jr. Th.D.
Epiphany, 2011

To my wife

Blanche

who encouraged me to keep at the task
until the book was finished.

Her love, support, and Christian witness
will always mean more to me
than my words can express.

Introduction

Everyone has a theology. The question is not whether we have a theology, but is our theology true or false, good or bad. Christians have a theology that is based on the person, teaching and deeds of Jesus as set forth in Scripture, on His person and work as the ultimate revelation of God, and supremely on His Cross and Resurrection. Anglicans have sought to build their theology on the supreme authority of the Holy Scriptures, with Jesus as the fulfillment, central climax and true perspective on the meaning of the whole of Scripture. In listening to the whole of Scripture, Anglicans have also listened to the traditions of the historic Church and the Fathers of the Church, who have sought to understand and apply the Scriptures. They have not thought it right or wise that they should read the Scriptures isolated from those who had gone before and those brothers and sisters who are speaking in the present. At the Reformation of the 16th Century, Anglicans stated in the Thirty-Nine Articles what they believe the Scripture to teach of essential importance, and that it should be held and taught by all Christians and particularly as binding upon all clergy and other teachers in Anglican churches. This necessitated a correction of some of the teachings then being taught in the Church. It is the contention of this book of doctrinal theology that the Thirty-Nine Articles are a superb statement of essential doctrine as found in Holy Scripture, and that all Christians should believe, live, and teach the doctrine that they set forth. The Articles provide for everyone the heart of the theology that we need to hold and be held by.

To help the reader make the best use of this book, I want to introduce the Articles from several perspectives and then state what I have attempted to do in writing this particular exposition of the Articles for use in seminaries and in congregations.

First, the several perspectives -

A key perspective for understanding of the Articles lies in the corporate worship of the Church. Anglicans have always confessed their Faith in, and through, their liturgy. This is largely true of all Christian bodies. Christian Churches have always expressed their grasp of the Faith in liturgy and song. Anglicans often say, *Lex credendi lex orandi est,* or "The law of belief is the law of prayer." Given the influence that a repeatedly used liturgy exerts upon the minds and hearts of the congregation, it is essential for a Church to ensure that its liturgy is faithful to Scripture.

In this matter, Anglicans have been remarkably blessed in *The Book of Common Prayer*. Thomas Cranmer, a genius in the formulation of liturgy, gave powerful expression to classical Patristic and Reformation theology in the rites found therein. Cranmer, both as the liturgist and as the author of much in the Articles, is in many ways the chief architect of Anglicanism. A great deal of godly theology is brought home to the heads and hearts of Anglicans via Cranmer's liturgy. Therefore, the Thirty-Nine Articles and *The Book of Common Prayer*, both official formularies of Anglicanism, are best read together.

However, the Church has never been content to make the liturgy the sole bearer, or even the primary bearer, of its doctrinal teaching. Preaching, creed and catechism have always had their place in conveying the Faith that the Church understands the Holy Scriptures to teach. While the Articles and *The Book of Common Prayer* agree theologically, the Articles provide a more precise interpretation of Christian doctrine than the less precisely worded liturgies and hymnody do.

Next, it is the theological perspective that is most decisive for understanding the Articles. At the time of the Reformation, painful differences about important theological matters existed between the Roman Catholic Church and those Churches that separated themselves from

Rome. Even within the Churches of the Reformation, critical theological differences arose. Since visible ecclesiastical unity and common proclamation depend upon common doctrine, it was crucial for each of the Churches to resolve their internal doctrinal differences and to state clearly the resultant common Faith. To do this, the various Churches added to the ecumenical creeds the catechisms and the confessions of the Reformation and of the early post-Reformation period. The Thirty-Nine Articles constitute the formal statement of the accepted, common teaching put forth by the Church of England as a result of the Reformation.

Some Anglicans, who are concerned to stress Anglicanism's "pre- and post-reformation catholicity," have denied that the Church intended for the Thirty-Nine Articles to serve as a document that authoritatively states the teaching of the Church of England on those matters that the Articles address. In this, they err. It is beyond historical doubt that the Thirty-Nine Articles were intended to serve as a confessional statement for the Church of England. The declaration of King Charles I, which has been printed alongside the Articles ever since their full adoption, makes their confessional character abundantly clear. The very title of the King's declaration makes the point:

Articles Agreed Upon By The Archbishops And Bishops Of Both Provinces, And The Whole Clergy, In The Convocation Holden At London In The Year 1562, For The Avoiding Of Diversities Of Opinions, And For The Establishing Of Consent Touching True Religion: reprinted by His Majesty's Commandment, with His Royal Declaration prefixed thereunto.

If the title itself were not sufficient, the content of the King's declaration makes the confessional character of the Thirty-Nine Articles undeniable.

Archbishop Cranmer with the help of Bishop Ridley

gave primary shape to the Articles' content as early as 1553. Later, such notables as Archbishop Parker and Bishop Jewel made some final adjustments. Historically the Thirty-Nine Articles took final official form in 1571, when they were ratified by the Convocation, the Queen, and Parliament.

The English Reformers sought to expound Scripture in the Articles. The Catholic Creeds and the early Councils of the Church, as well as the teaching of the Church Fathers, were all drawn upon. For additional and contemporary source material, they drew most heavily upon the Augsburg Confession of the Lutheran Churches, particularly as written in the Confession of Württemberg of 1552, which was prepared by the Lutheran Church for presentation to the Council of Trent. Alas, the Lutherans were not allowed to present the Confession to that Council.

In response to the Reformation, Pope Paul III convened the Council of Trent, which stretched from 1545 to 1563. During that period, the Articles of the Church of England were being formulated with the developing teaching of Trent clearly in mind.

The Articles were also written with an awareness of the teaching of certain radical Anabaptist groups that had appeared in England during that same period. The Articles make clear that Anglican teaching differs at various points from the teaching of the Roman Catholic Church as well as the Lutheran and the Reformed Churches and the radical Anabaptists.

You may ask, what is the status of the Thirty-Nine Articles in the Anglican Communion today? Do the Articles still function as a confession binding on the preaching and teaching of the clergy? The answer is "Yes and No"! Within the Anglican Communion, their status varies from Province to Province.

In the Episcopal Church in the United States of America, for example, the Articles are printed in the back of the *Book of Common Prayer* in a section entitled

"Historic Documents." This section includes documents of great significance in the history of the Western Church Catholic, and particularly of Anglicanism. Some of these documents continue to be highly influential throughout the Anglican Communion. However, since subscribing to the Articles is not required of the clergy of The Episcopal Church, USA, the Articles no longer hold the confessional status in The Episcopal Church that they once held in England, and that they still officially hold in a number of the Provinces of the Anglican Communion. It is important to note that the Thirty-Nine Articles do represent a vital, widely accepted theological position within worldwide Anglicanism. For example, most Provinces in Africa, which together comprise the largest number of Anglicans worldwide, affirm the Articles and require subscription to them prior to ordination. Moreover, the new Fellowship of Confessing Anglicans which has arisen from the Global Anglican Future Conference (2008) has taken as their theological norm that conference's *Jerusalem Declaration*, which states that the Thirty-Nine Articles are binding on its members.

This commitment to the Articles is part of the confessing movement among Anglicans everywhere. For example, the Reformed Episcopal Church has never abandoned the Articles, and a number of the churches that have left The Episcopal Church, often referred to as "Continuing Churches," hold them as binding, as does the Communion of Evangelical Episcopal Churches. The newly organized Anglican Church of North America (ACNA) refers to the Articles as "expressing the fundamental principles of authentic Anglican belief."

Nor is the influence of the Articles limited to Anglicans. One has only to read the history of the Intervarsity Fellowship to see how widely their impact has been in Great Britain, Australia and North America, not to mention the influence of the Reverend Doctors John R. W. Stott and J. I. Packer, whose amazing traveling, speaking and writing ministries have conveyed world-wide a theology shaped by the Thirty-Nine Articles. The Thirty-Nine Articles are having a well deserved renaissance.

One must emphasize, however that in the profoundest sense, the authority of the Articles rests not primarily upon their official status in the Anglican Churches but on their faithfulness to the Word of God written, the Holy Scriptures.

Theological Scope and Style -

What is the theological scope and style of the Thirty-Nine Articles? Even though the Articles were not written to provide a comprehensive, systematic treatment of all Christian doctrine, they do touch upon a remarkably wide range of topics. The central matters of the Faith are well treated in them. Therefore, the Articles do provide an excellent introduction to doctrinal theology in general, and to classical Anglican theology in particular. I have expanded my comments to cover, if briefly, all the areas of Christian Doctrine or systematic theology.

The Articles are modest in style, in the sense that they do not attempt to speculate, draw lines, or set limits beyond what is found in the Scriptures. As a humble, inclusive doctrinal statement, the Articles seek to include as wide a range of theological conviction as is compatible with the clear statement of biblical truth. They were carefully worded to be as inclusive as truth would allow. However, where matters of truth versus error are addressed, they provide a clear statement of the truth, without ambiguity or evasion. The Articles do not sacrifice truth in order to maintain visible unity. Quite the opposite is the case. The Articles state the truth for the sake of true Christian unity, even if visible institutional unity might be lost, which in fact happened. The reason for that strong stand is simple: true Christian unity is unity in Christ, in the truth of Christ and not otherwise. Mere organizational unity is not genuine Christian unity.

INTRODUCTION

Purpose and structure of this book -

Having indicated briefly several contexts and the nature of the Thirty-Nine Articles, I want to indicate the purpose of this book and how it will approach the exposition of the Articles.

First, I want to state more precisely the purpose of this book. It was written to provide an easily understood, reasonably concise exposition of the teaching of the Thirty-Nine Articles and in addition to indicate both their truthfulness and relevance to our faith in God and to the lives we live in His grace and service.

Over the years many fine, scholarly books on the Articles have been written; few remain in print today. The ones in print are written largely for scholars. I hope this book will prove thoughtful enough for scholars, readable enough for a wide range of readers, and practical enough to find a place in the educational work of congregations.

I am particularly concerned to point out the crucial, abiding relevance of the teaching of the Articles, especially today when things theological and moral are often relativized and when even the very foundations of the Christian Faith are held by some theological scholars to be fictional or outmoded.

I have written this book also because there is a pervasive ignorance of our Anglican Reformation heritage on the part of many in active leadership in Anglican Churches today. This condition makes it crucial to provide a book that can be read or referred to easily in the midst of busy lives.

As to the impact of the author's theology upon the interpretation of each Article, I can only say that I have not sought to advance or protect any school of Anglican theology. No doubt, my own evangelical leanings will have had some impact, but I have sought to let the Articles have their say, even if not all the readers will take joy in what I understand some of the Articles to teach.

A point of clarification is also in order. In this book I use statements like "Anglicans hold" or "Anglicans teach." The Anglicans I am referring to are those who agree with these Thirty-Nine Articles. I do not mean to imply that *all* Anglicans would agree with the affirmations that follow. Needless to say, there are Anglicans who do not abide by the Thirty-Nine Articles, just as there are Lutherans who do not abide by the Book of Concord and Roman Catholics who do not abide by the teachings of the Council of Trent.

Concerning the organization of the book, I have treated the Articles in numerical order. In this order I have grouped the Articles in sections that share a broad, common theme and then I have treated the individual Articles in that section in numerical order. Each section will begin with a short overview.

In discussing each Article, I quote the Article and outline its major teaching points. Each teaching point has an **Explanation**. Then I point out its **Biblical Foundations**. After that, I discuss **False Teachings Denied and Objections Answered**. Finally, in **Implications**, I consider some of the ways we ought or might apply the teaching of the Article to congregational life and mission, and to our lives and ministries. A brief **Conclusion** brings the discussion of the Article to an end. Because things do intertwine, it was not possible to keep these sections airtight. Also, since this is a book that will also be used as a reference, I have sought to make the comments on each Article able to stand alone. This has led to some repetition. I have also indicated, in a few places, where fuller treatment of a topic may be found in the book.

Historical considerations and other matters are subordinated to the theological teaching and practical application of the Articles in this commentary, in order to keep the book relatively modest in size, while being comprehensive in treatment.

Regarding the **Biblical Foundations** of the Articles, I wish to comment on the manner of citation of the Bible.

We will use the English Standard Version (ESV) because it is readable and seeks to be, as much as possible, a "word for word" translation. We will cite classic texts, which affirm the point being considered; most of the texts chosen are concerned to make in their original context the same point for which we cite them in this book. We will limit ourselves in the number of texts for each of the major points in the teaching of a particular Article. Therefore, it is important for the reader to keep in mind that a far more extensive case for the biblical faithfulness and truth of these Articles can be made than appears in the references chosen for this book. *The Topical Analysis of the Bible* by Walter A. Elwell, Baker Book House, Grand Rapids, 1991 or some other Topical Bible or Exhaustive Concordance can provide the interested reader with many more references.

God's revelation was given over an historical period, there is, therefore, a development of fullness and increasing clarity in the Scriptures. I have chosen texts that reflect the fuller development of the theme. However, I do draw upon the full range of the scriptural writings, Old and New Testaments. By such a careful citation of the Bible, I seek to avoid the charge of arbitrary "proof-texting," while at the same time citing Scripture to demonstrate the biblical rootedness and faithfulness of the Articles.

I have sought to keep technical terms to a minimum and to write clearly, so that this commentary can be read, understood, and used by anyone who has the interest to do so.

Introductions must end, so we turn to the Articles themselves to begin our journey through them. From these Articles, we can expect great things to come.

Section One
The Apostolic Faith: God and the Gospel
(Articles 1-5)

This first section of the Thirty-Nine Articles deals with the core of the Christian Faith. The assertions made in these first five Articles are so fundamental and so manifestly biblical that there was no controversy about them between the Church of England, the Roman Catholic Church and the other Churches at the time of the Reformation. In the present, when biblical authority is no longer given the supreme place in much theology, these central matters are disputed, or flatly denied, even within the historic churches. This is an indication of how far atheistic secularism has penetrated Western culture and the Churches dwelling therein. This contemporary situation makes it all the more critical for us to give very careful consideration to the teaching of these Articles.

In this first section, each of the first five Articles contributes to the theme of God and the Gospel. Article 1 describes the God of Creation and the Gospel. Article 2 speaks of the person and work of Jesus Christ, the center of the Gospel itself. Article 3 refers to His descent to Hades, an aspect of His redemptive work. Article 4 affirms the Good News of the reality and nature of His Resurrection from the dead. Article 5 affirms the full divinity of the Holy Spirit and implies the importance of His work in relation to the Gospel.

The fact that the Articles begin with God and the Gospel raises the question about the right place to start in expounding the Church's Faith. Many would hold that it would have been better had the Articles begun with teaching on the Bible as the Word of God, for the teaching about God in these Articles is largely drawn from the Bible and therefore presupposes the truth and reliability of the

Scriptures. Were we to pick up a typical contemporary systematic theology textbook, it would begin with the doctrine of revelation and the Bible. Considerable space would be given to justify confidence in the various sources of a true knowledge of God, and among these sources, the Bible would be given the place of prominence.

There are, however, at least five good reasons for beginning where the Articles do begin.

First, in once sense where one begins is not of critical importance, for no matter where one begins, a good deal must be presupposed, the content of which and the evidence for which must be discussed later. For example, if we begin with Scripture as the Word of God, we assume the reality of the God Who speaks in them and we also assume that we human beings can receive His Word by the illumination of the Holy Spirit. The Christian Faith is so interconnected in its major assertions that no doctrine can be considered without presupposing and drawing upon a number of other doctrines.

Second, in the light of our skeptical culture, which ignores and often denies the reality of the personal, triune God, the weakness of beginning with revelation and the Bible is that the Bible is regarded as an unreliable, human religious book, there being no personal God to have inspired it and to speak through it. Therefore, it is wise to state our view of God from the beginning as the doctrine that shapes all our other convictions.

A third advantage of beginning with the God of the Gospel is that it puts first things first. It is God and the Good News of His saving deeds in Jesus Christ and the Holy Spirit that we treasure, rejoice in, and honor above all else. Beginning there gives God the prominence He deserves and makes clear His graciousness. Ultimately, it is the reality and nature of God and His Gospel that makes the whole enterprise of Christian knowledge and teaching worthwhile. The Scriptures are instrumental to making Him, His Gospel, and His will known. The Bible is not an end in itself.

Fourthly, there is the fact that we know different things differently. How we know anything depends in no small measure on the nature of that which is known. For example, we know a person differently than we know a rock. In the same way, how we know God will depend greatly on Who God is, on the kind of God He is, and on what He has done "for us men and our salvation." Therefore, it makes sense to address the questions of the knowledge of God and Scripture only after we have made clear Who God is that we claim to know.

Fifth and lastly, aspects of the doctrine of how we know and what we know about God were controversial matters at the time of the Reformation. The English Reformers thought it important to begin on the common ground that all orthodox or right-thinking Christians shared at that time.

Therefore, in this section, we consider the Apostolic Faith, centering in God and the Gospel. First things first.

ARTICLE 1

Of Faith in the Holy Trinity

There is but one living and true God, everlasting, without body, parts, or passions, of infinite power, wisdom, and goodness, the Maker and Preserver of all things, both visible and invisible. And in unity of this Godhead there be three Persons, of one substance, power, and eternity, the Father, the Son, and the Holy Ghost.

Introduction

This Article is about God – the center of the Christian Faith. Everything in the Christian Faith is related to the reality, nature and character of God as He has revealed Himself in Jesus Christ in the Holy Scriptures.

This faith in God is controversial. It was so in the past. It is so today. For example, in the secular West, some people regard Christians as gullible or foolish for believing in God as He has revealed Himself in Holy Scripture, because they cannot "see or touch or weigh" Him. Such people claim to trust only scientific facts and what may be induced from them. Perhaps they also trust in some very well-authenticated and generally accepted evidences of history. They do not believe, however, that they are people who hold views by faith, views that go well beyond the obvious facts.

Those who hold this view err. They are naive. They too are believers. Everyone believes beyond what is obvious to all. There are no unbelievers or agnostics in the strictest sense. This is true because we all have a worldview, a view of reality, a view of the way things really are. For example, we have a view of what holds the world of things and persons in being. Secularists in the West tend to think of it as unconscious force or energy that acts without purpose in constant and predictable ways. They believe that to be so.

Every worldview has to make sense of certain common features of reality that we human beings all experience and know. We are all aware that people and the things we deal with are finite, limited, dependent and must be brought into being and held in being by a force or forces greater than they are. Therefore, in every worldview, there is a foundational reality from which or from whom all dependent beings draw their power to be. The foundational reality simply is; it is unique because it alone has within itself the power to be. Human religions, philosophies, and our informal worldviews display a variety of convictions as to what this fundamental reality is. Whoever or whatever is viewed as foundational is a matter of faith and cannot be proven. Of course, reasons for taking a particular view can be advanced, but they are never sufficient to amount to a proof in the strictest sense of that word.

We humans also are aware of conscience, truth, beauty, goodness. These too are part of the reality we know and experience. This awareness of truth, beauty, goodness, of right and wrong, and of an obligation to honor and be faithful to all of them, leads us to another crucial aspect of worldview. Every worldview holds or believes something to be of primary value or worth. Everyone has a view of what is the chief good in life, with an accompanying set of values and obligations. If this were not so, our life would have no direction and we would not be able to make decisions about what we want and ought to do. As one theologian, Emil Brunner, put it, "You can avoid making up your mind but not your life." What guides our decisions as we go about the business of living reveals what we really believe is right and worthy. Our convictions about what constitutes the supreme good and what is right and wrong are matters of belief. They cannot be proven. They are self-evident to the one holding them; he or she holds them by faith. There are other features of reality that must be included in our worldview, such as the inevitability of death, human society or community, human kindness and cruelty, and the meaning of history. The meaning of all of these cannot be proven, but must be believed.

Therefore, whether we are overtly religious or not, we are all believers. That being the case, the most important question to ask ourselves is not, "Am I a believer?" but rather, "In what or in whom do I put my faith? What or whom do I trust to be reliable and true?" Or to put it differently, "Who or what is my God or 'god'?"

In the religions of the world, the two central characteristics of every worldview, that which holds all else in being and that which is of supreme worth and obligation, are often held to be primary characteristics of "the divine" or of the "gods" or of "God."

Christians believe that we humans were not left to form our worldview on our own, but that God has revealed Himself. He has spoken by deed and word. In God's revelation in Israel and culminating in Jesus Christ, we find the foundational reality disclosed. He is the Creator and the Savior. This revelation of Himself makes sense of the hints or "general revelation" of Himself, hints that God has given us in the facts of nature and science, in our sense of being a finite self, and of having a conscience, reason, and an awareness of beauty. (For a brief treatment of the arguments for the existence of God, see Appendix A.)

God reveals Himself also as the Lord, the One Who is the good; Whose person, character, will, and purposes are worthy to be worshiped, relied upon, and emulated above all else. He is the One to Whom we are accountable, Who is sovereign, and the One Whose hand guides all history. He cares for us who are made in His image. Therefore, Christians seek to worship Him and obey Him, and Him alone.

Since God is the living center of all reality, and since He alone deserves and desires our utmost trust and allegiance, the Thirty-Nine Articles begin with Him. In beginning with God, the Articles follow the Bible. The Bible always begins with God.

There are two lessons in that practice. First, Scripture honors the fact that God can only be known rightly by His initiative, by His Self-revelation. God announces, introduces, and defines Himself. Moreover, as He does so, He distinguishes Himself from the false gods that arise from our fallen human imagination. Second, we learn that only when we see things in the light of their relationship to the living God do we rightly understand the things of creation and ourselves, for everything is the creation of the one true God, and exists only in relation to Him, by His power and for His purpose.

Article 1 gives a brief but comprehensive description of God as He is revealed in creation, in the history of Israel set forth in the Old Testament, and in Jesus Christ as presented in the New Testament.

Because so much is included in this first Article, as indicated by the teaching points listed immediately below, the reader is advised that this chapter is one of the longest in the book.

The Teaching of Article 1

Article 1 makes four chief teaching points concerning the being, character, and work of God:

1. God is one: the singularity and simplicity of God.

2. The attributes of God's being and character are listed.

3. God's relation to the universe as Creator, Preserver, and Providential Ruler is stated.
    Excursus: The doctrine of Providence

4. God's triune nature: the doctrine of the Trinity is taught.

1. God is one: the reality, singularity, and simplicity of God
Explanation
A. *There is only one God: His reality and singularity*

"There is… God." The Scriptures nowhere seek to prove that God is. His reality is too obvious in the light of mankind's innate and universal awareness of God, given by God in general revelation through creation, human nature and history, and particularly through saving revelation in His acts and deeds in biblical history. After all, a people that went through the Red Sea and that lives in relationship with the risen Christ can hardly be expected to deny the existence of God.

"There is <u>but one</u> living and true God." There are not many gods. There are not three gods. There is but one true and living God. The biblical Faith asserts the singularity of God. God alone is God; there is no one and no thing along side of Him, or with which He can be compared. He is the only God. He is not only the God of Israel or of the Church; He is the only God there is. He is the true God of the whole world and everyone in it. Therefore, He and He alone deserves our supreme devotion and confidence. Not to render supreme devotion to Him is to break the First Commandment: *"You shall have no other gods before me"* (Deut. 5:7).

Moreover, to violate the First Commandment immediately leads to idolatry, for we cannot live in a vacuum; if we do not worship the true God, we will worship someone or something else and something less. As noted above, "We can avoid making up our mind but we cannot avoid making up our lives."

B. *The simplicity of God*

God is also one in the sense that He is not composed of many parts. He cannot be subdivided. This is usually referred to as the simplicity of God. It is mentioned in the section that follows, that deals with the attributes of God.

Biblical Foundations

The singularity of God is taught pervasively in Scripture. Here are two texts:

Therefore you are great, O LORD God. For there is none like you, and there is no God besides you, according to all that we have heard with our ears. 2 Samuel 7:22

... we know that "an idol has no real existence," and that "there is no God but one." For although there may be so-called gods in heaven or on earth—as indeed there are many "gods" and many "lords"— yet for us there is one God, the Father, from whom are all things and for whom we exist, and one Lord, Jesus Christ, through whom are all things and through whom we exist. 1 Corinthians 8:4-6

False Teachings Denied/Objections Answered

1. This Article's assertion that there is only one true and living God together with the attributes of God listed in the Article and the description of His relationships with creation, exclude as erroneous all of the philosophical and religious views that conflict with biblical, monotheistic, Trinitarian theism.

2. There are only so many alternative views that are denied by the Christian Faith. They include
- *monism*, the view that there is only one substance in reality, or stated in terms of "God" *pantheism*, the view that God is all and all is God
- *dualism*, a view that holds that there are two eternal ultimate realities
- *atheism*, the view that there is no personal God
- *polytheism*, the view that there are many gods.

In one form or another, these erroneous beliefs comprise the core of all of the non-Christian worldviews. That means that all worldviews not shaped around biblical core beliefs are in profound error and will distort the various truths and the interpretations of the facts that all worldviews seek to include and understand. To see things rightly and to live rightly, we need to view things in the light of God's revealed being and nature.

One could enter into lengthy theological and philosophical debate with any or all of the above-mentioned philosophies, religions and concomitant worldviews. To do that would take us too far afield from the aim and intended scope of this book. The chief point to be made is that by so revealing Himself, God rightfully declares these other religious and systematic philosophies to be erroneous.

Implications

What difference does the oneness, the singularity, of God make to our thought and our lives? Here are four implications.

A. By affirming that God is one, we have the foundation of a unified view of reality. The fact that there is but one true and living God is the end, in principle, of all spiritual and mental "schizophrenia" which comes from the divided loyalties entailed in believing in several gods or fundamental realities, such as in dualism or polytheism. Where there are many gods or a plurality of ultimate authorities and values, the divided loyalties and consequent conflicts that accompany them are unavoidable. But since there is only one God, we can live our lives in relationship with the one true God, who is not in conflict with Himself. We live before an audience of One.

B. In addition, we can affirm that there is a universe, not a multi-verse. We rightly believe in the unity and the coherence of all things. Our minds can be and ought to be ordered and unified in the light of His wise, creative work and purpose.

C. The fact that there is but one God provides the foundation for the mission of the Church. Since God is the rightful God of all the earth and there is no other God, therefore, all people need to be restored to a right relationship with Him through the Gospel. To this end, the Church is sent forth into the world.

D. The existence and oneness of God and our unavoidable, implicit awareness of Him enable us to understand and account for humanity's universal sin and guilt before God. St. Paul points out in the first three chapters of Romans that when we suppress our intuitive knowledge of God and do not honor Him, but place our ultimate confidence and loyalty in something or someone else, we become guilty before God and corrupt in our behavior. The world's many and mutually contradictory religions, and the constant expressions of the pervasive cruelty and injustice of humanity are evidence of both the guilt and enslaving power of this rebellion and idolatry. It is because of this rebellious suppression of the knowledge of God that the Bible declares, "All have sinned and fall short of the glory of God" (Rom. 3:23).

2. The attributes of God's being and character
Explanation

The true God, in contrast to all idols or false "gods," is described as living, everlasting, without body, without parts, without passions, of infinite power, infinite in wisdom and goodness. Several of these attributes are self-explanatory, but several call for brief comment.

He is the living God. In Scripture to say that God is the living God is to contrast Him, the personal, active God, with dumb, inanimate idols. Idols do nothing and can do nothing. This is true whether they are graven images or mental constructs or our religious projections. They are not alive. They neither speak nor act. As the prophets loved to emphasize, these idols must be carried about or supported by their worshipers. In contrast God is alive. He holds the universe in His hands. He is not carried by His people, just the reverse, He protects and carries His people. He manifests His livingness by His action in Creation and in history, supremely in Jesus Christ and the Holy Spirit.

To say that God is without body is to affirm that He is pure spirit, and not located physically in one place as bodies are. Furthermore, the world is not His body nor is He the soul of the world. Both God's *transcendence*, by which He is beyond space and time and His creation, and His *immanence*, by which He upholds the universe, is omnipresent throughout it, and is active within it, require that God not be physically limited by having a body.

On the other hand, to say that God is not embodied does not exclude the fact that God the Son assumed human nature, and therefore assumed a human body in becoming Man in the *Incarnation*, or that due to the indwelling of the Church by the Spirit that the Church is in a very real sense the body of Christ. These are special redemptive actions of God and do not contradict the fact that in His eternal nature, He is pure, infinite spirit and has no physical body.

God is without parts. He is indivisible. He cannot be divided into smaller sub-units. This is often referred to as the simplicity of God, as was mentioned earlier. He is not a composite being and there are no parts more fundamental than Himself out of which He could be composed. His essence is one.

To say that *God is without passions* seems to contradict God's revelation of Himself in biblical history. The God of biblical revelation is surely not Aristotle's unmoved mover, contemplating only His own perfection because all else is unworthy of His notice. If there is passion, delight, and sorrow anywhere, it is found supremely in God. God cares. He grows angry. He loves so much that He comes and suffers in the person of the Son. This Article intends to deny none of these truths.

What then does it mean to say that He is "without passions"? This phrase is used in a specific and technical manner, drawn from philosophy. It means that God is "impassable" in the sense that there is no one and nothing greater than Himself that could compel Him to suffer. If He suffers, which He does, then it is not due to His being forced to suffer against His will. He suffers because He chooses to make Himself vulnerable, to create, to care for, and to relate personally to His creation. Above all, He relates to us who are made in His image, created in and for a relationship with Him. Perhaps we should also add that God is not driven by His passions but rather they are expressive of Himself in all of His attributes, and are thus shaped by His wisdom, righteousness, and goodness.

God is everlasting, eternal, without beginning or end. His utter uniqueness is seen in that He simply always is. It is His nature to be. We, and all we see and touch, do not have the power to exist in and of ourselves. We all are called into being from beyond ourselves. We begin and we are sustained and supported from beyond ourselves. Therefore to contemplate the God Whose nature it is to be, Who is eternal, leads us to bow in humility, awe, and wonder before Him.

While not specifically listed in the Article, we should also see in this reference to God's eternity a pointer to his *immutability* or *changelessness*. He is eternally the same. He does not begin, grow old, or improve in being and character. His changelessness does not mean that God is immobile and cannot act or do new things as some philosophers and theologians have wrongly taught. Rather it means that in all his actions, He is ever the same, everlastingly Himself. There is no fickleness nor "shadow of turning" in Him.

God has unlimited power, wisdom and goodness.

His power enables Him to do all that He desires to do. And what He desires to do will always be in accord with His character and His eternal purpose revealed in Jesus Christ.

His infinite wisdom enables Him to put His knowledge and power to work in effective actions to accomplish His great purpose. Wisdom in Scripture is essentially a practical attribute.

God is good, holy, and righteous altogether. He is of purer eyes than to behold evil. In Him there is no evil at all. He must and will judge evil and reward good. In all His ways He is just and righteous. Evil cannot abide in His presence.

A central part of God's goodness is His love. His love is a holy love. While He may set His love upon the sinner, He is not sentimental. He does not wink at evil. If His heart is a furnace of love, His love is always a fire of righteous love. His love is expressed in many and various ways: in His patience, in His benevolence to the just and unjust alike, in His mercy to those in need, and supremely in His grace. God's grace is His favor given to those who deserve His wrath and condemnation, favor given out of His sheer desire to rescue, to save, to forgive and to perfect. His grace is expressed most completely in His gift of His Son on the Cross in which His love and His justice are satisfied and fully expressed.

This description of God is one that affirms the greatness of His being and the purity and goodness of His character. It is drawn from His self-revelation in the history of Israel culminating in the full revelation of His being and character in Christ Jesus, the Incarnate Son, God with us. This revelation of Himself affirms and makes sense of our observations of creation and of ourselves.

Before the living and true God, we rightly fall down, "lost in wonder, love, and praise."

Biblical Foundations

It would be a joy and not difficult to quote a large number of texts of Scripture for each of the 11 attributes or perfections of God just discussed. However, space requires restraint.

In the Bible, all of the attributes of God's being and character taken together are often referred to as His glory and as His holiness. Therefore, first we will cite texts that refer to all of His perfections in those inclusive terms. Then we will cite a text or two that assert each of the attributes mentioned above.

Holiness and Glory

Who is like you, O LORD, among the gods? Who is like you, majestic in holiness, awesome in glorious deeds, doing wonders? Exodus 15:11

For God, who said, "Let light shine out of darkness," has shone in our hearts to give the light of the knowledge of the glory of God in the face of Jesus Christ. 2 Corinthians 4:6

The Living God, Everlasting God

But the Lord is the true God; he is the living God and the everlasting King. At his wrath the earth quakes, and the nations cannot endure his indignation. Jeremiah 10:10

Pure Spirit, without Parts, Immaterial

God is spirit, and those who worship him must worship in spirit and truth. John 4:24

Yet the Most High does not dwell in houses made by hands, as the prophet says, "Heaven is my throne, and the earth is my footstool. What kind of house will you build for me, says the Lord, or what is the place of my rest? Did not my hand make all these things?" Acts 7:48-50

See my hands and my feet, that it is I myself. Touch me, and see. For a spirit does not have flesh and bones as you see that I have. Luke 24:39

Transcendent/Immanent

Know therefore today, and lay it to your heart, that the Lord is God in heaven above and on the earth beneath; there is no other. Deuteronomy 4:39

Eternal

Lord, you have been our dwelling place in all generations. Before the mountains were brought forth, or ever you had formed the earth and the world, from everlasting to everlasting you are God. Psalm 90:1-2

"I am the Alpha and the Omega," says the Lord God, *"who is and who was and who is to come, the Almighty."* Revelation 1:8

Self-Existence

For as the Father has life in himself, so he has granted the Son also to have life in himself. John 5:26

Changelessness/Immutability

Every good gift and every perfect gift is from above, coming down from the Father of lights with whom there is no variation or shadow due to change. James 1:17

For I the Lord do not change; therefore you, O children of Jacob, are not consumed. Malachi 3:6

Unlimited Power

For I know that the Lord is great, and that our Lord is above all gods. Whatever the Lord pleases, he does, in heaven and on earth, in the seas and all deeps. Psalm 135:5-6

For nothing will be impossible with God. Luke 1:37

Unlimited Wisdom

Then the mystery was revealed to Daniel in a vision of the night. Then Daniel blessed the God of heaven. Daniel answered and said: "Blessed be the name of God forever and ever, to whom belong wisdom and might. He changes times and seasons; he removes kings and sets up kings; he gives wisdom to the wise and knowledge to those who have understanding; he reveals deep and hidden things; he knows what is in the darkness, and the light dwells with him. To you, O God of my fathers, I give thanks and praise, for you have given me wisdom and might, and have now made known to me what we asked of you, for you have made known to us the king's matter. Daniel 2:19-23

With God are wisdom and might; he has counsel and understanding. Job 12:13

Goodness/Holiness/Righteousness/Justice/Love/Mercy/Grace

And when the song was raised, with trumpets and cymbals and other musical instruments, in praise to the Lord, "For he is good, for his steadfast love endures forever," the house, the house of the Lord, was filled with a cloud. 2 Chronicles 5:13b

For you are not a God who delights in wickedness; evil may not dwell with you. Psalm 5:4

Righteousness and justice are the foundation of your throne; steadfast love and faithfulness go before you. Psalm 89:14

Whom God put forward as a propitiation by his blood, to be received by faith. This was to show God's righteousness, because in his divine forbearance he had passed over former sins. It was to show his righteousness at the present time, so that he might be just and the justifier of the one who has faith in Jesus. Romans 3:25-26

Beloved, let us love one another, for love is from God, and whoever loves has been born of God and knows God. Anyone who does not love does not know God, because God is love. In this the love of God was made manifest among us, that God sent his only Son into the world, so that we might live through him. In this is love, not that we have loved God but that he loved us and sent his Son to be the propitiation for our sins. 1 John 4:7-10

Nevertheless, in your great mercies you did not make an end of them or forsake them, for you are a gracious and merciful God. Nehemiah 9:31

So that in the coming ages he might show the immeasurable riches of his grace in kindness toward us in Christ Jesus. Ephesians 2:7

False Teachings Denied/Objections Answered

In one sense, it is sufficient to say here that any view of God that contradicts the list of attributes explained above is rejected as contrary to the true and living God. We will only mention false views that either have been widely held or that are presently being advocated.

1. Currently, the Mormon religion teaches that God has a body such as we have, only much larger. This is contrary to the Christian Faith and the teaching of Scripture. God, Who is infinite Spirit, has no material body, nor could He have, given all of His other attributes.

2. Recently, some theologians have taught views that deny the infinity of some of God's attributes. For example, some hold the view that God's knowledge is finite, limited by the free agency of human beings. Others have taught that His eternity and His transcendence are limited, that He is not above time and so He is limited by the unidirectional movement of time. Some process theologians and philosophers limit His power and speak of a finite God Who is limited by the choices of human beings and the stuff of the universe. None of these doctrines is acceptable. The infinite nature of all of God's attributes excludes all of these views. He is not a finite or limited God.

3. Some philosophers contend that the Mormons, the Bible and we Christians speak too anthropomorphically about God, that is, we speak of God too much as if He were a human being with hands and eyes and hearing.

This objection may well apply to the Mormon religion but it does not understand either the Bible's use of these metaphors or of their use by Christians. It is true that the Bible speaks of God's hearing, seeing, His hands and eyes, using human activity and body parts to point to God's nature and activity. Such speech, however, is meant to be understood as analogical speech. When we human beings wish to speak about God, our options are limited. It would not do, as some non-Christians do, for us to speak primarily in sub-human terms of God, for example, inorganically about God as if He were merely an unconscious force, or zoologically about God as though He were a life force that fell below the level of human personality.

To speak of God in analogy to human personality and human action is to use the highest analogy we have. God cannot be less personal than we are. Scripturally, just the reverse is true, since we are made in His image and not vice versa. He is not only personal but super-personal, more personal than we are. So the Bible speaks and so do Christians.

4. Others have complained that to speak analogically or metaphorically of God means that we do not know what we are saying. Why is that? Because any good comparison requires that we know both of the things we are comparing in order to know if the comparison fits. And since we do not have a direct knowledge of God that would enable us to know whether our comparisons fit, we really have no right to make these comparisons and do not know whereof we speak. For example, I know what my human father is like but how do I know if God is rightly compared to my father in any sense? Am I just guessing and hoping with no real guarantee of the truth of what I say?

What this objection overlooks is that it is not we who are making the comparison. It is God Who is drawing these comparisons. As our Creator, He knows us and the entire creation, and He knows Himself. He knows what in the universe and in our nature provides the best comparison to Himself and His activity. We can have confidence in the biblical descriptions of God since He is the one Who has chosen to reveal Himself to us in and by these biblical comparisons. And He is in the right position to know.

He has spoken throughout the history of revelation as recorded in Scripture and reveals Himself supremely in the person of Jesus Christ. The person, deeds, and teaching of Jesus Christ, both God and Man, therefore remains our fullest revelation of the being and attributes of God. Revelation is God's own Self-revelation in personal terms with which we are familiar.

The analogies hold. While God transcends our full comprehension, we do know Him truly, even if we cannot comprehend Him fully, in all of His greatness.

Implications

The being and character of God as described above will have consequences that will be seen in the other Articles as we consider them. Here are several important implications for our lives:

A. Awe.

If there is anything we Christians need to do, it is to recover a sense of awe before the reality, the greatness, and the goodness of God. We need to have our minds and hearts opened to the majesty of the living God. It is not for nothing that J.B. Phillips entitled his popular book, *Your God is Too Small*. Our tendency as sinners is to limit His powers and so to domesticate God; we tend to focus on ourselves and to view God primarily as our helper. We are often more concerned about how our faith in God benefits us than about desiring to honor God in all His glory and majesty and giving Him the glory He rightly deserves.

In a secular society that has little or no place for the living God in its view of reality, the Great Commandment to love God first and foremost is easily subordinated to the Second Commandment, which is to love our neighbor. It can even lead to neglecting the love of God altogether. In so doing, we invert reality and reverse the priority of Scripture. We are weak as Christians because of it.

How, then, are we to recover a vital sense of the reality and character of God? Surely the place to start is prayer. In conversation with God, as we meditate upon His attributes revealed in Holy Scripture, we will be moved to praise and adoration. Karl Barth reportedly once said that he was more certain of the existence of God than of his own existence. Such a comment reflects a profound, prayerful awareness of the greatness of God. It can be so for each of us.

B. Resting place.

Each attribute of God provides a profound resting place for the human heart and life. Our brief span of life on this earth rests in His eternity; our partial knowledge and ignorance draws upon His infinite knowledge and wisdom; our weakness relies on His power; our sin and failure are dealt with by His grace. It would be a helpful devotional practice to reflect on each attribute of God with our reliance on Him in mind. We are created to rest in God, "to glorify Him and enjoy Him forever," as the *Westminster Shorter Catechism* puts it. We would be wise to take the time to do so, intentionally and often.

C. Impact upon the wellsprings of our character.

In one of his television broadcasts, Bishop J. Fulton Sheen reportedly made the statement that we become in character like that which we worship. If we worship gold, we become hard and cold. That being the case, nothing is more important for us than the worship of the true and living God, so that in surrendering ourselves in worship to Him, both privately and corporately, we might be increasingly conformed to His image as He is revealed to us in Jesus Christ. The importance of worship underscores the blessing we Anglicans have in the godly liturgy given us by the work of the great Archbishop Thomas Cranmer.

3. God's relation to the universe as Creator, Preserver, and Providential Ruler
Explanation

The Christian doctrine of Creation is unique in human thought and among the world's religions. Philosophy tends to move between some form of monism that teaches that everything consists of one substance and some form of dualism that affirms that there are two eternal ultimate realities. Dualism holds that all actual things, finite and dependent, are but a momentary mixture or marriage of the two eternal realities. A careful reading of comparative religious literature will disclose that the religions of the world move between these same two positions. Left to ourselves, that is how we fallen human beings tend to think and worship. Apart from the Bible, there is really nothing like the biblical witness to God as the Creator of the universe. It is not dualistic for there is only one eternal God. It is not monistic because God does create a universe that is not Himself. The Creation exists as a reality dependent upon, but other than, God. The very uniqueness of the biblical doctrine of Creation amid human thought and religion points to its truth; it comes from above.

More specifically, what does it mean scripturally to speak of God as the Creator of the universe? A number of things are involved:

1. God alone is eternal; there is nothing eternal alongside of Him. The creation is freely called into being by Him and is sustained in being by His will and power.

2. God called or spoke the world into existence from nothing. He did not shape a preexistent material. When we create something we fashion what is already there; we fashion things out of some existing matter. Not so with God in Creation. He called the material into being from nothing, *ex nihilo*, and then fashioned it, gave it form.

3. The resultant world is dependent on Him for its continued existence; it has contingent being. God alone has the ground of His being within Himself. The biblical doctrine that God continues to hold the world in being through the power of His Word, affirms the dependent character of the creation, and the continuing goodness of God in upholding the world.

4. The universe is purposeful because it is the result of a wise, intentionally purposed act of God, Who is Himself the source and ground of all wisdom and purpose.

Further, since the universe is grounded in God's purpose, our life's purpose within it cannot be known apart from knowing God's purpose for creating the universe and us within it. It is not surprising that in a secular age, which marginalizes or denies the existence of God, and ignores

His revelation of Himself in Jesus Christ, people seek in vain for self-understanding and for purpose or meaning. Apart from God there is no ultimate purpose or meaning.

5. Since the created universe is created through the *Logos,* or Word of God, it is therefore orderly and rational. Science and technology are possible because God is such as He is. We, with a mind created by God, are able to observe and think after Him the thoughts that He embodied in the creation.

6. The creation is comprised of various kinds of things, inorganic and organic, personal and angelic, arranged in a hierarchy with human beings made in the image of God at the top. This order is God's work and is due to His purpose and plan.

7. Creation has a temporal or historical dimension as well. Creation is dynamic; God is working His purpose out though time. History is going somewhere, headed to God's conclusion.

8. This is not our creation but God's, therefore ecological responsibility and our accountability to God are anchored in God's act of Creation. We are His stewards, called to care for the creation, respect it, understand it, develop and use it in accord with God's purposes.

9. The work of Creation involves the three persons of the Trinity, the Father purposing and initiating, the Son being the Word through Whom all things were created, and the Spirit being the executor of the creative action.

Biblical Foundations

Texts that affirm the Creation and preservation of the universe by God abound. Here are three key passages:

You are the LORD, *you alone. You have made heaven, the heaven of heavens, with all their host, the earth and all that is on it, the seas and all that is in them; and you preserve all of them; and the host of heaven worships you.* Nehemiah 9:6

It is he who made the earth by his power, who established the world by his wisdom, and by his understanding stretched out the heavens. Jeremiah 51:15

In the beginning was the Word, and the Word was with God, and the Word was God. He was in the beginning with God. All things were made through him, and without him was not any thing made that was made. John 1:1-3

False Teachings Denied/Objections Answered
  1. Marcion (A.D. 150s) taught that the God of the Old Testament, the Creator, was a lesser and different God than the God of the New Testament, the God of Grace. This deprecation of God as the Creator and of the Old Testament witness to God is contrary to the Scriptures, was rejected by the Church after a struggle, and is rejected by this Article. It is the One God who is the Creator. The Scriptures never suggest a plurality of Gods. There is but one God. They clearly teach that God the Father created the world through the Son by the Spirit. It was such false teaching by Marcion and the practices that inevitably flow from it that led to Marcion's being designated a heretic despite his deep sense of the grace of God in Jesus Christ.
  2. Some have taught that modern natural science contradicts the biblical account of the Creation and makes any reference to God unnecessary when referring to Creation. That view of the relationship between natural science and divine revelation errs greatly. Such an assertion is due to a failure, on the one hand, to recognize the nature of modern natural science and on the other hand, to recognize the nature of the Biblical revelation of the Creator and Creation.
  Due to its nature, modern natural science has certain inherent limitations. It does what it does well but it does not do everything.
  A. It looks at the action of physical nature by observation, formulates hypotheses about the physical forces, and tests the hypotheses by repeated testing.

B. Further, modern natural science has certain beliefs or assumptions. It assumes our human existence and mental capacities, and it assumes the existence of physical nature. It assumes that nature and the natural forces are the same everywhere and at all times. It assumes that our senses are adequate for observing the natural physical phenomena and their repeated regular patterns of behavior and that our minds are of such a nature to understand the patterns through applied mathematics.

C. Since natural science requires the existence of an observer and of nature to be observed, it is at home in an existing universe. It cannot really speak about an absolute origin of the universe where there was no observer but God and nothing to observe. By observing the present expansion of the universe and reckoning backward it can point to a past moment of a beginning of the present state of the universe. It is a moment that it cannot fully comprehend. This view of the world's beginning is articulated in the "Big Bang" theory. But what exploded? Where did that come from? For these questions natural science has no answer.

D. In addition, since natural science is limited to objective physical matters, it cannot address the full personal character of the scientist himself, because personality involves more than an observable body and physical forces. It requires intentional purpose and moral fidelity to the data and these cannot themselves be physically measured. Natural science cannot explain or include the scientist who conducts natural science. And, if natural science cannot speak adequately of the scientist, or of human beings generally, it surely cannot speak of the personal God, the Creator. He is not an object in time and space. He is the almighty, personal, eternal Spirit Who transcends all that He has created. Therefore, natural science cannot speak of the purposed, intelligent, initial act of the Creator or of the absolute origin of the universe. These personal, unique, one-time divine actions lie outside of the limits of modern natural science.

E. We have not finished listing the limits of the natural scientific method. Modern natural science also cannot speak of miracles, which are special acts of God in time and space which, due to His action and energy, cause the behavior of physical things not to conform to the usual, repeatable patterns which natural science is designed to examine and test. They are not repeatable by the scientist for the purpose of testing and, if observed by the scientist, would appear as random data in his statistics or on his graph. Natural science does much superbly but it simply doesn't do everything. It doesn't do the personal, the one-time, morality, or beauty. It can't, therefore, deal with the whole of creation or the Creator.

Having spoken of the limits of natural science, it is important that we go on to say that there is, however, a great compatibility between Scripture and natural science. It is very important to note that the assumptions of modern natural science (i.e., that nature is orderly, constant, everywhere the same, that nature is knowable and worth knowing) were first brought into the world by people thinking within the worldview of biblical revelation. The early natural scientists believed that they were thinking God's thoughts after Him and that they were helping to fulfill the mandate given to humanity by God to understand, care for, and develop the use of nature. It is not accidental that modern natural science arose in the culture of the Christian West and not in the ancient Greek or Hindu or Asian cultures. Modern natural science is a child of the biblical revelation and of Greek mathematics. The point to be made is that there is no inherent contradiction between Biblical revelation and the proper findings of natural science.

To sum up, given the limitations and the birth of modern natural science in the Christian West, it is naive and wrong to suggest an inherent contradiction between natural science and the biblical account which speaks of

God and His purposive, creative action. Such a view fails to recognize the nature and limits of natural science and the nature of biblical revelation, which speaks primarily in terms of divine and human purpose in historical action. When we want to learn of the Creator's initial act of Creation, we are shut up to the Scriptural revelation; natural science can't get us there. It can, however, point in God's direction when its results are viewed in the light of God's revelation.

Implications

We have already indicated several ways in which God's creating and preserving work affects our lives. We stated that only in His purpose will we find the true purpose of our lives or the world. We spoke of our stewardship and of our accountability to God for our exercise of this stewardship. There are other implications as well. Here are some of the more important ones:

A. Nothing in all creation is to be worshiped: not the stars, the sun or moon, not reptiles or fish or any animal, nor human beings. God alone is to be worshiped, for as the transcendent Creator He exists on a different level than His creation. The Genesis account of the Creation takes pains to make clear that the "gods" of the world's religions, for example the sun and the moon, are really only creatures of the true and living God, and hence may be enjoyed with thankful hearts but may not be worshiped.

B. Further, it is incorrect to speak of human beings as having within us a "spark of divinity." Divinity doesn't spark! It is true that we are unique among the creatures of God, being made like God, in His image. We are precious and to be respected, having our dignity and value rooted in God, but we are not divine, and are not to be worshiped.

C. Concerning evil in the creation, there is good news and bad news. Evil includes so-called natural evils such as earthquakes, and it includes sin or moral evil. The good news is that evil, both physical and moral, is not eternal nor is it created. It is unnatural in the universe. God's character, purpose, plan, and action are good. He made, and makes, all things good, and sustains them in their created essence as good. Evil must therefore be a distortion of something, or someone, good. Moreover, if evil is not created, but rather a corruption of something or someone created good, then it can in principle be healed or restored.

If evil were created evil, that would imply, first, that God created evil and hence that He was evil, or at least partly evil. Second, it would deny the possibility of restoration; for that which is evil by nature, that is, by creation, would have no goodness to which to be restored. However, because evil is the distortion and corruption of something or someone created good, then that which has become corrupted may be redeemed or restored. That points us to God's solution in Christ.

The bad news is that evil in the universe is no make-believe. It is real. It does no good to deny it or to declare evil an illusion, as some worldviews do. Apart from Christ evil can be experienced as unbearable. It is to be dealt with by Christ and in Christ.

D. Since the world is God's world, created by Him, we can learn about God by looking at the universe that He has made and loves. Just as something of the artist or workman is reflected in his work, so it is with God. Jesus directs our attention to the flowers in the field clothed in beauty, the sparrows whose needs for food are supplied, to an anxious father looking out the back door for the return of a lost child, in order to see reflected in the creation the character and power of the Father, the Initiator and Creator of all. Because of the distorting effects of sin in the creation and in our hearts and minds, we need the lens of biblical revelation to see the world aright, but the signature of God is written there for those who have the glasses and the eyes to see.

E. Nothing is too hard for God, including miracles. If the world is His creation, and if the regular patterns of creation are maintained by His will as expressions of His dependability and orderliness, then it is surely not an impossible thing for Him to do the unusual, the miraculous, by an exercise of fresh creative power, should the well-being of mankind and the accomplishment of His fundamental purpose to save us call for such unusual action. Did not Jesus pray to the Father, "all things are possible for You"?

The fact that in a secular society many hold miracles to be impossible only discloses the fact that many start from anti-godly presuppositions. Let me use a humble analogy drawn from our experience. No one thinks it strange if I divert water from the river, where it naturally flows, to water my garden. This is done due to my decision, will, and power. The reason why such a redirection of the natural flow does not strike us as odd is because we assume that people can impose their will on the regularities of nature. We think and will; the body acts, and the water is pumped to my garden. But if we can alter the course of nature in some degree by our mental, spiritual purpose and will, how much more can God, the Creator of nature, Whose power is unlimited, do the same? If we can water our garden, we need not hesitate to pray to the Father for rain, for He can move the water in the heavens if it so pleases Him.

F. In creation there are also hints for ethics which receive further illumination and specificity from God's Word in Scripture. God has created the world with a certain shape and order. Certain constants keep appearing in every society and place: marriage, family, economic arrangements, and government. These are the orders of creation. While these orders are not fixed in form in every respect, they are there and cannot be avoided. The light of God's revelation helps us take note of them, respect them, and order them appropriately in the light of Scripture.

Further, the creation is structured in levels of kind and complexity, with mankind standing at the apex of God's creation. This too has ethical implications. It would surely be out of order to value a rock, even if it shines brilliantly as does the diamond, more than the life of a person made in the image of God. Alas, people often do.

The same ethical error and confusion is found in the recent charge of specie-ism made by certain extreme animal rights advocates against traditional ethics. They assume that it is inappropriate to value one species over another. A son, an acquaintance, a mouse, and a melon are all viewed as standing on the same level of value. This is egalitarianism gone crazy. Could anyone really live according to this ethical philosophy? In the case of a fire in the house, who would save the potted plants before the children? Only one with no conscience could really live out such a philosophy. This charge of specie-ism and so much contemporary ethical confusion illustrates the need for God's revelation in Scripture to renew and clarify our intuitive ethical awareness of the importance of the different orders of creatures in God's universe.

Excursus: Providence
Explanation

God's relation to the universe is not only that of Creator and Sustainer but also that of providential Ruler. While Article 1 does not specifically state this, it is implied in His being our Preserver, as well as in the reference to His infinite power and in the affirmation of the Creeds found in Article 8, in addition to the references to His sovereign grace found scattered through the Articles. Therefore, we will discuss His sovereign rule. It asserts the following points:

1. God is Lord and is constantly overseeing the outworking of His purpose in history. The chief point of the biblical doctrine of God's providential rule is that He is in charge and may be counted upon to keep His word, whether of promise or warning. In the end, His good purpose will surely be accomplished.

2. He makes all things work together for good to those who serve Him, who love Him, and who are called according to His purpose. Also, we read in Scripture that nothing in all creation will be able to separate His own from His love and power. These assertions must not be understood to imply that God makes all things pleasant for those who love Him and are called according to His purpose. It was not so for Christ.

3. Since He is actively working out His purpose in and through all things, He makes even the evil of men to serve Him and redeems the sufferings of the saints. The supreme instance of this is the Cross and Resurrection of Christ. Things therefore never get out of His control or fall from His sovereign hands and shepherding care.

Biblical Foundations

But Joseph said to them, "Do not fear, for am I in the place of God? As for you, you meant evil against me, but God meant it for good, to bring it about that many people should be kept alive, as they are today." Genesis 50:19-20

. . .having been predestined according to the purpose of him who works all things according to the counsel of his will. Ephesians 1:11

. . for truly in this city there were gathered together against your holy servant Jesus, whom you anointed, both Herod and Pontius Pilate, along with the Gentiles and the peoples of Israel, to do whatever your hand and your plan had predestined to take place. Acts 4:27-28

False Teachings Denied/Objections Answered

1. Deism teaches that God created the world but neither guides it nor interferes with its usual patterns by doing miracles. God is compared to a clockmaker who made a clock and then allows it to run on its own. At the end of time, God will distribute rewards and punishments to us, His moral creatures, according to how we have lived

in relation to the moral law built into the creation. So teaches the doctrine of Deism.

This view is in clear contradiction with the teaching of Scripture that God is in charge of, and intimately involved with, the world and history. It is also at odds with the fact that our final destiny at the consummation of all things is based primarily on our relation to Christ and not simply on our moral goodness.

2. Fatalism teaches that an impersonal power rules over human lives and history, directing history with no regard for human actions. This, too, is contrary to Scripture that teaches that God rules and that He does so in large measure by working in and through the choices of human beings, while not violating their wills and free agency.

3. That chance reigns is the view that nothing guides and controls the world and its history. All is mere chance, arbitrary happening, without purpose or guidance. Scripture teaches quite the opposite. It teaches that things happen according to the purpose and plan of God, which includes the decisions and actions of mankind, and that history will end in the consummation of His purpose revealed in Christ.

4. Some hold that the regular patterns discerned by modern natural science tell the entire story of reality so that the events of nature and history are determined by the interplay of impersonal, mechanical, and biological forces. This view simply fails to consider the limits of the natural scientific method. As said above, the scientist himself is a more complex reality than the natural scientific method can explore. And since we humans transcend the natural scientific method, how much more so does God, who is pure, sovereign Spirit and the very fountain of all created personality. The interplay of impersonal, physical, biological forces and human decisions are caught up in the providential guidance and purpose of God.

5. Others believe that Christians, when we call the Creator our Father, are merely projecting our desires onto an impersonal, chance-driven, temporal reality in order to

make ourselves feel better. They believe that there is no "Fatherly Hand" guiding history. Our response is threefold. First, we assert that God has often shown His hand in the events of nature and history in His mighty acts of salvation as recorded in Holy Scripture. These mighty acts of God reach a climax in the Cross and Resurrection of our Lord Jesus Christ. Second, we believe that God's hand has become visible in our lives as we pray and live out our faith, informed by the Scripture. Events have occurred, time and again, that compel us to see the hand of God, our Father, at work. Third, we respond that if we were simply projecting God onto an impersonal reality in order to feel comforted, we would have made up a much less demanding God than the God we know through Scripture. Nominal Christians, who neglect the Scriptures, often do just that.

6. Others hold that God cannot reign in history because human choice is real and therefore God is not sovereign in history. It is true that we human beings have some difficulty understanding how God's sovereign rule and human choice can fit together. We must not, however, deny the clear teaching of Scripture merely because it is difficult for us to fully comprehend how the teaching can be true.

Perhaps some light on this mystery is shed by the fact that if we really know the heart and character of someone, we can be pretty certain how that person will choose to act in a given circumstance. This is true because even though our choices are not determined by forces outside ourselves, they are determined by who we are, by our heart and character. If that were not true our choices would be sheer chance and utterly arbitrary and we would not really be responsible for who we are and how we behave. If we can read another's heart to a high degree, how much more can God know our hearts? Since God knows us completely, He can surely anticipate and guide our actions in history by directing the circumstances that we encounter.

Another part of the puzzle is that God can and does move our heart by His Holy Spirit to faith in Christ and is working within us to sanctify us. He is thereby also at work within us and works through us in history. Therefore, mysterious as it may remain, there is some light on the mystery of the compatibility between God's sovereignty and our personal choosing.

That being true, the attempt to make room for human choice by limiting the rule of God is an error. Limiting God's rule runs counter to the teaching of the Word of God written. It puts the authority and rule of God on the same plane as the decisions of mankind, thereby failing to realize that God can and does work precisely in and through our decisions, and it robs the believer of the comfort and encouragement of being able to trust God's reigning hand to be at work in all circumstances and to have ultimate control over all things.

Implications

The implications of God's providential rule are manifold. Here are some:

A. The chief benefit for the believer in God's providential rule is peace and security. This is particularly significant in difficult times. To know that amid suffering, pain, and frustration the living God is working in and through these events to bring about good, to bless those who love and work with Him to accomplish His great purpose, comforts the heart and makes continued work and effort meaningful. Historically, it is those with the strongest doctrine of the sovereign rule of God who have proven to be the most active and persevering in doing good, particularly in difficult times and against all odds.

B. If peace, security, and encouragement are chief benefits of the awareness of God's providential rule, humility and patience must also be added to its benefits. It is God who is in control. We are not. While we may work in His service we are not in charge; it is finally He who must give the increase and bring about the good in His time and in accord with His purpose and plan.

4. God's triune nature – the doctrine of the Trinity
Explanation

The God of Whom this Article has been speaking is the Triune God. In fact, it is only in the light of the revelation of the Triune God that we have been able to say what we have already said in the previous three teaching points of this Article. We could have discussed the Trinity first and then the other three teaching points, had we not followed the order of the Article.

What, you may ask, does it mean to say God is the Triune God? What grounds do we have for saying that He is Triune? And what are the implications of His Triune nature for our relationship with Him and for the wider range of our Christian life and witness?

A. The doctrine is neither speculation nor irrelevant

Before seeking to answer those questions, it is important to lay aside the two frequent misconceptions, that the doctrine of the Trinity is primarily a product of philosophical speculation and that the doctrine is an irrelevant theological abstraction. Quite the opposite is the case.

The doctrine of the Trinity arose out of the Church's desire to be faithful to the historical revelation that God has given of Himself in Israel and in Christ. The doctrine of the Trinity, while using philosophical reasoning and terminology, is actually a rejection of any philosophical speculation that distorts Who and What God has shown Himself to be in history.

Since the doctrine of the Trinity is rooted in God's historical, saving revelation, it is profoundly relevant, for it seeks to take seriously how God is specifically involved in our salvation. God the Father, God the Son, and God the Holy Spirit all jointly provide key elements in our salvation. Should we deny any of the persons of the Godhead, their full divinity and therefore their role in our salvation, we ourselves would need to take their place and, in effect, in part, save ourselves. Since self-salvation is impossible, given our creatureliness and our sinfulness, a denial of the Trinity would be bad news indeed.

For example, if Jesus were not the eternal Son of God Who assumed our human nature, how could His death upon the Cross be the atonement for the sins of the whole world? His death would be merely another human being's death, one martyrdom among many, a tragic window into the fallen state of mankind. We would then have to provide our own atonement. How could we? We could not. We need to be aware of the intensely practical relevance of this doctrine. We will sketch some of its other major implications later in this chapter.

B. The raw material of the doctrine is found in Scripture

The fully developed doctrine of the Triune nature of God is not found in Scripture. It took the Church hard work through trial and error over four hundred years to give the doctrine full and clear expression. The reality of God's triune nature, however, is clear in the Scriptural data and the formulation of a doctrine of the Trinity is demanded by that data. The closest we come to a direct statement of the Trinity in the Scripture is found in the words of the Risen Lord in the Great Commission, where we are commanded to baptize people in the Name (singular, one name) of the Father and the Son and the Holy Spirit (three-fold). The one Name includes three Names. We cannot speak rightly of the Name of God, the full revelation of Himself, unless we speak of the three Names, the Father, the Son, and the Holy Spirit (Matthew 28:19).

What are the data found in Scripture that require the doctrine of the Trinity? Here is a brief summary of the biblical data with a selection of supporting texts following:

1. *God is One*. This we have discussed above. It is the chief burden of the Old Testament teaching concerning God. It is a lesson that Israel learned the hard way in the midst of her polytheistic neighbors, whose polytheism she

was ever tempted to adopt. Finally it was driven home by the pain of the exile. The *Shema,* "Hear O Israel, the Lord our God is One," remains to this day the chief article of Faith in Judaism. Jews and Christians are passionately monotheistic. God is One.

2. *The Father is God. The Son is God. The Spirit is God.* This is taught both explicitly and implicitly in the biblical writings. This makes it impossible to say that God is only the Father or only the Son or only the Spirit. It also rejects any statement that the Son or the Spirit are less than fully divine

3. *The Father is personal. The Son is personal. The Spirit is personal.* Since each of the "persons" of the Trinity are personal or share in the personality of God, this means that the Spirit cannot be understood as an impersonal influence from God.

4. *The Father, the Son, and the Spirit are mutually interrelated to one another.* They invariably engage in joint action in saving history and are all simultaneously involved in the present experience and relationship of the Church and of individual Christians with God. This makes it impossible to teach that the Father, Son, and Holy Spirit are but temporary and successive ways of knowing God.

A selection of biblical texts that reveal the triune nature of God

Preparation in the Old Testament

Then God said, "Let us make man in our image, after our likeness. And let them have dominion over the fish of the sea and over the birds of the heavens and over the livestock and over all the earth and over every creeping thing that creeps on the earth. Genesis 1:26

The angel of the Lord found her by a spring of water in the wilderness, the spring on the way to Shur. And he said, "Hagar, servant of Sarai, where have you come from and where are you going?" She said, "I am fleeing from my mistress Sarai." The angel of the Lord said to her, "Return to your mistress and submit to her." The angel of the Lord also said to her, "I will surely multiply your offspring so that they cannot be numbered for multitude." And the angel of the Lord said to her, "Behold, you are pregnant and shall bear a son. You shall call his name Ishmael, because the Lord has listened to your affliction. He shall be a wild donkey of a man, his hand against everyone and everyone's hand against him, and he shall dwell over against all his kinsmen." So she called the name of the Lord who spoke to her, "You are a God of seeing," for she said, "Truly here I have seen him who looks after me." Genesis 16:7-13

By the word of the Lord the heavens were made, and by the breath of his mouth all their host. Psalm 33:6

For to us a child is born, to us a son is given; and the government shall be upon his shoulder, and his name shall be called Wonderful Counselor, Mighty God, Everlasting Father, Prince of Peace. Of the increase of his government and of peace there will be no end, on the throne of David and over his kingdom, to establish it and to uphold it with justice and with righteousness from this time forth and forevermore. The zeal of the Lord of hosts will do this. Isaiah 9:6-7

I saw in the night visions, and behold, with the clouds of heaven there came one like a son of man, and he came to the Ancient of Days and was presented before him. And to him was given dominion and glory and a kingdom, that all peoples, nations, and languages should serve him; his dominion is an everlasting dominion, which shall not pass away, and his kingdom one that shall not be destroyed. Daniel 7:13-14

God is One
Hear, O Israel: The Lord our God, the Lord is one. Deuteronomy 6:4

To you it was shown, that you might know that the Lord is God; there is no other besides him. Deuteronomy 4:35

See now that I, even I, am he, and there is no god beside me; I kill and I make alive; I wound and I heal; and there is none that can deliver out of my hand. Deuteronomy 32:39

I am the Lord; that is my name; my glory I give to no other, nor my praise to carved idols. Isaiah 42:8

How can you believe, when you receive glory from one another and do not seek the glory that comes from the only God? John 5:44

To the King of ages, immortal, invisible, the only God, be honor and glory forever and ever. Amen. 1 Timothy 1:17

The Father is God; the Son is God; the Spirit is God.
The Father is God

And the Word became flesh and dwelt among us, and we have seen his glory, glory as of the only Son from the Father, full of grace and truth. John 1:14

No one has ever seen God; the only God, who is at the Father's side, he has made him known. John 1:18

Do not labor for the food that perishes, but for the food that endures to eternal life, which the Son of Man will give to you. For on him God the Father has set his seal. John 6:27

According to the foreknowledge of God the Father, in the sanctification of the Spirit, for obedience to Jesus Christ and for sprinkling with his blood: May grace and peace be multiplied to you. 1 Peter 1:2

The Son is God (see Article 2 for a fuller treatment of this)

Behold, the virgin shall conceive and bear a son, and they shall call his name Immanuel (which means, God with us). Matthew 1:23

All things have been handed over to me by my Father, and no one knows the Son except the Father, and no one knows the Father except the Son and anyone to whom the Son chooses to reveal him. Come to me, all who labor and are heavy laden, and I will give you rest. Matthew 11:27-28

In the beginning was the Word, and the Word was with God, and the Word was God. John 1:1

And the Word became flesh and dwelt among us, and we have seen his glory, glory as of the only Son from the Father, full of grace and truth. John 1:14

Thomas answered him, "My Lord and my God!" John 20:28

Have this mind among yourselves, which is yours in Christ Jesus, who, though he was in the form of God, did not count equality with God a thing to be grasped, but made himself nothing, taking the form of a servant, being born in the likeness of men. Philippians 2:5-7

For in him the whole fullness of deity dwells bodily. Colossians 2:9

<u>The Spirit is God</u>

In the beginning, God created the heavens and the earth. The earth was without form and void, and darkness was over the face of the deep. And the Spirit of God was hovering over the face of the waters. Genesis 1:1-2

Where shall I go from your Spirit? Or where shall I flee from your presence? Psalm 139:7

And whoever speaks a word against the Son of Man will be forgiven, but whoever speaks against the Holy Spirit will not be forgiven, either in this age or in the age to come. Matthew 12:32

But if it is by the finger of God that I cast out demons, then the kingdom of God has come upon you. Luke 11:20

And I will ask the Father, and he will give you another Helper, to be with you forever, even the Spirit of truth, whom the world cannot receive, because it neither sees him nor knows him. You know him, for he dwells with you and will be in you. John 14:16-17

But Peter said, "Ananias, why has Satan filled your heart to lie to the Holy Spirit and to keep back for yourself part of the proceeds of the land? While it remained unsold, did it not remain your own? And after it was sold, was it not at your disposal? Why is it that you have contrived this deed in your heart? You have not lied to men but to God." Acts 5:3-4

These things God has revealed to us through the Spirit. For the Spirit searches everything, even the depths of God. For who knows a person's thoughts except the spirit of that person, which is in him? So also no one comprehends the thoughts of God except the Spirit of God. 1 Corinthians 2:10-11

The Father is personal. The Son is personal. The Spirit is personal.

The Father is personal

Then he said, "Do not come near; take your sandals off your feet, for the place on which you are standing is holy ground." And he said, "I am the God of your father, the God of Abraham, the God of Isaac, and the God of Jacob." And Moses hid his face, for he was afraid to look at God. Exodus 3:5-6

Then Moses said to God, "If I come to the people of Israel and say to them, 'The God of your fathers has sent me to you,' and they ask me, 'What is his name?' what shall I say to them?" God said to Moses, "I am who I am." And he said, "Say this to the people of Israel, 'I am has sent me to you.'" Exodus 3:13-14

I the Lord search the heart and test the mind, to give every man according to his ways, according to the fruit of his deeds. Jeremiah 17:10

On that day when, according to my gospel, God judges the secrets of men by Christ Jesus. Romans 2:16

The Son is personal

Therefore the Lord himself will give you a sign. Behold, the virgin shall conceive and bear a son, and shall call his name Immanuel. Isaiah 7:14

Now the birth of Jesus Christ took place in this way. When his mother Mary had been betrothed to Joseph, before they came together she was found to be with child from the Holy Spirit. And her husband Joseph, being a just man and unwilling to put her to shame, resolved to divorce her quietly. But as he considered these things, behold, an angel of the Lord appeared to him in a dream, saying, "Joseph, son of David, do not fear to take Mary as your wife, for that which is conceived in her is from the Holy Spirit. She will bear a son, and you shall call his name Jesus, for he will save his people from their sins." All this took place to fulfill what the Lord had spoken by the prophet: "Behold, the virgin shall conceive and bear a son, and they shall call his name Immanuel" (which means, God with us). When Joseph woke from sleep, he did as the angel of the Lord commanded him: he took his wife, but knew her not until she had given birth to a son. And he called his name Jesus. Matthew 1:18-25

And the Word became flesh and dwelt among us, and we have seen his glory, glory as of the only Son from the Father, full of grace and truth. John 1:14

No one has ever seen God; the only God, who is at the Father's side, he has made him known. John 1:18

And when Jesus finished these sayings, the crowds were astonished at his teaching, for he was teaching them as one who had authority, and not as their scribes. Matthew 7:28-29

Since therefore the children share in flesh and blood, he himself likewise partook of the same things, that through death he might destroy the one who has the power of death, that is, the devil. Hebrews 2:14

The Spirit is personal

And I will ask the Father, and he will give you another Helper, to be with you forever, even the Spirit of truth, whom the world cannot receive, because it neither sees him nor knows him. You know him, for he dwells with you and will be in you. John 14:16-17

And while Peter was pondering the vision, the Spirit said to him, "Behold, three men are looking for you. Rise and go down and accompany them without hesitation, for I have sent them." Acts 10:19-20

Likewise the Spirit helps us in our weakness. For we do not know what to pray for as we ought, but the Spirit himself intercedes for us with groanings too deep for words. Romans 8:26

All these are empowered by one and the same Spirit, who apportions to each one individually as he wills. 1 Corinthians 12:11

Do not quench the Spirit. 1 Thessalonians 5:19

The Father and the Son and the Spirit are mutually present to one another and are interrelated with one another.

And when Jesus was baptized, immediately he went up from the water, and behold, the heavens were opened to him, and he saw the Spirit of God descending like a dove and coming to rest on him; and behold, a voice from heaven said, "This is my beloved Son, with whom I am well pleased." Matthew 3:16-17

Go therefore and make disciples of all nations, baptizing them in the name of the Father and of the Son and of the Holy Spirit. Matthew 28:19

But when the Helper comes, whom I will send to you from the Father, the Spirit of truth, who proceeds from the Father, he will bear witness about me. John 15:26

This Jesus God raised up, and of that we all are witnesses. Being therefore exalted at the right hand of God, and having received from the Father the promise of the

ARTICLE 1

Holy Spirit, he has poured out this that you yourselves are seeing and hearing. Acts 2:32-33

To be a minister of Christ Jesus to the Gentiles in the priestly service of the gospel of God, so that the offering of the Gentiles may be acceptable, sanctified by the Holy Spirit. Romans 15:16

Now there are varieties of gifts, but the same Spirit; and there are varieties of service, but the same Lord; and there are varieties of activities, but it is the same God who empowers them all in everyone. 1 Corinthians 12:4-6

The grace of the Lord Jesus Christ and the love of God and the fellowship of the Holy Spirit be with you all. 2 Corinthians 13:14

But when the fullness of time had come, God sent forth his Son, born of woman, born under the law, to redeem those who were under the law, so that we might receive adoption as sons. And because you are sons, God has sent the Spirit of his Son into our hearts, crying, "Abba! Father!" Galatians 4:4-6

How much more will the blood of Christ, who through the eternal Spirit offered himself without blemish to God, purify our conscience from dead works to serve the living God. Hebrews 9:14

According to the foreknowledge of God the Father, in the sanctification of the Spirit, for obedience to Jesus Christ and for sprinkling with his blood: May grace and peace be multiplied to you. 1 Peter 1:2

But you, beloved, build yourselves up in your most holy faith; pray in the Holy Spirit; keep yourselves in the love of God, waiting for the mercy of our Lord Jesus Christ that leads to eternal life. Jude 20-21

From these texts and many others as well as from the Church's daily experience of God came the careful and precise doctrine of the Trinity. We will outline it below.

C. The Church's Doctrine: The classic doctrine asserting the oneness and threefoldness of God

How can all of the biblical teaching, just briefly summarized from Scripture, be true? After much discussion, trial and error, the classic doctrine of the triune nature of the One God was articulated. Article 1 states the classic Church doctrine most succinctly: "And in unity of this Godhead there be three Persons, of one substance, power, and eternity, the Father, the Son and the Holy Ghost." This statement involves the following points:

1. The Church's Doctrine of the Trinity asserts a *threefoldness* in God:

A. This threefoldness is of the very nature of God. It is not just a threefoldness in His revelation of Himself. What He shows Himself to be in His revelation is Who He actually is. His revelation does not distort but accurately conveys the truth about Himself. This is asserted against those who taught that the threefoldness in His revelation was a distortion of God's true nature made necessary because God had to adjust His Self-revelation due to the limits of our understanding as mere human beings. The Church said "no" to this error. God is true to Himself in His revelation of Himself.

B. Since God is triune in Himself, the personal distinctions within God are eternal and are not created; God is the Father, the Son, and the Holy Spirit by nature. He is eternally three-fold.

C. God's threefoldness is defined in terms of the internal relations of the persons within the Godhead. The Father is unique in being unbegotten and in eternally begetting the Son and breathing out the Spirit. The Son is unique in being eternally begotten of the Father. The Spirit is unique in being eternally generated by, or breathed out by, the Father Who is the fountainhead of all Divinity.

D. There is a difference in the way the Eastern Churches and the Western Churches developed this doctrine of the Trinity. Each approached the triune nature of God from a different starting point.

i. The Western Church approached the understanding of the Trinity from the starting point of the Oneness of God. The teaching of St. Augustine is dominant in the West. Augustine emphasized the mutuality of the Father and the Son in the inner life of the Trinity. He held that the Holy Spirit was the bond of mutual love in the Trinity, that is, the Spirit is the bearer of the Divine love from the Father to the Son and from the Son to the Father. The Western Church added to the Nicene Creed that the Spirit eternally proceeds from the Son to the Father as well as from the Father to the Son. The West did this by adding "and the Son" to the Nicene Creed, thereby underlining the fact that there is a mutuality of love within the Godhead.

This addition to an Ecumenical Creed was done unilaterally by the West without benefit of an Ecumenical Council or even consulting the Eastern Churches. This lack of communication and consensus has proven to be a serious cause of division between the Western and Eastern Churches, provoking the so-called *Filioque* ("and the Son") controversy. (See Article 5, Teaching Point 3, for a discussion of the *Filioque*.)

ii. The East approached the Trinity from the threefoldness in God. The Father is emphasized as the fountain of Divinity. The Father begets the Son and the Spirit proceeds from the Father to the Son only. There is an emphasis upon the eternal personal submission of the Son to the Father and of the Spirit to the Father and to the Son. It is a submission among equals, for each person shares in the one Godhead and participates fully in all the attributes of the one divine nature.

iii. Since the East more effectively articulates the threefoldness of God and the West the oneness of God, and in the light of the various emphases in Scripture, it is likely that the emphases of East and West are not contradictory in principle, that they are in fact mutually enriching and that we both have something to learn from the other in this matter. (See D, Analogies of the Trinity in creation, below.)

2. The Church's Doctrine of the Trinity also asserts the <u>Oneness</u> of God:

A. The "persons" in the Godhead are within the one God. There are not three Gods – only one.

B. The three "persons" so interpenetrate One another in an incomprehensible manner and degree that they are truly in One another, and imply One another. Each person of the Trinity eternally exists only in, with, and through One another.

C. When we consider the works of God in creating the universe and working within it, it is the One God who is acting; therefore all the persons of the Trinity are always involved appropriately in all of God's actions in the world.

We speak of the Father as the Creator, but He creates through the Son and by the action of the Spirit. It is the Son Who dies on the Cross, but it is the Father who sends Him and He obeys in the power of the Spirit. Thus the "Persons" of the Trinity cannot be separated, for they indwell One another, but neither are they absorbed by one another.

The points just mentioned above concerning the threefoldness and oneness of God, taken together, constitute a brief outline of the classical doctrine of the Church regarding the triune nature of God.

D. Analogies of the Trinity in Creation

Have we any analogies or models of such a tri-unity in our experience? St. Augustine wrote of the vestiges of the Trinity to be found in God's creation. Since only we as human beings are made in His image, it is likely that we ourselves would provide the most telling analogies. That seems to be the case. There are two primary analogies that modify one another. And both, taken together, illuminate the triune nature of God.

One analogy is the Divine Society. This is the emphasis of Eastern Christian thought. We may think of three human persons; they all share in the one human nature. In addition, these three can be of such agreement in all things that they think and act alike and act together as one. They are a profoundly intimate divine society. This model, when analogically applied to God, protects the personality of the Persons and the threeness in God, but it is weak in asserting the oneness of God and the interpenetration of the "persons." By itself it would tend toward tritheism, which is, having three "gods." The reason we sometimes put the "persons" of the Godhead in quotes is because they are not individuals in quite the way we are, for we do not interpenetrate one another by nature, as they do. Tom, Harry, and Dick may all be at one and think and act in agreement, but Tom does not require the existence of Dick or Harry to exist as do the "persons" in the Trinity. They are more One in nature than three of us can be.

The second analogy is more Western. It is the human self. Each of us is a kind of tri-unity. There is in each of us an I, the subject, a "me," the object, and the relationship that I have with me, which is the third reality in me. Each of us, therefore, is a "me, myself, and I," that is, a unity in which there is a threefoldness. This analogy when applied to God is strong on His oneness, but weaker on the threeness and the full personality of both the "me" and the "relationship." It falls short where the other analogy is strong.

The triune nature of God is, therefore, most adequately "pictured" or reflected when the two models are considered together and so qualify one another. God is more *three* than we are as individuals, and more *one* than are three of us who share the same nature and values. He is one with a threefoldness within His oneness. He is triune.

Biblical Foundations

Since we have given a large number of texts above, here we only cite a few texts that affirm the *triune* nature of the One Living God by bringing all three of the Persons before us:

And when Jesus was baptized, immediately he went up from the water, and behold, the heavens were opened to him, and he saw the Spirit of God descending like a dove and coming to rest on him; and behold, a voice from heaven said, "This is my beloved Son, with whom I am well pleased." Matthew 3:16-17

The grace of the Lord Jesus Christ and the love of God and the fellowship of the Holy Spirit be with you all. 2 Corinthians 13:14

. . . according to the foreknowledge of God the Father, in the sanctification of the Spirit, for obedience to Jesus Christ and for sprinkling with his blood. . . 1 Peter 1:2

False Teachings Denied/Objections Answered

A. As mentioned above, it has been taught that God is one in His nature and only appears to be three-fold in His revelation. This teaching is referred to as the "Economic doctrine of the Trinity." It is contrary to Scriptural teaching as indicated above.

B. It has also been taught that God appears in several successive modes. He appeared at first as the Father, the Creator, then as the Son, the Redeemer, and finally as the Holy Spirit, the Sanctifier. This has been called the "modalistic doctrine of the Trinity." It, too, is contrary to the Scripture as discussed above.

Implications

The triune nature of God influences in one way or another every doctrine of the Christian Faith. Here are some of the more important implications of the Trinity for our Christian life and thought:

A. God is love. *Anyone who does not love does not know God, because God is love.* 1 John 4:8

This is one of the few direct, definitional statements about the nature of God to be found in Scripture. It is not simply that God loves, but that God "is" love. The doctrine of the Trinity makes sense of that assertion. Love has many meanings, but love in all of its meanings is a relational word. Someone loves and thereby relates to something or to someone else. This is true of God as well. God is, by His nature, a relationship of love within Himself. The Father and the Son and the Spirit live in a life of divine love. God is not an isolated, undifferentiated, loveless monad; He is an eternal life of Holy Love. This love-in-relationship character of God's nature undergirds and shapes all of His relations with the world and with us who are made in His image. It is natural for God to love His world, and above all to love those whom He has made in His own image. It is hard to envision a more far-reaching and fundamental assertion about the nature of God than "God is love," keeping in mind that His love is holy love.

B. The freedom of God's actions and relationships with the world is rooted in His triune nature. Since God is love and since love requires a beloved, an object of love, some have concluded that God needs a world to love in order to be love or loving. In creating and redeeming, they would say, God is completing an inadequacy in Himself. His act of Creation would, therefore, not be free; it would be a necessity, a requirement of His nature if He is a God of love. This has led some to go on to assert that therefore the creation, like God, must be eternal, for God must eternally create in order to have a world to love if He is to be a God of eternal love.

This is clearly not what the Scriptures affirm. Creation in the Scriptures is a free act of God's love; it is not a necessity of His nature. His decision to create flows from the fullness and richness of His triune life and not from an assumed poverty. He does not require a world in order to love. In fact, just the reverse is the case; because He is love, He creates a world by love and to be known in love.

C. Because God is a relational God within Himself, when He calls forth a world and people with which and with whom to relate, He is doing what is compatible with and expressive of His own eternal nature. Relationships come naturally to God; they are not strange to His being. Views of God that describe Him as incapable of personal relationships abound in both Greek idealism and modern naturalism. Both miss the mark; neither sees the wonder of God, Who is related within Himself and Who therefore delights to relate to us and the rest of the world.

D. We are made in the image of God. This makes clear the relational character of human beings. We are made in and for a relationship with God and one another. We are a relationship within ourselves and between one another. We are born within a community of relationships, the family, the country, the world of peoples. It is impossible either to be conceived or born in an entirely unrelated manner. In all of this we reflect the nature of the triune God, who has made us in His likeness and for Himself.

E. One last implication: submission and subordination are honored in the life of the Trinity. Within the being and life of God, the Son is begotten by and responds obediently to the Father. In all the works of God, the Father sends the Son; the Son willingly submits in love and rejoices to obey. The Father and the Son send the Spirit. This order is never reversed. This sending and obeying reflect an internal subordination and submission in the very life and nature of God. It is clearly a subordination and submission between equals, for all the persons in the Trinity are equal in nature, sharing fully in all the attributes of the divine nature.

This sets a pattern for us. Fully shared dignity, mutual love, and respect can coexist with personal subordination and submission. We do not have to deny the social realities of subordination and submission to have our full personal equality and dignity recognized. One does not have to be the head of an organization to be fulfilled and fully affirmed by others.

The so-called "Western authority problem" may well lie here. We think we all have to be in charge in order to be equal in dignity. That conviction is actually quite ungodly. In fact, original sin consists of our asserting our equality with God and taking charge of our own lives. We thereby deny our creatureliness. We are not His equal. We are called to surrender and to submission. This denial of the goodness of submission to God and our rebellion against such submission constitutes the very heart of sin. How freeing it can be to know that submission and subordination are godly by nature and can be entered into with honor and gladness, both in relation to Him and in relation with one another.

Conclusion

Our comments on this Article have been extensive. This was necessitated by the fact that this Article says so much in so few words. Huge amounts of the Church's teaching lie behind these few key sentences in the Article.

Anglicans, in this Article, show that they stand firmly in the great classical tradition of the Church Catholic. None of what has been said is beside the point or could be ignored. We all do well to ponder deeply this biblical Self-disclosure of the living, triune God, and to respond to Him personally, in repentance and faith, with thanksgiving, praise, and adoration. And we all need to view all things in relation to Him and in His light.

ARTICLE 2

Of the Word, or Son of God, Which Was Made Very Man

The Son, which is the Word of the Father, begotten from everlasting of the Father, the very and eternal God, of one substance with the Father, took Man's nature in the womb of the blessed Virgin, of her substance: so that two whole and perfect natures, that is to say, Godhead and Manhood were joined together in one Person, never to be divided, whereof is one Christ, very God, and very Man; who truly suffered, was crucified, dead and buried, to reconcile His Father to us, and to be a sacrifice, not only for original guilt, but also for all actual sins of men.

Introduction

The Gospel is the center of the Christian revelation and the essential foundation of the Christian life and mission. The heart of the Gospel is set before us in this 2nd Article. Were we to get this wrong, then we could get nothing else right.

At the time of the 16th century Reformation, Rome, the Eastern Churches and the Churches of the Reformation all agreed on the central matters of the Gospel as they are stated in Articles 1-5.

Article 2 is written to make it clear that Anglicans in no way seek to depart from the ancient, Apostolic and Catholic Faith in these central doctrines. In brief compass Article 2 provides a brief statement of Christology and the Atonement.

Sadly, at the time of the Reformation some ancient heresies contradicting the Gospel reappeared among some smaller groups in England but these heresies were never widely accepted or influential in England at that time. Unfortunately, that has not remained the case within the Anglican Communion. Beginning with the 19th century and continuing to the present, even the Incarnation and the atoning work of Christ on the Cross have become matters of serious controversy. With such confusion and error being taught within the Communion, Anglicans and all faithful Christians can be grateful that this Article states things so clearly.

When Christians speak of the Gospel, they mean something very specific. Christianity rests upon something objective and done. The Gospel or Good News is first of all factual. It is "news" in the sense that we use the word "news" in "newspaper"; that is, the Gospel refers to historical events. It is anchored in history. The news that the Gospel announces is "good," good news, glad tidings. Further, the Gospel is not just any good news. It is the Good News, the Good News of what God has accomplished in the coming, the dying, the rising and the ascension of Jesus, Israel's Messiah, the long-awaited, promised and anointed Lord and Savior of the whole world.

As stated above, this Article addresses both the person and the atoning work of Christ. To treat both together is appropriate, for Christ's person and His work are interconnected. He can do what He did, does, and will do because of Who He is. And we know Who He is not only by His own testimony and His fulfillment of Scripture, but in large measure through what He has done, is doing, and will do. Because Jesus is the eternal Son Who became man, He is able to reconcile God and sinful human beings. And, in reconciling God and fallen humanity through the Cross, Jesus made it clear that He is the Divine Son Who came from above to seek and save the lost.

This Article does not discuss all that might be included under the work of Christ. For example, it does not discuss Jesus' fulfillment of the office of Prophet, as the Word Incarnate. Nor does it discuss Jesus as King, the Lord to whom all authority in heaven and earth has been given by the Father. What the Article does discuss is His priestly, sacrificial work upon the Cross whereby He makes atonement for the sins of the World. The prophetic and kingly aspects of Christ's work will be treated in later Articles.

The Teaching of Article 2

The teaching of this Article may be divided into two basic parts:

1. The Incarnation of the Eternal Son of God
    (Excursus: The Christological Doctrines of the First Four Ecumenical Councils)

2. The Atonement
    (Excursus: The Chief New Testament Themes concerning the Cross and the Classic Theories of the Atonement)

1. The Incarnation of the Eternal Son of God:

Teaching Point One concerns the Incarnation and involves four basic assertions concerning the person of Christ:

A. Jesus is an historic person.

B. Jesus is a fully human person, Who assumed human nature from the Virgin Mary.

C. Jesus is a fully divine person, being the eternal Word and only eternally begotten Son of the Father.

D. Jesus is utterly unique, being one person in two natures, divine and human.

We will treat these assertions in the order listed above.

A. Jesus is an historic person.
Explanation

Christians teach that Jesus is an historic person. Today few would doubt the historicity of Jesus. Historical realities, such as the Christian Church, require an historical cause; they don't just happen without a cause. All of the historical evidence makes it clear that Jesus was the chief historical cause of the Church. Both extra-biblical material and the writings of the New Testament attest to the historicity of Jesus and His giving birth to the Church.

We begin with evidence from outside of the Scriptures. One of the most striking extra-biblical witnesses to the historicity of Jesus comes from the Roman historian Tacitus, who was not a friendly witness. In the early 90s, he writes in his *Annals* concerning Nero and the great fire in Rome as follows:

> He (Nero) fastened the guilt and inflicted the most exquisite torture on a class held in contempt for their abominations, called Christians by the populace. Christus of whom the name had its origin, suffered the extreme penalty during the reign of Tiberius under one of our procurators, Pontius Pilate, and a most mischievous superstition, thus checked for the moment, again broke out, not only in Judea, the source of the evil, but even in Rome where all things hideous and shameful from all parts of the world find their center and become popular. (Annals xv, 44)

This statement not only attests the historicity of Jesus but also His crucifixion under Pontius Pilate, and the rise of the Christian movement or Church after Jesus' death. There are other non-Christian evidences of the historicity of Jesus in both Jewish as well as Roman sources.

To gain more intimate historical information about Jesus, however, we must turn to the writings of those who knew and followed Him and who cared enough about Him to record His words and deeds, as well as their impression of His person and His theological significance. This material is chiefly found in the synoptic Gospels, Matthew, Mark and Luke, and in the Fourth Gospel, John. Scattered confirmation concerning Jesus' historicity can be found in the rest of the New Testament as well.

It is true that the Gospels give us historical witness to Jesus as a figure of history. But, what sort of history do we find in the Gospels? The Gospels are more like portraits than photographs, more akin to popular history than to contemporary scientific or documentary history. In addition to being popular in style and less interested in strict chronology, for example, the Gospels were written with a purpose. They were written to invite all people to share in the Apostolic Faith through repentance and personal belief. That does not mean that the Gospels are not reliable history. Believing in someone and loving that person, and wanting everyone to do the same does not necessarily conflict with telling the truth about that person. Quite the opposite is often the case.

Several features of the Gospels indicate their historical reliability, given the popular, evangelistic kind of history they were concerned to write. First, there is the fact that the writers were followers of Christ. Christ calls for utter honesty from His followers. This applies to the early Christians and the writers of the Gospels as much as it does to us today.

Second, the "evangelists," the writers of the Gospels, were in a position to tell the truth. Many of those who were eye-witnesses of the events involving Jesus were still alive when the Gospels were being written. They could and would reject fanciful elaborations of the truth about Jesus. St. Luke tells us he canvassed their recollections. In fact, all of the Gospels claim to rest on a foundation of apostolic eye-witness.

Third, we note the fact that in these Gospels the writers were very honest about the faults and errors of the Apostles, despite the Apostles' exalted place as representatives of the Risen Lord. Such honesty speaks well for the reliability and trustworthiness of the Gospels when they speak about other matters, and particularly about Jesus.

Fourth, we find that in reading the Gospels a consistent picture of Christ's character and purpose is found, despite the variety of authorship and the diversity of the immediate audience to whom they were addressed. Such consistency is best accounted for by assuming they were telling the truth about Jesus.

Fifth and lastly, there is the fact that the issues that were alive in the Church when the Gospels were being written, which we find being discussed in the Pauline and Catholic Epistles, were not written back into the accounts of Jesus' history recorded in the Gospels. This too is best accounted for by their concern to be faithful to what was going on during Jesus' public ministry.

Taken together, all of these features give us strong reasons for trusting in the general historical trustworthiness and reliability of the Gospels. The Gospels thus provide convincing testimony that Jesus was a genuinely historical person.

The extreme historical skepticism of some contemporary biblical scholars seems to rest more on their secularist assumptions than on the data in the texts. This skepticism is, no doubt, influenced by the present anti-supernatural bias of Western culture. Agreeing with contemporary culture may make historical reconstructions popular, even sensational, in certain cultural circles; it does not, however, make such reconstructions reasonable or reliable historical scholarship.

We have said nothing, at this point, about the work of the Holy Spirit in biblical inspiration, which only deepens our confidence in Scripture. We will address that when we treat Article 6.

B. Jesus is a fully human person, Who assumed human nature from the Virgin Mary.

Jesus was not only an historical person. He was, according to the Gospels, a fully human person. It is important to affirm his full humanity, for to save us He must be one of us. "What is not assumed is not redeemed" is a saying of one of the early Fathers of the Church.

Being truly or fully human involves several things:

<u>First, Jesus was physically fully human.</u>

It is true that Jesus was supernaturally conceived in the Virgin Mary's womb by the Holy Spirit and had no human father, but it is also true that He assumed human nature from her and was born of the Virgin Mary with a normal birth. He grew through the common stages of development from childhood to manhood. He knew fatigue and hunger. He grew weary and thirsty. He died physically on a Cross by order of Pontius Pilate. He was no un-embodied phantom.

<u>Second, He was fully human in his mind, emotions and will.</u>

He thought and He taught. He taught like no man before or since. His parables were brilliant and stand apart. He knew tears and laughter, anger and joy. He obeyed the Father and carried out a sustained, costly and protracted ministry with great determination and perseverance.

<u>Third, He was fully human in his relational life.</u>

He was magnetic. He loved people and people loved Him. He gathered disciples and worked intensively with the Twelve.

<u>Fourth, He was fully human in His spiritual life</u>.

He had a life of prayer and attended worship. He knew and meditated on the Scriptures, just as each of us is called to do. He too needed a daily time apart with the Father.

<u>Fifth, He shared with us the limitations of being human.</u>

In His earthly body He could only be in one place at a time. He confessed to a certain limitation to His knowledge; He knew not the time of His return in glory. He was tempted in all things as we are, but without sinning.

In short, Jesus was not a momentary *theophany* – a form that God the Son assumed for a brief appearance, like the burning bush. He was not one who had only the appearance of humanity. His coming was far more radical. He assumed human nature. He became a man for our sake and remains so forever, as the incarnate Lord.

All of this is crucial to the second part of the teaching of this Article concerning the Atonement, for it was by becoming a sinless human that Jesus was able to be the "Lamb of God" and represent us on the Cross, as well as become our model or example in godly living.

Since Jesus was without sin, in Him our humanity is seen in its wholeness, as it was created to be. He was not only truly human; He was true humanity. For this reason, as part of our salvation, each of us is being conformed to His image. That is why Paul can urge us to imitate him as he, Paul, is imitating Christ. The Father would not be making us like His Son if His Son were not, in His humanity, what we are created and have been redeemed to be.

Biblical Foundations

Now the birth of Jesus Christ took place in this way. When his mother Mary had been betrothed to Joseph, before they came together she was found to be with child from the Holy Spirit. And her husband Joseph, being a just man and unwilling to put her to shame, resolved to divorce her quietly. But as he considered these things, behold, an angel of the Lord appeared to him in a dream, saying, "Joseph, son of David, do not fear to take Mary as your wife, for that which is conceived in her is from the Holy Spirit. She will bear a son, and you shall call his name Jesus, for he will save his people from their sins." All this took place to fulfill what the Lord had spoken by the prophet: "Behold, the virgin shall conceive and bear a son, and they shall call his name Immanuel" (which means, God with us). When Joseph woke from sleep, he did as the angel of the Lord commanded him: he took his wife, but knew her not until she had given birth to a son. And he called his name Jesus. Matthew 1:18-25

And while they were there, the time came for her to give birth. And she gave birth to her firstborn son and wrapped him in swaddling cloths and laid him in a manger, because there was no place for them in the inn. Luke 2:6-7

And rising very early in the morning, while it was still dark, he departed and went out to a desolate place, and there he prayed. Mark 1:35

And a great windstorm arose, and the waves were breaking into the boat, so that the boat was already filling. But he was in the stern, asleep on the cushion. And they woke him and said to him, "Teacher, do you not care that we are perishing?" And he awoke and rebuked the wind and said to the sea, "Peace! Be still!" And the wind ceased, and there was a great calm. Mark 4:37-39

So, whether you eat or drink, or whatever you do, do all to the glory of God. Give no offense to Jews or to Greeks or to the church of God, just as I try to please everyone in everything I do, not seeking my own advantage, but that of many, that they may be saved. Be imitators of me, as I am of Christ. 1 Corinthians 10:31-11:1

For we do not have a high priest who is unable to sympathize with our weaknesses, but one who in every respect has been tempted as we are, yet without sin. Hebrews 4:15

False Teachings Denied/Objections Answered

1. This Article affirms that Jesus existed as an historical and human person. From time to time some have denied that Jesus ever existed in history. He was declared to be a myth, in the sense of being a nonhistorical figure representing the divine. The sheer amount of historical evidence and research, however, has quieted such extreme skepticism. It would appear that today no responsible or respected scholar holds that position.

2. This Article denies the teaching of docetism (from

Greek, "to seem"), whether ancient or modern, that Jesus was not truly human with a physical body, but only assumed, for a time, the appearance of a man. Such tendencies arise in religion whenever religion is seen as an escape from the difficulties of human life in history and physical matter is seen as evil.

3. Article 2 also denies any teaching that Jesus was sinful and hence taught error in doctrine or ethics. "To err is human" is only true as a shortcut for saying that to err is inevitable for fallen human beings. Jesus was human and sinless.

4. This Article denies by implication the claim that the historical evidence in Scripture is so corrupted or so overlaid by the early Church's theological preaching and teaching that we can know very little of the actual historical Jesus. The Lutheran New Testament scholar Rudolph Bultmann took that view, as does a radical group of New Testament scholars called "The Jesus Seminar."

A) Reviewing what we have said above, we have agreed that the New Testament Gospels give us popular history. They were written to lead people to Christ and nurture believers in Christ. The Gospels and the writings of the Apostles are all written by believers. The authors loved and followed Jesus as Savior and Lord. However, as we said above, that does not mean the New Testament writings are not rooted in historical fact.

B) Popular history, told with love and to share the Good News, need not be indifferent to the factuality of the One of Whom they are speaking.

C) Finally, the New Testament authors claim to be relating historical fact. St. Paul tells us that we would be the most foolish of men were Jesus not actually raised from the dead. That would mean that the Apostles were all liars and had misrepresented what God had done. He then continues, "but in fact Christ has been raised from the dead" (1 Corinthians 15:20). He was clearly not indifferent to the facts about Jesus. St. Luke, in the Preface to his

Gospel, makes the same point affirming his concern to tell the factual truth about Jesus. They want us to know that they are being faithful to the truth about Jesus.

5. Article 2 rejects any doctrine that Jesus was not fully human. Some have held that Jesus assumed most but not all of human nature. The 2nd Ecumenical Council that met in Constantinople in A.D. 381 rejected the teaching of the godly Bishop Apollinarius, who held that Jesus had a human body but no human mind or soul because the 2nd Person of the Trinity already had a divine mind. In response, the Council declared Apollinarianism an error and affirmed that Jesus assumed the fullness of human nature from His Mother Mary.

6. Some object to the Christian conviction that Jesus is "true humanity," the One to Whom all persons are rightfully to be conformed. The philosopher Nietzsche referred to Christian ethics as "slave ethics," designed by the weak to limit the power of the strong. He held this view because as Christians we are called to love everyone, including the weak and needy, and even our enemies. Since Christian ethics are greatly dependent upon the example of Jesus, it is clear that Nietzsche speaks for those who did not and do not admire Jesus as being the one perfect human being. If such persons have really studied Jesus as He is revealed in the Gospels and still hold that view, we can only respond that we profoundly disagree with their fundamental values, and that we believe them to be repressing the witness of their own conscience. In love, we can only call them to repentance for their behavior and for their ethical blindness. They call evil good and good evil. If that is not abandoned it will become an unforgivable sin.

Implications

A. In the Christian Gospel we are in the realm of fact, not mere idea or unhistorical myth or free-flown speculation. That being the case, we must "learn of Jesus." We are not free to make Him up or fit Him into our prejudices, or see Him as only an accidental illustration of ideas and ideals which we already know. He is a "given," written into the reality of history. We are to rely on Him as Savior, and, at the same time, we are to adjust ourselves to Him as Lord, just as the disciples who became His apostles had to do.

B. In becoming human, Jesus thereby emphasized that each of us, as human beings, matters greatly to God. For God to take such extreme action for our salvation can only rest upon God's concern for us that passes all understanding and surpasses all expectation. The dignity of every human being is thereby revealed as grounded in God, in His creation of each of us and His redemption of mankind at such great cost. Our dignity and value are not based on whatever value any particular human society or group of persons might grant us. This high regard for each person has wide application. One immediately thinks of the practice of abortion, for example.

C. There are strong ethical implications in fact that Jesus is the picture of humanity as the Creator intends us to be. Ethics is largely a matter of imitation. We learn many of our values and moral practices by imitating our parents and other influential figures in our lives. Sainthood, too, has a large element of imitation, of imitating Jesus: *Imitatio Christi*. It is astonishing that people of all types and varieties find in Jesus the compelling model of true humanity. Conformity to Him does not restrict or limit us, but calls us into the fullness of what we know we are meant to be. In this, Jesus is the Universal Human Being, like no other.

C. Jesus is a fully divine person, being the eternal Word and the only eternally begotten Son of the Father.
Explanation

While few today would deny that Jesus was a fully human, historical person, many would doubt and even deny that Jesus is a truly divine person, fully God as well as fully man.

Before we go further, we need to be precise in defining what we mean when we say that Jesus is truly or fully divine. It may be helpful to begin by stating what Christians do not mean. We do not mean that He, like the rest of humanity, is made in the image of God, though it is true that human nature is so created. Nor do we mean that He is divine because we all are divine. We are not all divine. Only God is. Nor do we mean that because He was sinless, Jesus more fully reflects God than the rest of us do although that is true. And finally, we do not mean that, somehow, the human man Jesus became God, that is, was deified. No creature turns into God.

Rather, Christians mean something quite specific and utterly unique when we say that we are convinced and believe that Jesus is divine. We mean that He is the eternal, only begotten Son of God, God the Son. The eternal Word, Who while remaining God, assumed our human nature unto Himself and became one of us according to His human nature. He was and remains a member of the human race in and through His human nature, while remaining God the Son and retaining His full divine nature.

What Christians are stating is the exact opposite of the idea that a man could become God, an idea prevalent in Jesus' day in pagan religions and state politics. We are asserting that in Jesus, God became a man, which is something very different. For a man to become God is impossible. According to the biblical revelation, one is either always God or never becomes God. But for God to become man is not only possible, it actually happened! God, out of His great love and compassion, can and did become a man for the sake of our salvation. He assumed our human nature in order to do the work of seeking and saving the lost.

Such an assertion on the part of Christians, made from biblical times to the present, is based on the claims and evidence found in the Old Testament preparation and, supremely, in the person and ministry of Jesus Himself. It is attested in our hearts and consciences by the inner work of the Holy Spirit. The Incarnation of God the Son in Jesus is not a human idea, but rather it is a divine/human fact, lived out for human beings to see and recognize, despite its being so singular and astonishing.

What in the Old Testament preparation gives reason to assert the divinity of Jesus? Perhaps we can say that, above all, His unique fulfillment of the messianic expectation in Israel provides the evidence and revelation of the divine nature of Jesus. Israel was looking forward to the coming of the Messiah, the anointed one, or the "Christ," to use the Greek translation. In Jesus' day the expectations concerning the nature of the Messiah varied and ranged from a supernatural kingly figure of the Last Days who would come, trailing clouds of glory, to usher in a new and final age with cosmic consequences, all the way to being a mighty military warrior who would drive out the oppressive Roman invaders who held Israel captive. The common thread in all of the expectations was that the Messiah would publicly triumph, fulfill the promises of God to Israel, and establish God's universal reign. No one was looking for a Messiah who would be rejected, suffer and die, and be vindicated by God in a Resurrection, even though it was so written in the Scriptures if one had the eyes to see. Jesus had such eyes. It was the unexpected way in which Jesus fulfilled the messianic expectation that accounts for His reluctance to use the term "messiah" publicly, and for the fact that some thought He could well be the Messiah while others were quite certain that He was not. In the end, the latter group won; He was crucified as a blasphemer and a false messiah Who was misleading the people of God.

After Jesus was crucified and had risen, looking back in hindsight, we can see many promises and hints in the Scriptures concerning the Messiah as having been fulfilled by Jesus. Here are some: as the One Who spoke with divine authority, He fulfilled the promise of the final Prophet who, like Moses, would know God face to face and who would speak God's Word and lead His people out of bondage. As the One to Whom all authority in Heaven and upon earth was given, Jesus fulfilled the expectation of the Davidic King Who would sit forever on the Throne of David and restore Israel to her true spiritual place. On the Cross, as the "suffering servant," He fulfilled the prophecies of Isaiah, brought to perfection the various sacrifices of Israel, made atonement for the sins of the world, and instituted a foretaste of the great heavenly messianic banquet in the Lord's Supper. In His Resurrection and Ascension He was revealed as the divine figure, like the son of man, who came from above to receive a kingdom. In sending the Holy Spirit from the right hand of the Father, He bestowed on His disciples the power to live in the new age with God's laws written in their hearts. In sum, Jesus was the Mediator, uniting and fulfilling in Himself the Prophetic, Kingly and Priestly mediatory offices, while initiating the New Covenant promised by God through the prophets. The Jews were looking for the Messiah Who would come with supernatural dimensions, and Jesus came. In His coming, He revealed the true nature of the Messiah that they ought to have been expecting. The Old Testament helps us understand Jesus and His unique nature as God and man. And Jesus helps us understand the Old Testament as preparing for and pointing to Him. No one but the Jews was expecting the Messiah.

However, it is by attending closely to Jesus as depicted in the New Testament, read in the context of the Old Testament, that we encounter the most compelling reasons for acknowledging His divinity. Of those reasons, here are five of the most important:

1. Jesus' claims concerning Himself
2. Jesus' life
3. Jesus' mighty deeds
4. The claims of Jesus' witnesses
5. The inner testimony of the Holy Spirit to Jesus

1. Jesus' claims concerning Himself

The claims Jesus makes concerning Himself are both direct and indirect.

A. The chief direct claim

Directly, He claimed to be the Son. Jesus was the Son Who alone knew the Father and Who was truly known only by the Father. Because of this exclusive, mutual intimacy, the Son was in a position to reveal the Father to those to whom He, the Son, chose to reveal Him.

Jesus' unique sense of "Sonship" was first evidenced in the Temple at the age of twelve, when He confounded the Elders with His wisdom in spiritual matters. Jesus was surprised at His human parents' failure to anticipate His remaining in the Temple. Should they not have known that He must be in His Father's house? In Jesus' eyes the Temple was His Father's house.

Jesus used "Abba," the common family term of address of a child to its father, to address the Holy One of Israel, the Lord God and Creator of the world. This was striking, and we find it nowhere else in the New Testament, except on the lips of the followers of Jesus. The Lord's Prayer, in which we call God "Father," carries for us this family connotation. What was natural to Him is ours only by adoption and grace, ours only in Jesus.

The reality of His Sonship was also evidenced at the time of His baptism and at His transfiguration. In both events the Father refers to Him or addresses Him as the Son.

All through the Gospels, especially in John's Gospel, where Jesus openly and repeatedly asserts His Sonship, Jesus' filial consciousness sets Him on God's side of the great distinction between God and mankind, between God and creation. This claim to divine Sonship seems to be the most fundamental claim that Jesus makes. All of the other claims that He makes, He makes on the basis of His being the unique Son, sent into the world by the Father.

B. The key indirect claims

Indirectly, He claimed divine authority.

Jesus' claim to divinity is reflected in the fact that He both claimed and exercised absolute authority over mankind in a variety of ways. One thinks first of the authority of His teaching. Prophets prefaced their message with "Thus saith the Lord," but Jesus said, "Amen, Amen, *I* say unto you." Jesus thereby claimed to speak not only in the name of God but *as* God. He was more than a prophet. In some of His statements, He claimed to have superseded what had been told to them of old, by the Prophets. People commented on the authority in His teaching: "No one ever spoke like this man!" (John 7:46). Jesus went beyond the consciousness and authority of a prophet. But what, we may ask, goes beyond the authority of a prophet? What could be more authoritative than being a messenger chosen by God to speak His Word to His people? Surely St. John in the prologue to his Gospel stated it rightly; Jesus does not only speak the Word of God as a messenger, Jesus is the Word of God in person, incarnated in the flesh.

"In the beginning was the Word, and the Word was with God, and the Word was God....And the Word became flesh and dwelt among us, and we have seen his glory, glory as of the only Son from the Father, full of grace and truth" (John 1:1,14, ESV).

There are other clear indications of His claim to divine authority. He claimed the right as the Son of Man to forgive sins. He backed it up with a demonstration by healing a paralytic. And the Pharisees asked, "Who can forgive sins but God alone?" (Luke 5:21). Exactly!

He called disciples to follow Him, which Jewish teachers did not do. To call people to follow was what God had done in calling Moses, the Judges, and the Prophets.

Jesus said that for people to enter God's Kingdom they

had to come to Jesus, Himself, and become His disciples. He was claiming to be the King in the Kingdom.

In addition, Jesus claimed absolute loyalty and love of people, beyond all other relationships, even at the cost of their life. In one of His parables, He claimed that He would be the Judge in the final Day of Judgment, determining the eternal destination of everyone, dividing the sheep from the goats. It was a divine role that He was claiming.

In summary, we can only say that His explicit and implicit claims place Him above, beyond and over all humanity. He was claiming to be the promised One in Whom the very presence and reign of the Lord God had drawn near. Those around Him understood Him to have made such claims. In the end, He was crucified on charges that He had made Himself equal with God by calling God His Father and by admitting He was the Messiah and thereby blaspheming God.

To put this another way, there is no historical evidence at all that supports the view that Jesus was only a human religious teacher Who taught high morals and Who made no astonishing claims about Himself. All of the evidence points toward Him Who claimed, by word and deed, to be Immanuel, the Lord with us.

2. Jesus' Life

Jesus' life corroborates His claims.

In the context of Israel's firm conviction that there is only one God, Jesus' claims were so radical and offensive to the Jewish Faith that one would have to assume either that He was crazy or deluded, on the one hand, or that He was possessed of the Devil or was an evil liar and charlatan on the other, as C. S. Lewis has so eloquently stated.

His being crazy or deluded, however, is clearly unlikely. His life is marked by a lucidity and sanity of model quality. He was at every point in touch with reality, ever the master of the situations in which we find Him. He conducted a sustained, consistent and arduous ministry over a long period. There simply is no evidence of mental illness in the character and life of Jesus.

Nor can we suspect deliberate deception on Jesus' part. His is a life of astonishing righteousness in motive and deed. Honesty is a hallmark of Jesus' own person, and a claim He places upon all of His followers. His consistently caring behavior would make it hard to believe He was evil or possessed of the Devil. While His claims were exalted and authoritative, His life was one of remarkable humility and sacrificial love. He loved the Father and was totally surrendered to the Father. He loved those around Him. If His claims for His own person and work were high, His posture toward those around Him was low. He washed their feet. He forgave sinners and embraced outcasts. In the end He gave His life for us all, including His enemies. If it is true that "no one ever spoke like this man," then it is equally true that no man lived like Him before or since. His humility and love set Him apart and at the same time confirmed His claims. We must conclude that in His claims He was telling the truth.

3. Jesus' Mighty Deeds

His mighty deeds confirm His claims.

The signs and wonders done by Jesus throughout His ministry were not done only to confirm His implicit and explicit claims. They were genuine deeds of love expressing the inbreaking of the Kingdom of God in and through Him. But at the same time they also confirmed, to those who had the eyes to see, that Jesus was the promised Son sent by the Father as Jesus knew Himself and claimed to others to be.

The greatest mighty deed of all was Jesus' Resurrection from the dead. As we shall see in Article 4, the Resurrection vindicates and confirms not only His claims about His person but His work on the Cross as well.

The main point to be made here is that all of Jesus' mighty deeds confirm His claims to divinity. His actions confirm His claims. For those with eyes to see, the mighty deeds done by Jesus were done in the power with the blessing of the Father. The sad truth, however, is that those who had no eyes to see believed His deeds were done by the powers of darkness, despite the goodness of His life.

4. The claims of the witnesses to Jesus

Those who knew Jesus best worshiped Him.

It is impossible to over-emphasize the almost unbelievable fact that the worship of Jesus took place within Judaism and in Jesus' day. All of His disciples, especially those who became His Apostles, worshiped Him as Lord in the end, despite being Jews who were commanded to worship God alone. The rejection of the deification of human beings was particularly strong for the Jews after the exile. They had learned their lesson regarding pagan idolatry. Yet, it is precisely those Apostles who give us the New Testament picture of Jesus as Son, Word, Savior, Messiah and Lord.

There was no time for a deification of a purely human Jesus to take place. From the time of the Resurrection on, they all joined with Thomas saying, "My Lord and my God." Pagan deifications take time. The deification of the Buddha took 500 years in a culture that was sympathetic to religious exaltation of human beings. In Jesus' case it was immediate and in a Jewish climate utterly opposed to such a claim.

That the Apostles themselves were completely convinced of Jesus' divinity or Lordship cannot reasonably be doubted, for all the Apostles sealed their witness with their blood. They all died as martyrs.

Jews though they were, those who knew Him best worshiped Him as Lord. The Church has ever since.

5. The inner testimony of the Holy Spirit to Jesus

The Holy Spirit attests to the divinity of Jesus.

In addition to the objective grounds that confirm the

divinity of Jesus we have the inner witness of the Holy Spirit. The Spirit's witness confirms in our hearts the truth of the biblical witness concerning the person and work of Christ. Drawing upon the Gospel of our salvation and upon the whole biblical witness to Christ, the Spirit glorifies Christ in our hearts, pours the love that God has for us into our hearts, and assures us that in Him we are sons and daughters of God by adoption and grace. Therefore we too, in the Spirit, join with the Apostles in crying out from the heart, "My Lord and my God." The Christian's deep assurance that Jesus is Savior and Lord is not based on the external evidences alone. Such assurance is sealed in us by God's own voice within.

Given all of the above, it is no surprise that the earliest known credo or confession of Christians is "Jesus is Lord!" All of the above material on the divinity of Jesus Christ is summarized in this Article by these brief, carefully chosen words, "The Son, which is the Word of the Father, the very and eternal God, of one substance with the Father."

Biblical Foundations
Old Testament Preparation for Christ as a divine person

I saw in the night visions, and behold, with the clouds of heaven there came one like a son of man, and he came to the Ancient of Days and was presented before him. And to him was given dominion and glory and a kingdom, that all peoples, nations, and languages should serve him; his dominion is an everlasting dominion, which shall not pass away, and his kingdom one that shall not be destroyed. Daniel 7:13-14

The Lord your God will raise up for you a prophet like me from among you, from your brothers—it is to him you shall listen. Deuteronomy 18:15

Therefore the Lord himself will give you a sign. Behold, the virgin shall conceive and bear a son, and shall call his name Immanuel. Isaiah 7:14

For to us a child is born, to us a son is given; and the government shall be upon his shoulder, and his name shall be called Wonderful Counselor, Mighty God, Everlasting Father, Prince of Peace. Of the increase of his government and of peace there will be no end, on the throne of David and over his kingdom, to establish it and to uphold it with justice and with righteousness from this time forth and forevermore. The zeal of the Lord of hosts will do this." Isaiah 9:6-7

Behold, the days are coming, declares the Lord, when I will make a new covenant with the house of Israel and the house of Judah. Jeremiah 31:31

Rejoice greatly, O daughter of Zion! Shout aloud, O daughter of Jerusalem! behold, your king is coming to you; righteous and having salvation is he, humble and mounted on a donkey, on a colt, the foal of a donkey. Zechariah 9:9

And beginning with Moses and all the Prophets, he interpreted to them in all the Scriptures the things concerning himself. Luke 24:27

Christ's claims of divinity

All things have been handed over to me by my Father, and no one knows the Son except the Father, and no one knows the Father except the Son and anyone to whom the Son chooses to reveal him. Matthew 11:27

While walking by the Sea of Galilee, he saw two brothers, Simon (who is called Peter) and Andrew his brother, casting a net into the sea, for they were fishermen. And he said to them, "Follow me, and I will make you fishers of men." Matthew 4:18-19

You have heard that it was said, 'You shall love your neighbor and hate your enemy.' But I say to you, Love your enemies and pray for those who persecute you." Matthew 5:43-44

Now great crowds accompanied him, and he turned and said to them, "If anyone comes to me and does not hate his own father and mother and wife and children and brothers and sisters, yes, and even his own life, he cannot be my disciple. Luke 14:25-26

Christ's life as supportive of His claims

That evening at sundown they brought to him all who were sick or oppressed by demons. And the whole city was gathered together at the door. And he healed many who were sick with various diseases, and cast out many demons. And he would not permit the demons to speak, because they knew him. Mark 1:32-34

Then turning toward the woman he said to Simon, "Do you see this woman? I entered your house; you gave me no water for my feet, but she has wet my feet with her tears and wiped them with her hair. You gave me no kiss, but from the time I came in she has not ceased to kiss my feet. You did not anoint my head with oil, but she has anointed my feet with ointment. Therefore I tell you, her sins, which are many, are forgiven—for she loved much. But he who is forgiven little, loves little." And he said to her, "Your sins are forgiven." Luke 7:44-48

Christ's Deeds as corroborative of His claims

And when Jesus saw their faith, he said to the paralytic, "My son, your sins are forgiven." Now some of the scribes were sitting there, questioning in their hearts, "Why does this man speak like that? He is blaspheming! Who can forgive sins but God alone?" Mark 2:5-7

Jesus said, *"But that you may know that the Son of Man has authority on earth to forgive sins"—he said to the paralytic— "I say to you, rise, pick up your bed, and go home." And he rose and immediately picked up his bed and went out before them all, so that they were all amazed and glorified God, saying, "We never saw anything like this!"* Mark 2:10-12

And he said to them, "How many loaves do you have? Go and see." And when they had found out, they said, "Five, and two fish." Then he commanded them all to sit down in groups on the green grass. So they sat down in groups, by hundreds and by fifties. And taking the five loaves and the two fish he looked up to heaven and said a blessing and broke the loaves and gave them to the disciples to set before the people. And he divided the two fish among them all. And they all ate and were satisfied. And they took up twelve baskets full of broken pieces and of the fish. And those who ate the loaves were five thousand men. Mark 6:38-44

The witness of His followers to His Divinity

Thomas answered him, "My Lord and my God!" Jesus said to him, "Have you believed because you have seen me? Blessed are those who have not seen and yet have believed." John 20:28-29

Grace to you and peace from God our Father and the Lord Jesus Christ. Philippians 1:2

For in him the whole fullness of deity dwells bodily. Colossians 2:9

Long ago, at many times and in many ways, God spoke to our fathers by the prophets, but in these last days he has spoken to us by his Son, whom he appointed the heir of all things, through whom also he created the world. Hebrews 1:1-2

For in this way there will be richly provided for you an entrance into the eternal kingdom of our Lord and Savior Jesus Christ. 2 Peter 1:11

Now to him who is able to keep you from stumbling and to present you blameless before the presence of his glory with great joy. Jude 24

The internal witness of the Holy Spirit to His divinity

No one can come to me unless the Father who sent me draws him. And I will raise him up on the last day. John 6:44

One who heard us was a woman named Lydia, from the city of Thyatira, a seller of purple goods, who was a worshiper of God. The Lord opened her heart to pay attention to what was said by Paul. And after she was baptized, and her household as well, she urged us, saying, "If you have judged me to be faithful to the Lord, come to my house and stay." And she prevailed upon us. Acts 16:14-15

The natural person does not accept the things of the Spirit of God, for they are folly to him, and he is not able to understand them because they are spiritually discerned. 1 Corinthians 2:14

For by grace you have been saved through faith. And this is not your own doing; it is the gift of God, not a result of works, so that no one may boast. For we are his workmanship, created in Christ Jesus for good works, which God prepared beforehand, that we should walk in them. Ephesians 2:8-10

False Teachings Denied/Objections Answered

1. The false teaching of Arius was rejected by the first Ecumenical Council that took place in Nicaea in A.D. 325. Arius taught that the Son who became incarnate in Jesus was a creature, the first and greatest creature through which God created the rest of creation. Arius made the same point in another way. He said that "there was a time when the Son was not." The Council of Nicaea stated that the Son was fully divine. They agreed with the Epistle to the Colossians that "in Him the fullness of God was pleased to dwell" (Col. 1:19). The Catholic Faith has so confessed ever since. To deny the full divinity of Jesus is a heresy and places one outside the Church Catholic. Anglicans concur.

2. Another way of stating the same error in a more subtle manner is to say that the Son's eternal nature is generated from the Father's will but not from the Father's nature. That would imply that God is not by nature Triune and that the Son exists by God's choice and is not fully divine. This, too, is the heresy of Arius. It was taught at the

time of the Reformation by the Socinians and it is taught today by some of the cults.

3. Some have objected that because God and man are so different, and because man cannot become divine, it must also be true that God cannot become a man. But on what basis could we say that? Why cannot He assume unto His divine nature a human nature for the purposes of the salvation of human beings? There is a kinship of a sort. Were we not created for fellowship with God in the first place? And with God are not all things possible that are in agreement with His character? Actually, this debate has already been decided, for assuming human nature is precisely what God has done in and through the Son. It is a fact. A fact for which we give Him praise and thanks, for the assumption of our human nature was a profound act of humility on God's part, done out of His love for us in our great need.

Implications

There are numerous implications of the divinity of Christ for the life and work of Christians. Here are some of the more important ones:

A. Saint Athanasius pointed out that unless Christ is fully divine, worshiping Him would be idolatry. Christians do worship Him. It is instinctive with Christians. A day will come when all will bow the knee to Christ and worship Him. This is true because He is God the Son incarnate. He rightly deserves our worship.

B. Because Jesus is God incarnate, He is able to do the work of revelation and atonement. And since He is God the Son, we may rest in the sufficiency of the work which He has done. We have this confidence because God does all things well.

C. Since Jesus is not merely a human being teaching about God but the very presence and action of God Himself identifying with us and acting on our behalf, we can know how deeply God cares for us. He is not a God aloof and beyond compassion. He is *Emmanuel* – "God with us."

D. No one has ever seen God in His transcendent nature. He transcends the creation and our capacity of sight. But Jesus the Son incarnate has made Him known to us objectively, in a revelation suited to the limits of our human nature; we can see the glory of God in the face of Jesus Christ. He is God expressed in human terms!

D. That Jesus is utterly unique, being one person in two natures, divine and human.
Explanation

We need to be even more precise about the nature of the Incarnation of God in Jesus Christ. Christians do not teach that Jesus is a man with divine qualities, or God with human qualities. Nor do Christians hold that Jesus is the divinely indwelt man, thus being two persons, one divine and one human. Christians hold that He is at one and the same time fully God and fully man in the one person of God the Son. Jesus is one person existing then and now in two distinct natures united in Himself. In this union of His two natures within Himself, His natures are neither confused nor mixed together. Each nature retains its full being and characteristics.

To be sure, the Incarnation is mysterious and beyond our full comprehension. Jesus is unique, and we have nothing with which to compare Him to aid us in our understanding. He is the mystery of God bending low to become our Savior and Lord. God will always transcend our comprehension. This is particularly true in such a unique, singular action as the Incarnation.

Some have suggested that the Incarnation in Jesus is a logical absurdity, a contradiction in terms. One is either God or man but not both. To this we must reply that a mystery He may be, but a contradiction, He is not. We are not saying Jesus is divine and not divine or human and not human. Rather He is mysteriously human and divine.

In this respect, we do have analogies with which we

are familiar that we can draw upon. We as human beings are bodies, and share in all the realities of organic, biological life, but at the same time we are more. We are persons with self-awareness, judgment, values, emotions and creativity. To say we are both bodies and rational persons is neither illogical nor a contradiction. As a matter of fact, the analogy is even more apt, for how our thinking and our bodies interact is a mystery to us. We have two entirely different languages to describe the two aspects of our life, objective (my brain) and subjective (my mind). If our own unity is a mystery to ourselves, why should it be an offense that the unity of the two natures united in the person of Christ is a mystery, an even greater mystery, to us?

This uniqueness of Christ's being one person in two natures underlies the uniqueness and finality of His work, of what He has done and does for us. Because Christ alone exists as one person in two natures, divine and human, He alone is the divine-human mediator of the New Covenant. He alone has made atonement for the sins of the world reconciling God and mankind. He alone is the full revelation of the glory of God in human terms. He alone is the Risen Lord to Whom all authority in heaven and on earth has been given.

And in addition He is all of this "once for all." Who He is, He is forever. And what He has done, He has done once for all, for all people, and for all time. It is not that Jesus *was* Lord and Savior, but rather that Jesus *is* Lord and Savior, now and forever.

Biblical Foundations

In the beginning was the Word, and the Word was with God, and the Word was God. . . And the Word became flesh and dwelt among us, and we have seen his glory, glory as of the only Son from the Father, full of grace and truth. John 1:1,14

Have this mind among yourselves, which is yours in Christ Jesus, who, though he was in the form of God, did not count equality with God a thing to be grasped, but made himself nothing, taking the form of a servant, being born in the likeness of men. And being found in human form, he humbled himself by becoming obedient to the point of death, even death on a cross. Philippians 2:5-8

He is the image of the invisible God, the firstborn of all creation. Colossians 1:15

For in him all the fullness of God was pleased to dwell. Colossians 1:19

False Teachings Denied/Objections Answered
    1. The heretical teaching of Nestorius was addressed at the 3rd Ecumenical Council which met in Ephesus in A.D. 431. Nestorius taught that in Jesus we have two persons, the divine person of the Son and the human person of Jesus the man in His human nature. Therefore we have two persons in two natures, with the divine Son indwelling the human man Jesus. This is not different in principle from each Christian who is indwelt by the Holy Spirit. A consequence of such a view is that since we Christians are all indwelt by the Holy Spirit, Jesus differs from us only in degree. He is, in a way, a super-saint but not God incarnate. His true divinity and the unity of His person as the eternal Son were, in effect, denied. Nestorius was declared a heretic and his teaching declared inadequate to the facts and to the work of redemption and therefore false.
    2. The heretical teaching of Eutyches was addressed at the 4th Ecumenical Council meeting in Chalcedon, in A.D. 450, and was also denied. He taught that Jesus' humanity was absorbed into Jesus' divinity and a sort of mixed being, dominantly divine, came about. He was neither simply divine nor human in the usual sense. Jesus was a third thing, a mixture. This denied that Jesus remained fully God and fully man in one person. But this is not the Jesus of the

New Testament, the mediator of salvation, nor the Lord of the Church.

3. Some have concluded that this is all philosophical speculation and a waste of time. In fact it is not speculation at all but the Church's effort to understand the facts that are before us in the Scriptures and in our experience as Christians. It is "faith seeking understanding" as Augustine and Anselm have said. The Church's teaching on this is a faithful celebration of and witness to both the truth and the mystery of the Incarnation. At the same time, the Church's teaching gives us a clear indication of inadequate and false ways to understand Jesus. These we are to avoid, for they are not only false to the facts, but they also undercut the Gospel and its saving benefits.

Sadly, these false paths seem to keep on being reinvented in the history of the Church. There really is no excuse for our going down these false theological paths again.

Excursus: The Christological Decisions in the First Four Councils

It will be helpful if we briefly summarize the Christological decisions of the Church found in the first four Ecumenical Councils in historical order. We will list each council and where it took place, when it took place, the teacher whose teaching was rejected, the positive decision about Jesus the Christ, and the relevance of that decision for the Gospel of salvation

1. The First Ecumenical Council took place in Nicaea in A.D. 325. The heretical teacher was Arius who denied the divinity of Christ. The decision of the Council regarding Christ was that He was truly God. And the relevance to the Gospel is that only God in Christ could save us. If Christ were not God, He would be but our example and we would have to create our own righteousness before God, which is both impossible and a denial of the Gospel.

2. The Second Ecumenical Council took place in Constantinople in A.D. 385. The heretical teacher was the godly Bishop Apollinarius, who denied the full humanity of Christ. The Council's decision regarding Christ was that He was fully human. The relevance of that for the Gospel is that if He were not fully human, He could not represent us on the Cross nor serve as our example for godly living. In addition, such a view seems docetic. It suggests that for us to be saved we must finally deny some part of our humanity. "What is not assumed is not redeemed." A partially human Jesus is neither faithful to the Scriptures nor to the Gospel of grace.

3. The Third Ecumenical Council took place in Ephesus in A.D. 431. The heretical teacher was Nestorius, who presented a Jesus in whom were two persons and two natures. The unity of His person was lost and no incarnation really took place. He could only be understood as a sort of super-saint, who is at best an example for us to follow. The Council declared Nestorius' teaching to be a heresy and declared that Jesus was one person, the second person of the Trinity and not two persons. The relevance of this decision is that we have a Savior and not simply an example. Were Nestorius' teaching allowed to stand, we sinners are cast back again on our own righteousness which cannot stand before God, Who is "of purer eyes than to behold evil" (Habakkuk 1:13). This is a denial of the Gospel.

In addition, since no real union took place, no incarnation, a docetic tendency is also involved here, in that God did not really fully identify with us. Human life and the stuff of matter and history is either unworthy or incapable of redemption. Faith becomes an escape from life, not its redemption. This may apply to some Eastern mystic religions but it is contrary to the Gospel.

4. The Fourth Ecumenical Council took place in Chalcedon in A.D. 450. The heretical teacher was Eutyches, who taught that in the Incarnation Jesus'

humanity was absorbed into His divinity so that in the end He was neither simply God nor simply a man but some sort of "hybrid" or third thing. The Council declared that a heresy. Such a Jesus would be no mediator. He would be unlike both God and mankind and relate neither to God nor to mankind, like a bridge that abutted neither bank of the river. In essence divinity gobbles up humanity and salvation is absorption not redemption. This has little to do with the Gospel.

Concerning Jesus, the Fathers of the Council declared that in the Incarnation, Jesus remained and remains in both of His natures, divine and human, each undefiled and unmixed, both being unified in His Person, the Second Person of the Trinity.

The relevance for salvation is that in Him we find our entire humanity affirmed and redeemed, not absorbed into the divine infinity. Rather than obliteration, the Gospel brings about reconciliation with God in Christ. God as God unites us to Himself by the Holy Spirit in the Son, Who is divine and human in His one person.

As stated earlier, some have misunderstood the purpose of these controversies and what the Councils were seeking to do. They were not trying to remove the mystery of the Incarnation, but rather to describe its nature and relationship to the Gospel of salvation, as best they could, and thereby to protect it from being turned into something other than what God has actually accomplished in the Incarnation for the salvation of fallen mankind. These four decisions point out boundaries of understanding and block the ways that deny the Incarnation and the Gospel. They invite us to worship and to wonder at the mystery of the Lord Jesus and to receive His saving work on our behalf by faith with profound gratitude and praise.

Implications

Many of the implications of the Incarnation can be found in previous sections of this Article and in the excursus on the first four Ecumenical Councils. We will only emphasize the following two points:

A. It is important to keep in mind that the gracious self-humbling of the eternal Son in assuming our human nature was for the purpose of His saving work. His person and His saving work are all of one piece, all for us and our salvation. The grace that led Him to identify with us in the Incarnation, extends His identification with us into the waters of John's baptism for sinners and ultimately to the Cross where He bore our sins in His own body in our place. He came to do the work the Father had sent Him to do and bent low, even to the depth of the Cross to do it. Therefore thanksgiving must be added to wonder as we render to Him the praise that He so richly deserves.

B. There is an ethical dimension to keep in mind. We read in Scripture that we are to have that mind in us which is in Christ Jesus, Who became one of us, to take the form of a servant, humbling Himself even unto a despised and torturous death. Like Christ, we are invited to find meaning in humbly serving one another, placing others' interests before our own. We are even to be concerned for those who would harm us. This service, done in humility, includes our desire and effort to seek their reconciliation with God, Who in Christ has come seeking them.

2. The Atonement
Teaching Point 2 of this Article makes two basic assertions concerning Jesus' work upon the Cross:

A. Jesus truly suffered, was crucified, died and was buried.

B. Jesus bore the penalty of our sins on the Cross, propitiated the wrath of God, reconciled the Father to us, and offered a sacrifice, not only for original guilt, but also for all the actual sins of men.

A. Jesus truly suffered, was crucified, died and was buried.
Explanation

This first point is simple: it really happened. There should be little doubt that Jesus suffered, and suffered greatly. The final week of Jesus' earthly ministry is appropriately referred to as the "Passion Week," for there was no make-believe about the deep suffering of that last week. It was a week that included the agony in the Garden of Gethsemane, His rejection by the elders of Israel, the betrayal of Pilate, the mocking and humiliation by the soldiers, and the scourging. It was a week that culminated in the cruel agony of the Cross. His death followed and He was buried in the tomb of Joseph of Arimathea.

Popular Jewish expectation did not expect the Messiah to suffer and die a cruel death. In fact, the Gnostics held that the spirit of Jesus left Jesus and entered into another man before the actual crucifixion: Jesus did not suffer on the Cross. To this day, Islam denies that Jesus was actually crucified. They hold the view that God would not permit one of His holy prophets to undergo such pain and rejection. It was someone else that they crucified on the Cross, not Jesus.

Contrary to these views, the New Testament writers make the opposite point. God not only permitted His Son to suffer, the Father sent the Son to suffer at the hands of wicked men and to be crucified. And those who crucified the Lord of Glory did not act for themselves alone; they represent all of fallen mankind. It was by our hands that He was crucified and at the same time, it was for us that He died. Therefore the biblical writers and the early Christians did not suppress the fact of Jesus' crucifixion. Quite the opposite: the Passion and Cross of Christ Jesus became the center of their message, of the Good News. They "gloried" in the Cross. Jesus really did suffer and die.

For their news to really be news it had to be about something that actually happened. The truth of history is that Jesus truly did suffer, was crucified, died and was buried.

Biblical Foundations

And they crucified him and divided his garments among them, casting lots for them, to decide what each should take. And it was the third hour when they crucified him. Mark 15:24-25

This Jesus, delivered up according to the definite plan and foreknowledge of God, you crucified and killed by the hands of lawless men. Acts 2:23

Implications

A. The first point is to affirm once again that we are not dealing with mere theory or timeless mythology but objective, historic fact. Around two thousand years ago outside the gates of Jerusalem, for our sake, Jesus the Son of God, Who had taken human nature to Himself from the Virgin Mary, died a cruel, agonizing, criminal's death. Tacitus stated that Jesus "suffered the extreme penalty under one of our procurators." Christian Faith rests completely on the actuality of this event with all of its biblical meaning and accomplishment. He really suffered, died and was buried, and because He did the benefits of His death for us are also real.

B. Christ's Cross is a costly gift of grace. We can't help but be aware of the cost of that grace. God's grace in Christ is far from "cheap"; we have been purchased not with gold or silver but with the precious blood of the Son of God. Gratitude therefore becomes a central motive in the Christian life.

B. Jesus bore the penalty of our sins on the Cross, propitiated the wrath of God, reconciled the Father to us, and offered a sacrifice, not only for original guilt, but also for all the actual sins of men.

Explanation

Having affirmed the fact of the Cross, we turn to the theological meaning of the Son's death upon the Cross. Why did the Father, in love, will the Son to die on the Cross at the hands of sinful humanity? Why did the Son, in love, give Himself up to death for us?

It was not that the Father was wrathful toward the Son, for the Son was and is always well-pleasing in His sight. Nor was it that God did not love us while we were sinners and not yet reconciled to Him. In fact, just the opposite is the case. Several of the best-known biblical texts about the Cross stress that the Cross is an action proceeding from God's love and therefore revealing the fullness of God's love for sinful humanity. On the Cross, the Father commends His love to us by giving His Son to die so that we need not perish under His judgment. And the Son, loving us, gives Himself for us by dying on the Cross for the same reason.

The central meaning of the Cross is that, in His love, God substitutes Himself for us in the Son. And on the Cross, He deals with His wrath or judicial condemnation that rests upon us as sinners, and He does this for His name's sake as well as for our sake as sinners. Since God is holy, He is personally and morally offended by sin. And as the Judge of all the earth, He must see sin condemned and punished, justice done and righteousness honored. "Shall not the Judge of all the earth do right?" (Genesis 18:25, KJV). This stress on righteousness, justice and moral integrity is central in the biblical witness to the character and reign of God. Nowhere is it suggested that God can look upon and ignore or wink at moral evil. God even takes His own chosen people into exile, in judgment, because of their idolatry and consequent immorality. And ultimately in

His love, He sends His own Son to bear His judgment of sinful humanity upon the Cross.

Therefore Jesus, the incarnate Son, hung in our place on the Cross and bore our punishment under the judicial wrath of God. He did this so that reconciliation and judicial righteousness might be offered to us in Christ as a gift of God's mercy, utterly undeserved and unattainable by any works on our part.

The teaching that Jesus was taking our place under the judgment of God is repeated often in the New Testament. Its meaning is explained in a variety of rich metaphors, each of which is worthy of sustained meditation. The range of the metaphors is wide. The biblical writers take every area of human experience captive in order to interpret Christ's substitutionary work on the Cross.

They draw upon Israel's worship. Using terms of worship and sacrifice, Jesus is referred to as the sacrificial lamb, the Passover sacrifice, the great annual sacrifice of Atonement. Often we read of His blood being poured out. The blood of Jesus is mentioned often in our hymns.

The biblical writers also look to the judicial system, to the language of the law court. Jesus upon the Cross is seen as our judicial substitute, for He bore in His own body on the tree the judicial curse that was due to us who have transgressed the Law of God, in heart, mind and deed. We read that since, like sheep, we have all gone our own way and not God's way, the Lord laid on Him, the Suffering Servant, the iniquity of us all.

These writers look to Jews' and Gentiles' experience of slavery. Jesus' death on the Cross is viewed and interpreted in economic terms saying that on the Cross Jesus paid the ransom price that set us free from enslavement to sin and Satan and restored us to our rightful freedom that is found in God's ownership and our service to Him. This price was not silver or gold but the precious blood of Christ.

In a different metaphor of substitution, we read that He

drank the cup of the wrath of God that we might drink the cup of salvation.

The biblical writers use these various explanatory metaphors almost interchangeably, centering as they do in the solemn and glorious note of Christ dying in our place and for our salvation. All of the great Reformers, the classic Anglican Prayer Book tradition, and the Articles join together with the New Testament to make the sin-bearing work of Christ on the Cross central to the entire work of Christ.

Some have objected that the Article's phrase, "reconcile the Father to us," is misleading because in the New Testament the ministry of reconciliation refers to God's offer of reconciliation to us and not of His reconciling Himself to us. That observation is true, but one-sided. What the objectors fail to note is that God's offer of reconciliation to us is based on the already accomplished work of the Cross, in which God had first borne the price of His judicial judgment and had on the Cross reconciled Himself to us. If that were not true, we would have to reject vast tracts of the Old and New Testaments, and by far the largest part of the New Testament teaching on the Cross.

All of this teaching on the Cross sketched out above is what is involved when Article 2 asserts that Christ was crucified "to reconcile His Father to us, and to be a sacrifice, not only for original guilt, but also for all actual sins of men."

Biblical Foundations

Who has believed what they heard from us? And to whom has the arm of the Lord been revealed? For he grew up before him like a young plant, and like a root out of dry ground; he had no form or majesty that we should look at him, and no beauty that we should desire him. He was despised and rejected by men; a man of sorrows, and acquainted with grief; and as one from whom men hide their faces he was despised, and we esteemed him not.

Surely he has borne our griefs and carried our sorrows; yet we esteemed him stricken, smitten by God, and afflicted. But he was wounded for our transgressions; he was crushed for our iniquities; upon him was the chastisement that brought us peace, and with his stripes we are healed. All we like sheep have gone astray; we have turned every one to his own way; and the Lord has laid on him the iniquity of us all. Isaiah 53:1-6

But now the righteousness of God has been manifested apart from the law, although the Law and the Prophets bear witness to it— the righteousness of God through faith in Jesus Christ for all who believe. For there is no distinction: for all have sinned and fall short of the glory of God, and are justified by his grace as a gift, through the redemption that is in Christ Jesus, whom God put forward as a propitiation by his blood, to be received by faith. This was to show God's righteousness, because in his divine forbearance he had passed over former sins. It was to show his righteousness at the present time, so that he might be just and the justifier of the one who has faith in Jesus. Romans 3:21-26

But God shows his love for us in that while we were still sinners, Christ died for us. Romans 5:8

Therefore, we are ambassadors for Christ, God making his appeal through us. We implore you on behalf of Christ, be reconciled to God. For our sake he made him to be sin who knew no sin, so that in him we might become the righteousness of God. 2 Corinthians 5:20-21

Christ redeemed us from the curse of the law by becoming a curse for us—for it is written, "Cursed is everyone who is hanged on a tree." Galatians 3:13

He is the propitiation for our sins, and not for ours only but also for the sins of the whole world. 1 John 2:2

Knowing that you were ransomed from the futile ways inherited from your forefathers, not with perishable things such as silver or gold, but with the precious blood of

Christ, like that of a lamb without blemish or spot. 1 Peter 1:18-19

False Teachings Denied/Objections Answered
   1. There have been some New Testament scholars in the 19th century, even into the 20th century, who objected to using the word "propitiation" with reference to Christ's work on the Cross. It was seen to be a pagan concept and unworthy of the biblical picture of God. When we see in the Cross, however, that it is God, the Father in the Son, Who is dealing with His own righteousness and judicial judgment upon our sin on our behalf, due to His love for us, it is no longer necessary for us to explain away the biblical language that speaks of the Cross as directed toward God. We can let words that would naturally be translated as "propitiation" remain that way and not as "expiation" as was done in some translations in the 20th century (e.g. RSV).
   We hasten to underline the fact that the biblical understanding of "propitiation" is in great contrast to the understanding of "propitiation" in pagan religion. In pagan religion, man appeases the anger of an arbitrary and immoral god or gods using some form of external sacrifice, whether animal or grain or financial. That is not how "propitiation" is used in the New Testament. It is not we who propitiate God, but He Who does the propitiating. And certainly we are not dealing with an arbitrary, capricious God. It is God Himself in His righteousness Who acts in justice and love on the Cross, and reveals Himself to be just while justifying those who put their trust in the righteous, substitutionary work of Jesus on the Cross. Nor is the object of the propitiation the capricious anger of the gods, but rather the moral and judicial wrath of God against evil and sin. Further, the sacrifice is not some innocent third party but God Himself offering Himself on our behalf.
   You may ask, what then is the common point between the use of the term "propitiation" in pagan culture and its

use in biblical tradition? Why did the biblical writers want to use the word "propitiation" at all? The common point is that in both the biblical and the pagan use "propitiation" is directed to God and His wrath. Propitiation in biblical use assumes that God is the holy, righteous Judge of all the earth and that He must condemn sin. "Expiation" cannot replace "propitiation," for "expiation" speaks of God covering our sin and not dealing with His own wrath. In "expiation" the attention is upon us. In "propitiation" the attention is on God. Classic 19th century theological liberalism did not believe that God had any judicial wrath to be propitiated. The biblical writers tell us otherwise. Justice matters and it matters eternally.

What the liberal scholars did not take into consideration adequately is that when the biblical writers use a word drawn from the contemporary culture, they give it a bath, so to speak, to clean it up so they can use it in ways that are appropriate to the biblical way of viewing everything in the light of God as revealed in Israel and Christ. It is revelation, not culture, that has the last word in the Bible. Happily in this respect, contemporary translations of the New Testament are returning to the penetrating insight of the Church Catholic as well as the Continental and English Reformers and the teaching of Article 2, by reaffirming the place of propitiation in the work of Christ.

2. Some scholars in the "New Understanding of Paul" movement seem to suggest that Paul was not interested in "the justification of sinners" in the traditional sense, and therefore that he was not teaching the penal, substitutionary aspect of the atonement which provides the basis for "justification." The Apostle Paul, these scholars hold, was primarily, if not solely, interested in Gentiles and Jews being able to be united in table fellowship in Christ. And the good works against which Paul spoke were not moral works of self-justification, caused by an over-sensitive conscience. Rather, they were specific Jewish ceremonial

distinctive rites and practices that marked out Jewish Messianic believers in Jesus as distinct from Gentile believers in Christ and that separated them from Gentile Christians. These scholars believe that St. Paul was teaching that these Jewish practices had been fulfilled and done away in Christ, so that believers in Christ, whether Jew or Gentile, being united in Christ, could and should exhibit that unity at the Lord's Supper and in congregational fellowship. Paul himself practiced this.

We agree entirely that Paul was concerned that Jew and Gentile sit at table together. His great effort to see that the Gentile congregations sent help to the Jewish Mother Church in Jerusalem was to make that point, as well as offering needed help. We thank these scholars for emphasizing that deep concern of Paul, which has in large measure been lost to contemporary Western Church life. It is also true that the ceremonial laws, viewed as ways of keeping Israel distinct while Israel awaited the coming of the Messiah, are no longer binding and have been rendered optional; they may be freely observed, as Messianic congregations do today.

We deny, however, that Paul was not interested in the substitutionary, penal aspect of the Cross, which provides God's basis for His justification of sinners. Paul's letters to the Romans and to the Galatians make the point that it is precisely because both Jews and Gentiles are sinners, and are justified in and by Christ, that they may and must sit down together at the table of the Holy Lord. His righteousness is reckoned to both and is their wedding garment at the feast. It is the crucified and risen Lord Who invites us all to His table to partake of the Lord's Supper. It was He Who said, "Do this in remembrance of Me," referring to the dramatic reenactment of the Cross by which work, received in faith, we are all justified. Justification is not a minor point in Paul's mind or in Jesus' mind; justification is a precondition for anyone's sitting at the Lord's Table at all.

3. Perhaps the most repeated objection made to the penal substitutionary aspect of the Cross of Christ is that it is immoral of God to lay the punishment of our sins on an innocent third party, in this case on His Son. There are three things that need to be said in response to that objection.

First, Jesus became incarnate precisely to take our sins upon Himself. Having the wrath of God laid upon Him was neither arbitrary nor without His consent.

Second, He was not a third party but rather as God the Son, He is God taking our place. There is no third party, just God and us. Thus the penal substitutionary aspect of the Cross is appropriately compared to one person laying down His life in sacrificial love for another. We applaud that in human life. How much more should we applaud God and give Him the glory for doing that for us in Christ.

Third, consider the alternative to Christ being our judicial substitute. If God does not deal with our sin in Christ, as the Judge of all the earth He must deal with our sin directly with us. Those who object to the substitutionary penal aspect of the Cross must either deny the radical seriousness of sin, as did 19th and early 20th century liberalism, or stand before God in the final judgment in the tattered rags of their own righteousness. To deny the seriousness of sin is to be in for a terrible surprise at the final judgment. To stand in one's own righteousness is not to stand at all.

Implications

A. In the Cross, all the attributes of God receive full recognition. Righteousness and love are both affirmed as harmoniously working together in the Cross. Because God does not sacrifice righteousness in order to be loving and forgiving, we must not either. The present tendency to lower the standards in order to remove guilt will not work in a moral universe. The Christian Faith affirms both holiness and love in the ordering of society and life.

B. The penal judgment borne by Christ on our behalf is a completed work, full, sufficient and finished. This is the frequent emphasis of the Letter to the Hebrews. It is implied in the very concept of substitution. The peace with God on which Christian Faith rests is grounded on this sufficiency. To be anxious about one's right standing with God while trusting in Christ as one's Savior is to fail to grasp the sufficiency of the Cross or our union with, or being in, Christ. This sufficiency and union with Christ is such as to cover not only the guilt of the race into which we are born and of which we are members, but also to cover the guilt of our sinful hearts as well as our personal acts of sin, whether done by commission or omission, whether in the past, present or future.

We will discuss the doctrine of sin under Article 9. Suffice it to say here that the gracious work of Christ is utterly sufficient for all our needs as sinners. This sufficiency is not meant, however, to make light of sin. The Cross of Christ actually reveals the depth of its evil. The sufficiency of the Cross provides no excuse for sinning. This error of antinomianism will be treated under Article 7.

C. The Cross of Christ provides a tremendous affirmation of the value of human life. Only a humanity deeply treasured and loved by God would be rescued by God at such a great cost to Himself. It is by the precious blood of Christ that we can begin to measure both the depth of sin and the preciousness of human life to God. This of course has all sorts of moral implications about how we treat each other and particularly the weak, the marginalized and the lost.

Excursus: The Chief New Testament Themes concerning the Cross and the Classic Theories of the Atonement

There are four central themes concerning the Cross of Christ in the New Testament. These four are: 1) the love of Christ revealed; 2) the victory of Christ over Satan, sin and death; 3) the penal substitution of Christ dying in our place; and 4) the Cross as an example or pattern of life for believers to follow. The first three of these themes are intertwined in the apostolic writings and are different aspects of Christ's accomplishment on the Cross for us. The last theme has its focus on how we Christians are to live out our union with Christ by the power of the Spirit.

Each of the three classic theories of the atonement, "Christus Victor," "Penal Substitution," and "Moral Influence," builds on one of the first three themes.

The first of these classic theories of the atonement was taught by the early Fathers. It stresses the sovereignty of God and His victory over all created powers that warred against Him and His rule. It is called the "Christus Victor" theory of the atonement, for Christ as the victor defeated the worst that the fallen principalities and powers, sin, Satan and death could do. He triumphed by His life, His Cross and Resurrection. Jesus did not succumb to temptation. He did not avoid the battle and took the full onslaught of sin, Satan and death upon Himself, and in the end, He rose victorious, once for all and over all. The victory is ours in Him.

The second classic theory is the "Penal Substitution" theory of the Cross as we have set it forth above, Christ in our place, bearing the punishment of our sins in His own body on the Cross. It is often referred to as the Anselmian theory because after the Scriptures, it was first set forth by Anselm in the 11th century, in his book *Cur Deus Homo?* ("Why the God-man?"). Anselm used the feudal concept of honor to express the doctrine. Honor was owed by the inferior to those who were superior to him, the serf to the noble, all to the king, and everyone to God. When honor was not paid, then a price of restitution was owed and had to be paid. The nature and amount of restitution to be rendered was proportionate to the honor due the one offended. Since we had sinned against an infinite God our debt was infinite, which we as finite creatures could never pay.

Anselm taught that Christ assumed human nature and became the God-man, in order to take our place and pay our debt to God. Our debt was due to our sin in failing to give God the total reverence and obedience that is His right. The debt we owed was our death and eternal punishment since we had sinned against the God of infinite worth. Thus in dying in our place Christ, Himself divine and infinite and human, rendered to God, in our place and through our human nature, the infinite satisfaction and honor which was God's due.

This doctrine was stated in the more biblical terms of justice and righteousness by the 16th century Reformers, who sought in all things to conform their doctrine and thought to Scripture.

The third classic theory is usually referred to as the "Moral Influence" theory. It is also referred to as the Abelardian theory because Peter Abelard taught it in the 12th century. This view holds that in laying down His life for us, even while were still sinners and enemies, Christ so revealed the depth and fullness of the love of God toward us that upon our hearing of this sacrificial love of God through the Gospel, we are moved inwardly to a response of repentance and love to God. Love begets love. He thereby effected a reconciliation or at-one-ment between the loving God and us who, as sinners, had been estranged from God. Abelard had no place for the judicial wrath of God visited upon the Son in our place, which judicial wrath he denied.

Since each of these theories builds upon one of the biblical aspects of Christ's work on the Cross, they are biblical in their chief affirmation. However, in ignoring or even denying what the other two theories affirm, they err in what they deny or ignore. A truly biblical doctrine of the Cross will include all three aspects and will lead to our living a Cross-shaped life in gratitude.

Conclusion

This Article, like the second article of the Apostles' Creed, stands in the center of the Christian revelation. The objective, finished and sufficient work of Christ on the Cross provides the foundation for the new life of salvation in Christ in the Spirit. We shall find other Articles referring back to the content of this Article; we particularly think of Articles 15 and 31.

It would be hard to overestimate the importance of the content of this Article. It is very encouraging that there was no fundamental disagreement between our Anglican Reformers, Rome, Orthodoxy, and the other Churches of the Reformation on the main teaching concerning the person and the objective work of Christ on the Cross. Here we stand together on common ground.

ARTICLE 3

Of the Going Down of Christ into Hell

As Christ died for us, and was buried, so also it is to be believed that he went down into hell.

Introduction

At the time of the Reformation, this Article had been part of the Apostles' Creed in the West for some eight hundred years. Since it is probably referred to in Scripture and was an accepted part of the Catholic Faith, and since there was no controversy about it, the Anglican Reformers simply note their agreement with the Ancient Faith and make no further comment.

The Teaching of Article 3

1. After He died and before He was raised, our Lord in the Spirit went down to hell.

Explanation

The teaching of this brief Article seems straightforward. After He died and before He was raised, our Lord in His Spirit went down to hell. However, the meaning of "hell" is not clarified and nothing is said about what Christ did when He arrived there. This has led to a variety of interpretations of this statement found in both the Athanasian and Apostles' Creeds. It is not in the Nicene Creed.

A. This Article is not as weighty and central as the other Articles in this First Section of the Articles.

This event is ambiguously referred to in the New Testament and then in a somewhat marginal manner. Christ's going down to hell was not part of the central proclamation of the Gospel or *kerygma*. It only slowly found its way into the creeds of the Church, being first included in the Athanasian Creed in the middle of the 5th century and finding universal inclusion in the Apostles' Creed as late as the 8th century.

We ought not neglect it, however, for it was widely held in the Church long before it was included in the Creeds.

Perhaps we can best sum up the status of this Article by citing Thomas Rogers, the first commentator on the Articles. He wrote of this Article in 1607 as follows, "That Christ went down into hell all sound Christians, both in former days and now living, do acknowledge; howbeit in the interpretation of the Article there is not that consent as were to be wished" (p. 60).

B. What is meant by "hell"?

Is it *Sheol*, the realm of the dead, the place to which both the saved and the lost go? Or is it *Gehenna*, the place of final condemnation, that is, the hell in which only the lost go and finally dwell? This ambiguity in the word has led to the two main types of interpretation of the Article and of the Creeds.

Concerning this 3rd Article, the Latin edition of the Thirty-Nine Articles, issued at the same time as the English edition and possessing equal authority, uses the phrase *ad inferos*, which is best translated as "to those below." This would seem to point in the direction of Sheol or the realm of the dead. This view is strengthened by the wording of the Article in an earlier version of 1553 written by Cranmer, alluding to the account in First Peter, which most exegetes understand to refer to Sheol. However, this Article remains ambiguous.

C. The interpretations of the Article of the Creeds fall into two types.

The first type of interpretation holds that Jesus, in the

period between His death on the Cross, after His burial and before His Resurrection, went in the Spirit to Sheol, the place of the dead there to preach. This first type has a variety of interpretations concerning what Christ said and to whom in Sheol.

1. The Eastern Fathers tended to speak of Jesus as evangelizing the unbelieving dead, particularly the noble pagans who had not had the Gospel preached to them during their lifetime.

2. The Western Fathers tended to speak of Jesus declaring the Gospel and His victory to the patriarchs and prophets and the Old Covenant believers to bring them into His nearer presence or into paradise.

3. Continuing an early patristic tradition Luther and the Lutherans have tended to speak of the "harrowing of Hell" in which Christ completes his victory over Satan and makes clear to Satan and the damned their coming final state.

The second of the main types places Jesus in Gehenna or hell, the final destiny of the damned. Calvin held this interpretation. Calvin taught that Jesus' descent into hell was a reference to His having borne the hell of God-forsakenness in our place, as our substitute. The "Cry of Dereliction" (My God, My God, why hast thou forsaken me?) is cited in support of this view. The Reformed tradition has generally tended to follow Calvin in this matter.

More recently, a third type of interpretation has surfaced. It is based on the view that "hell" in the Creeds is really "Hades." Hades often refers simply to the grave. Psalm 16:10 and Acts 2:25ff are often interpreted to do so. Jesus really died, but the Father would not let the body of His holy One, the Son, undergo corruption in the grave. The meaning of this part of the Creed then would be to underline the reality of Jesus' death and to point forward to the fact of the Resurrection.

This more modern interpretation of the creedal statement has two difficulties. First, it seems to make the statement of the Creeds redundant, for in the Apostles' Creed it follows the statement that Christ "was crucified, dead, and buried." That seems a sufficient statement concerning the grave. Why then add another statement with the same meaning? Second, this interpretation would seem to contradict Scripture, particularly the statements of 1 Peter 3-4. However, a recent interpretation of the texts in 1 Peter 3-4 holds that these texts do not refer to Jesus going down to Sheol, hell or Hades, and therefore they are irrelevant to interpreting the Creed.

What then does this interpretation hold that 1 Peter 3:18-20 and 4:6 teach? It teaches that the pre-incarnate eternal Son came down in the Spirit to speak through Noah as Noah preached to his generation. Those of Noah's day who scoffed and rejected the Lord's preaching were imprisoned by sin (3:19) and dead to the Lord (4:6).

D. What is the Anglican interpretation of this Article?

It is likely that the Anglican Fathers were aware of the two main types of interpretation of the Creed, since they were circulating in the churches at that time, and had them in mind. Aware of the ambiguity of the statement in the Creed, they wished to allow for a variety of interpretations to be taught in the Church, since all of the usual interpretations were congruent with the main doctrines of the Faith and the references in Scripture. Therefore, they were content to simply affirm the event in this 3rd Article and leave its interpretation open. The new interpretation of 1 Peter would not have been known to them.

Biblical Foundations

For you will not abandon my soul to Sheol, or let your holy one see corruption. Psalm 16:10

For David says concerning him, 'I saw the Lord always before me, for he is at my right hand that I may not be shaken.' Acts 2:25

For you will not abandon my soul to Hades, or let your Holy One see corruption. Acts 2:27

He foresaw and spoke about the resurrection of the Christ, that he was not abandoned to Hades, nor did his flesh see corruption. This Jesus God raised up, and of that we all are witnesses. Acts 2:31-32

For Christ also suffered once for sins, the righteous for the unrighteous, that he might bring us to God, being put to death in the flesh but made alive in the spirit, in which he went and proclaimed to the spirits in prison, because they formerly did not obey, when God's patience waited in the days of Noah, while the ark was being prepared, in which a few, that is, eight persons, were brought safely through water. 1 Peter 3:18-20

For this is why the gospel was preached even to those who are dead, that though judged in the flesh the way people are, they might live in the spirit the way God does. 1 Peter 4:6

Implications

A. The first application would be for us to be charitable toward those whose interpretation does not agree with ours. While that is always a good policy, it is particularly appropriate in this case, since this is not about a core doctrine and since the texts cited above are susceptible to interpretations ranging from denying any descent of Jesus beyond entering the grave to the two major types outlined above.

B. Whatever else is affirmed here we can agree that Jesus' identification with us in the Incarnation was such as to undergo the full experience of death, as well as to bear the full judgment of God upon sinners in our place. While this may not have been the primary intention of this Article, it is surely assumed by it. When we die we do not tread a path in which our Savior has not gone before and redeemed for us.

C. There can be little doubt that, according to the New

Testament, those Old Covenant believers as well as all who now die in the Lord are joined with Christ in paradise. It is a great comfort to us to know that our loved ones who have died in Christ are now in His nearer presence.

D. Some have seen here the assertion of a first hearing of the Gospel to those who, due to our neglect in mission or for some other reason, have not had an opportunity to hear the Gospel. God is just; His love is for all mankind, and the Gospel has been sent to all. The doctrine of an after death "first chance," taught by some of the Fathers in connection with this creedal statement, seeks to give expression to the wideness of His love. It is hard to dismiss this concern out of hand. However, where Scripture makes no clear promises we dare not claim certainty.

Such "first chance" teaching needs to be clearly distinguished from the teaching of a "second chance," which holds that there is a second chance (or even unlimited chances) after death available to those who have knowingly rejected the Gospel in this life. The doctrine of a "second chance" is generally regarded by orthodox believers to be contrary to Scripture.

Conclusion

The assertion of Christ's descent in some sense is clear from Scripture. Its meaning is not clearly revealed. All of the above interpretations are in accord with the Gospel and of comfort to believers and may be taught.

ARTICLE 4

Of the Resurrection of Christ

Christ did truly arise again from death, and took again his body, with flesh, bones, and all things appertaining to the perfection of Man's nature; wherewith he ascended into heaven, and there sitteth, until he return to judge all men at the last day.

Introduction

In Article 4, we continue to address the heart of the Gospel and of the Apostles' preaching. Christ's Resurrection brings to conclusion the great finished work that our Savior has done for our salvation. Article 4 also directs us to His present kingly and priestly ministry in Heaven as well as to His future royal coming again in majesty to judge the living and the dead. The inclusion of so many very important themes makes the commentary on this Article rather extensive as is the case with Articles 1 and 2.

The Teaching of Article 4

Here are the teaching points for this Article:

1. Jesus Christ was actually raised from the dead.

2. His Resurrection was bodily and objective.

3. His Resurrection is of a final, or eschatological, nature, which led to His Ascension into glory in Heaven.

4. The Lord now sits at the right hand of God where He hiddenly governs the universe, reigns in grace over the Church, and intercedes for His own.

5. On the Last Day, He will return to judge all persons, both the living and the dead.

1. Jesus Christ was actually raised from the dead.
Explanation

As stated in earlier Articles, the Christian Faith is an historical Faith. It is related to events that have actually happened in history. If the Good News is really to be "news," it must declare what has actually happened. Just as Jesus actually died and was buried, so He did actually rise from death, raised by His Heavenly Father.

Historical events leave historical evidence. What is the historical evidence for the Resurrection of Christ? We possess a great wealth of evidence. Lee Strobel, the apologist, notes that the Resurrection of Christ is "the best attested event of ancient history." What we offer here is but a summary of the strongest lines of historical evidence.

Historical evidence comes in two types. The first type focuses on the consequences of an event, or what the event caused. The second type examines the testimonies of witnesses to the event. Both types of evidence exist and support the historical actuality of Jesus' Resurrection.

We will move toward the Resurrection from the present walking back to the event; that is, we will move from the consequences back to the cause. Therefore, we begin with the present, with effects of the Resurrection with which we are all acquainted.

The most fundamental consequence of the Resurrection of Jesus is the rise of the Church. What but the Resurrection of Jesus could cause a band of dispirited followers to emerge as a continuing fellowship, proclaiming Jesus as Lord, led by eleven of the original twelve disciples? Keep in mind that these were the same disciples who had had deserted Him and who went into hiding behind closed doors when Jesus was arrested. The change in the disciples itself requires explanation, for the Twelve appear immediately on the scene worshiping Jesus as the risen Lord, and proclaiming the Good News of Jesus in the very city where they once hid in fear. By their preaching, the Christian community grew and exists today. It is world-wide and growing, and this at a time when the great Roman Empire is no more.

Next, we note that this community worships on Sunday. This Church, originally composed entirely of Jews, not only worshiped on the Sabbath, as the Law required, but they worshiped on Sunday, or the First Day of the week, as well. The early Christians called this day "the Lord's Day." As Gentiles became Christians in large numbers and the community of Christ came to live increasingly outside Palestine, the Lord's Day replaced the Sabbath. What could explain this shift from observing the Sabbath on Saturday, in accordance with the Fourth Commandment, to observing Sunday, the First Day of the week, except the fact that Sunday is the day of the Resurrection of Jesus?

Then, there is the fact that every week, the Church gathers around the table of the Lord to celebrate the Lord's Supper, thereby to worship the living God: Father, Son, and Holy Spirit. This characteristic act of corporate worship is based upon the Last Supper of Jesus with the Twelve. One has to ask, how is it that the "Last Supper" did not prove to be the last of such gatherings? How has the Last Supper been changed into the Lord's Supper? In the life of the Church, it became and remains the Supper of the Risen Lord with His own. If Christ Jesus did not rise, what reason can we give for this liturgical transformation and continuing practice?

Reading the Scriptures, we find that in the New Testament writings, Jesus is worshiped as Lord. What would lead his disciples, being Jews and opposed to all idolatry, to join with Thomas in the act of worship, saying to Jesus, "my Lord and my God" except for His Resurrection? Is this not what St. Paul states in Romans when he declares that Jesus was "marked out" or declared

Son of God in power by Resurrection from the dead? If there is no Resurrection of Jesus, how then do we account for the high Christology of the New Testament that calls Jesus "Lord" in the fullest sense of that title?

To sum up, since historical consequences have an historical cause; we have listed abiding effects that we now know and experience that bear the signs of the historical Resurrection of Jesus etched deep within them as their cause and meaning.

Let us turn to the second type of evidence for historical events: personal witness. If we are to gain a clearer picture of Jesus' Resurrection and its nature we must ask the witnesses of key aspects of that event to tell us what they observed.

Personal witness is evaluated by three primary criteria: proximity, multiplicity, and reliability. Proximity deals with the nearness of the witness to the event. Were the witnesses at the scene or near the event so that they could give witness and not just hearsay? Multiplicity concerns the number of witnesses and whether they agree. Are there several or more witnesses whose testimony tells the same essential story? No two witnesses will tell the story in exactly the same way. We may expect differences of observation, wording, and of a sense of importance, but we should expect consistency in the essential contents. Reliability deals with the character and honesty of the witnesses themselves. Are the witnesses the sort of people who usually tell the truth? Would they have reason to lie in this situation?

First, let us consider the test of proximity. The best evidence is that of eye-witnesses and that is what we have in the New Testament.

We can arrive at the earliest eyewitness of the Apostles by a careful examination of 1 Corinthians 15:1-11, since it is the earliest historical account of the Resurrection of Jesus and of the preaching of the Apostles.

Paul was writing to a congregation that he founded in

approximately A.D. 55. This is some 25 years after the event of the Crucifixion and Resurrection of Jesus. He asserts that he is reminding them of the message he had brought to them some 10 years earlier when he first came to Corinth, preaching the Gospel in A.D. 44 or 45. This brings us to within 15 years of the event. Paul goes on to say that the message that he delivered to them then, so carefully and enthusiastically, was not peculiar to him; he had received it himself prior to bringing it to them. That which is written in 1 Corinthians 15 is pre-Pauline, prior to Paul. He received it.

When did Paul receive this Gospel? There are three points in Paul's life when he could have received the Gospel for the first time. The latest time is in A.D. 36; Paul tells us that after his encounter with the Risen Lord outside Damascus, he went to Arabia to reflect and to rethink his theology. His previous understanding had led him to persecute the Lord of Glory by persecuting Jesus' followers. At the end of three years, he went up to Jerusalem and there met with Peter and James. That meeting occurred in A.D. 36. So in that year, Paul was comparing his understanding of Jesus with Peter, the first of the apostolic eyewitnesses to the Resurrection. Paul tells us that all of the Apostles agreed on the Gospel and continued to preach it. Therefore it is certain that within six years of the events, Paul knew the common apostolic message of the Cross and Resurrection and proclaimed it. At this point Paul was personally aware of St. Peter's eyewitness which, along with the other original Apostles' eyewitness, is foundational to their life and preaching. Therefore, A.D. 36 is one point when Paul might claim to have first heard the apostolic Gospel.

However, we must step back to A.D. 33. This was but three years after the Resurrection. It was then that Paul encountered the Risen Lord outside Damascus. It was by this post-Ascension Resurrection appearance of Christ that Paul was made an eyewitness to the Resurrection and an

Apostle by the Risen Lord. Speaking of this event St. Paul said, "Am I not an apostle? Have I not seen Jesus our Lord?" (1 Corinthians 9:1). Only an eye-witness of the Resurrection could be an Apostle of the Risen Lord. Paul was then baptized by Ananias, who was sent to him by the Lord. Surely Ananias did not baptize him in utter silence. The early Church's practice was to catechize before baptizing. In addition, in the act of baptism, the Gospel was recited in a question and answer form. The statement of the Gospel found in 1 Corinthians 15:3-7 has a creedal shape and bears marks of its Jerusalem origins. Scholars believe it is likely that in this passage in 1 Corinthians we have the apostolic Gospel and witness to the Resurrection of Jesus already in a fixed baptismal formula that was used in Paul's baptism within three years of the events. Therefore, A.D. 33 is the second and most likely time when Paul could have said he had first received the apostolic Gospel.

But, we must go back earlier still, to A.D. 30. In that year, within weeks of the Resurrection of Jesus, we read of Paul's repeated encounter with the Apostles' eye-witness account of the Resurrection. Paul was present at the stoning of Stephen. Presumably even earlier he had already heard the apostolic claims, for he had become a persecutor of the Church, and one does not persecute without reason. At that time, Paul believed to his core that Jesus had been discredited by the crucifixion. Jesus had been shown to be a messianic pretender and blasphemer. Paul was offended and angered by the Apostles' claim that Jesus had been vindicated by the Father by His raising Jesus from the dead and that repentance and forgiveness of sins were being offered to all in His Name. As he sought out Christians in the synagogues to ban them as heretics, Paul must have heard the Gospel repeated time and again as the early Christians gave their testimony to the reason for the hope that was within them. Within weeks of the very events themselves, Paul heard the message of apostolic eye-witness through those early believers whom he was persecuting. He didn't believe them at that time, but he had heard the Gospel and heard of the Resurrection of Jesus.

We can summarize the above account as follows: within weeks of the events, through the early Christians and Stephen, Paul heard the claims of the apostolic witness to the Resurrection of Jesus. He was offended and did not believe that Jesus was the Christ. Three years later, while going to persecute Christians in Damascus, Paul met the Risen Lord, Who revealed to him the truth of the Gospel that he had already heard. At that time, he was baptized into the Gospel Faith and received the apostolic proclamation and eye-witness through a brief catechesis and through the fixed, creedal form used in his baptism, which we find written in 1 Corinthians 15. In the light of his encounter with the Risen Lord Jesus and his newfound faith, Paul spent three years in Arabia rethinking his understanding of the Old Testament Scriptures. He then went to Jerusalem to see those who were Apostles before him. He met with Peter and James in Jerusalem in A.D. 36. Having discussed with them their eye-witness and message, he was assured that he was in essential agreement with the preaching of all of the Apostles.

In this passage in 1 Corinthians, therefore, we have the earliest written account of the primitive, apostolic preaching of the Gospel, which contains the original Apostles' eye-witness to the Resurrection of Jesus. The Apostles' preaching of the crucifixion and Resurrection of Jesus is no "late tradition" that took decades to develop and become embellished in fanciful ways; this witness comes from the very events and from the Apostles themselves who were personally involved in the event.

We must add the witness of the Gospels, three of which were written before A.D. 70, and the Gospel of John, written some 20-plus years later. Matthew was himself an eye-witness, as was John. Peter's witness is the foundation of Mark's Gospel, Paul of Luke's, and the entire early community undergirds all four.

Therefore, taking Paul and the Gospels together, we have eye-witness testimony in rich measure. It is hard to imagine historical witness in closer proximity.

After proximity comes multiplicity. Do we have multiple witnesses that tell much the same story? Multiple witnesses are before us in 1 Corinthians 15:1-11. This Gospel summary ends with these words: "Whether, then, it was I or they, this is what we preach, and this is what you believed." Those who were Apostles before Paul and Paul himself all preached the same Gospel. The entire apostolic chorus sang the same song. Paul puts it in the present tense. The Apostles had been preaching the same Gospel for 25 years and were now preaching it at the time he wrote down this fixed summary statement of the Good News.

As one looks at the additional material in the other epistles, in the Acts of the Apostles where outlines of apostolic preaching are to be found, and in the Gospels where additional details are to be found, the same essential events are recounted. There are minor variations, i.e., how many angels are mentioned as appearing at the tomb and the locations of the various appearances of the Risen Lord are difficult to state in a simple chronological order, but the crucial details are the same. The eyewitnesses are multiple and tell the same essential story. Those who knew Him all agree: "He is risen! The Lord is risen indeed! He has appeared first unto Peter and then unto us all."

Finally, there is the test of reliability, of character. Are these witnesses truthful? Of that there can be little doubt. The apostolic witnesses all paid for their witness with their lives; they were all martyred, with the exception of John, and he was exiled. They sealed their witness, not only with honest lives and determined ministry, but also with their blood. People do not die for a witness that they have fabricated. One simply has to ask, what but the Resurrection of Jesus and His appearances unto them, along with His continued relationship with them in the Spirit could have changed these men from crushed, cowardly, frightened disciples into the bold witnesses and leaders that they became and persevered as such in the face of great opposition? There can be no doubt that the Apostles were utterly convinced that Jesus had risen and was their living Lord.

Article 4 sums up the evidence when it says, "Christ did truly arise from death." Only due to philosophical presupposition or prejudice can one deny or ignore the amount and the quality of this evidence that attests to the Resurrection of Jesus.

Biblical Foundations

For I delivered to you as of first importance what I also received: that Christ died for our sins in accordance with the Scriptures, that he was buried, that he was raised on the third day in accordance with the Scriptures, and that he appeared to Cephas, then to the twelve. Then he appeared to more than five hundred brothers at one time, most of whom are still alive, though some have fallen asleep. Then he appeared to James, then to all the apostles. Last of all, as to one untimely born, he appeared also to me. For I am the least of the apostles, unworthy to be called an apostle, because I persecuted the church of God. But by the grace of God I am what I am, and his grace toward me was not in vain. On the contrary, I worked harder than any of them, though it was not I, but the grace of God that is with me. Whether then it was I or they, so we preach and so you believed. 1 Corinthians 15:3-11

But in fact Christ has been raised from the dead, the first fruits of those who have fallen asleep. 1 Corinthians 15:20

Blessed be the God and Father of our Lord Jesus Christ! According to his great mercy, he has caused us to be born again to a living hope through the resurrection of Jesus Christ from the dead. 1 Peter 1:3

False Teaching Denied/Objections Answered

Some persons have denied the actual Resurrection of Jesus. They have offered other explanations to account for the proclamation of the Apostles. None are persuasive.

1. Some held that the women went to the wrong tomb, which was empty. That is unlikely, since the tomb of Joseph of Arimethea was a place known to them. Further, just the empty tomb by itself would not have sufficed to transform the disciples into Apostles and martyrs. They would still have been left with Mary's question, "Where have they laid my Lord?"

2. Others suggested that the Apostles were liars seeking personal benefits. But the personal benefits they received were hostility and death. And, besides, there were many who were still alive who had known Jesus and would spot a deception. Deceptions are hard to sustain over a period of time.

3. In the Scriptures we find an argument that the disciples paid the guards at the tomb to pretend to fall asleep, while the disciples stole and hid the body of Jesus. But how would that turn frightened disciples into bold Apostles?

4. Still others have suggested that Jesus was only wounded and that He revived in the tomb and came forth to revive the flagging spirits of the disciples. But a broken, wounded Jesus is not what would have transformed the disciples. Nor would such a recovery by a wounded Jesus have been a victory over the grave.

The conclusion to which we are driven, assuming one is open to the evidence, is that, as unique and amazing as it is, Jesus was actually raised from the dead. For Christians, this uniqueness is appropriate for Jesus Himself is unique and has carried out a unique, once-for-all-time and all-persons saving mission.

Implications

The applications of the historical fact of Jesus'

Resurrection are numerous. We state only some of the most significant implications:

A. The most obvious implication, already mentioned in the texts above, is Christian hope. The reality of death and the fear of ultimate loss of life are real, particularly in a secular age. To see one's loved ones die with no hope for eternity is excruciating. The fear of death for oneself can also be intense. Christians certainly know the grief and sadness of the loss of loved ones, but for Christians the experience of death is viewed in the context of ultimate hope. To die in Christ is to enter into the nearer presence of Christ, there to await the final Resurrection of the body and the cosmic fulfillment of God's purpose. We may grieve but not as those without hope, hope for others, for ourselves, and for God's final victory over all sin and evil, a victory already won once for all, in Christ's death, Resurrection, and Ascension.

B. Alongside of hope there is ultimate truth. It is in the Resurrection of Christ that the Apostles' eyes are opened to the true identity of Christ and to the final victory of God in Him. From the Resurrection on, things appear in a new light to the believers. Jesus is seen as the Son of God in power. The Cross can no longer be seen as the curse of a false messiah but is disclosed as Jesus' bearing our curse in His own body on the Tree. His entire ministry of teaching, exorcism, healing, and preaching of the Kingdom is now bathed in the light of the Father's vindication of the Son.

C. There are obvious hermeneutical or interpretational implications of Jesus' Resurrection as well. First, the Old Testament must now be read as fulfilled in the dying and rising of Jesus. And Jesus can only be fully understood as the One who fulfilled the promise of the Old Testament.

Second, in the risen Lord Jesus we have the key to a truer worldview. Everything must be seen in the light of His Resurrection and not the other way around. The Resurrection of Jesus does not fit into any frame of reference about reality of which His Resurrection itself is not the foundational revelation. The entire New Testament is written in the light of the Resurrection of Jesus.

Third, in the light of the Resurrection of Jesus, the contemporary worldview of secular Western culture must be seen as reductionist, incapable of dealing with the whole of reality, and in need of intellectual *metanoia* or repentance. Christians have an intellectual mission to the world, and not the least to the scholarly world. We must not hide the light of the Resurrection under a bushel or allow the Resurrection of Jesus to be pushed into a so-called private religious corner.

D. Reconciliation begins with the Resurrection of Jesus as Lord. In the Resurrection appearances to Apostles, Jesus forgives them and reconciles them to Himself. The Apostle Paul speaks of Jesus' being raised for our justification. It is only in the light of the Resurrection that the Cross is seen as the foundation of our forgiveness and reconciliation with God.

E. Mission flows from Jesus' Resurrection as Lord. It is as the Risen Lord that He sends the Apostles forth to proclaim the Gospel. The Resurrection of Jesus is the beginning of the sending and the missionary preaching of the Apostles and of the Church.

2. His Resurrection was bodily and objective.
Explanation

Having affirmed the historical fact of the Resurrection of Jesus, it is important to determine the nature of His Resurrection. Since so much depends upon the nature of the Resurrection, Article 4 is very explicit about it: Jesus rose bodily. Everything pertaining to our nature, that He had assumed in the Incarnation - body, soul and spirit – shared in His Resurrection.

The Resurrection of Jesus was bodily. It was not merely a subjective event that took place only in the hearts and minds of the Apostles, as some have interpreted it. The language of the New Testament Gospel is quite specific. He was crucified, died, and was buried, and on the third day, He was raised and then appeared to the Apostles. This parallelism in the Apostles' preaching as found in 1 Corinthians 15:3-7 is very important:

> *For what I received I passed on to you as of first importance: that Christ died for our sins according to the Scriptures, that he was buried, that he was raised on the third day according to the Scriptures, and that he appeared to Peter, and then to the Twelve. After that, he appeared to more than five hundred of the brothers at the same time, most of whom are still living, though some have fallen asleep. Then he appeared to James, then to all the apostles.*

This list speaks of distinct events: that Christ <u>died</u> for our sins in accordance with the Scriptures, that He was <u>buried</u>, that He <u>was raised</u> on the third day in accordance with the Scriptures, and that <u>He appeared</u> to Cephas, then to the Twelve. These events follow one another in chronological order and are reported in parallel couplets: died and buried, rose and appeared. Just as Jesus' dying is not the same as His being buried, so Jesus' Resurrection is not the same as His appearances to the women and the Apostles. His appearances reveal that He had already risen from the grave. The point is that the appearances did not constitute the Resurrection but were rather evidence of the Resurrection that had already happened in the tomb. Only the Father, the Son, and the Spirit observed the Resurrection itself. He had died and was buried and had risen and the tomb was empty. The Resurrection therefore must not be understood to be a vision seen as appearances, while Jesus' body lay moldering in the grave. Not one biblical writer viewed either the Resurrection of Jesus or the resurrection of ourselves in the final great day as something only subjective.

Such a view is so utterly foreign to the Apostles' witness that it should not be referred to as an interpretation of the New Testament. It is a substitution for and a denial of the Apostles' witness. According to the Apostles, it was Jesus Who was personally resurrected and Who appeared to His own. Just as Jesus' Resurrection is objective, so are His post-Resurrection appearances objective. He was really there.

An additional, interesting historical point that supports the bodily character of the Resurrection concerns the phrase "the third day." That is the day on which the women found the tomb empty. The body was gone. The tomb was empty. This was an objective fact that was seen by friend and foe alike. The empty tomb also supports the bodily, objective nature of Jesus' Resurrection.

Biblical Foundations

When the Sabbath was past, Mary Magdalene and Mary the mother of James and Salome bought spices, so that they might go and anoint him. And very early on the first day of the week, when the sun had risen, they went to the tomb. Mark 16:1-2

And looking up, they saw that the stone had been rolled back—it was very large. And entering the tomb, they saw a young man sitting on the right side, dressed in a white robe, and they were alarmed. And he said to them, "Do not be alarmed. You seek Jesus of Nazareth, who was crucified. He has risen; he is not here. See the place where they laid him. But go, tell his disciples and Peter that he is going before you to Galilee. There you will see him, just as he told you." Mark 16:4-7

Brothers, I may say to you with confidence about the patriarch David that he both died and was buried, and his tomb is with us to this day. Being therefore a prophet, and knowing that God had sworn with an oath to him that he would set one of his descendants on his throne, he foresaw and spoke about the resurrection of the Christ, that he was not abandoned to Hades, nor did his flesh see corruption. Acts 2:29-31

False Teaching Denied/Objections Answered

1. Some have suggested that the biblical account of the women discovering the tomb empty is fictitious. They believe that the account of the empty tomb is a later addition to the Gospels that the early Church fabricated in order to encourage confidence in the reality and importance of Jesus' Resurrection. This skeptical speculation cannot stand up to serious examination. A fabricated account of the women being the first to discover the tomb empty is highly improbable for several reasons:

First, the witness of women was not highly regarded in Jesus' day; women were not allowed to bear witness in court at that time. Why, then, would the disciples have made up a tradition dependent upon the witness of women?

Second, the early Church's preaching seems to have moved in the other direction, for in the earliest summary of the Gospel, which we examined above in 1 Corinthians 15, the list of official witnesses does not include the women at all. They were left out.

And third, having the women venture into danger to complete the burial preparations for Jesus, and thus to become the first witnesses to the Resurrection, while the Apostles were hiding behind closed doors in fear, certainly puts the Apostles in an unfavorable light. Such a tradition about the Apostles would hardly have been made up. It would have been both odd and foolish apologetics to do so. The only sensible conclusion is that the accounts of the empty tomb in the New Testament Gospels are true. As one biblical scholar said to this writer, "The reason the New Testament has the women discover the tomb empty is that the women discovered the tomb empty!"

The nature of Jesus' Resurrection was bodily; it was objective, not subjective or a mere vision. Jesus' bodily appearances to the Apostles and to others made the fact of His Resurrection known and explained why the tomb was empty. He, Himself, was raised. As the angel said, "He is not here. He is risen!"

2. Others have declared that Jesus' Resurrection could not be bodily because dead bodies simply do not rise. Therefore, the Resurrection is not an event involving Jesus' body; His body remained in the grave. Rather, His Resurrection was a God-sent vision that took place in the relationship between God and those disciples who had followed Jesus. This entire argument is based on the faith or presupposition that God could not and did not raise Jesus bodily from the dead.

Unfortunately, for that secularist, naturalistic worldview, all of the evidence points in a different direction. The evidence for the bodily Resurrection of Jesus as set forth in the New Testament simply bars the way to any purely subjective understanding of the Resurrection of Jesus. As someone put it, "The empty tomb is the rock upon which all subjective theories of the Resurrection dash themselves in vain."

Implications

The implications of Jesus' bodily Resurrection are important. Here we mention three of them:

A. The bodily Resurrection of Jesus points to its supernatural character. In the natural order of things, physical bodies ordinarily see corruption and decompose. Jesus' body in the Resurrection was transformed. He had predicted that His Father would vindicate Him by Resurrection, and the Father did so. It was a supernatural act of God, and a revelation of His purpose and power.

B. The bodily nature of Jesus' Resurrection points to the objectivity both of His past and of our future Resurrection. In God's good time, we and our loved ones shall all be raised from the dead and clothed with new bodies. We will not be unclothed spirits, nor will we be merely remembered by those who knew us best.

C. The bodily character of the Resurrection also points to the cosmic character of God's victory in Christ, and His purpose to redeem the entire natural order, now subject to decay and corruption. Jesus' body was and is made of the same basic elements of which the physical universe is composed, as are ours. The whole cosmos has been caught up in the Resurrection of Christ and waits His appearing for full consummation.

The Apostle Paul speaks of this in Romans 8:

For the creation waits with eager longing for the revealing of the sons of God. For the creation was subjected to futility, not willingly, but because of him who subjected it, in hope that the creation itself will be set free from its bondage to decay and obtain the freedom of the glory of the children of God. For we know that the whole creation has been groaning together in the pains of childbirth until now. And not only the creation, but we ourselves, who have the first fruits of the Spirit, groan inwardly as we wait eagerly for adoption as sons, the redemption of our bodies. Romans 8:19-23

What is involved in this final cosmic renewal is not yet fully revealed and we must wait for the consummation of all things in Christ to discover the full meaning and grandeur of it.

3. His Resurrection is of a final, or eschatological, nature, which led to His Ascension into heaven in glory.

Explanation

Of fundamental importance is that Jesus' Resurrection was not a resuscitation of a dead man back to earthly life. He was not raised backwards into the same life that He had left. His Resurrection was not another example of the sort of being raised from the dead that we see in Jesus' raising of Jairus' daughter, of the widow of Nain's son, or of Lazarus. These all died and were raised back into earthly life, only to die again. This is not what happened in the Resurrection of Jesus. "Jesus died unto sin once and He dieth no more." "Death hath no more dominion over Him." The final victory over death took place in Jesus' Resurrection. Just as His death was no ordinary death, but the atoning death of the Savior of the world, so His Resurrection is unique, for it is the beginning of the final Resurrection of all the living and the dead. He is the "first born of many brothers and sisters." In Him, the great Resurrection begins.

To put it graphically, Jesus was not raised backwards but forwards into glory and upward as Lord. As the Article states, "wherewith he ascended into heaven." In Him, in principle, the final or eschatological consummation of all things has begun, for us and for our salvation. We now know how it all ends; it ends in God's glory, in the bright, gleaming, and outshining of all God's purposes in a perfect completion that reconciles and redeems the entire universe in Christ.

Biblical Foundations

We know that Christ being raised from the dead will never die again; death no longer has dominion over him. For the death he died he died to sin, once for all, but the life he lives he lives to God. So you also must consider yourselves dead to sin and alive to God in Christ Jesus. Romans 6:9-11

So is it with the resurrection of the dead. What is sown is perishable; what is raised is imperishable. It is sown in dishonor; it is raised in glory. It is sown in weakness; it is raised in power. It is sown a natural body; it is raised a spiritual body. If there is a natural body, there is also a spiritual body. 1 Corinthians 15:42-44

False Teaching Denied/Objections Answered

Denied is any teaching that seeks to locate the Resurrection of Jesus entirely within the confines of history as we commonly know it. It is both historical and more than historical. There are historical elements in the Resurrection but the Resurrection itself transcends history and ushers in the beginning of the end of all things. The eschatological and triumphant character of the Resurrection must not be overlooked. And in that connection, the coming of the Holy Spirit, sent by the Risen Lord, is the first fruit and down payment of the "New Age" or the "Age to Come."

Implications

A. Christians view history in the light of its consummation in Christ. Living in Christ in the midst of history, we know where it is headed and thereby we are given a perspective on what is worth treasuring and serving in the present. This knowledge puts things into perspective. To serve Christ by serving His purposes in history is to move with the movement of God in history. It is to move with the tide. To serve some other end is finally to have spent one's life largely beside the point or swimming against the tide.

B. Viewing history from its consummation in Christ sets the Christian free to risk in the present. If the end is glory, we can dare great things for God in the present, and trust God to work all things together for good. Even though in this world we may have difficulties and troubles, God will use them to bless us, or others, and in the end, we have the victory in Christ. There is, therefore, a quiet serenity and optimism in the Christian Faith, which is neither sentimental nor naive but realistic, confident, and venturous.

4. The Lord now sits at the right hand of God where He hiddenly governs the universe, reigns in grace over the Church, and intercedes for His own.

Explanation

The Ascension marked the end of the post-Resurrection appearances of Jesus, with the exception of His one appearance to Paul that took place after the Ascension. Because of that exception, St. Paul calls himself "one born out of due time." The Ascension is not only the ending of one phase of Jesus' ministry, it is the beginning of a new phase. It is the transition to Jesus' sitting at the right hand of the Father, which is usually referred to as His heavenly session. Session comes from the Latin *sessio*, a "sitting." As the Father is pictured sitting upon the throne of the universe in sovereign majesty and authority, so now the crucified, risen, and ascended Son sits in the place of honor at His right hand, there to share in the honor and authority of the Father.

A number of things are signified by Jesus' sitting at the right hand of the Father:

First, it is significant with regard to Jesus' priestly ministry. His sitting signals that Jesus' work of atonement is complete. When a priest sits, the sacrifice has been made. When Jesus sits at the right hand of God as our High Priest, His atoning offering is finished and accepted by the Father; His very presence there speaks of the sufficiency and finality of His sacrifice for us all.

Secondly, it is the place of His intercession. As our High Priest, Jesus intercedes on our behalf, on behalf of all who have come and will come to the Father through Him. If the prayers of a righteous man avail much, how much more does the intercession of the Son of God avail for His own.

Thirdly, Jesus is seated not only as our High Priest but also as our King. His session is also a ministry of authority and reign. All authority in heaven and on earth has been given by the Father to the risen Son. He, in submission to the Father, is hiddenly in charge of the movement of history. Providence is part of His kingly work. Jesus will reign until the consummation of all things; then the Son will hand back the Kingdom to the Father.

This heavenly session of Jesus as King also refers to His reign of grace which is His particular reign over the Church. He is the Head of the Church, reigning over us by the Word and the Spirit. As King, reigning in grace, Jesus pours out the Spirit on His own, freeing us to respond in obedience to Him. At the same time, He assures us of our inheritance kept in heaven, undefiled and secure, of which the Spirit is a down payment. This points us to Article 5 on the Holy Spirit.

Biblical Foundations

But when Christ had offered for all time a single sacrifice for sins, he sat down at the right hand of God. Hebrews 10:12

Who shall bring any charge against God's elect? It is God who justifies. Who is to condemn? Christ Jesus is the one who died—more than that, who was raised—who is at the right hand of God, who indeed is interceding for us. Romans 8:33-34

And Jesus came and said to them, "All authority in heaven and on earth has been given to me. Go therefore and make disciples of all nations, baptizing them in the name of the Father and of the Son and of the Holy Spirit." Matthew 28:18-19

And he put all things under his feet and gave him as head over all things to the church, which is his body, the fullness of him who fills all in all. Ephesians 1:22-23

False Teaching Denied/Objections Answered

1. Some speak of the continuing propitiatory sacrifices of Christ. This has been addressed in Article 2 and will be addressed more directly in Articles 31 and 36. Here it is sufficient to simply state that such teaching is contrary to

the heavenly session of Christ.

2. Henry Ford is reported to have said, "History is one damned thing after another." William Shakespeare had his tragic figure Macbeth describing life as "a tale told by an idiot, full of sound and fury, signifying nothing." Both of these pessimistic opinions concerning the course of human events run contrary to the fact that Jesus is at the right hand of God reigning over the events of history. As the Cross and Resurrection make clear, God can use even the worst that man can do to advance His purposes.

Implications

A. Jesus as seated, having completed once for all His sacrificial work on the Cross, undergirds the confidence of the Christian that there is now therefore no condemnation for those who are in Christ Jesus by faith. We will discuss this basis of our confidence when we explore Article 11, "Of the Justification of Man." This completed sacrificial work of Christ will also be important when we discuss the sacrifices of the Masses in Article 31, "Of the one Oblation of Christ finished upon the Cross."

B. Intercessory prayer is a work of faith and a labor of love. It is also a sign of need. In the midst of life, we often ask people to pray for us and we promise to pray for others. Here we are taught that it is Christ Himself Who does this labor of love on our behalf, and even without our asking. It flows from His priestly office and His love for us. His prayer rests upon His finished work on the Cross, and applies God's forgiveness and sovereign power to our relationship with God and the events of our daily lives. We do well to pause and wonder that it is Christ Himself Who is now interceding for us in heaven.

C. The universal, kingly authority granted to the Risen Lord, whereby He is Lord of the Providence of God, teaches us to rest patiently in His care. We can expect to see, sooner or later, even in the most difficult of conditions, signs of His redemptive work, whereby "He makes all things work together for good for those who love Him and are called according to His purpose."

D. Jesus the Risen Lord is the rightful King and Lord of every nation and every person on the earth. That is the basis for the worldwide mission of the Church. As Lord of all, He sends us to all, and promises that by the Spirit we will be empowered to be His witnesses to the uttermost parts of the earth. We go, not in our own name, nor to export our culture, but to bring about the obedience of faith for Jesus' Name's sake and for the salvation of all.

E. The Christian life is a life lived intentionally under His gracious authority. That Jesus is our King, that we call Him "Lord," and are taught by Him to pray to the Father, "Thy will be done on earth as it is in heaven," means that we seek to serve Him in all things, come what may, cost what it will. We do this very imperfectly; hence we pray also, "Forgive us our trespasses as we forgive those who trespass against us."

5. On the last day, He will return to judge all persons, both the living and the dead.

Explanation

The purposes of God revealed and established in Christ will be consummated. God will be all in all, and things will come to a final conclusion. The present ambiguities of life and history will be done away with at the final coming of Christ in majesty and glory to judge the quick and the dead.

As we have noted above, the Resurrection of Jesus is eschatological; the great, final, and universal Resurrection of the dead has already begun in Him. This Article, therefore, places us in the midst of the Four Final Things.

Interestingly, this is the only Article which directly addresses these final events and then largely in the language of the Creeds. Apparently, the Anglican Reformers did not wish to venture explicitly into a full range of developed eschatology. This may be due to the fact that at the time these Articles were being written there was no great disagreement with Rome regarding final things, with the exception of the doctrine of purgatory which is addressed in Article 22. Also, interest in detailed schemes of eschatology was not characteristic of the Reformation period. It is in the 19th and 20th centuries that we find a strong interest in the development of such theories.

It would be accurate to say that Anglicans are instructed by the Articles and Prayer Book tradition only about the four Final Events. The four final events are: 1) the second coming of Christ, 2) the general resurrection of the dead, 3) the final judgment of mankind, and 4) the final states of Heaven and Hell.

Anglicans have never taken an official position regarding any particular detailed eschatological schema. This reticence on the part of Anglicans includes taking no definite position regarding the doctrine of the Millennium or the Lord's 1000-year reign. It is not explicitly mentioned in the Articles and is subject to various interpretations of the Book of Revelations and to various theories as to how Christ fulfilled a number of Old Testament prophesies.

For the sake of completeness, and because such theories are to be found alive in Anglican congregations, a few brief remarks about the main theories about the "thousand-year" millennial reign of Christ are in order.

There are three main views of His reign in relation to the four final things at the consummation of history. The theories are Amillennialism, Premillennialism, and Postmillennialism.

The Amillennial (or, present reign of Christ) view teaches that we are now living in the thousand-year reign of Christ. The thousand years are a symbolic number for a long time span with an undetermined number of years. At the end of this present reign, Christ will suddenly and unexpectedly return in glory and the other three final events will immediately follow.

The Premillennial view holds that Christ's Second Coming will take place unexpectedly. Christ will return in glory to Jerusalem and there He will initiate a literal one-thousand-year reign on the earth. At the conclusion of that reign, the other three final events will take place.

The Postmillennial view holds that, by God's Spirit, a thousand-year period of increasing conversion and blessing will come upon the earth. This is understood to be what is symbolized by the thousand-year reign of Christ. At the end of this period of remarkable blessing, Satan will break loose for a final devastating, brief period, after which Jesus will come in glory in His Second Coming to initiate the other three final events.

While nowhere in the Articles is the thousand-year reign of Christ mentioned, Article 4 does refer to 1) Jesus' Second Coming in majesty as Judge, 2) the Resurrection of the Dead as begun in Jesus, 3) the Final Judgment, and, implicitly, 4) the final states of Heaven and Hell as the result of Christ's judgment. Since these matters are either mentioned or implied in the Thirty-Nine Articles, we shall make a brief comment on each of the final four events.

First, we consider His Second Coming. In some respects, it will be like His First Coming; it will be personal and visible. In other respects, it will be unlike His First Coming, for it will be unmistakable, like a nearby lightning flash. And He will not come in humility and lowliness, but in majesty and with unmistakable authority. He will not come seeking the lost, but to consummate what had gone before. He will come as King and Judge of all.

There is no timetable we can use to calculate the time of His coming. He will come like a thief in the night. No human knows the hour, not even the Son Himself, only the Father. All we are told is that the Gospel must first be preached to all nations, that there will be cosmic signs, wars and rumors of wars, and a great turning to Christ among the Jews.

We are, therefore, not to seek to calculate the time but

rather to be desirous and ready at any time for His appearing. Taking our cue from the Lord's parable of the Wise and Foolish Virgins, if we are prepared all of the time, we will be ready at the right time.

Second, there is the general Resurrection of the Dead. At the appearing of the Lord, the dead will be raised and the living will stand before Him. The general Resurrection that began in Him in His Resurrection will then be consummated in all who have been created in the image of God. Those who are righteous through genuine faith in Him will receive glorified bodies, that will be perfectly suited to serve their regenerated spirits in the new heaven and new earth. Those who are not righteous through faith in Christ will receive bodies appropriate to existence in the place of eternal suffering.

Third is the final judgment. Jesus Himself will be the Judge in the Final Judgment. The judgments of God in history are partial and provisional until the consummation. In the Final Judgment they are completed and perfected. God is vindicated in His righteousness.

The purpose of the Last Judgment is to disclose the secrets of our hearts, to hold all of us accountable for our thoughts, attitudes, words, and deeds of omission and commission, and to assign each of us to a final state.

For Christians, united to Christ by faith, Christ has borne the final judgment concerning our eternal destiny; however, each of us, as Christians, must appear before the judgment seat of Christ to render an account of our lives to Him. The basis of His judgment will be the Law of God made known in conscience and in the Scripture and our cooperation with the gracious, redemptive, sanctifying work of Christ.

Finally there are the two final states: heaven and hell. The final states of those who are righteous in Christ through faith and of those who abide under the judicial wrath of God differ. For the saints, there is an unending life of fullness and perfection in communion with God and with the saints of God in the new heaven and new earth. The biblical writers describe this life in words of beauty, glory, worship, feasting, and fellowship.

There will be degrees of blessedness and honor proportionate to the fidelity, character, and service that each believer in Christ has rendered. Each will receive that measure of blessing, which he or she is able to receive, given the degree of sanctification each has attained.

For those who have rejected the Lord and His ways, there is an existence of sorrow, an unending loss of all good, combined with a guilty and painful conscience. Those in hell are banished from fellowship with God and the community of the saints, and dwell under God's condemnation forever. This terrible existence is endured in the place of banishment and in the presence of others with hardened and unrepentant hearts. Such suffering hardens and embitters; it does not lead to repentance. This suffering in hell is described in graphic language in Scripture as eternal punishment, eternal fire, a lake of fire, an everlasting pit, outer darkness, torment, the second death, weeping and wailing and gnashing of teeth. Jesus is the one Who most often warns about it. Here, too, there will be degrees of suffering and dishonor proportionate to the light rejected and the life lived.

To deliver people from such a destiny and to lead them in Christ into the new heaven and new earth is the reason that the Father sent the Son, and the reason the Son pours out the Spirit to empower us to preach the Gospel to all nations and every person.

Biblical Foundations

For the Lord himself will descend from heaven with a cry of command, with the voice of an archangel, and with the sound of the trumpet of God. And the dead in Christ will rise first. Then we who are alive, who are left, will be caught up together with them in the clouds to meet the Lord in the air, and so we will always be with the Lord. 1 Thessalonians 4:16-17

Do not marvel at this, for an hour is coming when all who are in the tombs will hear his voice and come out, those who have done good to the resurrection of life, and those who have done evil to the resurrection of judgment. John 5:28-29

So whether we are at home or away, we make it our aim to please him. For we must all appear before the judgment seat of Christ, so that each one may receive what is due for what he has done in the body, whether good or evil. 2 Corinthians 5:9-10

And these will go away into eternal punishment, but the righteous into eternal life. Matthew 25:46

False Teaching Denied/Objections Answered

1. There are those who deny the existence of hell. A loving God could consign no one to hell, they say. But it is Jesus, the very incarnation of the love of God, who speaks and warns most of hell in the New Testament. He has the inside word on this. We had better agree with Him and take hell seriously. Jesus tells us "to fear Him who can destroy both body and soul in hell."

2. There are also those who would limit hell in one of two ways. Some hold to the immediate extinction at death of all who are not going to Heaven. They do not deny hell but hold that it is empty. The others hold that hell is real and there are some who go there but only for a period of time. Since God has determined that they are beyond redemption, after sufficient suffering they go out of existence.

There is no hint of either of those views in Scripture. Hell and the sufferings of the punishments of hell are eternal in the same sense that eternal is used to describe the life in Heaven. Eternal is eternal in both cases. Only God is eternal by nature, but it would seem that God created us to have an eternal destiny. Each one of us needs to see that his or her destiny is a destiny to be desired.

(See Article 18, "of obtaining salvation only by the name of Christ," for a discussion of those who never get to hear the Gospel.)

Implications

A. We have been told by Christ not to seek to know the time of His return. In spite of Christ's caution, people do, from time to time, seek to predict the day, hour, and place of His return. This calculation is inevitably made known publicly and when it proves false it brings disappointment and discredit upon the Gospel. We are to flee all such speculation and seek to be ready for His return at any hour.

B. As we grow older, our bodies are no longer able to do all that they could do at the prime of our lives. The promise that at the end He will transform us, that we shall, in Him, have a body like unto His glorious body, is an encouraging word of hope and anticipation. Also, given this sure promise, we find the freedom not to pretend to be younger than we are. Such pretensions fool no one, are a delusion, and can cause us to miss the joys of each stage of life.

C. The Final State in Christ is glorious, beyond our imagining. Such glory to come puts the daily events of life in true perspective, and lets us view them in the light of their significant but passing character. This does not diminish their significance, for in them we do serve Christ and work out our salvation. In addition, we shall one day have to give to Christ an account of the deeds done in the body.

D. The least contemplation of the reality of hell should make passionate evangelists of us all. It has made evangelists of our Heavenly Father, of the Son, and of the Holy Spirit. The possibility that anyone we know, or might come to know, could end up in hell forever is horrible enough to move us to share the Gospel at every genuine opportunity. Jesus sets us an example. He came seeking the lost. He, the very incarnation of love, is the one in the Gospels Who warns openly and most frequently of the impending danger of hell. It can be no part of true love on our part to keep silent about or ignore the reality of hell.

Conclusion

The Resurrection of Jesus, the Christ, His Ascension and ministry of intercession and reign in Heaven, and His coming to judge the living and the dead are all part of the core of the Apostolic Faith. Their relevance to us is manifold and profound, as this Article 4 makes clear. Anglicans in no way depart from the Apostolic Faith and the Church Catholic in these central doctrines of the Faith.

ARTICLE 5

Of the Holy Ghost

The Holy Ghost, proceeding from the Father and the Son, is of one substance, majesty and glory, with the Father and the Son, very and eternal God.

Introduction

Who is the Holy Spirit? What does the Holy Spirit do? Are all Christians indwelt by the Holy Spirit? How would we know if that were true? These are questions that many Christians are unprepared to answer, even though they are fundamental to the core of the Christian Faith.

This Article briefly states the doctrine of the person of the Spirit. It is written in terms of the teaching of the Western Church. It is Western in that it teaches that the Spirit proceeds from both the Father and the Son, whereas the Churches of the East teach a single procession from the Father alone. We will discuss this difference at some length in our comments below in Teaching Point 3.

The Spirit of God is an active Spirit and much of what we know of the person of the Holy Spirit is learned from His activity, as recorded in Scripture. In addition, the work of the Spirit is touched upon in the various places in the Articles that address the application of salvation. Therefore, we will discuss the work of the Spirit and add a very brief comment concerning the scope of the work of the Spirit at the conclusion of our treatment of this Article. We do this in order to provide a framework for interpreting the references to the work of the Spirit in the later Articles. It will also give the reader a sense of the wide range and the central importance of the Spirit's work as found in Scripture.

We should take note that the person and the work of

the Holy Spirit are often neglected in the teaching of the Churches. For this reason, the Holy Spirit has been referred to as the "neglected person of the Holy Trinity." This neglect has happened despite the prominence given the work of the Spirit in the New Testament. This lack is now beginning to be redressed due to the world-wide influence of the Pentecostal Churches, and the Neo-Pentecostal or Charismatic movements in the historic Churches.

In our exposition of Article 1, in the section on the Trinity, we addressed several of this Article's points very briefly. Here we will treat those matters more fully.

The Teaching of Article 5
The teaching points of this Article concerning the nature of the Holy Spirit are threefold:

1. The Holy Spirit is the very and eternal God of the substance of the Godhead.

2. The Holy Spirit shares all the glory, majesty and attributes of the Godhead.

3. The Holy Spirit proceeds from the Father and the Son – The *Filioque*.
> **Excursus: The scope of the work of the Holy Spirit as described in Scripture is briefly stated.**

1. The Holy Spirit is the very and eternal God of the substance of the Godhead.
Explanation

The biblical writings affirm the full divinity and personhood of the Holy Spirit, in several ways. We will simply list these with relatively little comment.

A. The Spirit is named and referred to as "God" in Scripture.

In Acts 5: 3-4, the Apostle Peter declared to Ananias,

that when he lied to the Holy Spirit he lied to God. The Apostle Paul calls the Spirit "Lord" in 1 Corinthians 12:4-6. The Spirit is spoken of as "the Spirit" in the absolute sense. We are called God's temple because the Spirit dwells within us as God indwelt the Temple in Jerusalem. At times when the New Testament writers cite the Old Testament in passages where God is speaking, the New Testament will say, "the Holy Spirit said." All through the Scriptures we read of "His Spirit," "My Spirit," "the Spirit of God," "the Spirit of Him who raised Jesus from the dead," "The Spirit of the Sovereign Lord," and "The Spirit of Christ." The title "Holy Spirit" itself identifies the Spirit as essentially related to the One who is Holy.

B. In various texts the Spirit is explicitly linked with and placed on a par with the other persons of the Trinity.

We see this in the Trinitarian formulae in both the Great Commission in Matthew 28:19, "Go therefore and make disciples of all nations, baptizing them in the name of the Father and of the Son and of the Holy Spirit," and in the Apostolic Benediction in 2 Corinthians 13:14, "The grace of the Lord Jesus Christ and the love of God and the fellowship of the Holy Spirit be with you all," where the Father, the Son, and the Holy Spirit all appear together. The same happens at the key event of Jesus' baptism in Matthew 3:13-17: "Then Jesus came from Galilee to the Jordan to John, to be baptized by him. John would have prevented him, saying, 'I need to be baptized by you, and do you come to me?' But Jesus answered him, 'Let it be so now, for thus it is fitting for us to fulfill all righteousness.' Then he consented. And when Jesus was baptized, immediately he went up from the water, and behold, the heavens were opened to him, and he saw the Spirit of God descending like a dove and coming to rest on him; and behold, a voice from heaven said, 'This is my beloved Son, with whom I am well pleased.'"

C. The divinity of the Holy Spirit is revealed in the work that He does.

He creates; He recreates or regenerates; He resurrects; He unites us to Christ and the Father. He heals and exorcises. His actions are referred to by the Lord Jesus as the "finger of God." He inspires and speaks through the Scripture. He convicts of Sin. He produces Christ-like fruit in the character of the believer. He unifies the Church. He distributes spiritual gifts in the Church as He sees fit. He fills people and empowers them for ministry. In Him the Father and the Son come and indwell the Church. All of these works are the works of God.

D. The Holy Spirit is fully personal.

The Spirit is not an "it" but a "He." This is clear in Scripture. The personhood of the Spirit is clearly and extensively reflected in Scripture. Here are some of the ways:

1. Personal masculine pronouns are used of the Spirit where grammatically it would be more appropriate to use neuter pronouns (John 16:14). This is intentional and due to His personal nature.

2. Jesus compared the Spirit with Himself as another Comforter of the same kind or nature. In John 14:16, the Greek for "another" *allylos*, which means of the same kind, makes this point clear. In contrast, the Greek word for "another" referring to something of a different kind is *heteros*.

3. The Spirit is described as having personal characteristics. The Spirit has a mind. He makes decisions and carries them out; He has a will. He shows emotion.

4. The Spirit is affected as a person is affected. He can be blasphemed, grieved, lied to, obeyed, insulted, quenched or suppressed, and resisted.

5. The Spirit acts in personal ways. He commissions,

reveals truth, teaches, testifies to the Son, speaks, leads, searches the depths of God, encourages, intercedes, sanctifies, and strengthens.

6. The Spirit, given us by the Father and the Son, is Himself a giver and distributor of gifts in the Church as He sovereignly wills. In being a sovereign giver, He is distinct from and more than the gifts that He gives.

The conclusion is inescapable. Since there is but one God, and since the Spirit is fully God, it follows that the Spirit shares in the one substance of the Godhead. He is *homoousios*, of the same substance as the Father and the Son. He is the Third Person of the Trinity.

In biblical perspective, there are no gradations of divinity. One either is or is not God. And if one is God, then one is fully God. This reality and truth concerning the Holy Spirit was increasingly made evident to the Apostles and the early Church and is therefore widely attested in the New Testament Scriptures in biblical terms and receives doctrinal expression in the Ecumenical Councils of the Church.

Biblical Foundations
Named God
But Peter said, "Ananias, why has Satan filled your heart to lie to the Holy Spirit and to keep back for yourself part of the proceeds of the land? While it remained unsold, did it not remain your own? And after it was sold, was it not at your disposal? Why is it that you have contrived this deed in your heart? You have not lied to men but to God." Acts 5:3-4

Of the Trinity
The grace of the Lord Jesus Christ and the love of God and the fellowship of the Holy Spirit be with you all. 2 Corinthians 13:14
But, as it is written, "What no eye has seen, nor ear heard, nor the heart of man imagined, what God has

prepared for those who love him"— these things God has revealed to us through the Spirit. For the Spirit searches everything, even the depths of God. For who knows a person's thoughts except the spirit of that person, which is in him? So also no one comprehends the thoughts of God except the Spirit of God. 1 Corinthians 2:9-11

Does Divine works

The earth was without form and void, and darkness was over the face of the deep. And the Spirit of God was hovering over the face of the waters. Genesis 1:2

For no prophecy was ever produced by the will of man, but men spoke from God as they were carried along by the Holy Spirit. 2 Peter 1:21

The wind blows where it wishes, and you hear its sound, but you do not know where it comes from or where it goes. So it is with everyone who is born of the Spirit." John 3:8

While they were worshiping the Lord and fasting, the Holy Spirit said, "Set apart for me Barnabas and Saul for the work to which I have called them." Acts 13:2

Personal

And I will ask the Father, and he will give you another Helper, to be with you forever, John 14:16

And do not grieve the Holy Spirit of God, by whom you were sealed for the day of redemption. Ephesians 4:30

All these are empowered by one and the same Spirit, who apportions to each one individually as he wills. 1 Corinthians 12:11

False Teachings Denied/Objections answered

1. Some have taught that the Holy Spirit is a semi-divine or an exalted creature. Being convinced of the divinity of the Holy Spirit, the Church officially rejected any attempts to deny the full divinity of the Holy Spirit. For the same reason, the Church rejected the Gnostic, Neo-

Platonic, and popular pagan religious views affirming gradations of "the Divine." The Church affirmed the full Deity of the Spirit at the Second Ecumenical Council held in Constantinople in A.D. 381. Since the Church had already affirmed the divinity of the Son at the First Ecumenical Council held at Nicaea in A.D. 325, it needed only to extend its Christological reflection and language to refer to the Holy Spirit.

2. It is sometimes objected that since in Scripture we read that the Holy Spirit is subordinate to the Father and the Son, it is, therefore, impossible for the Spirit to be fully divine as the Father and the Son are. It is true that there is a subordination of the persons within the Godhead and in the work of God in relation to the world, but that does not imply a subordination of being in the Godhead. Personal submission is quite different from ontological inferiority, that is, of having a lesser nature or being.

Implications

We will discuss the implications for the teaching for points 1 and 2 at the same time, since the practical effects are the same. (See Point 2, Implications, below.)

2. The Holy Spirit shares all the glory, majesty and attributes of the Godhead.

Explanation

Since the Spirit is fully God, the Spirit shares in all of the glory, majesty, and attributes of the Godhead. Just as we have denied that the Father is not more divine than the Son, nor the Son more divine than the Spirit, so also no person in the Trinity lacks any of the divine attributes. The attributes are attributes of the Godhead and hence of all the persons in the Godhead.

As we will discuss more fully later, there is personal differentiation and personal subordination within the Godhead, but the subordination of the persons in the Trinity is a subordination of equals who share a common life and identity in the nature, substance, and singularity of the Godhead.

The Spirit's possession of all the attributes of the Godhead is clearly attested in the biblical writings. There the Spirit is referred to as glorious, majestic, one, living, eternal, omnipresent, omniscient, omnipotent, holy, righteous, good, loving, and gracious. These are the attributes of God. They are attributed to the Godhead and to each of the Persons quite specifically in the New Testament.

Biblical Foundations

And the Spirit of the LORD shall rest upon him, the Spirit of wisdom and understanding, the Spirit of counsel and might, the Spirit of knowledge and the fear of the LORD. Isaiah 11:2

And hope does not put us to shame, because God's love has been poured into our hearts through the Holy Spirit who has been given to us. Romans 5:5

If the Spirit of him who raised Jesus from the dead dwells in you, he who raised Christ Jesus from the dead will also give life to your mortal bodies through his Spirit who dwells in you. Romans 8:11

False Teaching Denied/Objections answered

1. Denied is any teaching that fails to affirm that all of the attributes of God are shared by the person of the Holy Spirit.

2. Most particularly, the Church denied the teaching that the Spirit is but an impersonal divine influence. Since the Spirit is referred to in Scripture as a "gift" and as "poured out" upon the Church, some have drawn the conclusion that the Spirit is only a power or influence and not God Himself, not the Third Person of the Trinity. A careful reading of the New Testament and the experience of the Church make such a view impossible. Therefore, this error has been officially rejected by the Church in the

Ecumenical Councils. Anglicans are in full agreement.

3. Consequently, since the Spirit is God and not merely a divine influence or power, it is quite wrong to refer to the Holy Spirit as "It," as one often hears people doing. In the Scriptures the Spirit is referred to as "He."

4. Our Lord teaches us to hallow the Lord's Name. We are to know and worship Him in accord with His revealed, Triune Name, that is, in accord with His nature as the Father, the Son, and the Holy Spirit. To neglect or demote the Spirit is to fail to honor the Lord according to His Triune Name (Matthew 28:19).

5. The Spirit is the vital link between the human heart and the living God. In and through the Spirit, God the Father and God the Son are present to us and within us. God acts in history providentially and redemptively by the Spirit. The Father and the Son come to indwell us, the people of God, and to manifest Themselves to us and through us by the Holy Spirit. All the means of grace are effective only by the presence and in the power of the Spirit.

Were the Spirit not God, we would be out of vital contact, union, and fellowship with the living God. Jesus and the Father would be remote from us. Therefore any doctrine that ignores or fails to affirm the present personal presence and vital action of the Spirit must be rejected.

We can put this point another way. If the Spirit within us were not fully God, then He could not mediate the Father and the Son to us, nor could He do the works of God within us and in our midst. In effect, to reduce His full divinity, or to depersonalize His relationship to us, would be to create a non-Christian religion of self-salvation in relation to a remote "God," a "spiritless" distortion of Christianity. Karl Barth referred to this as "flat tire theology."

6. Just as bad as having a religion without the Spirit is having a religion full of the wrong "spirit," a religion in which the "spirit" is not the Spirit of the Father and the

Son, not the Holy Spirit. Such religions lead to religious enthusiasm and vitality often with quite devastating consequences. For, when the "spirit" is not the Spirit of the Father and the Son, the "spirit" inevitably divinizes some aspect of creation with which the "spirit" is identified or closely connected. False gods produce terrible consequences for their adherents, in both the short and the long run. To mention just a few examples:

1) In some cases, the self is divinized which leads to individualistic tyranny.

2) In other cases, there is a loss of the self altogether, as in the Eastern mystic religions, in which the self is absorbed in the abyss of the divine mystery. A meditative quietism, largely indifferent to social life, is usually the result.

3) There is idolatrous tribalism and religious nationalism. In the case of the Nazi movement in Germany, the "spirit" was believed to be the "spirit of the Arian Race" and produced the national arrogance of German National Socialism, the Holocaust, and the Second World War. Many died because this spirit was not the Holy Spirit.

Implications

The Church recognizes the Spirit as the Spirit of the Father and of the Son and will worship no other.

3. The Holy Spirit proceeds from the Father and the Son – The *Filioque.*
Explanation

There is an historic controversy between the Eastern and the Western Churches over the procession of the Holy Spirit within the life of the Godhead. This controversy is unfamiliar to most Christians; therefore, we will need to make the issues and the practical implications of the controversy clear. This will require a somewhat fuller treatment than is usual in this commentary.

A. First, it is important to state the common ground, where there is no controversy

There is no controversy between the East and West concerning the sending of the Spirit to us by both the Father and the Son. John's Gospel clearly states that the Father will send the Spirit and that the Son will send the Spirit from the Father after the Son has been glorified, that is, after He has been crucified, has risen, and has ascended as Lord.

If we interpret the creedal phrase, "He proceedeth from the Father and the Son," to mean that the Spirit proceeds to us as sent by the Father through the Son for the purpose of uniting us to Christ and applying to us and manifesting in us the benefits won for us by the Son, there would be full agreement between East and West. This joint sending of the Spirit, however, is not what the West meant when it added "and the Son" to the Nicene Creed. The West was referring to the inner life of the Trinity, which is something different altogether.

Both the Eastern Churches and the Western Churches have also been careful to affirm the connection between the work of the Son and the work of the Spirit. In this sense, the Spirit is the Spirit of Christ, as Scripture asserts.

We should warn that some forms of contemporary theology quite wrongly view this linkage of the Spirit to Jesus as too restrictive of the Spirit's saving work. Where the connection between the saving work of the Spirit and that of the Son is weakened, ignored, or even denied, we find that the clear witness of Scripture to the sole, saving uniqueness of the work of Christ is lost. To put the matter positively, only in and through the Spirit is our union with Christ, and the benefits of the finished work of the Son and the certain future benefits of His victory, made real to our hearts and lives in the present. The Holy Spirit is a mediator of the present relationship we have with the Triune God, as well as a down payment, assurance, and anticipation of the glory to come.

B. Agreement ceases when we move from a consideration of the sending of the Spirit to us and turn to consider the internal life of God and the place of the Holy Spirit within the Triune Nature of God

This long-standing controversy between the Churches of the East and of the West has two aspects. On the one hand, the controversy is about a misuse of authority. It is about the lack of authority of the Church in the West to unilaterally change, or add to, an Ecumenical Creed apart from a decision by an Ecumenical Council. Specifically, this issue centers on whether the Pope and/or Western Councils called by the Pope had authority over the whole Church Universal. The Western Churches added the *Filioque* to the Nicene Creed without the consent or theological agreement of the Eastern Churches. That is one part of the controversy.

The second aspect of the controversy is theological. It concerns the theological correctness of the content of the *Filioque* clause, i.e. "and the Son" when it is understood to refer to the inner life of the Trinity. The West believes it is true; the East believes it is false. We will explore the theological issue shortly.

1. First let us consider the issue of authority. With regard to the controversy concerning papal authority, Anglicans today tend to side with the Churches of the East against the decision of the pre-Reformation Church of the West.

At the time the phrase was added, the Western Churches felt they had the authority to add the *Filioque* clause to the Creed without the agreement and authorization of an Ecumenical Council in large measure due to the Pope's support and authority. Anglicans do not acknowledge any divinely instituted jurisdictional authority of the Bishop of Rome over all of the Churches of the Universal Church. This does not mean that Anglicans do not listen respectfully and carefully to what the Bishop of Rome, the titular head of the world's largest visible body of Christians, has to say. But as a Communion, Anglicans do not acknowledge him to have been given either universal jurisdiction as the Vicar of Christ or to have infallibility in the exercise of his office.

Since many of the Western Churches of the Reformation, including the Churches of the Anglican Communion, deny that the Pope has ever had such authority, it would be appropriate for Anglicans world-wide to put the *Filioque* in the Nicene Creed in brackets as we use it in our liturgies. That would indicate that it is a Western use but not actually part of the Ecumenical Creed.

This bracketing should not be held to imply that Anglicans have concluded that it would be incorrect to add the *Filioque* to the Creed in a proper manner at a subsequent Ecumenical Council. Nor should it imply that the *Filioque* should be removed from our liturgies and our catechisms or not taught among us. The *Filioque* is a theological truth of which we are persuaded, even though it is not yet universally accepted by the whole Church. The question of its truth should be decided on the basis of theology not on the basis of procedure and that official discussion awaits a future Ecumenical Council..

The Ecumenical Creed in its original form neither asserts nor denies the theological substance of the *Filioque*. It is a matter therefore which deserves continued ecumenical discussion and debate.

2. This leads us to the second issue regarding the *Filioque,* which is the question of its theological correctness and relevance.

The Ecumenical Creed asserts that the Holy Spirit "proceedeth from the Father." This is a direct quotation from the Gospel according to St. John, which reads, "But when the Helper comes, whom I will send to you from the Father, the Spirit of truth, who proceeds from the Father, he will bear witness about me" (John 15:26). The Eastern

Churches rest their case on the simple fact that this is the only text which refers to the procession of the Spirit and it speaks of the Spirit's procession only from the Father.

The Churches of the East believe that this reveals that the fountain of divinity is the Father Who is unbegotten and Who eternally begets the Son and eternally "spirates" or "breathes out" the Spirit. This gives equal dignity to the Spirit and to the Son. It also protects the hierarchy in the Godhead, which involves personal submission within the Godhead. Both the Son and the Spirit are eternally dependent upon and submissive to the Father. It also makes clear that the substance of the Godhead is personal, for the persons of the Son and the Spirit are derived eternally from the person of the Father. There is no impersonal divine substance in which the persons of the Godhead exist.

The Churches in the West believe that the Scriptures teach that the Spirit proceeds or comes forth from the Father and the Son, even though the word "proceeds" is used only once, and only in reference to the Father. It is used in Scripture in the context of the Spirit's being sent to us and the text is not primarily referring to the inner life of the Trinity. As such that text does not tell the whole story regarding the inner life of the Trinity. Other texts clearly show that the Son as well as the Father sends the Spirit to us or pours out the Spirit upon us. What is true toward us mirrors what is true in the inner life of the Trinity. Scripture indicates that regarding His nature, the Spirit is the Spirit "of Christ" just as much as He is the Spirit "of the Father." Therefore, the Spirit is best understood as equally related to both the Father and the Son. As St. Augustine said, the Spirit is the bond of love in the life of the Trinity. As the bond of love in the life of the Trinity, the Spirit proceeds from the Father to the Son but also from the Son to the Father. Without denying personal subordination in the Godhead, it is important to emphasize the mutuality of love between the persons of the Trinity. The *Filioque* does that. It also models for us the mutual love we Christians are to have in the Body of Christ by the indwelling of the Spirit.

C. What, you may ask, is the relevance of these considerations? The relevance in part depends upon whether you view things from the Eastern or Western positions.

1. If we begin by looking at things from the Eastern Church's point of view, their theologians have noted that there is a Western tendency to approach the Godhead from the perspective of the Oneness or unity of God. To do this, the oneness of the divine substance or nature is emphasized and the persons are considered as divine by participating in the one divine essence or substance. This essence or substance is not itself "personal." In so approaching the Trinity, the West tends to depersonalize the Godhead as an impersonal substance that is more basic than the persons of the Trinity. It errs by not agreeing with the East that the Father, Who is personal, is the fountainhead of the Trinity. From Him, the Son is eternally generated and the Spirit is eternally spirated. By deriving from the personal being of the Father, the Son and the Spirit are therefore also personal realities, Who interpenetrate one another in a manner beyond our comprehension. This depersonalization of the divine essence accounts for the impersonal tendency that appears in the West's institutionalization of sacraments and authority in the Church.

This doctrinal depersonalizing of the divine substance has a number of consequences in the West, according to the East.

First, it leads to an understanding of the efficacy of the sacraments in terms of impersonal power.

Second, according to the East, the Church in the West lacks a sense of the Spirit's personal, authoritative, self-authenticating presence and guidance; therefore, the West institutionalizes divine authority. Divine authority comes to be seen in terms of the Church itself, as the extension of the

Incarnation, of its doctrinal authority, its jurisdictional authority, and institutional power. This institutional authoritarianism in turn has had cultural consequences in Western culture. It has prompted anti-authoritarianism in Western culture, a rebellion against institutional authority in all of its forms. Western culture is consequently individualistic, egalitarian, and rebellious, rejecting true authority and proper subordination.

This can be seen in the West in its loss of appreciation for the submission of the Son to the Father and the submission of the Spirit to both. Submission comes to be regarded as a bad thing in the Western culture, even though authority and submission are unavoidable in society.

According to the East, had we in the West a more personal and dynamic view of the person and work of the Spirit and a deeper appreciation of subordination of the Spirit within the life of the Godhead, these excesses and distortions would not have come about.

According to the theologians of the East, such have been the fateful, sad theological and cultural consequences of the addition of the *Filioque* to the Creed.

2. Looking at the *Filioque* from the Western Churches' point of view, things seem quite different. The Western theologians note that the East's approach to the Trinity is from the perspective of the Threeness and tends to weaken a proper emphasis on the unity of God. The East's emphasis upon the Father as the fountainhead of the Triune life and upon the submission of the Son and the Spirit to the Father causes the East to undervalue the mutuality of the love within the life of the Trinity. This leads to a hierarchical authoritarianism in the life of the Church that fails to place subordination in the context of mutual love and to affirm the equal dignity of all persons made in the image of God, lay and clergy, men and women. The same is true of the culture and society in the East. The lack of cultural productivity and venturous advance in the Eastern countries reflects a rigid authoritarianism in the Churches

of the East.

It also appears to the West that in the East the Threeness of God is so emphasized as to suggest a Divine Society, a near tri-theism rather than a Trinitarian Oneness. We dare not weaken the biblical revelation of the Oneness of God.

In addition, with a stress upon the Spirit proceeding only from the Father, there is also the danger that the work of the Spirit can be thought as separable from the work of the Son, with all of the idolatry and distortions such a separation produces, as we mentioned above. Theological liberalism often follows that erroneous path.

D. Evaluation

Which view is correct – the Eastern or the Western? The critique by the East is no doubt colored in part by the West's inappropriate action in adding the *Filioque* without due discussion and affirmation by an Ecumenical Council. The critique by the West is no doubt influenced by responding to the severe charges of the East. We need a calmer and longer discussion.

One is inclined to say that both the East and the West have strong points and that each has much right in what it affirms. Since both East and West draw upon emphases taught in the Scriptures, they must be fundamentally compatible.

It is hard to commend as methodologically sound basing an entire theology of the procession of the Spirit on a single text, although from it we see that the Father as the fountainhead of the Godhead and the submission of the Son and the Spirit are important truths and are inherent in the very Names the Lord has chosen to reveal Himself to us. There is much to be gained, however, by seeing all of that in the mutual love in the Godhead.

It is clear that more discussion between East and West is needed and would prove fruitful when conducted in the light of Scripture. Anglicans, with their love of both

Scripture and the Fathers of the Church, should take a lead in that conversation.

Biblical Foundations
But when the Counselor comes, whom I will send to you from the Father, even the Spirit of truth, who proceeds from the Father, he will bear witness to me. John 15:26

For all who are led by the Spirit of God are sons of God. Romans 8:14

And because you are sons, God has sent the Spirit of His Son into our hearts, crying, "Abba! Father!" Galatians 4:6

False Teachings Denied/Objections Answered
The objections and false teaching have been included in the "Explanation" section (just above) as part of the discussion between the East and the West.

Implications
The wide-ranging and profound implications of the *Filioque* are spelled out in the critiques of East and West above. One should add that both critiques probably assign more influence to the ecclesiastical and cultural consequences of adding the *Filioque* clause to the Creed than it actually deserves. Other factors have played a large role in shaping both Church and culture in the East and in the West. However, there is truth in both approaches, and the whole Church would benefit from serious joint reflection by both East and West on the Trinity and the person and work of the Holy Spirit.

Excursus: The scope of the work of the Holy Spirit as set forth in Scripture briefly indicated.

In Scripture, the work of the Spirit is wide-ranging and diverse. He is at work in the creation, giving actuality and order to the decision of the Father and the mediation of the Son.

In the Old Testament period within the Old Covenant, we find that the Spirit is the distributor of supernatural gifts, the source of power and strength to individuals, and the inspirer of prophecy. He comes upon people to enable their ministry. He is given to some, for some tasks, but only for some of the time. He does not yet indwell all of the members of the Covenant people, nor abide in them.

In the New Covenant prior to the death and Resurrection of the Christ, He is specially active in the conception of the Christ in the womb of the Virgin Mary. He indwells the Son's human nature and is manifest in Jesus' ministry. Jesus' life and ministry is a Spirit-empowered life and ministry.

After Christ is glorified on the Cross, and after His Resurrection and Ascension, the Spirit is poured out from the Father by the Son upon the believing community at Pentecost. He indwells abidingly all believers, uniting us to Christ as branches to the vine. In the Father's drawing people to the Son, the Spirit regenerates their hearts and illumines their minds to believe the Gospel. He abides in the believer to sanctify the believer, conforming the saints from one degree of conformity to Christ to another, until the believers are perfected in glory at the Second Coming of Christ.

In the Church, He is the Spirit of unity, Who empowers the members to love one another, bear one another's burdens, and disciple one another. He distributes the spiritual gifts within the Body of Christ as He sovereignly determines, for the up-building of the Body. He empowers the Church for mission. He is the One Who inspired the Holy Scriptures to be the "Word of God written" so that they are both the Word of God and the words of believing men. He did so in order for the people of God to hear the Lord speak afresh through them by the Spirit. He illumines the minds of those believers who hear and meditate upon them.

In the world, He sustains the creation and serves as the

executor of God's providential rule over history and Christ's gracious rule over the Church. He limits the degree of sinful expression in society. This wide and hidden work of the Spirit is often referred to as God's gift of "common grace." In conjunction with the Church's evangelistic work, the Spirit convicts sinners of their sin and glorifies Christ to them.

In summary, it is in and through the Spirit that the Father and the Son are present and active in the world. The Holy Spirit is ever the executor of the Godhead. Apart from the Spirit, there would be no union with Christ, nor Communion with the Father

Conclusion

In this Article, as well as in the other four Articles in this first Section, Anglicans declare their affirmation of the great Catholic tradition of the Church, East and West. The dispute about the *Filioque* invites further exploration and discussion. Our common affirmation of the Apostolic Faith provides the basis for that discussion and is the basis for the continuing fellowship among all the churches that share the Apostolic Faith.

Section Two

The Rule of Faith (Articles 6, 7 and 8)

Having stated common ground with the Church Catholic in the central matters of the Gospel in Section One, the Articles now turn in Section Two to the Rule of Faith, that is, to the Canonical Scriptures or inspired Writings and to the creedal Faith of the Church that has been believed and taught by and in the Church from the beginning in agreement with the Holy Scriptures.

Article 6 affirms the sufficiency of the Scripture for salvation. The *entire* Canon of Holy Scripture, which includes both the Old and New Testament writings, is declared to be sufficient for the whole range of salvation.

The apocryphal writings, though appreciated by and written by members of the Church, are not part of the Canon of Scripture and therefore do not form part of the Rule of Faith. This does not mean that the apocryphal writings are of no value, but it does mean that they cannot be used to formulate doctrine or test the truthfulness of any given doctrine or teaching of the Church.

The supreme authority of the Scripture as the revealed, inspired Word of God is implied in Articles 6 and 7 and clearly stated in Articles 20 and 21. Since the Scriptures are "the Word of God written" (Article 20) they are to be understood and interpreted in accord with their nature as God's Word. Articles 7, 20, and 21 point out ways required for the responsible interpretation of Scriptures. (See also Appendix B concerning Anglican Interpretation of Scripture.) Only when the Scriptures are faithfully and responsibly interpreted, can they rightly serve as the supreme authority in the Church.

In Article 8, the importance of the Catholic Creedal tradition of the Church is affirmed. The three classic creeds are affirmed as faithful to the Apostolic and Prophetic

Scriptures and are faithful summaries of the biblical Faith and guides to the Church and its interpretation of Scripture.

We turn now to an interpretation of each of the three Articles in this section.

ARTICLE 6

Of the sufficiency of the Holy Scriptures for Salvation

Holy Scriptures containeth all things necessary to salvation: so that whatsoever is not read therein, nor may be proved thereby, is not to be required of any man, that it should be believed as an article of the faith, or be thought requisite or necessary to salvation. In the name of Holy Scripture, we do understand those Canonical books of the Old and New Testament, of whose authority was never any doubt in the Church.

Of the names and number of the Canonical Books.

Genesis, Exodus, Leviticus, Numbers, Deuteronomy, Joshua, Judges, Ruth, The First Book of Samuel, The Second Book of Samuel, The First Book of Kings, The Second Book of Kings, The First Book of Chronicles, The Second Book of Chronicles, The First Book of Esdras, The Second Book of Esdras, The Book of Esther, The Book of Job, The Psalms, The Proverbs, Ecclesiastes, or the Preacher, Cantica, or Songs of Solomon, Four Prophets the Greater, Twelve Prophets the Less.

And the other books (as Hierome saith) the Church doth read for example of life and instruction of manners; but yet doth it not apply them to establish any doctrine; such are these following:
The Third Book of Esdras.
The Fourth Book of Esdras.
The Book of Tobias.
The Book of Judith.
The rest of the Book of Esther.
The Book of Wisdom.
Jesus the Son of Sirach.

Baruch the Prophet.
The Song of the Three Children.
The Story of Susanna.
Of Bel and the Dragon.
The Prayer of Manasses.
The First Book of Maccabees.
The Second Book of Maccabees.

All the books of the New Testament, as they are commonly received, we do receive, and account them Canonical.

Introduction

How important are the Holy Scriptures? What is their relation to the teaching of the Church? Who may read and interpret them? How do we know if we are interpreting them correctly? These are questions that require clear and thoughtful answers.

At the time of the Reformation and thereafter, in order to answer those questions, it became usual to discuss the unique nature and central role of Holy Scriptures in terms of their authority, sufficiency, clarity, and efficacy. Scripture's authority as the Word of God written refers to Scripture's supreme authority in the life, teaching and witness of the Church. Scripture's sufficiency refers to its adequacy to provide all that is needed for sharing in the salvation that God supplies in Christ. Scripture's clarity refers to its understandability and to the ability and responsibility of the Church and of each person in Christ to read and interpret it faithfully. The efficacy of Scripture refers to its unique suitability to be the supreme means of grace used by the Holy Spirit in His work of enlightening the minds and hearts of those attending to the Scriptures. This Article deals with the sufficiency of Scripture. Other Articles will treat the Scriptures' authority, clarity, and efficacy.

The Teaching of Article 6

There are three points in the teaching of this Article:

1. The sufficiency of the Holy Scriptures for salvation is asserted.

2. The books included in the Canon of Holy Scripture are listed.

3. The nature and names of the Books, referred to as the Apocrypha, are listed and their use described.

1. The sufficiency of the Holy Scripture for salvation is asserted.

Explanation

The fact that the Articles of Religion discuss the Scripture first in terms of its sufficiency for salvation is very instructive. This indicates that the salvation of sinners to the Glory of God is the central thrust and great theme of the Scriptures. One may read the Holy Scriptures with other concerns in mind, but until one reads them from the perspective of a lost sinner in need of God's salvation, one has not yet read them as they were written to be read.

Salvation in this Article refers to salvation in its full biblical extent, that is, 1) for justification, or salvation from God's condemnation and restoration to His favor in Christ Jesus, 2) for sanctification, or for deliverance from the enslaving power of sin by our being increasingly conformed unto the likeness of Christ, and 3) for glorification, or for us to be fully and finally transformed into the likeness of Christ and to share in the new life in the new heaven and earth at the great consummation of all things. Concerning this great divine work of salvation, the Scripture, as God's Word, is fully complete and sufficient. No individual person or corporate entity in or outside the Church need or may add or subtract any conditions for salvation beyond what is stated in Scripture.

This firm assertion of the sufficiency of Scripture raises a question as to the Anglican view of tradition. For if nothing may be added to Scripture, what then are we to make of tradition? Several comments about the Anglican regard for tradition are in order.

First, traditions cannot be avoided. No society or church can exist over time without forming traditional ways of doing things and of understanding and applying the Christian truth. Repeated ways of regarding, saying, and doing things form traditions. Given that fact, it is important to have a considered and clear attitude toward the place of traditions. To claim to have no traditions is simply to be blind to the traditions one has and to be unaware of their impact on the Church's life and mission.

Second, on the whole, Anglicans appreciate and treasure churchly traditions. At the Reformation, those traditions compatible with the teaching of Scripture were kept. They were viewed as the result of the work of the Spirit leading the Church into wise and helpful ways of understanding and of living out the Christian truth, life, and mission. Churchly traditions give stability and practical patterns to the life of the Church. This positive attitude to churchly traditions means that Anglicans, along with the Lutheran Churches, are part of the conservative stream of the Reformation.

Third, by saying the Scriptures are sufficient for salvation, the Article is not implying that traditions may be adopted or kept regardless of their content. Those traditions that are contrary to Scripture must be either reformed or removed altogether. This was no small part of the work of the Anglican reformers. Traditions must also be reformed or removed when, due to changes in the culture or due to cross-cultural missionary work, those traditions actually hinder the practical exercise of the ministry and mission of the Church. In such cases, practicality and mission are of more value than a specific tradition.

Thus, appreciation with caution and a need for keeping a careful eye on developing traditions remains an Anglican principle. At the time of the Reformation, this attitude was stated as "the Church reformed and ever reforming."

Other Christian Communions have taken a more radical and negative attitude to churchly traditions, claiming to retain only what is expressly required by Scripture. This attitude, however, robs them of much wisdom given by the Holy Spirit to the Church down through the ages, ignores changes in the culture and tends to obscure the fact that these churches have their own traditions as well. It is better to be open to tradition, to own one's traditions and to keep an eye on them in the light of an ever-renewed examination in the light of Scripture and in the context of living out the life and mission of the Church. (See Article 34 for a fuller discussion of Tradition and traditions.)

Biblical Foundations
Positive Comment on tradition
Follow the pattern of the sound words that you have heard from me, in the faith and love that are in Christ Jesus. By the Holy Spirit who dwells within us, guard the good deposit entrusted to you. 1 Timothy 1:13-14

But as for you, continue in what you have learned and have firmly believed, knowing from whom you learned it and how from childhood you have been acquainted with the sacred writings, which are able to make you wise for salvation through faith in Christ Jesus. 2 Timothy 3:14-15

Negative comment on tradition
He answered them, "And why do you break the commandment of God for the sake of your tradition? For God commanded, 'Honor your father and your mother,' and, 'Whoever reviles father or mother must surely die.' But you say, 'If anyone tells his father or his mother, What you would have gained from me is given to God, he need

not honor his father.' So for the sake of your tradition you have made void the word of God. You hypocrites! Well did Isaiah prophesy of you, when he said: 'This people honors me with their lips, but their heart is far from me; in vain do they worship me, teaching as doctrines the commandments of men.'" Matthew 15:3-9

I am astonished that you are so quickly deserting him who called you in the grace of Christ and are turning to a different gospel— not that there is another one, but there are some who trouble you and want to distort the gospel of Christ. But even if we or an angel from heaven should preach to you a gospel contrary to the one we preached to you, let him be accursed. As we have said before, so now I say again: If anyone is preaching to you a gospel contrary to the one you received, let him be accursed. Galatians 1:6-9

I warn everyone who hears the words of the prophecy of this book: if anyone adds to them, God will add to him the plagues described in this book, and if anyone takes away from the words of the book of this prophecy, God will take away his share in the tree of life and in the holy city, which are described in this book. Revelation 22:18-19

False Teachings Denied/Objections Answered

A. Adding to the Scriptures is not allowed. Whether consciously or unintentionally, we tend to take what is familiar to us in the life and work of the Church and to regard it as essential to salvation. This elevation of our customs and practices is declared unacceptable by this Article and we must guard against it. This becomes particularly significant in ecumenical discussions and in cross-cultural missions.

B. No syncretism is allowed. Searching outside of Scripture for additional instruction that is essential to salvation is excluded. In asserting the sufficiency of Scripture, this Article declares it wrong to expect the holy books of the world's religions, such as the *Koran*, or the collected writings of *B'hai,* to provide any necessary additional teaching or true wisdom concerning salvation. Salvation is found only in Christ as set forth sufficiently and authoritatively in Scripture.

C. Some have suggested that, in declaring the sufficiency of Scripture, the Church declares all other books to be of no value and thereby exalts ignorance and rejects scholarship and progress. This is a misunderstanding of the sufficiency of Scripture. Holy Scripture is neither sufficient for, nor intended to provide knowledge about, all sorts of matters important to human beings. Much knowledge that is not found in Scripture is both delightful to the inquiring mind and helpful to society and culture. Quite the opposite from encouraging ignorance, the Church has a divine mandate to take all thought captive to Christ, for He is both Creator and Redeemer. God is the author of both the Book of Nature and the Book of Scripture. All truth belongs to God and is to be valued and encouraged by Christians. The sufficiency of Scripture has to do with the knowledge of God, which is essential to salvation. For salvation, Scripture is the Book to which we may and must turn.

Implications

No doubt the greatest danger we face is our tendency to add to or subtract from the New Testament's conditions for salvation in Christ Jesus, whether consciously or unconsciously. As mentioned above, we tend to think our understanding and experience is normative and essential. Only knowledge of Scripture, frequent self-examination in the light of Scripture, and the enlightenment of the Holy Spirit can keep this tendency in us in check.

The terrible consequence of adding to what is essential for salvation is that we place upon ourselves and others false requirements which, in the end, we cannot bear. We bind upon their consciences and ours burdens that the Lord has not placed there. Jesus warned the Pharisees about this and called them "children of the Devil" for doing so.

Also, when we add a teaching to Scripture as part of the Faith, or subtract from Scripture what is taught therein, we impact and distort all of our teaching of Scripture, for the teaching of Scripture is interconnected and forms a coherent whole.

2. The books included in the Canon of Holy Scripture are listed.
Explanation

Until the time of the Reformation, there was no recent dispute concerning which books belonged in the New Testament Canon. The term "canon" derived from the word for reeds from which measuring rulers were made. From that connection, the "canon" came to mean the books and the list of books by which the teaching of the Church was measured or declared true, and which were permitted to be read and taught in the corporate worship of the Church.

We should point out that at the time of the Reformation the book of Lamentations was included in the book of Jeremiah and is thus included in "the four Prophets" in the Article's list of Books. Accordingly, at the time the Articles were written, First and Second Esdras were the names of the books now known as Ezra and Nehemiah.

The 27 Books of the New Testament were part of the Scripture from the early beginnings. These were books that were either written by Apostles, or by those who were personal disciples and followers of the Apostles, or by unknown members of the apostolic Church whose writings were apostolic in content and of such excellence and innate authority as to have been recognized by the Church to be God's Word written, and inspired by the Holy Spirit. One might say that the Canon (or the books that made up the New Testament Canon) simply imposed itself upon the Church by the books' inherent excellence and by the Holy

Spirit speaking through them, or as some would say, by the anointing of the Spirit resting upon them.

However, the Article's reference to the Canonical books of the New Testament as books about which there had "never been any doubt in the Church" raises a question, since the writers of the Article were aware of the debate about a few of the books that took place in the early stages of the Church's discernment of the limits of the Canon. Perhaps the authors of the Article were saying that none of the Canonical books had ever been doubted by all or even a majority of the Church. Nor had the Church officially or in any Council ever cast doubt on the divine authority of any of these books. In fact, these books had, from their appearing, been seen to be authoritative or Canonical by significant portions of the Church.

Actually, the problem that the early Church had in discerning the limits of the Canon was not in finding books to include but rather in discerning which books to exclude. More than 66 books were being read and exercising influence in the Church from almost the very beginning of the life of the Church. In a very real sense, the Church had a functioning Canon of Scripture before it knew its limits. As stated above with regard to the New Testament, it was essentially "apostolic" authorship, content, and relevance that commended the books and that enabled the Church to recognize which books belonged in the New Testament Canon. The books that took some time to receive universal recognition were James, 2 Peter, 2 and 3 John, Revelation, and Jude. Books such as the *Didache*, *The Shepherd of Hermes*, and *Barnabas* were admired by many, but were excluded from the Canon in the end.

Is the New Testament Canon closed? Yes and no. On the one hand, only the 27 Books of the New Testament constitute the Canon of the New Testament, and no others. Books not written by the Apostles or by the disciples of the Apostles or after the apostolic period, roughly the first Century, are not to be added to the Canon of Scripture. In this sense, the Canon is closed. On the other hand, if one were to discover some apostolic writing of possible universal importance, the Church, judging in the light of the existing Canon, would have to consider including it. In that limited sense the Canon is open.

Such a discovery and inclusion, however, is highly unlikely. For, to be included, a genuine apostolic writing would have to be discovered, and none has been found in several thousand years. Further, the writing would have to win the approval of the universal Church, which would be far from easy. It seems far more likely that God, in His Providence, has seen to it that the books belonging to the Canon have been included already, sufficient for the well-being of the Church and its mission in the world.

In the Church's history, persons such as Marcion have sought to reduce the number of books in the Canon. All such attempts have been rejected by the Church. Religious movements such as the Gnostics in early Church history or cults like the Mormons in present day history have sought to add non-apostolic writings to the Canon. These writings also have been rejected by the Church.

Things are a bit more complicated with regard to the Old Testament Canon, which is treated in the next teaching point.

3. The nature and names of the books, referred to as the Apocrypha, are listed and their use described
Explanation

The case regarding the Old Testament is different from that of the New Testament. With regard to the Apocrypha there was and is a significant difference between Rome and the Churches of the Reformation. The books listed in Article 6 as "the other books" were included in the Canon in the Roman Church but were excluded from the Canon by the Churches of the Reformation.

Why were they excluded from the Canon by the Churches of the Reformation, including Anglicans? There are several reasons: 1) These books were not originally written in Hebrew. They stemmed from synagogues outside of Israel, from the Jews living in Gentile lands and were written in Greek. 2) They were never included in the Hebrew Canon as recognized by the Jews in Israel. 3) Jesus never quoted them or referred to them. And 4) the writings excluded themselves by containing some things contrary to the teaching of the Apostles in the New Testament Canon. For these reasons, the Churches of the Reformation returned to the Hebrew Canon of Jesus' day as it was found in Israel and rejected the expanded Canon as found in the Synagogues of the Diaspora or Exile. The Apocryphal books were not recognized as God's inspired Word.

Rome retained these Apocryphal books which had been accepted in the Canon early in the Church's history after the Church had grown to include a majority of Gentile Christians coming from Greek-speaking lands. The Churches of the East did so as well.

This Article does make it clear that Anglicans do not reject these books in every sense. A few of the readings in the Anglican lectionary are drawn from these books and are allowed to be read in the services of the Church, though they are not to be introduced as "The Word of the Lord." These books are commended to be critically read in private for personal encouragement, piety, and manners. However, since they are not Canonical and are not the inspired Word of God, no doctrine may be based upon them. Like all tradition in the Church, they may be respected but must be evaluated in the light of the Canonical books.

Scholars study these books to learn about historical developments in the period between the closing of the Old Testament and the beginning of the New Testament. They are significant for gaining a better understanding of persons and institutions that grew up in that period and that are found in the New Testament.

The status of the Apocrypha remains a matter of dispute between Anglicans and the other Churches of the

Reformation, on the one hand, and the Churches of the East and the Roman Catholic Church on the other. Since the Canon is of fundamental authority in the life of the Church, this is a matter of grave importance and calls for serious ecumenical discussion.

Conclusion

The Scriptures of the Old and New Testament, taken together and read in the light of Christ, are sufficient for salvation in the full sense of salvation and for a coherent statement of the Faith. Nothing may be added to them or subtracted from them. Churchly traditions are significant, but they are subordinate to and must be tested by the Canonical Scriptures. The books of the Apocrypha are not part of the Canon and may be read only for matters of piety and manners, and must be judged by their agreement or disagreement with the official Canon of the Church.

ARTICLE 7

Of the Old Testament

The Old Testament is not contrary to the New; for both in the Old and New Testament everlasting life is offered to mankind by Christ, who is the only Mediator between God and Man, being both God and Man. Wherefore they are not to be heard which feign that the old Fathers did look only for transitory promises. Although the law given from God by Moses, as touching ceremonies and rites, do not bind Christian men, nor the civil precepts thereof ought of necessity to be received in any commonwealth; yet, notwithstanding, no Christian man whatsoever is free from the obedience of the commandments which are called moral.

Introduction

Now that Christ has come and fulfilled the Old Testament, why do we need the Old Testament? Isn't much in the Old Testament at odds with the teaching of Christ and the Apostles? If we do use the Old Testament in the Church, how do the Old and New Testaments fit together? Such questions as these keep rising in the Church's history and need a careful answer. This Article addresses them from the perspective of the unity of the Scriptures in Christ.

The Old Testament is a Christian Book! The Church has always read the Scriptures of the Old Testament in the light of Christ. The Church, from the beginning, affirmed that a true understanding of the Old Testament is found only in the light of Christ. It cannot be rightly understood in the light of the Law of Moses or the Pentateuch, as does Judaism. Nor can Jesus be properly understood apart from the Old Testament. For that reason, the New Testament is bound together with the Old Testament to form one Bible, or one Canon of Sacred Scripture.

Since the Old Testament is written prior to the coming of Jesus Christ and before the writing of the New Testament, it is important to state how the Old Testament Scriptures are rightly related to the New Testament writings to form one Canon.

Errors have occurred within the Church in understanding the relationship of the two Testaments. The errors have tended toward two extremes. On the one hand, there has been a neglect of the Old Testament, as if it were largely superseded by the New Testament. Some, for example the heretic Marcion in the 2nd Century, have even taught that the Old Testament is in fundamental respects contrary to the New Testament. On the other hand, there has been a failure on the part of some in the Church who treasure the Old Testament to see how the coming of Christ has affected the proper understanding of the Old Testament and its relationship to the New Testament. Where a rejection of a Christ-centered reading of the Old Testament has taken place, a legalistic tendency has influenced the Church, and the place of justification through faith in Christ has been weakened or ignored.

For these reasons, Article 7 briefly states how the Old Testament is properly understood to relate to the New Testament and how, as part of the Canon, the Old Testament is authoritative in the life of the Church.

The Teaching of Article 7

This Article teaches three main points:

1. The unity of the Old Testament and the New Testament is found in Christ Who offers eternal life in both.

2. That part of the Old Testament law that concerns rites, ceremonies and civil precepts is not of necessity binding on the life of the Church or of individual Christians.

3. Christians are of necessity bound by the Old Testament commandments called moral.

1. The unity of the Old Testament and the New Testament is found in Christ Who offers eternal life in both.

Explanation

Salvation of sinful man to the glory of God is the central theme of the Scriptures. In this central theme, the Old Testament and the New Testament agree. The Old Testament does not contradict the New Testament. Just the opposite is true. Salvation and its reception are the same in both. This is true because Christ is central in both Testaments. In the Old Testament, Christ is central as the promised and anointed One, the Messiah, through Whom salvation will come. In the New Testament, He is central as Messiah Who has come and is to come again. In Him, salvation or eternal life is now to be found and will be perfected.

The Old Testament believers who put their faith in God, in His Word and promises, were in effect putting their faith in the Christ who was to come and in His work on the Cross for sinners, even though they were not fully aware of it at the time. They were justified and received eternal life through faith in the promised One who was to come to be their atoning sacrifice and deliverer. God's previous acts of deliverance and the feasts, the sacrifices, and the ceremonial remembrances of those saving acts, and the explicit messianic promises all point to Christ. This means that the Old Testament believers were not limited to the temporary, earthly blessings that are recorded in the Old Testament history, but in, with, and through those saving acts and through their faith, they were receiving the gift of eternal life by anticipation. This Christ- centered approach to the Scriptures follows Jesus' and the Apostles' view and use of the Old Testament.

When we speak of Old and New Testament, we want to avoid any suggestion that since the New has come the Old is now superseded or out of date. Quite the opposite. We are speaking of stages in one single divine movement of salvation, one abiding purpose and history in which God is working His salvation of fallen humanity. Later stages build on and carry forward previous stages and there is no full understanding of any part of God's saving history without seeing how it fits into the whole of His saving history. Christ is the key to the whole story, to what has come before His first coming and to what follows it, as well as to what is still to come.

Since we have emphasized God's saving movement in history, it is important to have a sense of the whole. Here is a very brief outline of God's saving history as centered in, or as leading to and developing from, Christ, as it is set forth in Scripture:

History begins with God's Creation of the world and humanity, and with our fall into sin. Creation and Fall are the essential background and context of all that follows in salvation history. God calls into being a people through Abraham and makes a covenant with them to be their God, to bless them, and to use them to save or bless all the families upon the earth. This Covenant is called the Covenant of Grace because it has no conditions; it is simply a gift of His love and purpose to save lost sinners. God makes other covenants with Israel; particularly important is the covenant He made at the giving of the Law on Mount Sinai after He had delivered Israel from bondage in Egypt through the Red Sea. The covenant at Sinai is a covenant in which God did set conditions for Israel to keep: being faithful to Him, keeping His laws, following His leading, and trusting in Him. Israel consistently failed to keep these conditions, falling into idolatry and immorality, and misrepresenting God in the world. This failure of God's people to keep the Sinai Covenant and the failure of most of her kings, priests, and her false prophets, led to a hope in a Savior, a coming anointed One, a Messiah, Who would be the true King, the faithful Priest, and the true Prophet, and thus bring in and mediate the New Covenant, a covenant written in Israel's renewed heart by God's Spirit. This hope was based entirely on God, Who keeps His Word and His Covenant of Grace, and not on humanity's faithfulness. Jesus came and was the true Prophet; in fact, He was the Word Incarnate. He was the true Priest Who offered Himself as the atoning sacrifice. He was and is the true King, the Lord, as evidenced in the authority of His word, His mighty deeds, and by His enthronement in His Ascension to the right hand of God. Earlier, when Jesus appointed twelve disciples, He made it clear that He was calling for a renewal and reformation of Israel to be united to the Father through Him. After Jesus made atonement for sinners by His crucifixion, His overcoming death in His Resurrection, and His Ascension as Lord, He sent the Holy Spirit from the Father to indwell His people, the Church, to set them free from the power of sin, and to guide and empower them in world-wide mission. The mission is to call all people everywhere to come to the Father through Christ and be joined to Him and His people through faith in Jesus and repentance from sin. In Christ, God had not forgotten His Word to bless all the families on the earth through His people. Therefore, His people are on mission until Christ returns in glory to consummate God's purpose of salvation. Christ will return in glory and majesty. Those who reject Christ will dwell apart, in anguish, in the place of the lost. Those united to Christ will dwell in the new heaven and new earth in which righteousness will dwell, to the glory of God and to the joy of the saved.

As you can see, Christ is the high point and key to the whole story, and therefore the key to both Testaments, that is, to the two stages of the Covenant of Grace.

In addition to the two Testaments being part of one story there are numerous ways in which the Old and New Testaments draw upon one another, and interact. For example there are explicit prophecies in the Old Testament that are fulfilled in the New Testament. One thinks of Jesus' triumphal entry into Jerusalem, riding not on a white stallion, with drawn sword in hand, but humbly, meekly riding on the foal of a donkey. This He did in fulfillment of a prophecy in Zechariah 9:9. To take one more very important example, it is hard to miss that the prophecy of Isaiah the prophet concerning the suffering servant in chapters 52 and 53 is fulfilled by Christ in His crucifixion, burial, and Resurrection..

Another way the two Testaments interrelate are the Old Testament types that are repeated in the New Testament in a new way. A type is a foreshadowing event or person that has a later realization in the New Testament. For example the Passover lamb is a type of Jesus Who becomes our Passover Lamb on the Cross. And, the annual feast of the Passover is a type of the Lord's Supper or Eucharist that we Christians celebrate weekly on the Lord's Day. The Old Testament Temple in Jerusalem, where God dwelt, is a type of the Church, which the Holy Spirit indwells, and both are a type of the heavenly Temple where the saints come boldly into the very presence of the Lord. In typology, we see that which was said and done earlier is deepened and fulfilled in what was done at the coming of Christ. And what was done at the coming of Christ is better understood as a greater repetition in or by Christ, of what was done earlier.

Having emphasized the essential continuity and harmony between the Old and New Testaments, it is important to say that the coming of Christ does bring about some changes and some new ways of doing things in the New Covenant. This will be addressed in the next two teaching points.

The main idea in this first teaching point is that salvation and eternal life are given by God through faith in Christ in both Testaments. The two Testaments find their essential unity in Him. Justification by faith in God's grace through Christ, and not by our meritorious works, has been God's way of salvation from the beginning and remains so today. Christ Jesus is the key to understanding both of the Testaments and their unity.

Biblical Foundations

Do not think that I have come to abolish the Law or the Prophets; I have not come to abolish them but to fulfill them. For truly, I say to you, until heaven and earth pass away, not an iota, not a dot, will pass from the Law until all is accomplished. Matthew 5:17-18

And beginning with Moses and all the Prophets, he interpreted to them in all the Scriptures the things concerning himself. Luke 24:27

Then he said to them, "These are my words that I spoke to you while I was still with you, that everything written about me in the Law of Moses and the Prophets and the Psalms must be fulfilled." Then he opened their minds to understand the Scriptures. Luke 24:44-45

You search the Scriptures because you think that in them you have eternal life; and it is they that bear witness about me, yet you refuse to come to me that you may have life. John 5:39-40

This Jesus, delivered up according to the definite plan and foreknowledge of God, you crucified and killed by the hands of lawless men. Acts 2:23

Brothers, the Scripture had to be fulfilled, which the Holy Spirit spoke beforehand by the mouth of David concerning Judas, who became a guide to those who arrested Jesus. Acts 1:16

For what does the Scripture say? "Abraham believed God, and it was counted to him as righteousness." Romans 4:3

False Teachings Denied/Objections Answered

1. "The Old Testament is contrary to the New." A profound error is the view that the God of the Old

Testament is different from the God of the New Testament. From the earliest days to the present some have considered the Old Testament to present a different God from the New Testament. In the early Church, Marcion the heretic did this. Today, one hears in popular circles that the God of the Old Testament is full of wrath, whereas the God of the New Testament is full of love and mercy. This involves a misreading of both the Old Testament and the New Testament. God is the same holy and gracious God in both. In the Old Testament, He sets His love on Israel because of His grace alone. In the New Testament, it is Jesus, full of grace, Who will return to judge the living and the dead and Who warns, more than anyone else, of the danger of hell to the unrepentant. "Do not fear him who can destroy the body but beware Him who can destroy both body and soul in hell."

2. A related error is the view that one achieves salvation in the Old Testament by good works and in the New Testament by grace.

As pointed out above, salvation in both Testaments is always by grace received in faith enabling repentance and a life of obedience to God, albeit, of imperfect obedience. Salvation is never earned by our good works. Eternal life is always an undeserved gift and never a reward earned.

3. Some object, "Aren't you simply reading Christ back into the Old Testament Scriptures?" The answer is "No." The deepening sense of sin, the growing predictions of an anointed one who was to come and fulfill the offices of prophet, priest, and king, the promises of God for a final deliverance and the types and antitypes all find a unique and supernatural fulfillment in Christ. Moreover, to read the Old Testament as fulfilled in the Torah (the first five books of the Bible), understood only as centered in the Mosaic Law, misreads the Torah and leaves far too much of the Old Testament unaccounted for and without abiding meaning.

We have excellent warrant for reading the Old Testament Scriptures as centered in Christ. It is the way that Christ read the Old Testament Scriptures, and the Apostles after Him. As followers of Christ, Who is the Truth, we see light in His light, including His light upon the Old Testament.

Implications

When we read the Old Testament together with the New Testament, we find, to our joy, an essential preparation for and explanation of Who Christ is and what He came to accomplish. When we read the New Testament apart from the Old Testament, much of the meaning of the New Testament is lost and it is often misunderstood as a compilation of moral principles and timeless philosophy.

The main point is that we need the whole of Scripture and we need to read it as centered in Christ.

2. That part of the Old Testament law that concerns rites, ceremonies and civil precepts is not of necessity binding on the life of the Church or of individual Christians.

Explanation

The rites and ceremonies of the Old Testament are not binding on Christians for two reasons:

First, they are not binding because Christ has fulfilled these rites and ceremonies in Himself and has given them a new form of remembrance for His followers. A profound example is the Passover celebration. The Old Testament Passover ceremony is fulfilled and transformed into the Lord's Supper or Eucharist, because Christ has become our Passover Lamb. His blood is placed upon the lintels of our hearts rather than our doorposts. By His body broken and His blood shed for us, we have been passed over in the final condemnation. That being true, Christians are not bound out of necessity to celebrate the annual feast of the Passover, though Christians and Messianic Jewish believers may freely choose to do so, and many do. The same is true of the many Old Testament feasts and fasts. In fact, even the feasts and fasts of the Christian year that Anglicans treasure are not of necessity binding on Christian churches, though Anglicans commend them to all and require them among themselves.

Second, certain customs are no longer binding because Christ has declared some of the Old Testament practices to have fulfilled their purpose upon his arrival and are no longer in effect. For example, having declared that our problem is sinfulness and sinning against the holy love of God, He declared that the dietary laws of clean and unclean are no longer binding. They had served their purpose of keeping Israel distinct until the coming of the Messiah. Now, in the light of Christ, we can see that what is wrong with us is not what we take into our stomachs but what proceeds out of our fallen hearts. That is what makes a person unclean. So Christ declared all foods clean.

The Article also states that the civil precepts or laws that were binding on Israel as a nation are not of necessity binding on Christians. Israel was a theocracy, a nation governed by God. The Church is a theocracy but it is not a geographic, political nation. Rather, the Church consists of congregations united spiritually and spread among the nations of the earth. Therefore, on the one hand, the civil legislation of the Old Testament given to Israel is not directly binding on the nations or on the Christians in those nations. On the other hand, there is nothing that would bar a nation from considering Old Testament civil legislation to see what might be wise for the nation to adopt. Western civil law, for example, is greatly influenced by Old Testament civil laws, precepts, and principles.

It is important to note that the Article is careful and precise when it says that these customs and laws are "not of necessity binding." People in the Church may choose to keep some of the Old Testament ceremonies and rites if they wish and find them helpful, while giving them a

Christian or Messianic interpretation, but they may not bind them on the consciences of their fellow Christians as necessary to salvation. Messianic Jewish congregations today keep many of the Jewish feasts with a Christ-centered interpretation. This is quite acceptable and often very helpful spiritually. They are free to do this, provided that they do not require this as a necessity for all Christians. The largely Gentile Christian congregations would benefit greatly were they to learn of their Jewish roots from their neighboring Jewish Messianic congregations, and the Messianic congregations would benefit from getting to know and share with their Gentile brothers and sisters.

Biblical Foundations

And he said to them, "Then are you also without understanding? Do you not see that whatever goes into a person from outside cannot defile him, since it enters not his heart but his stomach, and is expelled?" (Thus he declared all foods clean.) Mark 7:18-19

[Jesus said] "Woe to you, scribes and Pharisees, hypocrites! For you clean the outside of the cup and the plate, but inside they are full of greed and self-indulgence." Matthew 23:25

And he said to them, "You yourselves know how unlawful it is for a Jew to associate with or to visit anyone of another nation, but God has shown me that I should not call any person common or unclean." Acts 10:28

Cleanse out the old leaven that you may be a new lump, as you really are unleavened. For Christ, our Passover lamb, has been sacrificed. Let us therefore celebrate the festival, not with the old leaven, the leaven of malice and evil, but with the unleavened bread of sincerity and truth. 1 Corinthians 5:7-8

False Teachings Denied/Objections Answered

1. Some hold that Old Testament rites and ceremonies are still binding upon all Christians if they are not expressly

cancelled in the New Testament. This overlooks the way in which much in the Old Testament is fulfilled in Christ.

2. Others would forbid Christians the freedom to practice certain Old Testament ceremonies if they so chose. This denies the freedom we have in Christ and the possibility of using these ceremonies with a Christ-centered interpretation.

3. Some have suggested that the teaching of this second point of the Article declaring rites, ceremonies, and civil laws not binding on Christians is designed to make being a Christian easy. Nothing could be further from the truth. The point of the Article is simply to be aware of the liberating and transforming effect of the coming of Christ and His fulfillment of the Old Testament for the life and mission of His followers. Actually, Christian faith and freedom call for a more searching, heart-felt obedience than the superficial manner in which some have observed and continue to observe ceremonies found in Scripture.

Implications

We are to be careful not to bind on our own conscience or the consciences of other Christians that which is not required in Christ. St. Paul makes this point in numerous places in his writings and St. Peter at the first Council of the Church made the same point. "For freedom Christ has set us free."

3. Christians are of necessity bound by the Old Testament commandments called moral
Explanation

The Ten Commandments are chiefly in view here; Jesus could sum them up as: love to God first and foremost, and second, love to the neighbor as to the self. The Ten Commandments are not optional - neither for God nor for us. They are not optional for God because they express the very nature and character of God Himself. They are not optional for us because the Ten Commandments are written in the depths of our conscience, as those created in the image of God to know Him and to worship and obey Him. And they apply God's holy character to our human relationship with Him and our neighbors. In short, they describe the moral order or structure in which we human beings live and move and have our being. "You shall be holy for I am holy."

But we must be very careful here. We need to ask, "In what way are we Christians bound by or under the Law, called moral?" First, it is essential to state that there is one sense in which we Christians are not under the moral law. We Christians are not under the moral law as a means of meriting or earning our salvation. Our justification, which is the abiding ground of our salvation, is provided to us by the grace of God in Christ Jesus, and is received by repentant faith. No Christian could ever rightfully claim to merit salvation or to keep the Law of Love from a sinless heart. Articles 11 and 12 will treat these issues specifically. If we get this wrong we have lost everything.

Christians, however, are under the Law as a mirror that shows us, in our conscience, our indwelling sin and our sinful actions. This diagnostic function of the Law leads us anew to Christ for renewed forgiveness and repentance. We need this use of the Law because we Christians are never free from indwelling sin and its effects in this life and because we are experts at self-deception. This use of the Law is actually gracious, albeit painful, and essential to our right relationship with God and to our growth in grace.

Christians are also under the revealed Law of God as giving us knowledge of the character of God and His will that shapes and informs our conscience. It gives us instruction in right or godly living. The Law, interpreted by the example of Christ and His teaching, serves as a guide that informs our renewed desire to love and serve the Lord and to love our neighbors as ourselves. Since our hearts are made new by the Holy Spirit, as new creatures in Christ, we delight in the Law of God which is more precious to us than silver and gold, sweeter than honey, even honey in the honeycomb. As believers, we walk in His ways in joy and in gratitude, at least in part. This instructional or guiding use or function of the Law is also essential to our life in the Lord and our growth in grace.

Therefore there are two ways in which we Christians are related to the Law of God called moral: it shows us our sin and it informs and guides our obedience. It is important to add that, as redeemed sinners, we Christians are under the Law in both of these senses simultaneously. Both are needed. This will remain true of us until Christ comes in glory to perfect us and to complete His work of salvation in us. Until then, we will have need to daily confess our sins and to rejoice in His moral instruction, guidance, and empowerment in the Spirit.

Biblical Foundations

The precepts of the Lord are right, rejoicing the heart; the commandment of the Lord is pure, enlightening the eyes. Psalm 19:8

Put false ways far from me and graciously teach me your law! Psalm 119:29

How sweet are your words to my taste, sweeter than honey to my mouth! Through your precepts I get understanding; therefore I hate every false way. Psalm 119:103-104

"Teacher, which is the great commandment in the Law?" And he said to him, "You shall love the Lord your God with all your heart and with all your soul and with all your mind. This is the great and first commandment. And a second is like it: You shall love your neighbor as yourself. On these two commandments depend all the Law and the Prophets." Matthew 22:36-40

Now we know that whatever the law says it speaks to those who are under the law, so that every mouth may be stopped, and the whole world may be held accountable to God. For by works of the law no human being will be justified in his sight, since through the law comes knowledge of sin. Romans 3:19-20

It is no longer I who live, but Christ who lives in me. And the life I now live in the flesh I live by faith in the Son of God, who loved me and gave himself for me. I do not nullify the grace of God, for if justification were through the law, then Christ died for no purpose. Galatians 2:20-21

But thanks be to God, that you who were once slaves of sin have become obedient from the heart to the standard of teaching to which you were committed, and, having been set free from sin, have become slaves of righteousness. Romans 6:17-18

False Teachings Denied/Objections Answered

1. Any doctrine that says that Christians are not under the moral law as convicting us of sin and as guiding our conscience, is to be rejected. Such teaching or theology is referred to as antinomianism (against-the-law-ism). This is a false application of the doctrine of justification by grace through faith and not by our merit or law-keeping. It is false because it denies that we, as Christians, are judged and shown by the Law to be sinners who need the abiding forgiveness of Christ and also that, as Christians who are justified, we are informed and guided by the Law, as we are moved by the Holy Spirit to gratefully obey the Lord's will for us, given in the Law. It separates faith from repentance and justification from sanctification, which is contrary to the New Testament and to the nature of God.

Antinomianism also errs because it leaves love blind. Love seeks the other's good and is even willing to sacrifice all for the other. But love needs to know what the good for the other is. The Law gives the moral perspective and principles that enable us to discern the good and to guide love's sacrifice.

2. The teaching that Christians are to keep all of the commands, rites, and ceremonies found in the Old Testament unless explicitly cancelled by Jesus Christ is

also to be rejected. This teaching is sometimes referred to as the doctrine of *theonomy,* from "the Law of God." It teaches that Christians and the civil authorities of the nations are to keep all of the laws found in the Old Testament unless they are explicitly cancelled by Jesus Christ or by the Apostles in His Name. This ignores the fact that the Christian Church is not a theocratic nation among the nations of the world and that the civil law of Israel is not binding on Christians or on the other nations of the world.

3. Some object that if we allow the Law a positive place in Christian life, it will lead us to believe that we are justified by our good works and not by grace. That is a danger. But such will not take place if the Law and Gospel are known in depth, for the Law penetrates deep within the heart and inevitably shows us our sin, calls for repentance and leads us to Christ our Savior for forgiveness, Who then leads us to a renewed dependence on His Cross and to follow Him.

4. Others will object that if we allow the Law a positive role in Christian life, and in our sanctification, that a self-righteous, joyless, judgmental form of Christianity will be the result. It must be admitted that this has at times been the case. Again, this can only take place when the Law is treated in a superficial manner and the super abundance of God's grace in Christ is overlooked. The antidote is the same as given in the objection just above.

It is clear that we need, and are given by the Lord, both the Law and the Gospel. To have the Law without the Gospel is to be led to self-righteous deception or to despair; to have the Gospel without the Law is to mock God's holiness and to live at ease in self-indulgent deception.

Implications

The most important implication is that, as Christians, we are to meditate on God's Word, and not least upon His Law, so that through it our Lord may convict us of sin, comfort us by the Gospel, and guide us in righteousness. Christians do well to memorize the Ten Commandments and to include them, deepened by the penetrating teaching and example of Christ, in their daily times of prayer and reflection before the Lord.

Conclusion

There is great freedom in Christ for Christians to be led by the Spirit, but the Spirit does not lead one to sin or to ignore or violate the moral Law of God, but rather to fulfill the Law in love.

ARTICLE 8

Of the Three Creeds

The Three Creeds, Nicene Creed, Athanasius's Creed, and that which is commonly called the Apostles' Creed, ought thoroughly to be received and believed; for they may be proved by most certain warrants of Holy Scripture. (Wording from 1662 Book of Common Prayer)

Introduction
The three creeds mentioned in this Article form part of the Rule of Faith in the Western Catholic Church. The Eastern Church and the Western Church both treasure and use the Nicene Creed, with the difference that the Western Church has added the *Filioque* clause. (See Article 5, Teaching Point 3.)

The Teaching of Article 8
This Article includes the following three teaching points:

1. Three Creeds are named: the Nicene, Athanasius's and Apostles'.

2. These Creeds are to be received and used as part of the Church's Rule of Faith.

3. The reason these Creeds are to be received is that they all may be proved by Holy Scripture.

1. Three Creeds are named: the Nicene, Athanasius's and Apostles'
Explanation

The Church has regularly used in its teaching and worship a summary of the Faith that is found in the Holy Scriptures. This practice arises from several perennial needs of the Church: First, there is the need to interpret the Scriptures in teaching and preaching. Second, there is the need to catechize the newly converted, the members and the children of the Church. Third, the Church is called to refute false teaching contrary to the Faith of the Scripture. And, fourth, the Church must clearly distinguish the Christian Faith from non-Christian religions and philosophies so that both Christians and non-Christians can see the difference and consider the unique claims of the Gospel and the errors of these religions and philosophies.

From the earliest days there was a common "rule of faith" found in the Church. It is found both in the Apostles' teaching and in the teaching of the Church. This "rule of faith" was a summary of the Apostolic Gospel set in the context of God as the Creator and the Consummator of all things. It was similar to what is found in the Apostles' Creed today. Thus the teaching of the Scriptures and the teaching of the Church were at one from the beginning.

As heresies arose and various philosophies were encountered the "rule of faith" was formally adopted and expanded as a creed. A creed, in this sense, functions as a statement of the central articles of the Faith to which the Church, its official teachers and members, are committed. The Creeds were also concisely expanded to reject false teaching that was influencing the Church.

The three Creeds listed in this Article are often referred to as the Ecumenical, or Catholic, Creeds, for they set forth the fundamental articles of the Christian Faith as accepted by the ancient, undivided Catholic Church and by almost all orthodox Christian bodies since.

It should be pointed out, however, that only the Nicene Creed has been officially accepted by both the Churches of the East and the West. It is therefore the most universal of the Creeds, having arisen from two Ecumenical Councils. The Athanasius' and Apostles' Creeds are official Creeds only of the West. They are in essential agreement with the Nicene Creed. The three Creeds are all Trinitarian in content and structure and they center in Christ and redemption.

A word about each of the Creeds is in order:

The Nicene Creed

The Nicene Creed was first adopted by the First Ecumenical Council of Nicaea in A.D. 325. It was probably based upon a local Eastern creed used in one of the churches, i.e. Jerusalem, Antioch, or Caesarea.

The local creed was adapted to assert the full divinity of the Son, Who was declared to be "very God of very God," "of the same substance of the Father," and that He was "begotten and not made." This truth the Council asserted against the teaching of Arius, who sought to preserve the oneness and transcendent nature of the true God, while honoring Jesus by teaching that Jesus was the first creation of the Father, through Whom the Father created all other creatures. Arius further taught that since the Son was a creature, "there was when the Son was not." To these assertions, the Council responded by affirming the full and eternal deity of the Son. The Council affirmed the oneness of God while at the same time declaring that the Father was God and the Son was also God, of the same nature as the Father (Greek, *homoousios*, "same essence" and not *homoiousios*, "similar essence" or "like essence"). In addition to the clear biblical statements that required these beliefs, the Council believed that only God could save us and that, since Jesus is our Savior, therefore Jesus the Son must be fully God.

At the next Ecumenical Council held in Constantinople in A.D. 381, the Nicene Creed was expanded to explicitly affirm the full divinity of the Holy Spirit against those who were denying the personhood and divinity of the Spirit.

The Nicene Creed was formally adopted again by the Fourth Ecumenical Council of Chalcedon in A.D. 451.

Later, beginning in A.D. 589, the Churches of the West unilaterally added the *Filioque* phrase ("and the Son") to the Nicene Creed, thereby declaring that the Holy Spirit proceeds from the Father <u>and from the Son.</u> This has been a matter of contention between the Churches of the East and the West ever since. The Churches of the East contend A) that the West had no right to unilaterally alter an Ecumenical Creed, B) that the *Filioque* is contrary to the teaching of Scripture, C) that it implies that there is an impersonal divine essence in the Godhead in which the three Persons of the Godhead share and D) robs the Holy Spirit from full personhood. The West denies these charges and claims A) that the *Filioque* is grounded in biblical teaching, B) expresses the full divinity of the Son and the Spirit, C) teaches the mutual love between the Father and the Son, D) prevents a separation of the work of the Spirit from the work of the Son, and E) while it may go beyond the earlier version of the Nicene Creed, it does not contradict it and only brings out the fuller biblical teaching behind the Creed. (For a fuller explanation of the *Filioque*, see Article 5, Teaching Point 3.)

The Nicene Creed
We believe in one God,
    the Father, the Almighty,
    maker of heaven and earth,
    of all that is, seen and unseen.

We believe in one Lord, Jesus Christ,
    the only Son of God,
    eternally begotten of the Father,

God from God, Light from Light,
true God from true God,
begotten, not made,
of one Being with the Father.
Through him all things were made.
For us and for our salvation
he came down from heaven:
By the power of the Holy Spirit
he became incarnate from the Virgin Mary,
and was made man.
For our sake he was crucified under Pontius Pilate;
he suffered death and was buried.
On the third day he rose again
in accordance with the Scriptures;
he ascended into heaven
and is seated at the right hand of the Father.
He will come again in glory to judge the living and the dead, and his kingdom will have no end.

We believe in the Holy Spirit, the Lord, the giver of life,
who proceeds from the Father and the Son.
With the Father and the Son he is worshiped and glorified.
He has spoken through the Prophets.

We believe in one holy catholic and apostolic Church.
We acknowledge one baptism for the forgiveness of sins.
We look for the resurrection of the dead,
and the life of the world to come. Amen.

The Creed of Athanasius

This Ecumenical Creed is sometimes referred to as the *Symbolum Quicunque* after the beginning of the Creed in Latin, *Quicunque vult salvus esse,* "Whoever will be saved." This Western Creed was not written by Athanasius (A.D. 297-373), who was an Eastern Father and the champion *par excellence* of Nicene theology against Arius and the Arians. The Creed bears his name because it sets forth Nicene theology with precision, embodying that for which Athanasius stood. It was written near the beginning of the 6th century in Southern Gaul by an unknown author who was clearly influenced by the theology of St. Augustine. The Creed clearly states the doctrine of the Trinity, the Incarnation of the Son, includes the *Filioque*, the saving acts of the Son, His return to judge the living and the dead, and declares that such belief is necessary for salvation.

At the Reformation of the 16th century, the Roman Catholic Church, the Lutheran Church, and the Anglican Church affirmed it as one of the Ecumenical Creeds.

The Creed of Saint Athanasius

Whosoever will be saved, before all things it is necessary that he hold the Catholic Faith.

Which Faith except everyone do keep whole and undefiled, without doubt he shall perish everlastingly.

And the Catholic Faith is this: That we worship one God in Trinity, and Trinity in Unity,

    neither confounding the Persons, nor dividing the Substance.

For there is one Person of the Father, another of the Son, and another of the Holy Ghost.

But the Godhead of the Father, of the Son, and of the Holy Ghost, is all one, the Glory

    equal, the Majesty co-eternal.

Such as the Father is, such is the Son, and such is the Holy Ghost.

The Father uncreate, the Son uncreate, and the Holy Ghost uncreate.

The Father incomprehensible, the Son incomprehensible, and the Holy Ghost

    incomprehensible.

The Father eternal, the Son eternal, and the Holy Ghost eternal.

And yet they are not three eternals, but one eternal.
As also there are not three incomprehensibles, nor three uncreated, but one uncreated, and
   one incomprehensible.
So likewise the Father is Almighty, the Son Almighty, and the Holy Ghost Almighty.
And yet they are not three Almighties, but one Almighty.
So the Father is God, the Son is God, and the Holy Ghost is God.
And yet they are not three Gods, but one God.
So likewise the Father is Lord, the Son Lord, and the Holy Ghost Lord.
And yet not three Lords, but one Lord.
For like as we are compelled by the Christian verity to acknowledge every Person by
   himself to be both God and Lord,
So are we forbidden by the Catholic Religion, to say, There be three Gods, or three Lords.
The Father is made of none, neither created, nor begotten.
The Son is of the Father alone, not made, nor created, but begotten.
The Holy Ghost is of the Father and of the Son, neither made, nor created, nor begotten,
   but proceeding.
So there is one Father, not three Fathers; one Son, not three Sons; one Holy Ghost, not three
   Holy Ghosts.
And in this Trinity none is afore, or after other; none is greater, or less than another;
But the whole three Persons are co-eternal together and co-equal.
So that in all things, as is aforesaid, the Unity in Trinity and the Trinity in Unity is to be
   worshiped.
He therefore that will be saved is must think thus of the Trinity.

Furthermore, it is necessary to everlasting salvation that he also believe rightly the
   Incarnation of our Lord Jesus Christ.
For the right Faith is, that we believe and confess, that our Lord Jesus Christ, the Son of
   God, is God and Man;
God, of the substance of the Father, begotten before the worlds; and Man of the Substance
   of his Mother, born in the world;
Perfect God and perfect Man, of a reasonable soul and human flesh subsisting.
Equal to the Father, as touching his Godhead; and inferior to the Father, as touching his
   Manhood;
Who, although he be God and Man, yet he is not two, but one Christ;
One, not by conversion of the Godhead into flesh but by taking of the Manhood into God;
One altogether; not by confusion of Substance, but by unity of Person.
For as the reasonable soul and flesh is one man, so God and Man is one Christ;
Who suffered for our salvation, descended into hell, rose again the third day from the dead.
He ascended into heaven, he sitteth at the right hand of the Father, God Almighty, from
   whence he will come to judge the quick and the dead.
At whose coming all men will rise again with their bodies and shall give account for their
   own works.
And they that have done good shall go into life everlasting; and they that have done evil into everlasting fire.
This is the Catholic Faith, which except a man believe faithfully, he cannot be saved.

The Apostles' Creed

This Creed is a Western Creed. It was not written by the Twelve Apostles, with each Apostle adding one line, as was once taught. It is named the Apostles' Creed because it states very briefly what the Apostles taught in words largely drawn from the Scripture. The Creed probably grew from the questions and answers used in the practice of baptism, mostly likely beginning in the Church in Rome. Its use in liturgy and instruction became widespread in the West by the 8th century. As it became known, it was widely used in the West in preparation for baptism and in the instruction of the faithful in general.

It is Trinitarian and begins with "I believe in" perhaps due to its origin in the liturgy for baptism, where the faith of the baptized, or his or her representatives, is called for. In contrast, the Nicene Creed in its earliest forms begins with "We believe in," stemming from its origin in the Councils, expressing the Faith of the Church.

The brevity of the Apostles' Creed is due to its containing very little theological elaboration of the biblical phrases it includes. As such, it reflects the primitive "rule of faith." It simply states the saving acts of Christ and sets them in the context of God as the Creator and the consummator of all things. The entire life of Christ is not mentioned and is covered by a comma. This does not mean that the life of Christ has no meaning to the Church, but that the life of Christ is to be understood and applied only in the light of the Gospel.

The Apostles' Creed
I believe in God, the Father almighty,
creator of heaven and earth.
I believe in Jesus Christ, his only son, our Lord.
He was conceived by the power of the Holy Spirit
and born of the Virgin Mary.
He suffered under Pontius Pilate,
was crucified, died, and was buried.

He descended to the dead.
On the third day he rose again.
He ascended into heaven,
and is seated at the right hand of the Father.
He will come again to judge the living and the dead.

I believe in the Holy Spirit,
the holy catholic Church,
the communion of saints,
the forgiveness of sins,
the resurrection of the body,
and the life everlasting. Amen

2. These Creeds are to be received and used as part of the Church's Rule of Faith.
Explanation

At the time of the Reformation when the teaching of the Church in the West was being criticized and reformed in the Church of England, it was important for all to know that there was no intent on the part of the Church of England, or the magisterial Reformers in general, to depart from the Faith of the ancient and undivided Church. Article 8 was written to make that point.

What was being changed by the Anglican Reformers was that part of the tradition of the Church that was contrary to the Scripture and was no part of the ancient Faith. The Anglican reformers continually make the point that Anglicans teach only that which is Apostolic and ancient.

Biblical Foundations

Follow the pattern of the sound words that you have heard from me, in the faith and love that are in Christ Jesus. By the Holy Spirit who dwells within us, guard the good deposit entrusted to you. 1 Timothy 1: 13-14

But as for you, continue in what you have learned and have firmly believed, knowing from whom you learned it and how from childhood you have been acquainted with the sacred writings, which are able to make you wise for salvation through faith in Christ Jesus. 2 Timothy 3:14-15

False Teachings Denied/Objections Answered

This 8th Article is an implicit rejection of any form of doctrine-less Christianity. The Church is by nature creedal and not creedless. The Church must state its core beliefs in creeds and other formularies if it is to remain faithful to its calling and responsibility for interpreting Scripture, teaching the faithful, engaging in faithful worship, defending the Faith against false teaching, and sharing the Faith with non-Christians.

This all seems obvious, but there have been some who have taught a "non-doctrinal Christianity," a creedless Christianity. They favor a religion of intuition and "religious experience." But Christianity is not, and never has been, a wordless experience of God. Orthodox (right thinking) Christians do not deny that the experience of standing in the presence of God does lead to awe, praise, and the awareness of one's sin. Isaiah saw the Lord high and lifted up and cried out, "Woe is me for I am lost; for I am a man of unclean lips, and I dwell in the midst of a people of unclean lips; for I have seen the King, the Lord of hosts!" (Isaiah 6:5). But far more is involved in knowing God than profound emotion and inexpressible awareness. At the heart of true Christianity is a Spirit-enabled response of repentance and trust in God, Who is known in and through His Word in Christ, known in and through the Gospel. God is a God of revelation through both His creation and His supernatural words and deeds, using Prophets and Apostles, Christ Jesus Himself being the chief revelation, the Word incarnate. God is not the "unknown God," nor the "wordless God," and the Church is not speechless, but is charged with the faithful proclamation of His Gospel and His truth to all. Creeds give expression both to God's Word to the Church and to the faithful response of the Church to God and to the world.

Implications

Rehearsing the core of the Faith, both as an act of worship and in order to teach the Church its doctrinal foundations, is essential. It is important that the members of the Church know the Ten Commandments, the Lord's Prayer, and the Creed by heart and also have a good understanding of the meaning and biblical foundation of these key summary parts of the Faith. For this to be true, the Creeds as well as the Lord's Prayer and the Ten Commandments have their place in the corporate worship of the Church and in churchly education for both adults and children. This needs to be taken far more seriously than is presently the practice in many congregations.

3. The reason these Creeds are to be received is that they all may be proved by Holy Scripture.

Explanation

Once again, the Articles make it clear that God speaking through the Scriptures is the supreme authority in the Church. The Creeds are to serve as part of the Church's "rule of faith" only because they are scriptural and not simply because they are ancient. They teach and summarize or lift up what is central in Scripture. They teach only what is found in Holy Scripture or may be deduced from the teaching of Scripture.

Biblical Foundations

Each article of the three Creeds can be documented from Scripture, as Article 8 claims. Here is one set of texts for the Apostles Creed. Many other texts could be added. (This selection of texts was compiled by the Rev. John Heidengren.)

One God (Nicene)
Therefore you are great, O LORD God. For there is none like you, and there is no God besides you, according to all that we have heard with our ears. 2 Samuel 7:22

Almighty God (All three creeds)
But Jesus looked at them and said, "With man this is impossible, but with God all things are possible." Matthew 19:26

Creator God (Apostles', Nicene)
By faith we understand that the universe was created by the word of God, so that what is seen was not made out of things that are visible. Hebrews 11:3

Your righteousness is like the mountains of God; your judgments are like the great deep; man and beast you save, O LORD. Psalm 36:6

Jesus is the Son of God begotten/of one being of the Father (All three creeds)
In the beginning was the Word, and the Word was with God, and the Word was God. John 1:1

And the Word became flesh and dwelt among us, and we have seen his glory, glory as of the only Son from the Father, full of grace and truth. John 1:14

Jesus is God (All three creeds)
He is the image of the invisible God, the firstborn of all creation. Colossians 1:15

Through Jesus all things were made (Apostles', Nicene)
For by him all things were created, in heaven and on earth, visible and invisible, whether thrones or dominions or rulers or authorities—all things were created through him and for him. Colossians 1:16

By the Holy Spirit's power, Jesus was born of the Virgin Mary (Apostles', Nicene)

In those days a decree went out from Caesar Augustus that all the world should be registered. This was the first registration when Quirinius was governor of Syria. And all went to be registered, each to his own town. And Joseph also went up from Galilee, from the town of Nazareth, to Judea, to the city of David, which is called Bethlehem, because he was of the house and lineage of David, to be registered with Mary, his betrothed, who was with child. And while they were there, the time came for her to give birth. And she gave birth to her firstborn son and wrapped him in swaddling cloths and laid him in a manger, because there was no place for them in the inn.

And in the same region there were shepherds out in the field, keeping watch over their flock by night. And an angel of the Lord appeared to them, and the glory of the Lord shone around them, and they were filled with fear. And the angel said to them, "Fear not, for behold, I bring you good news of great joy that will be for all the people. For unto you is born this day in the city of David a Savior, who is Christ the Lord. And this will be a sign for you: you will find a baby wrapped in swaddling cloths and lying in a manger." Luke 2:1-12

Jesus Christ suffered death and was buried (All three creeds)

When Jesus had received the sour wine, he said, "It is finished," and he bowed his head and gave up his spirit.

Since it was the day of Preparation, and so that the bodies would not remain on the cross on the Sabbath (for that Sabbath was a high day), the Jews asked Pilate that their legs might be broken and that they might be taken away. So the soldiers came and broke the legs of the first, and of the other who had been crucified with him. But when they came to Jesus and saw that he was already dead, they did not break his legs. But one of the soldiers pierced his side with a spear, and at once there came out blood and water. He who saw it has borne witness—his testimony is true, and he knows that he is telling the truth—that you also may believe. For these things took place that the Scripture might be fulfilled: "Not one of his bones will be broken." And again another Scripture says, "They will look on him whom they have pierced."

After these things Joseph of Arimathea, who was a disciple of Jesus, but secretly for fear of the Jews, asked Pilate that he might take away the body of Jesus, and Pilate gave him permission. So he came and took away his body. Nicodemus also, who earlier had come to Jesus by night, came bringing a mixture of myrrh and aloes, about seventy-five pounds in weight. So they took the body of Jesus and bound it in linen cloths with the spices, as is the burial custom of the Jews. Now in the place where he was crucified there was a garden, and in the garden a new tomb in which no one had yet been laid. So because of the Jewish day of Preparation, since the tomb was close at hand, they laid Jesus there. John 19:30-42

Jesus Christ descended to the dead (Apostles', Athanasian)

For Christ also suffered once for sins, the righteous for the unrighteous, that he might bring us to God, being put to death in the flesh but made alive in the spirit, in which he went and proclaimed to the spirits in prison, because they formerly did not obey, when God's patience waited in the days of Noah, while the ark was being prepared, in which a few, that is, eight persons, were brought safely through water. 1 Peter 3:18-20

Jesus Christ rose again on the third day (All three creeds)

Now on the first day of the week Mary Magdalene came to the tomb early, while it was still dark, and saw that the stone had been taken away from the tomb. So she ran and went to Simon Peter and the other disciple, the one whom Jesus loved, and said to them, "They have taken the

Lord out of the tomb, and we do not know where they have laid him." So Peter went out with the other disciple, and they were going toward the tomb. Both of them were running together, but the other disciple outran Peter and reached the tomb first. And stooping to look in, he saw the linen cloths lying there, but he did not go in. Then Simon Peter came, following him, and went into the tomb. He saw the linen cloths lying there, and the face cloth, which had been on Jesus' head, not lying with the linen cloths but folded up in a place by itself. Then the other disciple, who had reached the tomb first, also went in, and he saw and believed. John 20: 1-8

<u>Jesus Christ ascended into heaven and is seated at right hand of the Father (All three creeds)</u>

And when he had said these things, as they were looking on, he was lifted up, and a cloud took him out of their sight. Acts 1:9

That he worked in Christ when he raised him from the dead and seated him at his right hand in the heavenly places. Ephesians 1:20

<u>Jesus will come again (All three creeds)</u>

And while they were gazing into heaven as he went, behold, two men stood by them in white robes, and said, "Men of Galilee, why do you stand looking into heaven? This Jesus, who was taken up from you into heaven, will come in the same way as you saw him go into heaven." Acts 1:10-11

<u>The Holy Spirit is the giver of life (Apostles', Nicene)</u>

It is the Spirit who gives life; the flesh is no help at all. The words that I have spoken to you are spirit and life. John 6:63

But the Helper, the Holy Spirit, whom the Father will send in my name, he will teach you all things and bring to your remembrance all that I have said to you. John 14:26

The Holy Spirit proceeds from the Father [*and the Son*] (Nicene, Athanasian)

Jesus said, *"But when the Helper comes, whom I will send to you from the Father, the Spirit of truth, who proceeds from the Father, he will bear witness about me."* John 15:26.

There is one baptism (Nicene)

There is one body and one Spirit—just as you were called to the one hope that belongs to your call— one Lord, one faith, one baptism, one God and Father of all, who is over all and through all and in all. Ephesians 4:4-6

We believe in the resurrection of the dead/body (Apostles', Nicene)

Now if Christ is proclaimed as raised from the dead, how can some of you say that there is no resurrection of the dead? But if there is no resurrection of the dead, then not even Christ has been raised. And if Christ has not been raised, then our preaching is in vain and your faith is in vain. We are even found to be misrepresenting God, because we testified about God that he raised Christ, whom he did not raise if it is true that the dead are not raised. For if the dead are not raised, not even Christ has been raised. And if Christ has not been raised, your faith is futile and you are still in your sins. Then those also who have fallen asleep in Christ have perished. If in Christ we have hope in this life only, we are of all people most to be pitied. 1 Corinthians 15:12-18

One God in three persons (All three creeds)

Go therefore and make disciples of all nations, baptizing them in the name of the Father and of the Son and of the Holy Spirit. Matthew 28:19

The grace of the Lord Jesus Christ and the love of God and the fellowship of the Holy Spirit be with you all. 2 Corinthians 13:14

False Teaching Denied/Objections Answered

Some have objected to the Creed of Athanasius because of its strong assertion that those who do not so believe and teach will be lost forever. It seems to them that an affirmation of highly developed and abstract Trinitarian doctrine has replaced personal faith in the Gospel that involves a simple but true understanding of Jesus as God with us, a personal trust in Jesus as our Savior Who died and rose for us to take away our sin, and a repentance or a turning from sin to follow Him as Lord. In short, their objection is to the strongly rationalistic impression of the Creed and to the damnation clauses.

Since the purpose of these clauses can be misunderstood, it is important to understand what these damnation clauses seek to do. First, they do not intend to set forth the conditions for personal saving faith in Jesus Christ and individual salvation. If they were so interpreted, the vast majority of Christians down through history would be condemned, for they neither knew, understood, nor embraced the complicated and developed Trinitarian theology of this Creed.

What, then, do these damnation clauses intend? Essentially, they are about the importance of the teaching of the Church being faithful, based upon and in agreement with the Word of God written and in accord with the teaching of the Councils.

Second, they warn that those who do know and understand the Church's teaching on the Trinity and the Person of Christ as set forth in this Creed and who reject them and teach contrary to them, will surely be cast out of the Church and apart from repentance will lose their eternal salvation. Such heresy and even apostasy has appeared in the history of the Church. We think of the Arians in the 4th Century, the Socinians in the 16th Century, and some of the contemporary cults, not to mention the revisionist theologians and leaders in the present. These warnings in the damnation clauses are faithful because the doctrines set forth in the Creed are implicit in the Gospel itself and declare the crucial importance of faithful, biblical teaching in the Church, especially on core matters of the Faith.

Third and lastly, these damnation clauses warn of the terrible danger that false teachers are, first to the Church and second to the false teachers themselves. In view is the final judgment, as Jesus warned in the Gospels and as the Apostle Paul warned in his letter to the Galatians.

Given this understanding of the purpose of the condemnation clauses, their strong warning is to be welcomed.

We should add a word of caution. The final judgment concerning anyone's salvation lies with God. The Church's judgment is only proximate. There will no doubt be surprises both in Heaven and hell.

Implications

The Creeds are to be accepted as good and faithful summaries of the core of the Faith, and as faithful to the Scriptures. They are to be used in the life and work of the Church. Most churches are woefully inadequate in teaching the faithful the central doctrines of the Faith today.

Conclusion

Anglicans stand with the Roman Catholic Church and the orthodox Churches of the Reformation in affirming the rightfulness and usefulness of the three Ecumenical Creeds, since these Creeds are faithful to the Scriptures. The Eastern Churches affirm the Nicene Creed, without the *Filioque* clause.

Section Three

Salvation (Articles 9 to 18)

This Third Section addresses both our need for God's salvation and God's gift of salvation. Salvation involves the application of the Apostolic Gospel that is covered in Articles 1-5 in the First Section. Our knowledge of the truth of this Saving Gospel is conveyed through the Rule of Faith, covered in Articles 6-8 in Section Two. If we were to go astray in this Third Section, all of the teaching of the other Articles would be of little consequence to us.

Here we will consider some of the most controversial matters that arose and were addressed during the 16th Century Reformation. Also, this is no mere historical overview, because in many respects, these matters remain controversial today.

The theme of salvation covers a wide range of God's acts of deliverance in Scripture. These deliverances range from all sorts of human difficulties to the ultimate deliverance from sin and damnation. God's gracious salvation of sinners is wider than many people suppose. Scripture uses the term "salvation" in a three-fold manner. It uses the past tense, "I was saved," referring to our *justification*. It uses the present tense, "I am being saved," referring to the ongoing work of our *sanctification*. And it uses the future tense, "I shall be saved," referring to our complete and final salvation, *glorification,* which occurs at the consummation of all things in and by Christ.

The Articles in this Third Section relate to the theme of salvation from the condemnation and power of sin:

Articles 9 and 10 show the need for salvation. They develop a biblical understanding of the problem, the universality, and depth of sin.

Article 11 states the biblical teaching on justification, which is central to a sinner's salvation and is a key doctrine. The preaching and celebration of justification determines the difference between a standing and a falling Church.

Articles 12, 13, and 14 spell out the relation of all human works to our salvation in Christ.

Article 15 makes clear that the sinlessness of Christ is essential for His atoning work, and Articles 15 and 16 both make it clear that a doctrine of the perfection of sinners, prior to their final glorification, cannot be found in biblical teaching.

Article 17 concerns predestination or election and is a wonderful statement of the sovereign grace of God in our salvation. Election, along with justification, provides the basis of the Christian's assurance of eternal salvation.

Article 18 affirms that salvation is found in Christ alone and in no other name. It warns against false teaching on this matter.

In order to avoid the popular error that sees salvation only in terms of the individual person, Section Four immediately follows. It deals with the Church. God's salvation is not just concerned with the individual's salvation. People are human only in community. The "Fall" affects us in our social life. Therefore, there is a corporate aspect to God's saving work. The corporate aspect of God's salvation involves God's gift of the Church, of which Christ is the head. Various matters concerning the Church will be treated in Section Four.

For the sake of completeness, we should add that in biblical perspective God's ultimate salvation also involves the entire universe. Though referred to in Scripture, this theme is not specifically addressed in the Articles. It is implied in Jesus' bodily Resurrection. (See Article 4, Teaching Point 3.)

It would be difficult to find another place where such clear, essential, and profound theology concerning sin and salvation is so concisely stated, as in this Third Section of the Articles.

ARTICLE 9

Of Original or Birth Sin

Original sin standeth not in the following of Adam (as the Pelagians do vainly talk), but it is the fault and corruption of the nature of every man that naturally is engendered of the offspring of Adam, whereby man is very far gone from original righteousness, and is of his own nature inclined to evil, so that the flesh lusteth always contrary to the spirit; and therefore in every person born into this world, it deserveth God's wrath and damnation. And this infection of nature doth remain, yea, in them that are regenerated, whereby the lust of the flesh, called in Greek phronema sarkos (which some do expound the wisdom, some sensuality, some the affection, some the desire of the flesh), is not subject to the law of God. And although there is no condemnation for them that believe and are baptized, yet the Apostle doth confess that concupiscence and lust hath itself the nature of sin.

Introduction

What is sin? What do Christians mean by original sin? We know that alcoholism and cancer are serious problems, but just how serious is sin? Is there any way to get rid of sin once it infects us? This 9th Article and the next should answer these questions. Sin is a far more terrible problem that many people realize.

There is a precise correlation between our human predicament and the deliverance or salvation that God gives in Christ. Salvation presupposes a definite corruption of our human nature and a brokenness in our relationship with God with a fearful destiny to come, unless God intervenes. The radical nature of God's provision of salvation through the death of His Son upon the Cross reveals how profound and dangerous is our fallen or sinful condition and its consequences.

In short, Article 9 and Article 10 together spell out the nature of our fallen human condition and the chief consequences of our sinfulness. Here is a pit too deep for us to climb out of on our own. We will need a rescue from above.

The Teaching of Article 9
Here are the teaching points of this Article:
1. What original sin is not.

2. What original sin is.

3. Original sin that remains in the regenerate does not condemn us.

4. "Concupiscence" that remains in the believer has the nature of sin.

1. What original sin is not.
Explanation

The Article begins by rejecting an inadequate understating of "original sin." Some have taught that "original sin" consists merely of our being influenced by the bad example of Adam and Eve, of our society or of individuals who have had an ungodly impact upon our lives. Such a view holds that original sin consists only and entirely in our following the example of Adam and Eve, who did the original or first and the typical human sin. In this view, original sin today is original only in the sense that as an act of sin it copies the first or original sin done by Adam and Eve.

This "bad example" view was first made prominent by the monk Pelagius (A.D. 400). He taught that sin, once committed, did not affect our human nature in any sense.

There was no corruption of our nature, no bondage of our will in sin. Even when we have sinned by copying Adam, we retain the ability to immediately stop sinning by refusing to follow his bad example. Pelagius taught that we could and can and must obey God perfectly. Grace was sufficient to forgive past sins before baptism and to warn us of the penalty that would fall on future sins. But no grace was needed or given to overcome any damage to our human nature, for there was no corruption of our human nature.

Against this view of sin St. Augustine battled. He wrote several of his major theological writings against Pelagius. He argued that according to Scripture, which is confirmed in his own and general human experience, Adam's sin not only brought us as a human race into a state of guilt before God, and not only set a bad example which quickly spread to all human beings, but that in Adam's sin our human nature was corrupted and after the Fall we human beings were not able not to sin.

Sin is not only acts of sin or sins, but even deeper, it is sinfulness, a profound inclination of our heart, a bondage or enslavement of our self. It is a fallen state or condition of our central self that claims and distorts all our desires and wills.

As sons and daughters of Adam, we have inherited a fallen human nature, corrupted in the origin of our human race and passed on at our birth from fallen human parents. Original sin is therefore a present corrupting power in us and in the entire human race that puts us all in a condition of bondage and of guilt before God.

Article 9 agrees with St. Augustine. To limit "original sin" to copying the first bad example is superficial, unscriptural and contrary to the human experience of every individual and of all human societies. The nature and effects of sin are a far deeper matter than following a bad example, though bad example is a powerful force acting on the fallen heart.

Biblical Foundations

For texts that refute Pelagius' teaching see the texts listed in Teaching Point 2: "What original sin is."

False Teachings Denied/Objections Answered

1. This first point in the Article is intended to exclude any view of our sinful human condition that fails to see our human condition as one of a fallen state or condition, a condition that makes it impossible for us to consistently desire to, and to actually live in accord with God's will for us. It does not exclude the fact that we are also influenced by bad example. In fact, because we are in a sinful condition we find that we take to bad influences as "a duck takes to water." What is unnatural to our created human nature has become, in our fallenness, "natural" to us.

2. What are we to say to those who claim that this is an overly somber view of human nature as we know it? In fact some go farther and teach that the biblical view of our sinfulness is self-contradictory. The philosopher Kant said that if we ought to do something we must be able to do it. If that were not true, he held, we could not be held accountable to do it. Thereby Kant appeals to the very fact of our conscience as proof of our ability to do the right thing. He sided with Pelagius and denied that our nature was fallen or corrupted. For many people this still seems to be the common sense view of human nature.

Next to the clear teaching of Scripture, the strongest refutation of this superficial view of human fallenness is an appeal to our experience.

Here are several suggestions: let each of us commit to loving God with all of our heart, strength and mind and our neighbor as ourselves without fail for one week. How long do you think it would take us to fail? Could we even begin?

Another approach would be to ask the spouse of someone making a claim to have the ability not to sin to comment on the life of his or her partner after a trial week.

Or, we might read the newspaper or any book treating a period of human history in order to see that the human race consistently gives ample evidence of being profoundly fallen.

If we are honest with ourselves, we find that we often do not desire and are not inclined to be and do our best. Our heart isn't in it. Nevertheless, Kant not withstanding, we are responsible for what we desire as well as what we do as we act upon our desires. We know that we ought to live good lives as we understand good and yet we never live up even to our own fallen standards, much less to God's revealed standards found in Scripture and in the person and teaching of Jesus, Who is the picture of true humanity.

What is universally characteristic of all humanity must have a profound, gripping and universal cause. Original sin is far too powerful to be merely the influence of a bad example.

Implications

For God to save us, He will not only have to deal with our guilt before Him, which He does in the Atonement made on our behalf by the Son, but will also have to deal with the corruption of our nature or our bondage to sin. This He will do by the work of the Holy Spirit in us in regeneration and by the process of sanctification. As the hymn writer Toplady expressed it, speaking of salvation, "be of sin the double cure, save me from its guilt and power." We can rejoice that the Gospel contains God's gift and promise of both the removal of our guilt and the progressive freeing of our wills.

2. What original sin is.
Explanation

We will be helped by having the words of the Article that define "original sin" before us.

> *. . it is the fault and corruption of the nature of every man that naturally is engendered of the offspring of Adam, whereby man is very far gone from original righteousness, and is of his own nature inclined to evil, so that the flesh lusteth always contrary to the spirit; and therefore in every person born into this world, it deserveth God's wrath and damnation . .*

Original sin is defined in the Article as the "fault and corruption" of our nature so that we are far gone from the original righteousness in which we were created and that we are actively inclined to evil. The one leads to the other. What precisely is this corruption of our nature or sinfulness that has these characteristics in us?

One definition of sin is that it is any lack of conformity to God's will for us as expressed in creation. When Jesus was asked about God's will for us, He defined God's will in terms of love. "You shall love the Lord your God with all your heart and all of your strength and all your mind, that is the first and great commandment and the second is like unto it you shall love your neighbor as yourself." Original sin, then, is precisely the opposite of loving God first and foremost and the neighbor as much as we love ourselves; it is self-worship, the self-exultation of the self to be the center of the universe and the center of one's own life. It is making the self to be "god." It is an idolatry of the self. It is, as St. Augustine put it, "hubris" (i.e., the elevation of oneself above one's true place in the order of being), and such hubris or distorted pride is "an inordinate affection", literally "out of order". Luther said the same thing in different words; he said sin is essentially the "*cor incurvatus in se,*" that is, the heart turned in upon itself.

Original sin has a double face, for as original sin exalts the self, at the same time it rejects God as the rightful Lord of the universe and of our lives. Original sin is therefore not only something lost, such as our original righteousness, it is also something added: rebellion and idolatry. Original sin is active, rebellious enmity or hostility to God as Lord, whether we are conscious of this or not. The truth of this is inescapable. If we are our own "god," then God cannot be, as is His right. There is only room for one supreme "god" in our lives.

Original sin is therefore an orientation of our selves that, in principle, aims to subordinate to ourselves everything and everyone in the universe, including God. If I am the "lord" of my life, having and doing what I want when I want it, then everything and everyone I meet must in principle give way to my desires. I may not be able to compel everyone to worship me, but there is that within me that would do so if I could.

Original sin is universal in the human race. There is, of course, one exception, Jesus, who was without sin by the unique, miraculous work of the Holy Spirit. This work was done when the eternal Son assumed human nature from the Virgin Mary, who was herself fallen. He did this in order to save those who are dominated by original sin.

Original sin is universal not only because we all are fallen, but also in the sense that its corruption permeates all parts of our human nature: mind, emotion, desire, and will, so that, while we may not be as evil as we could be, we are in every respect very far gone from our original righteousness or created nature. That is why we read in *The Book of Common Prayer* that "there is no health in us."

Such a profound distortion of our nature with its rebellion against God has its effects or consequences.. Here are some of the chief consequences:

Consequences of original sin
1. Consequences in our relationship with God.
A. We come under the wrath of God and His judgment. We live East of Eden and life becomes more

difficult. A future and final judgment awaits us. Death becomes not only physical dissolution but it is spiritual separation from God and leads to eternal death or eternal suffering in Hell.

B. Idolatry arises. Since we are limited, dependent creatures, we are aware that we must be sustained from beyond ourselves to exist. The created self is not able to stand in its own strength. Having rejected the worship and love of God and His care, human beings must find a substitute. We project a "god" that we can depend upon and at the same time control. The world's religions serve to meet this need. So do secular forms of religious worship, such as extreme nationalism, tribalism, making one's family or career the purpose of life etc. The only serious alternatives to this fallen religiousness are a frantic busyness that avoids serious reflection, or some form of stoic, tragic despair such as one finds in the writings of Bertrand Russell and atheistic existentialists.

The demands of the idols, the exhaustion of the frantic activity, and the cosmic loneliness and the pointlessness are the cost and experience of living under the juridical wrath of God.

2. Consequences for our relationship with our neighbor.

A. Social difficulty and struggle is characteristic of fallen human life. "Being united in sin we are unable to be long united in anything else," said someone. It is true.

B. Difficulties often rise to the level of conflict and even war between groups, tribes and nations. For this reason armies, police, and law courts are essential to sustain fallen human society.

3. Consequences for our relationship with ourselves.

A. Hypocrisy becomes an unavoidable part of our life. With regard to our fellow human beings, we find that naked egotism is so destructive of social order and friendship that we must mask our self-enthronement and pretend to have a degree of concern and love toward others that we do not fully share. If we are religious, we find that we constantly bend all religion to serve ourselves while protesting to worship a greater cause or being than ourselves. We become life-long hypocrites.

B. We are captive and we find that we do not do what we know to be right and do what we know to be wrong. No one lives with a "good conscience." Even at our best, our motives are mixed and our goodness is always flawed; our bad conscience bears witness to it.

4. Consequences with nature.

We are to preserve and tend the garden and domesticate nature with care so that nature can serve humanity. But our greed and fear of other social groups or nations leads us to rape nature for profit and for security. We damage the "garden" for which we are to care.

Concluding Note on Original Sin

What is original sin? Original sin is self-worship and rebellion against the Lordship of God and the implicit subjection of everyone and everything else. And we live in the midst of its pervasive and devastating consequences.

Biblical Foundations

The LORD God took the man and put him in the garden of Eden to work it and keep it. And the LORD God commanded the man, saying, "You may surely eat of every tree of the garden, but of the tree of the knowledge of good and evil you shall not eat, for in the day that you eat of it you shall surely die." Genesis 2:15-17

So when the woman saw that the tree was good for food, and that it was a delight to the eyes, and that the tree was to be desired to make one wise, she took of its fruit and ate, and she also gave some to her husband who was with her, and he ate. Genesis 3:6

The Lord saw that the wickedness of man was great in the earth, and that every intention of the thoughts of his heart was only evil continually. Genesis 6:5

The fool says in his heart, "There is no God." They are corrupt, they do abominable deeds, and there is none who does good. The Lord looks down from heaven on the children of man, to see if there are any who understand, who seek after God. They have all turned aside; together they have become corrupt; there is none who does good, not even one. Psalm 14:1-3

The heart is deceitful above all things, and desperately sick; who can understand it? Jeremiah 17:9

For all have sinned and fall short of the glory of God. Romans 3:23

Therefore, just as sin came into the world through one man, and death through sin, and so death spread to all men because all sinned. Romans 5:12

For we know that the law is spiritual, but I am of the flesh, sold under sin. I do not understand my own actions. For I do not do what I want, but I do the very thing I hate. Romans 7:14-15

They are darkened in their understanding, alienated from the life of God because of the ignorance that is in them, due to their hardness of heart. Ephesians 4:18

Whoever believes in the Son has eternal life; whoever does not obey the Son shall not see life, but the wrath of God remains on him. John 3:36

False Teachings Denied/Objections Answered

1. Excluded is the Pelagian view as discussed in "Teaching Point 1: What original sin is not."

2. Also denied are the views that confuse Creation with sinfulness by suggesting that God made us sinful. Creation as it comes from God's hand has an original righteousness. Therefore, our sinful state after the Fall falls short of our true dignity and created nature.

3. Also rejected are all the views that are half-way measures. These views suggest that some part of our human nature remains unfallen, such as the will or the mind or the emotions. Similar are the views that teach that there are

some individuals or groups in the human race, other than Jesus the Savior, who are not sinners.

4. All views that diminish the seriousness of sin in the eyes of God and suggest that sinners are not under the wrath of God are wrong. Such views lead to the belief that those outside a saving relationship with Christ are not headed for eternal damnation and all will be in glory in the end. This is often referred to as "universalism." But universalism contradicts the Scriptures. Scripture teaches that death is the chief consequence of human sin. Since all die, all are reckoned as sinners in God's eyes and need the saving grace of God given in Christ Jesus.

However, there are those who believe that the universal sentence of death is not a judgment upon sin, but that death is a purely natural phenomenon and did not enter the human race because of sin. What are we to say to those who hold this naturalistic view that death is simply natural? We cannot resolve this problem scientifically because science can only observe human beings after the Fall; and after the Fall, death has become the universal or seemingly natural experience of all human beings. That being true, we are left to turn to Scripture for our understanding. Here are two considerations:

A. One aspect of God's general revelation to all humanity is the universal human sense that death is unnatural and unwelcome; it is a tragedy, an intruder in the midst of life, an enemy. It never seems natural when a loved one is dying. Life is always too short, as long as we are healthy and not in excruciating pain.

B. The matter is directly addressed in the Scripture. St. Paul, in Romans 6, states that death entered the human race by sin. And in Romans 8 he tells us that it is because of mankind's sin that the whole creation has been subjected to futility by God. The teaching of Paul is clear and in line with the account of the Fall in Genesis that recounts God's warning and later judgment that the punishment for sin is death, both physical and spiritual. In Scripture, death is more than physical dissolution. It is spiritual separation from God and ends in the eternal punishment and suffering of hell. Had there been no Fall, it is likely that we would all have been translated into glory without passing through death, like Elijah.

Implications

A. The teaching of this Article is in accord with the biblical teaching concerning God's holiness, His moral purity and righteousness, and His role as the Judge of all the earth. A weak view of sin and of the consequences of sin is at odds with both the holiness of God and the accountability of mankind. It is also contrary to the repeated teaching of Jesus concerning the final state of unrepentant sinners. It is indeed a fearful thing for a sinner to fall into the hands of the holy and living God.

B. This Article is also faithful to the biblical teaching concerning the chief benefits of the Gospel, which are deliverance from the wrath of God, exercised at the final Judgment, our deliverance from sin's enslavement, our restoration to His favor, and our entrance into glory. If we weaken the terrible nature and consequence of sin, we make the Gospel into something less than it is.

For example, if we make the chief benefit of the Gospel the peace and joy that it beings now in the midst of life, and obscure or even deny its gift of rescue from God's wrath on the Day of Judgment, then on what basis can we ask people to suffer for the sake of the Gospel now? If our present comfort is the main point of the Gospel, then suffering would be in direct contradiction to the purpose of the Gospel, so defined.

Quite the opposite is the case in Scripture. There we read that Christians are called to suffer for Christ's sake and for the Gospel's sake. Christ's suffering on the Cross is held up to us as a model for us to follow. The Gospel simply does not have in view our present comfort as its chief aim, but rather the Gospel gives glory to God, and secures the ultimate and final comfort and wholeness of our selves and of others.

3. Original sin that remains in the regenerate does not condemn us.
Explanation
A. Original sin does remain in the regenerated.

To discuss this teaching point we need to determine the meaning of "the regenerate." The meaning follows from the word itself. To generate is to cause something to come to be, for example, to give birth to a child. To re-generate is to cause something to come into being again, after it had died or been destroyed. When regeneration is applied to birth, to regenerate is to give a new or second birth to one who had died. To regenerate spiritually is to raise to spiritual life those who in the Fall had died spiritually, who were dead in their trespasses and sins and under the wrath of God. The regenerated are those who have been spiritually dead and been given new life or reborn.

Who are these regenerate? The regenerate are believers in Christ. Conversion, or repentance and faith in Christ as one's Savior and Lord, is the fruit of the inner, hidden, regenerating work of the Holy Spirit. This work of the Spirit is correlated with the Holy Gospel. That is, while repentance and faith are our response to the Gospel of Jesus Christ, our response is itself enabled by the regenerating work of the Holy Spirit, giving us a heart for God, a heart of flesh instead of a heart of stone. St. Paul put it this way in Acts 16:14, "And the Lord opened the heart of Lydia to attend the teaching of Paul." The only reliable visible sign of the hidden, inner regeneration of the heart by the Holy Spirit is the confession of faith in Christ as Lord and Savior, together with genuine repentance which intends serious discipleship. Therefore, we may take it that the regenerate to whom this Article refers are those who openly believe in Jesus Christ and seriously seek to live as His followers. The regenerated are the believers in Christ. All true believers are regenerate.

This 9th Article asserts that original sin does remain in the regenerate or the believer. It is true that there is a new heart in the regenerate; it is also true, however, that the old Adam still inhabits the believer's life. Our fallen human nature is dethroned, contradicted, and weakened by regeneration, but not erased or totally removed. A battle begins within us at regeneration.

B. This indwelling sin does not condemn us.

The truth is that the sin that abides in the regenerate does not condemn us. This is assumed in all of the portions of the New Testament that teach about the Christian life. How can this be true in our relationship with the holy God Who is of purer eyes than to behold evil? The answer to that is found in Articles 11, "Of the Justification of Man," and 12, "Of Good Works." We will discuss the "how" in those Articles. But at this point we do need to be aware that it is only because of the atoning work of Christ on the Cross accounted to us through our trust in Him, that the indwelling sin in us does not condemn us before the righteousness of God.

Biblical Foundations

Jesus answered him, "Truly, truly, I say to you, unless one is born again he cannot see the kingdom of God." John 3:3

Jesus answered, "Truly, truly, I say to you, unless one is born of water and the Spirit, he cannot enter the kingdom of God." John 3:5

And you were dead in the trespasses and sins in which you once walked, following the course of this world, following the prince of the power of the air, the spirit that is now at work in the sons of disobedience— among whom we all once lived in the passions of our flesh, carrying out the desires of the body and the mind, and were by nature children of wrath, like the rest of mankind. But God, being rich in mercy, because of the great love with which he loved us, even when we were dead in our trespasses, made us alive together with Christ—by grace you have been saved— and raised us up with him and seated us with him in the heavenly places in Christ Jesus. Ephesians 2:1-6

So I find it to be a law that when I want to do right, evil lies close at hand. For I delight in the law of God, in my inner being, but I see in my members another law waging war against the law of my mind and making me captive to the law of sin that dwells in my members. Wretched man that I am! Who will deliver me from this body of death? Romans 7:21-24

If we say we have no sin, we deceive ourselves, and the truth is not in us. If we confess our sins, he is faithful and just to forgive us our sins and to cleanse us from all unrighteousness. If we say we have not sinned, we make him a liar, and his word is not in us. 1 John 1:8-10

False Teachings Denied/Objections Answered

1. Any teaching that the sin that indwells the believer condemns him or her is denied.

2. The Council of Trent taught that baptism both conveys regeneration and washes away original sin. The remaining desires of the flesh are not sin but only become sin when we act upon them. Article 9 differs from Rome. Sin is any lack or want of conformity to God's will, both His will for us expressed in our created nature and His will revealed in His commands found in Scripture and in Christ Jesus. Therefore, even wrong desires are sinful. For example, Jesus taught that lust is an expression of adultery or anger an expression of murder, even when these desires are not acted upon.

In addition, Anglicans do not agree that baptism removes the presence of original sin. The Scriptures cited above and other places in Scripture clearly affirm that indwelling sin is not obliterated at our regeneration, baptism, or conversion but remains in the believer until glorification.

Implications

An honest admission of the reality of indwelling sin keeps us from having too exalted a view of our condition. Even at our best we remain "unprofitable servants." It also keeps us from falling into terror or despair when we do face the reality of continued indwelling sin in us. We are thankful that there is no condemnation to all who are in Christ Jesus, as the apostle Paul assures us in Romans 8:1.

4. "Concupiscence" that remains in the believer has the nature of sin.
Explanation

"Concupiscence" refers to a deep and profound desire, generally a wrongful desire. The Article here is referring to indwelling sin that distorts our desires and leads us to desire what is contrary to God's will or causes us to obey His will only from mixed motives. The point the Article is making is that the very desire is sinful and not just the actions that might spring from the desire. St. Augustine speaks of our disordered or inordinate affections.

Biblical Foundations

I do not understand my own actions. For I do not do what I want, but I do the very thing I hate. Romans 7:15

For the desires of the flesh are against the Spirit, and the desires of the Spirit are against the flesh, for these are opposed to each other, to keep you from doing the things you want to do. Galatians 5:17

But each person is tempted when he is lured and enticed by his own desire. James 1:14

Beloved, I urge you as sojourners and exiles to abstain from the passions of the flesh, which wage war against your soul. 1 Peter 2:11,

False Teaching Denied/Objections Answered

In the teaching of Trent, the Roman Catholic Church declared that concupiscence was not sinful. Anglicans disagree. Any view that states that "concupiscence" or the "desires of the flesh" that indwell us are not sin is an error. As stated in the explanation, these desires are not only the cause of sin when we act upon them – the very presence of these wrong desires in us is a mark of the Fall and a distortion of our created nature, and therefore sinful.

Implications

The chief implication of this point is a call to honesty concerning our motives. There is little room in genuine Christianity for boasting before the Lord, for moral pretensions. Such honesty about ourselves will serve to help us, as Christians, to seek the Lord's forgiveness, to be more forgiving of the sins of others, and to seek to grow in grace with the help of the Holy Spirit.

Conclusion

The Christian analysis of what is wrong with the human race, as set forth here in Article 8 and next in Article 10, is profound and realistic. It is neither naïve optimism nor ultimate pessimism but convicting, honest realism. On the one hand, our sinful condition allows for no self-help solutions. We all stand guilty before God. Sin is too corrupting and abiding for us to master it. We are enslaved to ourselves. We are sinful and therefore all that we think, will, desire, and do is distorted to some degree by that sinfulness. On the other hand, the Christian analysis does not leave us sitting in hopeless despair, for we, as the sons and daughters of Adam, were created good, and are delivered by divine grace from condemnation by Christ. In Christ, we participate in a process of sanctification, of being restored to wholeness by the Word of God and the Holy Spirit which will surely be completed in glory.

ARTICLE 10

Of Free Will

The condition of man after the fall of Adam is such, that he cannot turn and prepare himself, by his own natural strength and good works, to faith and calling upon God. Wherefore we have no power to do good works pleasant and acceptable to God, without the grace of God by Christ preventing us that we may have a good will, and working with us when we have that good will.

Introduction

Enslaved to whom or what? We have never been enslaved to anything or anyone. Of course we have free will; don't we make choices all day long? I can choose anything I want. Ah, but can you *want* to choose what you ought? Assertions that we have a free will with regard to loving God and the neighbor abound on the popular level, even among Anglican clergy and laity.

The concern of Article 9 is to define the nature of original sin and to make it clear that while indwelling sin persists in the believer, due to God's work in Christ, it does not condemn the believer in the eyes of God. Article 10 is concerned to show that indwelling sin binds the will of sinners, rendering them unable to choose God or to respond positively to the Gospel in their own strength. This condition of the "bondage of the will" shows the need for God to graciously address that inability in order to free mankind from enslavement to sin. Article 10 might have been better entitled "Of The Will Set Free in Christ".

The issue of the free will is of central importance and is greatly misunderstood. It was controversial as the Articles were being written and it is controversial now. To this day, Anglican, Lutheran, and Reformed Churches agree on this doctrine and stand over against the Semi-

Pelagianism of Rome and the Eastern Churches as well as those Protestant Churches influenced by Arminianism, commonly understood.

This Article, therefore, has two parts: first, the Article explains the enslaving power of Sin and then second, it turns to God's grace as that which sets the sinner free to respond to God in faith and repentance.

It is important to set this Article in its historical context, for is written at the consummation of a long development and debate.

This assessment of the radical nature of the power of sin taught by the Reformers was in conflict with late Medieval theology. Late Medieval theology taught that when sinners took the first step and did what they could do in their own strength, little though that might be, then God would respond and set their heart and will free. The initiative in turning to God was the sinner's.

This reliance upon man to take the first step in his own strength toward faith, however enfeebled by sin, is usually referred to as Semi-Pelagianism. It is in partial agreement with the teaching of Pelagius, the Scottish theologian, who taught that the will was not fallen or corrupted at all. In Semi-Pelagianism the will is damaged but not fully bound or enslaved. Man is spiritually sick, weak but not spiritually dead, and not fundamentally hostile to God. Saint Augustine (A.D. 354-430) argued effectively against Pelagius. Semi-Pelagianism is a weakened or compromised form of Augustinianism. Therefore, the pre-Reformation Western Church and, the Eastern Church ended up with a compromised doctrine. At the Reformation, this compromise was addressed from a biblical perspective. The major Reformers and their Churches – Lutheran, Anglican, and Reformed - restored Augustine's reading of Scripture.

Attributing the first step toward God to fallen sinners is also referred to as Arminianism, after the Dutch theologian, Arminius (A.D. 1560-1609). He is generally thought to have taught that it is man's self-initiated faith that God foresees and which provides the basis for God's saving election of the believer. In essence, it is the individual's choice of God that provides the basis for God's choice of that individual. This is a reversal of the biblical teaching that election is God's choice of sinners which enables the sinners to choose God. (The doctrine of election will be treated in Article 17.)

Arminius' teaching led to the calling of the Council of Dort (A.D. 1618-19), a Council of Reformed Churches, which included the Church of England. The Council of Dort rejected Arminianism as so understood, holding it to be contrary to the teaching of Scripture. This Article 10 of the Church of England is clearly in agreement with the Council of Dort.

It was not only the Reformed theologians and Reformed Churches that took this stronger view. Luther and the Lutheran Churches also held and continue to hold a view like that set forth at Dort. Earlier, Luther, in response to a book by Erasmus, wrote a book entitled *The Bondage of the Will* in which he states a view in full agreement with the teaching of this 10th Article. Confessional Lutheran Churches concur. The Roman Catholic Church, responding to the Reformation in the Council of Trent, continued the late medieval tradition; therefore it held, and appears to continue to hold, Semi-Pelagian views.

Having made clear the bondage of the will in all sinners, the Article turns to its second theme: grace, which includes both prevenient grace and accompanying grace. God's remedy to the bondage of the will is prevenient grace, whereby the fallen human heart and the enslaved human will are set free to choose to turn to God in faith and obedience. It is prevenient because it is grace given prior to the act of faith that it enables. Accompanying grace follows: it is the continuing, inner, gracious work of God enabling the believing sinner to remain and grow in faith and obedience. Grace in both actions is the undeserved gift of God in Christ and is applied by the inner work of the Holy Spirit. Salvation, therefore, is entirely of God's grace.

The Teaching of Article 10

We turn now to the teaching points of Article 10:

1. The human will is in bondage to sin and is not free to turn to God.

2. The prevenient grace of God is needed to set the will free to turn to God.

3. The abiding grace of God is needed to keep the will free to love and obey the Lord.

1. The human will is in bondage to sin and is not free to turn to God
Explanation

The first point deals with the problem of the enslaving power of sin. This is referred to as the "bondage of the will." What does the bondage of the will mean?

First, it will be helpful to make clear what it does not mean. It does not refer to a condition in which one is restrained physically or by other people from doing what one wills to do. There are times when we find ourselves simply bound by external forces and limits which we cannot alter. We cannot choose to jump over tall buildings or to force someone to love us or make all persons in society behave well. That the realities of external bondage and social limitation acting upon us limit our choices is not what is meant by the bondage of the will.

When we speak of the bondage of the will, we are referring to an orientation and power within ourselves that we are aware of precisely when we are physically able to choose what we want. The bondage of the will is found and encountered in the sphere of our wanting and choosing not in the absence of choice. It is an inner and not an external bondage.

But what sort of inner bondage is meant in this Article? The bondage of the will is found first and foremost in relation to God and other persons. This bondage is experienced as the fact that we cannot choose to love God with all of our heart, soul and mind and our neighbor as ourselves. At the deepest level of our heart or inner desire, we do not really want to love God or our neighbor that way and we cannot change this inclination and condition of our heart. We can, some of the time, choose not to express the selfish, self-preoccupation of our heart in our actions. We can appear to be loving persons and we can do the "loving" thing in the eyes of others. But God is not fooled; and even when we do the right thing, it is out of a mixture of love, fear of the opinion of others, and even self-righteous pride. We never act out of unalloyed love for God and for others. The truth about us and all human beings is that to a large extent, we are bound by inordinate self-exaltation and self-preoccupation that guides our choosing and actions. How thankful we must all be that others cannot read our minds and hearts.

In addition, as we noted in Article 9, we are often aware of a rebellious desire within us to do precisely what God has forbidden us to do simply because it is forbidden. We are rebels, wishing to throw off the claims of God and others and to be the Lord of our own lives.

Since at our core, in our heart, we are in rebellion against the Lordship of God and caught up in inordinate self-love, all of our choices reflect that rebellion and inordinate self-love. The problem, therefore, is not that we are not free to choose what we want; it is that we cannot really, totally and consistently want or desire what we ought to want and desire. Luther referred to this as the *cor incurvatus in se*, the heart curved in upon itself. Our will is led by our heart and our heart is captive to sin. God is not honored by half-hearted, hypocritical behavior, no matter how good it looks on the surface. His wrath is felt inwardly in our conscience in the present, and is experienced outwardly in the consequences of our behavior both individually and socially. God's wrath is also heard in Jesus' warnings of a final judgment to come, which warning is ignored by many. How many sermons have you heard about hell lately?

Another way of stating the same thing in more philosophical terms is to say that since our human nature is so corrupted that all of the functions of our human nature, our thinking, willing, and desiring are corrupted, inevitably we will act in ways that express that corruption. We cannot will, in any full and effective sense, to change our will because it is the corrupted self or fallen nature that does the willing.

If this seems to be too dark a view of human nature, let us be reminded that the Scriptures use the most radical language about our condition. 1) We read that the imagination of man's heart is evil continually. 2) We learn that we need God to give us a new heart, one of flesh and not of stone, one in which He will write His laws. We do not give ourselves a new heart nor write the Law of the Lord there. 3) We read that we are dead in our trespasses and sins, and dead people do not make themselves alive; they must be raised by another. 4) We hear that we need a new creation, and a new birth and we are not "self-creators" able to become a new creation. We are clearly beyond self-help.

To sum up, like the leopard we cannot change our spots; our bondage is beyond our ability to help ourselves because we ourselves are the problem and not the answer. All of our willing in one way or another expresses the bondage of our heart and every act of our will only digs the hole deeper. This is true even of our religious actions, as both the Sadducees and the Pharisees illustrated in their responses to Jesus.

We are in a Catch 22, a dilemma, for, on the one hand, until we accept the fact of the bondage of our heart and will, we will not see the need of God's grace to enable us to turn to Him. And, on the other hand, we will not accept our need for God's grace until God's grace is already at work in us setting us free to admit our need. That is why the Article states: "The condition of Man after the Fall of Adam is such, that he cannot turn and prepare himself, by his own natural strength and good works, to faith, and calling upon God."

Biblical Foundations

And when the Lord smelled the pleasing aroma, the Lord said in his heart, "I will never again curse the ground because of man, for the intention of man's heart is evil from his youth. Neither will I ever again strike down every living creature as I have done." Genesis 8:21

The heart is deceitful above all things, and desperately sick; who can understand it? Jeremiah 17:9

And you were dead in the trespasses and sins…among whom we all once lived in the passions of our flesh, carrying out the desires of the body and the mind, and were by nature children of wrath, like the rest of mankind. But God, being rich in mercy, because of the great love with which he loved us, even when we were dead in our trespasses, made us alive together with Christ—by grace you have been saved. Ephesians 2:1, 3-5

For this is the covenant that I will make with the house of Israel after those days, declares the Lord: I will put my laws into their minds, and write them on their hearts, and I will be their God, and they shall be my people. Hebrews 8:10

Jesus answered him, "Truly, truly, I say to you, unless one is born again he cannot see the kingdom of God." John 3:3

Jesus answered, "Truly, truly, I say to you, unless one is born of water and the Spirit, he cannot enter the kingdom of God." John 3:5

No one can come to me unless the Father who sent me draws him. And I will raise him up on the last day. John 6:44

False Teachings Denied/Objections Answered
1. The focus of this first teaching point is to exclude or reject Semi-Pelagianism. Fallen human beings cannot take the first step, without the prevenient grace of God enabling them. As stated above, this article excludes any view of humanity in its present fallen condition that teaches that human beings are free to turn to God in their own strength.

This applies to Roman Catholic teaching, Eastern Orthodox teaching and to such Evangelical Arminian theology, which continues to rely upon the sinners' ability in his or her own strength to choose God in response to the Gospel. God waits, so to speak, for the sinner to respond. Were that the case, the wait would be eternal.

2. Determinism is also at odds with this Article. Determinism teaches that our choosing is an illusion and not real. It is a total misunderstanding of Article 10 to interpret it as a form of determinism. Article 10 nowhere teaches that we human beings are entirely determined by something or someone other than ourselves, so that we do not actually choose. Both Scripture and our experience speak otherwise. We do choose and we are accountable to God for our choosing. Article 10 and the Scriptures throughout assume that we do choose and do so all of the time.

3. This article excludes any view of humanity that teaches that man is essentially evil by creation. Were that the case, grace could not redeem, restore, and renew the sinner. We would be by nature, by definition, beyond restoration. But people do repent and believe by God's grace, as Scripture and this Article affirm.

4. The Article also excludes indeterminacy, a view that holds that we humans make choices with no inclination whatsoever, as if we live in neutral and choose on no basis at all. This would make all choices nothing but a whim. But no one is neutral, living without an orientation of the heart and a shape to his or her character. We are either determined by our fallen heart and specific character or by the grace of God giving us a renewed heart. The bondage of the will is the unconverted sinner's condition.

5. It is sometimes objected and argued that we cannot be both bound and responsible at the same time. This was Kant's conviction. This objection fails to reckon with the fact that it is we ourselves who at the deepest level are bound by ourselves. We do not fully desire to turn in love to God as Lord. We desire and choose to be our own "lord" in life. It is not imposed upon us against our will. But we are bound by this profound desire or orientation of our self. We do choose and we are bound. And we choose wrongly until the Holy Spirit opens our hearts to the Gospel of Christ.

6. Some object we cannot be both bound and free. They see this as a simple logical contradiction. If we are bound we are not free and if we are free we are not bound. This is but another form of the previous objection, only now in terms of freedom. We have defined what we mean by bondage, but what do we mean by "free"? This objection presupposes a specific understanding of freedom that is in contradiction to all personal experience and that cannot withstand rational scrutiny. It defines freedom as the ability to choose anything at all, which is indeterminacy. But no one is ever free to choose anything at all. We are all claimed by our heart and character.

If you know a person well, you can almost certainly predict how he or she will "freely" choose in given moral circumstances. Why is that possible? It is possible because the person is of a certain moral sort; he or she has a specific moral character. Even though a certain choice might be physically or even socially possible, it would not be morally possible to a person of that moral character. We can say that the person is bound by his or her heart.

In what sense, then, is the person free? The problem with this objection is its false definition of freedom. We need a far better and more biblical definition of freedom than indeterminacy.

True freedom is not the ability to choose anything at all, for no one has that freedom. Freedom is the ability to choose what is right, and to want what we ought to want. True freedom is the freedom to wholeheartedly choose God because our heart is right. True freedom is to love God with all our heart, soul, strength and mind and our neighbor as our self, and then in that love to choose what we truly want. That is why St. Augustine can say that to serve God is "perfect freedom" and "love God and do what you will." It is for this true freedom that sinners need to be set free by God's gracious gift of a new heart and sustained therein by His progressive work of sanctification, that is, by accompanying grace.

Implications

One important implication of the bondage of the will has to do with the place and limitation of God's Law regarding fallen humanity. Three things are important to note:

A. There is both value and limitation in the civil use of the law. There is need of civil law to limit and punish antisocial behavior and to define, instruct and reward good social behavior. By causing fear and appealing to rational understanding as well as to personal reward, we can shape outer action. This is important in the family as well as in society in general. The limit of this function of the law is that it does not change the deepest desires of the heart or produce love as the central motive of human behavior. Under the law, fear and self-interest remain dominant in the fallen human heart. To recognize this limitation of the effect of the civil use of the law is not to belittle the importance of the civil use of the law. It is good that we obey traffic signals not only for safety but also for the fear of fines and the loss of a driver's license. And, one is reminded of Martin Luther King Jr.'s sentiment that he would like his neighbor to love him, but first he wanted his neighbor to quit lynching him (as required by law). There is a necessary role for civil law to play in society in a fallen world.

B. The place of the moral law with reference to the conscience becomes clear. When the law is "heard" as God's Law, penetrating to the conscience, it reveals our guilt for not loving God foremost and our neighbors as ourselves. This awareness of our guilt before God and of our condemnation is a good thing and is itself a gracious work of God in the heart and conscience. When God's moral law is seen in the context of the Gospel, it leads us to acknowledge our need for His forgiveness and His transforming work in us. We admit our need for a deliverance from the punishment due our sins and from the enslaving power of sin in our hearts and lives. It points us toward our need for Christ to be our sin-bearer and deliverer and the Holy Spirit to be our sanctifier.

However, the moral law by itself cannot give us a new heart or pay the price of sin. Given the bondage of the will, were the pastor to only exhort a congregation, or "carp" at the brothers and sisters week after week to do what is right, the results would show that such a ministry is foolish pastoral care. On the one hand, a moralistic ministry can produce an ignoring of the preacher and an avoidance of the law, as the Sadducees show us. Or, on the other hand, such a moralistic ministry will produce self-deceived self-righteousness, as the Pharisees exhibited. In fact, pastoral legalism will usually produce both results among the various members of the congregation at the same time.

Therefore, the grace of God must be proclaimed and embraced as the foundation of a new life in Christ, if new life is to be found. The Law can only be heard graciously in the context of the Gospel. Biblical exhortation always rests upon and follows the reassurance of the Gospel of grace. Pastors and parents both need to be reminded that the Ten Commandments were given to Israel after they had been set free from Egypt. The Covenant with Abraham is prior to and more basic than the Covenant with Moses, as the Apostle makes clear in Romans 4. We need to keep in mind that the Epistle of Paul was written to Christians who were aware of the Gospel when they read chapters 1 through 3 that set forth the depth of sin in both Jew and Gentile. Prevenient grace is essential, as the next point emphasizes.

2. The prevenient grace of God is needed to set the will free to turn to God.
Explanation

The Article speaks of prevenient grace as follows:

Wherefore we have no power to do good works pleasant and acceptable to God, without the grace of God by Christ preventing us, that we may have a good will...

What is meant by "preventing us"? The English word "prevent" has changed its meaning since the Article was written; "prevent" no long means what it did when the Article was written. It meant then "to precede," or " to come before." In this Article it means "to come before our response of faith." "Prevent" now means in common speech "to hinder" or "to stop." It has actually reversed its meaning.

By the phrase "the grace of God by Christ preventing us" the Article refers to the gracious work of the Holy Spirit within us preceding our choice to accept the saving gift of God in Christ Jesus. It refers to a work of the Holy Spirit enabling the opening of our hearts to choose to receive the Gospel in faith and repentance. This work of the Spirit "comes before," is prevenient, and enables our decision to turn to God, as He is revealed in Christ. We do choose, but we can take no credit for choosing, because it is a choice that was enabled by God's grace at work within us and it is also a choice in response to His prior work as Savior done for us on the Cross while we were still sinners rejecting God.

This work of the Spirit is referred to as grace because, on the one hand, it is entirely unmerited and undeserved and, on the other hand, because it is effective or empowering. In Scripture, grace has connotations both of being an undeserved gift and of effective spiritual power.

The Article's teaching concerning this prevenient work of the Spirit is required by the radical language of the bondage of the will with which this Article begins, as set forth in the first teaching point above. It is not possible for sinners dead in trespasses and sins to turn to or even to desire to turn to Christ. They are dead spiritually. Therefore it is only due to the prior action of God's gracious Spirit giving them spiritual life that sinners do turn to Christ.

It follows also that this work of the Spirit is efficacious where and when it pleases God. It is efficacious grace. The saving initiative and effectiveness lies with God. Left to our fallen nature, we would only resist all of His invitations to repent and believe. The things of the Spirit seem unreal or foolish, or impossible to fallen sinners. The "natural" man does not receive the things of the Spirit. But when God's prevenient grace is at work in us, we are set free to respond. We stop resisting Him; we see the light; we recognize our need and we embrace His gracious Gospel. We believe and repent or, to put it differently, we are converted and we convert.

This prevenient grace or work of the Spirit, enabling us to repent and believe, is also referred to in theology as "regeneration." Regeneration refers to God's giving a sinner a new birth, or a new heart; it is God Who generates us anew, or re-generates us. Regeneration is a hidden work of the Spirit deep within, in the heart. This work of regeneration becomes visible and conscious in us by the fruit of our conversion, by our faith in Christ and our repentance. (See Article 9, Teaching Point 3, for a fuller discussion of regeneration.)

Biblical Foundations

The natural person does not accept the things of the Spirit of God, for they are folly to him, and he is not able to understand them because they are spiritually discerned. 1 Corinthians 2:14

Jesus answered him, "Truly, truly, I say to you, unless one is born again he cannot see the kingdom of God." Nicodemus said to him, "How can a man be born when he is old? Can he enter a second time into his mother's womb and be born?" Jesus answered, "Truly, truly, I say to you, unless one is born of water and the Spirit, he cannot enter the kingdom of God. That which is born of the flesh is flesh, and that which is born of the Spirit is spirit. Do not marvel that I said to you, 'You must be born again.' The wind blows where it wishes, and you hear its sound, but you do not know where it comes from or where it goes. So it is with everyone who is born of the Spirit." John 3:3-8

Jesus answered them, "Do not grumble among yourselves. No one can come to me unless the Father who sent me draws him. And I will raise him up on the last day." John 6:43-44

"But there are some of you who do not believe." (For Jesus knew from the beginning who those were who did not believe, and who it was who would betray him.) And he said, "This is why I told you that no one can come to me unless it is granted him by the Father." John 6:64-65

that the God of our Lord Jesus Christ, the Father of glory, may give you a spirit of wisdom and of revelation in the knowledge of him, having the eyes of your hearts enlightened, that you may know what is the hope to which he has called you, what are the riches of his glorious inheritance in the saints," Ephesians 1:17-18

And you were dead in the trespasses and sins in which you once walked, following the course of this world, following the prince of the power of the air, the spirit that is now at work in the sons of disobedience— among whom we all once lived in the passions of our flesh, carrying out the desires of the body and the mind, and were by nature children of wrath, like the rest of mankind. But God, being rich in mercy, because of the great love with which he loved us, even when we were dead in our trespasses, made us alive together with Christ—by grace you have been saved— and raised us up with him and seated us with him in the heavenly places in Christ Jesus, so that in the coming ages he might show the immeasurable riches of his grace in kindness toward us in Christ Jesus. For by grace you have been saved through faith. And this is not your own doing; it is the gift of God, not a result of works, so that no one may boast. For we are his workmanship, created in Christ Jesus for good works, which God prepared beforehand, that we should walk in them." Ephesians 2:1-10

False Teachings Denied/Objections Answered

1. The false teaching of Pelagius, as set forth in Article 9, is clearly denied by this Article and so is every form of Semi-Pelagianism and popular Arminianism. Fallen human beings simply cannot, in their own strength, turn to God or even prepare themselves to turn to God. In their heart, they are enslaved to their self-idolatry and are at enmity with God. And we were also enslaved before the Lord drew us to Himself. The initial and enabling move lies entirely with God.

2. As stated earlier, it is sometimes objected that inability denies responsibility. The argument is as follows: since one is commanded by God to repent and believe the Gospel, and is held accountable by God for doing so, therefore one is able to do so. Responsibility proves ability and denies inability.

But that line of argumentation is simply not true. One can be unable, lack ability and be responsible at the same time. If your inability is such as to be due to your own fault or the fault of your forebears, then the responsibility for that inability continues to rest upon you.

No examples are adequate to fully explain the theological mysteries of sin and salvation but here are a few that are suggestive: If a man foolishly and drunkenly cuts off his arm in a sawmill, he becomes limited and cannot do what he could do as a two-armed person. He remains responsible for that limitation. Or, if a man rebelliously jumps off the Empire State Building in New York City and then, while falling, decides that he doesn't like the upcoming consequences, the responsibility for his present state and the coming consequences are still with the jumper. Or, to take another sort of example, if you are a spendthrift who places yourself and your family into great debt and cannot pay the income tax, you remain responsible for the debt and to the Internal Revenue Service, which will not forgive the debt, even though you do not have the ability to pay. In all of these cases, the resultant inability does not cancel accountability.

The same is true theologically concerning our fallen human condition. As sons and daughters of Adam, the inability is ours, and so, too, is the responsibility for our condition. We bear the responsibility for the resultant sinful choosing which we personally embrace and exhibit every day and for the constant accumulation of guilt leading to the final judgment. Inability before God does not cancel accountability, as our conscience bears witness. But God's grace does cancel bondage and damnation and bestows a renewed heart, enabling sinners to admit their need and turn to Christ.

Implications

The chief implication is that if one is lacking a heart for God, one needs to pray for a desire to seek God, and to ask for the inner work of the Spirit for the drawing of the Father to Himself.

Of course, that is precisely what most people will not do, sensing no need for God and having an aversion to God and to the Gospel. That means that we who have been drawn to God in Christ are called to pray for those who will not pray for themselves and who cannot because they will not turn to God in Christ on their own.

We are also called to show in our lives the love of Christ for them and to share with them the Gospel of God as occasion arises. All the while, we are to be praying that the Spirit will open their hearts to attend the Word of the Lord and to receive the grace which He offers them in the Gospel. He has done so with us; why not with them?

3. The abiding grace of God is needed to keep the will free to love and obey the Lord.
Explanation

God's grace initiates and His grace sustains. The Spirit indwells the faithful. Prevenient grace is followed by accompanying grace. The Article continues, "and working with us when we have that good will." The grace of God is described as "working with us" to maintain and strengthen that good will that is enabled in us by prevenient grace.

Accompanying grace might be called sanctifying grace. We are speaking of the abiding work of the Holy Spirit in the Christian's life to help us make right choices and to increase good desires in us. With this work of the Spirit, we as Christians cooperate. Since the power of sin remains at work in us, in our divided heart, we need God's strength and urging in us, in order to maintain our Christian life and to grow more and more in the likeness of Christ.

Even with our works of cooperation, this work of sanctification or accompanying grace remains grace. It is so because at no point do we deserve this work of God in us. The Spirit's indwelling work of sanctification is God's loving gift to us despite our abiding sin and is, in no sense, due to our merit or deserving. Further, it is grace because it empowers beyond our capacity our cooperative efforts of love to God and the neighbor.

Biblical Foundations

Abide in me, and I in you. As the branch cannot bear fruit by itself, unless it abides in the vine, neither can you, unless you abide in me. I am the vine; you are the branches. Whoever abides in me and I in him, he it is that bears much fruit, for apart from me you can do nothing. John 15:4-5

But by the grace of God I am what I am, and his grace toward me was not in vain. On the contrary, I worked harder than any of them, though it was not I, but the grace of God that is with me. 1 Corinthians 15:10

It is no longer I who live, but Christ who lives in me. And the life I now live in the flesh I live by faith in the Son of God, who loved me and gave himself for me. Galatians 2:20

And I am sure of this, that he who began a good work in you will bring it to completion at the day of Jesus Christ. Philippians 1:6

Therefore, my beloved, as you have always obeyed, so now, not only as in my presence but much more in my absence, work out your own salvation with fear and trembling, for it is God who works in you, both to will and to work for his good pleasure. Philippians 2:12-13

False Teachings Denied/Objections Answered

1. On the one hand, any view of the Christian life and of growth in the likeness of Christ that places the primary reliance upon our own ability, upon what we can do, is rejected by Article 10. Such approaches make light of the power and presence of remaining indwelling sin and, at the same time, fail to grasp the importance and full promise of God's gift of accompanying grace.

2. On the other hand, any view that indicates that growth in grace is not possible, that we are "stuck" where

we are, that God is not at work within us to help us grow in grace is a form of unbiblical pessimism. It rejects the hope and possibility of growth in the likeness of Christ. Such pessimism is to be rejected. We are not to make peace with our present state of holiness. We are not to yield our members as slaves to unrighteousness, as if we are not called to yield our members to righteousness and to follow the teaching and example of our Lord. True – we will find that our efforts to walk in the Spirit are often frustrated by indwelling sin, as St. Paul points out in Romans 7, but then in Romans 8, he goes on to discuss the new life in the Spirit in which, by the Spirit's power, our growth can be made and will be made. Sanctification does involve our response but its dynamic is the grace of God at work in us. It is for this reason that the various means of grace have been given to us by the Lord. More of this topic will come to discussion in Article 12.

3. One last objection that I have heard is that it is not good for us to be constantly measuring our growth in Christ. It is not good for two reasons: first, because our growth is so gradual as to be depressing and, second, because we are greatly inclined to self-preoccupation already. We so easily fall into false pride that if we could identify some improvement, however small, we would be inclined to take credit for it and boast in that instead of boasting in Christ alone.

There is much truth in this concern. There is a degree of self-forgetfulness in genuine holy love. Moreover, true progress in holiness always makes us more aware of our sinfulness. Bishop Ryle expressed that thought by comparing the saints to wheat. When the wheat matures and the heads of the wheat grow heavy, they bend low. So it is with the followers of Christ; to the extent that we do grow in grace we become more aware of how much more sin there is in our hearts than we ever thought possible and we can boast only in the Cross of Christ.

Nonetheless, there is a place for periodic thoughtful self-examination and particularly before we come to the table of the Lord for Holy Communion, as the Prayer Book encourages.

Implications

A. Clearly the main implication from accompanying grace is that we need to remain dependent on our union with Christ and on the Spirit, Who indwells us. The various means of grace such as Scripture, prayer, the sacraments, corporate worship, the fellowship of the saints, and the discipline of suffering are all given to us to assist us to rely and depend on the Lord.

B. We are to take conscious aim at godliness, seeking to walk in righteousness and in the Spirit, seeking in all things to please Christ, no matter the cost. In falling short of so true and proper a calling, we have the privilege of relying upon the justifying grace of our Lord, of fresh forgiveness and upon the grace to rise up to walk anew in His paths.

Conclusion

It is very significant that even when the Articles are dealing with sin they cannot avoid quickly shifting the focus to God's grace. Greater than the bondage of the will and the power of indwelling sin is the grace of God and the victory of Christ for us and in us. Our dependence upon Christ and our union with Him in the Spirit are the key to true freedom.

ARTICLE 11

Of the Justification of Man

We are accounted righteous before God, only for the merit of our Lord and Saviour Jesus Christ by faith, and not for our own works or deservings. Wherefore that we are justified by faith only is a most wholesome doctrine, and very full of comfort; as more largely is expressed in the Homily of Justification.

Introduction

What precisely is meant by "justification by faith"? How can we explain it simply? Is a doctrine that was crucially important in the 16th century still relevant in the 21st century? If "justification by faith" is true, what place do human works and deeds have? These are important questions. Without clear instruction, many Christians will remain poorly informed about this essential benefit of the Gospel.

Justification, as presented in the New Testament and in this Article, comes as a shock to many, due to the radical character of God's grace in justification. It is utterly contrary to how the "natural man" thinks.

Even though it is shocking, it is nonetheless true and crucial. Luther referred to "justification by faith" as the "Article of a standing or falling Church," by which he meant, if we err regarding this biblical teaching, we will have no right standing before God. We will have misunderstood the Gospel and will be unable to offer to anyone the comfort of the Gospel of Christ. Even worse, we will leave men and women to appear before God in the final judgment, clothed only in the rags of their own corrupted works. When all is said and done, it is hard to envision a more crucial doctrine than this.

The wording of this Article was drawn largely from the Lutheran Württemberg Confession. Its teaching is common to all the Churches of the Reformation and stands at the center of their teaching.

This recovery of the Pauline teaching contradicts and corrects the teaching of the unreformed Western Church and most probably the Eastern Church as well. The Council of Trent, for example, specifically condemns the teaching of this Article. Attempts have been made to reconcile Trent with this Article. Many are not convinced that they can be reconciled and believe that both the pre-Reformation teaching of the Western Church, as well as the post-Reformation teaching of the Roman Catholic Church, fail to grasp or agree with the radical nature of the grace of God in the biblical doctrine of justification. Ecumenically, there remains a need for extended discussion. Such conversations need to be conducted with a careful and constant appeal to the actual teaching of the Scripture, not just to previous churchly statements, and not with the primary aim to adjust traditions so as to achieve visible unity between churches, irrespective of the truth.

Aware of the critical significance of this doctrine, Anglicans gladly embrace justification by faith as central to the Gospel of Jesus Christ, to the teaching of Holy Scripture and to the Apostolic Faith.

The Teaching of Article 11

There are five main teaching points in this Article:

1. To be justified is to be declared judicially righteous by God.

2. We are not justified in the eyes of God due to our works or deserving.

3. We are justified on the basis of Christ's merit alone.

4. Faith is the instrumental means by which sinners receive justification.

5. The good news of justification is of crucial significance and full of comfort.

1. To be justified is to be declared judicially righteous by God.
Explanation

As created in the image and likeness of God in, and for, a relationship with Him, our relationship with God has a number of aspects. A fundamental aspect of our relationship with God is our accountability to Him as the Judge of all the earth. He is, in His character and position, the ground and guarantor of all morality and justice. As the supreme Judge, He guarantees final justice in the world. The biblical revelation sees all men as accountable to God and as fallen sinners guilty in His sight.

Justification has to do with our legal standing with God. It is a judgment by God, our Judge, about where we stand before Him. It is concerned with God's declaration to us about our state before Him. It does not address our personal transformation into the likeness of Christ. That is the concern of sanctification.

On one hand, we stand as guilty and condemned before God and cannot be in right standing with Him. On the other hand, to be justified is to be declared righteous by God, that is, to be declared to be in right standing with Him. In fact, in the fullest sense of justification, to be justified is to be declared righteous in His eyes forever, for justification in Christ includes God's declaration of our status in the final Judgment. "There is now therefore no condemnation to those that are in Christ."

If we, who are sinners, are declared by God to be righteous in His eyes, we must ask, "How can this be so"?

God is both omniscient and a just Judge. He cannot be fooled and He cannot lie. The biblical doctrine of justification through faith in Christ, as set forth in this Article, explains how God's declaration of our justification can be true of us despite our sin.

Biblical Foundations

Far be it from you to do such a thing, to put the righteous to death with the wicked, so that the righteous fare as the wicked! Far be that from you! Shall not the Judge of all the earth do what is just? Genesis 18:25

For you have maintained my just cause; you have sat on the throne, giving righteous judgment. Psalm 9:4

For it is not the hearers of the law who are righteous before God, but the doers of the law who will be justified. Romans 2:13

But now the righteousness of God has been manifested apart from the law, although the Law and the Prophets bear witness to it— the righteousness of God through faith in Jesus Christ for all who believe. For there is no distinction: for all have sinned and fall short of the glory of God, and are justified by his grace as a gift, through the redemption that is in Christ Jesus, whom God put forward as a propitiation by his blood, to be received by faith. This was to show God's righteousness, because in his divine forbearance he had passed over former sins. It was to show his righteousness at the present time, so that he might be just and the justifier of the one who has faith in Jesus. Romans 3:21-26

False Teachings Denied/Objections Answered

1. One way to deny the crucial importance of the doctrine of justification is to so weaken the view of our sinfulness as to render justification unnecessary. Since one of the effects of sin is to deaden our conscience to the reality and depth of our sin, the tendency to deny the depth of our sinfulness is common to us all. This tendency to

ignore or down-play sin increases wherever the biblical faith is unknown or ignored. Most of the world's religions have no doctrine of original sin or of the bondage of the will. A weak view of sin and final accountability is particularly characteristic of Western secular culture today.

2. Any view of God as less than holy in His character (and therefore capable of overlooking our sin) is rejected. Since sin is against God, a low view of sin usually indicates, at the same time, a low view of the righteousness, holiness, and purity of God. Only in the light of the biblical Prophets and ultimately in the light of the person, teachings, character, and death of Christ and by the convicting work of the Holy Spirit is the majesty of God's holy character revealed and appreciated.

In popular piety in the West, God's love is often so understood and emphasized as to greatly diminish His holiness; His forgiveness is seen as self-evident, requiring no atonement to ground it. As the German poet Heine said, "I love to sin and God loves to forgive; it is an admirable arrangement."

3. Any view that denies that all in Christ, even though they are sinners, are declared righteous in God's eyes is also to be rejected. The non-Christian religions that do take God's holiness seriously do not declare sinful people to be righteous before God, because the issue for them is never settled until the final judgment and then it is based on the surplus of their adherents' good works over their sinful deeds.

4. In some forms of Christianity, the justification of sinful believers is declared by God only after He sanctifies the believers to the point that they are no longer sinners. This view misses the entire point of the biblical doctrine of justification. In Scripture, it is the sinner who is justified. The believing sinner is *simul justus et peccator,* "at the same time just and a sinner."

5. Perhaps the main objection raised to the biblical teaching that sinners are declared righteous by the holy and

just God, is that it is an impossible contradiction. It cannot be a true declaration. It must be a legal fiction of some sort, a pretense on God's part. As we consider the other points in this Article it will become evident that justification of sinners is no pretense and is certainly not a "legal fiction." How this can be so is found in Christ.

Implications

Until persons come to see that they are sinners before a holy God to Whom they are accountable, and before Whom they are hopelessly condemned, the doctrine of justification will seem irrelevant, irrational and even offensive. No one comes to an awareness of his or her condition before God without seeing, as did Isaiah in the Temple, the holiness of God, and without hearing of the Cross and grace of Christ.

Therefore as witnesses we must declare the reality and the true character of God as the holy God and Judge of each of us. If, on one hand, we play down the holiness of God, obscure our sinfulness, and deny our condemnation, we err. If, on the other hand, we omit to make clear the radical grace of the Gospel of the Cross of Christ, we err, for we leave people in the error of their culture or in the errors of the world's religions or philosophies. Only the faithful preaching of our sinfulness and the clear declaration of righteousness given in justification can serve as the instrument the Holy Spirit uses to convict the world of sin, righteousness and judgment.

In justification by faith, amazing as it is, God declares us sinners to be right in His sight.

2. We are not justified in the eyes of God due to our works or deserving.
Explanation

The tendency to justify oneself, either by excuse or by effort of some sort, is so prevalent, profound, and natural in fallen humanity that the Article makes the point that we do not and cannot justify ourselves before God. It states this both positively and negatively. Putting it negatively, the Article states that "We are accounted righteous before God... not for our works or deservings." The ground of our being accounted righteous is not anything we have done, will do, could do or deserve. The Article also states the same truth positively with reference to Christ, "We are accounted righteous before God, only for the merit of our Lord and Savior Jesus Christ..." (emphasis mine). The words "not" and "only" exclude us from providing any part of the basis of our being accounted or declared righteous by God. It is simply beyond us. We are, after all, condemned sinners. It is, however, not beyond the merit or the Cross of Christ.

Biblical Foundations

For all have sinned and fall short of the glory of God. Romans 3:23

And you were dead in the trespasses and sins in which you once walked, following the course of this world, following the prince of the power of the air, the spirit that is now at work in the sons of disobedience— among whom we all once lived in the passions of our flesh, carrying out the desires of the body and the mind, and were by nature children of wrath, like the rest of mankind. Ephesians 2:1-3

For by grace you have been saved through faith. And this is not your own doing; it is the gift of God, not a result of works, so that no one may boast. For we are his workmanship, created in Christ Jesus for good works, which God prepared beforehand, that we should walk in them. Ephesians 2:8-10

False Teachings Denied/Objections Answered

1. Any teaching that affirms that we can make a positive contribution to our standing before God is rejected. This truth runs counter to the world's religions and to the natural inclinations and practice of all peoples everywhere.

2. Even the teaching that we must take the first step in returning to God by trust and repentance, which God then honors by providing the grace in Christ, is excluded. What could we think, will, say or do that is not tainted by indwelling sin and in need of justification? Nothing! As Archbishop William Temple once said, "What I have to offer God is only the sin from which I need to be redeemed," or words to that effect.

3. Some persons draw the false conclusion from justification by faith that God is indifferent to our sinful deeds. St. Paul was accused of teaching that since God is gracious and since justification does not rest on our merit, we could continue sinning, for justification makes our works of no significance. Some even concluded that if the Apostle were right, we should live all the more sinfully to provide the occasion for God to show even more grace. The Apostle responded, "God forbid!" That was not at all what he was saying. To say that our deeds are not the basis of justification is not the same thing as saying that our deeds do not matter to the Lord in any sense. Justification by faith in no way denies that a life built on the grace of justification will be affected in a transforming manner, by the Holy Spirit. We will discuss God's grace and our works in Article 12 which deals with sanctification. Article 11 is concerned to make very clear that God's accounting of us as righteous in Christ does not find its basis in our works.

Implications

The chief point is that we must look outside ourselves for the basis of our being in right standing, reconciled, and in positive fellowship with God. As the hymn puts it: "Nothing in my hand I bring." In the matter of being declared right with God, we come to Christ empty handed to receive, not to bring or offer.

This is severely humbling and impossible for the "natural man" to receive. It runs counter to almost everything else in life. Normally we get what we pay for.

Here, we get what we neither pay for nor deserve. Justification is not due to "our own works or deservings," as the Article puts it.

3. We are justified on the basis of Christ's merit alone.
Explanation

In Article 2, we expounded the biblical understanding of the Cross. Here in the biblical teaching about justification by faith, the penal substitutionary aspect of Christ's death on the Cross comes to the foreground. As Article 2 puts it, Christ "truly suffered, was crucified, dead and buried... to be a sacrifice, not only for original guilt, but also for all actual sins of men."

On the Cross, Christ Jesus bore our condemnation, paid the price for our sinfulness and our sins in His own body, and thus He laid the foundation for our justification. His righteousness, both in His life lived in full obedience to the Father and in His obedient death on the Cross as our substitute and representative, is credited to us, placed to our account, reckoned to us. Similarly, our sin and its guilt and deserved punishment were placed upon Him, accounted to Him, dying on the Cross in our place. Martin Luther referred to this as "the great exchange."

Thus the final, finished, full and sufficient sacrifice, satisfaction, or merit of Christ alone is the ground or basis of our justification. In Him, united to Him, we are accounted righteous before God, in a righteousness won for us and bestowed upon us by God in the Son. God looks upon us as robed in the righteousness of Christ, just as He looked upon the Son on the Cross as clothed in the unrighteousness of us fallen sinners.

Therefore, in direct opposition to the teaching of Rome, Anglicans hold that the sole meritorious cause of justification is not infused righteousness which properly refers to sanctification, but the merit of Christ's life and above all His atoning death on the Cross reckoned to us sinners as received by faith in Christ, which faith is not the foundation but the sole means or instrumental cause of justification.

Biblical Foundations

But now the righteousness of God has been manifested apart from the law, although the Law and the Prophets bear witness to it— the righteousness of God through faith in Jesus Christ for all who believe. For there is no distinction: for all have sinned and fall short of the glory of God, and are justified by his grace as a gift, through the redemption that is in Christ Jesus, whom God put forward as a propitiation by his blood, to be received by faith. This was to show God's righteousness, because in his divine forbearance he had passed over former sins. It was to show his righteousness at the present time, so that he might be just and the justifier of the one who has faith in Jesus. Romans 3:21-26

But the words "it was counted to him" were not written for his sake alone, but for ours also. It will be counted to us who believe in him who raised from the dead Jesus our Lord, who was delivered up for our trespasses and raised for our justification. Romans 4:23-25

For our sake he made him to be sin who knew no sin, so that in him we might become the righteousness of God. 2 Corinthians 5:21

Christ redeemed us from the curse of the law by becoming a curse for us—for it is written, "Cursed is everyone who is hanged on a tree." Galatians 3:13

He himself bore our sins in his body on the tree, that we might die to sin and live to righteousness. By his wounds you have been healed. 1 Peter 2:24

False Teachings Denied/Objections Answered

1. Denied is any doctrine that teaches that our righteousness in God's eyes is based on anything other than Christ's righteousness being imputed to us.

An example of such erroneous teaching is a popular teaching that we do not need to be declared to be righteous in God's eyes due to the Son's Cross, since as a kind and merciful God, our Father, He simply forgives us. The ground of our being declared righteous is His loving nature. This teaching fails to grasp Who God is, to grasp His attributes and His position as the Judge of all the earth. It does not measure the terrible seriousness of sin. It also fails to consider that, in forgiveness, the forgiver graciously chooses to pay the cost that underlies forgiveness.

2. Also denied would be any view that teaches that our righteousness in God's eyes is based upon Christ's righteousness being imputed to us, plus some contribution of ours. When the matter concerns our right standing with God and its basis, the foundation of our righteousness is found in Christ alone and not in any part in us.

This rejects any doctrine that makes our faith or any thing else we do the basis or part of the basis of our justification. We will discuss the place of faith in justification shortly.

3. As mentioned above, justification by faith does not render sanctification null and void. It does not mean that our good deeds and developing character as Christians mean nothing to God or others. Not at all, they mean a great deal and are the fruit of the work of the Spirit in the justified, but they are not the basis upon which we are declared to be righteous in God's sight and never become the basis of our justification.

We will discuss our "good works" in the next Article, "Of Good Works." However, it is important to emphasize from the beginning that there is an unbreakable connection between justification and sanctification. While utterly different and concepts that must be distinguished from one another, they are inseparable and belong together. One cannot have Jesus as Savior and not as Lord. There is just one Jesus Who is both. The writers of the Articles wisely placed the Articles on justification and sanctification next to one another in order to avoid a false separation while, at the same time, giving each its own distinct treatment so that they are not mixed or confused with one another.

Implications

We are to look to Christ's merits alone and not to ourselves as the ground of our salvation. Christian assurance rests upon the utter sufficiency of Christ's work on the Cross to place us right with God. We will explore that in the final teaching point of this Article.

This fixing of our minds on the merit of Christ alone as the basis of our right standing with God is of the greatest importance to those shepherding a congregation or to a parent or friend seeking to explain the Gospel to others or helping them grow in grace. For it is in the sufficiency of the Cross that the confidence and assurance of the Christian is to be found. (See Teaching Point 5 below.)

4. Faith is the instrumental means by which sinners receive justification.
Explanation

Faith, in the widest sense of the word, is a belief in or a trust in the truth or reliability of the word of another, in the ability and willingness of another person or institution to honor what they say. With reference to God's justification of us, faith is the belief in or trust in God's Word of promise given to us in the Gospel, despite our unworthiness. Such faith is called saving faith because it accepts salvation, in all its dimensions, as a gift from God in Christ.

Saving faith, as an act of a sinner, involves four aspects. First, it involves understanding. Unless we hear the Gospel and understand what is being offered by God in the Gospel, there can be no trust in the saving sense. We simply cannot act upon or trust a promise of which we are ignorant or do not understand. Second, there is the recognition of the truth concerning the Gospel promise.

The Gospel must be seen to be true, true in the facts concerning the person, death and Resurrection of Jesus upon which it rests, and true in the promise of salvation to sinners who repent and believe in the Gospel as God's gift. We cannot surrender ourselves to one whom we do not regard as truthful or to a word of promise that is not regarded as true and trustworthy. Third, saving faith includes the personal act and attitude of entrusting ourselves to Jesus as Savior and Lord to the glory of the Father. This is done in the light of an understanding of the Gospel and the belief that the Gospel as God's invitation and promise is true. Such trust allows us to rest in Christ's atonement as the basis of our right relationship with God and all that means for this life and the next. Fourth, while saving faith involves a turning to Christ as Savior and Lord, at the same time, it involves a turning away from false gods and evil. Repentance is an aspect of saving faith. "Repent and believe," we read in Scripture. These four aspects are all part of one act of saving faith.

Biblical Foundations

And he believed the Lord, and he counted it to him as righteousness. Genesis 15:6

But to all who did receive him, who believed in his name, he gave the right to become children of God. John 1:12

For God so loved the world, that he gave his only Son, that whoever believes in him should not perish but have eternal life. John 3:16

Now when they heard this they were cut to the heart, and said to Peter and the rest of the apostles, "Brothers, what shall we do?" And Peter said to them, "Repent and be baptized everyone of you in the name of Jesus Christ for the forgiveness of your sins, and you will receive the gift of the Holy Spirit. For the promise is for you and for your children and for all who are far off, everyone whom the Lord our God calls to himself." Acts 2:37-39

And they said, "Believe in the Lord Jesus, and you will be saved, you and your household." Acts 16:31

For I am not ashamed of the gospel, for it is the power of God for salvation to everyone who believes, to the Jew first and also to the Greek. Romans 1:16

But now the righteousness of God has been manifested apart from the law, although the Law and the Prophets bear witness to it— the righteousness of God through faith in Jesus Christ for all who believe. For there is no distinction: for all have sinned and fall short of the glory of God, and are justified by his grace as a gift, through the redemption that is in Christ Jesus, whom God put forward as a propitiation by his blood, to be received by faith. This was to show God's righteousness, because in his divine forbearance he had passed over former sins. It was to show his righteousness at the present time, so that he might be just and the justifier of the one who has faith in Jesus. Romans 3:21-26

False Teachings Denied/Objections Answered

1. One error is the teaching that faith is not necessary to God's justifying declaration. This view holds when Jesus died upon the Cross for the sins of the world, all men were justified in the eyes of God. That seems to be the teaching of Karl Barth. Faith is not seen as the necessary link between the objective work of Christ on the Cross and the personal participation of an individual in the benefit and promise of that work of Christ.

If this were true, the individual's salvation would be completed without the person's consent or knowledge. Such a view fails to consider that a person is not only an object, having a body, but is also a subject with a heart, a mind, a will and affections. Therefore, a person cannot be saved simply objectively as if he or she were a stick or a stone. The subjectivity of the person has to be involved and saved.

Most importantly, nowhere in the Scripture is justification made a universal description of all persons in the world. In Scripture, justification is a declaration by God regarding those who repent and believe in Christ and His saving work on the Cross and not otherwise.

2. Another false view regards saving faith as a meritorious work of the believer which is the basis for, or part of, the basis for justification. To hold that view means that we would either be saved by the merit of our faith or by the work of Christ on the Cross as well as by the merit of our faith. Such a view is in error; saving faith is essential, but it is not a meritorious work for several reasons:

First, faith is not a meritorious work because saving faith is the reception of a gift which the believer does not deserve. One does not earn a gift by simply receiving a gift. Saving faith is an empty hand that receives the gift of God and trusts in the promise of the Gospel. By trust a person takes God at His Word in Christ. Saving faith is an act in which a person gives up all attempts to merit justification and casts himself or herself on the merit of Christ alone. In saving faith, the eyes of the believer are on Christ alone. Faith does not look at itself.

Second, saving faith does not arise due to man's effort but comes from God. Saving faith is a response to the prior offer of God in Christ. Apart from the gift of the Gospel, there could be no saving faith. Moreover, saving faith is due to the inner work of the Holy Spirit regenerating the believer's heart and opening him or her to the Gospel. Apart from the gracious regenerating and illuminating work of the Holy Spirit, there would be no saving faith. Saving faith is a gift that accepts a gift.

Third, saving faith is not a meritorious work because our faith is mixed with weakness and false motives. It too is tainted by sin and must be justified by God on the basis of the saving work of Christ.

For all these reasons the Scriptures never speak of the merit of saving faith or of saving faith as a good work upon which, in part, our justification rests. Texts that say that we are saved by faith, are abbreviations and mean that it is through faith or by means of faith that we receive the salvation merited for us by Christ.

In sum, saving faith is instrumental not foundational. In saving faith, the believer looks only to Christ and not to himself or herself in any sense for justification. "Nothing in my hand I bring, only to Thy Cross I cling!"

Implications

One thing is needful for justification in Christ, that the atoning work of Christ is personally relied upon by the sinner, if he or she is to be justified by God. Saving faith is essential as the personal reception of God's gift in Christ.

Therefore, we are to invite, even command sinners everywhere to repent and believe or be lost and live under the wrath of God. Saving faith is not optional to salvation.

Since no one can turn to Christ unless the Father draws him, we need to pray that God will see that the Gospel is presented to the sinner through us and the whole Church, and that the Holy Spirit will so work in his or her heart that the gift of saving faith will be given and the sinner will receive that which Christ has accomplished on the Cross for all who turn to Him.

5. The Good News of justification is of crucial significance and full of comfort.
Explanation

By now it has become clear that justification due to the merit of Christ alone is of crucial significance. This last teaching point highlights the personal and pastoral importance of justification by emphasizing the assurance and strengthening that only justification can bring to the believing sinner.

To "comfort" someone is both to assure and to strengthen a person in a given situation of need. Wherein does Christian assurance of salvation find its basis? Justification is the only true basis of the assurance of salvation. Why is this so? It is so because our assurance before God rests on the perfection or complete satisfaction of Christ's work alone as applied or accounted to us by God Himself, as we turn to Christ in repentant faith.

His sacrifice is utterly sufficient. And on that sufficiency the Christian's faith and life rests. Nothing else will do! If I look to myself, there is nothing which is not tainted by sin, nothing perfect, nothing sufficient; but when I look to Him and His sacrifice, there is nothing lacking. It has been accomplished and done! The Resurrection and Ascension of Christ are God's "Yes!" to the Son's Cross and are God's Word to us.

Adding anything we might do, anything in addition to the sinless life of Christ and the sufficiency of the Cross as accounted to us by God would rob us of all assurance, for we would never know if we have done enough or have done what we have done with sufficient completeness and integrity. The mixed character of even our best actions and efforts would rightly leave us greatly troubled. Where then would be the joy of our salvation? It would be replaced by an uncertainty, or if we are honest about our sinfulness, by the certainty of our damnation. This is clearly not the note struck in the New Testament, and it is not the proper state of mind for anyone who places his or her faith in Jesus Christ.

Therefore this Article concludes by stating that this is a doctrine "very full of comfort."

It is important to emphasize that "comfort," as used in this Article, does not only mean to console or assure; it also means to encourage or strengthen as well. There is a strengthening of resolve and courage to serve Christ and the neighbor that comes with God's assurance of salvation. This aspect of comfort points us toward sanctification.

We should add one comment that points toward Section Four of the Articles. Since justification speaks of us as linked to Christ, we should not fail to see that justification also links us to Him as the head of His Body the Church with its life and mission. It is quite as wrong to treat justification by faith in an utterly individualistic fashion, as it is wrong to isolate justification by faith from sanctification.

Conclusion

The Apostle Paul writes in Romans, "Therefore, since we have been justified by faith, we have peace with God through our Lord Jesus Christ." Apart from justification by grace through faith in Christ, there is no peace with God, or with our brothers and sisters in Christ, or our neighbors, or, in the long run, within ourselves. Luther had it right—justification received by faith alone is "the doctrine of a standing or falling Church." We cannot over-emphasize the importance of justification through faith alone.

ARTICLE 12

Of Good Works

Albeit that good works, which are the fruits of faith and follow after justification, cannot put away our sins and endure the severity of God's judgement, yet are they pleasing and acceptable to God in Christ, and do spring out necessarily of a true and lively faith, insomuch that by them a lively faith may be as evidently known as a tree discerned by the fruit.

Introduction

The definition of a good work. What is a "good work"? Who can do them? If we are not justified by good works, do they matter? What significance do they have in a Christian's life?

As we shall see in the exposition to follow, the term "good work" must be qualified even for Christians, because our motives are always less than perfect.

We do need to state a definition of a "good work." In this Article the term "good work" refers only to the attitudes, thoughts, and actions of believers in Christ. A good work is the fruit of a living faith in Christ. A good work, in the sense of this Article, is enabled by the inner, transforming work of the Holy Spirit at work in believers. In addition, the action will be in agreement with or informed by the revealed will of God as found in Scripture.

The Teaching of Article 12

Here are the teaching points of this Article:

1. Good works follow after justification.

2. All of our good works are imperfect.

3. Our good works are pleasing to God.

4. True faith produces good works necessarily.

1. Good works follow after justification.
Explanation

When it speaks of good works, this Article is speaking of what is usually called the doctrine of sanctification or the transforming work of God, which begins by the regenerating work of the Holy Spirit in the heart of the sinner, freeing him or her to turn to Christ by faith and repentance, and continues in the life of the believer to enable his or her growth in grace. This 12th Article, therefore, is concerned with the character and active life of the Christian.

The Article is concerned with the relation of sanctification and justification. It seeks to indicate the nature of the relationship in the clearest manner.

Justification differs significantly from sanctification. Justification is God's gift of the state or status of being right with God. It is a state that is complete and perfect, which the believer simply receives by faith as a gift from Christ. Our works do not figure in justification at all. Sanctification, on the other hand, is a process, incomplete and imperfect in this life, in which the believer lives and works. The believer cooperates with God, being comforted, guided and empowered by the Holy Spirit. In sanctification, our works are significant as our contribution and participation in our progress in holiness.

It is of crucial importance that justification, previously discussed in Article 11, and sanctification, now discussed in Article 12, not be confused. They must be distinguished. Articles 11 and 12 are written as separate, distinct Articles in order to help the reader avoid confusing or blending the two. If they are confused or mixed, then our salvation would depend on the degree of our transformation and upon our good works. Christian assurance would be lost and justification denied. The Gospel would be perverted.

On the other hand, neither ought they be isolated from one another. Justification and sanctification belong together, because the faith that receives the promise of the Gospel necessarily bears fruit in good works. To make this mutual relationship clear, Articles 11 and 12 are placed side by side. Neither one should be considered without keeping the other in mind.

When Article 12 speaks of good works "following after justification," it is not only speaking of a temporal order, as in first justification at conversion and then in the following life of the Christian, we have the fruit of good works. The Article is also pointing out that good works follow after justification in the sense that they rest upon and take place within the status and resulting relationship of being right with God by being justified in Christ. Good works grow and bloom in the soil of the relationship with God that is anchored in justification. We never progress beyond justification in this life or the next, but rather are rooted in it. In both the temporal sense and foundational sense, "good works follow after justification."

Biblical Foundations

When you were slaves of sin, you were free in regard to righteousness. But what fruit were you getting at that time from the things of which you are now ashamed? The end of those things is death. But now that you have been set free from sin and have become slaves of God, the fruit you get leads to sanctification and its end, eternal life. For the wages of sin is death, but the free gift of God is eternal life in Christ Jesus our Lord. Romans 6:20-23

For those who live according to the flesh set their minds on the things of the flesh, but those who live according to the Spirit set their minds on the things of the Spirit. To set the mind on the flesh is death, but to set the mind on the Spirit is life and peace. For the mind that is set on the flesh is hostile to God, for it does not submit to God's law; indeed, it cannot. Those who are in the flesh cannot please God. You, however, are not in the flesh but in the Spirit, if in fact the Spirit of God dwells in you. Anyone who does not have the Spirit of Christ does not belong to him. Romans 8:5-9

For by grace you have been saved through faith. And this is not your own doing; it is the gift of God, not a result of works, so that no one may boast. For we are his workmanship, created in Christ Jesus for good works, which God prepared beforehand, that we should walk in them. Ephesians 2:8-10

And we all, with unveiled face, beholding the glory of the Lord, are being transformed into the same image from one degree of glory to another. For this comes from the Lord who is the Spirit. 2 Corinthians 3:18

False Teachings Denied/Objections Answered

There are two errors to keep in mind with regard to the relationship of justification and sanctification.

1. One error is to confuse the two and believe that good works belong to justification. This is the legalistic error. It teaches that we are saved by grace plus our works in one way or another. This error is clearly dealt with in Article 11. It is a profound distortion of the Gospel and robs the Christian of all assurance.

2. The other error is to so isolate sanctification from justification as to suggest that one can have justification without at the same time being caught up in the sanctifying work of the Holy Spirit, honoring Christ as Lord. This is tantamount to saying, "Let us go on sinning now that we are under grace and not law." This thought is regularly rejected in the New Testament. True faith not only surrenders to Jesus as Savior but in gratitude it desires and seeks to follow him as the Lord, aided and empowered by the Holy Spirit, with indwelling sin fighting against sanctification all of the way.

Implications

When teaching about our relationship with the Lord, we need to keep clearly in mind which aspect of our relationship with God we are discussing. If the question concerns whether we are in right standing with God, then justification, God's gift, is what needs to be taught and emphasized. This is particularly important when one is confronting a troubled conscience. We ought never to take up the active aspect of Christian living without a deep awareness of the utter sufficiency of Christ as one's Savior. Gratitude and thanksgiving provide the proper context for Christian ethics and living. To lose sight of that is to lose the joy of our salvation and to fail to truly honor Christ as Savior, while at the same time losing the freedom to live a new life in Christ.

If, however, the question concerns our active life in Christ, asking, "What am I to do?" or "How am I to act?" then the call and promise of sanctification is to be considered. There are good works in which we are to walk, which have been prepared for us by the Lord. Progress is to be made by the Holy Spirit dwelling within. Reinhold Niebuhr said something like, "There is always more *agape* that can be expressed than we have done to date."

2. All of our good works are imperfect.
Explanation

The Article states that our good works "cannot put away our sins or endure the severity of God's judgment." They could not put away our sins because, even were they perfect, they would only be what we owed God. Our previous sins and indwelling sin would still require atonement. But also, they cannot put away our sins because in fact our good works are not perfect but imperfect for they flow from a divided heart. As such our good works could not withstand God's judgment, should He be strict to count what is amiss in them.

This point emphasizes once again that our good works are not, in any sense, the basis of our right standing with God. They are expressions of a relationship founded solely on the righteousness of Christ reckoned to our account.

This second teaching point rejects any doctrine of perfectionism in this life. Even our best works must be humbly regarded as imperfect expressions of gratitude, love, and obedience, tainted by mixed motives and enacted often within imperfect options. Boasting or undue pride is excluded.

Biblical Foundations

Will any one of you who has a servant plowing or keeping sheep say to him when he has come in from the field, "Come at once and recline at table"? Will he not rather say to him, "Prepare supper for me, and dress properly, and serve me while I eat and drink, and afterward you will eat and drink"? Does he thank the servant because he did what was commanded? So you also, when you have done all that you were commanded, say, "We are unworthy servants; we have only done what was our duty." Luke 17:7-10

Two men went up into the temple to pray, one a Pharisee and the other a tax collector. The Pharisee, standing by himself, prayed thus: "God, I thank you that I am not like other men, extortioners, unjust, adulterers, or even like this tax collector. I fast twice a week; I give tithes of all that I get." But the tax collector, standing far off, would not even lift up his eyes to heaven, but beat his breast, saying, "God, be merciful to me, a sinner!" I tell you, this man went down to his house justified, rather than the other. For everyone who exalts himself will be humbled, but the one who humbles himself will be exalted. Luke 18:10-14

For I know that nothing good dwells in me, that is, in my flesh. For I have the desire to do what is right, but not the ability to carry it out. For I do not do the good I want, but the evil I do not want is what I keep on doing. Now if I do what I do not want, it is no longer I who do it, but sin that dwells within me. So I find it to be a law that when I want to do right, evil lies close at hand. For I delight in the law of God, in my inner being, but I see in my members another law waging war against the law of my mind and making me captive to the law of sin that dwells in my members. Wretched man that I am! Who will deliver me from this body of death? Thanks be to God through Jesus Christ our Lord! So then, I myself serve the law of God with my mind, but with my flesh I serve the law of sin. Romans 7:18-25

And we all, with unveiled face, beholding the glory of the Lord, are being transformed into the same image from one degree of glory to another. For this comes from the Lord who is the Spirit. 2 Corinthians 3:18

False Teachings/Objections Answered
    1. Some in the "Holiness tradition" have taught a doctrine of perfectionism. This has taken several forms, from a progressive perfectionism to a perfectionism enabled by a sudden work of the Spirit. In order to hold any doctrine of perfectionism, sin must be limited to the conscious violation of known commands of the Lord. Sinfulness in the heart is overlooked or denied to be sin. But, as discussed in Article 9, selfish and unloving desires of the heart are sinful even when they are not acted upon.
    2. This Article assumes the full, biblical view of sin. Sin is seen as including any departure from God's will for us as He created us in His image. Sin, therefore, includes unconscious sin, tainted motives, and sins of omission as well as intentional rebellion against the known will of God and His Lordship.
    While perfection is the proper aim of sanctification, it is not attained in this life. We do well to say with St. Paul, "Not that I have already obtained it."

Some would argue that in denying perfectionism we are limiting or denying the power and goodness of God. That is not true. It is not whether God could perfect us in this life that is denied, but rather that we have no scriptural evidence to support a doctrine that He has done so. He will do so in glory. However, if sin is allowed to be what it is in Scripture, and as is stated in Articles 9 and 10, then nothing in Scripture and human experience would support a doctrine of perfectionism. Jesus remains the sole exception to the declaration of the Apostle Paul that "all have sinned and continuously fall short of the glory of God."

Implications

Humility is the chief implication. We need to find ourselves alongside of the tax collector, not the Pharisee, in Jesus' parable cited above. The note of sincere honesty and self-awareness threads its way through this Article.

3. Our good works are pleasing to God.
Explanation

Our good works are imperfect "yet are they pleasing and acceptable to God in Christ," states this Article. What a joyful declaration that is. What an encouragement to us.

One might well ask, however, "How can it be possible that God should take pleasure in our imperfect good works?" The answer the Article gives is that He does this as our Father in Christ. Just as we, who are parents, delight in the imperfect first steps and deeds of our children and in the progress we see them making their whole life long, so our Heavenly Father delights in seeing us grow in grace by our imperfect steps.

In so doing, the Lord is delighting in the progressive accomplishment of His purpose of full salvation for us and in His own work of the Spirit within us, as well as our surrender and service in the Kingdom.

Biblical Foundations

And he who had received the five talents came forward, bringing five talents more, saying, "Master, you delivered to me five talents; here I have made five talents more." His master said to him, "Well done, good and faithful servant. You have been faithful over a little; I will set you over much. Enter into the joy of your master." Matthew 25:20-21

Pray then like this: "Our Father in heaven, hallowed be your name. Your kingdom come, your will be done, on earth as it is in heaven. Give us this day our daily bread, and forgive us our debts, as we also have forgiven our debtors. And lead us not into temptation, but deliver us from evil." Matthew 6:9-13

But when the fullness of time had come, God sent forth his Son, born of woman, born under the law, to redeem those who were under the law, so that we might receive adoption as sons. And because you are sons, God has sent the Spirit of his Son into our hearts, crying, "Abba! Father!" Galatians 4:4-6

I am the vine; you are the branches. Whoever abides in me and I in him, he it is that bears much fruit, for apart from me you can do nothing. John 15:5

Therefore, my beloved, as you have always obeyed, so now, not only as in my presence but much more in my absence, work out your own salvation with fear and trembling, for it is God who works in you, both to will and to work for his good pleasure. Philippians 2:12-13

False Teachings Denied/Objections Answered

At times, in devotional writings, one meets such a call to total surrender and complete devotion that it seems to suggest that anything less than perfection is unacceptable to God. If that were taken seriously, any sensitive saint would have to admit that nothing in his or her life could be acceptable to God. The Heavenly Father would relate to us only as a severe Judge and not as a Father. No doubt, some earthly fathers do relate to their children in such a judgmental manner, lacking love and mercy, but such is not the Heavenly Father we know in Christ. He does discipline us and sinful rebellion can darken our fellowship with Him, but our sinfulness does not remove our standing in Christ. He is quick to forgive and encourage us and to delight in our turning to him as we confess our sin and seek to walk in His paths. There is with Him an abiding sense of the joy in our salvation and in His fatherly care.

Implications

The joy of our salvation, a delight in our relationship with God, and the encouragement to walk in His ways are the implications of His delight concerning our efforts as we live under His Lordship. We live in Christ, aided and empowered by the Spirit, seeking in gratitude and thanksgiving to follow Him whom we worship and love. So we can live in honesty about our short-comings without gloominess and with joy without false pride, as we seek to follow Christ day by day.

4. True faith produces good works necessarily.
Explanation

Why do we believe that authentic faith in Christ as Savior and Lord will necessarily produce good works? Saving faith is made possible by the gift of the Spirit opening our heart to the Gospel. This act of regeneration, which changes a heart of stone to a heart of flesh, is both the inner means of justification and simultaneously the beginning of the work of the Spirit that enables the process of sanctification to begin. The believer's new heart seeks and wishes to honor and serve the Lord, Who is the Savior. Love and gratitude and a desire to do what is right are present from the beginning in authentic faith in Christ, due to the indwelling Spirit at work within the believer. Therefore, however feebly expressed and inadequate they might be, good works will appear. As the Article states, they appear necessarily. A new Creation has begun; a Resurrection has occurred. A good tree has been planted which is bearing fruit.

It is because of this necessary connection that the Article asserts that an observer can see the faith of an authentic Christian. The connection between faith in Christ and good works in the Christian's life is so inevitable that a fellow believer, given a sensitive eye, can see the fruit of the Spirit in the life of a Christian as a sure sign of the authenticity of the believer's faith. This is the point that James was making when he said, "So also faith by itself, if it does not have works, is dead... Show me your faith apart from your works, and I will show you my faith by my works" James 2:17-18. Bishop Ryle said much the same when he said that where he did not see grace in the life, he could not be certain of grace in the heart. God looks upon the heart, but we can only see what is visible in and through the body, and draw responsible but fallible conclusions.

Biblical Foundations

Either make the tree good and its fruit good, or make the tree bad and its fruit bad, for the tree is known by its fruit. You brood of vipers! How can you speak good, when you are evil? For out of the abundance of the heart the mouth speaks. The good person out of his good treasure brings forth good, and the evil person out of his evil treasure brings forth evil. Matthew 12:33-35

For God has done what the law, weakened by the flesh, could not do. By sending his own Son in the likeness of sinful flesh and for sin, he condemned sin in the flesh, in order that the righteous requirement of the law might be fulfilled in us, who walk not according to the flesh but according to the Spirit. Romans 8:3-4

Everyone who makes a practice of sinning also practices lawlessness; sin is lawlessness. You know that he appeared to take away sins, and in him there is no sin. No one who abides in him keeps on sinning; no one who keeps on sinning has either seen him or known him. 1 John 3:4-6

We love because he first loved us. If anyone says, "I love God," and hates his brother, he is a liar; for he who does not love his brother whom he has seen cannot love God whom he has not seen. And this commandment we have from him: whoever loves God must also love his brother. 1 John 4:19-21

So also faith by itself, if it does not have works, is dead. But someone will say, "You have faith and I have works." Show me your faith apart from your works, and I will show you my faith by my works. You believe that God is one; you do well. Even the demons believe—and shudder! James 2:17-19

False Teachings Denied/Objections Answered

1. Some seem to think that all obedience should be purely spontaneous, that there is to be no intentional effort and obedience in the Christian life. That is an error. We are to "strive after holiness" for several reasons: 1) life must be lived with some degree of purpose and focus; intentionality is unavoidable and to be desired. Aimlessness and half-heartedness are nowhere considered a virtue. 2) The key words we use as Christians to refer to God and our relationship with Him imply obedience: Father, Lord, King, Master. 3) The key words we use to refer to ourselves in relationship with God imply obedience: saints, servants, sons and daughters. Lastly, 4) the New Testament writings are filled with exhortations and warnings and commands addressed to us as Christians that call for intentional Christian living.

2. Another error is antinomianism (against-the-law-ism). Antinomianism is the view that the revealed will of God found in Scripture has no positive place in guiding the Christian's life in the process of sanctification. One is reminded that the Law was given to Israel after Israel was delivered from bondage. It is hard to read the New

Testament carefully and not take note of the many exhortations found therein.

Antinomianism has many subtle forms. It is sometimes held that any intentional effort to obey the declared will of the Lord or to keep a spiritual discipline is to fall back under the Law as a means of justification or being right with God. The danger is real, but love often takes willed, repeated, and steady paths.

In addition, to become aware of what God is asking us to do through the commands of God in Scripture does not automatically and always provoke rebellion and resentment on our part, though, because we are sinful, it may do so. Sometimes we consider it a privilege to serve the Lord as He commands. When the commands of the Lord do cause resentment and rebellion, we are directed by that sinful response to a fresh confession of our sin, a deeper reliance upon our justification, and a prayer for the grace to obey the Lord with a grateful heart.

3. Anglicans have never held to antinomianism as this Article 12 and Article 7 make clear. On the other hand, since the progressive transformation of the character of a Christian is enabled and empowered by the Holy Spirit, it would be a grave error to believe and teach that one could grow in Christ-likeness simply by human effort. We are to call upon God's power and presence, by making regular use of the various means of grace with a deep sense of His presence, mercy and empowerment.

4. In sanctification, our primary aim is not focused upon ourselves but on being thankful and obedient to the Lord, and upon being loving and helpful to our fellow human beings. God will see to our growth in Christ-likeness. There is a certain self-forgetfulness in the path of sanctification.

Scrupulosity is to be avoided. For some persons of strict conscience and earnest temperament, it is easy to become forgetful of the inherent imperfection of all our deeds or omissions, and become so caught up in self-examination and so demanding on oneself that the joy of the Gospel is lost and the love received from God and the neighbor are unappreciated. This blocks our growth in Christ and does not help the neighbor.

This is not to deny that self-examination before the Lord has its place when done in the context of gratitude and the peace with God that rests upon His grace.

Implications

Our Christian faith shapes our behavior and the behavior of our fellow Christians. While we are not to become judgmental, we do need to take note of the behavior of our brothers and sisters in Christ so that we may appropriately encourage them, learn from them or, if need be, confront them.

The Apostle Paul sets us an example of pastoral rebuke and encouragement in his epistles, showing his care for the congregations he founded and knew. This responsibility to care for one another is particularly appropriate between those who know one another well. If a brother or a sister in Christ knows us personally as one who cares for them, then that relationship provides the context for hearing, discussing, giving, and receiving needed words and acts of encouragement and rebuke.

Perhaps it needs to be clearly stated that if the above is true, then each of us must also be prepared to receive encouragement and rebuke from the brothers and sisters as well as to give it. Life in the body of Christ is a two-way affair, or better said, a three-way affair.

This Article does not spell out the means that the Holy Spirit uses to conform us to the likeness of Christ. It will be helpful if we merely mention some of the more usual means the Spirit uses in carrying out His sanctifying work. He uses the formal means of grace: the Holy Scriptures preached, read and meditated upon, prayer, the Sacraments of the Gospel, Baptism and Holy Communion, the occasional offices: confirmation, marriage, reconciliation of the penitent, ordination, anointing of the sick, and burial. He also uses the less formal means of self-examination, and the mutual encouragement and challenge of brothers and sisters in Christ. He uses our responsibilities in life and the experience of daily life as well as our personal experiences of suffering and joy and our experiences of communion with God that are unique to us as individuals in the providence of God.

Conclusion

The fundamental thrust of this Article on "Good Works" is that of joy and encouragement. Our joy is in our relationship with God Who works to assist and enable our growth in grace, enabling us to do the good deeds that He has prepared for us to walk in, and in the fact that God delights in us and our deeds, despite our and their imperfection. No matter the situation and condition, at its deepest level, the Christian life is one of thanksgiving, joy and hope in the Lord.

ARTICLE 13

Of Works before Justification

Works done before the grace of Christ and the inspiration of the Holy Spirit, are not pleasant to God, forasmuch as they spring not of faith in Jesus Christ, neither do they make men meet to receive grace, or (as the School authors say) deserve grace of congruity: yea, rather for that they are not done as God hath willed and commanded them to be done, we doubt not but they have the nature of sin.

Introduction

What about the "good works" of people who do not believe in Christ? Christians are not the only ones to take religion seriously or act caringly to one's family. Some have been known to show care to an enemy.

This Article considers human works of non-Christians in their relation to salvation. Article 13 is one of three consecutive Articles that deal with human works in their relation to salvation in Christ. The significance of the good works of believing Christians was discussed in Article 12. In Article 14, the works called "works of supererogation" are discussed. They are works done by Christians, which were thought in the pre-Reformation Western Church to deserve God's blessing because they were considered to go beyond a believer's duty. This Article 13 considers two specific questions: Do the "good works or deeds" of people who are not converted believers in Jesus Christ, whether inside the Church or outside the Church, please God? And do these "good works" prepare for, or merit in any sense, God's gift of justification? One can put this in the form of a question from a non-Christian: "I am not a believer in Christ. Will God save me or give me faith in Christ because I have sought to do good unto others as I would have them do unto me?"

The Teaching of Article 13

Here are the teaching points of this Article:

Introductory clarification: The definition of "works done before justification."

1. Works done before justification do not please God.

2. Works done before justification are powerless to deserve grace.

3. All works done before justification have the nature of sin.

Introductory clarification: The definition of "works done before justification."

A major concern in understanding this Article concerns the question about whom the Article is speaking. Is it speaking about all non-believers in Christ or is it only speaking about the extremely immoral unbelievers? The answer to that depends on what one means by "works done before the grace of Christ and the inspiration of His Spirit."

One reading of this Article sees an identity between the title which refers to "works done before justification" and the first sentence of the Article, which refers to "works done before the grace of Christ and the inspiration of His Holy Spirit." If we agree with that identification, the interpretation is as follows: the works that we are considering are those done before one is converted, that is, before one is led by the Spirit through the Gospel to place one's faith in Jesus Christ as Savior and Lord and is thereby declared justified by God. Therefore, the people doing these works would be any unbeliever and not just the extremely immoral unbelievers.

But this usual interpretation is challenged. It is challenged first, because the phrase "works of justification" never appears in the body of the Article, only in the Title.

Second, it is challenged because of God's common grace, which could be referred to as "the grace of Christ and the inspiration of the Holy Spirit." Common grace is experienced outside of faith in Christ and accounts for the "good works" of the non-Christians. It is absurd, so it is argued, to say that these good works are sinful and not pleasant to God. Therefore, the people referred to and the works referred to must be those works of extremely immoral non-Christians, the smaller group of utterly depraved persons who have rejected God's "common grace," the moral empowerment from God extended to all mankind in Creation and in His providence. It cannot refer to the larger group of persons who, though they are not Christians, live socially acceptable lives.

However, there are numerous convincing reasons for taking the first and usual interpretation, that "justification" and "the grace of Christ and the inspiration of the Holy Spirit" are referring to the same thing throughout this Article and hence to the works of all non-Christians:

1. It is what the title to the Article seems to say. If we think that "the grace of Christ and the inspiration of the Holy Spirit" refers to God's common grace and not to the gift of faith in Christ that leads to justification, then the title simply has nothing in the Article to which it refers. It simply hangs there. Further the "grace of Christ" is rather specific and would be an unusual and inappropriate way to refer to common grace. Whereas if we assume the author is coherent in his writing, then all our problems go away.

2. It is always right to give the benefit of the doubt to the author and to assume the author is consistent in what he or she is writing. Assuming the author to be consistent is especially appropriate when one is seeking to understand such carefully crafted writing as is found in these Articles. One should therefore assume that the title and the article are discussing "works before justification," which are also defined as "works before the grace of Christ and the inspiration of the Holy Spirit," or before conversion.

3. The practice of not repeating the exact terminology of the title of an Article in the body of the Article is not unique to this Article. Others in the Thirty-Nine Articles do not repeat the exact terminology of the title in the body of the Article. One finds this same practice in Article 10 entitled, "Of Free Will." The phrase "free will" never appears in the Article. In Article 4 entitled, "Of the Resurrection of Christ," the word "resurrection" does not appear in the body of the Article. Yet no one has any doubt about what these Articles are addressing. In fact, the language of the title can add a further nuance or specificity to the Article. Here, in Article 13, the title ties this Article to the preceding Article which addresses the works of Christians that follow after justification. Here the works are by non-Christians, before justification.

4. Most conclusively, there is an explicit contrast between the works that "spring not of faith" in this Article 13 and those works in Article 12 which "spring necessarily of a true and lively faith." The title ties the two Articles together and clarifies that the focus is on the relation of works to justification through faith in Christ.

5. The usual interpretation is in keeping with the concern of these three Articles which concern the relation of human works to salvation.

6. Lastly, the whole thrust of this Article is to reject any thought that works done before faith in Christ can contribute to our justification. This Article is not concerned with the value God might place on works done by common grace under His providential reign. That is a topic of significant interest and importance, but it is not in view here. The focus, as it is in all three Articles (12 through 14), remains specifically on the relation of human works to salvation in Christ.

Therefore we can, with confidence, assert that the works under review in this Article are those works done before justification; that is, before a person is converted and puts his or her faith in Christ as Savior and Lord. In this sense, "works done before the grace of Christ and the inspiration of His Spirit" are any works of non-Christians, insofar as these works are considered in their relationship to salvation.

This means that those commentaries that explore the relation of common grace and the providence of God and the relative value of works done by non-Christians to God's providential reign in history and society may have significant things to say, particularly for general ethics, but they are not dealing with the concern and meaning of this 13th Article.

1. Such works do not please God.
Explanation

In this Article, we are referring to those works done by non-Christians that, humanly speaking, would be counted "good works." They would be deeds of duty, of love and of religious observance, deeds done in good conscience and in agreement with accepted social standards. They could include deeds done to please "a god" as understood by non-Christians. Obviously immoral and consciously ungodly works would not raise the question of their worth in commending the doer to God for His saving grace.

Concerning such good deeds, the Article flatly states that they "are not pleasant to God." This affirms and expresses the constant teaching of Scripture that all fallen human beings have sinned and continually sin and that only those deeds done in faith in Christ please God. If, as Article 12 states, the best deeds of Christians could not withstand the severity of God's judgment apart from Christ, how could we think that the best deeds of non-Christians could please God or commend the non-Christians to God for salvation? With regard to salvation, God is not pleased by mixed motives, halfway measures, and false religion.

As stated above, this Article does not mean to say that God has no interest in the impact of human works as they are viewed from the perspective of His providential purpose and rule in history. Some deeds are better than others. For example, it is better to build a hospital than to ignore the sick, but none of the works of the unconverted are able to commend them to God for salvation. With regard to salvation, the good deeds of the unconverted "are not pleasant to God."

Biblical Foundations

Behold, I was brought forth in iniquity, and in sin did my mother conceive me. Psalm 51:5

The heart is deceitful above all things, and desperately sick; who can understand it? I the Lord search the heart and test the mind, to give every man according to his ways, according to the fruit of his deeds. Jeremiah 17:9-10

Then he began to denounce the cities where most of his mighty works had been done, because they did not repent. "Woe to you, Chorazin! Woe to you, Bethsaida! For if the mighty works done in you had been done in Tyre and Sidon, they would have repented long ago in sackcloth and ashes. But I tell you, it will be more bearable on the day of judgment for Tyre and Sidon than for you. And you, Capernaum, will you be exalted to heaven? You will be brought down to Hades. For if the mighty works done in you had been done in Sodom, it would have remained until this day. But I tell you that it will be more tolerable on the day of judgment for the land of Sodom than for you." Matthew 11:20-24

For all have sinned and fall short of the glory of God. Romans 3:23

And you were dead in the trespasses and sins in which you once walked, following the course of this world, following the prince of the power of the air, the spirit that is now at work in the sons of disobedience— among whom we all once lived in the passions of our flesh, carrying out the desires of the body and the mind, and were by nature children of wrath, like the rest of mankind. Ephesians 2:1-3

False Teachings Denied/Objections Answered

Some would draw a false conclusion from the teaching of this Article and teach, since human works of non-Christians cannot earn God's gift of salvation, that therefore all works of non-Christians are a matter of indifference to God in every respect. Such cannot be the case, for, as Scripture states, there are degrees of punishment in hell depending on the lives that were lived, and there are degrees of reward for the saved in Christ in Heaven depending on the lives they have led.

Implications

It is important for Christians to help non-Christians understand that their good works may have value in society but they in no way merit or contribute to receiving God's gift of salvation in Christ.

God may well be pleased with certain works with regard to His providential reign over history. There is no doubt that Christians should gladly cooperate in social works for the good of society.

2. Such works are powerless to deserve grace.
Explanation

At the time these Articles were being written, it was being taught in the Church in the West that by their good works the unconverted could commend themselves to God. That is, that such deeds would make it appropriate for God to give His gift of the Holy Spirit to draw those who had done what was in them to please God. The Holy Spirit would then lead them to faith in Christ. In the language of the time, there was a kind of merit to these works that made it congruous or in accord with God's nature as just and holy to grant them His saving grace. The phrase in the Article the "grace of congruity" refers to this. In Latin, the phrase is *meritum de congruo*, which means that these good deeds of the non-Christian had the merit of congruity - they had merit in the eyes of God and thus placed a claim upon

God's justice to lead such non-Christians to faith and hence to salvation.

This teaching of congruous merit errs. It errs in that it rests on a less-than-biblical view of the effects of the Fall and the depth of original sin. It builds upon a medieval teaching that, in the Garden of Eden, Adam's holiness consisted of two things: his unfallen human nature and an added gift of holiness, referred to as a superadded gift, a *donum superadditum*. In the Fall, it was the *donum superadditum*, the extra and protective gift of holiness that was lost, while Adam's human nature, though weakened and vulnerable to temptation, remained intact. It is the weakened but uncorrupted human nature that allows the unconverted to do such good works that make it appropriate for God to give the Holy Spirit to such a person to lead him or her to Christ.

Article 13, and Articles 9 and 10, flatly reject such a view of fallen human nature and deny man's ability, even in the slightest way, to merit or render himself in any sense deserving of the grace of God. The effects of the Fall have impacted the whole of human nature. We are profoundly corrupted and find our place deservedly under God's judgment and wrath. Consequently, no works done by fallen human beings have a *meritum de congruo*, a meritorious congruity that puts a claim on God's justice regarding salvation.

Biblical Foundations

The Lord saw that the wickedness of man was great in the earth, and that every intention of the thoughts of his heart was only evil continually. Genesis 6:5

The fool says in his heart, "There is no God." They are corrupt, they do abominable deeds, there is none who does good. The Lord looks down from heaven on the children of man, to see if there are any who understand, who seek after God. They have all turned aside; together they have become corrupt; there is none who does good, not even one. Psalm 14:1-3

The heart is deceitful above all things, and desperately sick; who can understand it. Jeremiah 17:9

For all have sinned and fall short of the glory of God. Romans 3:23

Therefore, just as sin came into the world through one man, and death through sin, and so death spread to all men because all sinned. Romans 5:12

For we know that the law is spiritual, but I am of the flesh, sold under sin. I do not understand my own actions. For I do not do what I want, but I do the very thing I hate. Romans 7:14-15

They are darkened in their understanding, alienated from the life of God because of the ignorance that is in them, due to their hardness of heart. Ephesians 4:18

Whoever believes in the Son has eternal life; whoever does not obey the Son shall not see life, but the wrath of God remains on him. John 3:36

False Teachings Denied/Objections Answered

In the explanation above, we discussed the false teaching that is to be avoided. There is no "merit of congruity." We cannot do anything to lay a claim upon God for His grace. His grace is freely given and in no sense earned.

Implications

It is obvious that the Churches of the Reformation, including the Anglican Churches, and the Roman Catholic Church continue to have significant differences and that there is need for continued theological discussion on grace in salvation in the light of the teaching of Scripture.

3. All such works have the nature of sin.
Explanation

Even the best works of the unconverted have the nature of sin. Why is that? Many find it difficult to consider a deed done for the good of society to be sinful and not pleasing to God. People are reluctant because they have not considered, as the Article states, that "they are not done as God has commanded them to be done." They are not done to the glory of God, out of wholehearted love for Him, and in accord with His Holy nature as set forth in Holy Scriptures and intuited in the human heart. They have not been done out of faith in Christ. Even when the works are more or less formally in accord with God's revealed will, the motives from which they spring will have been at best mixed with selfishness and pride and at worst have been evil.

Biblical Foundations

The texts listed just above under Teaching Point 2 substantiate this point:

The Lord saw that the wickedness of man was great in the earth, and that every intention of the thoughts of his heart was only evil continually. Genesis 6:5

The fool says in his heart, "There is no God." They are corrupt, they do abominable deeds, there is none who does good. The Lord looks down from heaven on the children of man, to see if there are any who understand, who seek after God. They have all turned aside; together they have become corrupt; there is none who does good, not even one. Psalm 14:1-3

The heart is deceitful above all things, and desperately sick; who can understand it. Jeremiah 17:9

For all have sinned and fall short of the glory of God. Romans 3:23

Therefore, just as sin came into the world through one man, and death through sin, and so death spread to all men because all sinned. Romans 5:12

For we know that the law is spiritual, but I am of the flesh, sold under sin. I do not understand my own actions. For I do not do what I want, but I do the very thing I hate. Romans 7:14-15

They are darkened in their understanding, alienated from the life of God because of the ignorance that is in them, due to their hardness of heart. Ephesians 4:18

Whoever believes in the Son has eternal life; whoever does not obey the Son shall not see life, but the wrath of God remains on him. John 3:36

False Teachings Denied/Objections Answered

The false teachings discussed in Points 1 and 2 apply here as well. They need to be reiterated.

In Point 1 we stated:

> Some would draw a false conclusion from the teaching of this Article and teach, since human works either of non-Christians or of Christians cannot earn God's gift of salvation, that all works of non-Christians are a matter of indifference to God in every respect. Such cannot be the case, for as Scripture states that there are degrees of punishment in Hell depending on the lives that were lived, and there are degrees of reward in Heaven for the saved in Christ depending on the lives they have led.

In Point 2, we said:

> This second point states the following: There is no 'merit of congruity.' We cannot do anything to lay a claim upon God for His grace. His grace is freely given and in no sense earned.

The teaching of condign merit is a form of Semi-Pelagianism.

Implication for all three points

There is perhaps no more widespread misunderstanding of Apostolic Christianity than the thought that we can commend ourselves to God for His salvation by our good works, at least in part. This view must be clearly denied so that people are invited to look exclusively to God in Christ for the undeserved gift of salvation and to give up any hope of deserving His grace. This point bears constant repeating, for it runs counter to all our inclinations as fallen sinners.

Conclusion

The Reformation Churches in general, and Anglicans in particular, hold a view of fallen human nature that makes it impossible for us as fallen sinners to initiate or to deserve, in any sense, the grace of God in Jesus Christ. This Article makes that explicit over against the wide-spread tendency on the part of humanity to seek to earn our salvation, at least in part if not totally. The Good News is that while we cannot deserve grace, God has taken and takes the initiative and extends to all the invitation to come to Him in Christ.

Not all Churches hold this biblical view consistently; therefore, more ecumenical, theological discussion is needed.

ARTICLE 14

Of Works of Supererogation

Voluntary Works besides, over, and above, God's Commandments, which they call Works of Supererogation, cannot be taught without arrogancy and impiety: for by them men do declare, that they do not only render unto God as much as they are bound to do, but that they do more for his sake, than of bounden duty is required: whereas Christ saith plainly, When ye have done all that are commanded to you, say, We are unprofitable servants.

Introduction
A "work of supererogation" defined

This is the last of the three Articles, 12, 13, and 14, that treat the subject of human works with reference to salvation in Christ. They deserve to be read together, though each is understandable when read alone.

What precisely is a "work of supererogation"? Before we can discuss its biblical possibility and its place in Western Christian theology, we need a clear definition of it. In essence, a work of supererogation is a work done by a Christian by his or her voluntary choice that goes beyond God's commands, or is above and beyond what God requires of us. It is extra and sacrificial.

The idea of a work of supererogation fits into a specific teaching of the pre-Reformation, Western Catholic Church, that was being taught at the time of the 16th Century Reformation while the Thirty-Nine Articles were being written. This doctrine is still taught in the Roman Catholic Church today. Such teaching affirms that if one chooses to do works of supererogation, works beyond those required of every Christian, works such as martyrdom, or the monastic vocation, which involves the taking of the vows of poverty, chastity, and obedience, one would earn merit that God was bound to recompense due to His justice. Then, the recompense or rewards from God due to these works could be gathered into the Church's Treasury of Merit. And, the Church could transfer these merits to the accounts of others who had died in a state of grace but had done too little to pay for their venial sins before they died so that they had penitential suffering that still needed to be done. This suffering would be done in purgatory. The transferred merits would allow those in purgatory, to whom they were applied, to have a greatly reduced period of suffering in purgatory. Such is the context and the importance of works of supererogation.

Article 14 deals only with the validity of works of supererogation. It does not address the entire merit system of the Western Church. Article 22 will address purgatory. The significance of this Article, however, is surprisingly great, for if the possibility of works of supererogation is denied, that would provide a devastating critique of the entire merit system of the unreformed Church. For, if there can be no works of supererogation, then the entire concept of the Church's Treasury of Merit and the transfer of merit collapses. Therefore, this Article raises a number of critical issues and questions and clearly calls for ecumenical discussions among all of the visible churches, and not just with those in the West.

The Teaching of Article 14

Here are the teaching points for this Article:

1. To teach that one can do more than is required by God is erroneous, dishonors God, and leads to arrogance.

2. Jesus explicitly taught against such a doctrine.

1. To teach that one can do more than is required by God is erroneous, dishonors God, and leads to arrogance.

Explanation

This Article states that works of supererogation cannot be taught without error, dishonoring God, and arrogance.

Such a doctrine of extra merit before God errs because it fails to recognize and teach the truth that all of one's heart and life is owed to God. While there are a variety of vocations, in each vocation, wholehearted obedience is owed to God. For example, persons in the married vocation are just as much called to the full service of God as those in the monastic vocation.

The doctrine of works of supererogation also errs in placing one vocation above another, as if one vocation went beyond what God requires of us and is more sacrificial in character than another. One vocation is not superior to another, for example, the monastic vocation is not superior to the married, secular vocation, nor is one vocation more costly to its members than another. Simply stated, 100% is 100% in both.

The teaching of works of supererogation dishonors God because it obscures and rejects His position as Lord of all, and denies His call for total discipleship given to each of us as His creatures.

And works of supererogation cannot be taught and claimed without arrogance, for it is arrogant to claim that we or anyone can do more than God requires or expects of us. The truth is that we are called to full obedience in whatever works God has prepared for us to walk in. Even more significant is that we, as fallen sinners who are redeemed in Christ, are far from doing what we ought to do, much less doing more than we are called to do. We cannot do even one acceptable work, apart from the atoning work of Christ covering our lives and deeds, as Article 12 makes clear.

Biblical foundations
Biblical foundations will be found in the next point.

False Teachings Denied/Objections Answered
1. Given the reality that we owe all of our heart and life to God, and the fact of the Fall that corrupts even our best deeds, the very approach to God in terms of our merit is misguided. Life in Christ is all a matter of undeserved grace as the Thirty-Nine Articles constantly remind us.

2. This is not to deny that there are various rewards in Heaven and degrees of punishment in Hell. These have to do with the inclination of our hearts and the seriousness with which we engaged in the calling which God has given each of us, whether in general providence or in the life and process of sanctification in Christ.

Implications
A. We are not to teach that there are works of supererogation. Nor are we to construe our relationship with God in Christ in terms of our merit, but rather in terms of undeserved grace and grateful obedience.

B. We are not to consider one vocation as superior to another. What is important is that we receive and obey the specific vocation God has for each of us, in the Body of Christ, the Church, and in the wider society and that we seek to do it wholeheartedly.

2. Jesus explicitly taught against such a doctrine.
Explanation
This point really needs little explanation. Jesus rejected any thought of works of supererogation in relation to God. His words are clear and explicit. With this St. Paul firmly agrees. The following texts show the Lord Jesus' and the Apostle Paul's renunciation of such teaching.

Biblical Foundations

Will any one of you who has a servant plowing or keeping sheep say to him when he has come in from the field, "Come at once and recline at table"? Will he not rather say to him, "Prepare supper for me, and dress properly, and serve me while I eat and drink, and afterward you will eat and drink"? Does he thank the servant because he did what was commanded? So you also, when you have done all that you were commanded, say, "We are unworthy servants; we have only done what was our duty." Luke 17:7-10

Two men went up into the temple to pray, one a Pharisee and the other a tax collector. The Pharisee, standing by himself, prayed thus: "God, I thank you that I am not like other men, extortioners, unjust, adulterers, or even like this tax collector. I fast twice a week; I give tithes of all that I get." But the tax collector, standing far off, would not even lift up his eyes to heaven, but beat his breast, saying, "God, be merciful to me, a sinner!" I tell you, this man went down to his house justified, rather than the other. For everyone who exalts himself will be humbled, but the one who humbles himself will be exalted. Luke 18:10-14

For I know that nothing good dwells in me, that is, in my flesh. For I have the desire to do what is right, but not the ability to carry it out. For I do not do the good I want, but the evil I do not want is what I keep on doing. Now if I do what I do not want, it is no longer I who do it, but sin that dwells within me. So I find it to be a law that when I want to do right, evil lies close at hand. For I delight in the law of God, in my inner being, but I see in my members another law waging war against the law of my mind and making me captive to the law of sin that dwells in my members. Wretched man that I am! Who will deliver me from this body of death? Thanks be to God through Jesus Christ our Lord! So then, I myself serve the law of God with my mind, but with my flesh I serve the law of sin. Romans 7:18-25

And we all, with unveiled face, beholding the glory of the Lord, are being transformed into the same image from one degree of glory to another. For this comes from the Lord who is the Spirit. 2 Corinthians 3:18

False Teachings Denied/Objections Answered

The teaching of this Article was a radical critique of the teaching of the unreformed Church in the West. Some persons then and some today would object that the Reformers had no authority to criticize the official teaching of the Church, because the official teaching had been developed over time under the guidance of the Holy Spirit. If the Reformers were merely standing on their own wisdom and stating their own opinions, that objection might carry weight, but they are standing on the Scripture, the Word of God written, and even on the explicit teaching of the Word Incarnate, the Lord of the Church.

Implications

We are to attend to the teaching of Jesus Christ, the Son of God. The Father says to us as He said to the Apostles at the Transfiguration, "This is my beloved Son, with whom I am well pleased, listen to Him!" Where the Church, in its official teaching, contradicts the clear teaching of Scripture and of the Lord Incarnate, we are, humbly but firmly, to seek to help the Church reform its teaching to embrace the "mind of the Lord."

Conclusion

There are no works of supererogation. The good news is that, in Christ Jesus, our lives are acceptable to God, being justified by grace alone through faith alone. In gratitude and praise, we do the works He has prepared for us to walk in. He assists us by the Holy Spirit and takes delight in us and finds our deeds pleasing in His sight, despite the imperfection inherent in them.

ARTICLE 15

Of Christ Alone without Sin

Christ in the truth of our nature was made like unto us in all things, sin only except, from which he was clearly void, both in his flesh, and in his spirit. He came to be the Lamb without spot, who, by sacrifice of himself once made, should take away the sins of the world, and sin, as Saint John saith, was not in him. But all we the rest, although baptized, and born again in Christ, yet offend in many things; and if we say we have no sin, we deceive ourselves, and the truth is not in us.

Introduction

Jesus is sinless. Scripture tells us that Jesus was like us in all things except for sin.

People are puzzled by this. It is hard for us, as sinners, to imagine what it would be like to be sinless or fully holy in character. We ask, "Just what does being sinless mean?" Even reflecting on the portrait of Jesus before us in Scripture, there is much about Jesus' sinlessness that remains mysterious. And even if Jesus is sinless, how important is that? What difference does it make?

While His sinlessness is important for His prophetic office and His kingly office, this 15th Article is specifically concerned with Jesus' full humanity and sinlessness in relation to His Priestly office, to His being our Savior by making atonement for our sins on the Cross.

In Article 2, there is a fuller discussion of Christ's Incarnation and of the atonement. The sinlessness of Christ is mentioned there but is not discussed with reference to the atonement as it is in this Article.

The Article also states that Jesus Christ is the only one of all humanity, after the Fall, who is sinless. The Article thereby rejects any claim to perfection by Christians in this life.

This would also deny any claims regarding the sinlessness of Mary, the Mother of our Lord, who, while being a virgin, conceived and bore the incarnate Lord. (For a fuller treatment of the Incarnation and of the Atonement see Article 2.)

The Teaching of Article 15

Here are the teaching points for this Article:

1. Jesus was and is sinless.

2. His sinlessness was essential for His atoning work for the whole world.

3. All mankind is tainted by sin.

1. Jesus was and is sinless
Explanation

When Christ, by the Holy Spirit, assumed the fullness of human nature from the Virgin Mary, He was made like us in every respect, with the exception of sin. He was void of sin in all aspects of His human nature, both in His human spirit and in His body or flesh. The Holy Scriptures make it clear that Christ alone is without sin. Article 15 simply records what Scripture teaches.

Since Christ is sinless from His conception on, we must conclude, along with St. Augustine and others, that the Holy Spirit worked in the Son's act of assuming human nature from the Virgin Mary in such a way that the Lord's resulting human nature was without sin. Because of this special work of the Holy Spirit, the Lord did not inherit fallen human nature from the Virgin.

There is no need to assert that the Virgin herself was sinless, as the Roman Catholic Church teaches. There are no biblical grounds for asserting such a doctrine. Indeed, we have evidence to the contrary. She paid the penalty for sin by dying, and she referred to her Son as her Savior. Further, by pushing the miracle back one generation to Mary's conception we still need a miracle, and we are forced to speculate that the Holy Spirit did His cleansing work in her conception to break the train of the corruption of human nature by sin. While Anglicans hold that Mary is the most blessed among all women and honor her, calling her blessed, we find no biblical evidence for a special work of the Holy Spirit at her conception. On the other hand, we do have biblical evidence of the Spirit's special work in the Son's act of assuming human nature from the Virgin Mary. Therefore, we Anglicans rightly hold to the biblical teaching that Christ alone is without sin.

Biblical Foundations

And the angel answered her, "The Holy Spirit will come upon you, and the power of the Most High will overshadow you; therefore the child to be born will be called holy—the Son of God." Luke 1:35

And he who sent me is with me. He has not left me alone, for I always do the things that are pleasing to him. John 8:29

Which one of you convicts me of sin? If I tell the truth, why do you not believe me? John 8:46

For our sake he made him to be sin who knew no sin, so that in him we might become the righteousness of God. 2 Corinthians 5:21

For we do not have a high priest who is unable to sympathize with our weaknesses, but one who in every respect has been tempted as we are, yet without sin. Hebrews 4:15

He committed no sin, neither was deceit found in his mouth. 1 Peter 2:22

You know that he appeared to take away sins, and in him there is no sin. 1 John 3:5

For all have sinned and fall short of the glory of God. Romans 3:23

False Teachings Denied/Objections Answered

1. This Article repeats the teaching of Article 2 in affirming the full humanity of our Lord. As such, it rejects any teaching that denies His full humanity, such as the Gnostics of early post-biblical days did. They held that matter or physical nature was inherently bad and limiting to the spirit or soul. In the scriptural worldview, there is no denigration of the physical. Physical matter is good and comes from God who is its Creator. In the end, there will be a new Heaven and new Earth.

2. Some hold that to be human is to sin. "To err is human." Therefore, it follows that if Christ is really human, He is, by definition, a sinner. But, to assert Christ's full humanity and at the same time to affirm His sinfulness would contradict Scripture and make it impossible for Him to be the model of humanity to which we are to be conformed. The popular saying, "To err is human," is a misleading and oversimplified form of a more complex truth. What it actually asserts is "To err is a common characteristic of fallen human beings." It applies to fallen humanity but not to humanity per se. To assert that Christ is fully human does not imply that He is by definition a sinner or has inherited fallen human nature. We must make a distinction between creation which is inherently good, and the corrupted state of creation after the Fall.

3. To hold that the Lord was sinful would deny that He could be the innocent Lamb sent by the Father. It would thereby render Him unfit to make the atonement for the sins of the world, as this Article asserts and the next teaching point develops.

Implications

A. We are to praise God for His love revealed in the Son's leaving glory above and bending low to assume our human nature, all for our salvation's sake.

B. We are to treasure the dignity of our human nature which is made in God's image and likeness, for which reason He came and assumed our nature into Himself.

C. Lastly, we affirm that, in assuming our human nature, the Lord Jesus is fit to carry out all of the offices of prophet, priest, and king as the Mediator of the new Covenant and, above all, to be the atoning sacrifice for sin.

2. His sinlessness was essential for His atoning work for the whole world.
Explanation

This Article approaches the Lord's work on the Cross from the perspective of His atoning sacrifice. A fuller treatment of the biblical perspectives on the Cross is found in Article 2, Part 2 with its Excursus.

The atoning sacrifices in the Old Covenant required a victim without blemish, innocent and perfect. The annual atoning sacrifice was offered by the High Priest once each year on Yom Kippur, the Day of Atonement. The prescribed sacrificial victim was sacrificed so that the shed, innocent blood could be sprinkled upon the mercy seat and upon the congregation, on the people of Israel, in whose place the victim had died. Thus, with this symbolic and anticipatory atonement made, the Holy God of Israel could and would dwell amidst His sinful people for the following year.

This was all done in anticipation and preparation for the true and final atoning sacrifice, which was rendered by the Lord Jesus upon the Cross. The blood of lambs, bulls, and goats could point ahead to the real and final atonement, but they could not make atonement for human beings in the final and full sense of atonement.

Jesus' sinlessness is essential to His atoning work since He, Himself, is to be the innocent victim, pure and unblemished and undeserving of death. Were He sinful, He would not have been qualified to be the victim and would, in fact, have needed atonement to be made on His behalf.

His having made the final atoning sacrifice in love as the innocent sacrificial victim, there is no longer a need for the atoning sacrifice to be repeated annually. It has been made once for all. The Atonement is His finished work. It is also His sufficient work. What is needed now is not the repetition of His sacrifice, but the reception by faith of the benefits of His atonement, which benefits are sufficient for all. The tearing of the curtain in the Temple that separated the holy of holies from the rest of the Temple when Jesus was sacrificed, allowing free access for believers to God, made this point dramatically.

Biblical Foundations

For all have sinned and fall short of the glory of God, and are justified by his grace as a gift, through the redemption that is in Christ Jesus, whom God put forward as a propitiation by his blood, to be received by faith. This was to show God's righteousness, because in his divine forbearance he had passed over former sins. It was to show his righteousness at the present time, so that he might be just and the justifier of the one who has faith in Jesus. Romans 3:23-26

For our sake he made him to be sin who knew no sin, so that in him we might become the righteousness of God. 2 Corinthians 5:21

For it was indeed fitting that we should have such a high priest, holy, innocent, unstained, separated from sinners, and exalted above the heavens. He has no need, like those high priests, to offer sacrifices daily, first for his own sins and then for those of the people, since he did this once for all when he offered up himself. For the law appoints men in their weakness as high priests, but the word of the oath, which came later than the law, appoints a Son who has been made perfect forever. Hebrews 7:26-28

For since the law has but a shadow of the good things to come instead of the true form of these realities, it can never, by the same sacrifices that are continually offered every year, make perfect those who draw near. Otherwise, would they not have ceased to be offered, since the worshipers, having once been cleansed, would no longer have any consciousness of sin? But in these sacrifices there is a reminder of sin every year. For it is impossible for the blood of bulls and goats to take away sins. Hebrews 10:1-4

But when Christ had offered for all time a single sacrifice for sins, he sat down at the right hand of God, waiting from that time until his enemies should be made a footstool for his feet. For by a single offering he has perfected for all time those who are being sanctified. Hebrews 10:12-14

But with the precious blood of Christ, like that of a lamb without blemish or spot. 1 Peter 1:19

False Teachings Denied/Objections Answered

1. Some see no necessity for Jesus to be a sinless victim and teach that Jesus was touched by sin just as all human beings are. Since we, as parents, can forgive our children without substitutionary sacrifice, why not our Heavenly Father?

This view simply flies in the face of large sections of biblical teaching on the Cross and on the sinlessness of Christ. It replaces the full teaching of God's Word with one theological model – that of our parental relationship with our children. In the light of God's Word, His relationship with us is not in every respect like our relationship with our children, for He is our Father in Christ and, at the same time, He is the Judge of all the earth and the ground of all morality and the One to whom all must render a final account. This view errs by oversimplification.

2. While the Roman Catholic Church does affirm the sinlessness of Jesus as essential to His sacrificial work on the Cross, they do teach that His sacrifice is to be repeated. The teaching on the sacrifice of the Mass, by the Council of Trent and by Rome to this day, affirms that during the Mass, the bloodless sacrifice of Christ is offered anew by

Christ through the Priest to the Father for the sake of merit and that those who deny this are condemned. This Article clearly rejects that teaching of Trent, as do the biblical texts cited above. The sacrifice found in the celebration of the Lord's Supper is the recalling of the completed and sufficient sacrifice of Christ for us and the sacrifice of the believers' praise, thanksgiving, and self-offering made not for merit, but rather in response to the abiding benefits of the Lord's finished sacrifice done once for all. No propitiatory sacrifice is offered in the Lord's Supper. (This is more fully treated in Article 31.)

Implications

Since Jesus alone is sinless, and since He alone has made the final atoning sacrifice for our sins and the sins of the whole world, we respond to Him with praise and thanksgiving and self-offering. In addition, we are to rest upon the sufficiency of His sacrifice for us. It is the basis for our justification and assurance (see Article 11).

Since Jesus is unique and His sacrifice is sufficient and final, we are to invite all to come to Him in faith and to partake of the benefits of His atoning work. There is salvation in no other name but that of Jesus. (See Article 18, where this is developed more fully.)

3. All mankind is tainted by sin

There is really no surprise in this assertion here in Article 15. It simply repeats what is found in Articles 9 and 10. The reader is referred back to those Articles where sin is treated more fully.

Conclusion

The uniqueness of Christ, His Incarnation and sinlessness, as well as His work on the Cross, is meant to evoke faith, peace, reverence, and self-surrender in us. Can we ever thank God sufficiently for His unspeakable gift to us in Christ?

In the light of His Cross, we see also our own sinfulness and are thankful that we can stand before the Lord clad in the righteousness of Him Who, as our Lamb without spot, has made the full and final atonement for us.

ARTICLE 16

Of Sin after Baptism

Not every deadly sin willingly committed after Baptism is sin against the Holy Ghost, and unpardonable. Wherefore the grant of repentance is not to be denied to such as fall into sin after Baptism. After we have received the Holy Ghost, we may depart from grace given, and fall into sin, and by the grace of God we may arise again, and amend our lives. And therefore they are to be condemned, which say, they can no more sin as long as they live here, or deny the place of forgiveness to such as truly repent.

Introduction

If you sin after conversion and repent can you be forgiven? If you sin after having been baptized is forgiveness possible? If you have been excommunicated from the congregation for some gross and shocking public sin can you be reconciled and restored to membership if you repent? Not all Christians have been of one mind on these matters. Where do Anglicans stand?

The concern of this Article is to reject any teaching and practice in the Church, past or present, that refuses forgiveness to baptized, repentant sinners.

Who would deny the availability of forgiveness, we ask? Such refusal of forgiveness is usually rooted in a doctrine of perfection that affirms that truly converted Christians are able not to sin after their conversion and/or baptism. Therefore, if they sin, particularly in some obvious and public manner, they are to be refused forgiveness and restoration to the Church, even if they repent.

In clear contrast to that teaching, this Article affirms that there is always forgiveness of sin available for baptized, repentant sinners. These Articles recognize the fact of indwelling sin in believers, and that indwelling sin leads to actual sin in the life of faithful Christians. This Article (as well as Articles 9, 12, 14, and 15) denies all doctrines of Christian perfectionism in this life.

The Teaching of Article 16

Here are the teaching points for this Article:

1. Believing Christians can and do sin after baptism.

2. Not all sins committed after baptism are the unforgivable sin against the Holy Spirit.

3. Sins committed after baptism, when repented of, can and should be forgiven.

1. Believing Christians can and do sin after baptism.
Explanation

In the history of the Church there have arisen various doctrines of perfectionism that teach that, at baptism or conversion or at some later stage of sanctification, genuine Christians reach a state in this life in which they are able not to sin. These doctrines sometimes teach that there is no forgiveness for those believers who sin subsequent to baptism or conversion or whenever total sanctification is thought to occur. Such doctrines are contrary to Scripture and unrealistic. They are denied by this Article.

In fact, all doctrines of perfectionism in this life are implicitly rejected by this Article and earlier Articles mentioned above. This is not to deny the reality and importance of the work of God in the sanctification of the believer and the work of the believer, striving after obedience or holiness of life by the Spirit. It does affirm, however, that the process of sanctification is never complete or perfect in this life.

Biblical Foundations

Pray then like this: "Our Father in heaven, hallowed be your name. Your kingdom come, your will be done, on earth as it is in heaven. Give us this day our daily bread, and forgive us our debts, as we also have forgiven our debtors. And lead us not into temptation, but deliver us from evil. For if you forgive others their trespasses, your heavenly Father will also forgive you, but if you do not forgive others their trespasses, neither will your Father forgive your trespasses. Matthew 6:9-15

If you then, who are evil, know how to give good gifts to your children, how much more will the heavenly Father give the Holy Spirit to those who ask him! Luke 11:13

If we say we have no sin, we deceive ourselves, and the truth is not in us. If we confess our sins, he is faithful and just to forgive us our sins and to cleanse us from all unrighteousness. If we say we have not sinned, we make him a liar, and his word is not in us. 1 John 1:8-10

Now the Lord is the Spirit, and where the Spirit of the Lord is, there is freedom. And we all, with unveiled face, beholding the glory of the Lord, are being transformed into the same image from one degree of glory to another. For this comes from the Lord who is the Spirit. 2 Corinthians 3:17-18

False Teachings Denied/Objections Answered

1. As stated above, this Article rejects the erroneous doctrine that teaches that at baptism or at conversion or at some definite point later in the Christian life one is totally sanctified and therefore could and should live a sinless life thereafter.

2. There is a long history of the false doctrine that there is no forgiveness for sins committed after baptism. This doctrine led some to delay baptism until they were on their death bed. The Montanists taught such a view in the

2nd century. Even Tertullian, the great Latin theologian, became a Montanist in his latter years and held this view.

Later, the Donatists exhibited the same tendency in the 5th century. They believed that those who denied Christ by surrendering the Holy Scriptures under persecution should not be allowed to repent, be forgiven, or be permitted to rejoin the Church after the persecution was past. The influence of the Donatists was defeated in the Church largely through the theological teaching of St. Augustine, who held the biblical doctrine of indwelling sin and hence of our imperfect obedience, along with a high doctrine of the sufficiency of God's grace and availability of forgiveness to those who repent.

An inclination to legalistic perfectionism appeared during the 16th century Reformation and was held by some Anabaptist groups. It appeared again in the 18th century in Wesleyan circles and is still taught today in some "Holiness" Churches, though they do allow people to be restored to the Church after repentance.

3. Most, if not all, perfectionist views require a denial of indwelling sinfulness, a redefinition of sin that limits sin to intentional sins and a misunderstanding of the lifelong, progressive character of sanctification.

4. Those who hold perfectionist views must misinterpret key texts found in the New Testament. They believe that the New Testament teaches that Christians do not sin. For example, they find this taught in 1 John 3: 6, where we find these words: "No one who abides in him keeps on sinning; no one who keeps on sinning has either seen him or known him." Surely that text is clear, say the perfectionists. But the perfectionists overlook the fact that in the same letter we find the words "If we say we have no sin, we deceive ourselves, and the truth is not in us." When we take both statements together it becomes clear that the phrase, "no one who abides in him keeps on sinning," refers not to a sinless life but to a life in which repentance, forgiveness, and renewed obedience is characteristic. A life

simply given over to sin is a life which no genuine Christian could accept.

Implications

The biblical and Anglican view of the Christian life is as follows: When one becomes a believing Christian, a struggle against sin begins and continues throughout the life of the believer. In this struggle, Christians are aided by the power of the indwelling Holy Spirit. Total victory over sin lies outside of our life in history as we know it. Our lives will be fully perfected at the triumphant return of Christ, at which time He will bring God's saving purpose to fulfillment. If the believer dies before the return of Christ, his or her purgation and perfection is completed at death, so that he or she goes to reside in the nearer presence of Christ, to await the resurrection of the body and the final judgment and fulfillment of all things.

The fact that genuine Christians can and do sin is not a permission to sin, or to take sin lightly, or to consider any particular sinful act or sinful omission to be inevitable. We are to seek to obey Christ, to love God and the neighbor, in all things. However, knowing that we are justified sinners, we can admit it when we sin, repent, and turn to the Lord for forgiveness and for the strength to rise and to walk anew in the power of the Spirit.

It is also true that, as we live together with our Christian brothers and sisters, we will not be surprised that they, too, sin and fall short of the glory of God. We who are forgiven in Christ are called to forgive them as we seek their forgiveness for our failings.

2. Not all sins committed after baptism are the unforgivable sin against the Holy Spirit.
Explanation

What is the unforgivable sin? Is there such a thing? Can one commit the unforgivable sin unknowingly and be lost forever? At times these questions become serious pastoral problems. Therefore, we need to give this matter some careful consideration.

First, we need to clarify our terminology. On the one hand, before God, "coram Deo," all sins are deadly, mortal. We read in Scripture that "the wages of sin is death." Sins are evidence of our spiritual death, for as we read in Scripture, "dead in your trespasses and sins" and "for in the day that you eat of it you shall die." Each sin is an expression of our spiritual rebellion against God, against His loving, holy reign over our lives. James said, "For whoever keeps the whole law but fails in one point has become accountable for all of it" (James 2:10). Any sin of commission or omission is sufficient to reveal our spiritual state, our indwelling sin, and our condemnation under the wrath of God, where we would remain were it not for the atoning work of Christ. In that sense, there are no minor or venial sins.

On the other hand, in reference to our fellow human beings, with reference to society, it is true that not all sins are equal in the consequences that they may have for those around us. In that sense, some sins are worse or weightier than others. Martin Luther King Jr. is reputed to have said, "I want my neighbors to love me, but until they do, I would like them to stop lynching me." Passive "not loving" is usually not as bad as the active expression of hate.

There is before God, one sin that is set apart by the Lord. As this Article puts it, "not all sins are the unforgivable sin against the Holy Spirit." What is the unforgivable sin against the Holy Spirit?

In the history of the Church there have been a number of explanations of this saying of the Lord or of the sayings of the Apostles which refer to "a sin unto death" or an "eternal sin," which seem to refer to the same thing. Our understanding of "the unforgivable sin" depends upon careful examination of our Lord's words, so we will discuss them after citing the biblical foundations in the next section.

Biblical Foundations

Then a demon-oppressed man who was blind and mute was brought to him, and he healed him, so that the man spoke and saw. And all the people were amazed, and said, "Can this be the Son of David?" But when the Pharisees heard it, they said, "It is only by Beelzebul, the prince of demons, that this man casts out demons." Knowing their thoughts, he said to them, "Every kingdom divided against itself is laid waste, and no city or house divided against itself will stand. And if Satan casts out Satan, he is divided against himself. How then will his kingdom stand? And if I cast out demons by Beelzebul, by whom do your sons cast them out? Therefore they will be your judges. But if it is by the Spirit of God that I cast out demons, then the kingdom of God has come upon you. Or how can someone enter a strong man's house and plunder his goods, unless he first binds the strong man? Then indeed he may plunder his house. Whoever is not with me is against me, and whoever does not gather with me scatters. Therefore I tell you, every sin and blasphemy will be forgiven people, but the blasphemy against the Spirit will not be forgiven. And whoever speaks a word against the Son of Man will be forgiven, but whoever speaks against the Holy Spirit will not be forgiven, either in this age or in the age to come." Matthew 12:22-32

"Truly, I say to you, all sins will be forgiven the children of man, and whatever blasphemies they utter, but whoever blasphemes against the Holy Spirit never has forgiveness, but is guilty of an eternal sin"— for they had said, "He has an unclean spirit." Mark 3:28-30

And everyone who speaks a word against the Son of Man will be forgiven, but the one who blasphemes against the Holy Spirit will not be forgiven." Luke 12:10

For it is impossible to restore again to repentance those who have once been enlightened, who have tasted the heavenly gift, and have shared in the Holy Spirit, and have tasted the goodness of the word of God and the powers of the age to come, if they then fall away, since they are crucifying once again the Son of God to their own harm and holding him up to contempt. Hebrews 6:4-6

For if we go on sinning deliberately after receiving the knowledge of the truth, there no longer remains a sacrifice for sins, but a fearful expectation of judgment, and a fury of fire that will consume the adversaries. Anyone who has set aside the law of Moses dies without mercy on the evidence of two or three witnesses. How much worse punishment, do you think, will be deserved by the one who has spurned the Son of God, and has profaned the blood of the covenant by which he was sanctified, and has outraged the Spirit of grace? Hebrews 10:26-29

If anyone sees his brother committing a sin not leading to death, he shall ask, and God will give him life—to those who commit sins that do not lead to death. There is sin that leads to death; I do not say that one should pray for that. 1 John 5:16

Explanation Continued

Jesus tells us that to blaspheme the Holy Spirit is the unforgivable sin. The context of this statement is the Pharisee's statement that Jesus' exorcisms were done in the power of Satan. Jesus' reply made it clear that He understood that He was casting out demons by the finger of God or the power of the Holy Spirit. Therefore, the Pharisees were blaspheming the Holy Spirit and calling good "evil" when they accused Jesus of being in the service of the Devil.

Jesus refutes the Pharisees with two statements that further illumine the nature of the "unforgivable sin." First, He tells the Pharisees that their explanation that He was driving out demons by the power of the Devil was self-contradictory. Were that to be the case, the Devil would be robbing himself, for he would be driving out his own servants. Such a divided kingdom of evil would surely collapse. Actually, Jesus sees His exorcisms as the strong man robbing Satan of his victims. Jesus' mighty deeds were part of the in-breaking of the reign of God, not the power of Satan. The Pharisees had so hardened their hearts to Jesus that they would call good "evil" and blaspheme the Holy Spirit rather than admit the truth of Jesus' claims and the goodness of what they were seeing happen. They had done the same thing when Jesus asked them about whether John the Baptist had come from God. The unforgivable sin arises from a heart set against Jesus and His mission and is expressed in calling the work of the Spirit "evil." The Pharisees knew better. After all, when the Pharisees saw their sons driving out demons, they did not attribute that obviously good work to the Devil. They were sinning against the light and the inner witness of the Spirit.

Secondly, Jesus draws a distinction between speaking against Himself, the Son of Man, which was forgivable, and blaspheming the Holy Spirit, which was not. This is not to suggest that the Holy Spirit is more important than the Son, but rather that the Son is more difficult to recognize than the obviously good work of the Spirit in setting people free from demonic possession. Jesus had not come in clouds of glory, as Daniel 7 promises concerning the Son of Man. The glorious coming belongs to Jesus' second coming. Rather, now before the Pharisees He has come in humility and vulnerability. To speak against the Son of Man seen in His humble appearance could be, at least for a time, a failure of discernment and not a rejection of the light. Whereas, the unforgivable sin is a rejection of the clear and obvious work of the Holy Spirit.

We note that Jesus did not say that the Pharisees had committed the unforgivable sin but He is warning them against it. The unforgivable sin, therefore, seems to be something of a process leading to a final rejection of God. To persist in calling "evil" the good work of the Spirit done by Jesus, or in Jesus' name, is to harden the heart to the point that the Spirit will no longer strive with that person (Genesis 6:3), but will withdraw and all hope of forgiveness will be gone. One would be hardened in rebellion and left there. Only God knows when and where that state has come to be the case. In essence, Jesus seems to be saying to the Pharisees and to all of us: "But be warned, do not call the good work of the Holy Spirit done by Me or in My name evil! Do not sin against the light; do not call evil what you know to be good. And since I am doing the obviously good work of exorcising in the power of the Spirit, take a closer look at Me!"

To sum up what we have said, blasphemy against the Spirit reveals that one is tending to become hardened or settled in the rejection of the good work of the Spirit in Jesus ministry or by others in Jesus name, even to the point of suppressing the truth of what one knows to be true and good, and thereby putting oneself beyond forgiveness. Jesus, in effect, warns the Pharisees that the Spirit will not always strive in the heart of a sinner, and that to declare the Spirit to be evil is to court being given over by God the Spirit to a reprobate mind.

The same intentional rejection of the Spirit working in Jesus' name seems to be in the mind of the Apostles when they warn Christians against the danger of apostasy as an eternal sin or sin unto death. To taste the Spirit Who glorifies Christ and then to reject His works is to run the great risk of becoming hardened in that state.

False Teachings Denied/Objections Answered
1. The chief error is rejecting the obviously good work of the Spirit that honors the Son. We are to take seriously the warning of Jesus and the Apostles not to declare as evil the present work of the Spirit in Jesus' name. To so blaspheme the Spirit is to court a final withdrawal of the Spirit from one's life and consequent eternal condemnation.

Some object that there is no sin that cannot be forgiven in the light of the Cross. That is true, if the sinner repents and believes. Here, however, we are considering a warning that the blasphemy against the Holy Spirit, by calling His obviously good work in Jesus' name evil, is so serious a hardening of one's heart that if persisted in God could withdraw His Spirit, leaving the sinner in a final unrepentant state. We have no right to assume that the Spirit of God will always strive with any given person (Genesis 6:3). Jesus means this warning to be taken seriously by us all.

2. Some fear or even declare that they have, in the past, committed the unforgivable sin and are eternally lost. They anguish about it. However, if they are concerned about this in a troubled spirit, they can be certain that they have not entered into a sustained state from which the Spirit has withdrawn. If that were the case, they would not be troubled. Therefore, they have not yet committed the unforgivable sin. They need only repent and believe or renew their repentance and faith in the Lord Who has borne their sin, to know the release and joy of His salvation.

Implications

We are to take great care never to violate our conscience by suppressing the truth. We are not to sin against the light by declaring what we know to be the good work the Spirit of God has done in Jesus' name, whether around us or within us, is the work of evil.

We are to heed the warning of Jesus that to harden one's heart to the inner or outer work of the Holy Spirit can lead to eternal condemnation.

3. Sins committed after Baptism, when repented of, can be and should be forgiven.
Explanation

There are two types of situations requiring repentance and forgiveness to which this Article applies. One is sinning in such a way that, while one's relationship with the Lord is troubled, it is not broken. Confession and forgiveness are called for. This is similar to the situation when a husband and wife have hurt one another and forgiveness is called for, or when a child has disobeyed his parents and needs to be restored to favor.

The other type of situation is far more radical; it involves a break in the relationship itself. The relationship is not merely disturbed, but has been severed and needs to be restored. Here, it is as if a divorce has taken place and a restoration by remarriage is needed. It is as if the child has rejected the parents and family and has been disinherited and needs to be restored to the family.

Christians are familiar with the first situation in our relationship with the Lord. Personal confession of sin and God's absolution in the Christian's life is the daily experience of every Christian on his or her knees. And it is the weekly experience of every Anglican congregation in corporate worship. This degree of sin and forgiveness requires no further treatment here. If one is particularly troubled, then auricular confession is what is needed.

There is, however, the more radical falling from grace. Two examples come to mind: apostasy and the great excommunication. Excommunication is treated extensively in Article 33, therefore we will not address it here. We will, however, make a few remarks about apostasy.

Apostasy is the deliberate rejection and falling away from the orthodox Faith which was previously believed. It is so serious as to entail a departure from the Church and it opens the apostate to abandonment by the Holy Spirit, as was discussed above. Apostasy is addressed in the two warnings found in the Epistle to the Hebrews, that are cited in the Biblical Foundations just below. It is a very serious situation. It is beyond the ability of purely human resources to overcome.

This Article clearly states that as long as the Spirit works within us, we may turn from sin, repent, and by the grace of God be forgiven, restored to faith and to the Church. While apostasy is a very dangerous form of sin, it need not be a final condition in every case. Judas and Peter both denied Christ. Restoration was available for both. Peter trusted the mercy of God in Christ, and Judas did not. One was restored, the other committed suicide. The call to the apostate is to repent, believe, and return. Delay is dangerous.

This Article condemns those who would refuse to give forgiveness and restoration to those who, having abandoned the Lord, the Faith, and the Church, have been moved by the Spirit to repent and return. Since God's mercy is great and Christ has died for the sins of the world, genuine repentance is to be respected always and forgiveness extended.

Biblical Foundations

Thus it is written, that the Christ should suffer and on the third day rise from the dead, and that repentance and forgiveness of sins should be proclaimed in his name to all nations, beginning from Jerusalem. Luke 24:46-47

Whoever believes in the Son has eternal life; whoever does not obey the Son shall not see life, but the wrath of God remains on him. John 3:36

And Peter said to them, "Repent and be baptized every one of you in the name of Jesus Christ for the forgiveness of your sins, and you will receive the gift of the Holy Spirit." Acts 2:38

Repent therefore, and turn again, that your sins may be blotted out. Acts 3:19

To him all the prophets bear witness that everyone who believes in him receives forgiveness of sins through his name. Acts 10:43

Let it be known to you therefore, brothers, that through this man forgiveness of sins is proclaimed to you, and by him everyone who believes is freed from everything from which you could not be freed by the law of Moses. Acts 13:38-39

For godly grief produces a repentance that leads to salvation without regret, whereas worldly grief produces death. 2 Corinthians 7:10

For it is impossible to restore again to repentance those who have once been enlightened, who have tasted the heavenly gift, and have shared in the Holy Spirit, and have tasted the goodness of the word of God and the powers of the age to come, if they then fall away, since they are crucifying once again the Son of God to their own harm and holding him up to contempt. Hebrews 6:4-6

For if we go on sinning deliberately after receiving the knowledge of the truth, there no longer remains a sacrifice for sins, but a fearful expectation of judgment, and a fury of fire that will consume the adversaries. Anyone who has set aside the law of Moses dies without mercy on the evidence of two or three witnesses. How much worse punishment, do you think, will be deserved by the one who has spurned the Son of God, and has profaned the blood of the covenant by which he was sanctified, and has outraged the Spirit of grace? Hebrews 10:26-29

If we confess our sins, he is faithful and just to forgive us our sins and to cleanse us from all unrighteousness. 1 John 1:9

False Teachings Denied/Objections Answered

1. One common error concerning the giving of forgiveness denies the responsibility of the Church to evaluate the sincerity of repentance and to exercise ecclesiastical discipline. This view regards forgiveness as automatic and immediate whenever a person verbally declares that he or she has repented and asks the Church for forgiveness and restoration, irrespective of how they have behaved and are presently living.

That is a superficial understanding of repentance and faith. The clear teaching of this Article, and of the Scripture that we are to forgive all who repent and believe, is not to be understood to mean that the mere saying of words is sufficient, or that there is no place for official discipline in the wlife of the Church.

Repentance, particularly for open and public sins, must be seen to be genuine and often that can only be done by a period of discipline assigned by the Church (see the discussion in Article 33 for a fuller treatment). In the personal relationship between individual Church members, repentance also needs to be seen to be genuine for full fellowship to be restored. In some cases, that may take some time.

On the other hand, we are reminded that we are to forgive as we have been forgiven by the Lord, not just seven times but seventy times seven times, that is, without limit. A concern that repentance be real or genuine is not an excuse for an unforgiving spirit on the part of the one sinned against.

God looks upon the heart in a way we cannot; He does not need any external proof and can extend His forgiveness as soon as repentance and faith are genuine. For us human beings, trust may take some time to develop.

It is clear from this Article that anyone who is unwilling to forgive the truly repentant believer is greatly in need of repentance and forgiveness himself or herself.

Implication and Conclusion

The inevitability of sin in the life of Christians is admitted. Repentance and forgiveness are daily realities to us as Christians. Therefore, the importance of repentance and forgiveness is underlined.

There is a reference to "the unforgivable sin," which is blasphemy against the Holy Spirit. We cannot turn from the Lord, blaspheme His Name, and particularly call the good work of His Holy Spirit done in the name of Christ to be evil, with impunity. We are not to tempt the Lord to withdraw His Spirit from us.

The central emphasis of this Article is that we are called and enabled to be a forgiving people, for we have all been forgiven much, yea, everything. Being a forgiving people is so important, and the temptation to fall prey to a legalistic, unforgiving spirit is so prevalent, that we all need to take to heart the emphasis of Article 16, both as members of the body of Christ and as leaders in congregations charged with the exercise of ecclesiastical discipline.

ARTICLE 17

Of Predestination and Election

Predestination to Life is the everlasting purpose of God, whereby (before the foundations of the world were laid) he hath constantly decreed by his counsel secret to us, to deliver from curse and damnation those whom he hath chosen in Christ out of mankind, and to bring them by Christ to everlasting salvation, as vessels made to honour. Wherefore, they which be endued with so excellent a benefit of God be called according to God's purpose by his Spirit working in due season: they through Grace obey the calling: they be justified freely: they be made sons of God by adoption: they be made like the image of his only-begotten Son Jesus Christ: they walk religiously in good works, and at length, by God's mercy, they attain to everlasting felicity.

As the godly consideration of Predestination, and our Election in Christ, is full of sweet, pleasant, and unspeakable comfort to godly persons, and such as feel in themselves the working of the Spirit of Christ, mortifying the works of the flesh, and their earthly members, and drawing up their mind to high and heavenly things, as well because it doth greatly establish and confirm their faith of eternal Salvation to be enjoyed through Christ, as because it doth fervently kindle their love towards God: So, for curious and carnal persons, lacking the Spirit of Christ, to have continually before their eyes the sentence of God's Predestination, is a most dangerous downfall, whereby the Devil doth thrust them either into desperation, or into wretchlessness of most unclean living, no less perilous than desperation.

Furthermore, we must receive God's promises in such wise, as they be generally set forth to us in holy Scripture: and, in our doings, that Will of God is to be followed, which we have expressly declared unto us in the Word of God.

Introduction
The very term "predestination" seems to irritate many and confuse others. What is really involved in this doctrine? Is it referring to the same reality as "election" and, if so, what is involved in "election"? How is this doctrine related to salvation in Christ? Is it Good News or a "horrible decree" as one theologian called it? How does it differ from the many false assumptions about it?

This Article presents a carefully stated summary of the content and purpose of the biblical doctrine of predestination and election. Some theologians have tended to draw unwarranted inferences from this doctrine. In our comments we will endeavor to remain within the bounds of biblical teaching and not draw inferences or offer conjectures which usually lead to a contradiction with other major biblical themes. Nor do we assume that we will be able to remove all of the difficulties that surround this doctrine of God's electing grace.

The Teaching of Article 17
Here are the teaching points for this Article:
1. Predestination to Life is defined.

2. The blessed benefits of Predestination to Life are stated.

3. The consequences of meditation upon Predestination to Life are explored.

4. An interpretational (hermeneutical) exhortation to receive and teach God's promises as found in Scripture is set forth.

1. Predestination to Life is defined.
Explanation

Article 17 describes predestination in four specific ways: 1) as predestination to life, 2) as the everlasting purpose of God, 3) as a decision or decree He made within Himself, before the foundations of the world were laid, necessarily secret from us, and 4) as persons chosen in Christ from out of mankind in order to deliver them from the curse and damnation and to bring them by Christ to everlasting salvation, as vessels made to honor Him.

First, predestination involves the destiny of believers in Christ. "Predestination to Life" concerns God's sovereign plan, by which He determines the glorious, final destiny of those whom He will save in Christ. It is a positive doctrine of life and brings positive benefits which give confidence and joy to the believer. It also humbles us, for it is all by grace and is not due to our achievement.

The second characteristic of predestination to life is that this determination is eternal and everlasting. God has always had this purpose for the people He has chosen out of fallen mankind. And, as everlasting, it has no end. It is not a secondary backup plan.

Third, the "pre" in predestination refers to God's decision as prior to Creation. Before God began the works which He does outside of His inner life, the first being Creation. It was also before any decision that we, as His fallen creatures, might make. It leads to faith; it is not based on our faith.

Even though this is a decision made by God in eternity, it is important to note that this election or choice by God concerns human beings after the Fall and in the bondage of sin, as the Article so clearly states.

Fourth, this predestination to life is redemptive. God decided to choose or elect the persons that He would save in Christ Jesus from out of the whole of fallen humanity. He chose them in Christ in order to deliver them from damnation and to lead them to salvation or eternal life, as vessels made for honor. So the Scriptures teach, so this Article states, and so Anglicans confess.

Two controversial matters arise from this definition with its four characteristics.

First, universalism, which is the doctrine that in the end all will be saved, is clearly denied by the Article, for it says that God chose out of mankind those whom He will save. It does not say that God chooses to save all mankind. All sinners are loved, but only some are chosen for salvation, not all. This choosing of some and not of all is underlined when the Article speaks of the two responses to the doctrine, the response of the godly in their happy meditation on the biblical teaching of predestination to life and the response of the carnal and curious who are driven to despair by the same.

In the several texts that appear in the various Biblical Foundation sections to follow, it is clear that the "elect," are referred to in Scripture as a distinct group chosen out of mankind. Moreover, the elect are chosen in Christ, which means that the choosing of the individual by God is in the context of the chosen people of God which is Israel as renewed and gathered in Christ, the Church. As members of the Church, the elect share in a relationship with God involving worship, mutual fellowship with one another in Christ, and the Spirit empowered mission to seek, serve and save the lost. This too sets the elect apart as distinct among mankind.

The second controversial matter is that the Article does not tell us the basis upon which God makes this choice. It clearly says it is "secret to us." It is important to take note that the Article does not say that there is no basis for God's choice, as if God were arbitrary, which He is not. However, the Article leaves the basis of His choice secret to us. "The secret things belong unto the Lord." Alas, some have not been content to let the secret things remain so and several suggestions as to the basis of His choice have been offered in the history of the Church. These have led to controversy and have given rise to false understandings of what the Scriptures actually teach about Predestination or Election. We will deal with those unfortunate conjectures in the section on false teaching and objections.

Biblical Foundations

And if those days had not been cut short, no human being would be saved. But for the sake of the elect those days will be cut short. Matthew 24:22

For false christs and false prophets will arise and perform great signs and wonders, so as to lead astray, if possible, even the elect. Matthew 24:24

And he will send out his angels with a loud trumpet call, and they will gather his elect from the four winds, from one end of heaven to the other. Matthew 24:31

All that the Father gives me will come to me, and whoever comes to me I will never cast out. John 6:37

And when the Gentiles heard this, they began rejoicing and glorifying the word of the Lord, and as many as were appointed to eternal life believed. Acts 13:48

For those whom he foreknew he also predestined to be conformed to the image of his Son, in order that he might be the firstborn among many brothers. And those whom he predestined he also called, and those whom he called he also justified, and those whom he justified he also glorified. Romans 8:29-30

What if God, desiring to show his wrath and to make known his power, has endured with much patience vessels of wrath prepared for destruction, in order to make known the riches of his glory for vessels of mercy, which he has prepared beforehand for glory. Romans 9:22-23

Blessed be the God and Father of our Lord Jesus Christ, who has blessed us in Christ with every spiritual blessing in the heavenly places, even as he chose us in him before the foundation of the world, that we should be holy and blameless before him. In love he predestined us for adoption through Jesus Christ, according to the purpose of his will, to the praise of his glorious grace, with which he has blessed us in the Beloved. Ephesians 1:3-6

In him we have obtained an inheritance, having been predestined according to the purpose of him who works all things according to the counsel of his will. Ephesians 1:11

For God has not destined us for wrath, but to obtain salvation through our Lord Jesus Christ. 1 Thessalonians 5:9

False Teachings Denied/Objections Answered

1. One of the false teachings concerning this doctrine is one understanding of a range of views referred to as Arminianism, named after the Dutch theologian Arminius of the late 16th century. It is increasingly clear that Arminius did not teach Arminianism as it was understood at the Council of Dort and as it has been understood by a number in the Wesleyan, Holiness tradition. There is scholarly debate on that subject. It is even dubious that John Wesley held such a view, since he and George Whitefield, a strong Calvinist, came to agreement. Be that as it may, one understanding of election claims to know the basis God uses for His election. Accordingly, since God is omniscient, He knows from all eternity how each of us will respond to the Gospel, and so God elects or chooses those who, by their own power, will repent and believe the Gospel. This interpretation, therefore, teaches that the basis for God's choice of those to be saved is His foreknowledge of their faith in response to the Gospel. The problem with this teaching, as Article 10 makes clear, is that fallen persons of themselves cannot and will not turn from sin or repent and believe the Gospel. They are dead in their

trespasses and sins and hostile to God. If we understand God's foreknowledge as a mere foreseeing what we would do, and not as His redeeming love whereby He determines to send His Holy Spirit to give the elect the ability and will to turn to Christ in faith, then all God could foresee looking down the corridors of history, is that the entire fallen human race would reject the Gospel. Any doctrine of election that depends on sinful humanity's ability to respond to God by our unaided will in our fallen condition fails in its doctrine of sin, and also, in its understanding of the saving effectiveness of God's grace.

2. Another error related to the biblical teaching on predestination speaks of "Predestination to Hell." There is no teaching of predestination to hell in Article 17 or in Scripture. Hell is a destiny mankind has chosen for itself in the Fall. And we, as children of Adam, reiterate the Fall by our own sin. Anglicans have generally held that a doctrine of predestination unto Hell, or double predestination, is a false teaching. To teach that God created persons in order to condemn them, so as to have occasion to reveal His justice, is foreign to Scripture, dishonors God, and is a false doctrine. Predestination to life envisions mankind after the Fall, in a fallen state, and is therefore an election unto eternal life of those already lost and spiritually dead. It is good news for sinners, a positive doctrine and not a horrible decree, as Calvin referred to the idea of predestination to hell.

3. Another objection often raised against the biblical teaching of election unto life is that it teaches that God is arbitrary, teaching that He chooses for no reason but His good pleasure. "His good pleasure" is language drawn from Ephesians that some use to speak of the basis of God's election. However, "His good pleasure" does not mean that there is no reason for God's choosing as He does. The phrase merely says that the basis of God's choice does not lie in us, that is, in our ability to choose Him or to commend ourselves to Him on the basis of our good works.

The basis is His; it lies entirely in His wisdom and holy love. He has not revealed to us what that basis is, so it remains secret to us, as the Article states. We are creatures, made in His image to know Him, but not to fully comprehend Him. We will never be able to comprehend Him fully. However, since in Christ we know Who God is, we are called and able to trust Him to be the very fountain of goodness and wisdom in this as in all other things as well.

Implications

The fundamental implication of predestination or election to life, as set forth in this first teaching point of the Article, is the fact that in the gift of salvation God is sovereign and we are utterly dependent upon Him. This both assures us and it humbles us. It assures us, for His sovereign decision is our blessed necessity; it is what it is prior to our decision or approval. And it gives us our assurance of salvation and yields us our freedom to live and walk in His ways.

At the same time, it humbles us and removes from us any basis for pride, for we are not allowed to find in ourselves and our choice the partial basis for our salvation. It is all of God and all His doing, even though He does not bypass our response but rather enables our response of faith in Christ Jesus and of repentance.

In also humbles us because we are called to trust Him beyond our understanding and to be willing to "let the secret things belong to the Lord" and remain so. Our fallen, inordinate pride hates this. It is particularly offensive to have to accept the fact that there are limits to our human understanding. Whole philosophies have been built on the omni-competence of human reason. In that they err.

There is another aspect of the humbling of our understanding in this biblical teaching. There is the seeming contradiction between the wideness of God's love for all, displayed in the atoning death of Christ for all, on the one hand, and, on the other hand, the particularity of the Spirit's saving application of election in Christ in some sinners and not in all. It seems to suggest that God is of two minds. However, since God is not double-minded the apparent contradiction must be seen to be just that, an apparent and not a real contradiction. This too, humbles us, for we cannot comprehend their harmony in the mind and will of God.

2. The blessed benefits of Predestination to Life are stated.
Explanation

The benefits of predestination to life, as listed in this Article, are 1) effectual calling, 2) justification, 3) adoption, 4) sanctification, and 5) glorification or eternal blessedness. Having determined in His decree to bestow these benefits, God will surely accomplish them in the elect. The language of the Article concerning these benefits is so excellent that it is worth having them immediately before us:

> *Wherefore, they which be endued with so excellent a benefit of God be called according to God's purpose by his Spirit working in due season: they through Grace obey the calling: they be justified freely: they be made sons of God by adoption: they be made like the image of his only-begotten Son Jesus Christ: they walk religiously in good works, and at length, by God's mercy, they attain to everlasting felicity.*

Effectual calling is to be distinguished from general calling. General calling refers to God's invitation or even command given to all who hear the Gospel to repent and believe. Effectual calling refers to the Holy Spirit's application of the general call to the heart of the elect, granting regeneration and leading to conversion, that is, to repentance and belief in Christ.

Justification, on the basis of the merits of Christ, is granted to those who repent and believe.

Adoption into the family of Christ as sons and daughters of God is granted to all who believe in Christ as Savior and Lord.

Sanctification is described here in terms of conformity to Christ, of our being made more and more like Him by the work of the Holy Spirit within us and our intentional commitment to follow the Lord. In the process of this transformation or sanctification, we are carried along by and walk in the Spirit and in the good works which God has prepared for us to walk in, albeit imperfectly.

At the end of all things, the great and final conclusion of all of these benefits to the elect is everlasting blessedness, sharing in glory in the New Heaven and New Earth with all of the saints. These benefits will surely come to pass for they are rooted in the sovereign election and grace of God.

Biblical Foundations

Since the doctrine of predestination or election is confusing and even disturbing to many, we have included more biblical references than is usual in this commentary. Please read them carefully.

And he said to them, "Go into all the world and proclaim the gospel to the whole creation. Whoever believes and is baptized will be saved, but whoever does not believe will be condemned. Mark 16:15-16

For many are called, but few are chosen. Matthew 22:14

One who heard us was a woman named Lydia, from the city of Thyatira, a seller of purple goods, who was a worshiper of God. The Lord opened her heart to pay attention to what was said by Paul. And after she was baptized, and her household as well, she urged us, saying, "If you have judged me to be faithful to the Lord, come to my house and stay." And she prevailed upon us. Acts 16:14-15

For by grace you have been saved through faith. And this is not your own doing; it is the gift of God. Ephesians 2:8

Since you have been born again, not of perishable seed but of imperishable, through the living and abiding word of God. 1 Peter 1:23

And to the one who does not work but trusts him who justifies the ungodly, his faith is counted as righteousness. Romans 4:5

But to all who did receive him, who believed in his name, he gave the right to become children of God. John 1:12

Now the Lord is the Spirit, and where the Spirit of the Lord is, there is freedom. And we all, with unveiled face, beholding the glory of the Lord, are being transformed into the same image from one degree of glory to another. For this comes from the Lord who is the Spirit. 2 Corinthians 3:17-18

I give them eternal life, and they will never perish, and no one will snatch them out of my hand. My Father, who has given them to me, is greater than all, and no one is able to snatch them out of the Father's hand. John 10:28-29

The Lord will rescue me from every evil deed and bring me safely into his heavenly kingdom. To him be the glory forever and ever. Amen. 2 Timothy 4:18

Therefore, brothers, be all the more diligent to make your calling and election sure, for if you practice these qualities you will never fall. 2 Peter 1:10

And he told them many things in parables, saying: "A sower went out to sow. And as he sowed, some seeds fell along the path, and the birds came and devoured them. Other seeds fell on rocky ground, where they did not have much soil, and immediately they sprang up, since they had no depth of soil, but when the sun rose they were scorched. And since they had no root, they withered away. Other seeds fell among thorns, and the thorns grew up and choked them. Other seeds fell on good soil and produced grain, some a hundredfold, some sixty, some thirty. He who has ears, let him hear." Matthew 13:3-9

For it is impossible to restore again to repentance those who have once been enlightened, who have tasted the heavenly gift, and have shared in the Holy Spirit, and have tasted the goodness of the word of God and the powers of the age to come, if they then fall away, since they are crucifying once again the Son of God to their own harm and holding him up to contempt. Hebrews 6:4-6

For if we go on sinning deliberately after receiving the knowledge of the truth, there no longer remains a sacrifice for sins, but a fearful expectation of judgment, and a fury of fire that will consume the adversaries. Anyone who has set aside the law of Moses dies without mercy on the evidence of two or three witnesses. How much worse punishment, do you think, will be deserved by the one who has spurned the Son of God, and has profaned the blood of the covenant by which he was sanctified, and has outraged the Spirit of grace? Hebrews 10:26-29

They went out from us, but they were not of us; for if they had been of us, they would have continued with us. But they went out, that it might become plain that they all are not of us. 1 John 2:19

False Teachings Denied/Objections Answered

1. Romans 8:29-30 states, *For those whom he foreknew he also predestined to be conformed to the image of his Son, in order that he might be the firstborn among many brothers. And those whom he predestined he also called, and those whom he called he also justified, and those whom he justified he also glorified.* If we take these words seriously, then these benefits will surely be accomplished by the Lord in the elect. Therefore, any doctrine that denies that certainty is thereby false. To be one of the elect of God is to receive the fullness of salvation in Christ. This includes God's preservation of the saints through the Spirit-enabled perseverance by the saints.

2. This leads us into the controversial doctrine of the "Perseverance of the Saints," for the texts that assert the character and benefits of election clearly teach the fullness of salvation for the elect. Some teach that the elect may fall away and be lost forever. That is clearly denied in Scripture.

Perhaps a distinction between kinds of faith may help us in this matter. Superficial believers are not of the elect. In the parable of the soils Jesus does warn of a surface faith that initially responds positively to the good seed of the Gospel only to prove superficial and temporary. Jesus mentions seed sown on the path and eaten by the birds, seed that fell on rocky soil that could not put down deep roots and withered, seed that fell among the thorns that were choked out as contrasted with seed sown in fertile soil that produced abundantly. In three out of four cases the faith was not saving faith. What looked like saving faith was revealed not to be as time went on. There are texts in Hebrews that speak of falling away and not being able to be restored to faith. Here apostasy, the denial of a previously held faith, is in view. The author is warning against committing apostasy, lest it prove to be a persistent state. John in his First Epistle writes of such apostates: "They went out from us because they were not of us." That is, they were never really of the elect; their "faith" had never been saving faith. They did not have the kind of faith that Jesus compared to the "good soil." The elect will never finally fall away. They may be backsliders for a time, but in the end, they will return and persevere since God has chosen them and will preserve them in salvation. The confidence of the elect is not in themselves but in the God Who found them and brought them home on His shoulders, rejoicing. He will complete what He has begun in them.

3. Others have taught that it is impossible to know if you are one of the elect. That too is an error; otherwise why would we be urged in the Scripture to make our "calling and election sure"?

How, you may ask, are we to become sure of our calling and election? The answer first and foremost, is that assurance comes by faith in Christ. Faith in the Lord Jesus is the primary sign of election. Therefore our focus as elect of God is to be upon the excellence of Jesus as Savior and Lord. Faith rests upon Him, His work, His initiative, and His trustworthiness. We trust neither ourselves nor our faith; rather we trust Him, Who found us, to keep us and never let us go.

Second, there is given to all who are in Christ Jesus a painful inner struggle against indwelling sin. This is a lesser or subordinate sign of our election. In the First Epistle of John, there are a number of signs of the New Birth mentioned: faith in the Son who has come in the flesh, the love of God, sacrificial love for the brethren, sanctification or walking in the light and keeping the commandments of God, confessing sin and receiving forgiveness from God. These are all signs of election.

However, because we are all imperfectly sanctified and since, therefore, all signs observed in us are ambiguous in varying degrees, the chief assurance remains that Christ has claimed us to be His own. Our election rests in His excellence and His sacrificial love that will not let us go. Election is anchored not in us but in Him. The words of the old Gospel hymn tell it all: "Blessed assurance, Jesus is mine, Oh what a foretaste of glory divine, heir of salvation, purchase of God, born of His Spirit, washed in His blood, This is my story, this is my song, trusting my Savior all the day long."

4. Another objection frequently raised is that God's sovereign election robs us of our free will. Much depends upon what one means by "free will." If, on the one hand, by free will we mean free agency, that is that we live by choosing and making decisions and are responsible for the choices we make, then it is clear that election does not rob us of our responsible free agency. The Holy Spirit does not bypass our choosing and deciding, but rather, the Spirit sets

us free from the bondage of sin to choose to respond to the Lord in repentance and faith.

On the other hand, if by free will one is claiming that we fallen sinners are free to change our heart so as to love God with all our heart and soul and strength and our neighbor as ourselves, free to repent and believe in the Lord in our own strength, then one has not taken the depth and slavery of sin with Christian seriousness. We refer the reader to Article 10 where the matter of the bondage of the will is treated more fully. Freedom in the full sense of being free to chose and live rightly, is by grace alone. Such freedom is the fruit of election, not its cause.

Implications

The benefits of election are so encompassing and wonderful that the awareness of our election can only lead to praise, thanksgiving, and a renewed desire to serve the Lord in all things. This is developed in Teaching Point 3.

3. The consequences of meditation upon Predestination to Life are explored.
Explanation

For the Christian, there are particular benefits to meditating on the nature and benefits of election. In such meditation, our eyes are opened and our awareness of God's work in us is deepened.

This Article refers first to a godly consideration of predestination and our election in Christ. What is meant by a godly consideration of election unto life? It is meditation caught up in the power and perspective of personal faith in Christ. It is meditating on our being elect in Christ, as one of the elect. It is meditation in the perspective of the assurance of our calling and election, assured because Christ has claimed us as His own forever. As we consider the benefits of election as one of the elect, an unspeakable assurance and comfort fills us. And, we begin to discern something of the working of the Spirit of Christ within us, changing us, killing the sinful inclinations and desire, and elevating our hearts and minds to godly desires and matters. All of this work of the Spirit is imperfectly achieved in us, no doubt, but it is going on nonetheless.

As the Lord opens our eyes to His electing grace, our love for the Lord is deepened and refreshed and our faith in Him is rendered more and more certain. For this reason, the Article encourages us to know, receive, and meditate on this great theme of our being elect in Christ.

On the other hand, the Article goes on to say that it is no help at all to meditate on predestination unto life unless we can do so in Christ, that is, as one of the elect. To meditate on election from the position of one outside of faith in Christ, apart from the assurance of being one of the elect is counter-productive. To believe the doctrine to be true and at the same time not to believe oneself to be elect, could only lead to despair or resentment or rejection of the doctrine. This could lead either to severe depression or to wild, profligate living, believing that one was lost no matter how one lived.

Of course, there is the question as to how anyone could know himself or herself not to be of the elect, since all persons, as long as they are alive, no matter how sinful, are invited to come to Christ through the Gospel.

If a person were convinced that the doctrine of election was untrue, then it would be prudent to leave the doctrine alone. Why? To meditate upon the doctrine would be unfruitful, for it would be examining something of no personal significance. That is why the unbelieving perspective is referred to as "curious and carnal." This is not a matter for mere curiosity but for spiritual encouragement. Moreover, to hold what is taught in Scripture to be untrue is a denial of the authority and inspiration of Scripture, which only drives one farther from faith. It would be far better spiritually to consider the prior and foundational matter, the claims of Christ to be the Savior and Lord.

The Article goes on to solemnly warn that to contemplate election apart from faith in Christ, is to open oneself to the work of the Devil. Just as God works positively in the elect through a godly meditation on the doctrine of predestination to life, so the Devil works through an unbelieving reflection on the doctrine to deepen his grip on the unbelieving sinner.

The truth of the matter is that the doctrine of predestination to life is a Christian doctrine and has its proper place in the Christian's heart and mind. In Bunyan's *Pilgrim's Progress*, one is reminded of the gate that is the entrance to the road that leads to the Celestial City. From outside, approaching the gate, one sees written on the gate: "Enter here all ye who will." It is the general invitation of the Gospel, declared to all. All who will are invited. After passing through the gate and looking back at the gate from the inside, one sees written on the Gate: "Chosen from before the foundation of the world." It is only when a person is already on the road to the Celestial City that he or she is meant to consider and delight in the grace of Predestination to Life. It is not a doctrine designed for the unbeliever to consider.

Biblical Foundations

You shall therefore lay up these words of mine in your heart and in your soul, and you shall bind them as a sign on your hand, and they shall be as frontlets between your eyes. Deuteronomy 11:18

But his delight is in the law of the Lord, and on his law he meditates day and night. Psalm 1:2

We have thought on your steadfast love, O God, in the midst of your temple. Psalm 48:9

My eyes are awake before the watches of the night, that I may meditate on your promise. Psalm 119:148

But when you pray, go into your room and shut the door and pray to your Father who is in secret. And your Father who sees in secret will reward you. Matthew 6:6

Let us then with confidence draw near to the throne of grace, that we may receive mercy and find grace to help in time of need. Hebrews 4:16

False Teachings Denied/Objections Answered

Someone might object that it is good for the unbeliever to meditate on predestination to life in order to be convicted of his or her sin and desperate condition and be led to the Gospel. That would be true and desirable, only if along with the doctrine of predestination to life, the Gospel were clearly set forth and taken seriously.

In fact, the importance of the general call of the Gospel to everyone is the chief concern of the fourth and last teaching point of this Article. It is God's will that the promises of the Gospel are to be offered to all who will repent and believe. This is not to be obscured or in any sense weakened or denied by the doctrine of predestination to life.

Implications

Make your calling and election sure. As believers in Christ, we are to meditate upon the benefits and the wonder of our election in Christ!

4. An interpretational (hermeneutical) exhortation to receive and teach God's promises as found in Scripture is set forth.

Explanation

We are taught in Scripture that the Gospel is to be preached to all nations, to all persons. Just as all have sinned and continually fall short of the glory of God, all are to hear the invitation of the Gospel and to be invited to repent and believe and to be reconciled to God in Christ. On the one hand, no one is beyond the reach of God's saving grace or the sufficiency of Christ's atoning work on the Cross. All who come will be received and those who come will never be cast away. Nothing in the doctrine of predestination to life is to be permitted to discourage, obscure, weaken, or deny this general preaching and promise of the Gospel!

Also, the doctrine of predestination to life is not to be used to deny the Christian's call to holy living. When we read of warnings in the Scriptures that those who give themselves over to sinful things will not inherit the Kingdom of God, and when we are exhorted to live in conformity with the will of God revealed in Scripture, we are not to say: "Well, as the elect, I can't be lost, so I can do what I want and live as I want." That very thought is a denial of election, for election is unto life not to death, to holiness and not to lasciviousness. And, nothing in the doctrine of predestination unto life is intended to obscure, weaken, or deny the exhortations and the warnings of the Scripture.

The Scriptures are to be taken at their face value. This is a general rule of interpretation for all of Scripture, but it particularly applies where there are intellectual tensions which we cannot reconcile, such as that between the wideness of God's mercy, shown in the general invitation to come to Christ, and the particularity of election. In such cases, we do well to follow the maxim of Charles Simeon who said, "I will allow each verse of Scripture to carry its natural meaning and weight." If we cannot entirely reconcile in our minds the universality of God's love, work, and offer in Christ with the particularity of the election, then let it be so. Both are true and both are to be taught.

One thing is certain: we have no right to make up some teaching that will reconcile the two by altering the clear meaning of either or both. Truths hard to reconcile are often encountered in human thought. Created reality in all sorts of areas is found to be mysterious and paradoxical to our minds. Consider the fact that we cannot understand how our minds and our bodies inter-face. We actually need two entirely different types of language to speak of ourselves. We describe color in terms of a reading on a dial or in terms of the beauty that we see in our mind's eye. Which is it? We speak of our brain, something objective in time and space, which can be pictured, weighed and measured. We also speak of our mind as our thinking and thoughts which cannot be seen, weighed or measured. The inter-relation of the two is beyond us. If, at times, we are perplexed when we speak of ourselves, how much more will that be the case when we are considering the mystery of God and His work?

Conclusion

This Article concerning predestination to life, and the truth about God and ourselves that it summarizes, is a wonderful statement of God's sovereign grace in our salvation. It is a joyful and positive doctrine. Therefore, let nothing deter us from rejoicing in God's Word concerning our election to eternal life in Christ Jesus. We are invited and called to meditate upon it day and night and grow in gratitude, wonder, and praise, living it out daily, "making our calling and election sure."

ARTICLE 18

Of Obtaining Eternal Salvation Only by the Name of Christ

They also are to be had accursed that presume to say, That every man shall be saved by the Law or Sect which he professeth, so that he be diligent to frame his life according to that Law, and the light of Nature. For Holy Scripture doth set out unto us only the Name of Jesus Christ, whereby men must be saved.

Introduction

Are Christians narrow-minded? Why is salvation to be found in Christ alone? Didn't the historian Arnold Toynbee say that Christian exclusiveness was the one thing in Christianity that needed to go? Where did this exclusiveness in Christianity come from?

Also, there is an historical limitation or narrowness to the Gospel. The Good News of salvation is rooted in and based upon the person and work of Jesus Christ, Who was born, lived, died, and rose again in the early part of the first century A.D. His historical particularity raises a number of questions. How can this very particular message of the Gospel be God's universal means of salvation addressed to all humanity? What of those people who lived before Jesus came? What of those persons who never hear the Gospel at all? What of people who sincerely follow other religions or non-religious moral paths? This 18th Article is clear and does not equivocate. It is only through faith in Jesus Christ that Salvation is to be found.

The Teaching of Article 18
Here are the teaching points for this Article:

1. No one is saved by sincerely following a non-Christian religion or non-Christian religious morality or philosophy.

2. Scripture teaches that only in the Name of Jesus is salvation to be found.

3. Those who teach otherwise are to be excommunicated.

1. No one is saved by sincerely following a non-Christian religion or non-Christian religious morality or philosophy.
Explanation

There are many religions and many philosophies that a person might sincerely embrace and endeavor to live by. Some religions would allow a believer to embrace one or more at the same time. However, according to this Article and Scripture, no one can be put right with the true and living God by such flawed religions and/or philosophies or by the sincerity of their erroneous belief and practice.

Why is this true? There are three primary reasons. First, it is true because no one can be set right with God based upon his or her own efforts. As Articles 9 and 10 make clear, sin has too deep a grasp on our human nature and behavior to permit any form of self-salvation. We are simply beyond self-help.

Second, it is true because the world's religions and philosophies, while they may contain some elements of truth, are themselves full of error and distorted by sin. The Apostle Paul states that the world's religions arise from worshiping the creature rather than the Creator. They give expression to ungodliness and are largely designed to compel "God" or the "gods" to provide for our needs and to reward us for our good works and deeds. In short the world's religions all seek to domesticate "God" and make Him serve us.

Philosophy shares the same condition. Philosophical reflection rarely, if ever, can discern or admit the depth of human corruption, particularly with regard to human reason itself, or to offer a solution to the same. Further, human reason is unable to soar to the heights to speak of the transcendent, holy God who reveals Himself in Christ. God must condescend to us, for apart from His revelation we cannot rise to Him, much less know His saving plan. "His ways are too high for us." To exalt human reason beyond its human limits is itself sinful hubris and a denial of the need for saving revelation. To rescue us from sin and error is the reason why God became incarnate in the first place. So, neither religions nor philosophies can save us.

Third, it is true because to be sincerely wrong is still to be wrong. Only relativism, the denial of objective truth regarding God, could ever suggest that sincerity is a sufficient basis for a right relationship with God or for life in any of its aspects for that matter. One can, for example, sincerely drink poison thinking it to be a healing medicine and die. One can write checks, thinking there is money in the bank, and still be overdrawn. As the Prophets frequently pointed out, false gods really do not do anything, being the creation of human minds and hands. No matter how sincerely they are worshiped, idols, philosophies, and the world's religions are not salvific and no one is saved by them.

Biblical Foundations

The reader is directed to the texts found in Articles 9 and 10 as well as these texts.

Jesus answered him, "Truly, truly, I say to you, unless one is born again he cannot see the kingdom of God." John 3:3

For the wrath of God is revealed from heaven against all ungodliness and unrighteousness of men, who by their unrighteousness suppress the truth. For what can be known about God is plain to them, because God has shown it to them. For his invisible attributes, namely, his eternal power and divine nature, have been clearly perceived, ever since the creation of the world, in the things that have been made. So they are without excuse. For although they knew God, they did not honor him as God or give thanks to him, but they became futile in their thinking, and their foolish hearts were darkened. Claiming to be wise, they became fools, and exchanged the glory of the immortal God for images resembling mortal man and birds and animals and reptiles. Therefore God gave them up in the lusts of their hearts to impurity, to the dishonoring of their bodies among themselves, because they exchanged the truth about God for a lie and worshiped and served the creature rather than the Creator, who is blessed forever! Amen... Though they know God's decree that those who practice such things deserve to die, they not only do them but give approval to those who practice them. Romans 1:18-32

Where is the one who is wise? Where is the scribe? Where is the debater of this age? Has not God made foolish the wisdom of the world? 1 Corinthians 1:20

The natural person does not accept the things of the Spirit of God, for they are folly to him, and he is not able to understand them because they are spiritually discerned. The spiritual person judges all things, but is himself to be judged by no one. "For who has understood the mind of the Lord so as to instruct him?" But we have the mind of Christ. 1 Corinthians 2:14-16

And we know that the Son of God has come and has given us understanding, so that we may know him who is true; and we are in him who is true, in his Son Jesus Christ. He is the true God and eternal life. Little children, keep yourselves from idols. 1 John 5:20-21

False Teachings Denied/Objections Answered

1. One of the erroneous doctrines and consequent religion by which people have sought to be saved is deism. Deism of the 17th and 18th centuries taught a religion of moral duty. Moral discernment was to be drawn from the light of nature found in conscience and the surrounding cosmos, and it was believed that such light would suffice to guide mankind into the right path. Special revelation from God was not needed, and if provided by God, it could only serve to agree with and emphasize what we humans already know. God, for His part, created the world and then He stood apart from it, until the final judgment when He will render the last verdict determining our final destiny, based on our previous moral behavior. If an individual has kept these moral laws faithfully, he or she will be rewarded in the end by God with blessing, and if not, then he or she will be judged and condemned by God forever.

This deistic view of things errs in a number of respects: A) It fails to take the distorting fact of sin seriously. Sin distorts our understanding, our desires and actions. We can neither easily agree on what is universally right nor do it. B) It falsely exalts human moral reason. In actuality, the deists were naïve about what they thought they found naturally in the conscience, for much of the moral content of their conscience was not based on general moral awareness. It was based on the moral content that was due to the inherited moral teaching of Western Christianity. C) Underestimating the impact of sin, deism fails to treasure God's provision by the Cross of Christ. In fact, this view of religion has little to do with the truth as God has revealed it in Christ. It is contradicted by biblical revelation. Deism is a distorted form of Christianity, a form of Christianity that has lost its nerve to be different and has conformed itself to the culture around it. One scholar compared deism to the smile on the disappearing Cheshire cat in "Alice in Wonderland." Deism is the last gasp of a dying religion, once rooted in the Prophets of Israel, and in God's revelation in Jesus Christ.

2. Others have taught that all religions are essentially the same and differ only in superficial ways. Therefore, all who are conscientious followers of any religion will, in the end, reach the same final blessing. Often cited in support of this teaching that all religions in their essence are the same, is the metaphor of different roads that are far apart at the bottom of the mountain, but which all converge at the top of the mountain. While religions look different in many respects in their origins, as they mature they become more and more alike until they merge into one in the end. This is possible because they have been essentially the same all along.

This view of the essential unity and sameness of all religions makes several false assumptions. They are: A) that the religions are all heading to the top, B) that all of them will reach the top, and C) that their teachings and morals are more or less the same, or are at least compatible.

This seemingly egalitarian evaluation of all religions is A) contradicted by the profound contradictions that are actually found between the different world's religions. They cannot all, at the same time, be true. B) In addition, they cannot deal with the reality of sin and of God's judgment upon sin and, hence, none reach the top. C) What a contrast is found in the Gospel in which the top, God, comes down to us in grace and Incarnation. That is quite a different story.

The most recent and consistent religious form of this view that all religions are essentially the same, is found in the Baha'i religion, an offshoot of Shi'ite Islam. Baha'i views the founders of all the major religions as prophetic manifestations of God. It holds that the founders and their subsequent religions differ only in non-essentials and it seeks to incorporate all that is good in all of the various forms of religion, so that only the essence of religion is embraced. This, of course, assumes that someone (one of the key leaders of Baha'i, no doubt) is in a position to determine what is good in each religion, and knows what the essence of religion is. Secondly, it assumes that we could live rightly were we able to identify such a pure religion. Given the limits of human nature and the corruption of sin, neither of these assumptions is true.

When Christians declare the world's religions and/or philosophies to be flawed, we do not mean to say that there are no elements of truth in them. The truth in Christ incorporates and fulfills any elements of truth embraced in them. Truth, wherever it is found, is God's truth. We do mean to assert, however, that the world's religions are as a whole and in many parts misleading and in error.

Implications
Salvation is not to be found in the world's philosophies or religions. The way of salvation is to be found in Christ or better finds us through and in Him, or not at all. The obvious implication is to turn to Christ, Who has already turned to us and invites us to respond.

2. Scripture teaches that only in the Name of Jesus is salvation to be found.
Explanation
There are two claims made here: first, that salvation is to be found in the Name of Jesus and, second, that salvation is to be found only in the Name of Jesus. A word about each point is in order.

Salvation is to be found in the Name of Jesus. What is meant by the "Name of Jesus"? "Name" in biblical use involves three aspects: 1) historic revelation, 2) divine-human fellowship, and 3) mission or godly representation.

1. We make a name as we reveal ourselves by word and deed. So it is with God in the biblical history of salvation. He has revealed Himself by words and deeds over time, in the midst of His people, reaching a climax in Jesus Christ, Who is God Incarnate, crucified, risen, and

ascended, and Who poured out the Holy Spirit from the Father upon us.

2. When we give our name to another, we invite communication and communion. This is true of God as well. Scripture tells us that He made His name to dwell in the Temple, where His people could come to sacrifice and pray and hold fellowship with Him. Jesus is the Name in which we are invited to pray. It is Jesus Who promises to be with God's people until the end of the ages and Who indwells us by the Holy Spirit.

3. And when we wear a blazer with the name of our school or country upon it, we become representatives of the school or our nation. It is so with Christians, signed with the Name of Jesus Christ in baptism; we belong to Him, and are sent forth by Him in His Name to represent Him to our fellow human beings throughout the whole world. It is in Jesus' Name, in this rich biblical sense of the word, that salvation is to be found.

Since salvation is found in Jesus' Name, it is important to ask what is meant by salvation. The Articles include the full biblical content of God's saving work, for us and in us: justification, sanctification, and glorification (see Articles 11 and 12).

What does the second claim, that it is only in Jesus that salvation is to be found, actually mean? It means exactly what it says. It is only in Jesus that salvation is made available to human beings. With all of the human race having fallen into sin and being alienated from God and condemned in His sight, God sent His only begotten Son to earth, to assume human nature to save us. He entered our fallen history and did the saving work that had to be done. He comes now in the Spirit chiefly through the means of grace and His community of faith. God the Father comes to unite us to Himself in the Son by the Spirit. And thereby He bestows salvation upon those who humbly and undeservingly place their faith in Christ Jesus, those who, in repentance, follow Him as Savior and Lord. In so responding to Christ, they are united to Christ, adopted into the family of Christ, made sons and daughters of God, members of His body the Church, and are called into His world mission.

This assertion that it is only in Christ that salvation is mediated raises a number of questions and some objections. We will deal with these following the biblical foundations.

Biblical Foundations

All things have been handed over to me by my Father, and no one knows the Son except the Father, and no one knows the Father except the Son and anyone to whom the Son chooses to reveal him. Matthew 11:27

And Jesus came and said to them, "All authority in heaven and on earth has been given to me. Go therefore and make disciples of all nations, baptizing them in the name of the Father and of the Son and of the Holy Spirit, teaching them to observe all that I have commanded you. And behold, I am with you always, to the end of the age." Matthew 28:18-20

For God so loved the world, that he gave his only Son, that whoever believes in him should not perish but have eternal life. For God did not send his Son into the world to condemn the world, but in order that the world might be saved through him. Whoever believes in him is not condemned, but whoever does not believe is condemned already, because he has not believed in the name of the only Son of God. John 3:16-18

Jesus said to them, "I am the bread of life; whoever comes to me shall not hunger, and whoever believes in me shall never thirst." John 6:35

Again Jesus spoke to them, saying, "I am the light of the world. Whoever follows me will not walk in darkness, but will have the light of life." John 8:12

Jesus said to them, "Truly, truly, I say to you, before Abraham was, I am." John 8:58

My sheep hear my voice, and I know them, and they follow me. I give them eternal life, and they will never perish, and no one will snatch them out of my hand. My Father, who has given them to me, is greater than all, and no one is able to snatch them out of the Father's hand. I and the Father are one. John 10:27-30

Jesus said to her, "I am the resurrection and the life. Whoever believes in me, though he die, yet shall he live, and everyone who lives and believes in me shall never die. Do you believe this?" John 11:25-26

Jesus said to him, "I am the way, and the truth, and the life. No one comes to the Father except through me." John 14:6

And there is salvation in no one else, for there is no other name under heaven given among men by which we must be saved. Acts 4:12

False Teachings Denied/Objections Answered

1. The fundamental overarching objection that is raised to this biblical exclusivity is that to restrict the mediation of salvation to Jesus alone as the Mediator is too narrow and leaves out too many people. This objection takes several forms:

A. One misunderstanding of the particularity of God's salvation in Christ alone is to see it as a reluctance on God's part to reach out to all. That cannot be. "The Son of Man came to save sinners." He "so loved the world that he gave His only begotten Son." "He died not for our sins only but for the sins of the whole world." And we, His Church, are to bear the message to the uttermost parts of the earth, and we are to invite everyone to repent and believe the Gospel, to receive Christ. All are invited to the great feast of the Lord.

It is precisely because we are in a lost and fallen condition that He Who loves us comes in Christ to be our Savior. There is no reluctance on the Savior's part. The problem lies not with Christ but with us. The reluctance and refusal is on our part, not His. We need to put the blame where it belongs, on our sinful condition, our behavior and our rejection of the Gospel.

If everyone in the world had a deadly disease and if an antidote were discovered by a doctor and offered by him to all and if many refused to take it, preferring their home remedies or denying that they are sick, it would not be appropriate to blame the doctor. Rather than blaming God, we need to thank God that an antidote is provided and to urge all to receive it.

B. What some people seem to want is salvation by general revelation, a universal salvation available to all without historical mediation, without a Cross, and without the possibility of final refusal on the human side. That, of course, is not possible. It could only be possible if we had not fallen, and if people did not live by personal willing and choosing and could be saved purely externally.

C. If we were to hold that other paths than Christ were sufficient for salvation, we would need to ask ourselves, "Why then did God take the costly path of salvation that He did take in Christ? Why would He save believers by sending His only begotten Son to suffer great humiliation and to die for us, if any other way were possible?" Surely the very radical nature of the remedy points to the depth of our need and the necessity of the path God has taken.

This still leaves us with a number of questions of various sorts.

2. What about the believers in the Old Testament prior to the coming of Jesus as the Christ or Messiah? The answer is that the saints of the Old Covenant exercised faith in God and were viewed by God in the light of Christ Who was to come. Their faith in God's Word was implicitly, and later explicitly, trust in the Messiah Who was to come and through Whom God's saving reign would come in power. They believed in His Word and God counted it to them as righteousness.

3. What are we to think about those who have been personally hurt or made skeptical by unloving, hypocritical Christians, and for that reason do not trust the Gospel? Or what about the many who have never had and will never have a chance to hear the Gospel in this life? To questions like these we can only answer that God has not revealed to us the state of those who, for whatever reason, have not, could not, or cannot consider the claims of the Gospel. There is a difference between having no second chance after death and never having a first chance in life. God is both just and merciful. Christ's Cross is sufficient for all. Where Scripture is silent we do well to admit our ignorance. One thing is clear, however: there is salvation in no one but in Jesus Christ.

What we can say with certainty is that we are charged with sharing the Gospel with everyone. That is the high calling and mission of the Church. It is our calling, on the one hand, because salvation is only in and through Jesus Christ. It is our calling, on the other hand, because of the deep need of every person for God's deliverance and reconciliation. We will never meet a person who does not need Christ. And it is our calling, because the love of Christ constrains us, to minister the Gospel to them in their need.

Finally, we do well to remember that it is God who determines the fate and destiny of all persons, not we; we leave the fate of those who never really hear the Gospel in God's righteous, just, and merciful hands. Our part, our calling, is clear: we are to preach the Gospel to the whole world.

Implications

The Christian claim is that salvation is found in Christ alone. There are all sorts of alternatives to the Gospel. And while there are good reasons for us to become familiar with those alternatives, one does not need to wait to share the Gospel until one has examined them all, for if the Christian claim is true, then all the others are in serious error and cannot provide what all of us sinners so greatly need.

For Christians, the chief implication is that we need to be about our calling to love and preach the Gospel to the whole world. It is not without meaning that at the conclusion of each of the four Gospels we find the risen Lord commissioning us to go make disciples of all nations.

3. Those who teach otherwise are to be excommunicated.

Comment

The topic of excommunication is dealt with in Article 33. We will not treat that point here, except to say that among the grounds for excommunication is false teaching that distorts a key doctrine of the Faith. Teaching matters. Ideas have consequences. And it is a terrible, false teaching to encourage people to deny or ignore the Gospel and to believe themselves secure while they are sitting in sinking boats. All of this is done when Christians deny that salvation is found only in Jesus Christ.

False teachers are to be required to stop their false teaching and repent. Should they refuse and persist in spreading error, they are to be cut off from the community of Faith. Note the urgency with which St. Paul makes this point in the first chapter of his Letter to the Galatians (Galatians 1:8-9). In Matthew 18: 6, the Lord Himself speaks most solemnly when He says that it would be better not to have been born than to cause one of the little ones (His followers) to sin or perish.

Conclusion

With this gracious and grand theme of God's gift of salvation, found only in Jesus Christ, we are brought to the end of Section Three of the Thirty-Nine Articles. It has dealt with personal salvation in its various aspects. Our salvation, however, is also corporate or communal, so we now turn to an extensive Fourth Section of the Articles, which addresses the community of Faith, the Church, which section also includes a consideration of the ordained ministry and the sacraments.

Section Four

The Church, Ministry and Sacraments
(Articles 19-36)

Articles 19-36 are concerned with the Church, the family of God, the Body of Christ. This section deals with the corporate or communal dimension of salvation in Christ. It is the longest section of the Thirty-Nine Articles. This is due, in part, to there being many matters of controversy connected with the Church, its worship, sacraments, ministry and discipline at the time the Articles were being written. It is also the case because, when speaking of the Church, there are a larger number of topics to be covered.

The Church is of greater importance than is often appreciated. The concern for the individual's personal faith in Christ on the part of Evangelicals and other Christians, combined with the influence of contemporary Western individualism often tends to diminish our awareness of and even to obscure the Lord's gift and love of the Church. A careful study of these Articles should help restore a biblical understanding of and appreciation of the nature and importance of the Church.

Article 19 sets forth the essential marks of a visible church. Based on a careful reading of the Scriptures, Anglicans hold a definite view of what constitutes a visible church. It is important to know what it is and how it differs from the views of other Christian bodies.

Article 20 treats of the authority of the Church in relation to the authority of Holy Scripture. Article 21 does the same for the authority of General Councils. Article 22 indicates teachings and practices in which the Church has abused her authority and erred in her teaching.

Article 23 addresses the issue of the authority to minister in the Church as an ordained minister. Article 24 affirms that worship is to be intelligent worship and so should be conducted in a language that the people who are worshiping can understand.

Articles 25-31 are concerned with the Sacraments of the Church. Article 25 outlines an Anglican understanding of the chief characteristics of the two sacraments of the Gospel. Article 26 points out that the efficacy of the sacraments lies not in the worthiness of the human minister but in Christ in whose name the sacraments are administered. Article 27 sets forth the nature and blessings of Christian Baptism. Article 28 does the same for the Lord's Supper. Article 29 makes clear that personal faith is necessary for the right reception of the Holy Communion and to receive its blessings. Article 30 insists that the Lord's command to share both bread and wine in the Eucharist is to be obeyed. Article 31 makes it clear that the Lord's Supper is not a meritorious, bloodless, re-sacrifice of the Lord Jesus.

Articles 32-36 deal with various matters concerning the life, discipline and ministry of the Church. Article 32 declares that it is biblical to allow Bishops, Presbyters, and Deacons to marry, if they are so led by the Lord. Article 33 treats the solemn matter of excommunication. Article 34 allows for variety in the traditions of the visible churches, provided that the Faith is kept entire. Article 35 speaks of the value and the use of *The Homilies*. And Article 36 asserts that the Anglican ordinal, by which Bishops, Priests, and Deacons are consecrated and ordained, is faithful to Scripture and contains nothing superstitious.

Taken together, these Articles set forth a clear and distinct Anglican view of the Church, its worship, and ministry.

ARTICLE 19

Of the Church

The visible Church of Christ is a congregation of faithful men, in the which the pure word of God is preached and the sacraments be duly ministered according to Christ's ordinance in all those things that of necessity are requisite to the same. As the Church of Jerusalem, Alexandria, and Antioch have erred: so also the Church of Rome hath erred, not only in their living and manner of ceremonies, but also in matters of faith

Introduction

When we say the word "Church" what do we mean? Is every group that calls itself a Church really a Church? What do Anglicans mean by "Church"?

This 19th Article concerns the visible Church, the Church existing in time and space that can be seen. Letters can be sent to this Church and received and read by the Church.

Questions arise concerning the visible Church. How, for example, would you know whether a local congregation is a visible manifestation of the Church of Christ or a cult? What marks would need to be present? This question became all the more urgent during the time of Reformation and realignment in the 16th century. The same questions could be put to the larger expressions of the Church such as a National Church or an International Communion. What are the essential characteristics of a visible Church of Christ in any of its manifestations?

Before we turn to the teaching of this Article, in order to set the Article's comments about the visible Church in proper perspective, it is important to discuss several aspects of the Church that are not directly mentioned in this

Article, but are implied therein. We have in mind the invisibility of the Church and the Creedal marks of the Church.

When we speak of the visible Church, we imply a distinction between the visible and the invisible Church. How does invisibility apply to the Church? First, there is an invisible aspect of the visible Church due to the inherent invisibility of faith. This concerns the boundaries of the Church. The Church is a believing community. Invisibility is therefore occasioned by the fact that genuine faith is not always easy to distinguish from its counterfeits. False teachers can be part of the visible Church. Hypocrites can join the visible Church for false reasons. Persons can be members of the visible Church out of family custom but never come to personal faith. St. Paul said of the visible community of Israel, "no one is a Jew who is merely one outwardly" (Romans 2:28-29). This is true of the visible Church as well. Not all in the visible Church are genuine believers in Christ. St. Augustine made this point by saying, "There are some of the body of the Church that are not of the soul of the Church and some of the soul of the Church not yet of the body of the Church." The invisibility of true faith makes the boundaries of the believing Church impossible for us to discern.

A second characteristic of the Church's invisibility lies in the fact that genuine believers are found among all of the present visible communions and denominations of the Church. There is therefore a unity in the Spirit that is deeper than the divisions of the visible Church. The contemporary Ecumenical Movement seeks to bring that unity to light and to enable a greater visible unity among the visible Churches.

A third implication of the invisibility of the Church is that some of the statements and promises in the New Testament regarding the Church are best understood to refer to the believing or invisible Church existing in, with, and under the various visible Churches and do not pertain exclusively or even primarily to any one particular visible Church. For example, there is the promise that Christ will present His Church, His Body, as perfected, without spot or wrinkle, to the Father in the end. This is true of the Church comprised of the believing elect in all of the churches, but no visible church has the right to claim that for itself. In Heaven there will be no denominations, just the Church triumphant.

A final aspect of the invisibility of the Church is that some in Christ have died and are in the nearer presence of Christ in Heaven. This leads to a distinction between the Church triumphant and expectant in heaven, invisible to us, and the Church militant and visible here on earth.

In addition to the distinction between the invisible and visible aspects of the Church, there are four creedal marks or notes of the Church. These marks are: one, holy, catholic, and apostolic. They are affirmed by all of the historic Churches of the Reformation. Much could be said about each of these creedal marks or notes. We will simply mention the essential nature of each.

The Church is "one" in that it worships one God, has one Savior and Lord, one faith, one baptism, one Holy Spirit. Its unity lies in its being united with its one Head.

The Church is "holy" in its being set apart from all other societies or communions by its relationship with the Lord Whom it worships and serves alone. It is also holy as it walks in His ways by His Holy Spirit, manifesting the fruit of the Holy Spirit.

The Church is "catholic," or universal, in that it is the community into which everyone in the world is invited through repentant faith in Christ Jesus. All are invited, for Christ's Cross is sufficient for all. None of the world's usual divisions apply to the Church. Early in the Church's life, the term "catholic" also took on the connotation of "Creedal Faith" and "Catholic Order" in the ordained ministry. Anglicans treasure this Creedal Faith and Catholic Order and commend it to all Christian bodies. However,

Anglicans do not deny the presence of the Church where the ordained ministry of a visible church is ordered in some other pattern, as long as the Gospel is truly preached and the sacraments of the Gospel are rightly celebrated.

The Church is "apostolic" in that it is "sent" by the Risen Lord to the world. Global mission lies at the heart of the Church. It is sent to do works of mercy and, above all, to share the Gospel with and make disciples of all peoples. The Lord of the Church is on mission, therefore His Church is on mission or it is unfaithful. In addition, the Faith of the Church is in accord with the teaching of the Apostles. A body or community that does not hold to the teaching of the Apostles and is not on Apostolic mission is neither Apostolic nor the Church.

Anglicans have among themselves some differences in their understanding of the ordained ministry; however, Anglicans see the historic Episcopate, the orders of Presbyters or the Priesthood, and the Diaconate as growing out of and giving expression to the apostolic and catholic character of the Church.

Lastly, there are certain essential activities of the Church which reflect its nature. These are first, the corporate worship of the Father through the Son by the Spirit, second, fellowship with one another that involves the exercise of sacrificial care for one another in Christ, which includes teaching and discipling one another, and third, obeying the Great Commission together, being on mission to the world. These three essential activities are deeply interrelated. To lose, suppress or distort any one of them is to lose or distort all of them, sooner or later.

With these general remarks about the nature of the Church in mind, we turn to consider the specific points of this Article concerning the visible Church.

The Teaching of Article 19
Here are the teaching points for this Article:
1. The nature of the visible Church of Christ is defined.

2. The identifying marks of the visible Church are stated.

3. The visible Church of Christ can and does err.

1. The nature of the visible Church of Christ is defined
Explanation

"The visible Church of Christ is a congregation of faithful men." Four important assertions are found in the opening language about the visible Church. First, there is one visible Church. We do not read first of "<u>a</u> visible church" or "the visible church<u>es</u>" but of <u>the</u> visible Church. Second, the visible society referred to is called "The Church of Christ." Third, the visible Church is defined as a congregation. Fourth, the visible Church is a congregation of believers in Jesus Christ. Each of these references tells us something important about the nature of the visible Church.

First, there is one visible Church. This oneness does not refer to institutional unity but to a unity that is present wherever professing believers in Jesus Christ are gathered into congregations around apostolic preaching and the celebration of the sacraments of the Gospel. They are all expressions or manifestations of one thing: the one visible Church of Christ.

Second, these visible congregations are referred to as expressions of the "Church of Christ." While the word "Church" probably comes into English from the Greek word *kuriakos* meaning "of the Lord," that is not the chief meaning of the word "Church" in the New Testament. The primary meaning of the word "Church" in the New

Testament refers to Christian congregations as communities in Christ. The word translated "Church" in our translations is *ekklesia* in Greek. The connotations of the term *ekklesia* are as follows: first, in Hellenistic society, *ekklesia* referred to any public assembly; second, more specifically in the Greek Old Testament Septuagint translation, *ekklesia* referred to Israel solemnly assembled before God, and third, in the New Testament, the *"ekklesia* of Christ" connotes the believers assembled around the risen Christ, the Head of the Church, Who is its Savior and Lord.

Ekklesia, therefore, emphasizes that the relationship and worship of God the Father, in Christ, by the Spirit is essential to the nature of the Church. To be the "Church of Christ" is to be that community that is called out of fallen humanity by God through the Gospel and assembled around Jesus Christ in an intimate relationship of solemn hearing and responding in faith and obedience to God, which constitutes the heart of worship.

Third, these visible Christ-centered churches are called "congregations." The term "congregation" is particularly appropriate for it not only reflects the gathering or assembled nature of the Church; it also refers to the family life of the Church. It catches up the sacrificial love for one another and the discipling of one another that lies at the heart of being the Church. In addition, the word "congregation" is flexible enough to cover the various groupings of the Church, whether local or regional or global societies. In the New Testament, the Church is described as a local congregation, as a regional group of congregations, and sometimes as all Christians past, present, and future. In principle, it can refer to all of the congregations of the visible Church world-wide.

Lastly, these visible congregations of Christ are composed of "faithful men"; that is, of men and women and their children who believe in Christ and confess Him as Lord and Savior. A personal relationship with Christ and with one another in Christ stands at the heart of the nature of the Church. The Church visible is essentially a community that believes in Christ.

Biblical Foundations

And King Solomon and all the congregation of Israel, who had assembled before him, were with him before the ark, sacrificing so many sheep and oxen that they could not be counted or numbered. 1 Kings 8:5

Bless God in the great congregation, the Lord, O you who are of Israel's fountain! Psalm 68:26

For as in one body we have many members, and the members do not all have the same function, so we, though many, are one body in Christ, and individually members one of another. Romans 12:4-5

Paul, Silvanus, and Timothy, To the church of the Thessalonians in God the Father and the Lord Jesus Christ: Grace to you and peace. 1 Thessalonians 1:1

To the church of God that is in Corinth, to those sanctified in Christ Jesus, called to be saints together with all those who in every place call upon the name of our Lord Jesus Christ, both their Lord and ours. 1 Corinthians 1:2

For in one Spirit we were all baptized into one body—Jews or Greeks, slaves or free—and all were made to drink of one Spirit. 1 Corinthians 12:13

And they devoted themselves to the apostles' teaching and fellowship, to the breaking of bread and the prayers. Acts 2:42

And Jesus came and said to them, "All authority in heaven and on earth has been given to me. Go therefore and make disciples of all nations, baptizing them in the name of the Father and of the Son and of the Holy Spirit, teaching them to observe all that I have commanded you. And behold, I am with you always, to the end of the age." Matthew 28:18-20

False Teachings Denied/Objections Answered

1. People are often misled by the fact that we use the word "church" to refer to buildings. To call a building a "church" is, strictly speaking, an error. For 300 years, the Church was not permitted to build or own public buildings. The Church assembled in homes, in groves, in the fields and, when necessary, met in secret in the catacombs. The buildings that we refer to as "churches" are simply the buildings that the Church uses.

2. No existing denomination is the only true, visible Church. Anglicans consider it to be an error when the Roman Catholic Church, the Orthodox Churches of the East and some Protestant Churches identify themselves as the only true Church. They then claim that the references to the Church in the New Testament apply exclusively to them.

This Anglican position is held and applied in a variety of ways. First, the visible Church as this Article defines the visible Church, was and is called into being by a movement of the Spirit of God and has never been entirely contained in any single institutional entity. To document this point, let us take a New Testament example: the Church in Rome. When the Apostle Paul wrote his epistle to the Christian congregations in that city, as far as we know, no Apostle had ever visited them. In fact, no one knows who first brought the Gospel to Rome or when these congregations came into being, yet the Apostle considers them to be expressions of the visible Church and addresses them as such. From that day to the present, the Holy Spirit is using Christians, ordained and not ordained, to spread the Gospel and plant visible churches. We have never kept up with the Spirit in this matter of the expansion of the Church.

Second, it was a joy for Anglicans to hear the Roman Catholic Church announce, during Vatican II, that it has begun to see some elements of "ecclesial (Churchly) reality" in the "separated brethren," though in Rome's eyes we are still too severely deficient as congregations of baptized Christians to be called churches in any outright sense of the word. St. Paul had a less institutional vision of what constituted a visible church.

Thirdly, there are various denominations or communions of the Church that manifest the creedal notes of the Church and that exhibit the marks of the visible Church. Anglicans refer to all such as churches. Notably, Anglicans have done this officially and repeatedly in the Lambeth Conferences of the Anglican Communion. These conferences are comprised of all the active Anglican Bishops world-wide and are held every 10 years.

Fourthly, the fact that the Church finds expression in all the visible churches is a precondition of the Ecumenical Movement. The modern Ecumenical Movement assumes that all of the visible churches, where the marks of the visible Church are present, share in an inherent spiritual unity which is obscured by our divisions, by our competition, and by any exclusive claims. If such a unity were not already present, we could not hope to give fuller, visible expression to our unity in Christ by the means of consultation and cooperation and where appropriate by institutional merger. Were no unity already present, it would not be an ecumenical movement that was called for but evangelism.

Anglicans, being concerned about the unity of the visible churches, have been leaders in the ecumenical movement from its inception to the present. Some believe, due to our reformed Catholicism, that Anglicans have a special fitness and calling for ecumenical ministry.

In sum, to claim that one institutional expression of the visible Church is the only true Church is an error. Article 19 has a less institutional scope.

3. The visible churches often tend to do things on their own and fail to cooperate with other churches where it is possible and practical. That, too, is an error in practice. There is great wisdom in the Lund Principle, named after the Ecumenical Gathering in Lund, Sweden, that states that

the churches should do together all that they can in good conscience. Churches can and should support one another in the Great Commission.

Implications

While we treasure and commend our Anglican distinctives, and want to share them with all who are willing to receive them, we hold that it is essential that people come to know Christ and find their ecclesiastical home in a congregation where the marks of a visible Church are present, whether Anglican or not.

2. The identifying marks of the visible Church are stated.
Explanation

What are the identifiable, visible signs or marks of a visible church that give expression to its nature? What must one be able to see and discern to consider a particular group an expression of the visible Church? This is a crucial question because there are all sorts of religious groups that claim to be in contact with the divine and to be able to help their members be in communion with God, some of them referring to themselves as Churches. There are cults that claim to be Christian groups and expressions of the visible Church of Christ which, in fact, are not.

This need for clear identity marks is not just a modern reality. It was true early in the life of the primitive Church. Also, various heterodox and heretical groups were present when the Church of England declared itself to be independent of the oversight of the Bishop of Rome.

Therefore it became necessary for the Church of England to state clearly what were the marks that distinguish true congregations of the visible Church of Christ from pretenders or false claimants. Stating what these marks are is the main concern of this Article.

In essence, three marks are identified: 1) the faithful preaching of the pure Word of God, 2) the due celebration of the sacraments of the Gospel and 3) the proper exercise of ecclesiastical discipline(implied in this Article). Each of these visible marks of a true Church requires a brief word of explanation.

1. In the visible Church of Christ, the "pure word of God is preached." This refers to the preaching and teaching of the Gospel of Christ and the whole counsel of God, that is, of the whole of Scripture read in the light of Christ.

In Anglican practice, this preaching of the pure Word of God includes the use of the lectionaries for the Daily Office and for the Holy Communion to guide the reading of the Scripture and the preaching of Scripture in the congregation. The Articles commend *The Homilies* to be read to the congregation and to serve as godly examples of faithful preaching of the pure Word of God (see Article 35). Offices of Instruction and the Catechism of the Church are found in *The Book of Common Prayer*; they are also aids for the faithful teaching of the pure Word of God. The Thirty-Nine Articles were subscribed to by the clergy to guide the preaching and teaching of the pure Word of God. They are still subscribed to in many Provinces of the Anglican Communion today. A further means of proclaiming the pure Word of God is *The Book of Common Prayer* itself, for it is, in large measure, composed of material drawn from the Scripture. This range of material and practice when taken seriously and used well, makes it possible for Anglicans to be well instructed and able to evaluate whether what is being preached and taught in the congregations of which they are members is the Word of God or something else.

2. The sacraments of the Gospel have several Articles devoted particularly to them (see Articles 25, 27, and 28). Article 19 insists that the sacraments be administered in accordance with Christ's institution. Future Articles will discuss failings on the part of some churches in regard to their administration of the Sacraments. For a congregation or communion to depart from Christ's institution of

Baptism and the Lord's Supper challenges that congregation's claim to be a visible church of Christ. The sacramental liturgies of *The Book of Common Prayer* assist the Anglicans to celebrate the sacraments of the Gospel faithfully and thus, by practice and familiarity, to instruct the congregations so they are able to judge whether the sacraments are being administered in accordance with Christ's ordinance.

3. Anglicans see a third mark of a true visible church implicitly present in the two visible marks of a visible church mentioned in the Article. This third mark is the proper use of ecclesiastical discipline. Someone is needed to see to it that the right preaching and the right administration of the sacrament are actually occurring and, if not, to take action to set things right. This mark, which is implicit in Article 19, is explicit in the Homily for Whitsunday where all three visible marks are listed as follows:

> The true church is a universal congregation or fellowship of God's faithful and elect people, built upon the foundation of the Apostles and Prophets, Jesus Christ himself being the head corner-stone. And it hath three notes or marks, whereby it is known: Pure and sound doctrine; the sacraments ministered according to Christ's holy institution; And the right use of ecclesiastical discipline (pg 322).

It is important to note that Article 35 states that *the Homilies* are part of the official teaching of the Church of England.

This concern for proper ecclesiastical discipline is of great importance, for its neglect allows false doctrine to overtake a congregation. This can be so severe that the congregation ceases to be a visible Church. Ecclesiastical discipline is treated in Article 26 and in Article 33. We will discuss it more fully there. Given the concern for the supremacy of the Holy Scripture that permeates these

Articles, it remains surprising that ecclesiastical discipline was not explicitly listed in this Article.

Biblical Foundations

And they devoted themselves to the apostles' teaching and fellowship, to the breaking of bread and the prayers. Acts 2:42

Let the word of Christ dwell in you richly, teaching and admonishing one another in all wisdom, singing psalms and hymns and spiritual songs, with thankfulness in your hearts to God. And whatever you do, in word or deed, do everything in the name of the Lord Jesus, giving thanks to God the Father through him. Colossians 3:16-17

For I received from the Lord what I also delivered to you, that the Lord Jesus on the night when he was betrayed took bread, and when he had given thanks, he broke it, and said, "This is my body which is for you. Do this in remembrance of me." In the same way also he took the cup, after supper, saying, "This cup is the new covenant in my blood. Do this, as often as you drink it, in remembrance of me." For as often as you eat this bread and drink the cup, you proclaim the Lord's death until he comes. Whoever, therefore, eats the bread or drinks the cup of the Lord in an unworthy manner will be guilty of profaning the body and blood of the Lord. Let a person examine himself, then, and so eat of the bread and drink of the cup. For anyone who eats and drinks without discerning the body eats and drinks judgment on himself. That is why many of you are weak and ill, and some have died. 1 Corinthians 11:23-30

If your brother sins against you, go and tell him his fault, between you and him alone. If he listens to you, you have gained your brother. But if he does not listen, take one or two others along with you, that every charge may be established by the evidence of two or three witnesses. If he refuses to listen to them, tell it to the church. And if he refuses to listen even to the church, let him be to you as a Gentile and a tax collector. Matthew 18:15-17

I wrote to you in my letter not to associate with sexually immoral people— not at all meaning the sexually immoral of this world, or the greedy and swindlers, or idolaters, since then you would need to go out of the world. But now I am writing to you not to associate with anyone who bears the name of brother if he is guilty of sexual immorality or greed, or is an idolater, reviler, drunkard, or swindler—not even to eat with such a one. 1 Corinthians 5:9-11

False Teaching Denied/Objections Answered
1. The Quakers hold that neither preaching the Word of God nor the celebration of the Sacraments of the Gospel are necessary to sustain a congregation or to serve as identification marks of a true visible church. Their meetings have no preachers, no set readings, nor any necessary Bible readings at all, no sacraments of the Gospel, and no clergy. They rely on the "inner light" or the inner word of the Holy Spirit speaking in and through all gathered. Historically, a Quaker meeting is built around prayer and sharing by the members of the congregation.

One Quaker congregation actually called a Presbyterian clergyman to be its leader of worship and teacher. When the Presbyterian clergyman protested that to call him was a very "un-Quaker-like" thing to do, they said, "When our forefathers sank within in prayer, they found the Spirit shining on the pages of the King James Bible that they had memorized, but when we sink within in prayer, we bump into the stock market averages. We need a teacher of the Word." All of which points to the need for biblical content. It is not clear why the Quakers feel free to ignore the biblical practice of the reading and expositing the Scriptures or Jesus' command to "do this in remembrance of me" with regard to the Lord's Supper. In any case, the result is that it has been hard for the Quakers to remain orthodox in doctrine down through history. In departing from the marks of a visible church, they do err and lose their right to claim to be visible churches.

2. The Salvation Army has done something similar. They are happy to read and preach the Scriptures in their worship services, but they see no need for the Sacraments of the Gospel, despite Jesus' clear command. Anglicans would have to judge that the Salvation Army is Christian in its intent, but has abandoned a key mark of a visible church. What are they then? Perhaps they are best viewed as gatherings of Christians encouraging one another, and doing much-needed good works among the needy, but lacking the full status of visible churches.

3. Needless to say, a number of congregations in the Anglican Communion would not measure up to the definition of a visible church, given the radical departure from the doctrines of the Scripture in the preaching and teaching that is found in their life and in their moral practice. Some have declared their doctrinal indifference by inviting non-Christians to receive Holy Communion, in contradiction to Jesus' institution of the Sacrament.

Not all groups who call themselves a "church" truly qualify for the name they claim the right to bear.

Implications

If the "church" in which you are a member does not have the marks of a true visible Church, challenge the leaders of the church to repentance and the restoration of the visible marks or transfer to one that does treasure and manifest them.

3. The visible Church of Christ can and does err.
Explanation

The Article states: "As the Church of Jerusalem, Alexandria, and Antioch have erred: so also the Church of

Rome hath erred, not only in their living and manner of ceremonies, but also in matters of faith."

This third teaching point of the Article asserts the fallibility and denies the infallibility of all visible churches, the Orthodox Churches of the East, the Roman Catholic Church and the Pope, and the Church of England as well. It would be well into the 19th century before the Roman Catholic Church would officially declare itself, through the office of the Pope, to be infallible. Already at the time these Articles were being written in the 16th Century, however, there were tendencies, both in the Roman Catholic Church and in the Orthodox Churches of the East, to declare the Church, at least in its conciliar pronouncements, to be infallible. Anglicans believe that the Scriptures make no such promise to visible churches, composed, as they are, of sinful human beings; nor does the history of the Church support such a claim, when it is honestly examined.

The denial of infallibility raises several questions:

First, what are we to make of Christ's claim that even the gates of hell will not be able to defend themselves against the Church? Does that saying not imply the infallibility of the Church? It does not. But it does imply the indefectibility of the Church, as do other biblical statements about God's final victory over evil and Satan. The doctrine of the indefectibility of the Church teaches that the visible Church will not so err as to be utterly corrupted or destroyed. Rather, the visible Church will be preserved and renewed by the Lord through the Word by the Spirit. Thus the Church will triumph over Satan, sin and death and will be the Church triumphant in the end. The visible Church may fall into grievous error for a time, but not in all its members and not finally. Reform will surely come.

Second, if the visible Church can err, including the Church of England, what then is the status of these Thirty-Nine Articles? How do we know that they, too, are not in error? The answer lies in the comparison of their teaching with the Scriptures of the Old and New Testaments. In addition, consulting the teaching of the ancient Church in the Councils of the undivided Church as well as the general consensus of the Fathers of the Church is wise, for they are worthy witnesses, subordinate to the teaching of the Scriptures. Anglicans invite the comparison of their doctrine with the clear teaching of the Holy Scriptures and the general consensus of the Ancient Church and Councils.

Anglicans believe that such a comparison will show that these Thirty-Nine Articles do conform to both the Scriptures and the general consensus of the Councils, the Catholic Creeds, and the Fathers of the Church. Since the Thirty-Nine Articles state the official teachings of the Anglican Church and are binding where they are officially endorsed by a Province, if an individual clergyman or lay person believes them to be in error in any respect, that matter must be brought before the councils of the Church and argued there. In principle, the Articles are revisable, but until they are revised officially by renewed comparison with the Scriptures and shown to be in error, they are to be honored in the preaching and teaching of the Anglican Churches (Provinces) that recognize them.

Biblical Foundations

I therefore, a prisoner for the Lord, urge you to walk in a manner worthy of the calling to which you have been called, with all humility and gentleness, with patience, bearing with one another in love, eager to maintain the unity of the Spirit in the bond of peace. There is one body and one Spirit—just as you were called to the one hope that belongs to your call— one Lord, one faith, one baptism, one God and Father of all, who is over all and through all and in all. Ephesians 4:1-6

I am astonished that you are so quickly deserting him who called you in the grace of Christ and are turning to a different gospel— not that there is another one, but there are some who trouble you and want to distort the gospel of

Christ. But even if we or an angel from heaven should preach to you a gospel contrary to the one we preached to you, let him be accursed. As we have said before, so now I say again: If anyone is preaching to you a gospel contrary to the one you received, let him be accursed. Galatians 1:6-9

False Teachings Denied/Objections Answered

1. It is obvious that the claims of Rome to be infallible are denied by this Article. So, too, are the similar claims of the Orthodox Churches of the East and of certain Protestant Churches.

2. Any teaching that the visible Church, in any of its expressions, can err only in matters ceremonial and practical living but not in doctrine is denied.

3. On the other hand, it is not to be thought that every doctrine of the Church is erroneous. The teachings of the churches that are in agreement with the Scriptures are true and to be accepted as such. That we can err, and do sometimes err, does not mean that truth always escapes us. We need not fall into skepticism. While orthodox believers do differ in some areas, they do not generally differ on the fundamentals of the Apostolic Faith, for the Scriptures are clear on the essentials and any honest attempt to understand their teaching leads to a common understanding. The Thirty-Nine Articles are themselves such an appeal to the clear teaching of Scripture.

Implications

The chief implication is that all doctrine and all ethical instruction of any visible Church is to be measured by the official teaching of that Church which itself is to be in accord with and compared with Holy Scripture.

This places a solemn obligation upon all of the members of the Church to be serious students of Scripture and of the teaching of their respective churches. It also places a solemn obligation upon the clergy to see that the laity are well-instructed in both.

Conclusion

It is easy to underestimate the significance of the visible Church. God's gift of a community of salvation in Christ is a gift of great worth. United to Christ and in Christ to one another, we worship and serve the Lord together and have fellowship with one another in Christ. We draw upon His faithfulness and power and as we turn to Him, day by day. We disciple one another; we grow up in Christ, lead our children into personal faith in Christ, and together undertake the mission of Christ to the world. As visible churches, rooted in Scripture and the Sacraments of the Gospel, we often fall short of what we are called to be as Christ's people, but His promises are that He will reform and renew us and finally will complete what He has begun in us. As Christians, we are called to love all people, but especially those of the Household of Faith.

ARTICLE 20

Of the Authority of the Church

The Church hath power to decree rites or ceremonies and authority in controversies of faith; and yet it is not lawful for the Church to ordain anything contrary to God's word written, neither may it so expound one place of Scripture, that it be repugnant to another. Wherefore, although the Church be a witness and a keeper of Holy Writ: yet, as it ought not to decree anything against the same, so besides the same ought it not to enforce anything to be believed for necessity of salvation.

Introduction

Just what kind of authority does the Church have? Can it add to the revelation in Holy Scripture? Can it correct material in Holy Scripture, when it has come to disagree with it? What about traditions in the Church - can the Church change them?

Article 20 is concerned with the proper exercise of the Church's authority. The Church does have authority; that is, it has both the right and the power to carry out specific responsibilities. The authority given the Church by God is to be exercised and not neglected, because the responsibilities it has are important ones. On the other hand, the authority of the Church has limits and its authority is not to be exaggerated or abused, as has sometimes happened in the history of the Church.

Anglicans approach this matter of the proper use of the Church's authority by examining the nature and relation of the Church's authority in relation to the supreme authority of the Holy Scriptures as the Word of God written. The significant but less fundamental question of the Church's authority to change its traditions is dealt with in Article 34.

The Teaching of Article 20

Here are the teaching points for this Article:

1. What the Church has the authority and power to do is stated.

2. What the Church must not do regarding Scripture is declared.

3. What the Church must do regarding Scripture is set forth.

1. What the Church has the authority and power to do is stated.

Explanation

There are certain things pertaining to the life and witness of the Church that must be done. Since that is the case, then someone or some institution in the Church has to have the authority and power to decide and to do these things. When Article 20 states that the Church has the authority to decide and do certain things, it affirms that the Lord of the Church has given this specific right and power to the Church and not to some other society.

What decisions and actions has the Lord given the Church the authority to undertake? The Article mentions two: the authority and power to decree rites or ceremonies and the right and power to decide controversies of Faith, that is, controversies about doctrine, including ethical doctrine. It belongs to the Church to define both its worship and its teaching. It does this in obedience to its head, Jesus Christ, in accordance with His truth and will made known in and through the Scriptures.

With reference to rites or ceremonies, each province or local church in the Anglican Communion has a Book of Common Prayer which sets forth the rites or ceremonies of that local Anglican Church. Until the mid 20th Century, all of the Anglican Provinces and Churches had Books of

Common Prayer which were very similar. This was the case because all of the Books of Common Prayer being used in the Anglican Communion had descended with only small alterations from the classic 1662 *Book of Common Prayer and Ordinal*. In fact, a number of the Provinces still use the 1662 *Book of Common Prayer* and Ordinal as their designated means of worship. In the 1960s and 70s, this common usage was lost as several of the Provinces of the Anglican Communion revised their prayer books extensively and also permitted the use of alternative services.

This authorized variety does not violate the stated position of the Anglican Communion because Anglicans have long held that the forms of prayer may vary from church to church, provided that the substance of the Faith is kept entire.

What about the doctrines officially held and taught by the Church? Once again, until fairly recent times, this too has been rather uniform in the Anglican Communion, for all the Anglican Churches or Provinces recognized and subscribed to the historic Anglican formularies. These classic formularies are the Holy Scriptures of the Old and New Testaments; the Three Catholic Creeds, i.e. the Nicene, Apostles', and Athanasian Creeds; the Thirty-Nine Articles of Religion; *The Book of Homilies*; and the 1662 *Book of Common Prayer,* and Ordinal. It is important to note that *The Book of Common Prayer* and Ordinal are considered to be doctrinal norms along side of the Creeds and Thirty-Nine Articles and *The Book of Homilies*. What a congregation regularly sings and prays does teach and communicate doctrine. This general uniformity of Anglican doctrine was weakened and then compromised, first, by the influence of the Enlightenment in the late 17th and 18th centuries and, second, by the rise of the Romantic Movement and Anglo-Catholic Movements in the 19th century. In the 20th century, Anglican doctrinal unity had become profoundly compromised, if not totally lost with the appearance of secular relativism in the 20th and 21st centuries, to which many in the Anglican Provinces in the West have surrendered. This has created a crisis for the Anglican Communion, which it is presently attempting to address.

Such crises are not new in the life of the Church. Time and again, differing interpretations of scriptural teaching and departures from the same have arisen within the Church. Here are two major examples:

In the 4th century, a difference concerning the divinity of Christ arose between Arius, who believed and taught that the Word or the Son was the first and great creature through Whom God created all of the rest of creation. In opposition, Athanasius and the Nicene Fathers, in dependence upon the Apostles, confessed Jesus to be the incarnation of the eternal Son of God. After due consideration, the Church in the Council of Nicaea, A.D. 325, declared that the Son or Word, Who became incarnate in Jesus, was of the same nature as the Father. He was not a creature. He was God the Son.

In the 5th century, there arose another great conflict between St. Augustine and Pelagius. They differed as to the reality and effects of original sin, particularly regarding the bondage of the will. Pelagius believed that the human will was untouched by sin, whereas Augustine believed that it was profoundly corrupted by sin. Pelagius was declared a heretic, and the Church followed Augustine in large measure, though not completely. In such matters, the Church through the study of Scripture and prayer has decided official doctrine and rejected error in the light of the Scriptures.

Anglicans agree with St. Athanasius and recognize the Nicene Creed as one of the main formularies of the Church as well as affirming the Christological affirmations of the first four general councils of the Church, declaring Jesus to be God the Son incarnate. Anglicans clearly affirm this in the Thirty-Nine Articles of Religion and in the liturgies in *The Book of Common Prayer*.

With regard to original sin, Anglicans agree with St. Augustine and affirm the doctrine of the bondage of the will in Article 10, and in many prayers in *The Book of Common Prayer*.

The main point is that when the Scriptures give us sufficient material to make a responsible decision concerning true doctrine, and when differing interpretations arise, or false doctrines arise, the Church has to address the problem and declare the truth. The Church is not to neglect this responsibility and allow false doctrine to grow in its life like leaven, increasing in influence, obscuring the truth, misleading and finally dividing the Church. This responsibility to teach faithful doctrine includes the moral teaching or the moral doctrine of the Church.

The resolution of such controversies of Faith is not to be left to individuals. The Lord has given the right, the power, and the responsibility to the Church to address controversies of Faith. However, each individual is invited to compare the teaching of the Church with the Scriptures in order to satisfy himself or herself that the Church holds right doctrine (see Article 19).

Biblical Foundations

For the time is coming when people will not endure sound teaching, but having itching ears they will accumulate for themselves teachers to suit their own passions. 2 Timothy 4:3

And when he had said this, he breathed on them and said to them, "Receive the Holy Spirit. If you forgive the sins of anyone, they are forgiven; if you withhold forgiveness from anyone, it is withheld." John 20:22-23

But Peter, standing with the eleven, lifted up his voice and addressed them, "Men of Judea and all who dwell in Jerusalem, let this be known to you, and give ear to my words. For these men are not drunk, as you suppose, since it is only the third hour of the day. But this is what was uttered through the prophet Joel: 'And in the last days it shall be, God declares, that I will pour out my Spirit on all flesh, and your sons and your daughters shall prophesy, and your young men shall see visions, and your old men shall dream dreams.'" Acts 2:14-17

And after Paul and Barnabas had no small dissension and debate with them, Paul and Barnabas and some of the others were appointed to go up to Jerusalem to the apostles and the elders about this question. Acts 15:2

When they came to Jerusalem, they were welcomed by the church and the apostles and the elders, and they declared all that God had done with them. But some believers who belonged to the party of the Pharisees rose up and said, "It is necessary to circumcise them and to order them to keep the law of Moses." The apostles and the elders were gathered together to consider this matter. Acts 15:4-6

For it has seemed good to the Holy Spirit and to us to lay on you no greater burden than these requirements: that you abstain from what has been sacrificed to idols, and from blood, and from what has been strangled, and from sexual immorality. If you keep yourselves from these, you will do well. Farewell. Acts 15:28-29

I appeal to you, brothers, to watch out for those who cause divisions and create obstacles contrary to the doctrine that you have been taught; avoid them. Romans 16:17

If anyone teaches a different doctrine and does not agree with the sound words of our Lord Jesus Christ and the teaching that accords with godliness, he is puffed up with conceit and understands nothing. He has an unhealthy craving for controversy and for quarrels about words, which produce envy, dissension, slander, evil suspicions, and constant friction among people who are depraved in mind and deprived of the truth, imagining that godliness is a means of gain. 1Timothy 6:3-5

For I received from the Lord what I also delivered to you, that the Lord Jesus on the night when he was betrayed took bread, and when he had given thanks, he broke it, and said, "This is my body which is for you. Do this in remembrance of me." In the same way also he took the cup, after supper, saying, "This cup is the new covenant in my blood. Do this, as often as you drink it, in remembrance of me." For as often as you eat this bread and drink the cup, you proclaim the Lord's death until he comes. 1 Corinthians 11:23-26

False Teaching Denied/Objections Answered
1. At the Reformation, the question of the proper exercise of Church authority was raised in several ways by the congregations of the Radical Reformation:

A. The Anabaptist movement was comprised of various groups with rather diverse beliefs. They are referred to as the "Radical Reformation" because their departure from the Faith, order, and practice of the pre-Reformation Church was quite radical. The two doctrines upon which they were all agreed were: 1) that baptism should only be given to believers and 2) that believers should live separated or holy lives, very distinct from and often isolated from the surrounding culture and society.

At the time of the Reformation, some Anabaptists held that the Church had little or no authority at all; it was the responsibility of the individual believer to discern the truth. Such a view errs, for it fails to recognize that the Church is responsible before the Lord for the public teaching and behavior of its members.

Because the Church is commanded to preach the Word of God within its life and to the world, it must therefore have the authority to declare what it understands the teaching of the Word to be. The same applies to the moral life of the members of the Church. That doctrinal responsibility of the Church is, by itself, sufficient to refute the view that denies any authority to the Church.

Also, the Church must order its worship in some clear fashion. Considered from a biblical perspective, not just anything is acceptable worship of the Triune God.

In addition to the internal need of Anglicans to make these decisions, the extreme views held by those of the Radical Reformation concerning baptism and holy living required authoritative responses by Anglicans and the other more conservative Churches of the Reformation.

The exercise of authority in the Church is simply unavoidable in practice.

B. Not all Anabaptists took the view that the individual alone had to determine true doctrine. Others took quite the opposite view, giving supreme authority to the collective voice of the congregation or the voice of its designated leader. Isolated from the traditional wisdom of the Church, and often being unlearned in Scripture, such groups were frequently led into bizarre life-styles, strange teachings and unrealistic expectations. It is an error to isolate Scriptural authority from the subordinate standards of the Church's traditions.

2. It is also an error for the Church to hold first-century institutions, traditions, and cultural applications of Scripture to be as final and authoritative as the doctrines and principles of Scripture themselves. To attempt to return to and thus to freeze the Church's teaching and practice in the Hellenistic culture of the 1st century or any other past period in history is called "repristination." An attempt at such repristination took place when some Puritans felt that Cranmer had not gone far enough in conforming the liturgy of the Church and Church order to the example of the New Testament Church. Rather than requiring the Church's teaching and morals to be in agreement with the doctrine of the Scriptures, while allowing a retention of godly church traditions that had developed after the 1st century, these Puritans wanted a far more rigid conformity to Scripture. They believed that only what was actually stated in and required by Holy Scripture should be allowed in worship.

This, in effect, denied the Church authority and discretion in shaping the forms of worship. It left no room for the Spirit's leading the Church into wise and good traditions in the light of Scripture, or for the Church to adjust to changing circumstances as the times changed, or to exercise cross-cultural sensitivity, which was important as soon as the Church moved into the different parts and cultures of the world.

This restriction was both impractical, and unbiblical and is repudiated by Anglicans in this 20th Article. The learned Richard Hooker wrote his famous "Laws of Ecclesiastical Polity" in large part to refute the extreme narrowness of that particular school of Puritans. This Article clearly affirms the Church's right to decide these matters in accord with Scripture. And Anglicans have done so ever since.

3. In many very free-thinking congregations in the West today, a relativistic and permissive mood concerning doctrine prevails. Members and preachers in such churches would balk at being told by the Church what one was to believe or preach. The same would apply to being confined to an official, specific liturgy. This relativism denies objective truth and hence denies the Church's responsibility and rightful authority in the area of doctrine. Usually such bodies hold that the Church is not defined by doctrine but by the loving inclusion of all persons who are interested in belonging, no matter their beliefs and moral lifestyle. "Doctrine divides, love unites" is their "doctrinal" motto.

This "doctrine" of the Church that denigrates doctrine for the sake of including all and for the sake of institutional unity overlooks the fact that Jesus is the narrow way. He has come to invite all to enter through Himself, the narrow gate, by means of faith and repentance. Institutional ecclesiastical unity apart from repentant faith in the redemption through the Cross and Resurrection of the Lord is an illusion. It ignores sin and its power, biblical revelation, and the power of the Holy Spirit. Right doctrine is set forth by the Church to make the Good News of the "Way" clear and correct so that sinners may hear, repent, believe and enter.

4. Another error with regard to the authority of the Church is to give the State the right to determine the worship and/or teaching of the Church. This is referred to as Erastianism, named after a 16th century Swiss theologian, Thomas Erastus, who advocated such a view. The Orthodox Churches of the East from the days of Constantine onward have leaned in this direction. However, the State is in no position to tell the Church what it is to preach and how it is to order its worship. What norm would the State use to make such decisions? God did not give the State such authority.

Moreover, Erastianism renders the Church incapable of exercising a proper biblical critique of the State when the State violates biblical standards for society. Some theologians have suggested that it was due to the Erastianism of the Orthodox Church in Russia that the State under the Czars was left largely without criticism. That lack of criticism allowed the State, unchecked, to so mistreat its citizens that it actually prepared the way for the Communist takeover in the 20th century.

The churches that were reformed by the Word of God in the 16th century in the West largely rejected Erastianism, in any full sense of that word, and have sought to act as salt and light in the societies wherein they are set. (The Church of England is unique among the churches of the Anglican Communion in being somewhat "Erastian." See Article 37 for a fuller discussion of this.)

Implications

The Church has the authority and the responsibility to determine its doctrine in the light of Holy Scripture. Neglect of this responsibility can only lead to disastrous consequences.

It is true that private judgment is both necessary and unavoidable. St. Paul tells us that we are to "test all things." Each believer should satisfy himself or herself that what the Church requires in doctrine and worship is faithful to Scripture. No individual, however, has the right to insist on purely personal preferences in the teaching or liturgy of the Church.

No State has the authority to dictate to the Church concerning matters of morals, doctrine and worship. The Church does have a responsibility to preach to the State when it violates universal moral principles or the role of the State as set forth in creation and taught in Scripture.

2. What the Church must not do regarding Scripture is declared.
Explanation

Article 20 states three things that the Church must not do in relation to Scripture:

First, it declares that the Church must not ordain anything contrary to Scripture. Anglicans thereby assert the supreme authority of the Scripture over the Church. When the Church is deciding matters of doctrine, ethics, or ceremony, nothing may be ordained that contradicts Scripture. Where Scripture is clear it is to be followed. This Article repeats this point because the authority of Scripture is crucial to an Anglican view of the Church and its authority, that is, to the subordination of the Church to Scriptural authority in doctrine and in practical discipleship.

Second, the Article declares that the Church may not expound one place of Scripture as repugnant to, or contradictory of, another place of Scripture. This is a rule for the proper interpretation of Scripture. This rule is not optional for Anglicans, for it arises from the nature of the Scriptures. The doctrine of Scripture behind this rule is that the Scriptures are inspired by the Holy Spirit, by the one Divine mind, therefore they are coherent in their teaching. This coherence of the Scripture is, however, not always obvious. This is true because the different biblical writers use the same words differently, write in various styles and types of literature, and in various historical periods. It is necessary to look carefully in order to discern the harmony or coherence underneath the different use of the same terms and to consider where the writing fits into God's history of revelation and salvation as found in the Scripture. If this is carefully done, the coherence will be found. (See Appendix B for a brief treatment of Anglican hermeneutics.)

Since the inspiration of Scripture is assumed in this Article, a brief word about the inspiration of Scripture is in order. Our Lord and St. Paul and St. Peter very clearly affirm that the Scriptures are God's Word, as do the biblical writings generally, that is, its human authors, chosen from among God's people, were so inspired or empowered and directed by the Holy Spirit that they wrote what God wished them to write to His people. The Word of God is expressed in the words of man. It is not taught that the personal thoughts and characteristics of the human writers were bypassed, but rather their gifts and thoughts were used and heightened by the Holy Spirit. Therefore we have in Scripture God's Word in human words, a dual authorship. Because of this the Scriptures are unique, and they have a coherence and supreme authority.

Third, the Article makes a statement about the sufficiency of Scripture. The Church is not to require anything to be believed for salvation that is not required by the Holy Scripture itself. This point is familiar to most Anglican clergy, for Anglican clergy at their ordination state, "I do believe the Holy Scriptures of the Old and New Testaments to be the Word of God and to contain all things necessary for salvation." (Article 6 discusses the sufficiency of Scripture more fully.)

Biblical Foundations

But as for you, continue in what you have learned and have firmly believed, knowing from whom you learned it and how from childhood you have been acquainted with the sacred writings, which are able to make you wise for salvation through faith in Christ Jesus. All Scripture is breathed out by God and profitable for teaching, for reproof, for correction, and for training in righteousness, that the man of God may be competent, equipped for every good work. 2 Timothy 3:14-17

But he answered, "It is written, 'Man shall not live by bread alone, but by every word that comes from the mouth of God.'" Matthew 4:4

For truly, I say to you, until heaven and earth pass away, not an iota, not a dot, will pass from the Law until all is accomplished. Therefore whoever relaxes one of the least of these commandments and teaches others to do the same will be called least in the kingdom of heaven, but whoever does them and teaches them will be called great in the kingdom of heaven. Matthew 5:18-19

And he said to them, "O foolish ones, and slow of heart to believe all that the prophets have spoken! Was it not necessary that the Christ should suffer these things and enter into his glory?" And beginning with Moses and all the Prophets, he interpreted to them in all the Scriptures the things concerning himself. Luke 24:25-27

The apostles and the elders were gathered together to consider this matter. And after there had been much debate, Peter stood up and said to them, "Brothers, you know that in the early days God made a choice among you, that by my mouth the Gentiles should hear the word of the gospel and believe. And God, who knows the heart, bore witness to them, by giving them the Holy Spirit just as he did to us, and he made no distinction between us and them, having cleansed their hearts by faith. Now, therefore, why are you putting God to the test by placing a yoke on the neck of the disciples that neither our fathers nor we have been able to bear? But we believe that we will be saved through the grace of the Lord Jesus, just as they will." Acts 15:6-11

False Teaching Denied/Objections Answered

1. In churches where the Scriptures are not given their proper authority, tradition can be given equal authority or even higher authority than that of Scripture.

In the Eastern Orthodox tradition, the teachings of the Ecumenical Councils of the undivided Church are assumed to be without error, not on the basis of their accurate exegesis of Scripture, but on the basis of their being the teaching of the undivided Church which, it is assumed, God would not let err. This in effect places them on a par with Scripture, if not above the Scripture, for they control all further interpretation of Scripture. Anglicans disagree. Article 8 makes it clear that we accept the creeds because they agree with Scripture not the other way around. This Article declares that even Councils can and have erred. We can find no promise in Scripture that God will not let the visible Church err.

In the West, the Roman Catholic Church, in the Council of Trent, declared that the Church regarded the Scriptures and the unwritten Apostolic teaching in the Church with "equal affection." This has opened the door to doctrines that Anglicans, on the whole, cannot support. Tradition, while worthy of great respect and consideration under Scripture, must not be held with equal affection to the Scriptures.

The relation of Scripture and tradition remains a serious point of discussion between Anglicans and the Orthodox and Roman Churches.

2. In extremely liberal churches, a doctrine of development of doctrines can lead to all sorts of teachings that are extraneous to or even contradictory of the Scriptures. Often these doctrines are justified by an appeal to the conviction that God is leading His people by the

Holy Spirit into new truth that goes beyond Scripture and even contradicts and corrects the Holy Scriptures.

In essence, this view assumes either that the Holy Spirit contradicts Himself, or that the Scriptures were in significant places a flawed reading of God's truth all along. In either case this is clearly at odds with the teaching of the Thirty-Nine Articles and the other Anglican formularies regarding the inspired nature, the supreme authority, and sufficiency of the Holy Scriptures in the visible Church. It is not an Anglican position and contradicts the teaching of Jesus and the Apostles as well as numerous texts of Holy Scripture (see the texts listed above).

3. Another abuse of the Church's authority is done when it is taught that one portion of Scripture contradicts another passage of Scripture. This is taught, not in the sense of a paradox, truths that seem to the finite human mind to conflict but since both are true cannot ultimately conflict, but is taught in the sense that a simple contradiction of theologically significant texts exists in Scripture. In contemporary liberal churches and theological colleges, the assertion that biblical passages are in contradiction to one another is taught with little or no sense of impropriety. The result is that in the light of some extra-biblical norm, either of the passages is, or both passages are, viewed to be in error. Portions of Scripture are thereby declared to be without authority.

One recent example involves the two descriptions of the Creation found in the first and second chapters of Genesis. In the debate about homosexual behavior, one scholar, who was in favor of homosexual intimacy, argued that the first account was not acceptable for it contained the command of God to the man and woman "to be fruitful and multiply and fill the earth" whereas the second account was to be preferred because it did not. The first account seemed to suggest that the chief purpose of sexual intimacy was to produce offspring which would unduly limit the purpose of sexual intimacy and exclude homosexual intimacy;

therefore it was in error and in contradiction to the preferred second account that contained no such charge.

If one affirms the coherence of Scripture as does this Article, and interprets the whole of Scripture in the light of Christ, such picking and choosing in the light of some part of Scripture or an extra-biblical norm is avoided and the coherent contours of biblical theology become available.

4. Lastly, this Article states that to add anything as necessary to "salvation" except that which Scripture declares to be necessary is an abuse of the Church's authority.

If we take "salvation" in this article to refer to coming into a right relation with God in Christ through conversion and justification and baptism, then the biblical requirements are the hearing of the Gospel and personal repentance and faith in the Lord of the Gospel. Should the Church add anything else to that, it would abuse its authority.

On the other hand, if we take "salvation" in the wide sense which includes justification, sanctification and glorification, and thereby involves the Christian's whole life in the Church, a wider range of necessary doctrine comes into play. Life in the Church for Anglicans involves confirmation, which includes personal faith in Christ and repentance, the acceptance of the Faith as received by the Anglican Church of which one is a member, and coming under the oversight of the local Bishop. To add any doctrine to the Faith to be received and believed at confirmation or reception except what can be "proved by warrant of Holy Scripture" would be an unwarranted addition and an abuse of the Church's authority.

Implications

Any teaching that is contrary to Scripture is erroneous and has no place in the Church. Further, since the Scriptures are the Word of God written, all of the Church's teaching, no matter how ancient, or taught by whom or what council, must be tested by Scripture and supported by the Scripture's teaching. Since the Scriptures are inspired by God, they are theologically coherent and must be interpreted as such. No church has the authority to add conditions to salvation beyond those clearly stated in the Scriptures. The reverse is also true – the Church may not reject those biblical conditions and doctrines found in Scripture.

Some churches, both in the East and West, seem to Anglicans to have added doctrines not rooted in the Scriptures which are to be accepted in confirmation or reception. This remains a matter for ecumenical discussion.

3. What the Church must do regarding Scripture is set forth.
Explanation

Since the Holy Scriptures are a chief means of grace, the Church has a number of positive responsibilities regarding the Scriptures.

According to Article 20, the Church is to be a "witness and keeper of Holy Writ." What does it mean for the Church to be a "witness of Holy Writ"? It means several things.

First, it means that the leaders and members of the Church are to know the Scriptures and to treasure their excellence. Second, the Church is to speak of the excellence of Scripture, to witness to it. The Church is to speak to its own members by Christian education, by sermon and song, and through the content and shape of the liturgies used in worship. The Church is also to speak to its young people through their parents, who are to teach the content and remarkable qualities of Scripture to its children in the home. As the primary witness to the Scriptures under the Holy Spirit, the Church is also to speak of the attributes or excellencies of Scripture openly to the world as well.

What are the excellencies of Scripture? The Church usually lists them as 1) their supreme authority, 2) their sufficiency, 3) their clarity, 4) their efficacy, and 5) their necessity. These are sometimes referred to as the perfections of Scripture or the attributes of Scripture. They are the qualities of Scripture given them by God so that He might speak His Word to us ever anew through them.

When the Church is sound, there is a great love in the heart of the Church for the Scriptures. They are treasured as "the Word of God written" and are read in the light of Jesus, the Word of God, incarnate, crucified, risen, and ascended, as their organizing center and as the One who speaks through them today.

The attributes of Scripture are discussed more fully in Article 6. Here we will discuss the authority of Scripture and only mention the leading idea of the other attributes of Scripture.

With regard to the authority of Scripture, it is important to explain the sense in which Anglicans embrace the Reformation slogan *Sola Scriptura* that is, "Scripture alone." This slogan is a statement about the unique authority of Scripture. The phrase "Scripture alone" does not mean that the Scriptures are isolated from subordinate standards in the life of the Church. All churches inevitably have a tradition of what the Scriptures are discerned by the Church to teach. It is better by far when this official interpretation is written down for all to see. Anglicans have the Three Catholic Creeds, the Thirty-Nine Articles of Religion, the 1662 *Book of Common Prayer* and Ordinal and *The Homilies* as subordinate standards. Anglicans have never taught "Scripture alone" in the sense of an isolated Scripture. Rather "Scripture alone" means that Scripture has a unique level of authority of its own. It alone is the supreme authority in the life of the Church and nothing else is on the same level as Scripture. All aspects of tradition are to be tested by what is taught in Scripture. For Anglicans, the Scriptures are the norming norm, i.e. the *norma normans*, while the subordinate formulae are the normed norms, or *norma normata*, for they are normed by Scripture and draw their authority from their agreement with Scripture.

This view of the supreme authority of Scripture lies at the heart of Anglicanism. This is evidenced by the fact that all of the subordinate authorities recognized by Anglicans are exegetical in nature and make obvious reference to their dependence upon and deference to the Scriptures.

The clarity of Scripture refers to the clear teaching it gives of the essential matters of the Faith. There are passages that are hard to understand, but the central matters are clear to all who take the pains to read the Scriptures.

The sufficiency of Scripture regards its sufficiency for our knowledge of God and seeing all things in relation to God.

The efficacy of Scripture lies in its capacity to be used by the Holy Spirit to address us in our heart and to call us, convert us and transform us.

The necessity of the Scripture lies in its fixed form so that it travels with the Church down through time and history until the consummation of all things. It provides the Church with the abiding means through which God can and does regularly renew His people in Apostolic Faith and witness.

To sum up, when we speak of the Church as a "witness" of the Scripture, we declare that it is incumbent upon the Church to bear witness within and without the Church to the content of Scripture and to the excellence of Scripture, in all of its attributes, and above all to the unique and supreme authority of the Scripture.

The Church is also referred to as a "keeper of Scripture." What does it mean for the Church to be a "keeper of Scripture"? It means the Church is called to protect the Scriptures. It means treating the Scriptures with great respect and care. It involves hiding the Scriptures during times of persecution. It also means that the Church is to see that copies of Scripture are made available to its members wherever and whenever possible and in a translation that is in the native tongue of the congregations.

To be a "keeper" of the Scriptures involves the Church in the scholarly attempt through textual study to recover the original wording of the various books of the Bible. This work of textual criticism has been very successful, due to the unusually large amount of early biblical manuscript evidence. Scholars suggest that we have, in the modern reconstructed manuscripts of the Bible, 99% of the original wording of the original texts of the various books of the Bible. And, further, these scholars assert that of the 1% a large part is variant readings and does not directly affect any of the teachings of the Scripture.

By God's provision and providence and by the Church's faithful preservation and protection of the Scriptures, we have, to all intents and purposes, the Bible as the various books were initially written. The Church has indeed been mindful of its calling to be a keeper of the Scriptures.

Biblical Foundations

And how from childhood you have been acquainted with the sacred writings, which are able to make you wise for salvation through faith in Christ Jesus. 2 Timothy 3:15

But Jesus answered them, "You are wrong, because you know neither the Scriptures nor the power of God." Matthew 22:29

Now these Jews were more noble than those in Thessalonica; they received the word with all eagerness, examining the Scriptures daily to see if these things were so. Acts 17:11

How can a young man keep his way pure? By guarding it according to your word. Psalm 119:9

I have stored up your word in my heart, that I might not sin against you. Psalm 119:11

I will meditate on your precepts and fix my eyes on your ways. I will delight in your statutes; I will not forget your word. Psalm 119:15-16

How sweet are your words to my taste, sweeter than honey to my mouth! Through your precepts I get understanding; therefore I hate every false way. Your word is a lamp to my feet and a light to my path. Psalm 119:103-105

False Teaching Denied/Objections Answered
1. The Church is to witness faithfully to the inspired nature and Canonical authority of Scripture. Any teaching in the Church concerning the nature and authority of the Scripture that detracts from its true nature and authority is a false teaching and contradicts the Church's calling to be a witness to Scripture. This repeated prohibition seeks to prevent such additions to official Anglican teaching or to any part of the church.

2. The liberal tradition in theology in the 19th and 20th centuries increasinglu saw the Holy Scriptures as only a human book about God, possessing only human authority. This is not the view of Jesus, the Apostles and the Church down through the centuries. The Church has consistently taught that the Scriptures are the Word of God in written form. They are the Word of God in the words of human authors. It was written by members of the chosen people of God, who were inspired and guided by the Spirit of God and who wrote in specific times and places. Therefore the Scriptures have dual authorship, with God as the supreme author. As Karl Barth once said: "The Bible is not man's word about God but God's Word to man." And we might add "through man." We can thank historical, critical biblical scholarship for its recovery of a concern for the human, historical nature of the Scriptures. But we cannot be thankful that so many of these scholars, being too influenced by the Enlightenment, often denied the divine authorship of the Scriptures. This denial of the dual

authorship of Scripture is found in the works of a number of biblical scholars and preachers from the late 18th century to the present.

Implications

In Anglican circles, one seldom hears a sermon or attends an adult education class in which the attributes of the Scriptures are explained and celebrated. There is a deep respect for Scripture among Anglicans, but it is often held with insufficient understanding and intellectual grounding. This should be remedied.

The responsibility of the families of the Church to be witnesses of the Scripture within the family and to friends and neighbors is also far too often neglected. It is a great calling and privilege and needs to be taken to heart.

The science of textual criticism has served the Church well as a key part of the Church's faithfulness in preserving the Scriptures with such fidelity.

Conclusion

The Anglican Churches have, on the whole, respected the reality, the responsibility, and the limits of the Church's authority as set forth in this Article 20. We, in our time, are called to continue this faithfulness and, where necessary, to reaffirm it. Congregations are called to commend the Scriptures within and without and need to do this more faithfully than has recently been the case.

ARTICLE 21

Of the Authority of General Councils

General Councils may not be gathered together without the commandment and will of princes. And when they be gathered together, forasmuch as they be an assembly of men, whereof all be not governed with the Spirit and word of God, they may err and sometime have erred, even in things pertaining to God. Wherefore things ordained by them as necessary to salvation have neither strength nor authority, unless it may be declared that they be taken out of Holy Scripture.

Introduction

What is a General Council? Do any of the present international ecclesiastical gatherings qualify as a General Council? Could a General Council ever be called under our present political and ecclesiastical conditions?

This 21st Article deals first with the question concerning who has the authority to call a General Council. It also denies that a General Council is protected from all error by the Holy Spirit. The Holy Scriptures are declared to be the norm and determiner of what is true in the pronouncements of a General Council. This assertion about the authority of Scripture and the derived and subordinate authority of the Church on all levels including a General Council is repeated here for the fourth time in the Thirty-Nine Articles (see Articles 6, 8, 20, 22).

The Teaching of Article 21

Here are the teaching points for this Article:

1. General Councils must be duly called.

2. General Councils can err and have erred.

3. Decrees of Councils concerning salvation have authority only when in agreement with Holy Scripture.

1. General Councils must be duly called.
Explanation

Both in Scripture and in Church history, General Councils have played an important role. Historically they have been called by the Emperor or by Kings, Princes, or National Heads of State. But now that we are in a divided Church spread among the nations of the world, who has the authority to call a General Council? That was the question facing the churches at the time of the Reformation and faces us still.

The Bishop of Rome has claimed this right from the 11th century onwards, and continues to do so. The Orthodox Churches of the East have never recognized the Pope's unilateral authority to do so. Nor have the Protestant Churches. The Orthodox Churches of the East looked to the Christian Emperor and today would most probably look to one of the Eastern Patriarchs or to several of them together to do so, now that there is no single Empire and no Emperor. At the time of the 16th century Reformation, the Anglicans turned to Christian kings or princes of the Christian nations to do so. Most Protestant Churches are not Erastian and therefore they are not submissive to the various national governments. They generally hold the doctrine of the separation of Church and State. Therefore the Protestant Churches would, most probably, look to the official leaders and/or the chief constitutional governing conventions of the several churches acting together to call a General Council.

Despite all of the modern means of electronic communication, in the divided world of many nations and of local or national churches, connections are difficult and are made more difficult because only some of the Churches are members of a world-wide Communion such as the Anglican Communion. It would have to be the collective heads of the several historic Churches that could call a General Council. Given the differences that exist between the Churches, it would take a miraculous work of the Holy Spirit for all the Churches to come together to take counsel together, with the express purpose of making decisions that would have binding authority upon the whole Church, that is, upon all of the churches taking part.

In short, there is no single and direct authority that could call a true General Council today. The modern Ecumenical Movement does point suggestively in that direction, but the World Council of Churches can only facilitate mutual discussion and cooperation and make declarations which have no binding authority on the member Churches.

Biblical Foundations
And after Paul and Barnabas had no small dissension and debate with them, Paul and Barnabas and some of the others were appointed to go up to Jerusalem to the apostles and the elders about this question. Acts 15:2

When they came to Jerusalem, they were welcomed by the church and the apostles and the elders, and they declared all that God had done with them. But some believers who belonged to the party of the Pharisees rose up and said, "It is necessary to circumcise them and to order them to keep the law of Moses." The apostles and the elders were gathered together to consider this matter." Acts 15:4-6

Then it seemed good to the apostles and the elders, with the whole church, to choose men from among them and send them to Antioch with Paul and Barnabas. They sent Judas called Barsabbas, and Silas, leading men among the brothers, with the following letter: "The brothers, both the apostles and the elders, to the brothers who are of the

Gentiles in Antioch and Syria and Cilicia, greetings. Since we have heard that some persons have gone out from us and troubled you with words, unsettling your minds, although we gave them no instructions, it has seemed good to us, having come to one accord, to choose men and send them to you with our beloved Barnabas and Paul, men who have risked their lives for the sake of our Lord Jesus Christ. We have therefore sent Judas and Silas, who themselves will tell you the same things by word of mouth. For it has seemed good to the Holy Spirit and to us to lay on you no greater burden than these requirements: that you abstain from what has been sacrificed to idols, and from blood, and from what has been strangled, and from sexual immorality. If you keep yourselves from these, you will do well. Farewell." Acts 15:22-29

False Teachings Denied/Objections Answered

The Roman Catholic Church has continued to call councils which she regards as General Councils or Ecumenical Councils. This is due to her conviction that the Pope is the Vicar of Christ and head of the one, holy, catholic, and apostolic Church on earth. Therefore, in their view, the Pope has the right to call General Councils. The Papal claim has never been universally recognized by all Christian bodies and is not so recognized today. While the Councils called by the Roman Catholic Church are taken seriously by most Christian bodies, they have not been recognized by the other Christian churches as General Councils binding on all Christian churches. These Councils do, of course, have binding authority upon the congregations of the Roman Catholic Church itself.

Implications

The visible Church is divided into various Bodies today. The various visible churches or visible expressions of the One, Holy, Catholic, and Apostolic Church can only regard the calling of an Ecumenical Council as one of hope for an act of God, a work of the Holy Spirit.

Meanwhile, the various visible expressions of the Church should be 1) praying for such a Council, 2) determined to be as open to one another as is compatible with truth and a good conscience, 3) be ready to work together whenever and wherever possible, and 4) seek together to show Christ's love to one another and to the world. In this form of "active waiting," we will best be able to carry out our mission to the lost in the world.

2. General Councils can err and have erred.
Explanation

This second point in Article 21 denies General Councils are infallible on two grounds:

First, it points out that General Councils are composed of men who are fallen and therefore are not fully governed by God's Word and Spirit and hence are men who can and do err. If the individuals who compose a Council can err and do err, then the Council itself can err and is very likely to err.

The second reason given is that General Councils have in fact actually erred, even in matters of theological importance. This second reason moves from theory to actual fact and proves that General Councils can err and do err. If these two grounds be true and if General Councils can err and have erred in the past, then it is incumbent on the Church in all of its visible manifestations to continually test all things by their agreement with Holy Scripture, particularly the theological and moral statements of General Councils.

The canons of all the General Councils do not possess the same importance and authority as do their dogmatic pronouncements; however, they too should be weighed by their conformity to Scripture.

Biblical Foundations

"'In vain do they worship me, teaching as doctrines the commandments of men.' You leave the commandment of God and hold to the tradition of men." And he said to them, "You have a fine way of rejecting the commandment of God in order to establish your tradition!" Mark 7:7-9

Thus making void the word of God by your tradition that you have handed down. And many such things you do. Mark 7:13

The natural person does not accept the things of the Spirit of God, for they are folly to him, and he is not able to understand them because they are spiritually discerned. 1 Corinthians 2:14

And count the patience of our Lord as salvation, just as our beloved brother Paul also wrote to you according to the wisdom given him, as he does in all his letters when he speaks in them of these matters. There are some things in them that are hard to understand, which the ignorant and unstable twist to their own destruction, as they do the other Scriptures. 2 Peter 3:15-16

False Teachings Denied/Objections Answered

1. As mentioned above, the Roman Catholic Church holds that General Councils do not and cannot err if they are affirmed by the Pope and/or are called by the Pope, who is gifted with infallibility when he speaks from his seat, *ex cathedra*. The Orthodox Churches of the East hold that the seven General Councils of the undivided Church are without error.

Both of these views are directly contradicted by this 21st Article. Anglicans see no biblical grounds for such assertions and believe that the implications of sin abiding in believers as well as the actual history of the General Councils of the Church offer compelling reasons to deny that claim.

To find examples of errors taught in a General Council in the Western Church, the Anglican authors of this Article needed to go no further back than the sessions of Trent which had recently taken place and were still taking place as these Thirty-Nine Articles were being written. The differences on justification and on the relation of Scripture and church tradition and on the relation of the sacrifice of Christ on the Cross to the Holy Eucharist were prominent matters of dispute in which Anglicans held and hold that Rome had erred according to Scriptural teaching, and there are others as well. Tridentine errors are discussed directly or by intimation in the following 20 Articles: 6, 9-14, 19-22, 24, 25, 28-32, 36, and 37. Clearly the writers of the Thirty-Nine Articles were convinced that the Council of Trent could, had, and was erring, for Trent was not yet over when the Articles were being written.

2. With reference to the Orthodox Churches of the East that hold to inerrancy of the first seven Councils of the undivided Church, Anglicans differ as well. Anglicans have generally received the teaching of the first four General Councils and the Christological clarifications of the Fifth and Sixth Councils of the undivided Church. They have been reluctant to endorse the full dogmatic teaching of the Seventh Council because the teaching on icons of the Seventh Council has seemed to many Anglicans to go well beyond Scripture, and to allow a degree of veneration to the icons that is unbiblical. Beyond the doctrines of the Seventh General Council, there are a number of items in its canons with which Anglicans do not agree.

3. This Article is not intended to deny the ultimate indefectibility of the One, Holy, Catholic, and Apostolic Church, for this is taught by Jesus in His statement that the very gates of hell shall not be able to withstand His Church (Matthew 16:18). Anglicans understand Jesus to mean that all visible churches, expressions of the One, Holy, Catholic, and Apostolic Church, will never at the same time lose the truth of the Gospel. And Anglicans hold that His words

affirm that, in the end, it is the Church of Christ and not the power of Satan that will prevail and be triumphant.

Implications

While the teachings of General Councils of the early Church are to be treated with great seriousness and respect, their teaching is to be evaluated by their faithfulness to Holy Scripture.

3. Decrees of Councils concerning salvation have authority only when in agreement with Holy Scripture.
Explanation

This is now the third time that the warning against adding things to be believed for salvation beyond what is required in Scripture is asserted in the Articles. In addition to its affirmation here, it appears in Articles 6, 8, and 22. It is repeated here because the authority of General Councils and all ecclesiastical councils is ultimately derived from their faithfulness to Scripture.

This prohibition once again affirms the utter sufficiency of the Scripture for salvation. The chief purpose of Scripture is to "make us wise unto salvation through faith in Christ Jesus our Lord." It also reaffirms that the teaching of the Church, and most particularly in its official teaching in General Councils, is to make clear the teaching of the Holy Scripture concerning salvation in Christ and not to add to it.

Since this warning is repeated three times, we must conclude that a tendency to add requirements beyond what is taught in Scripture as essential for salvation has appeared in the visible Church. This repeated prohibition must be seen as a warning to the Roman Church which was then meeting in Trent, as well as a warning to Anglicans themselves, since Anglicans are not immune to the same tendency.

Biblical Foundations

But as for you, continue in what you have learned and have firmly believed, knowing from whom you learned it and how from childhood you have been acquainted with the sacred writings, which are able to make you wise for salvation through faith in Christ Jesus. 2 Timothy 3:14-15

Since you have been born again, not of perishable seed but of imperishable, through the living and abiding word of God. 1 Peter 1:23

He answered them, "And why do you break the commandment of God for the sake of your tradition? For God commanded, 'Honor your father and your mother,' and, 'Whoever reviles father or mother must surely die.' But you say, 'If anyone tells his father or his mother, What you would have gained from me is given to God, he need not honor his father.' So for the sake of your tradition you have made void the word of God. You hypocrites! Well did Isaiah prophesy of you, when he said: 'This people honors me with their lips, but their heart is far from me; in vain do they worship me, teaching as doctrines the commandments of men.'" Matthew 15:3-9

I am astonished that you are so quickly deserting him who called you in the grace of Christ and are turning to a different gospel— not that there is another one, but there are some who trouble you and want to distort the gospel of Christ. But even if we or an angel from heaven should preach to you a gospel contrary to the one we preached to you, let him be accursed. As we have said before, so now I say again: If anyone is preaching to you a gospel contrary to the one you received, let him be accursed. Galatians 1:6-9

I warn everyone who hears the words of the prophecy of this book: if anyone adds to them, God will add to him the plagues described in this book, and if anyone takes away from the words of the book of this prophecy, God will take away his share in the tree of life and in the holy city, which are described in this book. Revelation 22:18-19

False Teachings Denied/Objections Answered

1. In the Council of Trent, the Roman Catholic Church taught that it held the unwritten apostolic teachings found in the Church's tradition and the apostolic teaching found in the New Testament with equal affection. This opens the door to adding all sorts of additions to the Faith that is found in the Scriptures. We see the results of this in the various Marian dogmas that were later affirmed in the Roman Church as well as the dogma of the Infallibility of the Pope. This repeated prohibition seeks to prevent such additions to the official teaching of any expression of the visible Church.

2. The contemporary views of doctrinal development which embrace progressive, continuing, normative revelation held by some in the non-Roman Western Churches, in which the Spirit is assumed to lead the Church beyond the Scripture into new truth, and even in contradiction to the teaching of Scripture, are clearly rejected by this repeated point in the Articles. Such views are clearly not Anglican, even when they appear in Anglican Churches.

Implications

This teaching point is an affirmation of the supreme authority and sufficiency of Scripture for salvation in Christ Jesus. It includes a solemn warning to avoid the tendency found in the history of the Church to add, as necessary to salvation, beliefs that are not stated to be necessary in the Scriptures.

Conclusion

The seven General Councils of the undivided Church, as well as the Councils referred to as General Councils by Rome, are worthy of our careful consideration and our grateful acceptance, when they are in accord with Holy Scripture. Councilliar teaching is intended to be explanatory of the teaching of the Scriptures and is to be judged by its faithfulness thereunto. Anglicans have traditionally accepted as biblical and binding the teaching of the first four General Councils and the dogmatic clarifications of their Christological teaching that are found in the next three. This describes the usual way in which Anglicans have affirmed the Councils of the undivided Church. All other so-called General Councils beyond those seven are actually local or denominational Councils and should be studied and appreciated as such.

ARTICLE 22

Of Purgatory

The Romish doctrine concerning Purgatory, Pardons, worshipping and adoration as well of Images as of Relics, and also Invocation of Saints, is a fond thing vainly invented, and grounded upon no warranty of Scripture; but rather repugnant to the word of God.

Introduction

If the Church has erred and added to her doctrine that which is contrary to Scripture, what doctrines might they be? Were these doctrines adequately dealt with by the Reformation and the Counterreformation?

In Article 21, we encountered for the third time the prohibition against adding anything as necessary to be believed for salvation other than what is found or implied in Holy Scripture. Now, here in Article 22, we find a list of doctrines and practices that have been added by the Church to be officially taught as doctrines of the Church. They are presently continued in the Roman Catholic Church and are held as necessary to be believed by the faithful, despite, according to Anglicans and other churches, their lack of any foundation in Scripture and being contrary to the teaching of Scripture (see Ratzinger 1994; Clarkson et al. 1995).

But is purgatory, and are these practices and their assumed doctrine, really condemned? Some Anglicans seek to avoid this conclusion by suggesting that Article 22 refers only to the pre-Reformation, Western understanding and use of these doctrines and practices. They hold that while the pre-Reformation distortions of these things are rejected by this Article, it is not the present Roman Catholic interpretation of purgatory with its attendant pardons, the veneration of the saints and relics, and the invocation of the saints that are rejected as vainly invented, lacking warrant of Scripture and repugnant to Scripture. Those pre-Reformation popular teachings and practices may well deserve to be rejected, but not the doctrine of purgatory and the attendant practices themselves. To apply such a criticism to the doctrines and practices themselves is too radical and would go too far in breaking with such long standing traditions in the Church. So have some Anglicans viewed this Article.

Several things militate against such an interpretation of the Article. First, the Article refers to the doctrines and practices as "Romish" as being taught and practiced by Rome.

Second, there was nothing particularly unique about the understanding and doctrine of purgatory and all of the practices listed in the Article at the time the Articles were being written. The teaching and exercise of these things had been more or less the same for some 900 years. And they continue the same in understanding and practice today.

Third, a key requirement in the Articles is that things must rest upon or be warranted by Scripture. But, it is the doctrines and practices themselves, and not any supposed crude popular views of them, that lack biblical warrant. When one considers the attempts to find biblical warrant for the traditional doctrine of purgatory and the accompanying practices it becomes evident that these are doctrines and practices hunting for a text and not the other way around.

Fourth, as one considers the practices in their essence, one can see that they are contrary to or repugnant to the Scriptures, as the following texts in the Biblical Foundations sections and the commentary will make clear.

Fifth, perhaps most convincing, is the fact that all of the churches of the Reformation rejected the traditional doctrine of purgatory and all of these practices. It was not just any abuses of these things but the things themselves that were rejected. Since the Church of England is part of this Reformation, it seems likely that in this Article they did what the other Churches of the Reformation did and continue to do.

We conclude, then, that it is the very theology and practice of purgatory and the practices listed and their presumed doctrines that are rejected by this Article and not just some abuses of them or a corrupt manner of teaching and practicing them. This Article does constitute a serious critique and break with long-standing doctrines and practices within the Church. There was need for the 16th Century Reformation.

The Teaching of Article 22

Here are the teaching points for this Article:

1. Purgatory with its attendant pardons is contrary to Scripture.

2. The worship and adoration of images and relics is contrary to Scripture.

3. The invocation of saints is contrary to Scripture.

1. Purgatory with its attendant pardons is contrary to Scripture

Explanation

The Roman Catholic Church taught and teaches that all who die in a state of grace will surely go to heaven and share in the final New Heaven and New Earth. However, since a person is not morally perfect at the time of death, he or she must undergo a cleansing or purgation in order to attain that holiness necessary for entering into glory or the beatific vision of God. This purgation is at the same time both a cleansing fire and a punishment for those venial, forgivable sins not already paid for by penance during the sinner's lifetime.

Purgatorial suffering, though temporary, is not to be taken lightly. St. Thomas of Aquinas taught that the least pain in purgatory is worse than the greatest pain on earth. Further, purgatorial suffering consists of long periods of hundreds and thousands of days. It was and is a truly horrible thing to contemplate, either for one's loved ones or for oneself.

However, a person's time in purgatory, undergoing such cleansing punishment and suffering, could be greatly shortened or even canceled by the application of the Church's Treasury of Merit, built up on the basis of the works of supererogation accumulated by the saints. These merits could be placed by the Church to the account of the believer suffering in purgatory. This amelioration or pardoning of days of suffering could also be achieved by Masses offered and prayers said on behalf of the dead as well as by visiting certain shrines and attending to certain relics of martyrs and saints, often as assigned by a confessor or local authorities. These, too, add to the basis for the pardons related to purgatory. Indeed, a plenary indulgence, the cancellation of all purgatorial suffering, can be granted under certain conditions.

This entire system of merit is rejected by this Article for several reasons. First, salvation is by grace and not by works of merit. The merit approach to dealing with our sins by temporal suffering and punishment in purgatory demeans the completeness and sufficiency of Christ's work on the Cross. The merit of Christ's sacrifice on the Cross is infinite and cannot be added to. Second, this arrangement involves the transfer of works of supererogation and Article 14, "Of Works of Supererogation," has already declared that works of supererogation are both impossible and unbiblical. Finally, third, in the Scriptures the saints who have died are depicted as in the nearer presence of Christ, not as suffering in purgatory.

In rejecting purgatorial punishment, Anglicans do not deny that a purgation is required for believing sinners to enter the nearer presence of Christ. While there is no dogma about this, it is generally held that this gracious work that completes sanctification takes place at the point of death by the agency of the Holy Spirit.

Biblical Foundations

For by grace you have been saved through faith. And this is not your own doing; it is the gift of God, not a result of works, so that no one may boast. For we are his workmanship, created in Christ Jesus for good works, which God prepared beforehand, that we should walk in them. Ephesians 2:8-10

Will any one of you who has a servant plowing or keeping sheep say to him when he has come in from the field, "Come at once and recline at table"? Will he not rather say to him, "Prepare supper for me, and dress properly, and serve me while I eat and drink, and afterward you will eat and drink"? Does he thank the servant because he did what was commanded? So you also, when you have done all that you were commanded, say, "We are unworthy servants; we have only done what was our duty." Luke 17:7-10

Two men went up into the temple to pray, one a Pharisee and the other a tax collector. The Pharisee, standing by himself, prayed thus: "God, I thank you that I am not like other men, extortioners, unjust, adulterers, or even like this tax collector. I fast twice a week; I give tithes of all that I get." But the tax collector, standing far off, would not even lift up his eyes to heaven, but beat his breast, saying, "God, be merciful to me, a sinner!" I tell you, this man went down to his house justified, rather than the other. For everyone who exalts himself will be humbled, but the one who humbles himself will be exalted. Luke 18:10-14

For I know that nothing good dwells in me, that is, in my flesh. For I have the desire to do what is right, but not the ability to carry it out. For I do not do the good I want, but the evil I do not want is what I keep on doing. Now if I do what I do not want, it is no longer I who do it, but sin that dwells within me. So I find it to be a law that when I want to do right, evil lies close at hand. For I delight in the law of God, in my inner being, but I see in my members another law waging war against the law of my mind and making me captive to the law of sin that dwells in my members. Wretched man that I am! Who will deliver me from this body of death? Thanks be to God through Jesus Christ our Lord! So then, I myself serve the law of God with my mind, but with my flesh I serve the law of sin. Romans 7:18-25

The poor man died and was carried by the angels to Abraham's side. The rich man also died and was buried, and in Hades, being in torment, he lifted up his eyes and saw Abraham far off and Lazarus at his side. Luke 16:22-23

And he said to him, "Truly, I say to you, today you will be with me in Paradise." Luke 23:43

And such were some of you. But you were washed, you were sanctified, you were justified in the name of the Lord Jesus Christ and by the Spirit of our God. 1 Corinthians 6:11

For to me to live is Christ, and to die is gain. If I am to live in the flesh, that means fruitful labor for me. Yet which I shall choose I cannot tell. I am hard pressed between the two. My desire is to depart and be with Christ, for that is far better. Philippians 1:21-23

But if we walk in the light, as he is in the light, we have fellowship with one another, and the blood of Jesus his Son cleanses us from all sin. 1 John 1:7

False Teachings Denied/Objections Answered

Since this Article is itself a rejection of false teaching there is no need for a special section on this topic.

Implications

We may trust completely in the sufficiency of the merits of Christ in His atoning work and the cleansing work of the Spirit done immediately at our death to cover us with the righteousness of Christ and to purge us so completely as to complete our sanctification. The result is that at our death we will enter into the closer presence of the Lord Himself. Has He not promised that He would meet us at the door of death and take us to be where He is (John 14:1-3)? Therefore, purgatory as a place of extended suffering and punishment for our venial sins has no place in biblical religion.

2. The worship of and adoration of images and relics is contrary to Scripture.
Explanation

There is every reason to thank God for the saints. We are to honor those who have preceded us and have set an example of godly life for us. This is particularly true of the martyrs who laid down their life for Christ. There is no reason, however, to find special merit in gazing upon or touching some portion of their clothing or body that continues to exist after their death. Nor are we to fall back into a religion of earning merit by such actions.

"Holiness" of character is not communicated simply by physical contact. Holiness of character is enabled through the means of grace and by the gracious work of the Spirit within believers. Holiness grows in the life of faith and obedience enabled by grace.

Also, there is no biblical reason to worship the saints or physical images of God. Worship is to be given to God alone. That is a fundamental biblical principle. With regard to icons, a longstanding controversy came to a head in the 8th and 9th centuries of the Church. The Second Council of Nicaea in A.D. 787, which is the Seventh Ecumenical Council, allowed their use and their veneration but refused to them the kind of worship (*latreia*) that is to be given to God alone. Anglicans have never officially bound themselves to the Seventh Council. Many wonder if the subtle difference between veneration and *latreia*, or divine worship, can actually be maintained in the human soul. The recurring teaching that icons have special powers indicates a recurring failure to maintain the distinction.

Can there be a proper use of icons? The Greek Orthodox tradition tends to describe icons as "Windows into Heaven," suggesting that they are not to be directly worshiped but are to be used as aids to the worship of God. With few exceptions, Protestant Churches have used stained glass and church ornamentation to do the same. The use of symbols to speak of God and our relationship with Him is all through the Scripture and the history of Christian worship. Moreover, the use of symbols is unavoidable, if we are to worship in accordance with the witness of Scripture. However, a clear line must be drawn between aids to worship and the Lord Whom we worship, Who has chosen to reveal Himself in Christ and in His Word written.

Yes, in principle icons can be used properly, provided that their character as aids to worship is duly respected. It is important also to note that, unlike the means of grace instituted by Christ, they are human helps and should not be seen as divinely instituted means of grace for the universal Church. They have never been widely used in the West.

Biblical Foundations

You shall not make for yourself a carved image, or any likeness of anything that is in heaven above, or that is in the earth beneath, or that is in the water under the earth. You shall not bow down to them or serve them, for I the Lord your God am a jealous God, visiting the iniquity of the fathers on the children to the third and the fourth generation of those who hate me. Exodus 20:4-5

Every man is stupid and without knowledge; every goldsmith is put to shame by his idols, for his images are false, and there is no breath in them. They are worthless, a work of delusion; at the time of their punishment they shall perish. Jeremiah 10:14-15

And Jesus answered him, "It is written, 'You shall worship the Lord your God, and him only shall you serve.'" Luke 4:8

Do not be idolaters as some of them were; as it is written, "The people sat down to eat and drink and rose up to play." 1 Corinthians 10:7

Therefore, my beloved, flee from idolatry. 1 Corinthians 10:14

Little children, keep yourselves from idols. 1 John 5:21

False Teachings Denied/Objections Answered

Since the Article and the explanation of this point just given is itself a rejection of false teaching there is no need for further comment in this section. Perhaps we should point out explicitly that the veneration of relics, particularly when indulgences are attached to such veneration, is excluded by this Article and the teaching of Scripture.

Implications

We are indeed surrounded by a great cloud of witnesses in the history of the Church. We do well to become familiar with the saints who have gone before us, with their lives and be encouraged by their witness. We tend to be too little aware of what God has done in them and through them. Reading the biographies of the saints can serve us well. It is right and proper to give God thanks for them. But their physical remains should not be thought to hold special powers or take the place of the Holy Spirit's work in our lives. The idea of using relics to earn merit before God is to be avoided.

We can, and no doubt should, use aids to worship the living God, but worship is to be given to the living, Triune God alone. Aids are to be used, God is to be worshiped.

3. The invocation of saints is contrary to Scripture.
Explanation

This Article clearly teaches that to address the saints who have died and entered into the nearer presence of the Lord and to ask them to intercede for us, i.e. to invoke the saints, is "a fond thing, vainly invented, grounded upon no warrant of Scripture and repugnant thereto." It would be hard to imagine clearer language. We mention this because invoking the saints is practiced not only in the Roman Catholic and Eastern Orthodox Churches but by many Anglicans as well. The bold language of this Article will come as a shock to many Anglicans.

Communicating with the dead in a variety of ways has been part of the practice of religion from the earliest known days of mankind. On the one hand, this practice is rooted in the love one has for the departed and in the reluctance to lose contact with the one who has died. On the other hand, communicating with the dead is also often rooted in fear and the desire to control the power of the spirits of the departed through religious ceremonies and shamans, because the dead are believed to still have influence in this life.

In biblical religion, all contact with the dead is forbidden. Saul increases his guilt in the sight of God by seeking the services of the "medium" of Endor (1 Samuel 28:7ff). In Deuteronomy 18:9-14, the people of Israel are forbidden to engage in the practices of consulting the dead that were prevalent in the Promised Land into which they were entering. In the New Testament, it is Christ Himself Who is the great intercessor. In the Old or New Testament, there is no example of anyone in God's people having permission or encouragement to pray to anyone but God.

Despite the biblical command against such, the practice of the invocation of the departed saints slowly grew in the Church. It was thought that, because of their godly lives and deaths, the saints had special influence with God. The invocation of the saints was and is sometimes justified by an appeal to the Communion of the Saints. The Scriptures never use the Communion of the Saints in that way. In the end, such invocation of the saints eclipsed invoking the intercession of Christ on the popular and practical level. To go directly to Christ was thought too presumptuous; better to speak to one of the departed saints who were in the nearer presence of Christ.

We can observe the application of the theology of this Article in the limitation of Saints' Days in *The Book of Common Prayer* to those saints that are mentioned in Scripture and then only to honor them but not to pray to them. The collect for All Saints' Day sets forth the Anglican view of our honoring the saints. It reads as follows:

> O ALMIGHTY God, who hast knit together thine elect in one communion and fellowship, in the mystical body of thy Son Christ our Lord; Grant us grace so to follow thy blessed Saints in all virtuous and godly living, that we may come to those unspeakable joys, which thou hast prepared for them that unfeignedly love thee; through Jesus Christ our Lord. Amen.

We have no biblical warrant for thinking that we can have or should have direct contact with those who have gone before. Nor does Scripture teach that they, who are finite and limited, have the capacity or the permission to listen to many persons addressing them from this side of the grave. We do well to follow the examples of the saints, to thank God for them, but not to seek to address them directly.

Since Christ is our Lord, Savior, and Intercessor, we may invoke Him instead of the saints.

Biblical Foundations

To the place where he had made an altar at the first. And there Abram called upon the name of the Lord. Genesis 13:4

When you come into the land that the Lord your God is giving you, you shall not learn to follow the abominable practices of those nations. There shall not be found among you anyone who burns his son or his daughter as an offering, anyone who practices divination or tells fortunes or interprets omens, or a sorcerer or a charmer or a medium or a wizard or a necromancer, for whoever does these things is an abomination to the Lord. And because of these abominations the Lord your God is driving them out before you. You shall be blameless before the Lord your God, for these nations, which you are about to dispossess, listen to fortune-tellers and to diviners. But as for you, the Lord your God has not allowed you to do this. Deuteronomy 18:9-14

Then Saul said to his servants, "Seek out for me a woman who is a medium, that I may go to her and inquire of her." And his servants said to him, "Behold, there is a medium at En-dor." So Saul disguised himself and put on other garments and went, he and two men with him. And they came to the woman by night. And he said, "Divine for me by a spirit and bring up for me whomever I shall name to you." The woman said to him, "Surely you know what Saul has done, how he has cut off the mediums and the necromancers from the land. Why then are you laying a trap for my life to bring about my death?" 1 Samuel 28:7-9

And call upon me in the day of trouble; I will deliver you, and you shall glorify me. Psalm 50:15

But when you pray, go into your room and shut the door and pray to your Father who is in secret. And your Father who sees in secret will reward you. Matthew 6:6

Pray then like this: "Our Father in heaven, hallowed be your name. Your kingdom come, your will be done, on earth as it is in heaven. Give us this day our daily bread, and forgive us our debts, as we also have forgiven our debtors. And lead us not into temptation, but deliver us from evil." Matthew 6:9-13

A devout man who feared God with all his household, gave alms generously to the people, and prayed continually to God. Acts 10:2

About midnight Paul and Silas were praying and singing hymns to God, and the prisoners were listening to them. Acts 16:25

False Teachings Denied/Objections Answered

1. As regards the "Communion of the Saints," we are right to believe that we are united with those who are in the nearer presence of the Lord in Christ. But being united with them in Him is not the same as having direct communication with them. The Scottish theologian Peter Taylor Forsyth, concerning his loved ones now with the Lord, said, "I can no longer speak with my loved ones, for they are in heaven. But I talk daily with the Captain of that place, and He assures me that they are well."

How blessed we are to be able to rely upon the intercession of Christ. If "the prayers of a righteous man availeth much," how much more does the intercession of Our Lord Who sits at the Right Hand of the Father avail!

2. When we ask fellow Christians here on earth, whom we are able to address, to pray for us and with us, we do so seeking their fellowship and encouragement in this matter, knowing that it pleases God to use us all in the ministry of intercession. And knowing also that our intercession is carried to the Father by the intercession of Christ Himself.

Implications

We are to pray only to God the Father, the Son and the Holy Spirit. We are to honor the saints and praise God for them, be encouraged and learn from them, but we are not to invoke them. Rather, in the Spirit, we invoke Christ Himself, Whose intercession avails for us and bears our intercessions to the Father.

Conclusion

In this Article, we have examined instances in which the Church has erred and abused its authority. We are aware that this Article will be something of an offense to a number of Anglicans as well as Roman and Eastern Catholics. However, the Church has no authority to practice or teach that which is not in accord with Holy Scripture and must reject that which contradicts the teaching of Scripture. As we have said before so we say again, there is need for further sustained ecumenical discussion in the light of Scripture on this and other matters.

ARTICLE 23

Of Ministering in the Congregation

It is not lawful for any man to take upon him the office of public preaching or ministering the sacraments in the congregation, before he be lawfully called and sent to execute the same. And those we ought to judge lawfully called and sent, which be chosen and called to this work by men who have public authority given unto them in the congregation to call and send ministers into the Lord's vineyard.

Introduction

Are Anglican clergy truly ordained? What about the clergy of the other Churches of the Reformation? Who is in position to answer that question? Does it matter?

During the 16th century Reformation, when churches were declaring their independence from the jurisdiction of the Bishop of Rome, the question arose as to who would have the authority to ordain and appoint clergy to the several congregations of the Church of England. If the Pope was no longer to do this, then who was to do it? Would it be the King? Could the congregations simply call whomever they wished? Could individuals simply announce they were divinely called to preach and preside in a given congregation and take the office by force of personality or by personal connections or by the influence of wealth? What was the order of the Church of England to be? This Article answers that question for Anglicans in a surprisingly general way.

The Teaching of Article 23
Here are the teaching points for this Article:

1. No one may assume the office of preaching and administering the sacraments unless that person be lawfully called and sent.

2. Only those who have had authority given to them in the Church to do so can lawfully call and send ordained ministers into the Church.

1. No one may assume the office of preaching and administering the sacraments unless that person be lawfully called and sent.

Explanation

First, we note that this teaching point assumes the existence of an ordained ministry. The Article speaks of "the office of public preaching or ministering the sacraments in the congregation"; it thereby presupposes an ordained ministry of Word and Sacrament in the Church that is called to exercise this ministry. We need, therefore, to make a brief comment on the ordained ministry in the visible Church.

The people of God have always had persons set apart in authorized orders of ministry connected with the worship of God. In the Old Testament, we find that God set apart Priests and Levites through His leader, Moses.

In the period of the Exile and in the inter-testamental period, when many of the Jews were isolated from the Temple, the institution of the synagogue arose. The synagogue functioned as a meeting place in which a local congregation could meet for worship. The worship consisted largely of Scripture, read and explained, and common prayers. The synagogue also served as a gathering place for civic affairs. It was governed by a board of Elders led by the Ruler of the Synagogue.

In the New Testament, we find Jesus, Himself sent by the Father, calling and sending the Apostles. The Apostles, after the Resurrection of Jesus, appointed Elders in each of the congregations that the Apostles had founded through the Gospel. In Jerusalem, Deacons were set apart with the approval of the Apostles. Later, we find both Elders/Presbyters and Deacons in the various congregations.

From this New Testament beginning, the three-fold ordained ministry of Bishops, Presbyters or Priests, and Deacons developed in the Church and became the universal pattern by the end of the 2nd century.

Initially, the New Testament Elders/Bishops/Presbyters were understood primarily as a pastors-teachers-leaders. In relation to pagan religions, the Church said we do not have an earthly altar or priest, for our High Priest and Altar is in heaven. However, after some 100 years or so, a change took place and the Church began to teach that we too have priests and altars, a better priesthood and a better altar. The doctrine developed that the Presbyters are Priests, successors in Christ of the Old Testament Priests who offered sacrifices for the people at the Altar of God. In the mid-third century in Africa, the martyr Bishop Cyprian was the first to speak in this fashion and a fundamental change in perspective took place and became the teaching of the Church in both the East and the West. In this development, the ministry of Bishops and Presbyters or Priests was viewed in sacerdotal perspective, that is, that the Bishop and Priest were intermediaries between God and the people, through whom Christ at the Lord's Supper offered Himself bloodlessly for merit in the sacrifice of the Mass or Eucharist. This view persisted unchallenged until the 16th century Reformation.

At the Reformation of the 16th century, the various churches moved in different directions concerning the ordained ministry.

The Anglicans retained the three-fold ministry in historic succession, but with an understanding that these ministries were not sacerdotal. The New Testament never speaks of the ordained ministry in sacerdotal terms. This was clearly an intentional break with Old Testament usage and was due to the fact that Christ had made the one and final meritorious or atoning sacrifice on the Cross. That sacrifice was not to be repeated, as Article 31 makes clear. Rather, Bishops and Presbyters had as their primary responsibilities the public ministry of preaching and teaching the Word of God, of administering the Sacraments of the Gospel which centered in and recalled the atoning and completed sacrifice of Christ, of enabling the laity in their ministries, and of giving pastoral care and oversight to the congregations where they served. We will give more attention to the Anglican view of the ordained ministry in the discussion of Article 36, which concerns the Ordinal (see also Appendix C).

The Lutheran Church kept the three-fold ministry in some of its churches, particularly in Scandinavia. However, the Lutherans usually understood the local Pastor to combine in himself the Episcopal and Priestly offices, as is found in the New Testament period. In their view, there is really only one pastoral office of Word and Sacrament and oversight. This view is based on the fact that in the New Testament "Elder" or "Presbyter" and "Bishop" or "Overseer" are terms used interchangeably to refer to the same persons or order of ministry. They believe that the distinction between Bishop and Presbyter is a post-Canonical development, whereas Anglicans see the beginnings of the distinct episcopate within the New Testament. In addition, in many parts of Europe, the Bishops rejected the Reformation and were not available to the Lutheran churches. The result is that some Lutheran

Churches have Bishops, Pastors, and Deacons, and some have no Bishops at all. Generally, Lutherans are concerned only that the pastoral office be maintained and see its form as a matter that is not mandated by God and is therefore open to a variety of forms.

The Reformed or Presbyterian Churches broke with tradition and reshaped the ordained ministry around the office of Presbyter or Elder. They distinguish between the ruling Elders of the congregation who comprise the Board of Elders and the Teaching Elder or Pastor who is the preacher, teacher, and pastor, and who generally administers the sacraments of the Gospel. He or she shares in the oversight of the congregation with Board of Elders.

Some of the Anabaptists held that there was no need for being sent to minister in the congregation. They held that the individual's sense of inner call from God gave to the individual the right and authority to exercise the ministry of preaching, administering the sacraments, and overseeing the congregation, should the congregation recognize and receive him in such a ministry.

Even more extreme were some groups, such as the Quakers, who denied any place for an ordained ministry at all. In the case of the Quakers, they also denied that the sacraments of the Gospel, as well as that the Canonical Scriptures were objective, were means of grace. Everything rested upon the inner work of the Spirit Who was at work in each believer and in the congregation as a whole.

As this brief survey shows, the Anglicans were the most conservative of the churches that participated in the Reformation with regard to the ordained ministry, keeping both its traditional form and historic continuity. They did, however, reform the understanding of the ordained ministry in the light of Scripture, returning to a more pastoral and non-sacerdotal understanding.

Second, the Article asserts that the matter of sending ministers must be done in an orderly or lawful manner. Only persons "lawfully called and sent" may enter the public ministry of Word and Sacrament. Why did Anglicans insist on persons being lawfully called and sent? There are several reasons for this to be done lawfully:

1. Anglicans seek to be biblical and they see in the Holy Scriptures God's institution of an officially recognized ordered ministry, as we have briefly outlined above. It is God's will that there be an ordained ministry in the Church.

2. Since God is a God of order, all is to be done officially and in an orderly, accepted manner in the Church. This concern for recognition and orderly procedure is not unique to the Church, for all communities, sacred or secular, require accepted and orderly ways of designating ministry and leadership in their life and work.

3. The chief means of grace, the preaching and teaching of the Word of God, the administration of the sacraments of the Gospel, and the oversight of the Church are far too important for the life and work of the Church to be left to unauthorized, unexamined, and unprepared persons to minister.

4. Anglicans, as part of the Church Catholic, are appreciative of the work of the Spirit in the developing life of the Church and hence of the developed traditional institutions and patterns of the Church, as long these are compatible with the Holy Scriptures and are effective for the Church's life, ministry and mission. The traditional pattern of lawfully or officially calling and sending ordained ministers fits these criteria.

5. God calls persons to this ministry. The Article refers to these persons being both "called and sent." When the Article speaks of "called" it has several aspects in mind:

A. A person is called into ordained ministry in at least three senses. First, the Article assumes that an inner call by God has been discerned by the individual seeking ordination. This is clear from the Anglican rites for ordination in which the ordinand is asked explicitly, "Do you believe that you are called by God to this ministry?" to which the ordinand must answer, "Yes."

Second, "called" also has an external aspect, and the chief emphasis of this Article falls upon the external aspect of "call." This external aspect of a call to ordained ministry is the Church's part. It includes both the judgment of the Church upon the validity of the individual ordinand's sense of call and readiness for ministry. It also includes the Church's need for additional ordained ministers, for calling is directly linked to ordination and the sending of the ordained to a place to minister.

The Church's judgment involves an examination of the person's readiness in several areas: in theological knowledge, gifts for ministry, and personal piety and moral integrity. The Church completes the call by an act of ordination, which takes place when the Church is satisfied that it sees a genuine call from God in this person, who is also seen to be ready to begin to exercise an ordained ministry in the life and work of the Church and when the Church has a place to send the ordinand once ordained.

There is a third sense in which we use "called" in relation to the ordained ministry today. This third sense may be implied in this Article. It refers to the congregation's invitation of an individual, about to be or already ordained, to take up a ministry within the congregation.

B. "Sent" is the other concept that is mentioned. "Sent" refers to a person who is about to be or already is ordained, being sent into a particular congregation or institution to minister by those in the Church who have that authority. This is treated under the next teaching point of this Article, which treats of the authority to ordain and send.

Biblical Foundations
Priests and Levites
Then bring near to you Aaron your brother, and his sons with him, from among the people of Israel, to serve me

as priests—*Aaron and Aaron's sons, Nadab and Abihu, Eleazar and Ithamar.* Exodus 28:1

And the Lord spoke to Moses, saying, "Bring the tribe of Levi near, and set them before Aaron the priest, that they may minister to him. They shall keep guard over him and over the whole congregation before the tent of meeting, as they minister at the tabernacle." Numbers 3:5-7

Synagogue

Then came one of the rulers of the synagogue, Jairus by name, and seeing him, he fell at his feet. Mark 5:22

Jesus and the Twelve

Sanctify them in the truth; your word is truth. As you sent me into the world, so I have sent them into the world. John 17:17-18

These twelve Jesus sent out, instructing them, "Go nowhere among the Gentiles and enter no town of the Samaritans." Matthew 10:5

Whoever receives you receives me, and whoever receives me receives him who sent me. Matthew 10:40

Apostles and Elders

And when they had appointed elders for them in every church, with prayer and fasting they committed them to the Lord in whom they had believed. Acts 14:23

Deacons

Paul and Timothy, servants of Christ Jesus, To all the saints in Christ Jesus who are at Philippi, with the overseers and deacons. Philippians 1:1

Spiritual Qualifications

You then, my child, be strengthened by the grace that is in Christ Jesus, and what you have heard from me in the presence of many witnesses entrust to faithful men who will be able to teach others also. 2 Timothy 2:1-2

External Call
And when they had appointed elders for them in every church, with prayer and fasting they committed them to the Lord in whom they had believed. Acts 14:23

False Teachings Denied/Objections Answered
1. We have mentioned above that some Christian bodies have decided that there is no need for an ordained ministry. We think of the Quaker meeting, in which the entire congregation sits in silence until the Spirit moves someone to make a contribution. There is no written liturgy, no lectionary, and no ordained ministry. While there is a general pattern, the worship and instruction is all spontaneous under the leadership of the Spirit. While this Article does not bar Anglicans from including such additional services in the life of a congregation, or even including spaces of silence and openness to the Spirit within the liturgy, this Article does expect that a congregation will have a duly ordained and sent minister exercising pastoral care and oversight in the congregation and its worship. The ordained minister would be serving under the pastoral care and oversight of a Bishop. Anglicans hold that communities that have rejected all forms of ordained ministry have strayed from God's provision and will.

2. It is sometimes objected by some that institutional ordinations and authorized placements kill the Spirit. Spontaneity alone, they say, is the proper vehicle for the Spirit of God. To this, it must be objected that while institutional arrangements may sometimes quench the Spirit, not all that is spontaneous is of the Spirit of God and that not all official, institutional sending inhibits the Spirit; those who are ordained and serving in the offices of the Church are intended to be, can be, and often are instruments of the Spirit.

3. Some Church bodies, or at least some of their theologians, have taught that the external call alone is all that really matters. Calling is not primarily a matter of an inner sense of being called by God into the ordained ministry. The inner sense may be utterly lacking when God calls through the Church, and is, in any case, far too subjective to be relied upon. It is better to let all rest upon the call of the Church, as God's instrument, by which He calls the individual. So the argument goes.

There is some truth in that view, and it may be the case that the external call may be that which comes first to an individual; however, it would appear that the individual would personally have to see the hand of God in the call of the Church in order to consent to the call. Therefore, an inner call is both unavoidable and essential. Both ultimately are involved and it is best if both are strong and clear.

4. The Roman Catholic Church has judged the ordained ministries of the Churches of the Reformation to be invalid. This is held by Rome to be true of the Anglican ministry even though it has kept the three-fold ministry in historic succession with the pre-Reformation ministry. Why is this so? Rome holds that all of these ministries, including the Anglican ordained ministries, have a common and fundamental lack. The lack is that none of them intend to set men apart through whom Christ will offer Himself to the Father bloodlessly for merit in the sacrifice of the Mass or Lord's Supper.

In this judgment, Rome is accurate. None of the churches do so intend. However, the point that all of the Churches of the Reformation make to Rome is that they do not ordain persons to such a sacrificing ministry, precisely in order to honor Christ, in faithfulness to His once for all sacrifice on the Cross. They do not do so because the Apostolic Scriptures do not allow it. And therefore, they would add, Rome should not do so either. (This matter is discussed in Articles 15, 31 and most fully in Article 36.) Here again we see the need for ecumenical conversation.

Implications

The chief implication is that no one who is not properly ordained and sent is to accept or be permitted to exercise the public ministry of Word and Sacrament in the Church.

Other implications are that there must be clear standards for ordination in the Church and someone or a group in the Church must be given the responsibility to discern the call and readiness of persons for ordination and finally to ordain and send such persons when they are ready and when the Church needs them.

2. Only those who have had authority given to them in the Church to do so can lawfully call and send ordained ministers into the Church.

Explanation

It is in this teaching point that we find a "surprising generality" in this 23rd Article. As we noted above, the Church must ordain and send an individual into a specific place of ministry. Who is to do this? Both the congregation and the person being sent need to know that this has been done lawfully, in a manner recognized by the Church, and that someone is ultimately accountable for that placement.

The answer given by Anglicans to the questions concerning the authority both for ordination and for sending is the Bishop of the Diocese. The Bishop is the one who ultimately holds the authority. He is the one who finally authorizes and does both the ordination and the sending and is therefore the one accountable for overseeing the relationship between the ordained minister and the congregation. If that is the case, why did this Article not simply say so? Instead, it uses the general term "by men who have public authority given unto them in the Congregation to call and send Ministers into the Lord's vineyard."

The answer to this is related to the nature of the visible Church and to Anglican ecumenical concern. In defining the visible Church in Article 19, no mention is made of any specific form of ordained ministry. Further, Anglicans were in ecumenical relations with the other Churches of the Reformation. Those shaping the Articles knew that the Lutherans and Reformed Churches had no bishops over many of their churches, so they wished to state the principle concerning authority for ordination and sending in general terms so as to include as far as possible the patterns of ordained ministry and the ordaining and sending arrangements of all the Churches of the Reformation. They viewed the other Churches of the Reformation as expressions of the One Holy, Catholic, and Apostolic Church, even though they did not retain the traditional three-fold order in historic succession. In addition, they did not want to give grounds to any who might think that Anglicans, because we have retained the traditional ordained ministry in historic succession, teach or ought to teach that those Churches of the Reformation that had adopted other patterns of ordained ministry were no longer expressions of the visible Church.

This Anglican ecumenical concern, however, is not to imply that all arrangements of ordained ministry are equal in Anglican eyes or that the departure from the historic order of ministry is of little significance. (See Article 36.)

In addition the phrase, "and those we ought to judge lawfully called and sent," has another significance or application altogether. It makes it clear that only those who are called and sent by the recognized authority in the Church are to be permitted to serve in a given or particular congregation or place of ministry. This shuts the door to unauthorized, ordained ministers who by force of personality or upon some other ground would seek to intrude themselves upon the faithful. Clear, recognized public authority to ordain and send allows for proper order, discernment, discipline, and oversight in ordained ministry, without which there could be chaos in the life of the Church.

Biblical Foundations

And when they had appointed elders for them in every church, with prayer and fasting they committed them to the Lord in whom they had believed. Acts 14:23

False Teachings Denied/Objections Answered

1. What of Congregationalism? What are Anglicans to think of those congregations or local churches that would adopt a congregational polity, who say we need no authority over us and need no one to send us ordained ministers?

We note: first, that St. Paul insists that his call and his being sent as an Apostle to the Gentiles was not subjective but was by the Risen Lord in a Resurrection appearance, given out of due time. He thereby models and underlines the importance of ministers of the Gospel having both an internal and external aspect to their call and in their being sent by one having the authority to send. Paul was not a self-based volunteer.

Second, we find that congregations in the New Testament normally had elders and recognized apostolic authority over them. Congregations were devoted to the Apostles' teaching, whether heard in person, by memory, or in and through apostolic writings and visitations, or through their delegates.

Third, we see that Timothy and Titus were apostolic delegates who exercised a ministry of oversight over several churches and their elders. Anglicans find here the beginning and foreshadowing of the later episcopate with the authority of oversight, ordaining and sending and as serving as the link to the other Bishops of the Church by regional meetings and eventually by Councils.

Therefore it seems to Anglicans that a careful reading of Holy Scripture points toward the traditional patterns for lawfully calling and sending clergy to minister and not in the direction of congregationalism.

2. Some deny that a congregation can really be a visible church if it does not have bishops. They hold that Anglicans err in recognizing the Churches of the Reformation to be visible churches and in having ecumenical relations with them, since they have departed from the historic pattern of the ordained ministry in historic succession. To this we reply: first, that there are similar situations in the New Testament. When the Apostle Paul wrote to the congregations in Rome there had been no Apostle over them, yet they had grown in size and maturity. As the Apostle to the Gentiles, the Apostle Paul seeks to establish his authority in relation to them and to use them as a base for his wider travels. At no point, however, did he deny that they constituted a visible church of the Lord from their beginning, and he addressed them as such. Second, we note that in Article 19, which treats of the marks of a visible church, no particular form of ecclesiastical ministry and oversight is mentioned. And third, this ecumenical openness is characteristic of the practice of Anglicans both at the time of the Reformation and subsequently in the language of the Lambeth Conferences in which Anglicans refer to the Churches of the Reformation as Churches or expressions of the Church Catholic.

Implications and Conclusion

The chief implication is that congregations are not to receive ordained ministers who are not sent to them by the authority of those in the Church having that authority.

The other implication of this Article is that churches are to recognize and exercise ecumenical sharing in mission, as far as possible, with other visible churches, even when the arrangements concerning ordination differ, assuming that the conditions of a visible church as indicated in Article 19 are met.

This is not to be understood to imply that Anglicans believe all forms of ordained ministry are matters indifferent.

ARTICLE 24

Of Speaking in the Congregation in such a Tongue as the People Understandeth

It is a thing plainly repugnant to the word of God and the custom of the primitive Church, to have public prayer in the Church, or to minister the sacraments in a tongue not understanded of the people.

Introduction

Is worship defined in Scripture? Does worship require understanding, or is it primarily a matter of mood or subliminal awareness? Anglicans are noted for their concern for corporate worship. What do they believe about it?

Worship is central in the Christian life. It is to be wholehearted and the whole person is to be involved. The Apostle Paul refers to it as our *logikein*, or reasoning worship (Romans 12:1).

What was the need for this Article? Why was it written? At the time when these Articles were being written, the Mass was the chief service of corporate worship in the congregations of the West and it was said in Latin. The vast majority of the people did not read or understand Latin. Lacking both a solid grasp of the comfort of the Gospel and not being able to comprehend the Gospel to the extent it is embedded in the Latin of the Mass, many people, as a result, did not receive the sacrament. This non-communicating practice led to the use of more private devotions during the Mass, usually the saying of the rosary. The high point of the Mass or Eucharist, for the laity and even the clergy, shifted from communicating or receiving the consecrated elements as the gift of and communion with the crucified, risen, and present Lord, to observing the visible action of the Priest in the elevation of the miraculously transubstantiated host. Observation replaced sacramental communion. In addition, the Word was often not preached at the Mass or if preached it was often very brief, poorly done, and with dubious content.

The result was that the use of Latin, after it was no longer understood by the congregation, greatly contributed to a loss of the proper use of the Eucharist. It also contributed to a loss of the transforming impact of the Word of God. The Reformers felt it was time to address this practice in a principled manner.

The Teaching of Article 24

Here is the teaching point for this Article:

1. It is contrary to the Word of God written and the practice of the early Church to have common worship in a language the people cannot understand.

Explanation

There are three primary reasons for conducting the corporate worship of the Church in the common tongue.

The first reason is that understanding is inherent in and foundational to the Christian Faith. Understanding is not universally prized in all religions. There are religions that stress mystical intuition and felt inner experience to the exclusion of the mind. These religions ignore teaching or doctrine altogether and seek to awaken a sense of awe and wonder by their ritual practices. In some of the Eastern mystic religions all that we can see and know is regarded as "Maya" – an illusion and not worthy of our serious attention. Even the individual self is an illusion. All is one. All is God and God is all. This ineffable, wordless monism is utterly foreign to the biblical revelation and Christian Faith.

Even monotheistic Islam does not have the passion for intelligible communication that the Christian Faith does.

The contrast is illustrated in the slogan: "The language of Islam is Arabic while the language of Christianity is translation." It could hardly be other than "translation" for a Faith that centers in the Incarnation of the Word of God through whom the World was made. The Word became incarnate in Jesus Christ to express Himself in human terms in order to be known and understood. Jesus taught publicly. He acted meaningfully, carrying out the Father's purpose and plan. He died intentionally and rose in fulfillment of revealed divine promises. He sent His Apostles to go forth into the whole world to preach, teach and heal. All of this takes clear communication very seriously.

Consequently, while Islam tells us that only if we learn Arabic can we understand the Koran, Christianity seeks to translate the Scriptures into every language and dialect in the world, so that all may read, mark, learn, and inwardly digest the revelation of God and the good news of the Gospel.

While it is true that total comprehension of God is impossible for human beings and that mystery remains in our knowledge of God and His ways, nonetheless, understanding what is revealed lies at the heart of the Christian Faith.

Others have missed the importance of understanding in Christianity by stressing the moral dimensions of Christian Faith to the neglect of its doctrinal teaching about God and the Gospel. This "ethical" Christianity has been given the name, *Undogmatishes Christentum,* "non-dogmatic Christianity," or doctrine-less Christianity. Such a view of Christianity cannot appeal to the Old or New Testaments, for both Testaments ground ethics in the nature of God and in what He has said and done for us in Creation and in salvation history.

Given the rational character of God and His revelation in Christ, the Christian act of believing or faith involves the mind. Believing in Christ includes: 1) understanding what God has revealed in the Gospel, 2) assent to its truth, and 3) heart-felt repentant trust in the Lord who offers us His complete forgiveness, the Holy Spirit, and eternal life in His Son through the Gospel. Through this trust in Christ, the Lord gives us His Spirit to assure us of our forgiveness and to transform us and set us increasingly free from the bondage of sin. By His grace, we turn from ungodly living and walk in His ways in the fellowship of His Church and in the mission of the Lord to the world.

There is, therefore, a balance and participation of the whole person in believing in Christ. All of our human nature is involved: our mind, will, emotions, and senses. While it is not only a matter of understanding, still the Christian faith involves understanding at its heart. The Christian grows in understanding in order to mature and as we mature in Christ.

The importance of understanding is further reflected in the fact that the Church treasures theology and scholarship to a high degree. Judaism, its parent Faith, has never embraced systematic theology as has the Church. From its inception to the present, the Church has invested and continues to invest a large amount of its energy in teaching the faithful and preparing its members to go forth to share the Gospel with the world. It refers to its endeavors of thought as "Faith seeking understanding." That is, theology seeks a greater understanding of the riches found in God's revelation in Scripture and seeks to see how all things in Scripture, creation and history fit together in Christ. Therefore, we worship with the mind as well as witnessing in word and deeds.

A second reason for "worshiping in a tongue understanded of the people" is the example of the Church recorded in Scripture. In the Bible we see that biblical teaching, worship, and witnessing is generally done in the common language. What is true of the nature of Christian Faith is naturally expressed in the practice of the Church. From the institution of the Tabernacle to the building of the Temple, worship in the Old Testament was in the common tongue of the people. The Prophets and Priests spoke and taught in the language of the people.

It is true that after the Exile, at the return of Israel to Jerusalem, there was need for translators and interpreters when the Law was read to the people, because not all who returned understood the Hebrew of the Scriptures. But the very fact that such translation and interpretation was given indicates the continuing concern for understanding. So, too, does the translation of the Old Testament into Greek in the Septuagint for the use of Greek-speaking congregations located outside of Israel.

In the New Testament Jesus taught in the language of the people and worship in the congregations founded by the Apostles was in a language understood by the members. The lengthy treatment by the Apostle Paul in 1 Corinthians 12-14 which concerns the building up of the congregation by speaking in a tongue "understood of the people" is a case in point. The exhortation of the Apostle Peter to all of us to be ready to give a reason for the hope that is within us makes the same point concerning witnessing to the unbeliever.

A third reason for worshiping in the common tongue is that the early Church continued the biblical practice and worshiped and taught in the language of the people. We see this deep concern for understanding in the various liturgies of the early Church and the Church of the Fathers; they were in the local common tongue. This is true also for the catechetical instruction given by the Bishops of the Early Church and Patristic Church, who taught in the language of those in their diocese whom they were addressing.

In summary, worshiping in a common tongue simply expresses the nature of the Christian Faith. When the passion for "understanding" weakens in visible churches, a sacred language of the liturgy emerges. Such a development is generally not a good one.

Biblical Foundations

In the beginning was the Word, and the Word was with God, and the Word was God. He was in the beginning with God. All things were made through him, and without him was not any thing made that was made. John 1:1-3

No one has ever seen God; the only God, who is at the Father's side, he has made him known. John 1:18

Also Jeshua, Bani, Sherebiah, Jamin, Akkub, Shabbethai, Hodiah, Maaseiah, Kelita, Azariah, Jozabad, Hanan, Pelaiah, the Levites, helped the people to understand the Law, while the people remained in their places. They read from the book, from the Law of God, clearly, and they gave the sense, so that the people understood the reading. Nehemiah 8:7-8

I appeal to you therefore, brothers, by the mercies of God, to present your bodies as a living sacrifice, holy and acceptable to God, which is your spiritual worship. Do not be conformed to this world, but be transformed by the renewal of your mind, that by testing you may discern what is the will of God, what is good and acceptable and perfect. Romans 12:1-2

Nevertheless, in church I would rather speak five words with my mind in order to instruct others, than ten thousand words in a tongue. 1 Corinthians 14:19

False Teaching Denied/Objections Answered

1. For many years, the Church in the West taught that translations are risky and that the unlearned laity can easily misinterpret the Scripture. It was thought that it is better to leave the Scriptures and liturgy in the traditional Latin and let the Priests interpret in teaching and in sermons. This led to a situation that is similar to what happened in the return of the exiles to Jerusalem, where interpreters were needed. We note that, when this Article was being written, the Council of Trent had anathematized all those who said that the Church should celebrate the Mass in the common tongue (Session 22, Canon 9).

There is some truth in this caution about translations. Some of the newer translations of both the Scriptures and the newer liturgies reflect such an influence from contemporary theological currents as to weaken their faithfulness to Scripture. Moreover, there is a great advantage in having one official translation of the Scriptures and a common liturgy in a language with which all of the members of the Church are familiar. Further, the Church does produce biblical commentaries and study Bibles with notes that can help make the Church's teaching clear. Also, the Church can authorize liturgical aids that place the Latin liturgy and the common language of the people side by side so that the laity can understand as they follow along. The people will soon become familiar with the Latin of the liturgy.

This supplementing of a Latin or ethnic liturgy seems to apply to the liturgy but is less persuasive with regard to a refusal to translate the Scriptures. In either case, the primary concern of the Church should be to have a Bible translation and a liturgy that is faithful to Scripture, and to make available sufficient aids that will enable the laity to come to a true understanding and growing appreciation of their content. Translation in one form or another in order to be "understanded by the people" must remain central.

2. The phrase "a language understood of the people" also applies to another matter that is frequently debated in the present. It is the tension that arises between the mandate of the Church to reach out to the unchurched, for whom the language and terminology of Scripture and the traditional liturgy in the Church are increasingly unfamiliar on the one hand, and the mandate of the Church to help the faithful believers mature in the faith and to grow in their understanding of the Scripture through study and worship on the other. If we worship in a language already understood by the unchurched, we often weaken the depth, riches, and faithfulness of the language of the traditional liturgy, and if we abide by the traditional language of the

liturgy we make contact difficult with those unchurched persons who might be persuaded to attend one of the services. It is a tension not easily resolved.

Perhaps it is important to say that worship is not primarily an act of evangelism and that we should let the liturgy attend to its primary purposes and find other ways and means for outreach, instruction and evangelism in a culturally more accessible language, such as is done in courses such as *Alpha* or *Christianity Explained*. In addition, there are a number of ways for the Church to help make the traditional liturgical worship of the Church easier for new-comers without changing the language and content of the liturgy itself. For example, such a simple thing as a clear service sheet with helpful instructions can go a long way toward that goal. Of course, a warm reception of the "visitors" is essential.

Implications and Conclusion

Understanding is central to saving faith, the act of believing in Christ. Worship is therefore to be entered into with understanding. This was the practice of the Early Church and the Church of the Fathers. It should be our practice as well. Therefore, the liturgy and the worship of the Church should be in the language understood by the members of the Church. This, however, need not mean a wholesale abandonment of the riches, beauty and depth of the traditional vocabulary of the liturgy. The long history of the Anglican *Book of Common Prayer*, with just minor changes from 1662 to the present, remains an outstanding testimony that this can be done, and calls us to make its riches available to all.

If a Church determines to worship in a liturgical language not understood by the people, such as is done by the Eastern Churches and Rome, it behooves the Church to have available copies of the liturgy with translations side by side, and to preach in the common tongue.

ARTICLE 25

Of the Sacraments

Sacraments ordained of Christ be not only badges or tokens of Christian men's profession, but rather they be certain sure witnesses and effectual signs of grace and God's good will towards us, by the which He doth work invisibly in us, and doth not only quicken, but also strengthen and confirm, our faith in Him.

There are two Sacraments ordained of Christ our Lord in the Gospel, that is to say, Baptism and the Supper of the Lord.

Those five commonly called Sacraments, that is to say, Confirmation, Penance, Orders, Matrimony, and Extreme Unction, are not to be counted for Sacraments of the Gospel, being such as have grown partly of the corrupt following of the Apostles, partly are states of life allowed in the Scriptures; but yet have not the like nature of Sacraments with Baptism and the Lord's Supper, for that they have not any visible sign or ceremony ordained of God.

The Sacraments were not ordained of Christ to be gazed upon or to be carried about, but that we should duly use them. And in such only as worthily receive the same, have they a wholesome effect or operation: but they that receive them unworthily, purchase to themselves damnation, as Saint Paul saith.

Introduction

What exactly are sacraments? Why are they necessary? Can we replace their physical elements or signs with more modern elements that we use in every day life? Why have they become such matters of contention between churches?

This 25th Article begins a series of seven Articles (25 to 31) that concern the sacraments of the Gospel. There is inescapable mystery involved with the sacraments, as well as a good bit of ignorance and confusion about them, not to mention a good deal of theological argumentation. This Article seeks to dispel the ignorance and confusion, to clarify the argumentation, to help us appreciate the mystery, and to help prepare us to participate in the sacraments more fully and with greater understanding.

These seven Articles concerning the sacraments are placed in Section Four, a section concerned with the Church, because: 1) the sacraments are administered by the Church in Christ's name; 2) through the sacraments God admits members into the Church and nourishes them; and 3) while the sacraments are more, they are also visible signs of one's membership in the Church, for both the other members and the world to see.

In the Anglican tradition, which treasures both "Word and Sacrament," the sacraments are administered with the Word read and preached. They are usually administered to the whole congregation, since the sacraments are by nature corporate events.

What exactly is a "sacrament"? The term "sacrament" is actually an unusual word. The term is of obscure origin. It is usually thought to take its meaning from the cultural use of the word to refer to a Roman soldier's oath of loyalty to his unit and commander. It found its way into Western theology through the Latin translation of the Bible by Ambrose in which he translated the Greek *mysterion* (mystery) into Latin *sacramentum*. The word *mysterion* referred to many things in the Eastern Church including the sacraments of the Gospel. So "sacrament" became the Western word for the mysteries of Baptism and the Lord's Supper and the five sacramental acts of confirmation, marriage, ordination, reconciliation of a sinner, and anointing for burial. Because of this obscure path, the word itself does not tell us a great deal about the nature of the sacraments except that they involve our commitment and mystery in our relationship with God in Christ.

We need, therefore, a more specific statement of what the Church means by the term. As Anglicans, we find an excellent, brief definition in the Catechism of the 1662 *Book of Common Prayer*. It reads as follows:

Question: What meanest thou by this word Sacrament?
Answer: I mean an outward and visible sign of an inward and spiritual grace given unto us, ordained by Christ himself, as a means whereby we receive the same, and a pledge to assure us thereof.

We will treat most of the aspects of this definition in the teaching points below. At this point we want to note that this Anglican definition defines the sacraments of the Gospel as one of the means of grace. Since the sacraments are means of God's grace, there are three important implications that deserve brief comment:

The first implication is that, since the sacraments are means of God's grace, it is God Who is the chief actor in the sacraments and not we. Grace, in and through the sacraments, is His gift, His favor shown to us. As a means of saving grace, the sacraments are instruments of His undeserved favor and rescue shown to us who deserve quite the opposite for having rejected His sovereign authority over us and His love of us.

That God in Christ by His Spirit is the chief actor in the sacraments is also emphasized by the fact that the sacraments are administered at the command and in the name of Christ. He is the giver in and through the sacrament.

Anyone who does not begin with the fact that in the sacraments it is God in Christ Who is the initiator and giver will never be able to appreciate the full meaning and significance of the sacraments.

Since God in Christ is the chief celebrant and the Lord of the sacrament, it follows that we do not cause Him to act. In fact, God has the priority and preeminence in all of the means of grace and not just in the sacraments of the Gospel. For example, having a sermon touch you deeply, open your heart to the Lord, and illumine your mind, is not something the preacher or you did. It is the gift of God. It is the same with the sacraments of the Gospel as means of grace.

The second implication is that, as means of grace, the sacraments are highly personal and relational. They are not mechanical and impersonal. Grace is the gift of God's love and favor and God's favor is to be received by us sinners in repentance, faith, gratitude and humility in response to God. Celebrating a sacrament is not a matter of merely going through a ritual. "This people honors me with their lips, but their heart is far from me" (Mark 7:6). Even though the chief actor in the sacrament is God, we have our part to play, our subordinate and enabled, personal participation.

The third implication is that a "means" of a thing is not the same thing as that of which it is the means. The telephone is a means for us to converse, but the telephone is neither the speaker nor listener nor the conversation. So too the sacraments have their function or efficacy only as instruments or as means of a vital relationship between God and His people. As previously stated, they are relational and communal by nature. The sacraments are misused when abstracted from that relational context and misunderstood when viewed as things in themselves apart from the relationship of which they are a means.

The Teaching of Article 25

Here are the teaching points for this Article:

1. Four characteristics of the Sacraments of the Gospel are listed in this Article.

2. Two Sacraments of the Gospel and the Five Sacramental Acts are generally accepted by the visible Churches.

3. The right use of the sacraments is by repentant faith which alone receives a beneficial effect.

1. Four characteristics of the Sacraments of the Gospel are listed in this Article.
Explanation

This Article lists four characteristics of the sacraments of the Gospel. They are:
 1. "Ordained by Christ"
 2. "Badges or tokens of Christian men's profession"
 3. "Certain and sure witnesses"
 4. "Effectual signs of grace and God's good will towards us by which he doth work invisibly in us and doth not only quicken, but also strengthen and confirm our faith in him."

We will discuss these characteristics in order.

 1. Sacraments of the Gospel are "ordained by Christ."

The sacraments were instituted by Christ. Therefore by definition, any thing or event that was not expressly instituted by Christ is not a sacrament of the Gospel. Christ instituted the sacrament of Holy Baptism in the Great Commission with the words: "Baptizing them in the name of the Father and the Son and the Holy Spirit." He instituted the Holy Communion, or the Lord's Supper or Eucharist, at the Last Supper with the words: "Do this in remembrance of me."

Limiting the number of sacraments to those explicitly instituted by Christ sets Anglicans apart from Roman Catholic teaching which holds to seven sacraments, even though five of them were not expressly initiated by Christ.

Because Christ explicitly ordained the Lord's Supper and Christian Baptism, they are sometimes referred to as "ordinances," the Ordinance of Holy Communion and the Ordinance of Holy Baptism. The term "sacrament" is avoided by some denominations and the word "ordinance" is used to make it clear that these denominations do not believe that every time a baptism is done or the Lord's Supper is celebrated, God's grace is conveyed simply by the doing of the ceremony, irrespective of the faith and disposition of the participants. These denominations would also hold that a right disposition on the part of the recipient also applies to listening to the preaching of the Gospel or to the reading of Scripture for them to be effective in deepening our relationship with God.

Unfortunately, the use of the term "ordinance," while accurate, is inadequate, for it fails to refer to these ordinances as means of God's grace and to convey that God is the chief actor in the sacraments of the Gospel. Therefore, this use tends to obscure and weaken a right understanding and use of the sacraments in the Churches that use the term exclusively.

Further, such an avoidance of the term "sacrament" is unnecessary and is based on a misunderstanding. It is incorrect to assume that the term "sacrament" implies that merely going through a rite automatically bestows the Lord's blessing. That is not the teaching of any part of the Church. Even the Roman Catholic Church, which teaches that the sacraments convey their blessing *ex opere operato*, that is "by their being done," qualifies that principle by adding that the blessing is bestowed as long as the participant does not place a block to the reception of the blessing of the sacrament. Anglicans stress that faith is needed for a "right use" of the sacraments, that is, to receive the grace of God given through them.

2. Sacraments are "not only badges or tokens of Christian men's profession." It is true that the sacraments

are not first and foremost about our faith in Christ; however, the sacraments are also, in fact, public badges and tokens of a Christian's profession of faith. If faith in Christ is a condition for a right participation in the sacraments, then by participating in the sacraments we are declaring to the Lord, to other believers, and to the world that we are believing Christians.

It is important for other Christians to know where we stand with the Lord. The author of the Letter to the Hebrews tells us not to neglect meeting together, but to gather together to encourage one another to good works (Hebrews 10:24-25). It is also important for the world to see that we are Christians and that we want them to become Christians as well.

Naturally, all of this assumes that one ought not to participate in the sacraments of the Gospel if one is not a believing Christian. To do so without faith is hypocritical and offends God.

3. The sacraments are "certain and sure witnesses." This point is tied closely to the next point that the sacraments are effective signs. Perhaps all we need to say at this point is that, because these sacraments are ordained by Christ, they stand alongside us and witness to us. They are not the voice of the Church, not our own voice, but rather they are Christ's voice, His enacted Word and action, witnessing to us of His grace and love for us. What could be more certain and sure than these Word-actions lovingly instituted and commanded by the Savior Himself? Coming from Him as they do, they speak to us as "sure and certain witnesses."

4. The sacraments are "effectual signs of grace and God's good will towards us by which he doth work invisibly in us and doth not only quicken, but also strengthen and confirm our faith in him."

First, we note that the sacraments are signs: "signs of grace and God's good will towards us." A sign signifies something, conveys a meaning or a rich fullness of meaning. The sacraments are enacted signs using physical elements, actions and words that convey meaning.

The physical elements that are part of the signs of the sacraments have a natural appropriateness for what the sacrament is signifying. Think of the associations with the water in Baptism, such as dying and rising, life-giving, and cleansing. Consider the wine and bread as food in the Lord's Supper. Food nourishes life, and eating together is a profound act of fellowship; red wine suggests His blood shed; the bread broken suggests Christ's body broken.

Going beyond the natural associations of the elements, there is an essential historical connection. The fact is that the physical elements, actions and words are anchored in the history of Jesus and the Gospel. They bring Christ to our minds and hearts as He is revealed in those crucial events that enacted and speak of God's love and grace that are set before us in and through the sacraments.

In addition, the sacramental signs are personally appropriated by each of the participants, the words are spoken to each, the water is applied to the person being baptized, and the bread and wine are taken and eaten by each of the communicants. Sacraments are signs, powerful, rich and vivid signs, to say the least.

Second, the sacraments are not only signs but they are effective signs; that is, they are instruments or means through which something is effected, something happens. Through them the Lord gives Himself to us. Let me repeat that, through them He gives Himself to us! He communicates His love and favor to the believers and thus He works invisibly in our hearts and lives, to enliven and stir up, strengthen and confirm our faith in Himself.

This work that God does in us through the sacraments of the Gospel is appropriate to each specific sacrament of the Gospel. (See Article 27 on Baptism, Article 28 on the Lord's Supper.)

His work in us does not always produce a vivid emotional experience; it can be at times a deep, almost hidden, work of the Spirit. On the other hand, at times, it can be quite emotional, provoking us to awe and wonder and tears. It can bring to our understanding entirely new insights into the Gospel and the grace of the Lord. By His presence and the Spirit, the Lord does His gracious work within us and within the congregation as we participate in faith. The sacraments of the Gospel are efficacious (effective) signs by God's design and sovereign action.

Biblical Foundations

I baptize you with water for repentance, but he who is coming after me is mightier than I, whose sandals I am not worthy to carry. He will baptize you with the Holy Spirit and with fire. Matthew 3:11

Go therefore and make disciples of all nations, baptizing them in the name of the Father and of the Son and of the Holy Spirit, teaching them to observe all that I have commanded you. And behold, I am with you always, to the end of the age. Matthew 28:19-20

Now as they were eating, Jesus took bread, and after blessing it broke it and gave it to the disciples, and said, "Take, eat; this is my body." And he took a cup, and when he had given thanks he gave it to them, saying, "Drink of it, all of you, for this is my blood of the covenant, which is poured out for many for the forgiveness of sins. I tell you I will not drink again of this fruit of the vine until that day when I drink it new with you in my Father's kingdom. Matthew 26:26-29

For I received from the Lord what I also delivered to you, that the Lord Jesus on the night when he was betrayed took bread, and when he had given thanks, he broke it, and said, "This is my body which is for you. Do this in remembrance of me." In the same way also he took the cup, after supper, saying, "This cup is the new covenant in my blood. Do this, as often as you drink it, in remembrance of me." 1 Corinthians 11:23-25

And Peter said to them, "Repent and be baptized every one of you in the name of Jesus Christ for the forgiveness of your sins, and you will receive the gift of the Holy Spirit. Acts 2:38

And now why do you wait? Rise and be baptized and wash away your sins, calling on his name. Acts 22:16

Do you not know that all of us who have been baptized into Christ Jesus were baptized into his death? We were buried therefore with him by baptism into death, in order that, just as Christ was raised from the dead by the glory of the Father, we too might walk in newness of life. Romans 6:3-4

For in Christ Jesus you are all sons of God, through faith. Galatians 3:26

False Teachings Denied/Objections Answered

1. Some in the history of the Church have placed all the emphasis upon the believer in interpreting the sacraments. They speak primarily about our activity. The sacraments are our badge and the token of our profession. This man-centered view of the sacraments is sometimes called Zwinglianism and is attributed to the teaching of Zwingli at the time of the Reformation. Whether Zwingli actually believed and taught that is disputed. Be that as it may, the view called Zwinglianism fails to grasp the sacraments at the core. It ignores the priority and action of God and exalts man's role. It fails to grasp the nature of Jesus' institution of the sacraments and the biblical teaching about them. It fails to understand the Word as a means of grace. It is right in what it affirms, but wrong in what it ignores or rejects.

2. Even further from a right understanding and use of the sacraments are those Christian bodies that reject the sacraments altogether, thinking them unnecessary or

magical in nature. The Quakers and the Salvation Army are examples of faith communities that reject the sacraments. In this they are in error and are, at best, on the edge of the life and witness of the historic Church. They do not measure up to the marks of a visible Church according to Article 19.

Implications

God, in and through Christ, has instituted the Sacraments of the Gospel and works in us, by His Spirit, through them. We are to treasure them and use them rightly, in faith.

2. Two Sacraments of the Gospel and Five Sacramental Acts are generally accepted by the visible Churches.
Explanation

"There are two Sacraments ordained of Christ our Lord in the Gospel, that is to say, Baptism and the Supper of the Lord."

This Article makes it clear that, for Anglicans, there are only two sacraments of the Gospel: Baptism and the Lord's Supper. These two sacraments are set apart in several ways:

1. They alone are expressly instituted by the Lord Jesus, and have their physical elements and the words of administration mandated by Him.

2. They are also unique in that they are "of the Gospel," uniquely centered on the Gospel. They are rehearsals of the center of the Gospel.

3. In addition, they were instituted for the participation and benefit of all of the people of God and apply to the whole of the Christian life. The five sacramental acts are either for some or are related to specific states of the Christian life.

In this sense, by definition, there are only two sacraments of the Gospel. Since each of these two

ARTICLE 25

sacraments of the Gospel has an Article or Articles expressly dedicated to them, we will not elaborate on them at this point. (See Baptism Article 27, Holy Communion Article 28.)

There are five sacramental acts that are treasured by almost all Christian bodies. When Anglicans assert that there are but two sacraments of the Gospel, this does not mean that the other five sacramental actions, referred to as sacraments in the pre-Reformation Western Church, are not of great significance in the Church's life. The Article briefly states: *"Those five commonly called Sacraments, that is to say, Confirmation, Penance, Orders, Matrimony, and Extreme Unction, are not to be counted for Sacraments of the Gospel, being such as have grown partly of the corrupt following of the Apostles, partly are states of life allowed in the Scriptures."*

These sacramental actions find some basis in the work of the Apostles and draw upon the grace of God in Christ. They call for the Lord's blessing and empowerment upon significant aspects of the life of Christians within the life and ministry of the Church.

Confirmation assumes Baptism and is administered by the Bishop in Anglican practice. It serves to mark a time in the life of a Christian, when after serious instruction in the Faith, the individual: 1) confesses his or her faith in the Lord; 2) states his or her agreement with the teaching and practice of the Church; 3) declares his or her readiness to be responsible for service in the life and ministry of the Church and in society, in accordance with his or her gifts and sense of calling; 4) declares a readiness to accept the authority of the Bishop and local leaders; and lastly, 5) asks for a fresh anointing of the Holy Spirit for the strength to do all the above and to grow in grace until his or her life's end. The Bishop lays hands on the confirmand and prays for the strengthening gift of the Holy Spirit to that end. Confirmation also gives all of the members of the congregation an opportunity to reaffirm their own baptismal and confirmation vows and to commit themselves to help the newly confirmed to keep his or her vows as well.

Penance or the reconciliation of a penitent provides a private, formal context in which a Christian may confess his or her sins or a particularly burdensome sin to a Priest of the Church and upon genuine repentance receive the declaration of the forgiveness of Christ for the same. Among Anglicans, auricular confession to a Priest of the Church is said to be "required of none, open to all, and pastorally needed by some."

Holy Orders refers to the ordination of Bishops, Priests or Presbyters, and Deacons. The Ordinal provides the rite and the Bishops administer ordination to the Diaconate and to the Priesthood, and the consecration of Bishops. Article 36 will discuss "Holy Orders" more fully.

Matrimony as a sacramental act is an act in which a man and women solemnly exchange vows and thus marry one another in public before God and the Church. The Church is represented by the congregation gathered and by the officiating clergy. The clergy ask and declare the Lord's blessing on the newly married couple, in which act of marriage they become one and will need the Lord's blessing to keep the vows that they have taken.

Extreme unction refers to the anointing with prayer of Christians near death and points to the burial service to come. In the burial service, thanks are expressed for the redemption and life of the departed Christian and for God's grace and victory over death in Christ into which the soul of the departed is commended. Prayers are offered for those who mourn.

While these five sacramental acts are not sacraments of the Gospel, as defined by Anglicans, they are sacramental actions that are treasured by Anglicans and provision is made for each in *The Book of Common Prayer*. It is instructive that all of the historic Churches of the Reformation have also provided for their use. Anglicans treasure these important means of grace. While some distinction in language about the sacraments of the Gospel and the five sacramental acts is preferable, there is a reason why the five sacramental acts were commonly called "sacraments"; it is that they are all means of grace and use outward and visible signs. There seems to be no essential reason why they may not be referred to as the lesser sacraments today, if one so prefers, provided one understands that they lack all of the marks of a sacrament of the Gospel as stated above.

Biblical Foundations

For I received from the Lord what I also delivered to you, that the Lord Jesus on the night when he was betrayed took bread, and when he had given thanks, he broke it, and said, "This is my body which is for you. Do this in remembrance of me." In the same way also he took the cup, after supper, saying, "This cup is the new covenant in my blood. Do this, as often as you drink it, in remembrance of me." 1 Corinthians 11:23-25

And Jesus came and said to them, "All authority in heaven and on earth has been given to me. Go therefore and make disciples of all nations, baptizing them in the name of the Father and of the Son and of the Holy Spirit, teaching them to observe all that I have commanded you. And behold, I am with you always, to the end of the age." Matthew 28:18-20

False Teachings Denied/Objections Answered

1. The Council of Trent condemned those who denied that the five sacramental acts are sacraments of the Gospel. The Roman Catholic Church holds that while they were not explicitly instituted by Christ, they are rooted in His earthly ministry and in the Gospel, and are indirectly instituted by Him and thus are sacraments of the Gospel. They thereby expand the number of sacraments to seven. This obscures the unique character of the two sacraments of the Gospel.

As mentioned above, some distinction of language is preferable.

2. While Anglicans do limit the sacraments of the Gospel to those intentionally instituted by Christ with the certain promise of Christ given in their institution, Anglicans do treasure and make use of the five sacramental acts, so it seems that much of the quarrel is beside the point, even if the Council of Trent anathematizes all who disagree with Rome.

Perhaps part of the reason for the strong language of condemnation by the Roman Church lies in the fact that Anglicans did not and do not recognize the authority of the Church of Rome over Anglican teaching, but rather submit all teaching to the Word of God written.

Implications

Anglicans recognize and celebrate the central and special place of the Sacraments of Baptism and Holy Communion as sacraments of the Gospel. They, along with all of the Churches of the Reformation, also treasure and make use of the five sacramental acts.

3. The right use of the sacraments is by repentant faith which alone receives a beneficial effect.
Explanation

The Article states: *"The Sacraments were not ordained of Christ to be gazed upon or to be carried about, but that we should duly use them. And in such only as worthily receive the same, have they a wholesome effect or operation: they that receive them unworthily, purchase to themselves damnation, as Saint Paul saith."*

The right use of the sacraments of the Gospel has two aspects. The first aspect is that the sacraments should be used as Christ intended them to be used. The second aspect is that they be received in a worthy manner. We need to examine each of these aspects briefly.

First, we ask, "What is the intended use of the sacraments?" In the pre-Reformation Western Church in the Middle Ages, a shift took place in the use of the sacrament of the Lord's Supper; it was a shift away from its proper and intended use as a participatory sacramental meal, instituted by Christ. It became in large measure a non-communicating, miraculous object of observation. The sacramental sign was lifted up as something or Someone to be gazed upon in adoration, or carried about in procession within the Church building and in and through the streets on festive occasions.

Several factors were involved in this shift of focus from communion to observation. One was the fact that many felt themselves too sinful to receive the sacrament. A second and more influential factor was the doctrine of transubstantiation which taught that the substance of the sacramental sign had actually and miraculously been changed into the Body and Blood of Christ, so that to see the sacramental sign after the consecration of the elements was to see Christ Himself under the accidents or appearance of bread and wine.

This 25th Article states that the non-communicating use of the sacrament of the Lord's Supper is not why the sacraments were instituted by Christ. The sacrament of the Lord's Supper is to be celebrated and taken and eaten in faith as Christ intended. It was not intended to become service for the observation of the sacramental signs. Believing sinners were to participate and receive in humble repentant faith, and not to abstain unless there was some unusual unease of spirit, which should then be addressed with godly counsel as soon as possible.

Article 28 addresses the doctrine of transubstantiation and rejects it as unscriptural and contrary to the nature of a sacrament. Thus these Articles take away the fundamental theological reason for gazing upon and carrying the sacramental sign in procession.

To be precise and fair, the Article does not expressly forbid the extra-Eucharistic practices of procession and the "Adoration of the Blessed Sacrament"; it simply states that these were not the purposes for which the Eucharist was instituted. On the other hand, the phrase "that we should duly use them" does seem to discourage such practices.

The second aspect of a right use of the sacraments, according to the Article, is the "worthy reception" of the sacraments. Since the sacraments are for sinners, what could possibly be meant by "worthy reception"? If we were worthy, we would not need the sacraments or even Christ for that matter. Of course, "worthy" in this sense does not mean that we deserve the grace that we receive from Christ in and through the sacraments, but rather that we take part in the sacrament in an appropriate manner, that is, with an intentional, humble, repentant faith in Christ as our Lord and Savior, seeking His forgiveness and intending to follow Him as Lord. We receive as the Publican and not the Pharisee (Luke 18:9-14). It is only when received in this way that the benefits of the sacraments are given and received.

Following St. Paul, the Article also states to receive them with some other disposition is to court disaster and condemnation (1 Corinthians 11:17-34).

Anglicans take this matter of worthy participation seriously and *The Book of Common Prayer* provides exhortations to be read to the congregation that, in uncompromising terms, call the congregation to humble, believing participation in the sacrament of the Lord's Supper.

Biblical Foundations

And Peter said to them, "Repent and be baptized every one of you in the name of Jesus Christ for the forgiveness of your sins, and you will receive the gift of the Holy Spirit." Acts 2:38

And on the Sabbath day we went outside the gate to the riverside, where we supposed there was a place of prayer, and we sat down and spoke to the women who had come together. One who heard us was a woman named Lydia, from the city of Thyatira, a seller of purple goods, who was a worshiper of God. The Lord opened her heart to pay attention to what was said by Paul. And after she was baptized, and her household as well, she urged us, saying, "If you have judged me to be faithful to the Lord, come to my house and stay." And she prevailed upon us. Acts 16:13-15

And all ate the same spiritual food, and all drank the same spiritual drink. For they drank from the spiritual Rock that followed them, and the Rock was Christ. Nevertheless, with most of them God was not pleased, for they were overthrown in the wilderness. 1 Corinthians 10:3-5

Whoever, therefore, eats the bread or drinks the cup of the Lord in an unworthy manner will be guilty of profaning the body and blood of the Lord. Let a person examine himself, then, and so eat of the bread and drink of the cup. 1 Corinthians 11:27-28

False Teachings Denied/Objections Answered

1. The Roman Catholic teaching of Trent does not require faith as essential to the right use of the sacraments. They do speak of the recipient not providing a block to the sacrament. It is not entirely clear what is meant by a "block"; however, in not requiring faith to receive the benefit of the sacrament, Anglicans believe that the Council of Trent erred and failed to grasp the personal and relational nature of the sacraments and the biblical place of faith in salvation.

2. It is also true that Rome did not follow Christ's institution of the Lord's Supper in the celebration of the Mass, for Rome withheld the cup from the laity. That, too,

contradicted the right use of the sacrament. It is a happy matter that the cup has been restored to the laity by the Roman Catholic Church.

Implications

In the celebration of the sacraments of the Gospel, the Church is to do what Christ commanded in His institution. In addition, faith in Christ as Savior and Lord is essential for a right use of the sacraments and to receive the Lord's grace in and through the sacraments.

Conclusion

The sacraments of the Gospel are of great significance. They have been instituted by Christ and are to be celebrated as He prescribed. In order to use them rightly, we participate in humble, repentant faith.

The five sacramental acts, while not expressly instituted by Christ, apply the Gospel and grace of Christ to ministries and stages in the Church's life and the individual Christian's life. They have been blessed by the Holy Spirit as they are used in faith. Anglicans treasure them.

ARTICLE 26

Of the Unworthiness of the Ministers, which Hinders not the Effect of the Sacraments

Although in the visible Church the evil be ever mingled with the good, and sometime the evil have chief authority in the ministration of the word and sacraments; yet forasmuch as they do not the same in their own name, but in Christ's, and do minister by His commission and authority, we may use their ministry both in hearing the word of God and in the receiving of the sacraments. Neither is the effect of Christ's ordinance taken away by their wickedness, nor the grace of God's gifts diminished from such as by faith and rightly do receive the sacraments ministered unto them, which be effectual because of Christ's institution and promise, although they be ministered by evil men.

Nevertheless it appertaineth to the discipline of the Church that inquiry be made of evil ministers, and that they be accused by those that have knowledge of their offences; and finally, being found guilty by just judgement, be deposed.

Introduction

Can we receive the sacrament from the hands of a minister who is known to be a public notorious sinner? This is even more a question now that we have lay Eucharistic ministers, for a larger number of people are involved.

All human beings, with the singular exception of Jesus Christ, are sinners. No one is perfect, not one. This applies to ordained persons in one or more of the Holy Orders of the Church as much as anyone else. This Article is written with clergy primarily in mind.

However, some clergy are not only sinners, but they are unrepentant, public, and notorious sinners. By their actions they not only sin egregiously, but in addition, by their example and indifference, they bless and promote sin. There have been times in the Church's history, when those in authority were either very slow in disciplining such clergy or did not discipline them at all. Such failure in discipline led to a scandalous state of many of the clergy and the Church.

Clergy who are flagrant and open sinners, serving actively in the ministry of God's Word and sacraments, are an offense to the faithful laity. Their behavior and presence unavoidably raises painful questions in the minds and hearts of the laity and their fellow clergy. What are we to think of their ministry, of the sermons they preach, the sacraments they administer, their sacramental acts, the counsel they give? Does not their sin render their preaching and the sacraments they administer null and void? Have those whom they have served really been baptized, truly received Holy Communion or have the clergy actually been ordained through their ministry?

The contradiction between their profession of faith and their immoral behavior has led some to deny the validity and efficacy of the sacraments of the Gospel that such clergy have administered, as well as of their sacramental acts such as marriage and ordination.

Article 26 addresses this issue with pastoral concern, first for the congregation and then for the "evil ministers" themselves.

The Teaching of Article 26

Here are the teaching points for this Article:

1. The unworthiness of the minister does not hinder the effect of the sacrament.

2. Evil ministers are to be identified, accused and, being found guilty, deposed.

1. The unworthiness of the minister does not hinder the effect of the sacrament.

Explanation

Clergy are to order their lives and the lives of their families in such a manner as to be godly examples to the congregations committed to their care. If they are Anglican clergy, they have promised to do this in their ordination vows. Alas, not all clergy do this very well. Some do not do live godly lives at all. They are open sinners who offend the godly consciences of their flock, and who are indifferent to that fact. This has been true from the days of the Church in the New Testament period onward and continues to be true today. Article 26 assumes this to be a sad fact.

The personal evil of such ministers does not weaken or cancel the grace and benefits of the Word and Sacraments administered in Christ's name. The validity and efficacy of God's Word proclaimed and of the Sacraments celebrated is grounded not in the sanctity of the clergy but in the authorization, gift, and promise of God in Christ, and by the present work of the Holy Spirit. Therefore, when the sermon is preached in conformity to God's Word written and when the sacraments and sacramental acts are administered using the Church's faithful liturgy and received rightly by faith, their validity and efficacy may be trusted, no matter the spiritual and moral condition of the clergy administering them.

This declaration of confidence in God's Word and Sacraments is not intended to deny the fact that the open sinfulness of clergy is a painful scandal that makes faith more difficult and hurts the effectiveness of numerous aspects of the ministry of such persons.

The opposite is also true; the faithfulness and godly lives of the clergy help to strengthen the faith and growth in grace of the congregation and assist the Church in being a witness to the world. This applies to the lives, witness and ministry of laity as well.

Biblical Foundations

The one who hears you hears me, and the one who rejects you rejects me, and the one who rejects me rejects him who sent me. Luke 10:16

And when Peter saw it he addressed the people: "Men of Israel, why do you wonder at this, or why do you stare at us, as though by our own power or piety we have made him walk?" Acts 3:12

What then is Apollos? What is Paul? Servants through whom you believed, as the Lord assigned to each. I planted, Apollos watered, but God gave the growth. So neither he who plants nor he who waters is anything, but only God who gives the growth. 1 Corinthians 3:5-7

For what we proclaim is not ourselves, but Jesus Christ as Lord, with ourselves as your servants for Jesus' sake. For God, who said, "Let light shine out of darkness," has shone in our hearts to give the light of the knowledge of the glory of God in the face of Jesus Christ. But we have this treasure in jars of clay, to show that the surpassing power belongs to God and not to us. 2 Corinthians 4:5-7

False Teachings Denied/Objections Answered

1. It is hard to conceive of anyone denying that evil clergy have and do exist, unless one holds a doctrine that ordination places the clergy beyond the possibility of sin which, as far as the author knows, no one has ever held in the Church. Some laity who do not know the clergy very intimately find it hard to believe that any of the clergy could take their ordination vows so lightly as to live in utter contradiction of them. However, those who know Church history and are well-acquainted with the clergy will not have difficulty accepting the truth of the Article at this point. As the old saying goes, "Clothes do not a gentleman make." That applies to clerical garb as well.

2. There are two errors that have appeared and reappeared in the history of the Church concerning the

trustworthiness of the Word and sacraments administered by evil ministers. One error denies the efficacy of the sacraments and sacramental acts that obviously sinful clergy administer. The second error concerns doubts in some believers' minds due to uncertainty about the secret intentions of scandalous clergy when they are administering the sacraments or preaching the Word.

A. The first error, in effect, denies that grace is conveyed in and through the Word, sacraments, and sacramental acts administered by scandalous clergy. This error has arisen numerous times, beginning in the early centuries of the Church. The famous African theologian Tertullian in the 2nd Century became a Montanist and had apocalyptic, ascetic, and legalistic tendencies. He denied the efficacy of baptisms administered by heretics. Cyprian, a Bishop in the 3rd century, denied the validity of the baptisms administered by the Novatians, who were Christian believers and separatists who had compromised under persecution and handed over the Holy Scriptures to their persecutors. Cyprian required them to be rebaptized when they returned to the Church. St Augustine in the 5th Century fought with the Donatist sectarians who had separated from the Church over the election of a Bishop who had been consecrated by a Novatian. St. Augustine affirmed that their baptisms were valid and that persons baptized in the Triune Name and with water outside of the visible Church did not need to be and should not be baptized again when they were accepted in the Church. In the East, St. Chrysostom took the same position as St. Augustine did in the West. At the Reformation of the 16th century, some Anabaptists held that the efficacy of the sacraments depended upon the worthiness of the minister as well as upon the one baptized being of consenting age and the mode of baptism being immersion.

In the present day, people are often so devoted to the clergy of their congregations as to fall into this error without realizing it. Their disappointment is so great when a beloved minister is revealed to be seriously compromised by sinful behavior that these laity leave the congregation.

We all need to be reminded that the chief Shepherd of the congregations is the Lord Christ Himself and He is Lord of the Word and the sacraments that are administered in His name. Our confidence is in Christ Himself. He honors His Word and sacraments.

B. The second error has to do with doubt regarding the intention of scandalous clergy when they are administering the Word or the sacraments or a sacramental act. The Council of Trent had laid down that for a sacrament to be valid and efficacious the administering clergy had to "intend what the Church intends." But how can we know what the personal intention of a clergyman is? The answer cannot be found in trying to penetrate into the inner mind of the clergy. That would land us in a sea of speculation and uncertainty. The answer is found in taking seriously the action itself. When the sacrament is administered by a proper minister, in accordance with the Scriptures, using the rite of the Church, which rite expresses the Church's intention, that action by the clergy constitutes an adequate expression of the public intention of the clergy and of the intentionality of the sacrament. What is thus done and said is the public intent which can be known by all believers and about which there needs to be no doubt.

Implications

While it is entirely appropriate to be scandalized by clergy who are leading ungodly lives, it is wrong to let their condition and behavior cast doubt upon the Word of God rightly preached or the Sacraments of the Gospel and sacramental acts rightly administered. They are given to us by Christ for our comfort and strengthening.

Further, when the Word is preached in accordance with the Scriptures and the Sacraments are administered as Christ intended, the very fact that they are done so publicly in the Church using the liturgy of the Church and in the name of Christ constitutes a clear expression of the public intention of the clergy administering them and of God's intention to bless us through their use. There is no need to be concerned about any secret intention of the administering clergy.

2. Evil ministers are to be identified, accused, and, when found guilty, deposed.
Explanation

At the time of the Reformation when this Article was being written, discipline in the Church had been lax for some time, the Bible had not been widely read, and the clergy were often openly degenerate. Ignorance, superstition and greed characterized the time and a large part of the clergy as well.

While we are not to expect Christian clergy to be perfect, we may, and should, expect them to live and work as godly examples to those whom they serve. When the lives of clergy become a public scandal, ecclesiastical discipline is clearly needed.

Even though notoriously sinful clergy may not cancel the grace of the Word preached and Sacraments celebrated, they are not thereby excused from the responsibility of discharging their ministry in accordance with Scripture and in faithfulness to their ordination vows. Such scandalous clergy bring discredit upon the Church and dishonor the Lord. They are an offense in the eyes of the world as well as of the congregation. Obvious immorality and hypocrisy are offensive to all. Blatant, unrepentant heresy, neglect of pastoral responsibilities, sexual misconduct, addiction to drugs or alcohol, and financial dishonesty are obvious grounds for clergy to be suspended and, if not repentant, deposed or removed from the active exercise of ordained ministry.

Those who are responsible for their supervision and care, when they hear or see that these clergy are notorious sinners, are to call them to repentance and exercise appropriate ecclesiastical discipline. Should the sinful clergy fail to repent and to reform their behavior and attitude by God's grace, they are to be brought to trial and deposed.

Biblical Foundations

I am the true vine, and my Father is the vinedresser. Every branch of mine that does not bear fruit he takes away, and every branch that does bear fruit he prunes, that it may bear more fruit. John 15:1-2

Do not admit a charge against an elder except on the evidence of two or three witnesses. As for those who persist in sin, rebuke them in the presence of all, so that the rest may stand in fear. 1 Timothy 5:19-20

Do not be hasty in the laying on of hands, nor take part in the sins of others; keep yourself pure. 1 Timothy 5:22

False Teachings Denied/Questions Answered

1. Some people object to disciplining the clergy. They believe that since we are all sinners and live only by the grace and forgiveness of God, we should not discipline notoriously sinful clergy, much less depose or remove them from active ministry. This sort of thinking denies 1) the sanctifying or liberating work of the Holy Spirit in the Christian's life, and 2) the responsibility for leaders in the Church, both lay and ordained, to live as godly examples to the flock. Those who are unwilling or unable to live as examples are disqualified from ordained or lay leadership in the Church. It is the responsibility of the ordination committees and ultimately of the Bishop or the ordaining person to present and ordain only suitable persons for the ordained ministry.

Implications

The place of ecclesiastical discipline is essential to the life of the Church. Clergy that are a scandal to the Church must be dealt with pastorally, appropriately and without undue delay.

Conclusion

Sermons preached in accordance with the Word of God written and the sacraments of the Gospel and sacramental acts that are administered in the name of Christ, with the use of faithful liturgies, are to be trusted as valid and efficacious when received in faith, irrespective of the moral or spiritual state of the clergy who administer them.

Evil, scandalous clergy are to be disciplined appropriately by those under whose oversight and care they serve.

ARTICLE 27

Of Baptism

Baptism is not only a sign of profession and mark of difference whereby Christian men are discerned from other that be not christened, but is also a sign of regeneration or new birth, whereby, as by an instrument, they that receive baptism rightly are grafted into the Church; the promises of the forgiveness of sin, and of our adoption to be the sons of God, by the Holy Ghost are visibly signed and sealed; faith is confirmed, and grace increased by virtue of prayer unto God. The baptism of young children is in any wise to be retained in the Church as most agreeable with the institution of Christ.

Introduction

Who should be baptized? Who should do the baptizing? Under what conditions should it be done? What must be done for a baptism to be properly done? Must baptism be an immersion in water? Into what name are we to baptize? What happens in baptism? How can the infant children of believers be baptized when the infants don't know what is taking place? These questions and more have never been settled to the satisfaction of all Christian Churches. Anglicans have taken a clear position.

During the 16th century Reformation, several questions arose. There were some, such as the Anabaptist Communities, that rejected the baptism of infants born to members of the Church. The Roman Catholic Church taught a doctrine of baptismal regeneration that needed careful consideration in the light of Scripture and in the light of the recovery of the place of faith in salvation.

The issues that arose at that time continue today. Anglicans believe the Scriptures are sufficiently clear to affirm the sacramental character of baptism. Since views vary, it is important therefore to give careful attention to the teaching of this Article.

The Teaching of Article 27

Here are the teaching points for this Article:

1. Baptism is a public sign of the profession of Faith in Christ and a mark of difference whereby Christians are discerned from other persons not baptized.

2. Baptism is a visible sign, seal, and promise of the full scope of Christian salvation.

3. Baptism is God's means or instrument by which those who receive baptism rightly, in faith, are grafted into the Church.

4. The baptism of infants of believing members of the visible Church is to be retained as agreeable to the institution of baptism by Christ.

1. Baptism is a public sign of profession of Faith in Christ and a mark of difference whereby Christians are discerned from persons not baptized.

Explanation

Baptism is a public act of profession of faith on the part of a person and/or of the person's sponsors. It is not to be done except where genuine faith is present. If an infant is to be baptized, the parent(s) and sponsors are to be believers and active participants in the life of the Church. They are to agree to raise the child in the love and nurture of the Lord, until such time as, after due instruction and preparation, the child can make its own profession and be brought to the Bishop for confirmation.

Baptism has its natural setting in a public service of the congregation, in the midst of whom those being baptized will be nurtured and grow to serve as lay or ordained ministers of Christ. This setting also gives the members of the congregation an occasion to reaffirm their own faith and to welcome the newly baptized and to accept its obligation to love, help and serve those being grafted into the Church by baptism.

There may be pastoral reasons why a private baptism is appropriate. However, private baptisms ought to be the exception and not the rule.

In addition, since Holy Baptism is a public act, it makes known to the world the faith of the congregation and of those being baptized and of their sponsors.

In some societies and cultures baptism is a dangerous action, one that will socially mark all those who are baptized. At certain times and places, being baptized has led and still leads to death, to loss of jobs, to limitations in education, and to rejection by the family. This cost can be so high that some believers choose to practice "secret belief," hiding their faith, a situation which is far from ideal. Martyrdom is a gift of the Spirit and is never wasted; it is often the seed-bed of the Church, as the early Church found to be true and has been found to be true time and time again in the history of the Church.

Biblical Foundations

And Peter said to them, "Repent and be baptized every one of you in the name of Jesus Christ for the forgiveness of your sins, and you will receive the gift of the Holy Spirit. For the promise is for you and for your children and for all who are far off, everyone whom the Lord our God calls to himself." And with many other words he bore witness and continued to exhort them, saying, "Save yourselves from this crooked generation." So those who received his word were baptized, and there were added that day about three thousand souls. And they devoted themselves to the apostles' teaching and fellowship, to the breaking of bread and the prayers." Acts 2:38-42

While Peter was still saying these things, the Holy Spirit fell on all who heard the word. And the believers from among the circumcised who had come with Peter were amazed, because the gift of the Holy Spirit was poured out even on the Gentiles. For they were hearing them speaking in tongues and extolling God. Then Peter declared, "Can anyone withhold water for baptizing these people, who have received the Holy Spirit just as we have?" And he commanded them to be baptized in the name of Jesus Christ. Then they asked him to remain for some days." Acts 10:44-48

False Teaching Denied/Questions Answered

1. In a nation which is officially Christian and where there is a State Church, it can come to be assumed that all citizens of the State have the right to Holy Baptism. Infants can then be "done" or brought to baptism by parents and sponsors who have no Christian Faith and have no intention of living up to the promises made in the rite of Holy Baptism.

This practice makes a mockery of baptism, and it ignores the role of faith that is essential to a right use of the sacraments. In the case of infants, such faith is to be present in the sponsors and parents as representatives of the infant. Therefore, it is important that those administering the sacrament of baptism in Christ's name, examine those bringing an infant to baptism to see if assurances can be given that the promises they will make during the baptism will be kept.

Implications

The administration of Holy Baptism is to be done only when faith in Christ is present in those being baptized or, in the case of infants, in their sponsors. Further the sacrament of holy baptism is to be administered normally in a congregation's corporate worship.

2. Baptism is a visible sign, seal, and promise of the fullness of Christian salvation.

Explanation

Baptism in the New Testament embodies the full range of the Gospel and of salvation. The fullness of salvation in Christ is signed and sealed in baptism, just as the full range of salvation is celebrated in the Lord's Supper or Holy Communion. It is for this reason that these two are referred to as Sacraments of the Gospel.

Article 27 makes this point by itemizing what is signed and sealed in the Sacrament of Holy Baptism. The following are listed: regeneration or new birth, being grafted into the Church, the promises of forgiveness of sin, adoption as sons of God, faith confirmed, and grace or the inner work of the Holy Spirit increased.

Just as the full range of salvation – justification, sanctification, and glorification – is signed and sealed, so also the full range of human participation and response to God is required on the part of the one to be baptized for a right use of the Sacrament of Holy Baptism. That is, being regenerated by the Spirit, repentance, faith in Christ, being grafted into His Body the Church, being filled daily with the Spirit, and walking in the Spirit.

Baptism therefore, as Luther pointed out, initiates a life-long pattern in the life of the believer that involves daily dying to sin and rising to new life, putting off the old sinful ways and putting on obedience to Christ by the power of the Holy Spirit.

The proper administration of the sacrament of baptism on the part of the Church involves the following: the administration of the sacrament to proper recipients, the commitment to receive the baptized as brothers and sisters in Christ, to assist them to grow in Christ and to take their place in the Christian life, ministry and mission of the

Church. This includes a commitment to prepare them for and to provide the ministry of confirmation in due time.

Biblical Foundations

Baptism, which corresponds to this, now saves you, not as a removal of dirt from the body but as an appeal to God for a good conscience, through the resurrection of Jesus Christ. 1 Peter 3:21

He saved us, not because of works done by us in righteousness, but according to his own mercy, by the washing of regeneration and renewal of the Holy Spirit. Titus 3:5

And Peter said to them, "Repent and be baptized every one of you in the name of Jesus Christ for the forgiveness of your sins, and you will receive the gift of the Holy Spirit." Acts 2:38

Do you not know that all of us who have been baptized into Christ Jesus were baptized into his death? We were buried therefore with him by baptism into death, in order that, just as Christ was raised from the dead by the glory of the Father, we too might walk in newness of life. Romans 6:3-4

There is one body and one Spirit—just as you were called to the one hope that belongs to your call— one Lord, one faith, one baptism, one God and Father of all, who is over all and through all and in all. Ephesians 4:4-6

False Teachings Denied/Questions Answered

1. One question that is sometimes raised is: why is justification by faith not explicitly mentioned in this Article? Actually, the reality of justification is present both in this Article and in the Baptismal liturgy in *The Book of Common Prayer*. Forgiveness is used in Scripture for justification and for the whole of redemption. For example, see Colossians 2:13-15 and Ephesians 1:7. Forgiveness is simpler and easier to grasp than the more technical term

"justification" and is more suitable for liturgical usage. This Article is following the language of the baptismal rite.

2. Some people question where sanctification is to be found in the Article. Regeneration and justification by faith are prerequisites of and lead necessarily to sanctification. Sanctification is referred to in the Article by the phrase "and grace increased." The faith which alone receives the gift of justification is never alone. The Holy Spirit Who regenerates us and thus enables our faith in the Gospel also begins the progressive transformation of our heart and character. All of this is signed and sealed in Baptism.

3. The language of two baptisms, one of water and one of the Spirit, is an error and is misleading. Some persons refer to the sacrament of Holy Baptism as "water baptism" in distinction from "the Baptism in the Holy Spirit," thereby emptying the sacrament of baptism of the Holy Spirit. St. Paul tells us clearly in Ephesians 4:5 that there is but "one baptism." The phrase "water baptism" can appropriately refer to the lustrations of the Jews or to the baptism of John but it never refers to Christian Baptism in the Scriptures. The sacrament of baptism is never just "water baptism" for, as St. Paul tells us, we are made to drink of the one Spirit in baptism.

If those who speak of "water baptism" are awkwardly trying to distinguish between the administration of the sacrament at a given point of time and the timing of the sovereign work of the Spirit in applying what is signed and sealed to the persons being baptized, one can be sympathetic with their intention, but not with the language. The language of two baptisms is unfortunate, unbiblical, and misleading.

The "two baptisms" language also appears in the charismatic renewal movement which often defines "Baptism in the Spirit" as an event distinct from the one Christian baptism. They do this to account for the loss of the manifestation of the gifts of the Spirit in much contemporary Christian life and the low level of much

Christian living. The observation about a good portion of contemporary Christian living is accurate, but the reference to two baptisms is not. It would be better were we to retain St. Paul's use and speak of one baptism and then speak of life in the Spirit, of the release of the Spirit and/or of continuing and repeated fillings of the Spirit (Ephesians 5:18).

It is important for all in the congregation to know that when they were baptized they were made to drink of the one Spirit. There cannot be some of the baptized believers in the congregation that have received the Spirit and others of the baptized believers who have not. That assumed division is what Paul is explicitly denying. "For in one Spirit we were all baptized into one body—Jews or Greeks, slaves or free—and all were made to drink of one Spirit" (1 Corinthians 12:13).

Since all have received the Spirit, then all are blessed and called to live in the Spirit, to surrender to His leading and empowering, and daily to be filled with the Spirit. All are to be open to the manifestation of the gifts of the Spirit as the Spirit sovereignly wills. There is no evidence in the New Testament that the gifts of the Spirit have been withdrawn.

4. Some err in thinking that St. Paul demeans the importance of baptism in 1 Corinthians 1:10-17, where he thanks God that he did not come to Corinth to baptize. His point is that he came to preach and lead non-Christians to faith in Christ. His preaching then led others to do the baptizing of the new believers and their children. He does, however, recall that he did a few baptisms. But he is pleased that, since he did not exercise a major ministry of baptism, no one could think that he was baptizing people into himself or his own name or group. This concern of the Apostle Paul was due to the fact that the Corinthian Christians had formed themselves into warring groups in the Church. Paul is speaking against this schismatic tendency. Moreover, all through his writings, the Apostle

Paul assumes that all believers and their children have been baptized as Christ commanded.

Implications

The sacrament of Holy Baptism is a sacrament which is rich in meaning. It is the sign, seal, and initiation of full salvation in Christ. This is richly symbolized in the action of Baptism and is well-expressed in most rites for the sacrament of baptism.

There is need to give significant instruction to those to be baptized and their sponsors about the meaning of baptism and the rite being used. An understanding of the gift given in baptism should be thoroughly taught. Given the low level of the understanding of the sacrament of baptism among Christians, preaching and teaching on baptism and the Prayer Book rite should be given to the entire congregation from time to time. It is one thing to have a precious gift; it is another to understand why it is precious and to savor it.

3. Baptism is God's means or instrument by which those who receive baptism rightly, in faith, are grafted into the Church.

Explanation

In baptism, the water and the words and action are not just bare signs but are efficacious signs. Something is happening. It is important to understand Who the chief actor in baptism is and what He is doing. Anglicans believe and teach that the chief actor is God. The Scriptures and the 25th and 27th Articles of Religion make the point that the chief actor in the sacraments of the Gospel is the Lord himself and not the Church or the believer. Anglicans do not deny that both the believer and the Church have a role to play, but theirs is a dependent and responsive one. Baptism, therefore, is an act of God done in and through the sacramental ministry of the Church and involves the appropriate participation of those being baptized and their sponsors.

God's acts are usually through an instrument, whether it be in and through preaching, the Eucharist, Baptism, or the five sacramental acts, or through His acting in less formal ways in evangelism, deeds of charity, etc. At times, He acts without an instrument, but these are usually either private or obviously miraculous.

That God uses the sacrament of Baptism as an instrument is also affirmed by the fact that we administer the Sacrament of Baptism in the name of Christ.

The question arises as to what is implied by the phrase "in the name of Christ"?

"Name" is a rich concept in Scripture. First, to act in Christ's name is to act in obedience to His command and as His agents. We baptize in His name as His agents because He told us to do so. It is a sacramental act in which He, as the Baptizer, acts. John the Baptist states that "He shall baptize you" not "the Church shall baptize you."

Secondly, to act "in His Name" means that the action done is in accord with His revealed character and purpose. He has made a name for Himself, revealed Himself, by what He has said and done, and most particularly by what He has done in His Cross and Resurrection and Ascension as Savior and Lord. His character and the key events of the Gospel are embodied, revealed afresh, and rehearsed in the sacrament of Baptism.

Thirdly, as baptized persons, we henceforth bear His name as Christians. It is into His ownership, His likeness, and His service that we are baptized. This is a result of being baptized into His name. As such we also become His representatives in the world.

Lastly, Jesus' name can only be understood as part of the Triune name of God (Matthew 28:19). To be joined to Jesus is to be joined to the Father and the Spirit: the One God. There is, in the end, only one divine Name, the triune Name of God the Father, God the Son, and God the Holy

Spirit. As the risen Lord makes clear in His institution of baptism, it is into the triune Name that we are baptized.

In the sacrament of Holy Baptism, the Article states that those being baptized are being grafted into the visible Church and through the visible Church into the One, Holy, Catholic, and Apostolic Church of which it is a visible manifestation. The persons' names are entered on the rolls of the local congregation. The records of the Church are kept. A Certificate of Baptism is given to those baptized and can be used as a legal means of identification. This is clearly and finally done, signed, and sealed at the moment of baptism.

From that time on, baptized persons are either living out their baptism and membership in the Church in the Spirit, albeit never perfectly, or they are living as apostates, in rejection of their baptism and membership in the Church, whether by indifference or by conscious intention to depart the Faith and the Church. In the lives of faithful, baptized Christians, the Spirit has brought and brings to actuality all that is signed and sealed at baptism, in such timing and in a manner as the Spirit sovereignly wills and that is appropriate to each individual in the fellowship of the Church.

As stated several times above, the right use of the Sacraments is by faith in Christ. To receive baptism rightly and be grafted into the Church is to receive it in faith. This, of course, raises the question about the baptism of the infants of believers who cannot have or express faith in Christ. That question is treated in the next teaching point.

Biblical Foundations

I baptize you with water for repentance, but he who is coming after me is mightier than I, whose sandals I am not worthy to carry. He will baptize you with the Holy Spirit and with fire. Matthew 3:11

For in one Spirit we were all baptized into one body—Jews or Greeks, slaves or free—and all were made to drink of one Spirit. 1 Corinthians 12:13

For in Christ Jesus you are all sons of God, through faith. For as many of you as were baptized into Christ have put on Christ. Galatians 3:26-27

What shall we say then? Are we to continue in sin that grace may abound? By no means! How can we who died to sin still live in it? Do you not know that all of us who have been baptized into Christ Jesus were baptized into his death? We were buried therefore with him by baptism into death, in order that, just as Christ was raised from the dead by the glory of the Father, we too might walk in newness of life. Romans 6:1-4

And now why do you wait? Rise and be baptized and wash away your sins, calling on his name. Acts 22:16

For if the sprinkling of defiled persons with the blood of goats and bulls and with the ashes of a heifer sanctifies for the purification of the flesh, how much more will the blood of Christ, who through the eternal Spirit offered himself without blemish to God, purify our conscience from dead works to serve the living God. Hebrews 9:13-14

False Teachings Denied/Questions Answered

1. Any view of baptism that sees it only as the profession of faith on the part of a believer has missed the central point of baptism and is therefore a deficient teaching.

2. Any view of baptism that sees it as a blessing only to the individual but does not see its innate connections to the Church as the Body of Christ is a deficient teaching. It is for this reason that so-called "private baptisms" must be the exception and done only due to urgent health or other pastoral needs.

3. Some want to be re-baptized either because they want to be immersed or to be baptized due to their own intention as contrasted with having been baptized as an

infant without their personal desire or permission. Rebaptism, actually, cannot be done. If one has been baptized then one has been grafted into the Church, and the fullness of salvation has been signed and sealed by the Lord upon the baptized. It has been done. It can be ignored, contradicted, and personally rejected but it cannot be undone or redone. The liturgical rite can be repeated but the repetition of the rite, by whatever mode of administration, cannot be a baptism any more than repeating one's wedding ceremony every 10 years is a marriage. The two who do so are already married in the eyes of God, the Church, the State, and themselves.

4. Some want to make a particular mode of the application of water in baptism to be essential to genuine baptism. This is hard to defend, either from the word "baptism" or from practice in Scripture. All of the modes – sprinkling, pouring, or immersion – emphasize some part of the meaning of salvation in Christ that is signed and sealed in baptism. Immersion highlights the significance of dying and rising in Christ. Pouring emphasizes being cleansed in the blood of the Lamb. Sprinkling recalls the sprinkling of the blood of the sacrifice on the Altar and upon the believer, providing atonement and justification. Anglicans have said that whatever mode of application of water in the baptism the person to be baptized desires should be made available.

Implications

It is important to realize that Jesus is the Baptizer, that the Triune God is the chief actor in baptism and that He is using the sacrament of baptism as an instrument to sign and seal the fullness of salvation upon the baptized. Salvation includes being grafted into the Church; therefore baptism is the sign of initiation into Christ and life in the Spirit in the body of Christ. Baptism is a solemn and precious gift of eternal proportions. Given what baptism is, the Church is called to teach and prepare people for baptism far more faithfully, thoroughly, and carefully than it presently does.

Needless to say, the grace of baptism and the continuing application of its riches by the Holy Spirit can be rejected and denied or repudiated by those who either never come to faith or who consciously reject the Faith as apostates.

4. The baptism of infant children of members of the visible Church is to be retained as agreeable to the institution of baptism by Christ.

Explanation

The statement of this Article that "the baptism of young children is in any wise to be retained in the Church, as most agreeable with the institution of Christ," is true and rests on the following biblical grounds:

1. Foundational to the baptism of the infants who are the children of believers is the inclusion of children in the Covenant of grace. The inclusion of children as members of God's covenant people was made clear when circumcision, the sign of membership in the Abrahamic Covenant, or the covenant of grace, was extended to the children of Covenant (Genesis 17:9-14). The "new" Covenant prophesied by Jeremiah (Jeremiah 31:41) and declared by Jesus at the Last Supper (Matthew 26:28) is not new as a different covenant, but rather new as the fulfillment of the Abrahamic Covenant, so that there is but one Covenant of Grace expressed in two dispensations: the Old as type and anticipation of the New, and the New the fulfillment of the Old.

While the signs of the dispensation of the Covenant of Grace change from those of the Old dispensation to those of the New, the one Covenant of Grace remains for believers and their families. Since baptism is the sign of initiation into and membership in the Covenant of Grace in the New dispensation it replaces circumcision in the Old.

Baptism, like circumcision, is to be administered to the children of the Covenant in the new dispensation just as circumcision was in the old dispensation.

A mark of the "newness" of the New Covenant is that baptism, as the new sign and seal of the covenant, is administered to the female children as well as to the male children.

This first point is straightforward, since there is one Covenant of Grace in two dispensations, and since children were members of the Covenant in the old dispensation, so also are they members of the covenant in the new dispensation and they rightly receive the sign and seal of the New Covenant membership, which is baptism. It would be odd, would it not, if the old dispensation were more generous and gracious than the new?

2. Very important also for determining the basis for the baptism of the children of believers are the statements of Christ and His attitude toward children. He regarded them as members of the Covenant and precious to Him and the Father: "Suffer the little children to come unto me and do not hinder them for of such belongs the Kingdom of God" (Mark 10:14-16; cf. Matthew 19:13-15, Luke 18:15-17). What is right for Christ, regarding children, is right for the Church.

3. The same attitude and teaching that we find in Christ, we find also in the attitude and the practice of the Apostles. Their view is seen: first, in the statement by Peter in Acts 2:38-41, where he calls upon all to repent, be baptized for the forgiveness of sins, be filled with the Holy Spirit and declares that the promise was to the hearers and their children and to those far off; second, in the household baptisms cited of Lydia's household and that of the Philippian jailer (Acts 16:15, 33), and Stephanus in 1 Corinthians 1:16; third, in the statement of Paul in 1 Corinthians 1:7-14 in which the children of a believer in a mixed marriage are declared holy unto the Lord through the faith of the parent; and fourth, in the typological references

to baptism as the Ark in the flood (1 Peter 3:21) and as a circumcision not made with hands (Colossians 2:11), both of which have referents involving children.

4. Lastly, in Christ's institution of baptism we find an implicit inclusion of children. In the Great Commission (Matthew 28:18ff), He sends the Apostles to go to all nations to baptize. By usual usage, "nations" include children; there is no biblical reference to nations that excludes children.

Given all of these points, it seems that the burden of proof lies at the feet of those that would refuse baptism to the infant children of believers in Christ who are members of the Covenant of Grace.

Anglicans take it that the above evidence and argumentation does clearly establish that the sacrament of baptism is to be given to believers in Christ and their children.

This does leave one further question to be addressed. What about faith? How does this practice cohere with the right use of the sacraments, which includes personal faith? Salvation is through faith in Christ and the infant children of believers are not capable of faith in any usual sense of that word.

For Anglicans, this situation is met by the requirement that there be sponsors, usually the believing parents and godparents chosen from among believers, who will make the response on the infant's behalf and promise to raise the children in the fear and nurture of the Lord.

Also, the rite of Confirmation is provided as a necessary subsequent rite to assure the congregation that the one being confirmed has, by the Holy Spirit, been given the gift of faith and has personally come to faith in Christ. The one being confirmed has claimed what has been signed and sealed and promised by the Holy Spirit and by the sponsors on his or her behalf in baptism. Confirmation is also used by the Holy Spirit to strengthen the faith and gifts for ministry of the one to be confirmed, by prayer, calling upon the Holy Spirit, and by the laying on of hands.

If the believing parents and the Church do not baptize their infants, a serious question arises. What then is to be done with them? If we refuse them baptism, we thereby declare that they are not members of the Covenant people, of the Church. Do we really want to say that? In addition, the usual alternative for the children is a service of dedication. But the fact is that the Scriptures make no provision for a general practice of the dedication of the infants of believers. Even more telling is the fact that the infants that were dedicated in the Old Testament were all previously circumcised and thus had already received the sign of the Covenant. The practice of replacing baptism with a service of dedication is simply in contradiction to the analogy of Scripture.

To hold that infants of believers are to be baptized requires the belief that the Holy Spirit enables the baptized infants to appropriate what is signed and sealed in baptism in stages and that the appropriation of all that is signed and sealed in the act of baptism does not immediately take place during the administration of the rite of baptism itself.

Personal responses appropriate to salvation can precede, be simultaneous with, or follow the administration of baptism. In the case of the baptism of adult converts, for example, regeneration and faith precede the administration of baptism, even though regeneration and faith are signed and sealed in baptism. In the case of the baptism of the infants of believers, the sacrament of baptism precedes personal faith, which is signed and sealed in the sacrament and is promised on behalf of the infant by the parents and godparents. Since the Lord, by His Spirit, deals with us as individuals in the context of His people, it is impossible to say more about timing of the actualization of what is signed and sealed other than that it is the sovereign work of the Holy Spirit and cannot be scheduled by us.

What we can say with assurance is that we have two patterns of the relationship of faith and baptism in the New Testament and in the life of the Church. There is the pattern of conversion unto baptism. This is dominant in missionary situations but it is never absent from the Church. The other pattern is baptism unto conversion which takes place within the life of the Church and for Anglicans is affirmed in confirmation. This pattern is dominant in populations which are largely churched. It is important to note that in both patterns, personal faith in Christ is central and is essentially linked to baptism.

Biblical Foundations

And God said to Abraham, "As for you, you shall keep my covenant, you and your offspring after you throughout their generations. This is my covenant, which you shall keep, between me and you and your offspring after you: Every male among you shall be circumcised. You shall be circumcised in the flesh of your foreskins, and it shall be a sign of the covenant between me and you. He who is eight days old among you shall be circumcised. Every male throughout your generations, whether born in your house or bought with your money from any foreigner who is not of your offspring, both he who is born in your house and he who is bought with your money, shall surely be circumcised. So shall my covenant be in your flesh an everlasting covenant. Any uncircumcised male who is not circumcised in the flesh of his foreskin shall be cut off from his people; he has broken my covenant." Genesis 17:9-14

But when Jesus saw it, he was indignant and said to them, "Let the children come to me; do not hinder them, for to such belongs the kingdom of God. Truly, I say to you, whoever does not receive the kingdom of God like a child shall not enter it." And he took them in his arms and blessed them, laying his hands on them. Mark 10:14-16

And after she was baptized, and her household as well, she urged us, saying, "If you have judged me to be faithful to the Lord, come to my house and stay." And she prevailed upon us. Acts 16:15

And he took them the same hour of the night and washed their wounds; and he was baptized at once, he and all his family. Acts 16:33

(I did baptize also the household of Stephanas. Beyond that, I do not know whether I baptized anyone else.) 1 Corinthians 1:16

Baptism, which corresponds to this, now saves you, not as a removal of dirt from the body but as an appeal to God for a good conscience, through the resurrection of Jesus Christ. 1 Peter 3:21

In him also you were circumcised with a circumcision made without hands, by putting off the body of the flesh, by the circumcision of Christ. Colossians 2:11

And Jesus came and said to them, "All authority in heaven and on earth has been given to me. Go therefore and make disciples of all nations, baptizing them in the name of the Father and of the Son and of the Holy Spirit, teaching them to observe all that I have commanded you. And behold, I am with you always, to the end of the age." Matthew 28:18-20

False Teachings Denied/Objections Answered

1. Anglican teaching differs from Roman Catholic teaching on baptism at two major points. The first point is that, in Roman Catholic teaching, should a child fail to be baptized and die, he must go to limbo because his inherited indwelling sin has not been removed in baptism. Anglicans do not believe that baptism removes indwelling sin. This is explicitly discussed in Article 9. Nor do Anglicans believe in limbo. It is not the lack of baptism but the despising and abuse of baptism that offends the Lord.

2. The second point at which Anglicans differ with the teaching of Rome is that Roman teaching on baptism, as found in Trent, holds that regeneration is not only signed and sealed at baptism and the baptized grafted into the

Church but that regeneration is effectively and immediately effected in every one baptized. Thus, everyone baptized is held to be inwardly regenerated. In the light of subsequent experience when some of the baptized commit apostasy, Roman teaching must take the line that regeneration and the full blessings of salvation can be lost, thus weakening the doctrine of God's sovereignty in both regeneration and the perseverance of the saints.

Anglicans take a hopeful and charitable attitude regarding the baptized, but do not seek to say more than can be said, realizing that not every child of the covenant or every adult who is baptized is of the good soil that produces a harvest. The mystery of election runs through the Church as well as through the world at large (see Article 17).

3. Some denominations hold that in the New Testament the baptism of adult believers alone is envisioned. However, since there is only one baptism, and since the New Testament does assume the baptism of infants of believers, it cannot be true that the New Testament practice and teaching on baptism refers only to adult converts. Since the New Testament writers were largely in a missionary situation it might be fair to say that their practice has primary reference to the baptism of adult converts but not exclusively so, as we have indicated above.

Implications

No Anglican congregation faithful to the Articles of Religion can fail to teach the appropriateness of baptizing the infant children of believers and to provide the sacrament of holy baptism for them. "Suffer the little children to come unto Me." Naturally, in a secular culture, the Church finds itself in a missionary situation, and where the Church is active in evangelism, the baptism of adult believers will greatly increase.

A particular issue concerning the baptism of the infants of believers does arise in pastoral ministry. What are Anglican clergy to do with those believers who are not persuaded of the biblical appropriateness of the baptism of their infant children and who want to mark the unique situation of the birth of their children with some sort of public ceremony of dedication? It seems to the author that this Article requires that the biblical grounds for infant baptism of the children of believers must be carefully and fully presented to them as clearly and persuasively as possible.

If they are not thereby persuaded, then, with the Bishop's permission, a dedication ceremony of some sort may be conducted during corporate worship on the Lord's Day, done in pastoral care for the children and the parents. However, since the baptism which is withheld is the instrument of grafting into the visible Church, the names of the children cannot be listed as members of the Church until they come to such time as they are rightly baptized, nor can the full nature and promises of salvation be signed and sealed to them. If the parents do not believe it is right to include the children in the covenant and thereby the Church, then we must not pretend that they are so incorporated. At the same time, one can't help but wonder if this "waiting period" of the unbaptized children is really doing justice to the fact that God has sent these children into the hearts and families of believers.

Conclusion

The Sacrament of Holy Baptism is the gift and work of Christ and is of great importance. It needs to be boldly and vividly celebrated and taught in the congregation. The baptism of the infants and young children of believers is in accord with Scripture and is to be carefully taught and celebrated. Baptism of the young is to lead to the confirmation of those who have come to personal faith in Christ. Confirmation is done after serious preparation. The baptism of adult believers, quite as much as of infants, should lead into a serious time of learning and preparation for confirmation.

ARTICLE 28

Of the Lord's Supper

The Supper of the Lord is not only a sign of the love that Christians ought to have among themselves, one to another, but rather it is a sacrament of our redemption by Christ's death: insomuch that to such as rightly, worthily, and with faith receive the same, the bread which we break is a partaking of the body of Christ, and likewise the cup of blessing is a partaking of the blood of Christ.

Transubstantiation (or the change of the substance of bread and wine) in the Supper of the Lord, cannot be proved by Holy Writ, but is repugnant to the plain words of Scripture, overthroweth the nature of a Sacrament, and hath given occasion to many superstitions.

The body of Christ is given, taken, and eaten in the Supper, only after an heavenly and spiritual manner. And the mean whereby the body of Christ is received and eaten in the Supper is Faith.

The Sacrament of the Lord's Supper was not by Christ's ordinance reserved, carried about, lifted up, or worshipped.

Introduction

Some churches invite all Christian believers to receive Holy Communion; some allow only members of their denomination to receive. Why? Some Churches are presently inviting anyone present at the celebration of the Eucharist to receive, even if they are not committed Christians; that seems generous, but can that be right? What is given and received in the Lord's Supper? There seems to be a good bit of theological argumentation about that.

It is true that in the history of the Church many controversies have arisen about the Lord's Supper or the Holy Communion. Some have led to divisions in the Church. This strife over the Lord's Supper is particularly sad, for while the Lord's Supper is far more than an expression of our love, it is a visible sign of God's love to us and of the love we are to have for God and for one another in Christ.

The chief cause of these controversies lies in different convictions concerning the nature of the presence of the Lord in and through the sacrament and the relation of the Lord's Supper to the finished work of Christ on the Cross.

Anglicans have rejected transubstantiation as a faithful understanding of the manner of the Lord's presence in the Sacrament and believe that the doctrine of transubstantiation has proven to be the cause of many of the erroneous practices, problems, and divisions that have arisen around the sacrament.

In addition, Anglicans have opposed any understanding of the Lord's Supper that would suggest that Christ is being bloodlessly sacrificed anew for merit under the forms of bread and wine as the sacrament is being celebrated.

One last comment concerns the title of this 28th Article. The title of this Article refers to the sacrament as "The Lord's Supper." That is but one of the several names that the Church has used to refer to this sacrament. The title "The Lord's Supper" reflects the founding of the sacrament in the Last Supper. After the Resurrection of the Lord Jesus, the Last Supper became the risen Lord's Supper with His disciples; it centers on His atoning Cross. Other names include the Mass, the Holy Communion, the Sacrament of the Altar, and the Eucharist. Each has its own emphasis. "The Mass" comes from the Latin phrase *Ite, missa est,* "It is finished. Go, you are sent." It points to the Christian life and mission for which the sacrament strengthens us. "Holy Communion" speaks of the sacred communion between Christ and His people and between the members of the Body of Christ. "The Sacrament of the Altar" emphasizes the reception of the broken Body and shed Blood of Christ and "the Eucharist" emphasizes the thanksgiving and praise which we offer for so great a redemption.

The Teaching of Article 28

Here are the teaching points for this Article:

1. The Lord's Supper is a sign of the love that Christians are to have among themselves.

2. The Lord's Supper is a sacrament of our redemption by Christ's death and is to be received in humble faith.

3. Transubstantiation contradicts Holy Scripture, overthrows the nature of a Sacrament, and gives rise to superstitions.

4. The body of Christ is given, taken, and eaten in the sacrament of the Lord's Supper in a spiritual manner, by faith.

5. The sacrament of the Lord's Supper was not ordained by Christ to be reserved, carried about, lifted up, or worshiped.

1. The Lord's Supper is a sign of the love that Christians are to have among themselves.
Explanation

There can be no doubt that the Lord's Supper is a sign of God's love for us in Christ and a sign of the love we Christians have and ought to have for one another in Christ.

This is the case for several reasons. First, the Lord's Supper is a symbolic, community meal and eating together is inherently expressive of fellowship and love. This is true in all cultures but it was particularly true in biblical times. Second, St. Paul emphasizes this community of mutual love when he speaks of us as Christians being one because we eat of the one loaf, who is Christ. Third, the early Church celebrated the Lord's Supper as part of a meal. This meal came to be referred to as an *agape* meal, or "love" feast. Therefore, we celebrate our love for the Lord and for one another in this sacramental meal.

Biblical Foundations

A new commandment I give to you, that you love one another: just as I have loved you, you also are to love one another. By this all people will know that you are my disciples, if you have love for one another. John 13:34-35

The cup of blessing that we bless, is it not a participation in the blood of Christ? The bread that we break, is it not a participation in the body of Christ? Because there is one bread, we who are many are one body, for we all partake of the one bread. 1 Corinthians 10:16-17

Whoever, therefore, eats the bread or drinks the cup of the Lord in an unworthy manner will be guilty of profaning the body and blood of the Lord. Let a person examine himself, then, and so eat of the bread and drink of the cup. For anyone who eats and drinks without discerning the body eats and drinks judgment on himself. That is why many of you are weak and ill, and some have died. But if we judged ourselves truly, we would not be judged. But when we are judged by the Lord, we are disciplined so that we may not be condemned along with the world. So then, my brothers, when you come together to eat, wait for one another. 1 Corinthians 11:27-33

False Teachings Denied/Objections Answered

1. The Holy Communion is clearly a corporate sacrament. The development of private or Chantry Masses in the Church is a contradiction of the communal nature of the Lord's Supper. The Anglican Reformers forbade all private masses. If no one comes to a stated celebration of the Lord's Supper, the Priest may not celebrate the Sacrament beyond the ministry of the Word.

2. Since the Lord's Supper is a sign of the love of God to those in Christ and of the love Christians have for one another, it is utterly inappropriate to invite those to receive the Sacrament who are not Christians. This is being done in some places and is now being referred to as "Open Communion." This recent practice is not to be confused with inviting Christians of a different branch of Christ's Church to receive communion, which is also referred to as "Open Communion." The practice of inviting non-Christians to receive communion flies in the face of the nature of the Sacrament and the Apostles' teaching, and violates Anglican doctrine and discipline. It is a scandal and an abuse of the sacrament.

3. Some having rightly held that the Lord's Supper is a sign of the love that Christians are to have for one another, have made our human response the entire meaning of the sacrament, teaching that the Lord's Supper is only, and nothing more than, a sign and expression of our thanksgiving to God and of our love for Christ and for one another. This "man-centered" teaching is usually referred to as Zwinglianism, after the teaching of the Swiss reformer Ulrich Zwingli (1484-1531). It can be argued that Zwingli's teaching was more complex and orthodox than that. Be that as it may, it is clear that that the Article rejects what has come to be called Zwinglianism. Zwinglianism is true in what it affirms, but false in what it denies and leaves out. Its very focus is wrong. The chief actor in the Sacraments of the Gospel is God, and believers respond to Him, not the other way around.

Implications

A. The right use of the sacrament as an expression of God's love for us and our love for God and for one another in Christ calls us to participate in faith and love. The Prayer Book invitation to receive the sacrament in a worthy fashion bids us to receive the sacrament in faith, intending to lead a holy life, walking in the commandments of God, and being in love and charity with the brethren and our neighbors. It is therefore contradictory of the right use of the sacrament for persons in the congregation who are estranged from one another and unforgiving of one another to receive the sacrament. They should first seek reconciliation and then receive the sacrament. Should reconciliation be sought by one and not the other, the one who has extended forgiveness and sought to be reconciled is in a state to receive the sacrament rightly.

B. The 1662 *Book of Common Prayer* has three Exhortations which make the right use of the Sacrament clear. One of these is appointed to be used in every celebration of the Lord's Supper. The present practice in many congregations is to use an Exhortation very infrequently, if at all. This neglect is happening at the same time that the Lord's Supper is being celebrated more and more frequently. The result is a superficial and even unworthy participation in the sacrament by many in the congregation. St. Paul warns us that unworthy participation is to invite judgment on oneself.

2. The Lord's Supper is a sacrament of our redemption by Christ's death and is to be received in humble faith.

Explanation

Here we come to the heart of this 27th Article. In the briefest of terms, it touches upon the nature of the Lord's Supper: "it is a Sacrament of our Redemption by Christ's death." There are at least four themes that are of special significance in the celebration of the Lord's Supper. They intermingle and cannot be kept entirely separate from one another. They are 1) remembrance, 2) sacrifice, 3) Christ's presence, and 4) Christ's words of institution referring to His Body and Blood. As we discuss these themes it will be helpful to have St. Paul's statement of the institution of the Last Supper (1 Corinthians 11:23-29) immediately before us:

> *For I received from the Lord what I also delivered to you, that the Lord Jesus on the night when he was betrayed took bread, and when he had given thanks, he broke it, and said, "This is my body which is for you. Do this in remembrance of me." In the same way also he took the cup, after supper, saying, "This cup is the new covenant in my blood. Do this, as often as you drink it, in remembrance of me." For as often as you eat this bread and drink this cup, you proclaim the Lord's death until he comes. Whoever, therefore, eats the bread or drinks the cup of the Lord in an unworthy manner will be guilty of profaning the body and blood of the Lord.*

First, we consider "remembrance." "Do this in remembrance of me." These words of our Lord are in the imperative mood and are a command of the Lord to His disciples to do this after His death and Resurrection. The "this" refers to the eating of the consecrated bread and the drinking of the consecrated wine in remembrance of His body broken and His blood shed for us sinners on the Cross.

The word "remembrance" is a rich word in biblical usage. It refers most fundamentally to recalling to mind and heart an event of the past. In this case it refers to recalling the once for all, completed act of Christ on the Cross by which Jesus made atonement for the sins of the world and thereby provided the basis for our justification through faith in Him. It is a recalling of a deed done. It is not a repetition of the act.

Remembrance also has a present sense. By recalling the Last Supper and its interpretation of Good Friday, we are bringing the event into the present in a sense. This is true today in our secular society; some very significant events that we recall are so vividly remembered that they almost seem to be taking place now. Those of us from the United States think of Fourth of July parades and the impact on us when the bandaged soldiers carrying the flag of the colonies, accompanied by the drummer and fife player, march by. This is our story. We were there.

This was particularly true in biblical times. A ceremony or celebration brought a past event to the present so vividly that it was almost as if the original event were taking place now, in the present. One thinks specially of the Passover celebration in Israel. Jews celebrate Passover still. And we celebrate our Passover in the Lord's Supper now. This too is our story.

Remembrance also has an important role in meeting and knowing other persons in the present. For example, we identify the character and the nature of our relationship with the person who is before us, when we recall key things from our previous relationship with them. We do this to recognize our friends and acquaintances. If we did not remember them, we would not know who they were, what they were like, and what would be an appropriate way for us to relate to them.

We do this even more intentionally as we meet with our Lord Who is present with us in the Lord's Supper. How does He desire for us to remember Him in order to recognize Him? He tells us; He asks us to remember Him in this eating and drinking of the bread and wine and to know Him now as our Savior Who has made atonement for us on the Cross. And, as we do that, we also identify and know ourselves as His disciples, forgiven by His grace. The Lord's Supper has its center and focus precisely on Him in this atoning deed. Secondarily, the focus is on us as the recipients of His costly grace. He is giving Himself to us in this sacrament of His Body and Blood.

Second is the theme of "sacrifice." There are two sacrifices involved in the Lord's Supper. The primary sacrifice is the sacrifice of Christ made once for all time on the Cross. It is vividly recalled and rehearsed. It is remembered as a finished and completed sacrifice. It is not and cannot be repeated. The pervasive and central argument of the Book of Hebrews emphasizes that the sacrifice of Christ on the Cross brings to an end all bloody, atoning sacrifice by perfecting it, so that Christ's death is the final and sufficient atonement for all sin. The author points out that the very act of continuing the sacrifices in the Temple in Jerusalem made it clear that those sacrifices did not and could not put away sin. They were only to prepare for and to point to the final sacrifice made by Christ. Article 31 makes this point more extensively so we will not develop it further here.

There is a second sacrifice in the Lord's Supper; it is our responsive sacrifice of praise and thanksgiving and our offering of ourselves to the Lord as a living sacrifice, which is our bounden duty and our spiritual worship. Our sacrifice rests upon and responds to Him in His all sufficient and completed sacrifice. It is offered by us only by the grace and in the power of the Holy Spirit. Its character is one of thanksgiving. It is not, in its nature, a meritorious work.

Third, there is the "presence of the Lord" in the celebration of the Lord's Supper. If God is the chief actor and initiator in the Sacrament, then He is present. In a very real sense, it is the Risen Christ and the congregation who celebrate this sacrament, and the Priests or Presbyters are but servants of both. If it is God the Holy Spirit in whom the Father and the Son draw near, and if it is God who thus speaks in the Word read, and preached, then surely it is Christ Who administers the bread and the wine to each communicant in and through the clergy who are administering the sacrament in His name. Just as Christ is present in our midst when two or three of His disciples draw near to God in prayer, so in this eating and drinking in obedience to Christ's command, we draw near to Christ, Who has already drawn near to us, as we eat and drink with

ARTICLE 28

Him in the in-breaking Kingdom of God. Christ is in our midst as the host of this meal.

Fourth, there is the meaning of Christ's words of institution to consider. "This is my Body broken for you," and "This is my Blood shed for you," spoken as He passed out the bread and the cup. With these words of institution, the question arises as to the nature of the relation between Christ's presence by the Spirit and the consecrated elements of bread and wine.

There are five basic views or doctrines about the relationship of the Presence of the Lord with the consecrated elements. 1) There is the Anglican view as set forth in the formularies, 2) there is the Roman Catholic and Orthodox view, 3) there is the Zwinglian View, 4) there is the Lutheran view, and 5) there is the Reformed view.

1. We consider the Anglican view first. It is what may be called an instrumental view. The Article states: "insomuch that to such as rightly, worthily and with faith receive the same, the bread which we break is a partaking of the Body of Christ and likewise the Cup of Blessing is a partaking of the Blood of Christ." The identification of receiving the bread and wine with "partaking" indicates an instrumental receiving in and through the consecrated elements of Christ's self-giving addressed to the heart and soul of the faithful recipients. The Anglican theologian Richard Hooker put it this way, "The real presence of Christ's most precious Body and Blood is not to be sought for in the sacraments but in the worthy recipients of the sacraments." This statement, however, is not to be understood in a purely subjective or receptionist sense, for Hooker also said of the sacraments, "Christ doth truly and presently give His own self in His sacraments: in baptism that we may put Him on; and in His supper that we may eat Him by faith and spirit" (see the "Laws of Ecclesiastical Polity" 5.50-67).

This view is confirmed by the Catechism of the 1662 *Book of Common Prayer* which states: "Question: What is the outward part or sign of the Lord's Supper? Answer: Bread and Wine, which the Lord hath commanded to be received. Question: What is the inward part or thing signified? Answer: The Body and Blood of Christ, which are verily and indeed taken and received by the faithful in the Lord's Supper." The partaking of the outward and visible sign of Bread and Wine is both the assurance of and also the instrumental means of taking and receiving the Body and Blood of Christ. In taking the bread and wine in faith we are taking and receiving the Body and Blood of Christ.

Such an instrumental understanding distinguishes between the sacramental sign, which is the consecrated bread and wine, and that which is signed, the Body and Blood of Christ. The two are not identified, as in transubstantiation, nor are they so related as to convey the Body and Blood to those that partake unworthily and without faith, for only those who take and receive in faith, spiritually, receive Christ's self-giving of His Body and Blood. Christ gives His Body and Blood spiritually in and through the signs of so great a thing. Archbishop Cranmer makes this point in the following words: "We do not pray absolutely that the bread and wine may be the Body and Blood of Christ, but that unto us, that they may be so in that Holy Mystery, that is to say, that we may so worthily receive the same that we may be partakers of Christ's Body and Blood and that therewith in Spirit and truth we may be spiritually nourished." (Works vol 1, pg 79, Parker Society)

2. The Roman Catholic and Eastern Orthodox view identifies the sign with the thing signified so that the essence of the bread and wine become the Body and Blood of Christ. After the consecration there is no bread or wine but only Christ's Body and Blood, though the elements retain the outward appearance of bread and wine to human sight. This assumes that the "is" in Christ's words of institution involved a transformation of the elements and was not referring to them as a sign of His Body that was to

be broken and His Blood to be shed on Good Friday. As Roman Catholic writers sometimes put it, at the Last Supper Christ held Himself in His hand, as does the Priest hold Christ's Body and Blood in his hands in the Mass.

3. The Lutheran view distinguishes between the sign and the thing signified but so connects the two that even those who partake in unbelief and unworthily, receive the Body and Blood of Christ. There is a tendency in Lutheran Eucharistic theology to stress the objective, physical nature of the glorified Body and Blood of Christ present in, with, and under the sacramental signs of bread and wine. Lutheran confessional writings therefore speak of a *manducatio oralis*, an oral eating of the Body and Blood of Christ and of a *manducatio indignorum*, an eating of the Body and Blood of Christ by the unworthy and unbelieving who receive the Body and Blood of Christ to their condemnation. In Article 29, Anglicans explicitly reject the teaching that unbelievers receive the Body and Blood of Christ.

4. The Reformed view and the Anglican view are similar. The Reformed view distinguishes between the thing signified and the sign, but the sacramental connection is left undefined. The Reformed Confessions sometimes speak of a sort of parallelism, saying that as surely as we partake of the sign of bread and wine in faith and repentance so we can be certain that we are also truly receiving the Body and Blood of Christ. Since the glorified Body of Christ is believed to be exclusively in Heaven, Calvin and Reformed theologians speak of the hearts of the believers being raised up into Heaven into Christ's presence in the Sacrament.

Anglicans are far more cautious about pronouncements concerning the mystery of the risen Lord's glorified body than either the Reformed or the Lutherans.

5. The Zwinglian view is non-sacramental and uncomplicated. It holds that Jesus was speaking figuratively in the words of institution. "This represents my

Body and Blood" is what He meant and that is all that He and the later statements of the Apostles meant. Hence, the Lord's Supper is not a sacrament of His presence, but rather serves as a reminder to us of His Cross and as a vehicle for giving expression of our love and gratitude to Him and to one another in Him. Anything more goes beyond Scripture and ignores the fact that Jesus' risen and glorified Body is in Heaven and we are on earth, according to the Zwinglian view. This is a non-sacramental view of the Lord's Supper and makes us the chief actors in the ordinance.

In summary, Anglicans do not seek to explain the mystery of Christ's presence beyond the strong affirmation of His presence with us in the sacrament and of His giving Himself in His atoning virtue, His Body and Blood, only to believers, for they are received by faith, in and through the sacramental signs of the consecrated bread and wine.

Lastly, the Article speaks of partaking of the sacrament rightly, worthily, and with faith. The sacraments of the Gospel are instruments of grace, instruments that are effective in the relationship between God and man in Christ by the Holy Spirit. Christ gives Himself and the virtue of His atonement to the individual and the congregation to sustain, assure, nurture, and strengthen a living, growing faith in Christ. To participate in unbelief, or in any other unworthy manner, is to profane the sacrament, to dishonor God and to bring judgment upon oneself. Repentant faith is essential to a right use of the sacrament because the nature of Christ's self-giving is personal and because the Lord's Supper is for sinners who receive unmerited grace therein.

Jesus speaks about the importance of humble, repentant faith in connection to worship. The Apostle Paul warns us that to profane the Sacrament will bring serious consequences. It is far better to judge oneself and partake of the sacrament only in a worthy manner, in repentance and faith, than to offend the Lord.

Biblical Foundations

For where two or three are gathered in my name, there am I among them. Matthew 18:20

Go therefore and make disciples of all nations, baptizing them in the name of the Father and of the Son and of the Holy Spirit, teaching them to observe all that I have commanded you. And behold, I am with you always, to the end of the age. Matthew 28:19-20

Now as they were eating, Jesus took bread, and after blessing it broke it and gave it to the disciples, and said, "Take, eat; this is my body." And he took a cup, and when he had given thanks he gave it to them, saying, "Drink of it, all of you, for this is my blood of the covenant, which is poured out for many for the forgiveness of sins. I tell you I will not drink again of this fruit of the vine until that day when I drink it new with you in my Father's kingdom." Matthew 26:26-29, with parallels in Mark 14:22-25 and Luke 22: 13-20

For I received from the Lord what I also delivered to you, that the Lord Jesus on the night when he was betrayed took bread, and when he had given thanks, he broke it, and said, "This is my body which is for you. Do this in remembrance of me." In the same way also he took the cup, after supper, saying, "This cup is the new covenant in my blood. Do this, as often as you drink it, in remembrance of me." For as often as you eat this bread and drink the cup, you proclaim the Lord's death until he comes. Whoever, therefore, eats the bread or drinks the cup of the Lord in an unworthy manner will be guilty of profaning the body and blood of the Lord. Let a person examine himself, then, and so eat of the bread and drink of the cup. For anyone who eats and drinks without discerning the body eats and drinks judgment on himself. 1 Corinthians 11:23-29

The cup of blessing that we bless, is it not a participation in the blood of Christ? The bread that we break, is it not a participation in the body of Christ? Because there is one bread, we who are many are one body, for we all partake of the one bread. 1 Corinthians 10:16-17

For anyone who eats and drinks without discerning the body eats and drinks judgment on himself. 1 Corinthians 11:29

Examine yourselves, to see whether you are in the faith. Test yourselves. Or do you not realize this about yourselves, that Jesus Christ is in you? —unless indeed you fail to meet the test! 2 Corinthians 13:5

False Teachings Denied/Objections Answered

1. We have already made it clear that Zwinglianism is right in what it affirms and wrong in what it denies. In addition, it has things upside down by giving believers the initiative. Also, how odd to hold that God Himself in the Spirit graciously and sovereignly draws near to speak to us through the Word read and preached, as most churches who hold this view do believe, but that the Lord does not draw near and is not present with us and to us in the Supper of the Lord.

2. Anglicans differ seriously from the Roman Catholic and Eastern Orthodox in doctrine and practice in several ways. Teaching Point 3 of this Article will deal with transubstantiation so we will not address that here.

However, there are other points at which Anglicans differ from Roman Catholic and Eastern Orthodox teaching.

First, one very important difference concerns the matter of the Sacrifice of the Mass. Roman Catholics taught at Trent that in the Mass Christ through the Priest offers Himself in a bloodless manner for merit to the Father. Eastern Orthodox teaching, while less dogmatic and less concerned with merit, seems to move along the same general lines regarding sacrifice in the Eucharist. Anglicans believe that this doctrine is contrary to the Scripture. It takes away from the sufficiency of Christ's sacrifice on the Cross. It reverses the whole movement of grace in the

Sacrament, so that Christ ends up offering to God what He is offering to us. It introduces the accumulation of merit into our relationship with God, in which relationship we have no merit, but are saved by grace alone. And lastly, it redefines the nature of the ordained priesthood from that found in the New Testament. In the New Testament, we find a pastoral priesthood, whereas in Rome and Eastern Orthodoxy, we find a sacerdotal priesthood like that of the Old Testament. In the Old Testament, Priests did offer atoning sacrifices to God. The New Testament redefinition of the Old Testament priesthood to that of a pastoral Presbyterate arises from the fact that in Christ the atonement has been made, once for all. It is clear that further ecumenical discussion is in order as well as discussion between Anglicans.

Second, there is also a difference between Anglican and Roman Catholic teaching on a right use of the Sacrament. For Anglicans, it is a matter of repentant faith, coming humbly to the table without one plea, with empty hands. Apart from that manner of participation, no grace is received. In the case of Rome the Sacrament is effective *ex opera operato*, by the very doing of it in the correct and churchly manner, provided one does not put a block (*obex*) to receiving, or to receive when one is not in a state of grace. A lack of faith is not expressly stated to be a block to receiving the grace of the sacrament. Whereas, in a biblical and Anglican understanding, faith is essential to a right use of the sacrament.

Third, the practice of communicating infants in Eastern Orthodoxy seems to be at odds with the right use of the sacrament which requires repentant faith. Anglicans are divided about the practice of communicating young children and at a minimum require that the child be instructed and of such an age as to be aware of the uniqueness of what he or she is doing. The necessity of repentant faith is also clearly at odds with a recent growing tendency in secularized Anglicanism to practice "Open

Communion" in the sense of inviting non-Christians to receive the Holy Communion.

3. Anglicans differ from the Lutherans with reference to their seemingly physical view of the present glorified Body and Blood of Christ and on the Body and Blood of Christ being communicated to unbelievers, scoffers, and those that receive the sacrament unworthily. Anglicans accept that an unworthy eating of the bread and wine of the Sacrament blasphemes the Lord, dishonors the Sacrament, and brings judgment on those who do so, but Anglicans deny that unbelievers and unworthy participants ever receive the Body and Blood of Christ. Unbelievers only receive the sign of "so great a thing."

On the other hand, there is much for Anglicans to admire in Lutheran Eucharistic theology: its strong emphasis on grace, its affirmation of the partaking of the Body and Blood of Christ in, with, and under or through the sacramental signs of bread and wine, and its clear teaching that Christ is present at all of the celebrations of the Lord's Supper to give Himself to us.

4. With the Reformed, Anglicans can rejoice in the strong sense of assurance that what God promises in the Sacrament He surely gives. God keeps His promises. Anglicans are less comfortable with the limiting of Christ's glorified body to Heaven. It is good to allow what is mysterious to remain mysterious.

Implications

Anglicans affirm the objective and real presence of Christ in the Lord's Supper. To "take and to receive" implies the presence of the Giver, the existence of that which is given and received, as well as the presence of believers who take and receive.

As sinners approaching the Lord's Supper in repentant faith in Christ, we hold fellowship with the Lord and with fellow believers. We are present to one another.

In the Sacrament, we are assured that our standing with God rests upon Christ's completed work on the Cross. We eat spiritually of His Body and drink of His Blood and receive anew the virtue and benefits of His atoning work in our relationship with the present Lord.

The Lord's Supper is a sacred gift. We do well to examine ourselves before we come to the table in order to partake worthily.

3. Transubstantiation contradicts Holy Scripture, overthrows the nature of a sacrament, and gives rise to superstitions.
Explanation

The Reformers strongly rejected the Tridentine Roman Catholic doctrine of transubstantiation. An early form of that doctrine had been taught by the Abbot Paschasius Radbert as early as the 9th century, causing a great controversy. The controversy broke out again in the 11th century when the increasingly popular view that taught a physical change of the elements took place at the consecration was challenged by Archdeacon Berengarius. In the end, it was the conviction that the elements underwent a change of essence at consecration that prevailed. This doctrine of transubstantiation was given its finest and final formulation by St. Thomas Aquinas in the 13th century. In it, he taught that the accidents, that is, the appearances of bread and wine remain after the consecration of the elements, but that the essence or substance of the elements, that which makes something what it is, was changed into the Body and Blood of Christ. Therefore, we have in the Eucharist the actual Body and Blood of Christ, though it retains the appearance of bread and wine.

St. Thomas offered several reasons why the Lord chose to leave the accidents or appearances unchanged: one reason was that God did this so that non-believers would not be offended and charge us with cannibalism as had happened in the early days of the Church. Another reason was so that we ourselves would not be offended by having to eat what looked and tasted like flesh and drink what looked and tasted like blood. A third reason was that in so hiding the Body and Blood under the appearance of bread and wine, God gave our faith something to believe on the basis of Christ's Word that went beyond sight and reason.

Our Reformers offered five reasons why they rejected this teaching of St. Thomas and of the Council of Trent.

Firstly, they held that transubstantiation cannot be proved by Holy Scripture. In Scripture, there is no hint that the essence of the bread and wine undergo a change. It is dangerous to teach anything as necessary to be believed for salvation that cannot be proven by the clear and explicit teaching of Holy Scripture.

Secondly, the Reformers held that transubstantiation is actually contrary to the teaching of Holy Scripture. The Scriptures refer to the consecrated elements as bread and wine. If it is dangerous to teach what cannot be proved by Scripture, it is clearly wrong to teach anything contrary to what the Scriptures do teach.

Thirdly, they said that the doctrine overthrows the very nature of a sacrament. A sacrament is comprised of three parts: the outward and visible sign, and the inner and spiritual grace or virtue, and the sacramental union or relationship between the two. In transubstantiation, the thing signified and the sign become the same thing. The relationship is identity. We no longer have a sign of Christ's Body and Blood; we only have the Body and Blood. This is not a sacrament but a simple identity under misleading appearances. The very nature of a sacrament has been overthrown.

Fourthly, they were convinced that God would not ask us to violate the sight and taste with which He had endowed us. Cranmer wrote: "We see, smell, taste and touch bread and wine. We are asked to believe clear contrary to our senses. Christ never made any such article of our Faith. Our Faith teaches us to believe things we cannot see but it does not bid us that we should not believe what we do see... rather our senses confirm our faith."

Fifthly, the Reformers held that because the Church taught this error a number of objectionable and superstitious practices sprang up in the Church. They had in mind such things as the shift in the focus of the sacrament from communication by the faithful to the observation of the miracle of the change in the bread and wine by those attending the Mass; also in mind was the practice of some people who secretly took the consecrated host home to work healings, to ensure success in crops, and other similar superstitious uses.

Other Reformers had their objections as well. Luther objected that it was dangerous to wed the teaching of the Bible and the Church to any given philosophy, for philosophies come and go but the Word of God abides forever. In addition, he felt that the doctrine of transubstantiation necessitated numerous unnecessary miracles. Others, including the Anglican Reformers, pointed out that the doctrine was contrary to the "old authors of the Faith." It was a teaching not held "always, everywhere, and by all."

Biblical Foundations

The cup of blessing that we bless, is it not a participation in the blood of Christ? The bread that we break, is it not a participation in the body of Christ? Because there is one bread, we who are many are one body, for we all partake of the one bread. 1 Corinthians 10:16-17

For I received from the Lord what I also delivered to you, that the Lord Jesus on the night when he was betrayed took bread, and when he had given thanks, he broke it, and said, "This is my body which is for you. Do this in remembrance of me." In the same way also he took the cup, after supper, saying, "This cup is the new covenant in my blood. Do this, as often as you drink it, in remembrance of me." For as often as you eat this bread and drink the cup, you proclaim the Lord's death until he comes. Whoever, therefore, eats the bread or drinks the cup of the Lord in an unworthy manner will be guilty of profaning the body and blood of the Lord. 1 Corinthians 11:23-27

False Teachings Denied/Questions Answered

Much false teaching has been discussed above. We have already explained why non-sacramental Zwinglianism, whether past or present, is inadequate; it is true in what it affirms and false in what it denies. We have stated at some length why the doctrine of Transubstantiation is a teaching to be rejected as contrary to Scripture and for other reasons as well. Having said that, however, we do not want to be understood to deny that these doctrines were serious attempts, though inadequate and even erroneous, to teach about aspects of the Lord's Supper that are of great importance.

Implications

There is much that is mysterious about the sacraments of the Gospel. The biblical teaching in Scripture on the Lord's Supper is actually not very extensive and is largely aimed at our right use of the Sacrament. Given this, we do well to keep our teaching close to the word of the Scriptures. The saying concerning the Lord's Supper attributed to Queen Elizabeth I is wise and can serve as a good guide for us all: "What the Word of God doth make it; I do believe and thus do take it."

4. The body of Christ is given, taken, and eaten in the Sacrament of the Lord's Supper in a spiritual manner, by faith.
Explanation

Anglicans hold that the Sacraments of the Gospel take place in the personal relationship between God and His believing people. In this personal or spiritual relationship, the giving and the taking and eating of the Body and Blood of the Risen and Glorified Lord is spiritual. It involves the self, the heart, as well as the body.

As Jesus said:

There is nothing outside a person that by going into him can defile him, but the things that come out of a person are what defile him... Do you not see that whatever goes into a person from outside cannot defile him, since it enters not his heart but his stomach, and is expelled... What comes out of a person is what defiles him, For from within, out of the heart of man come evil thoughts, sexual immorality, theft, murder, adultery, coveting, wickedness, deceit, sensuality, envy, slander, pride, foolishness. All these evil things come from within and they defile a person. Mark 7:15-23

If the sign of bread and wine are instrumental to the Lord's Body and Blood, then as the sign of the Sacrament is given to the person through the mouth, so the Body and Blood of Christ are addressed to and received by the heart. The Body and Blood of Christ in the Sacrament of the Lord's Supper are given, taken and eaten after a heavenly or spiritual manner by faith.

St. Augustine made this point when he said, "To what end do you prepare teeth and tongue, just believe and you have eaten." He also said of unbelievers, "They neither eat Christ's flesh nor drink His blood, although they eat the sacrament thereof, to the condemnation of their presumption (Works Vol. I pg 205). St. Augustine makes the same point by distinguishing three manners of eating: 1) spiritual only, that is, by faith in Christ apart from the Sacrament, 2) spiritual and sacramental, that is, by the sacrament in the mouth and Christ in faith, and 3) sacramental only, that is, with the sacrament in the mouth and no reception of Christ in faith.

Archbishop Cranmer agreed: "We receive with a pure and sincere faith" (Works Vol. I pg 43). Therefore, as an expression of the personal relationship between Christ and His members, the Body and Blood of the Lord is given, taken, received, and eaten in a spiritual and heavenly manner through faith and the soul is nourished and strengthened.

Biblical Foundations

But the Lord said to Samuel, "Do not look on his appearance or on the height of his stature, because I have rejected him. For the Lord sees not as man sees: man looks on the outward appearance, but the Lord looks on the heart." 1 Samuel 16:7

Jesus said, *"There is nothing outside a person that by going into him can defile him, but the things that come out of a person are what defile him." And when he had entered the house and left the people, his disciples asked him about the parable. And he said to them, "Then are you also without understanding? Do you not see that whatever goes into a person from outside cannot defile him, since it enters not his heart but his stomach, and is expelled?" (Thus he declared all foods clean.) And he said, "What comes out of a person is what defiles him. For from within, out of the heart of man, come evil thoughts, sexual immorality, theft, murder, adultery, coveting, wickedness, deceit, sensuality, envy, slander, pride, foolishness. All these evil things come from within, and they defile a person."* Mark 7:15-23

Therefore, brothers, since we have confidence to enter the holy places by the blood of Jesus, by the new and living way that he opened for us through the curtain, that is, through his flesh, and since we have a great priest over the house of God, let us draw near with a true heart in full assurance of faith, with our hearts sprinkled clean from an evil conscience and our bodies washed with pure water. Hebrews 10:19-22

False Teachings Denied/Objections Answered

1. The Roman Catholic and Eastern Orthodox position teaches the physical presence of the Body and Blood of Christ in the sacramental elements that were once bread and wine. This both overthrows the nature of a sacrament and makes the presence of the Lord in the Sacrament physical in nature.

2. Lutherans do not teach the transubstantiation of the bread and wine and so do not overthrow the nature of a sacrament. However, they do teach that the glorified body of Christ is physically present in, with, and under the sacramental signs of bread and wine, which is why they insist that unbelievers unworthily receive the Body and Blood of the Lord, albeit to their shame and condemnation. Faith, then, is not the means to receive the glorified Body and Blood of Christ; instead, faith in Christ is only the way to receive it for benefit. This seems 1) to understand the glorified presence of the Lord and His Body and Blood in the sacrament in too physical a manner and 2) to change the role of faith from being the means whereby one may take and eat the glorified Body and drink the Blood of Christ until He comes again in glory to being the way to receive the Body and Blood for salvific benefit. This entails the further teaching that unbelievers receive the Body and Blood of the Lord just by physical eating and drinking.

Anglicans hold to a real spiritual presence of Christ, a real giving, taking and receiving of His glorified Body and Blood in and through the sacrament, but this is done in the Spirit and is received only in a spiritual manner, by faith in Christ. (See the discussion in Article 29.)

Implications

While Anglicans do affirm the "objective" or real presence of Christ in the Lord's Supper and a real giving, taking, eating, and drinking of His Body and Blood, this is affirmed in the sense that the giving and receiving is interpersonal and addressed to the human heart. The proper preparation for partaking of the Lord's Supper is a preparation of the heart in repentance and faith. The Sacramental signs are received physically and they are instrumental to our partaking spiritually of Christ's Body and Blood. The bread and the wine are the sacramental sign and instrument of the inner grace received in faith. The Body and Blood of Christ are not physical objects available to all who partake of the Sacrament regardless of their spiritual condition. They can be received, eaten, and drunk only by faith.

5. The sacrament of the Lord's Supper was not ordained by Christ to be reserved, carried about, lifted up, or worshiped.

Explanation

The purpose for which the sacrament of the Lord's Supper was instituted by the Lord Jesus was for giving, taking, eating, and drinking in the Spirit. It was not for observing but for partaking, for active participation involving the whole self and the community of faith.

The teaching of transubstantiation caused a shift of the focus of the congregation from communication to observation. Non-communicating masses became legitimate and people increasingly attended the Eucharist to see the miracle rather than to receive Christ in and through the Sacrament in repentance and faith.

The doctrine of transubstantiation led to the practices listed in this section of the Article: processions with the consecrated elements such as *Corpus Christi*, the elevation of the elements in the celebration of the Mass for all to see "the Lamb of God" hidden under the appearances of bread and wine, and the development of such extra-Eucharistic services as the Adoration of the Blessed Sacrament, in which the elements were and are worshiped because they are believed to be the transubstantiated Body and Blood of the Lord.

These practices were not intended by the Lord in His institution of the Sacrament. And once transubstantiation is denied, these practices lose much of their foundation and purpose.

Reservation is quite different. It was practiced early in the life and history of the Church. Justin Martyr mentions it in the 1st century. The consecrated elements were reserved to be taken to the sick that could not attend the community celebration on that Lord's Day. They were not reserved to be adored but to be consumed in faith. This practice is in line with the intention of the Lord's institution of the Sacrament. The other practices of procession, elevation and adoration came only much later in the life of the Church beginning around the 10th century in some parts.

Some Anglicans point out that the Article does not forbid these practices which are listed in the Article. The Article only teaches that they are not the purpose for which the Lord instituted the sacrament and that therefore these practices may be retained in the worship of a congregation.

It is true that the practices are not explicitly condemned. On the other hand, given the context of the previous paragraph of the Article, which rejects transubstantiation as overthrowing the nature of a sacrament and as giving rise to many superstitions, it is hard to see how these practices are not, at least, viewed in the Article with grave suspicion.

If they are to be continued in Anglican circles, surely a clear biblical explanation of their theological rationale must be provided so that transubstantiation is not implied and taught when they are practiced. If they are continued without a clear biblical explanation, they will implicitly teach transubstantiation, since they arose from that perspective in the first place.

Biblical Foundations

Now as they were eating, Jesus took bread, and after blessing it broke it and gave it to the disciples, and said, "Take, eat; this is my body." And he took a cup, and when he had given thanks he gave it to them, saying, "Drink of it, all of you, for this is my blood of the covenant, which is poured out for many for the forgiveness of sins. I tell you I will not drink again of this fruit of the vine until that day when I drink it new with you in my Father's kingdom." Matthew 26:26-29

The cup of blessing that we bless, is it not a participation in the blood of Christ? The bread that we break, is it not a participation in the body of Christ? Because there is one bread, we who are many are one body, for we all partake of the one bread. 1 Corinthians 10:16-17

For I received from the Lord what I also delivered to you, that the Lord Jesus on the night when he was betrayed took bread, and when he had given thanks, he broke it, and said, "This is my body which is for you. Do this in remembrance of me." In the same way also he took the cup, after supper, saying, "This cup is the new covenant in my blood. Do this, as often as you drink it, in remembrance of me." For as often as you eat this bread and drink the cup, you proclaim the Lord's death until he comes. Whoever, therefore, eats the bread or drinks the cup of the Lord in an unworthy manner will be guilty of profaning the body and blood of the Lord. 1 Corinthians 11:23-27

False Teachings Denied/Objections Answered

Some Anglicans would deny that the previous paragraph of the Article rejected all forms of transubstantiation but only the Roman Catholic form as stated by St. Thomas and the Council of Trent. And therefore, the listed practices can be continued with no biblical rationale needed.

This is not convincing for two reasons: 1) The Article defines transubstantiation as "the change of the substance of the bread and wine," and it is hard to think of what any doctrine of transubstantiation might be that did not include such a change. It is the heart of the doctrine. Also, 2) the doctrine as Rome holds it was formulated by St. Thomas of Aquinas and is the finest expression of transubstantiation to be found. The Council of Trent gave official stamp to the doctrine as formulated by St. Thomas. If it is rejected, the very concept is rejected.

Therefore, the conclusion we must come to is that these practices, if they are continued, will need to be accompanied with a clear biblical rationale.

Implications

This last teaching point of this Article warns us that liturgy and ceremony are inherently related to doctrine; that is, services and ceremonies express what one believes the Lord's Supper to be, and what its purpose is. What one does, one liturgically teaches. Ceremony is not prescribed except in a minimal way in the rubrics of the Prayer Book. This restraint, however, should not be interpreted to mean that ceremony is of no importance. Ceremony involving the Lord's Supper and the sacramental signs of the Lord's Supper should give expression to what the Lord's Supper is meant to be and do, according to the Lord's purpose in instituting it.

Conclusion

The Lord's Supper is richly symbolic and centrally significant in the worship of the Lord. It is a great gift of Christ and is to be treasured and entered into with penitent faith, thanksgiving, and anticipation. The Lord's purpose in giving us the Lord's Supper should control our celebrations of the Lord's Supper and use of the elements or the signs of the Sacrament. If extra-Eucharistic practices are continued, they should be subordinate to Christ's intention in the institution of the Lord's Supper and the congregation should be taught their meaning in the light of Scripture.

ARTICLE 29

Of the Wicked Which Do Not Eat the Body of Christ, in the Use of the Lord's Supper

The wicked and such as be void of a lively faith, although they do carnally and visibly press with their teeth (as S. Augustine saith) the sacrament of the body and blood of Christ, yet in no wise are they partakers of Christ, but rather to their condemnation do eat and drink the sign or sacrament of so great a thing.

Introduction

What are we to think regarding the unworthy reception of the Lord's Supper? What, if anything, is communicated to those who receive the sacramental signs of the Lord's Supper in an unworthy manner? These questions arise when the doctrine of transubstantiation is denied. Rome taught that all received but not all benefited. Anglicans took a different view.

This Article seems to be an appendix to the previous Article 28. It emphasizes and restates what is to be found there. It would be profitable to read Article 28 first and then continue with the reading of this Article.

The Teaching of Article 29

Here are the teaching points for this Article:

1. The wicked and unbelieving do not eat the body nor drink the blood of Christ in the use of the Lord's Supper.

2. They do physically eat and drink the sacramental signs of bread and wine only and bring condemnation upon themselves.

1. The wicked and unbelieving do not eat the body nor drink the blood of Christ in the use of the Lord's Supper.

Explanation

The main point of this Teaching Point 1 has already been stated in Teaching Point 4 of the previous Article, Article 28. Those who partake of the Lord's Supper in an unworthy manner, whether by unbelief or unrepentant wickedness, do physically consume the sacramental signs of the consecrated bread and wine, but since it is repentant faith that spiritually receives the glorified Body and Blood of the Lord, they do not receive His glorified Body and Blood. This eating and drinking is spiritual and an action of the heart. A heart closed to the Lord cannot receive or partake the Body and Blood of the glorified Lord.

The opposite may also be said, that whoever partakes of Christ's Body and Blood in the Sacrament of the Lord's Supper by faith, is united to Him and abides in Him through faith.

In this Article, the phrase "in no wise" drives the point home with absolute clarity. Unbelievers are "in no wise partakers of Christ." In Article 28, the same emphasis is present in the word "only" as in "The body of Christ is given, taken, and eaten in the Supper, only after an heavenly and spiritual manner. And the means whereby the body of Christ is received and eaten in the Supper is by faith." Articles 28 and 29 leave us no uncertainty about this.

Biblical Foundations

But the Lord said to Samuel, "Do not look on his appearance or on the height of his stature, because I have rejected him. For the Lord sees not as man sees: man looks on the outward appearance, but the Lord looks on the heart." 1 Samuel 16:7

[Jesus said,] "There is nothing outside a person that by going into him can defile him, but the things that come out of a person are what defile him." And when he had entered the house and left the people, his disciples asked him about the parable. And he said to them, "Then are you also without understanding? Do you not see that whatever goes into a person from outside cannot defile him, since it enters not his heart but his stomach, and is expelled?" (Thus he declared all foods clean.) And he said, "What comes out of a person is what defiles him. For from within, out of the heart of man, come evil thoughts, sexual immorality, theft, murder, adultery, coveting, wickedness, deceit, sensuality, envy, slander, pride, foolishness. All these evil things come from within, and they defile a person." Mark 7:15-23

[Jesus said,] "This is the bread that comes down from heaven, so that one may eat of it and not die. I am the living bread that came down from heaven. If anyone eats of this bread, he will live forever. And the bread that I will give for the life of the world is my flesh." The Jews then disputed among themselves, saying, "How can this man give us his flesh to eat?" So Jesus said to them, "Truly, truly, I say to you, unless you eat the flesh of the Son of Man and drink his blood, you have no life in you. Whoever feeds on my flesh and drinks my blood has eternal life, and I will raise him up on the last day. For my flesh is true food, and my blood is true drink. Whoever feeds on my flesh and drinks my blood abides in me, and I in him. As the living Father sent me, and I live because of the Father, so whoever feeds on me, he also will live because of me." John 6:50-57

Therefore, brothers, since we have confidence to enter the holy places by the blood of Jesus, by the new and living way that he opened for us through the curtain, that is, through his flesh, and since we have a great priest over the house of God, let us draw near with a true heart in full assurance of faith, with our hearts sprinkled clean from an evil conscience and our bodies washed with pure water. Hebrews 10:19-22

False Teaching Denied/Objections Answered

1. Trent having affirmed transubstantiation taught that all who receive the consecrated elements in the Mass did receive the Body and Blood of Christ. In so doing, those who were not in a state of grace profaned the sacrament and offended God. As stated earlier, Anglicans have rejected transubstantiation.

2. The Lutherans, while they did not teach that the consecrated bread and wine were transubstantiated, teach that the Body and Blood of Christ are present in, with, and under the sacramental signs in such a manner that all who receive the consecrated elements do receive the Body and Blood of Christ. The unbelieving receive the Lord, only to bring judgment upon themselves. As this Article makes clear, Anglicans do not agree with the Lutherans at this point.

3. Anglicans note that the language about eating, drinking, and feeding on Christ in the Scriptures is consistently linked to repentant faith, and to being united to and abiding in Christ, and not merely to physical eating and drinking. There is no biblical teaching of a partaking of the Body and Blood of Christ that is not beneficial. There is, however, a teaching that asserts that to eat and drink of the Supper unworthily, that is, taking the sacramental signs of consecrated bread and wine without repentant faith, is to eat and drink judgment upon oneself.

Implications

Those who take the sacrament of the Lord's Supper apart from repentant faith, in an unworthy manner, can have no confidence that they have received the nourishment of the Body and Blood of Christ or that they are united to Christ thereby. The assurance of the Sacrament does not belong to them. What they can be certain of leads us to the dire warning in the Teaching Point 2 of this Article.

2. They do physically and visibly eat and drink the sacramental signs of bread and wine only, and bring condemnation upon themselves.

Explanation

The connection between the sacramental signs of bread and wine and the Body and Blood of Christ, His self-giving to us, is spiritual. Therefore to take the sacramental sign in a unspiritual manner, without repentant faith, is to receive only the outer signs of the sacrament and not the inner grace of the sacrament.

The incurring of judgment follows from unworthy participation. If you profane the sacrament by receiving it unworthily, then you offend the Lord of the sacrament and bring judgment upon yourself. It is no light matter to profane Holy things and most particularly the sacrament of the presence and gift of the Risen Lord Himself.

It is for this reason that there are three exhortations concerning the seriousness of participation in the Lord's Supper and the need for self-examination to be found in *The Book of Common Prayer*.

Biblical Foundations

Jesus said, "But when the king came in to look at the guests, he saw there a man who had no wedding garment. And he said to him, "Friend, how did you get in here without a wedding garment?' And he was speechless." Matthew 22:11-12

You cannot drink the cup of the Lord and the cup of demons. You cannot partake of the table of the Lord and the table of demons. 1 Corinthians 10:21

Whoever, therefore, eats the bread or drinks the cup of the Lord in an unworthy manner will be guilty of profaning the body and blood of the Lord. Let a person examine himself, then, and so eat of the bread and drink of the cup. For anyone who eats and drinks without discerning the body eats and drinks judgment on himself. That is why many of you are weak and ill, and some have died. 1 Corinthians 11:27-30

False Teaching Denied/Objections Answered

There is a difference of opinion about the interpretation of 1 Corinthians 11: 27-30:
> Whoever, therefore, eats the bread or drinks the cup of the Lord in an unworthy manner will be guilty of profaning the body and blood of the Lord. Let a person examine himself, then, and so eat of the bread and drink of the cup. For anyone who eats and drinks without discerning the body eats and drinks judgment on himself. That is why many of you are weak and ill, and some have died."

Some interpret "without discerning the body" to refer to a cavalier partaking of the sacrament. The Corinthians were not taking the sacrament seriously as the gift and presence of the Lord.

However, a more careful reading of the text seems to move in another direction. To what, then, does "discerning the body" refer? Given the context in the Epistle, it is by far more likely that the "body" to which the Apostle is referring is the congregation and not the sacramental elements. The Corinthians were not so much indifferent to the sacrament as they were indifferent to each other in the very midst of celebrating the sacrament of their unity in Christ. The offense was not a failure to discern the sacramental elements to be instruments of Christ's self-giving to them, but a failure to discern the body that they themselves were in Christ. This is such a serious contradiction and abuse of the sacrament that the Apostle Paul almost denies that they are celebrating the Lord's Supper at all. "And when you come together, it is not the

Lord's Supper that you eat. For in eating, each one goes ahead with his own meal. One goes hungry, another gets drunk" (1 Corinthians 11:20-21).

It was due to this indifference to one another and quarreling among themselves while partaking of the sacrament that the Lord visited punishment upon them by illness and even death. If this is an accurate interpretation of this text, it stands in line with Jesus' teaching to leave our gifts and the altar and first be reconciled and then return to worship. And it applies to congregations and not just individuals.

There are, therefore, several unworthy ways to partake of the Lord's Supper. To partake without repentance or without faith in Christ are ways to abuse the sacrament, as is partaking while harboring unforgiveness or indifference with regard to fellow Christians. St. Paul is surely right to say that a man should judge himself before partaking in the Holy Communion. The alternative is to run the risk of offending the Lord and to come under His judgment for unworthy participation.

Implications

The abuse of the sacraments involves consequences. To partake of the sacrament in an unworthy manner can bring God's judgment not only on oneself, but also upon a congregation that does the same. As the Apostle Paul and the Prayer Book Exhortations tell us, we are called to examine ourselves so that we do not eat and drink God's judgment upon ourselves.

This Article raises a serious question about the easy and often superficial manner in which we frequently partake of the sacrament of the Lord's Supper.

Conclusion

We are to glorify and honor the Lord by the worthy use of the sacraments and of all of the means of grace that He so freely and lovingly gives us.

This is particularly true with regard to the Lord's Supper, given to nourish us both as individual Christians and as members of one another in Christ.

Those who partake of the Lord's Supper in an unworthy manner do not receive the Body and Blood of the Lord, but only the sacramental sign of so great a thing. In so doing, they eat and drink judgment upon themselves.

ARTICLE 30

Of Both Kinds

The Cup of the Lord is not to be denied to the lay people; for both parts of the Lord's sacrament, by Christ's ordinance and commandment, ought to be ministered to all Christian men alike.

Introduction

Some Churches give the laity only the bread while other Churches share both the bread and the wine in the Lord's Supper. Which is right and why?

As the Articles were being written, all things were being tested anew by their conformity to Scripture. The practice, in the Western Church, of communicating the faithful in one kind only, by the consecrated bread, came up for evaluation.

The Teaching of Article 30

Here is the teaching point for this Article:

1. The sacrament of the Lord's Supper is to be administered in accordance with Christ's institution. Therefore, the laity, as well as the clergy, are to receive in both kinds.

Explanation

The Sacrament of the Lord's Supper was instituted for all the people of God. For 10 centuries it was the custom of the Church to administer the bread and cup to all. However, beginning about A.D. 1100, the Church began to withhold the cup from the laity. Initially, it was largely a matter of convenience, because it is far more difficult to carry the wine; also, wine is easy to spill during the communion of the faithful. In addition, the practices of procession, elevation and adoration gave a certain priority to the consecrated host.

The practice of withholding the Cup from the laity, and later from all of the clergy except the celebrant, was endorsed by the Council of Constance in 1415 and again by the Council of Trent in 1562. Trent also anathematized those who reject this practice and those who thereby deny the doctrine of concomitance.

The doctrine of concomitance was devised to give theological justification for this departure from Jesus' explicit command that all should eat and drink, as recorded by the Apostle Paul. The doctrine of concomitance teaches that since the two natures in Christ, while distinguished from one another, cannot be separated from one another because they are unified in the one person of the Son, so also the Body and Blood of Christ cannot be separated from one another and therefore both are present in the Host as well as in the Cup. Consequently, the laity and the clergy that are not celebrating are not really being deprived of the Blood of Christ when they receive only the consecrated Host, since both the Body and the Blood of Christ are present in the Host. So the doctrine of concomitance teaches.

The Reformers took seriously Jesus' command and intention and rejected this practice. The consecrated bread and the wine were to be administered to all, to all of the clergy and all of the laity alike. Moreover, having rejected transubstantiation, they thereby rejected the foundation for the doctrine of concomitance as well.

This departure from the institution and intention of Christ in the administration of the Lord's Supper by withholding the Cup becomes a critical matter since, as Article 19 states, the administration of the Sacraments according to Christ's institution is one of the essential marks of a visible Church. It is therefore a matter of rejoicing among Anglicans to note that Rome has restored the cup to the faithful.

Biblical Foundations

And he took a cup, and when he had given thanks he gave it to them, saying, "Drink of it, all of you." Matthew 26:27

And he took a cup, and when he had given thanks he gave it to them, and they all drank of it. Mark 14:23

For I received from the Lord what I also delivered to you, that the Lord Jesus on the night when he was betrayed took bread, and when he had given thanks, he broke it, and said, "This is my body which is for you. Do this in remembrance of me." In the same way also he took the cup, after supper, saying, "This cup is the new covenant in my blood. Do this, as often as you drink it, in remembrance of me." For as often as you eat this bread and drink the cup, you proclaim the Lord's death until he comes. Whoever, therefore, eats the bread or drinks the cup of the Lord in an unworthy manner will be guilty of profaning the body and blood of the Lord. Let a person examine himself, then, and so eat of the bread and drink of the cup. 1 Corinthians 11:23-28

False Teaching Denied/Objections Answered

1. The doctrine of concomitance assumes and builds upon the doctrine of transubstantiation. As stated above, the teaching of Trent in the doctrine of concomitance, presupposing transubstantiation which teaches that the consecrated Host is the actual body of Christ and the consecrated Cup the actual blood of Christ, draws the further conclusion that since the divine and human in Christ cannot be separated from one another, therefore both the Body and Blood are in both the Host and the Cup.

Anglicans, having rejected transubstantiation (see Articles 28 and 29), also reject the doctrine of concomitance as contrary to Jesus' intention and practice. Jesus makes the distinction between the signs by speaking of the bread as His Body and the wine as His Blood. To obscure this sacramental distinction is contrary to Scripture.

2. It is highly instructive that the Roman Catholic Church has abandoned the practice of withholding the Cup from everyone but the celebrant of the Mass. Now, all present at the Mass who are in a state of grace, are invited to receive in both kinds. There is no indication, however, that the doctrine of concomitance has been abandoned.

3. Perhaps there is a reluctance to change this doctrine because to question it would endanger the doctrine of the infallibility of Roman teaching. When a doctrine has been given authoritative Papal approval, i.e. when the Pope has spoken *ex cathedra,* and most assuredly when he speaks *ex cathedra* in agreement with an Ecumenical Council, the Church does not and cannot err. The official, infallible doctrine may be improved or set in a fuller context, but cannot be declared to be in error. The doctrine of the infallibility of the Pope speaking *ex cathedra* makes ecumenical conversations difficult. The doctrine of infallibility is itself a matter that needs ecumenical discussion, for Anglicans and most other Christian bodies do not accept it. (See the discussion in Article 21, Teaching Point 2.)

4. In addition, this Article reflects the strong Anglican concern for the communal nature of the sacraments, as discussed in Article 25. Consequently, there were to be no private masses in which only the celebrant was present and who, therefore, would receive in both kinds alone. There is no example anywhere in Scripture of a private Mass or Chantry Mass. Such a practice seems to arise not from the Scriptures or Christ's institution of the sacrament as much as from the Roman Catholic understanding of sacrifice of

the Mass and the sacerdotal understanding of the priesthood. (See Articles 31 and 36.)

Implications

The implications of this Article are simple and direct. We are to obey Christ's institution and administer the consecrated bread and wine to all. We are to have no private celebrations of the Lord's Supper and we are to conform our theology to what is taught in Holy Scripture.

Conclusion

In all things, we are to obey Christ and certainly in the administration of the Lord's Supper as well as in all of our sacramental theology and practice. The Church has no authority to ordain anything contrary to God's Word written.

ARTICLE 31

Of the One Oblation of Christ Finished upon the Cross

The offering of Christ once made is the perfect redemption, propitiation, and satisfaction for all the sins of the whole world, both original and actual, and there is none other satisfaction for sin but that alone. Wherefore the sacrifices of Masses, in the which it was commonly said that the priests did offer Christ for the quick and the dead to have remission of pain or guilt, were blasphemous fables and dangerous deceits.

Introduction

What are we to think about the sacrifice of Christ in relation to the Lord's Supper? Its place in the Lord's Supper seems to be a matter of controversy. Does it matter one way or another. If so, why does it matter?

For the Roman Catholic Church, the sacrifice of the Mass lies at the heart of the Mass. Trent taught that the sacrifice of the Mass is an act of the Risen Lord by which He offers Himself to the Father through the priest for propitiation, the merit of which may be applied to believers through the treasury of the Church.

Anglicans rejected this doctrine because of the teaching of Scripture. Anglicans agreed that in the Lord's Supper there is a recalling of the Lord's completed sacrifice on the Cross, and that in response to the completed Sacrifice of Jesus rehearsed in the Lord's Supper, there is a sacrifice of praise and thanksgiving and a sacrifice of ourselves on the part of the congregation, offered to the Lord in gratitude for so great a salvation. But to the claim that there is a bloodless, propitiatory offering of Christ in the Lord's Supper, offered for merit, is at odds with

Scripture, contrary to the finality and sufficiency of the Savior's Cross, and obscures the fact that in the sacrament it is Christ Who is giving Himself to us.

Since everything in the Gospel of our salvation depends upon our reliance on the sufficiency of the Cross done once for all, this Article and our continuing disagreement with Rome on this matter is of the gravest significance and concern.

The Teaching of Article 31

Here are the teaching points for this Article:

1. Christ's sacrifice on the Cross done once for all for all time, is the one and only perfect sacrifice, sufficient for the redemption, propitiation and satisfaction for the sins of the whole world.

2. The doctrine that in the sacrifices of the Masses Christ offers Himself for merit for the remission of the guilt of the living and the dead is both an error and spiritually destructive.

1. Christ's sacrifice on the Cross done once for all, for all time, is the one and only perfect sacrifice, sufficient for the redemption, propitiation and satisfaction for the sins of the whole world

Explanation

The emphasis of this Article does not lie in this first teaching point, concerning the atonement made by Christ on the Cross, but in the second point in which the offering of Christ in the Mass is rejected. This is evident from the fact that this Article is placed amid the Articles dealing with the Lord's Supper as well as from the fact that the Atonement has already been rather fully dealt with in Article 2 and is also referred to seriously in Article 15. (For the fuller treatment of the Atonement we refer the reader to Article 2, Teaching Point 2.)

Teaching Point 1 is dealt with first in this Article because it sets forth the foundation for Teaching Point 2. It sets forth Christ's atoning work on the Cross with a special concern for its finality, sufficiency, and un-repeatability. It thereby provides the theological foundation for the criticism found in the following teaching point.

"The offering of Christ" refers to His one supreme offering or sacrifice on the Cross. "Once made" stresses that it is not made over and over again, but is made once, for all time and for all persons, and that the accomplishment of Christ's sacrifice is total. It is "that perfect redemption, propitiation and satisfaction for the sins of the whole world, both original and actual." It is perfect because by this sacrifice Christ has 1) fully paid the ransom price to set us free, 2) has completely propitiated the judicial Wrath of God, and 3) has entirely satisfied both God's righteousness and His love. There is therefore no need for, nor any room for, additional sacrifices or for any repetition of His sacrifice. "It is finished" both in the sense of having been done once for all and of being fully completed.

Since His sacrifice has been perfectly accomplished, to seek to add to it or to repeat it, is actually a detraction of and an attack upon the sufficiency of His sacrifice once made. Any renewed offering of His finished sacrifice would teach that Christ's sacrifice was not perfect and complete. This is one of the chief themes of the Letter to the Hebrews, to mention but one example. According to the Epistle to the Hebrews, the repetition of the sacrifices in the Temple in Jerusalem reveals that they are not final, in contrast to Jesus' sacrifice, which is final and sufficient and is therefore not to be repeated. Therefore, to speak of additional meritorious offerings of Christ in the Mass contradicts the clear teaching of the Scriptures on this matter.

This sufficiency and finality of the Cross is central to the Gospel, for the Gospel declares that on the Cross God has done all that needs to be done. Our part is not to add to His atoning work, but rather to gratefully receive its benefit as an utterly undeserved gift, which we did not and cannot earn and to which we cannot add anything.

Finally, to make its point absolutely clear, the Article declares that there is no other sacrifice that makes final satisfaction for sin; there is just this one sacrifice which has been done once for all, by Christ. His sacrifice is to be celebrated and honored, and relied upon by sinners; it is not to be repeated nor added to, nor competed with. The biblical texts in the following Biblical Foundations section make this very clear.

Biblical Foundations

Because this matter of the complete sufficiency and hence un-repeatability of the Cross is so important to the Gospel and because it is still a matter of dispute among Christians, we have added more texts than usual. We have also underlined a number of key words and phrases that underscore the sufficiency, finality and finished character of Christ's Atonement.

He was despised and rejected by men; a man of sorrows, and acquainted with grief; and as one from whom men hide their faces he was despised, and we esteemed him not. Surely he has borne our griefs and carried our sorrows; yet we esteemed him stricken, smitten by God, and afflicted. But he was wounded for our transgressions; he was crushed for our iniquities; upon him was the chastisement that brought us peace, and with his stripes we are healed. Isaiah 53:3-5

Pay careful attention to yourselves and to all the flock, in which the Holy Spirit has made you overseers, to care for the church of God, which he obtained with his own blood. Acts 20:28

For while we were still weak, <u>at the right time Christ died</u> for the ungodly. Romans 5:6

For the death <u>he died he died to sin, once for all</u>, but the life he lives he lives to God. Romans 6:10

Or do you not know that your body is a temple of the Holy Spirit within you, whom you have from God? You are not your own, for you <u>were bought</u> with a price. So glorify God in your body. 1 Corinthians 6:19-20

For our sake he <u>made him</u> to be sin who knew no sin, so that in him we might become the righteousness of God. 2 Corinthians 5:21

Christ <u>redeemed us</u> from the curse of the law by becoming a curse for us—for it is written, "Cursed is everyone who is hanged on a tree." Galatians 3:13

For it was indeed fitting that we should have such a high priest, holy, innocent, unstained, separated from sinners, and exalted above the heavens. He has <u>no need</u>, like those high priests, <u>to offer sacrifices daily</u>, first for his own sins and then for those of the people, since <u>he did this once for all when he offered up himself.</u> Hebrews 7:26-27

But when Christ appeared as a high priest of the good things that have come, then through the greater and more perfect tent (not made with hands, that is, not of this creation) <u>he entered once for all</u> into the holy places, not by means of the blood of goats and calves but by means of his own blood, thus securing an eternal redemption. Hebrews 9:11-12

...for then he would have had to suffer repeatedly since the foundation of the world. But as it is, he has appeared once for all at the end of the ages to put away sin by the sacrifice of himself. And just as it is appointed for man to die once, and after that comes judgment, so <u>Christ, having been offered once to bear the sins of many</u>, will appear a second time, not to deal with sin but to save those who are eagerly waiting for him. Hebrews 9:26-28

And by that will we have been sanctified through <u>the offering of the body of Jesus Christ once for all</u>. And every *priest stands daily at his service, offering repeatedly the same sacrifices, which can never take away sins. But when <u>Christ had offered for all time a single sacrifice for sins, he sat down at the right hand of God</u>, Waiting from that time until his enemies should be made a footstool for his feet. For by a single offering, he has perfected for all time those who are being sanctified.* Hebrews 10:10-14

knowing that you <u>were ransomed</u> from the futile ways inherited from your forefathers, not with perishable things such as silver or gold, but <u>with the precious blood of Christ</u>, like that of a lamb without blemish or spot. 1 Peter 1:18-19

For <u>Christ also suffered once for sins</u>, the righteous for the unrighteous, that he might bring us to God, being put to death in the flesh but made alive in the spirit. 1 Peter 3:18

<u>He is the propitiation for our sins</u>, and not for ours only but <u>also for the sins of the whole world.</u> 1 John 2:2

False Teaching Denied/Objections Answered

1. Some in the Reformed tradition seem to teach that Christ died on the Cross not for the sins of the whole world, but only for the elect. There is no such limitation in the teaching of St. Paul and St. John. It was not for our sins only but for the sins of the whole world that the Lord was content to die. That the Cross is only effective for some persons, in the plan of God, does not mean that His sacrifice was not sufficient for all persons nor offered for all and to all. Therefore the benefits of the Cross can be openly and honestly proclaimed to all, and all be urged to repent and believe. Sufficient for all, efficient for the elect is a good summary of the biblical teaching.

2. Some teach that Christ's sacrifice was for original sin only and not for actual sins. But where would that leave us as sinners, who constantly fall short of the glory of God by our sins of commission and omission? The Article is right to say that the Cross of Christ avails for both original and actual sins: past, present, and future.

3. There are several classic theories of the Atonement that fall outside the scope of this Article. The reader is directed to Teaching Point 2 of Article 2 for their treatment.

Implications

Christ's sacrifice is final, utterly sufficient and avails for our sinfulness as well as for our actual sins. This is the heart of the Gospel and the foundation of our confident relationship with God. We are to receive His gift, honor Him for it, and rest ourselves for time and eternity in its sufficiency. As the hymn says, "Nothing in my hands I bring, only to Thy Cross I cling."

2. The doctrine that in the sacrifices of the Masses Christ offers Himself for merit for the remission of the guilt of the living and the dead, is both an error and spiritually destructive.

Explanation

The Council of Trent wrote its statement on the Sacrifice of the Mass some 10 years after this Article was written. The Council was fully aware of this Anglican Article and saw that this Article was a rejection of the official Roman Catholic teaching on the sacrifice of the Mass and rejected the teaching of this 31st Article. This is what Trent wrote:

> If anyone shall say that the Mass is a Sacrifice of praise and thanksgiving only, or a bare memorial of the sacrifice made on the Cross and not a propitiatory offering, or that it only benefits him who receives it and ought not be offered for the living and the dead for sins, punishment, satisfaction and other necessities, let him be accursed.

It is clear that Trent accurately understood the teaching of this 31st Article. This Article reforms pre-Reformation teaching in the Western Catholic Church and is at odds with the teaching of Rome formulated in the Council of Trent, which remains the teaching of Rome to the present.

Therefore this Article is an important part of our continuing difference and discussion with Rome regarding the sufficiency of grace and the place of merit in our relationship with God in Christ.

Since the Cross of Christ, once offered, is sufficient for the salvation of all sinners, past, present, and future, there is no propitiatory sacrifice done or offered in the Lord's Supper. It has been made. God has been propitiated on the Cross. There is the recalling of the Cross wherein propitiation was made once for all and which is the basis of our assurance and profound gratitude. There is the presentation of bread and wine which is regarded by some Anglicans as part of our thank offering, to be used by God in the Supper as the sacramental signs of, and vehicles of, the Lord's giving Himself, His Body, and His Blood to us. There is our sacrifice of praise, sung and said. And there is our offering of ourselves, our souls and bodies, in gratitude to be a living sacrifice, which is our spiritual service. But none of these are propitiatory. Nor is Christ offering Himself to the Father anew in the Lord's Supper but rather He is giving Himself, His Body and Blood, to us on the basis of His sacrifice on the Cross once made.

The whole question of merit and the doctrine of the Treasury of Merit and Masses being offered to shorten time in purgatorial punishment has been discussed and rejected by Anglicans in Article 22. (Articles 12 and 14 are also pertinent in this regard.)

This Article uses rather strong language in saying that the doctrine of "the sacrifices of the Masses... (offered)... for the quick and the dead, to have remission of pain or guilt are blasphemous fables and dangerous deceits."

"Fables" is used because the doctrine finds no support in Scripture and in fact contradicts it. It is a doctrine based on human fancy. It is "blasphemous" in the sense that it detracts from the sufficiency of the Cross and thereby undercuts the assurance of the believer. It is precisely this assurance that is being nourished in the Lord's Supper. It was "dangerous" because it led to the various calculations of merit in our relationship with God which we can never satisfy. As Article 11 states it, "We are accounted righteous before God, only for the merit of our Lord and Savior Jesus Christ by Faith." And, in the end, this doctrine of a propitiatory Eucharistic sacrifice is profoundly misleading or a "deceit," for it denies the biblical teaching that there is only the one sacrifice and none other that can satisfy for sin. Therefore, the doctrine of a propitiatory Sacrifice of Christ in the Mass as held by Rome, and by any others, is rejected by Anglicans as contrary to Scripture and dangerous spiritually, a serious error indeed. Clearly, further ecumenical discussions are greatly needed.

Biblical Foundations

The former priests were many in number, because they were prevented by death from continuing in office, but he holds his priesthood permanently, because he continues forever. Consequently, he is able to save to the uttermost those who draw near to God through him, since he always lives to make intercession for them. Hebrews 7:23-25

For it was indeed fitting that we should have such a high priest, holy, innocent, unstained, separated from sinners, and exalted above the heavens. He has no need, like those high priests, to offer sacrifices daily, first for his own sins and then for those of the people, since he did this once for all when he offered up himself. Hebrews 7:26-27

Now the point in what we are saying is this: we have such a high priest, one who is seated at the right hand of the throne of the Majesty in heaven. Hebrews 8:1

But when Christ appeared as a high priest of the good things that have come, then through the greater and more perfect tent (not made with hands, that is, not of this creation) he entered once for all into the holy places, not by means of the blood of goats and calves but by means of his own blood, thus securing an eternal redemption. Hebrews 9:11-12

For Christ has entered, not into holy places made with hands, which are copies of the true things, but into heaven itself, now to appear in the presence of God on our behalf. Nor was it to offer himself repeatedly, as the high priest enters the holy places every year with blood not his own, for then he would have had to suffer repeatedly since the foundation of the world. But as it is, he has appeared once for all at the end of the ages to put away sin by the sacrifice of himself. Hebrews 9:24-26

False Teachings Denied/Objections Answered

The Early Church, for some 200 years, did not speak of an offering of the Body and Blood in the Lord's Supper or Eucharist. It is first during the time of Cyprian that we find sacrificial language appearing concerning the Body and Blood of Christ in the Lord's Supper. Such language became increasingly popular. By the time we come to the 16th century Reformation, Rome, Anglicans, Lutherans, Reformed, and other bodies needed to clarify their positions. Rome, and the Orthodox in their own way, affirmed that Christ's Body and Blood were offered for propitiation in the Mass; all the other Churches rejected any propitiatory offering in the Lord's Supper.

1. The Roman Catholic Church, at Trent, understood Article 31 as we have set it forth above. Rome continues to take that view and holds Anglicans to be in grave error. While painful, such a state of affairs is actually promising, for if we can agree as to what the disagreement is, we can and should engage in prayerful and honest discussion in the light of careful biblical exegesis, in order to seek to come to a common mind for the Lord's sake.

2. Anglicans among themselves, however, have not all agreed on the right understanding and application of this 31st Article.

Some have followed Cardinal John Henry Newman, who sought to read the Article as disagreeing with pre-Tridentine popular teaching in the Western Catholic

Church. He taught that it was not the sacrifice of the Mass as taught in Trent that was being rejected by Article 31, for Trent had not yet written its statement on the Sacrifice of the Mass. Rather, the Article rejects the crude popular teaching of the sacrifices of the masses, a view quite different from that careful doctrine taught by Trent. Newman later renounced that position and said that Article 31 was precisely antagonistic to Trent's teaching that the Sacrifice of the Mass is propitiatory.

In addition, there is no doubt that Trent was fully aware of Article 31 as well as Bishop Jewel's Apology, when Trent wrote its statement some 10 years after Article 31 was written. Trent's language seems to echo the language of the Article.

Here is how Trent defined the Sacrifice of the Mass; it is hard to see how this and Article 31 can be seen to be in agreement in any sense:

> In the divine sacrifice that is offered in the Mass, the same Christ, who offered himself once in a bloody manner on the altar of the cross is present and is offered in an unbloody manner. Therefore, the holy Council teaches that this sacrifice is truly propitiatory, so that if we draw near to God with an upright heart and true faith, with fear and reverence, with sorrow and repentance, through the Mass we may obtain mercy and find grace to help in time of need (Heb. 4:16). For by this oblation the Lord is appeased....

3. Some Anglicans have sought to find a propitiatory sacrifice in the Lord's Supper, in connection with Christ's pleading of His sacrifice to the Father in Heaven, as part of His heavenly priestly ministry.

The doctrine is somewhat complicated. It is as follows: the analogy is that of the High Priest in the Old Testament sprinkling the blood on the Altar or the Mercy Seat on the Day of Atonement, thus presenting the sacrifice of the life offered. In this view, the focus of the sacrifice is not in the dying under judgment for sin but rather in a life offered and in being presented before God through the sprinkled blood.

This would mean that in Jesus' heavenly pleading or presentation, in some sense His sacrifice would be continually offered by Christ to the Father in His heavenly ministry in a propitiatory way by His pleading or presentation of His final sacrifice.

This ongoing heavenly action is related to the celebration of the Lord's Supper. At the consecration of the Bread and Wine, His death is signified by the separation of the Body and the Blood through separate actions of consecration of the bread and the wine in the Eucharistic consecration and is offered to God, which offering participates or shares in Christ's eternal offering or pleading of the Cross in heaven. Thus the Eucharistic sacrifice that we celebrate on earth is joined to or participates in Christ's continuing heavenly pleading of His sacrifice on the Cross.

There are a number of serious objections to this doctrine. The first and crucial difficulty with this is that we have no text in Scripture that teaches that Christ is pleading His sacrifice in Heaven. It seems to be made up of whole cloth. We are taught in Hebrews that He has sat down. Sitting is what a priest does when the sacrifice has been made and is finished. The Letter to the Hebrews clearly states that the atoning sacrifice of Christ, both on the Cross and in His entrance into the Heavenly Temple, is a finished work. To be sure we are taught by the writer of Hebrews and St. Paul that Christ as our heavenly High Priest continually intercedes for us who are His, as part of His priestly ministry. But it is nowhere said that He continually pleads the Cross as part of His heavenly intercessory, priestly ministry. The language of Scripture, and particularly in Hebrews, speaks only of His being seated, of His finished work on the Cross and of His intercession in Heaven.

Second, this is a novel doctrine. It is novel for Anglicans. There is not a hint of it in the historic *Book of Common Prayer* or Articles. Further it is a novel doctrine not only to Anglicans but to the whole Christian Church; it is certainly not a doctrine believed and taught by everyone and everywhere. Also, it is novel regarding its understanding of the general nature of Jesus' bloody sacrifice in Scripture. The Cross is referred to as a payment for sins, as the bearing of our sins in His own body, and as having the iniquity of us all laid on Him. It is not simply a life offered but an atonement for sin. And finally it is novel as regarding Christ's sacrifice to be continued forever through a heavenly presentation.

This theory of Christ continually pleading or presenting His Body and Blood is at odds with Article 31 and with Scripture. It is far better to abide by the clear teaching of the Articles, *The Book of Common Prayer* and the Epistle to the Hebrews and St. Paul. It seems that Anglicans have need for serious discussion among themselves.

Implications

We do not propitiate God. That has been done. We are not to offer to Him what Christ has offered once for all. We are not to offer to God what Christ is giving to us in the Lord's Supper. Rather, we do well to receive in repentant faith what Christ is offering to us in His Supper, Himself, His Body and Blood. We recall His great sacrifice finished, and are assured, and we take quite seriously the offerings that we make by grace in response: the sacrifice of praise and thanksgiving and of ourselves, our life, and labor as living sacrifices to God.

Conclusion

Anglicans officially and gratefully abide by Apostolic teaching regarding the finished character of the sacrifice of Christ as set forth in Scripture, as this Article clearly requires us to do.

ARTICLE 32

Of the Marriage of Priests

Bishops, Priests, and Deacons are not commanded by God's laws either to vow the estate of single life or to abstain from marriage. Therefore it is lawful also for them, as for all other Christian men, to marry at their own discretion, as they shall judge the same to serve better to godliness.

Introduction

May the clergy marry? Do all of the clergy have a call to the single life? Are only those who have a call to the single life called to ordination? Is it true that in every or even most cases it is better for the conduct of a fruitful ministry if those called and ordained to it are single? What do the Scriptures say?

This Article, measuring things in the light of Scripture and experience, takes the position that clergy may marry.

The Teaching of Article 32

Here is the teaching point for this Article:

1. Since the Scripture permits it, it is permissible for the clergy to marry in accordance with their discernment of their calling and giftedness.

Explanation

There is nothing in the Scriptures to forbid the marriage of the clergy. In fact, there is much to commend it. The Priests of the Old Testament married and had families. The Apostles married and had families. The Presbyters and Deacons in the New Testament married and had families. In the early Church, the clergy married and had families.

The general teaching of Scripture exalts marriage as a divine ordinance given by God in Creation, blessed by God, and honored by Christ. The Letter to the Hebrews and St. Paul commend marriage to all.

This is not to deny that some are called to be celibate. Jesus tells us that some are called to be eunuchs for the Kingdom of God's sake; some, but not all. The language of Scripture indicates that celibacy is a divine gifting and should not be imposed upon all. Nor is it held to be a higher way. It is a particular calling and gifting given to some for the sake of the ministry to which they are called.

Much suffering and immorality has come about in the history of the Church from binding celibacy upon those who do not have that gifting.

In this Article, Anglicans clearly declare that this matter is best left up to the discernment of the individual. The clergy may or may not marry as they discern God's calling in this matter.

Biblical Foundations

When anyone brings a grain offering as an offering to the Lord, his offering shall be of fine flour. He shall pour oil on it and put frankincense on it and bring it to Aaron's sons the priests. And he shall take from it a handful of the fine flour and oil, with all of its frankincense, and the priest shall burn this as its memorial portion on the altar, a food offering with a pleasing aroma to the Lord. But the rest of the grain offering shall be for Aaron and his sons; it is a most holy part of the Lord's food offerings. Leviticus 2:1-3

And I declare to him that I am about to punish his house forever, for the iniquity that he knew, because his sons were blaspheming God, and he did not restrain them. 1 Samuel 3:13

In the days of Herod, king of Judea, there was a priest named Zechariah, of the division of Abijah. And he had a wife from the daughters of Aaron, and her name was Elizabeth. Luke 1:5

And when Jesus entered Peter's house, he saw his mother-in-law lying sick with a fever. Matthew 8:14

But because of the temptation to sexual immorality, each man should have his own wife and each woman her own husband. 1 Corinthians 7:2

Do we not have the right to take along a believing wife, as do the other apostles and the brothers of the Lord and Cephas? 1 Corinthians 9:5

Now the Spirit expressly says that in later times some will depart from the faith by devoting themselves to deceitful spirits and teachings of demons, through the insincerity of liars whose consciences are seared, who forbid marriage and require abstinence from foods that God created to be received with thanksgiving by those who believe and know the truth. For everything created by God is good, and nothing is to be rejected if it is received with thanksgiving, for it is made holy by the word of God and prayer. 1 Timothy 4:1-5

Let marriage be held in honor among all, and let the marriage bed be undefiled, for God will judge the sexually immoral and adulterous. Keep your life free from love of money, and be content with what you have, for he has said, "I will never leave you nor forsake you." Hebrews 13:4-5

False Doctrines Denied/Objections Answered

Some Churches require the clergy to be celibate. This is the case in Rome. Some permit the Presbyters to be married but forbid marriage to Bishops. This is the case in Orthodoxy.

These decisions are not made on the basis of Scripture but are pastoral decisions made by the various Churches based on their own wisdom. In one sense there is no problem in this. Article 34 affirms that traditions need not be alike in all Churches, provided that nothing is ordered contrary to Scripture and all is done for edification or the building up of the Church.

Not all traditions, however, are good or wise; Anglicans avoid both extremes by staying close to Scripture in this matter.

Has the decision of Rome to require singleness of all the clergy born the fruit that was desired? In many cases, it has been helpful and fruitful. But in other cases, it has led to immoral behavior, apparently in a number of cases, and it seems to have greatly restricted the number of vocations in recent years. It has also tempted laity and clergy alike to believe that clerical singleness is a higher state of life and involves a greater sacrifice than marriage and the raising of a family. That view is both unbiblical and dubious to say the least.

Some have offered various pragmatic arguments for clerical celibacy. First, some claim that celibacy allows the clergy to accomplish more, given the fact that they have no family for which to care, except the congregation itself. However, the loneliness of those that are not gifted with the gift of celibacy can render them inefficient in many respects.

Second, some point out that there is a greater expense involved when the clergy have a family for which to provide. The economics are no small matter and cannot be denied, but by themselves would be an insufficient reason to bind celibacy upon all clergy. In addition, the clergy will need costly domestic help. If the clergy were to do all the domestic requirements themselves that would greatly reduce the time they have to minister.

Implications

We should not make this a matter of division between Church bodies. However, Anglicans do well to give marriage the honor it has in Scripture and to permit the freedom granted in Scripture to allow the clergy a personal choice in the matter of marriage.

Conclusion

The wisdom of binding nothing on Christians but what is bound in the Scriptures is both liberating and beneficial. We can see this clearly in the case of the marriage of clergy.

ARTICLE 33

Of Excommunicate Persons, How They are to be Avoided

That person which by open denunciation of the Church is rightly cut off from the unity of the Church and excommunicated, ought to be taken of the whole multitude of the faithful as an heathen and publican, until he be openly reconciled by penance and received into the Church by a judge that hath authority thereto.

Introduction

Does the Church have the right to cast people out of its fellowship? Who in the Church could make such a decision? How can such an action be a loving action that is in accord with the Gospel and the grace of Christ? If so, under what conditions and to what end can this casting out or excommunication be done? Is there a greater and a milder form of excommunication?

The Teaching of Article 33

Here are the teaching points for this Article:

1. The Church may exercise discipline over its members, including excommunication in both a mild and a severe form.

2. The purpose of excommunication is disciplinary, preventive and hopeful.

3. The attitude of the congregation in relating to excommunicated persons is to be in accord with the Gospel, both while those members are in excommunicate status and also when they are reconciled to the fellowship.

1. The Church may exercise discipline over its members, including excommunication in both a mild and a severe form.

Explanation

Excommunication is an official act of discipline by the Church that bars a member from partaking of Holy Communion and includes other deprivations that may be included in the act of discipline.

There are two forms of excommunication in the practice of the Church. One is a milder form, usually referred to as "the lesser excommunication." It generally consists of being barred from receiving the consecrated elements at the Lord's Supper and from exercising leadership in the congregation, until a period of time has passed and some form of penance has been completed to show the genuineness of repentance on the part of the offending member of the Church. The believer is not barred from worship and participation in the life of the Church. It lies with the leaders of the Church as to whether this lesser excommunication should be publicly announced or not.

The other form of excommunication is the one directly referred to in this Article. It is referred to as the "great excommunication" in which one is publicly banned from the Lord's Supper, from the worship of the Church, and from all contact with the common life of the Church, until such time after repentance when he or she is restored to membership by a public declaration made by the leaders of the Church.

Excommunication is an exercise that every social group has the right and responsibility to do. Every gathered community must define what are the standards for its membership, must discipline its own members in the light of those standards, and in extreme cases remove those, having been admitted to membership, who unrepentantly violate the essential standards for membership.

In this Article, Anglicans declare that the Church has the right to exercise such discipline. Anglicans do not need the State's permission nor the permission of any other visible Church to do so.

Who in the Church actually exercises this discipline? Generally in Anglicanism it is the Bishop of the Diocese who makes the final decision for the great excommunication, though in that decision the Bishop usually depends, in large measure, upon the advice and council of the local clergy of the congregation from which the member is being excommunicated.

The lesser excommunication is generally done by the local Rector or senior pastor, operating within the guidelines given by the Bishop and informing the Bishop of the action taken.

With regard to the history of the practice of excommunication, the Church took over the ancient practice of Israel and of Judaism at the time of Jesus. They did this with the encouragement and instruction of Jesus Himself. It is a biblical practice.

Biblical Foundations

For seven days no leaven is to be found in your houses. If anyone eats what is leavened, that person will be cut off from the congregation of Israel, whether he is a sojourner or a native of the land. Exodus 12:19

But the person who eats of the flesh of the sacrifice of the Lord's peace offerings while an uncleanness is on him, that person shall be cut off from his people. Leviticus 7:20

And that if anyone did not come within three days, by order of the officials and the elders all his property should be forfeited, and he himself banned from the congregation of the exiles. Ezra 10:8

If your brother sins against you, go and tell him his fault, between you and him alone. If he listens to you, you have gained your brother. But if he does not listen, take one or two others along with you, that every charge may be established by the evidence of two or three witnesses. If he refuses to listen to them, tell it to the church. And if he refuses to listen even to the church, let him be to you as a Gentile and a tax collector. Matthew 18:15-17

His parents answered, "We know that this is our son and that he was born blind. But how he now sees we do not know, nor do we know who opened his eyes. Ask him; he is of age. He will speak for himself." (His parents said these things because they feared the Jews, for the Jews had already agreed that if anyone should confess Jesus to be Christ, he was to be put out of the synagogue.) Therefore his parents said, "He is of age; ask him." John 9:20-23

But now I am writing to you not to associate with anyone who bears the name of brother if he is guilty of sexual immorality or greed, or is an idolater, reviler, drunkard, or swindler—not even to eat with such a one. 1 Corinthians 5:11

God judges those outside. "Purge the evil person from among you." 1 Corinthians 5:13,

Among whom are Hymenaeus and Alexander, whom I have handed over to Satan that they may learn not to blaspheme. 1 Timothy 1:20

As for those who persist in sin, rebuke them in the presence of all, so that the rest may stand in fear. 1 Timothy 5:20

As for you, brothers, do not grow weary in doing good. If anyone does not obey what we say in this letter, take note of that person, and have nothing to do with him, that he may be ashamed. 2 Thessalonians 3:13-14

Everyone who goes on ahead and does not abide in the teaching of Christ, does not have God. Whoever abides in the teaching has both the Father and the Son. If anyone comes to you and does not bring this teaching, do not receive him into your house or give him any greeting. 2 John 9-10

False Teaching Denied/Objections answered

1. Some persons hold that since the Lord loves both the just and the unjust and the Lord died for all, the only

standard the Church can have is to accept all into its membership, no matter their beliefs or behavior. Therefore, any act of excommunication is a violation of the one standard of the Church. Such a view has never been the official teaching of any Church that takes the Scriptures seriously.

While it is true that God loves both the just and the unjust and that He sent His Son to die for the sins of the world, His universal love is not the same as His acceptance or salvation. The world is lost and under condemnation. God accepts and saves those who, by His grace and by consequent faith and repentance, are united to His Son and are reckoned righteous in His sight and made members of His Church. The Lord is actively conforming these members more and more into the likeness of Christ by the work of His Spirit. The Church therefore does rightly have both standards of faithfulness to His Word and to the moral standards found therein and that were exhibited by Christ in His ministry on earth. The Church rightly expects a commitment from its members to seek to live in accord with these standards.

Therefore, the excommunication of those who knowingly and unrepentantly violate those standards is not contrary to the Gospel, for the Gospel includes both justification and sanctification. Excommunication is a necessary form of the discipline of the Church.

2. Some hold that excommunication is impractical in our contemporary world of many denominations. A person excommunicated by one denomination can and will simply go over to another denomination and be received.

While that may be true, that does not excuse each denomination, diocese, or congregation from doing what is right and from doing what it can do. Also, the names of people who have been excommunicated by the great excommunication can be shared with the headquarters of the other churches and passed out to the local congregations.

3. Some misunderstand the limits of excommunication. The Church does not condemn to hell those who are excommunicated. Excommunication is a pastoral judgment on behavior. The ultimate state of the soul is God's alone to judge. Nor does the great excommunication sever the soul from the Church; one remains related to the Church as a baptized member in a state of exclusion and in the hope of restoration. Only in the final judgment will it be fully and finally revealed who are the sheep and who are the goats.

Implications
Ecclesiastical discipline is essential and needed. If a practice is left undisciplined, not only the individual but over time the entire congregation will be corrupted. There never has been a time when God's people did not have the need for the practice of discipline. In some parts of the Anglican Communion, discipline has been greatly neglected and is being so in the present. Without fail the result of such neglect has proven disastrous.

2. The purpose of excommunication is disciplinary, preventive and hopeful.
Explanation
The attitudes and behaviors that require the lesser excommunication are various. The use of this form of discipline calls for the pastoral judgment of the clergy. The great excommunication is appropriate only for obvious, public, and sustained violation of the morals, doctrine, and discipline of the Church.

Is excommunication loving? The answer is "yes." It is loving to the individual being disciplined, to the congregation of which he or she is a member, and is honoring to God.

Therefore, the aims of excommunication are threefold: First, excommunication honors God. It affirms those doctrines and standards given by God to the Church that are being disobeyed and discredited. If one is permitted to preach and teach heresy, or to act immorally in a public and obvious manner, then the truth of the Gospel, God's moral commands, and the consequent sanctification of the people are being rejected, and if nothing is done, these matters will soon be regarded as of uncertain authority or reduced to a matter of personal opinion.

If God's standards are obscured and lost, then all is lost. For when there is no truth by which to call people to repentance and when there is no Divine Word to preach and to carry forth in mission, then the Church ceases to be the Church. In Scripture, we read that God is jealous for His honor and for His Word; therefore, excommunication is essentially an act of worship, of faithfulness to Him and of thanksgiving to the Lord for His Word and calling.

Second, the act of excommunication is loving to the individual being disciplined. As we read in Scripture, excommunication is to be done for the sake of the repentance and restoration of the one being disciplined. It is never the first act of discipline, as our Lord's instructions in Matthew 18 make clear. It is always a last choice, addressed to the stubborn and unrepentant member. It should never be done in anger and vindictiveness, but always in love and hope. We read in Scripture that the Lord disciplines those whom He loves.

If the individual is not disciplined, the individual will come to the false conclusion that he or she is not wrong or that the matter is of no great consequence in the eyes of God and the Church. If friends do not let friends drive when drunk, then the saints do not let fellow saints sin grievously without the needed rebuke in love.

Thirdly, the act of excommunication is loving to the congregation. In Scripture the analogy that is used is leaven. Heresy, immorality, and public rebellion against those in authority all are catching and, like leaven, will penetrate and permeate the entire congregation. That which is permitted becomes accepted, and that which is accepted is ultimately recommended. If we take Article 19 seriously and also the Homily on Whitsunday, a congregation without discipline is soon corrupted and ceases to be a visible church, even if it retains the name "Church" on its signs, stationery, and on the lips of its members. As the Lord put it, what good is salt when it loses its savor? It is useless! This condition is devastating to all the members, and to all of the generations to come, who will be raised in such a corrupt congregation.

Excommunication, rightly exercised, prevents this downward spiral into falsehood and ecclesiastical oblivion.

Biblical Foundations

For seven days no leaven is to be found in your houses. If anyone eats what is leavened, that person will be cut off from the congregation of Israel, whether he is a sojourner or a native of the land. Exodus 12:19

If your brother sins against you, go and tell him his fault, between you and him alone. If he listens to you, you have gained your brother. But if he does not listen, take one or two others along with you, that every charge may be established by the evidence of two or three witnesses. If he refuses to listen to them, tell it to the church. And if he refuses to listen even to the church, let him be to you as a Gentile and a tax collector. Matthew 18:15-17

I appeal to you, brothers, to watch out for those who cause divisions and create obstacles contrary to the doctrine that you have been taught; avoid them. Romans 16:17

You are to deliver this man to Satan for the destruction of the flesh, so that his spirit may be saved in the day of the Lord. Your boasting is not good. Do you not know that a little leaven leavens the whole lump? 1 Corinthians 5:5-6

But now I am writing to you not to associate with anyone who bears the name of brother if he is guilty of sexual immorality or greed, or is an idolater, reviler, drunkard, or swindler—not even to eat with such a one. 1 Corinthians 5:11

Among whom are Hymenaeus and Alexander, whom I have handed over to Satan that they may learn not to blaspheme. 1 Timothy 1:20

As for those who persist in sin, rebuke them in the presence of all, so that the rest may stand in fear. 1 Timothy 5:20

As for a person who stirs up division, after warning him once and then twice, have nothing more to do with him. Titus 3:10

False Teaching Denied/Objections Answered
1. It has been objected that we ought not use excommunication because excommunication can be and has been misused to exert political influence. An example of such abuse took place when the Church leaders used excommunication to exercise authority over the State (Emperor etc.). This objection is accurate. In the New Testament, excommunication is not a State or political discipline but rather an ecclesiastical and pastoral one. It was misused by the Church in the Middle Ages to control the State and was thereby brought into disrepute. However, a misuse of something does not negate its proper use.

Today we cannot misuse excommunication politically in the West, for in the democratic West, the Church no longer claims to have jurisdictional authority over both Church and State.

2. Some reject excommunication on the grounds that the Church is a hospital for sinners, and that one sinner should not be disciplined above others. Sin is sin and all sins are sufficient to separate one from the approval of God. So why be strict with a particular sinner?

In one sense it is true that there are no minor sins. We read in Scripture that if one violates any part of the law, one violates the entire law. However, there is a difference between those sinners who are faithful Church members seeking to follow Christ and the standards of the Church and those sinners who reveal by their public, unrepentant behavior that they are not willing to follow the teachings of Christ as set forth by the Church. It is not simply a matter of committing sin, but of publicly practicing and commending or blessing sin. Profound rebellion involves open and persistent rejection of the Word of God and the Church's teaching and morals demonstrably drawn from it. It is one thing to have a divided heart and to sin and repent; it is another thing to persist in rejecting the truth as held by a given Church and to do so openly and unrepentantly, even after coming under ecclesiastical warning and discipline. Such is the rebellion that leads to the great excommunication

It is important to repeat that the great excommunication is not in and of itself the unforgivable sin. The great excommunication is always done in hope. (See Article 16 for a discussion of the unforgivable sin.)

Implications

As discipline is needed in the family, so excommunication is needed in the family of God. And while discipline and excommunication are important and necessary in the Church, their usefulness is in part dependent upon the proper intent of the leaders exercising the discipline and the response of the congregation. Excommunication is always to be done in love and hope and always as the last option, all else having failed.

3. The attitude of the congregation in relating to excommunicate persons is to be in accord with the Gospel both while those members are in excommunicate status and when they are reconciled to the fellowship.

Explanation

Excommunication involves three different actions on the part of the Church. One set of actions involves gentle contact and rebuke seeking repentance and reconciliation. These attempts call the person or persons to repentance short of excommunication. They are done first by one, then by two or more fellow members. But when that fails, serious violations of the standards of membership must be brought to the Church, to those in authority, to be addressed (Matthew 18:15-17).

A second set of actions takes place when the person is excommunicated and when the great excommunication has been publicly announced. The excommunicated person is excluded from the gathered life of the Church. The one excommunicated is to avoid entering into the gathered life of the Church until he or she is reconciled by the public announcement of the leaders. The purpose of this is, first, to honor the threefold purposes of excommunication discussed above and, second, to give the one excommunicated an experience of life excluded from the Body of Christ. This experience is meant to make clear to the one excommunicated what his or her behavior is actually doing, dishonoring Christ and violating the Body of Christ. It also seeks to make the person aware of what he or she is missing, that is, the worship and fellowship of the Body of Christ. Hopefully, this will encourage the excommunicated member to repent and seek reconciliation and restoration.

The third set of actions concerns the behavior of the whole congregation. It is two-fold. First, it calls for the members of the Church to treat the excommunicated person as one who is under discipline and not to relate to him or her as though nothing had happened. This is not to be understood as being forbidden to even speak with the one who is excommunicated, should one meet outside of the gathered community or to be in any way impolite, but rather that the fact of the excommunication is to be mentioned, defended, and honored on such occasions.

Second, the congregation has a very different call when the period of excommunication has ended and the person has been publicly reinstated. The Congregation is then called to extend to the formerly excommunicated person full forgiveness, acceptance, encouragement, and warm fellowship.

In some situations, such forgiveness and reconciliation is far from easy. The pain, embarrassment, and shame of the congregation caused by the person who was excommunicated often remain vividly in the consciousness of the members of the congregation. Being an angry elder brother comes easily to us as fallen and redeemed sinners. Therefore the call to the members of the congregation to extend full forgiveness and restoration is mentioned a number of times in Scripture, as well as in this Article. As we have been forgiven, so are we to forgive. As the Father welcomed home the prodigal with open arms, so we are to welcome home those who have been restored to membership with open hearts. Harboring unforgiveness is itself sinful.

The leaders of the Congregation are responsible to oversee the process of integration into the congregation of the restored member and the pace of the restored member's possible return to previous positions of leadership in the congregation. No doubt, distrust, due to the previous serious violations of trust, will take some time to be overcome. And the standards of the Faith must be seen to be honored before the privilege of serving in positions of leadership should be restored.

Biblical Foundations

But now I am writing to you not to associate with anyone who bears the name of brother if he is guilty of sexual immorality or greed, or is an idolater, reviler, drunkard, or swindler—not even to eat with such a one. 1 Corinthians 5:11

If your brother sins against you, go and tell him his fault, between you and him alone. If he listens to you, you have gained your brother. But if he does not listen, take one or two others along with you, that every charge may be established by the evidence of two or three witnesses. If he refuses to listen to them, tell it to the church. And if he refuses to listen even to the church, let him be to you as a Gentile and a tax collector. Matthew 18:15-17

So you should rather turn to forgive and comfort him, or he may be overwhelmed by excessive sorrow. So I beg you to reaffirm your love for him. 2 Corinthians 2:7-8

Brothers, if anyone is caught in any transgression, you who are spiritual should restore him in a spirit of gentleness. Keep watch on yourself, lest you too be tempted. Galatians 6:1

False Teaching Denied/Objections Answered

1. Some in the Church object that to exclude people from the life of the congregation is too severe and unchristian and they would not be willing to shun a fellow Christian. The use of the term "shunning" is incorrect. Excommunication is not the same as shunning. Shunning is actually more severe than excommunication, for shunning bars any personal relationship with those under discipline, even in encounters outside the common life of the community.

Actually, shunning assumes a closed, somewhat isolated community, whereas the Church exists in the midst of society. Being publicly barred from the life of the gathered community of the Church is severe enough.

2. Another objection is that the great excommunication won't work because of the inevitable self-righteous, unforgiving spirit of the congregation. It is true that in cases when the behavior of the one who was excommunicated brought great shame and embarrassment or other severe damage upon the congregation, the greatest danger is that when the excommunicated person is penitent and reconciled, the community will not welcome the person back in any convincing way. Forgiveness is hard work. It rests on a Cross, so it is supposed to be costly. But it is an

essential mark of Christian faith. The leadership of the congregation is called to teach about this whenever public excommunication is exercised. By grace, all things are possible.

3. A final objection is that excommunication can be conducted as an instrument of personal vindictiveness, to secure the leaders' own authority or to remove those who are raising legitimate objections about the leaders in the congregation. What recourse does the congregation have against such an utter abuse of excommunication? Such an abuse of excommunication can, has, and does happen. Institutional avenues of appeal need to be clearly established, to which those being excommunicated as well as other congregational members can appeal in such cases. In Anglicanism the Bishop is one avenue of appeal. In addition, there are usually other constitutional avenues of appeal available. They, too, are necessary in case the offender is the Bishop himself.

Implications

None of the behaviors that are connected with discipline and excommunication come easily to us. Nevertheless, they remain our calling. With God's grace, we can exercise the discipline that is needed in the love that is needed.

Conclusion

When discipline and excommunication are done in humility, with prayer and love, we avoid legalistic harshness as well as sentimental permissiveness, both of which are destructive of the Church's life and mission in Christ.

ARTICLE 34

Of the Traditions of the Church

It is not necessary that traditions and ceremonies be in all places one or utterly alike; for at all times they have been diverse, and may be changed according to the diversity of countries, times, and men's manners, so that nothing be ordained against God's word. Whosoever through his private judgement willingly and purposely doth openly break the traditions and ceremonies of the Church which be not repugnant to the word of God, and be ordained and approved by common authority, ought to be rebuked openly that others may fear to do the like, as he that offendeth against common order of the Church, and hurteth the authority of the magistrate, and woundeth the conscience of the weak brethren.

Every particular or national Church hath authority to ordain, change, and abolish ceremonies or rites of the Church ordained only by man's authority, so that all things be done to edifying.

Introduction

What are we to think of traditions? Is being traditional good or bad? How do traditions in the Church relate to the need to be effective in the present? What impact did the Reformation have on the traditions of those Churches that participated in the Reformation?

When the Church of Rome no longer determines the acceptable traditions and ceremonies of the various visible Churches and local congregations of the Church in the West, all sorts of questions arise. Who, for example, has the authority to decide which traditions should be kept and which should be changed? What room is there for national, regional and congregational diversity in the traditions and ceremonies of the Church Catholic? Wherein do the preferences of an individual or a small group within a congregation find a limit?

These questions had to be addressed at the period when the Articles were being written as they do today. Local provinces, dioceses and congregations continue to raise these questions as do cross-cultural church planting and ecumenical discussions.

The Teaching of Article 34

Here are the teaching points for this Article:

1. Traditions and ceremonies need not be the same in all places as long as they are agreeable to God's Word.

2. No person due to personal preference may publicly violate the local traditions and ceremonies of the local church that are agreeable to God's Word.

3. National Churches have authority to command, change, or abolish ceremonies or forms of worship that are appointed only by men's authority, provided everything is done for the building up of God's people.

1. Traditions and ceremonies need not be the same in all places as long as they are agreeable to God's Word.
Explanation

We need to be clear about what is meant by tradition or traditions. There are at least three uses of the word "tradition." First, the word "tradition" is used in a wide or inclusive sense to refer to all that the Church does, prays, says, and sings in order to pass on the Gospel and its life and witness over time. Tradition in this sense is unavoidable. Whatever the Church does more than once soon becomes customary, part of a developing tradition that expresses the identity of a particular visible church. This is true whether the traditions are written down or not.

In fact, it is better to have the important traditions written down so that they are not violated unknowingly by the newly initiated. It also makes the content of the official tradition clearer to all involved.

The second use of "Tradition," with a capital "T", is used to refer only to things essential. This use is less common. It appears in formal theological documents in phrases such as "the Tradition and the traditions." Still, it is important to be aware of this use so we are not misled or confused when we see it used in this way. Tradition, in this sense, refers to the essential aspects of the Church's Faith and practice that are common to all orthodox or biblical Christian Churches. At the center of "the Tradition" is the Scripture and at the center of the Scripture is the Gospel and the sacraments of the Gospel; these are essential to the life, witness, and mission of the Church everywhere.

In their fundamental elements, essential things are to be alike in all places. The Creeds, the Canon of Scripture, and the sacraments of the Gospel, i.e. Baptism and the Lord's Supper, are essential parts of the tradition of the Church. It is a sign of the basic unity of the Church that all of the historic Churches share the Canon of Holy Scripture, the three Catholic or Ecumenical creeds, and the two dominical sacraments of the Gospel as basic to their Tradition. (See Articles 1-4, in Section One: The Apostolic Faith.) The Confessional documents of the various visible churches are also part of this core, since they state how that church understands the Scriptures. For Anglicans, that includes the 1662 *Book of Common Prayer* and Ordinal, the Thirty-Nine Articles, and *The Homilies*.

It is a serious ecumenical problem that there is a disagreement about the limits of the Canon. The apocryphal writings have a differing status as regards their authority as Scripture among the Roman Catholic and Eastern Orthodox

Churches, on the one hand, and the Churches of the Reformation on the other. This is a most serious disagreement about essentials since God speaking through Scripture is the supreme authority in the Church.

The third use of "tradition" is used to refer to non-essential things, things that are repeated and become standard or expected in a local or particular visible church. Traditions in this sense can and often do vary from place to place. In this 34th Article, "traditions and ceremonies" refer to the things that are not required by Scripture as essential to the life and work of the Church. They are *adiaphora* – meaning things neither commanded nor forbidden by Scripture. There are many things that local churches do, say, and sing, including matters of style and ethos, that are not universal and do not need to be so. For example, the Eastern Churches and the Western Churches have differed in their calendar of the Church year. While this, at times, has caused awkwardness and difficulties between the Churches, it is not something over which the Churches should break communion.

Another example of permissible diversity would be the variety of the liturgies of the Lord's Supper that have arisen in the Church's life. In their essentials they are alike, but they differ in many ways: in length, in prayers, in prescribed ceremony, and in structure.

The manner of baptism varies; some immerse in water, some pour water, and some sprinkle the water. Some, for example Anglicans, permit all three modes of administration. Some churches pass the kiss of peace, some do not. The hymnals of the various churches differ. The hour on the Lord's Day when the main corporate worship of the Church takes place varies from congregation to congregation.

These non-essential things in the practice of the Church have never been alike, as the Article states. The reasons for this diversity are various: geographic diversity, differing native languages, cultural differences, and developments in the customs of the local churches that have taken place over time, particularly at a time when close contact and frequent communication between churches was difficult.

However, as this Article points out, there is a limit to allowable diversity in the teaching and practice of the Churches. The limit is that the Scriptures be rightly taught and that nothing can be ordained or permitted that is contrary to the Holy Scriptures. This point is made most strongly in several Articles. And nothing is to be omitted that the Scriptures make clear belongs to what is to be required in a visible Church.

Biblical Foundations

For truly, I say to you, until heaven and earth pass away, not an iota, not a dot, will pass from the Law until all is accomplished. Therefore whoever relaxes one of the least of these commandments and teaches others to do the same will be called least in the kingdom of heaven, but whoever does them and teaches them will be called great in the kingdom of heaven. Matthew 5:18-19

And he said, "Woe to you lawyers also! For you load people with burdens hard to bear, and you yourselves do not touch the burdens with one of your fingers." Luke 11:46

And the voice came to him again a second time, "What God has made clean, do not call common." Acts 10:15

Now, therefore, why are you putting God to the test by placing a yoke on the neck of the disciples that neither our fathers nor we have been able to bear? Acts 15:10

Do not be idolaters as some of them were; as it is written, "The people sat down to eat and drink and rose up to play." 1 Corinthians 10:7

But even Titus, who was with me, was not forced to be circumcised, though he was a Greek. Galatians 2:3

For he himself is our peace, who has made us both one and has broken down in his flesh the dividing wall of hostility. Ephesians 2:14

Therefore let no one pass judgment on you in questions of food and drink, or with regard to a festival or a new moon or a Sabbath. Colossians 2:16

False Teaching Denied/Objections Answered

1. The most fundamental and important question raised by this Article is how to determine what is basic or essential to the Tradition and what things are *adiaphorous*, non-essential, and up to the discretion of the local Church. The Article states that nothing may be allowed that is contrary to Scripture. This implies that all that is essential according to Scripture would be essential in the life of the Church. But who is to decide what is mandated by Scripture and what is contrary to Scripture?

The answer to that, for the Reformation Churches generally, and Anglicans particularly, lies firstly in the perspicuity, or clarity, of Scripture - the *claritas Scripturae*. God's Word written is sufficiently clear in stating the things essential that by the careful reading of Scripture in faith, God, speaking through it, will lead the Church to a common mind in essential matters. Thus, the Church of England and these Articles constantly appeal to the Scripture.

Secondly, under Scripture, there is an appeal to the Faith of the undivided Church, and particularly to the Three Catholic Creeds and the first Four Ecumenical Councils. Due consideration is taken of the consensus of the Fathers of the undivided Church as well.

Thirdly, the determination of what is essential and what is not, is made in the light of these standards and by prayer for the leading of the Holy Spirit. This is done by the leaders in the councils of the various churches that have been established to serve as the Church's *magisterium* or "authority" in matters of doctrine and morals.

Therefore, when differences still exist between visible churches, the fundamental call is to renewed biblical exegesis, ecumenical discussion, and prayer.

This is essentially a corporate appeal to Holy Scripture read with an eye to the consensus of the Church Catholic. Any other approach is an error in Anglican judgment.

The different Churches of the Reformation have made various arrangements concerning the form and manner of this authoritative process. For Anglicans, it varies somewhat between the several national churches of the Anglican Communion, but is usually some form of council or synod involving representative Bishops, other clergy, and laity. From earliest days this decision has been made by a council or synod, beginning with the Jerusalem Council, recorded in Acts 15.

2. The Roman Catholic Church holds that the answer to the question as to who determines what is essential for all expressions of the Church throughout the world is the Pope acting in consort with the Bishops of the Church in Council. In addition, since 1870, the Pope, as the Vicar of Christ on Earth, is held to have the right and authority in his office to speak on matters of Faith and morals with final and infallible authority, even apart from a council, when he speaks *ex cathedra*, "from the Chair of St. Peter." With this position the Eastern Orthodox Churches, the Anglicans, and the Churches of the Reformation did not and do not agree.

3. The Eastern Orthodox Churches find their theological norm in the Scriptures read in the light of the seven Ecumenical Councils of the undivided Church, which they seem to hold did not and could not err. They also consult the teaching of the Eastern Fathers, for further light upon subsequent issues while they await the next Ecumenical Council. Therefore, they make few if any changes in the tradition. It is clear from Article 21, which states that general Councils can and have erred, that

Anglicans do not agree with the position of the Eastern Orthodox Churches.

4. There is little doubt that an ecumenical council seriously committed to Scripture as the Word of God written and recognized by all is greatly needed. As discussed in Article 21, it is difficult to see how such a General or Ecumenical Council could come about or reconcile our differences. The Roman Church is unlikely to submit the authority of the Pope to the authority of a council, even an Ecumenical Council. In addition, it is clear that among the Churches of the Reformation, the various councils of the national churches have not all remained faithful to Holy Scripture or to the Faith of the undivided Church. The general councils of some churches, particularly in the West, have been unduly influenced by the spirit of the age and have approved things contrary to Holy Scripture.

The World Council of Churches has done some excellent work in theology, but has no magisterial authority.

What then is to be done? In the author's opinion, what is needed for Anglicans, if we are to remain true to our historic Anglican identity, is for us first to subscribe to our historic formularies. These are: the Scripture as the supreme authority, the three Ecumenical Creeds, the Thirty-Nine Articles of Religion, and the 1662 *Book of Common Prayer* and ordinal and Homilies. Second, Anglicans united in the Anglican Communion need to adopt or reaffirm these standards, agreement with which is essential to membership in the Anglican Communion. And finally, Anglicans need the Anglican Communion to so restructure itself as to become a Communion overseen by an authoritative Council with binding authority in matters essential, to which the several national churches of the Anglican Communion would be submitted. Provincial autonomy in matters non-essential is one thing, but autonomy is inappropriate and destructive in matters essential. Having done that, and thus coming again under Scripture, in the light of which all can be constantly reviewed and reformed, we Anglicans should be able to be of some help through continuing prayer and ecumenical discussions to point toward the next General or Ecumenical Council, and at the very least to model in some measure what is needed by all.

Implications
Upon serious and sufficient reasons, churches may change their traditions and ceremonies in secondary matters as they see fit, as long as the Faith is kept entire and that they do not require of their members anything contrary to the teaching of Holy Scripture. We can be thankful that we have been given the freedom and responsibility to allow for diversity in things not essential. However, we will surely lose our way if we are not deeply rooted in and obedient to the clear teaching of Holy Scripture.

2. No person due to personal preference may publicly violate the local traditions and ceremonies of the local Church that are agreeable to God's Word.
Explanation
Each Christian in every congregation has his or her preferences about a whole range of matters concerning the life and practice of the local church. It is certainly right and proper for each person to make his desires and insights known to those in authority in the congregation, so that the leaders can make decisions regarding the affirmation or alteration of non-essential traditions and ceremonies of the congregation or the diocese or the province. However, when those matters have been officially decided and instituted, it is required of all of the members to respect the common customs of the church that are agreeable to the Holy Scripture, for God is a God of order.

For example, when a church has determined that its worship shall be in accord with the official *Book of Common Prayer*, which is faithful to Scripture, it would be unacceptable for one of the clergy to lead Morning Prayer on Sunday morning or to preside over the Lord's Supper using some non-Anglican liturgy just because the officiant or some portion of the congregation did not like the service in the Prayer Book, unless the Bishop gave permission for worthy liturgical experimentation.

The Article states that a person or group in the congregation that violates the approved common patterns and customs of the church should be publicly rebuked, so that they and the other members of the congregation will be reminded of the obligation that rests on all of us to respect the common order of the church and the authority of those in leadership.

The Article gives two reasons for respecting the common order. First, it refers to "hurting the authority of the magistrate." That was the case when the civil authorities were responsible for seeing that the rules and institutions of the established Church were observed. In most of our situations today, the State or government is secular and is not properly concerned with such matters. A disregard of the official customs and practices of the Church, however, would weaken the authority of those who are in official positions of leadership in the Church.

Second, the Article states that such personal rejection of public order would "wound the consciences of the weaker brethren." Should one or more in the church, who are not persuaded of the value of the present customs and practices, violate them in some public manner, with disregard of the due authority of the leaders of the church, that violation would offend the conscience of those more dependent upon the tradition and more respectful of due order. St. Paul, in Romans, bids us restrain our personal freedom so as not to offend those whose consciences are bound in rules concerning eating meat offered to idols. The Article concurs with the Apostle on this point.

Biblical Foundations

The scribes and the Pharisees sit on Moses' seat, so practice and observe whatever they tell you— but not what they do. For they preach, but do not practice. Matthew 23:2-3

I know and am persuaded in the Lord Jesus that nothing is unclean in itself, but it is unclean for anyone who thinks it unclean. Romans 14:14

I appeal to you, brothers, to watch out for those who cause divisions and create obstacles contrary to the doctrine that you have been taught; avoid them. Romans 16:17

What then, brothers? When you come together, each one has a hymn, a lesson, a revelation, a tongue, or an interpretation. Let all things be done for building up. 1 Corinthians 14:26

But all things should be done decently and in order. 1 Corinthians 14:40

Now we command you, brothers, in the name of our Lord Jesus Christ, that you keep away from any brother who is walking in idleness and not in accord with the tradition that you received from us. 2 Thessalonians 3:6

As for those who persist in sin, rebuke them in the presence of all, so that the rest may stand in fear. 1 Timothy 5:20

False Teaching Denied/Objections Answered

This Article was written around 1549, with the third paragraph being added in 1553. Some 10 years after that, some of the Puritans in the Church who were unhappy with matters concerning church order and several doctrinal Articles, principally, on Predestination (Article 17) and on *The Homilies* (Article 35), sought not to conform to all of the Articles, to be non-conformists, while remaining in the Church of England. This, they were not allowed to do. They had to conform or leave, and many left. It was a tragic loss to the Church of England of many godly clergy; on the other hand, without respect for order and authority, soon all common life and true spiritual unity are lost. In addition, disregard in matters of common order concerning nonessential issues soon spills over into essential issues.

Implications

For the common good we are to be content to abide by the official common traditions of the Church, unless they contradict the Scriptures, or hinder the building up of the Church and the exercise of its mission.

3. National Churches have authority to command, change, or abolish ceremonies or forms of worship that are appointed only by men's authority, provided everything is done for the building up of God's people.

Explanation

Prior to the Reformation, there had been only two major expressions of the Church: the Orthodox Churches of the East with their several Metropolitans and Archbishops and diverse liturgical rites, and one Church in the West united under the Pope and governed by him and such councils that he called. At the time of the 16th century Reformation, these two great expressions of the One, Holy, Catholic, and Apostolic Church, East and West, were not in communion with one another and had not been so since the 11th century. There had been no national churches in the West because, on the one hand, nations were just coming into their own and, on the other hand, the Pope was the ruling head of the Church in the West.

After the Reformation, when Churches in the West came out from under the authority of the Pope, we can speak, as this Article does, of national Churches in the West. Anglicanism at first consisted solely of the Church in England; but soon the Church of England spread to various nations, largely by following the colonial outreach of England and the development of the British Commonwealth. With the churches planted by the Church of England and by other Churches of the Reformation in several nations, it became necessary to address the issue of unity and diversity in these various expressions of the One, Holy, Catholic, and Apostolic Church in the several nations.

Since the various visible expressions of the one Church (see Article 19), i.e., the national Churches, found themselves in varying cultures, and since in being reformed by the Word of God, the various visible Churches took somewhat divergent paths in reforming the pre-Reformation customs and ceremonies, significant diversity in secondary matters was present.

This Article affirms that each national church has the right and authority, within limits, to ordain, change, or abolish ceremonies and rites as it best sees fit within its circumstances. Today each denomination continues to have that right.

Two limitations with regard to such diversity of ceremonies, rites, and customs are listed. The first limitation is that the freedom to authorize, change, or abolish rites and ceremonies applies only to things that have been or could be established by human authority. Put positively, whatever had been mandated by God in Holy Scripture must be honored.

The second limitation is that changes being introduced on the local or national level must serve to build up or edify the Church. Appropriate change is to be welcomed, but it is to be principled change. It is to be change that is in accord with the Holy Scripture and would serve the life and mission of the Church. It is not to be change for change's sake, nor diversity for diversity's sake. Continuity, commonality, and stability are important in the Church as they are in society as a whole.

Biblical Foundations

Then it seemed good to the apostles and the elders, with the whole church, to choose men from among them and send them to Antioch with Paul and Barnabas. They sent Judas called Barsabbas, and Silas, leading men among the brothers, with the following letter: "The brothers, both the apostles and the elders, to the brothers who are of the Gentiles in Antioch and Syria and Cilicia, greetings. Since we have heard that some persons have gone out from us and troubled you with words, unsettling your minds, although we gave them no instructions, it has seemed good to us, having come to one accord, to choose men and send them to you with our beloved Barnabas and Paul, men who have risked their lives for the sake of our Lord Jesus Christ. We have therefore sent Judas and Silas, who themselves will tell you the same things by word of mouth. For it has seemed good to the Holy Spirit and to us to lay on you no greater burden than these requirements: that you abstain from what has been sacrificed to idols, and from blood, and from what has been strangled, and from sexual immorality. If you keep yourselves from these, you will do well. Farewell." Acts 15:22-29

So then let us pursue what makes for peace and for mutual upbuilding. (Romans 14:19,

What then, brothers? When you come together, each one has a hymn, a lesson, a revelation, a tongue, or an interpretation. Let all things be done for building up. 1 Corinthians 14:26

Follow the pattern of the sound words that you have heard from me, in the faith and love that are in Christ Jesus. 2 Timothy 1:13

False Teaching Denied/Objections Answered

1. One extreme position concerning the right of national churches to change non-essential parts of the tradition was to deny it altogether and to declare that almost everything had to be standardized or approved by a supreme office over all of the churches. The phrase "need not be the same" with regard to traditions and ceremonies implies that there was such an insistence upon uniformity and centralized authority on the scene, to which this Article objected. It was in disagreement with this insistence on uniformity by some Anabaptists and some in what would become the Puritan party, and by Rome, that the material in the Article in this third teaching point, was written. Anglicans claimed the right for local churches to determine local tradition.

The Council of Trent had claimed that the Pope, as the Vicar of Christ on earth, had direct authority over all of the churches, East and West. While it was not until 1870 that the Roman Catholic Church declared that the Pope was infallible when speaking *ex cathedra* on matters of Faith and morals, the seeds of such a claim and authority were already present in the 16th century and earlier. This claim had long been rejected by the Orthodox Churches of the East and was also rejected by those Churches of the West that embraced the 16th century Reformation. Since then, a general uniformity in the West has been replaced by diversity and, unfortunately, by a degree of isolation and a lack of unity even in matters essential in some cases.

2. Anglicans, or the Church of England, affirmed that the Archbishop of Canterbury stood on a par in terms of his authority over the Church in England with the Bishop of Rome over the churches under his care. In England, the pattern of the exercise of authority was complex, involving the Bishops in the chapters of both Canterbury and York, as well as the King and the Parliament. As the Anglican Communion arose, instruments of unity or consultation arose, but each national Church or Province was accorded

autonomy to such an extent that when matters essential are being violated by any member church of the Communion, there is no authoritative way to address that serious problem. The Anglican Communion is presently seeking to address that problem.

3. The Reformation also produced groups, largely Anabaptists, that allowed for little change from Scripture. These radical groups ended up seeking to reproduce or repristinate the customs and cultural conditions of the first-century Church that are found in Scripture. In so doing, they created a tradition at odds with all the other churches and at odds with the culture of their time. Believing this to be biblical and therefore essential, they held that all the Churches should be like them. They tended to live apart from the cultures and societies wherein they were set. Here, too, the visible unity of the wider Church is damaged.

4. If Rome and certain radical groups tended toward central authority, some Anabaptist groups at the time of the Reformation and groups such as the Quakers, went to the other extreme, tending to leave almost everything to the perceived leading of the Spirit. The Quakers so feared authority that they allowed neither a normative place to Scripture nor a place for clergy in the Church.

In contrast, Anglicans, along with the Lutherans, are conservative and seek to avoid both extremes by declaring essential beliefs in formularies or confessions, while allowing local or national churches the freedom to be diverse and to make changes in the non-essential traditions of the Church. They allow national churches to fix certain standard customs and ceremonies or liturgies as required within their bodies. The question now before both Anglicans and Lutherans as global expressions of the Church Catholic is how discipline is to be carried out when national churches depart from essential doctrine as commonly understood.

Anglicans find significant help in this matter of local diversity in matters non-essential in the writings of Richard

Hooker. The struggle with a sizable number of the Puritans, mentioned above, led to his writing of *Ecclesiastical Polity*. In the fifth book of *Ecclesiastical Polity*, he suggested a number of principles for judging the place of traditions and ceremonies in areas where the teaching of Scripture did not clearly teach or command. Where Scripture speaks clearly, it is to be followed. He suggested four principles to be applied where it does not. A ceremony or outer form might well be kept if: 1) it tended to incline people to godliness, 2) if it had been approved in the judgment of antiquity, or the ancient Church (this was his adoption of the ancient Vincentian Canon, *quod semper, quod ubique, quod omnibus*, i.e., "that which is believed always, everywhere and by all"), and 3) if the leadership of the Church commended it. He added a fourth point that, in certain cases where circumstances demanded or situations of necessity arose, exceptions could always be allowed. If these principles are applied, decisions about matters non-essential become principled.

In summary, we can say that the Anglican principle regarding non-essential traditions would seem to be: if a custom or a tradition is not forbidden by Scripture and is agreeable to Scriptural principles, and if it has been widely accepted in the Church over a long period of time, and if it has proven to be fruitful in building up the Church, it is to be kept. If a custom or tradition is contrary to Scripture, or seems a hindrance to the building up of the Church and the mission of the Church, then it should be reformed or dropped. Anglicans held then and still hold now that national churches should have the freedom and responsibility to apply those principles in their own situations.

Implications

National Churches have both the freedom and responsibility to make principled decisions about non-essential or secondary traditions, customs, ceremonies, and rites. Local circumstances are best addressed by those Christians who live in them and who, in prayer and reflection upon Scripture, seek God's wisdom for their common life and witness. Such change, however, is to be done carefully and with the oversight of those in the local church who have been set apart and given authority to oversee such changes.

Conclusion

In all of the expressions of the One, Holy, Catholic, and Apostolic Church, there will be a similarity or family likeness in the basic teachings of the Faith and morals and in sacramental celebration. Between the various bodies, there will also be significant diversity of rites and ceremonies and other aspects of the local traditions. As long as the diversity is in accord with Scripture and the essentials of the Faith are kept entire, such diversity will provide a richness in which we can all rejoice and from which we all can learn. If we depart from Scripture, the diversity will become increasingly disruptive, corrupting, and divisive.

ARTICLE 35

Of Homilies
The second Book of Homilies, the several titles whereof we have joined under this Article, doth contain a godly and wholesome doctrine and necessary for these times, as doth the former Book of Homilies which were set forth in the time of Edward the Sixth: and therefore we judge them to be read in Churches by the ministers diligently and distinctly, that they may be understood of the people.

Of the Names of the Homilies.
1. Of the right Use of the Church.
2. Against Peril of Idolatry.
3. Of repairing and keeping clean of Churches.
4. Of good Works: first of Fasting.
5. Against Gluttony and Drunkenness.
6. Against Excess of Apparel.
7. Of Prayer.
8. Of the Place and Time of Prayer.
9. That Common Prayers and Sacraments ought to be ministered in a known tongue.
10. Of the reverend Estimation of God's Word.
11. Of Alms-doing.
12. Of the Nativity of Christ.
13. Of the Passion of Christ.
14. Of the Resurrection of Christ.
15. Of the worthy receiving of the Sacrament of the Body and Blood of Christ.
16. Of the Gifts of the Holy Ghost.
17. For the Rogation-days.
18. Of the State of Matrimony.
19. Of Repentance.
20. Against Idleness.
21. Against Rebellion.

Introduction

What is to be done when the preaching is poor? Who can address this? What can be done? Is it important to deal with this? If it is, why?

In the transition occasioned by 16th century Reformation, the Word of God took a central place. This change found the clergy poorly prepared to preach and teach and largely ignorant of the Scriptures. Therefore, Cranmer and others thought it wise to provide sermons, *The Homilies*, for the clergy to use in public as well as for their own learning. Luther had the same problem and addressed it by writing the *Larger Catechism* and by making available collections of his sermons. Later, the Methodists provided guidance and training for their preachers by publishing John Wesley's *Standard Sermons*.

The *First and Second Books of the Homilies* have been printed as one volume since 1623 and are still available in print. They are well worth reading today. In addition to their excellent content, felicitous Elizabethan expression, fine exegesis, and logical presentation, they show the theological mind-set of those who shaped and wrote the Thirty-Nine Articles. They thereby provide a rich commentary on the themes of the Articles and on *The Book of Common Prayer*.

Since their style is too time-conditioned to be widely read in the Church, a simplified and modestly modernized version of *The Homilies* would be a great practical help to the Church today.

The Teaching of Article 35

Here are the teaching points for this Article:

1. The First and Second Books of *The Homilies* contain only godly and wholesome doctrine.

2. *The Homilies* are authorized and urged to be read clearly to the congregations.

1. The First and Second Books of *The Homilies* contain only godly and wholesome doctrine.

Explanation

The aims of this Article are: 1) to officially commend the theology found in *The Homilies*, 2) to require that the clergy read *The Homilies* to the congregations, and to do so in an understandable fashion, and 3) in so doing, to set forth a model of expositional and thematic preaching that would instruct the clergy in biblical theology and in the art of preaching.

Archbishop Cranmer and the other early Anglican Reformers were convinced that the Word of God is essential to the Christian life and to the well being of congregations. They were faced with a body of clergy that had not been trained in preaching or in biblical theology but only in pre-Reformation theology, and often very little of that. Therefore, it was clear that something had to be done.

What they did regarding preaching was two-fold. First, they determined that preachers needed to be licensed to preach. Not all ordained persons were immediately permitted to preach. To be licensed to preach required some preparation and continuing training. Second, they placed in the hands of the clergy the First and then the Second Books of Homilies to be studied and read to the congregations.

The title *Homilies* comes from the root of the Greek word for "a crowd" and refers to a popular address or talk as contrasted with a technical address. A homily is a talk that the people could understand. To be popular does not imply that the Sunday sermons or homilies were to be superficial or merely entertaining; rather, they were to open up the Scriptures in a manner that would instruct the congregation so that their heads and hearts would be filled with the knowledge of God that is in Christ Jesus as found in God's Word written.

By expounding the Scriptures in the light of Christ and the Gospel, the clergy were to proclaim the whole council of God. In a real sense, Archbishop Cranmer, Bishop

Ridley, later Bishop John Jewel, and others, in writing these homilies, were serving as teachers of the whole Church in and through the homilies. In so doing, they were communicating and commending the biblical theology that lay at the heart of the Reformation and renewal of the Church. Their vision and aim was large: it was the evangelical education of the whole of England, clergy and laity alike.

For the sake of the unity of the Church, and to settle any disputes on basic theological matters, the Thirty-Nine Articles were written and officially adopted. The Articles give a more concise, doctrinally precise statement of the Church's theology than do *The Homilies*. Therefore, it was required of the clergy that they subscribe to the Articles as providing much of the content as well as the context and perspective of their teaching and preaching, They were also required to study and read *The Homilies* to the congregation.

On the one hand, *The Homilies* are to be understood in the light of the Thirty-Nine Articles of Religion. On the other hand, since the authors of the Articles and of *The Homilies* are largely the same people and since *The Homilies* are authoritatively commended in the Articles (Articles 11 and 35), they are rightly consulted, where helpful, to clarify the meaning and application of the Thirty-Nine Articles. Needless to say, the Articles remain the chief source for determining the Anglican Faith on any given subject treated therein, but *The Homilies* are of value and instructive in their own right.

Biblical Foundations

But how are they to call on him in whom they have not believed? And how are they to believe in him of whom they have never heard? And how are they to hear without someone preaching? Romans 10:14

For if I preach the gospel, that gives me no ground for boasting. For necessity is laid upon me. Woe to me if I do not preach the gospel! 1 Corinthians 9:16

And we also thank God constantly for this, that when you received the word of God, which you heard from us, you accepted it not as the word of men but as what it really is, the word of God, which is at work in you believers. 1 Thessalonians 2:13

And what you have heard from me in the presence of many witnesses entrust to faithful men who will be able to teach others also. 2 Timothy 2:2

False Teachings Denied/Objections Answered

1. Some of the Puritans objected to reading *The Homilies* in the place of the sermon, for they held that only the fresh preaching of a biblical text, not the reading of a standard, written sermon, was honoring to God and sufficient to sanctify the faithful. In their view, reading was different than preaching, even reading an excellent sermon written by someone else. No service should have the Scripture read without being expounded in a lively fashion by a preacher. No reading of a written sermon, no matter how sound its theology, was an adequate substitute for a fresh exposition of the Word.

They were strongly opposed to the reading of *The Homilies*. In the end, their objection to the reading of *The Homilies* was one of the reasons the "nonconformists" were forced to leave the Church of England.

2. Others held that only Scripture, the inspired Word of God written, should be read in Church. No non-Canonical writings should be read. It would be an act that gave the human written word far too much authority. They, too, opposed the reading of *The Homilies*.

Obviously, the Anglican Reformers did not agree. Both the study of these soundly biblical Homilies and the act of reading them in Church are enjoined on the clergy. As the

Reverend Thomas Rogers, the earliest commentator on the Thirty-Nine Articles, said, "The Apostles were to teach as well by the pen as by lively voice." If the Apostles could teach in both methods, so too could Archbishops and all the clergy.

3. Some extremists in the Anabaptist movement held that no merely human writings should be read at all, either in or outside of the worship of the Church. Thus, they rejected *The Homilies*. They burned their books in public in rejection of human wisdom and turned simply and solely to the Holy Scriptures. They held that the Scriptures were not only the supreme norm in the light of which we are to judge all claims to truth wherever found, but that truth can be found only in the Scripture and nowhere else.

One can appreciate their zeal to be biblical, but not their confusion and narrowness. They erred in confusing the unique authority of Scripture with its being the sole means whereby God's truth may be conveyed and found. Sermons and even conversation can serve to bear the Word of God to others. Nor is God's truth limited only to saving revelation. The Heavens declare the glory of God. Anglicans have always held that God speaks through both the book of Creation and the book of Holy Scripture. And the two books ultimately agree and cohere, for the Word of God, through Whom all creation is created, is the same Word that became incarnate in Christ Jesus for our salvation and through Whom God reveals Himself redemptively. We are to receive truth wherever it is to be found, but to test all by God's Word in Christ.

Implications

A. Anglicans do well to adopt Cranmer's great aim to instruct the entire Church in wholesome and godly doctrine through the expository and thematic preaching of the Scriptures.

B. The practice of licensing clergy or learned laity to preach is wise, for what is preached and how it is preached is very influential in the building up or tearing down of a congregation.

C. In many professions and callings, an updating of essential skills and learning is required on a given schedule. It would be appropriate for those who are called to preach regularly to take part in some such arrangement with regard to preaching. It is an art that is never perfected.

D. In the preparation for ordination, a careful and required reading of *The Homilies* would be both wise and appropriate.

2. *The Homilies* are authorized and urged to be read clearly to the congregations.

Explanation

Initially, and then later from time to time, the Archbishops would set forth schedules according to which *The Homilies* were to be read Sunday by Sunday in the parish churches. Not all of the clergy rejoiced in this. Some were of the pre-Reformation theological persuasion still and did not agree with the biblical theology of *The Homilies*. And others, like those Puritans mentioned above, did not believe that *The Homilies* should be read at all. One of the things the clergy did to observe the letter of the law while violating its intention was to read *The Homilies* so softly or so indistinctly that they were not understandable by the congregation. This Article requires not only that they be read, but that they be read "diligently and distinctly," so that they could be understood by the people.

Biblical Foundations

[Jesus said,] "What do you think? A man had two sons. And he went to the first and said, 'son, go and work in the vineyard today.' And he answered, 'I will not,' but afterward he changed his mind and went. And he went to the other son and said the same. And he answered, 'I go, sir,' but did not go. Which of the two did the will of his

father?" They said, "The first." Jesus said to them, "Truly, I say to you, the tax collectors and the prostitutes go into the kingdom of God before you." Matthew 21:28-31

But above all, my brothers, do not swear, either by heaven or by earth or by any other oath, but let your "yes" be yes and your "no" be no, so that you may not fall under condemnation. James 5:12

False Teaching Denied/Objections Answered

This requirement came to be the downfall of many, forcing them to leave the Church of England. There is nothing wrong with making one's disagreement known to those who are in authority. However, having done so and failing to persuade those in authority, there are only two acceptable paths. One can resign one's position under that authority, or one can accept being under that authority and do what one is required to do with a good heart and in accord with the intent of the requirement.

Mumbling a required reading was no obedience to authority. The Article is right to exclude that rebellion and evasion of responsibility.

Implications

We are to deal honestly with one another in love. If we are under the authority of others in the Body of Christ, then we are to respect that authority. Should we come to a point of conscience, then we must pay the price and make our stand, but we cannot evade difficult decisions by undue compromise, on the one hand, or by deceptive evasion of responsibility, on the other. This is all the more true with regard to the ministry of God's Word and sacraments.

Conclusion

Preaching is of great importance. Not just everyone who is willing should be licensed to preach. It is important that what is preached be true and preached in a way that is understandable by the congregation. Preaching is to touch minds and hearts with the Gospel and the whole counsel of God. To this end a careful reading of *The Homilies* remains an excellent help.

Leaders in the Church would do well to evaluate the content and quality of preaching of those under their oversight and take such action as would help the preachers to continually improve and thereby also help the congregations that are being served by those preachers.

ARTICLE 36

Of Consecration of Bishops and Ministers

The Book of Consecration of Archbishops and Bishops and ordering of Priests and Deacons, lately set forth in the time of Edward the Sixth and confirmed at the same time by authority of Parliament, doth contain all things necessary to such consecration and ordering; neither hath it anything that of itself is superstitious or ungodly. And therefore whosoever are consecrate or ordered according to the rites of that book, since the second year of King Edward unto this time, or hereafter shall be consecrated or ordered according to the same rites, we decree all such to be rightly, orderly, and lawfully consecrated or ordered.

Introduction

Who is to be ordained? What is needed for a valid ordination? Who has the authority to ordain Deacons, Priests, and consecrate Bishops in the One, Holy, Catholic, and Apostolic Church? These are questions that must be answered, and particularly at a time such as the Reformation in the 16th century, when previous answers were no longer adequate. Much of this is treated in Article 23, where it is discussed in more general terms. This Article is more limited, for it discusses the validity and adequacy of the ordinal, or rites of ordination in the Church of England's Ordinal, which is usually bound with *The Book of Common Prayer* and is seen as part of our formularies. This Article, however, goes beyond the specifics of the Anglican Ordinal and raises fundamental and general questions about the nature of the ordained ministry in the Church in all of its expressions when viewed in the light of the Scriptures.

The Papal Church did not approve of the departure of the Church in England from under its authority at the time of the Reformation. The Pope claimed and continues to claim to be the universal Vicar of Christ on earth. The separation by the Church of England cast doubt, in the eyes of the Roman Catholic Church, on the validity of the ordinations and Holy Orders of those subsequently ordained in the Church of England without the Pope's approval or consent.

Later, the Church of Rome, in an official judgment, declared Anglican Orders to be invalid due to the inadequacy of the Anglican Ordinal.

This 36th Article responds to the objections to the Anglican Ordinal from Rome and to objections regarding the Ordinal from some Puritans and Anabaptists in England. Article 36 asserts both the adequacy and the biblical faithfulness of the Anglican Ordinal. It thereby affirms the validity of Anglican orders in the One, Holy, Catholic, and Apostolic Church and of those clergy ordained in and through the ordinal of the Church of England.

The Teaching of Article 36

Here are the teaching points for this Article:

1. The Ordinal approved in the Church of England contains all that is necessary for the right ordering of Bishops, Priests and Deacons in Christ's One, Holy, Catholic and Apostolic Church.

2. The Anglican Ordinal contains nothing ungodly or superstitious.

3. All who have been or shall be ordained or consecrated through the Anglican Ordinal are rightly and lawfully ordained.

1. The Ordinal approved in the Church of England contains all that is necessary for the right ordering of Bishops, Priests and Deacons in Christ's One, Holy, Catholic and Apostolic Church.

Explanation

At the time of the Reformation everything was being considered in the light of the Scriptures. Therefore the question is posed, "What do the Scriptures say and teach by example about what ordination rites need to include to be acceptable to God and used by Him?" Because the adequacy of the Anglican Ordinal, or the Anglican rites used for ordination of Deacons, Priests or Presbyters, and the consecration of Bishops, was questioned by Rome and others on theological grounds, this became a question about the very nature of the ordained ministry as well. Rome's objections were particularly concerned with the nature of the ordained ministry as related to the celebration of the Eucharist or Lord's Supper.

Anglicans, in the Articles, seek to build their doctrine and practice on the Holy Scripture and only on such developments in the history of the Church that are congruent with the Scriptures. Also, as the Articles frequently assert, the Church has no authority to ordain anything that is contrary with Scripture. Therefore, this Article gets us deep into matters about which Christians do not at present agree. Anglicans seek to make an ecumenical contribution here as in other places in these Articles.

It is interesting that the New Testament never uses the term "ordain," but the substance of ordination is found under such terms as "called," "chosen," "appointed," and "set apart." Jesus chose and called the Twelve Apostles; the Apostles appointed elders or presbyters in the congregations they founded, and the elders seem to have set apart deacons in the several congregations.

Actually, we have little information about the ceremonies that were used to ordain or consecrate people into these offices or orders. The fullest description we have is found in Acts 6 where the deacons were set apart by the Apostles. There we find that they were set apart by public prayer and the laying on of hands. In addition, in a number of places in Acts and in the letters of Paul and particularly in the pastoral epistles, we hear of the laying on of hands as involved in the way people were set apart for specific ministries and offices.

Therefore, it would satisfy biblical teaching and practice if an ordination rite or an ordinal consisted of public prayer and the laying on of hands by those with authority to ordain or consecrate persons into a particular order or office.

No doubt, as the Church grew and expanded and developed in different parts of the world, the rites of ordination expanded and what was included in one part of the Church was not necessarily included in the rites of other churches. All ordination rites, however, as far as we know, included and continue to include the biblical elements of public prayer and the laying on of hands by those with the authority to ordain.

The Anglican ordinal from the time of Edward the Sixth onwards contained these essential elements. Anglicans, therefore, are confident that the services of ordination in the Anglican Ordinal, from the beginning, contained the necessary elements to ordain persons for the godly ministry of the Word and sacraments in God's One, Holy, Catholic, and Apostolic Church.

In the New Testament, the dominant language about the office of Presbyter or Priest and of Bishop is that of humble service in pastoral oversight and teaching. Little is said about who presides in the celebration or administration of the Holy Communion, though one can surmise with a high degree of confidence that it was one of the elders or presbyters who presided when an Apostle was not present.

At the Reformation, the Church of England through Archbishop Cranmer recovered the biblical emphasis on the reading, preaching, and teaching of the Word, while retaining a high regard for the ministry of the Sacraments of the Gospel celebrated in the context of the ministry of the Word. Because of this Scriptural emphasis, the Anglican Ordinal has the giving of the Bible to the ordinand during the ordination serve as a sign that the order into which the ordinand was entering was a biblical order, that it would be carried out in the power of the Spirit speaking through the Scriptures, and would be conducted in accordance with the Word of God written.

Several traditional statements and the items traditionally given when a Priest or Presbyter was ordained were omitted in the Anglican Ordinal as being either secondary or contrary to the nature and calling of Christian Priesthood, as set forth in Scripture.

Biblical Foundations

And the Holy Spirit descended on him in bodily form, like a dove; and a voice came from heaven, "You are my beloved Son; with you I am well pleased." Luke 3:22

So also Christ did not exalt himself to be made a high priest, but was appointed by him who said to him, "You are my Son, today I have begotten you." Hebrews 5:5

In these days he went out to the mountain to pray, and all night he continued in prayer to God. And when day came, he called his disciples and chose from them twelve, whom he named apostles. Luke 6:12-13

Now in these days when the disciples were increasing in number, a complaint by the Hellenists arose against the Hebrews because their widows were being neglected in the daily distribution. And the twelve summoned the full number of the disciples and said, "It is not right that we should give up preaching the word of God to serve tables. Therefore, brothers, pick out from among you seven men of good repute, full of the Spirit and of wisdom, whom we will appoint to this duty. But we will devote ourselves to prayer and to the ministry of the word." And what they said pleased the whole gathering, and they chose Stephen, a man full of faith and of the Holy Spirit, and Philip, and Prochorus, and Nicanor, and Timon, and Parmenas, and Nicolaus, a proselyte of Antioch. These they set before the apostles, and they prayed and laid their hands on them. Acts 6:1-6

And when they had appointed elders for them in every church, with prayer and fasting they committed them to the Lord in whom they had believed. Acts 14:23

For those who serve well as deacons gain a good standing for themselves and also great confidence in the faith that is in Christ Jesus. 1 Timothy 3:13

Let the elders who rule well be considered worthy of double honor, especially those who labor in preaching and teaching. 1 Timothy 5:17

For this reason I remind you to fan into flame the gift of God, which is in you through the laying on of my hands. 2 Timothy 1:6

False Teaching Denied/Objections Answered

There are several objections raised by the Roman Catholic Church to the Anglican Ordinal.

1. Rome objected that there was not sufficient differentiation in the words of ordination for the different orders of ministry, since the same words for ordination and/or consecration were used for both the Priesthood and Episcopate.

However helpful this differentiation might be at the point of the laying on of hands, the earliest known ordinals of the ancient Church did not include any such differentiation. Therefore, if that expression of differentiation at the moment of ordination were declared essential for valid ordinations, all ordinations would be invalid, for no one was validly ordained since the undifferentiated formula was commonly used. Those who were later ordained using the fuller formula would not have been validly ordained either, for they would have been ordained by those who were not truly ordained. This is a conclusion no one was or is willing to embrace. That objection was eventually dropped.

Anglicans gladly added words of differentiation in the ordinal, agreeing that it was a wise, though not an essential, thing to do. In 1662 the words: "for the office and work of a Deacon," "for the office and work of a Priest," and "for the office and work of a Bishop" were added to the words of ordination and consecration in the Anglican Ordinal.

2. Rome also objected and continues to object that the words "to offer sacrifice for the living and the dead" were missing in the ordination of the Priest. This is by far the most important issue and question raised concerning the ordinal.

This omission was intentional on the part of Cranmer and the Anglican Reformers. These words were omitted because they assumed and taught that Priests offered, or that Christ offered Himself through the Priests, as a propitiatory sacrifice in the Mass, which Anglicans denied. (See the discussion of this point in Article 31.)

It should be stated that the word "Priest" in *The Book of Common Prayer* is a shortened form of Presbyter or Elder; *Presbuteros* and not *hieirus* (the word for the Old Testament priest, who did offer sacrifices for sin). The word *hieirus* is never once applied to the ordained ministry in the New Testament. That could hardly have been accidental. It was due to the fact that Jesus had made the final and sufficient propitiatory sacrifice. It was not to be repeated. Further, Jesus remains in office eternally, interceding for us as our High Priest in heaven.

For this reason, not only does Rome have serious reservations about the Anglican Ordinal, Anglicans have and should have serious reservations about the Roman Ordinal, which has included a sacrifice and sacerdotal view of the ordained ministry which is contrary to the teaching of Scripture. These are matters for serious ecumenical discussion.

3. Rome asserted her sense of being the Church by objecting that the Anglican Ordinal did not intend to do what the Church was doing. This is a valid point only if one holds that the Pope is the Vicar of Christ on earth with jurisdiction over all Christians and that the Roman Catholic Church is in fact the One, Holy, Catholic, and Apostolic Church, rather than one visible member church or expression of the One, Holy, Catholic, and Apostolic Church (and one, from the Anglican perspective, that needs reformation in a number of areas, not least in its understanding of Priesthood).

According to Anglican doctrine, what Rome does, does not *per se* define what the Church does or ought to do. Therefore, Anglicans hold that this objection is based on false premises.

4. Rome also believed that in failing to anoint the Priest's hands for blessing and by failing, in the service of ordination, to give the traditional implements of office, such as a paten, chalice, and chasuble, the Anglican rites were essentially deficient. Anglicans point out that the early ordinals did not include the giving of these implements and that they were omitted because they implied, at the time of the Reformation, a sacerdotal or sacrificing priesthood, which is foreign to the New Testament priesthood or presbyterate. They still carry that sacerdotal meaning in the Roman Ordinal. Anglicans hold that the authority of the Priest to preside over Word and Sacrament is sufficiently and clearly signified in the giving of the Holy Scriptures, and by words of the Ordinal.

In addition, a stole is usually given and the ordinand is vested with it at the ordination as well. Stoles are generally worn by Anglican clergy when they are celebrating and administering the sacraments. Eucharistic vestments are also worn by some Anglicans. These ceremonial matters are matters of some debate among Anglicans.

Implications

We can summarize the heart of all these objections by saying that the Anglican Ordinal differs from the Roman Catholic Ordinal both by not acceding supreme authority to the Roman Catholic Church and by having a different and biblical understanding of the nature of the priesthood. In the Mass, the Roman Catholic Priest intends to offer, Christ acting through him, a meritorious, propitiatory sacrifice for the living and the dead. The Anglican Priest does not, but rather recalls the once-for-all, completed, and finished propitiatory sacrifice of Christ and presides over the Holy Communion in which Christ gives Himself, His Body and Blood, to the repentant faithful for their nourishment in their relationship to Him and to one another and for their part in His mission to the world. The ordinals reflect and express this difference.

2. The Anglican Ordinal contains nothing ungodly or superstitious.
Explanation

One wonders, what would one object to in the Anglican Ordinal as superstitious or as ungodly? We turn from objections coming from Rome to objections coming from groups of believers, largely in England. Some of the Anabaptists that were involved with the radical wing of the Reformation and later some Puritans raised these objections. It seems that Bishops were a matter of contention.

Some of the Anabaptist groups were inclined to reject all practices and traditions that developed after the closing of the New Testament Canon. As such, their reading of the New Testament led them to deny all authority in the Church beyond the authority of the congregation and its authority to choose its own leaders, both governing elders and teaching elders. They were congregational in polity or governance. To them, the Anglican Ordinal was seen to include instruments of oversight, i.e., Bishops, that were not instituted by God.

They objected to the office and the authority of the Bishop on two grounds. First, they objected to the fact that the Ordinal sees Bishops as being an order and exercising an office distinct from Presbyters because, in the New Testament, the roles of Bishops and Presbyters/Priests referred to the same people. The distinction of Bishop from Presbyter was a purely post-Canonical development, in their mind.

Anglicans disagreed, holding that the rise of the monarchical Episcopate took place along lines already found in Scripture in Timothy and Titus and was a development fully in accord with Scripture.

A second reason they objected to Bishops was that the Bishop, representing the wider Church, exercised an authority over the several local congregations in a diocese. For example, the permission of the Bishop was required for an ordination to take place. Congregations could recommend whom they would like to see ordained and serve them, but they did not have the authority to ordain or simply to choose whomever they wanted as their leaders. Such authority these nonconformists did not find in Scripture.

Both of these elements in the Ordinal were considered by the Anabaptists to be unwarranted and false additions to biblical teaching and simplicity. Therefore the Anglican Ordinal was considered ungodly by the Anabaptists, who held to a congregational polity.

As mentioned above, the Anglican response to these objections comes from a closer reading of Holy Scripture. In the Scriptures, the Apostles held authority over the congregations. However, as the Church was rapidly expanding and the Apostles were being martyred, some new form of unifying oversight was needed. Anglicans see the beginning of a developing episcopate in figures such as James, who was something of a monarchical figure in Jerusalem, and Timothy and Titus who were apostolic deputies, presbyters answerable to the Apostles and who had several congregations with their clergy placed under their oversight by the Apostles. By A.D. 180, the monarchical Episcopate had become universal in the Church. This was a development that made explicit what was implicit and even beginning to emerge in Scripture in the New Testament period.

Somewhat later, some Puritans who were clergy in the Church of England also believed that the office of Bishop was an improper retention, a remainder of unreformed tradition, that needed to be removed so that the reformation of the Church could be properly completed. The response to the Anabaptists just outlined above also describes the Anglican response to those Puritans.

In addition, those Puritans were also offended by the words of the Ordinal: "Receive the Holy Ghost for the office and work of a Priest (Bishop) in the Church of God, now committed unto thee by the imposition of our hands. Whose sins thou dost forgive, they are forgiven; whose sins thou dost retain they are retained." These words were retained from the pre-Reformation Ordinal.

The Puritans held that these words were superstitious, for in their opinion, man cannot claim to bestow the Holy Spirit by the laying on of hands, nor can any man forgive sins. God alone does both.

They held this despite the fact, as Anglicans pointed out, that the words quoted are those of Christ spoken to the Apostles. The incarnate Son did and does have the authority to forgive sins, and it is in His Name and service that the Presbyter or the Bishop authoritatively declares to repentant believers the forgiveness of Christ.

In essence, the objections of both the Puritans and the Anabaptists are answered by observing that the elements in the Ordinal to which they objected are actually developments in the Church's history that have their foundation and beginning in the New Testament and are in accord with the Scripture. Given this, Anglicans believe that there is nothing superstitious or ungodly in the Ordinal.

Biblical Foundations

Jesus said to them again, "Peace be with you. As the Father has sent me, even so I am sending you." And when he had said this, he breathed on them and said to them, "Receive the Holy Spirit. If you forgive the sins of anyone, they are forgiven; if you withhold forgiveness from anyone, it is withheld." John 20:21-23

After they finished speaking, James replied, "Brothers, listen to me. Simeon has related how God first visited the Gentiles, to take from them a people for his name. And with this the words of the prophets agree, just as it is written, " 'After this I will return, and I will rebuild the tent of David that has fallen; I will rebuild its ruins, and I will restore it, that the remnant of mankind may seek the Lord, and all the Gentiles who are called by my name, says the Lord, who makes these things known from of old.' Therefore my judgment is that we should not trouble those of the Gentiles who turn to God, but should write to them to abstain from the things polluted by idols, and from sexual immorality, and from what has been strangled, and from blood. For from ancient generations Moses has had in every city those who proclaim him, for he is read every Sabbath in the synagogues." Then it seemed good to the apostles and the elders, with the whole church, to choose men from among them and send them to Antioch with Paul and Barnabas. They sent Judas called Barsabbas, and Silas, leading men among the brothers. Acts 15:13-22

Paul, an apostle of Christ Jesus by command of God our Savior and of Christ Jesus our hope, To Timothy, my true child in the faith: Grace, mercy, and peace from God the Father and Christ Jesus our Lord. As I urged you when

I was going to Macedonia, remain at Ephesus that you may charge certain persons not to teach any different doctrine, nor to devote themselves to myths and endless genealogies, which promote speculations rather than the stewardship from God that is by faith. The aim of our charge is love that issues from a pure heart and a good conscience and a sincere faith. 1 Timothy 1:1-5

In the presence of God and of Christ Jesus and of the elect angels I charge you to keep these rules without prejudging, doing nothing from partiality. Do not be hasty in the laying on of hands, nor take part in the sins of others; keep yourself pure. 1 Timothy 5:21-22

You then, my child, be strengthened by the grace that is in Christ Jesus, and what you have heard from me in the presence of many witnesses entrust to faithful men who will be able to teach others also. 2 Timothy 2:1-2

To Titus, my true child in a common faith: Grace and peace from God the Father and Christ Jesus our Savior. This is why I left you in Crete, so that you might put what remained into order, and appoint elders in every town as I directed you— if anyone is above reproach, the husband of one wife, and his children are believers and not open to the charge of debauchery or insubordination. For an overseer, as God's steward, must be above reproach. He must not be arrogant or quick-tempered or a drunkard or violent or greedy for gain, but hospitable, a lover of good, self-controlled, upright, holy, and disciplined. He must hold firm to the trustworthy word as taught, so that he may be able to give instruction in sound doctrine and also to rebuke those who contradict it. Titus 1:4-9

False Teaching Denied/Objections Answered

1. Anglicans have ever treasured the historic Episcopate, that is, Bishops in historic succession, as a pastoral sign and servant of the wider apostolic succession of the Church. The apostolic succession of the Church is

not just Bishops in succession through time, as is sometimes taught, but also all the various ways the Church passes on the Apostolic Faith, life, and mission from one generation to the next generation.

The historic Episcopate must never be isolated from that which it serves and from which it draws its meaning. For example, as a servant of the Apostolic life, Faith, and mission of the Church, a reality that is broader than his office, an Anglican Bishop in historic succession who is teaching contrary to the Apostolic Faith and contrary to the Thirty-Nine Articles of the Anglican Church is unfaithful first and fundamentally as a Bishop in the Church Catholic, and in particular as an Anglican Bishop. Apostolicity in the Episcopate cannot be isolated from the Apostles' teaching.

2. Having asserted that the order of Bishops in historic succession has its roots in Scripture and has ever been treasured by Anglicans, it is important to go on to say that Anglicans have not un-churched those Churches of the Reformation that did not continue with Bishops in historic succession. Some churches did not continue the historic Episcopate because the Bishops in their areas refused the Reformation. Others did not continue the historic Episcopate because they saw no great value in the office of Bishop as they had experienced it and therefore replaced the traditional forms of ministry with other patterns, and some others, following Calvin, thought that Scripture mandated a different form of oversight and governance. It is instructive that it was the Calvinists, not the Anglicans, that insisted, along with Rome and the Orthodox, that a specific pattern of ecclesiastical oversight is essential and not just desirable.

3. In ecumenical relations, Anglicans have sought to avoid two extremes. On the one hand, Anglicans want to commend the historic Episcopate to all the Churches; they affirm the biblical roots, the divine leading, and the practical value and importance of that form of ministry. Many Anglicans are convinced that it was the Lord Who

led the whole Church into use of the Episcopate by the end of the 2nd century. Moreover, Anglicans can see no way to recover the full visible unity of the whole Church apart from the historic Episcopate. So Anglicans encourage all the churches to consider receiving the historical Episcopate.

On the other hand, they do not want to deny that those churches are truly churches and expressions of the One, Holy, Catholic, and Apostolic Church that at present neither have, nor presently desire to have, Bishops in historic succession.

This concern to affirm the place of Bishops in historic succession and at the same time to affirm the Catholicity of all the historic Churches of the Reformation has led to the three classic views of the importance of the historic Episcopate that are presently found in Anglicanism. A small number of Anglicans hold to the *esse* position. The name is taken from the Latin verb "to be." This view holds that the historic Episcopate is essential to the being of the Church. Since it is held to be essential, without it there can be no Church. Rome, the Eastern Churches, and some Anglo-Catholic Anglicans share this view. This view does not really fit the language of the Anglican formularies or the statements of the Lambeth Conferences. In essence, it denies that those Churches of the Reformation without the historic Episcopate are truly churches and views them as communities of baptized Christians living under the uncovenanted mercies of God.

A second view is referred to as the *plene esse* position and holds that the historic Episcopate belongs to the fullness of the Church. Churches without the historic Episcopate are missing something that belongs to the wholeness of the nature of the Church, but they are still churches, assuming that they exhibit the marks listed in Article 19. The historic Episcopate is a gift of God given through the guidance of the Holy Spirit. It is a treasure when done in godly faithfulness. And Anglicans commend it to all churches.

A third view is called the *bene esse* view. It teaches that the historic Episcopate is a good and godly way of ordering the Church, and is rightly to be prized by those churches that have it. However, it is seen as a development in the life of the wider Church that all churches do not share, and most certainly ought not be imposed upon them if they do not see its goodness and desire it. Not all have had a good experience with Bishops. From experience at the time of the Reformation and subsequently, as well as in the present, it can be seen that Bishops in historic succession of office can fail to remain in the succession of Apostolic Faith, and have led in the wrong direction. We have to confess that the Houses of Bishops of a number of Anglican Provinces have failed dismally in keeping the Faith in recent history. The indefectibility of the Church cannot rest only or ultimately on the Bishops of the Church.

The second and third views, *plene esse* and *bene esse*, both fit within the language of the Articles and of the Lambeth Conferences and the practice of the Anglican Communion.

The experience of the Ecumenical Movement has shown that the historic Episcopate cannot be forced upon others; if we Anglicans live it out with faithfulness, we may hope that its value will become apparent to all.

Implications

There is nothing superstitious or ungodly in the Anglican Ordinal, and Anglicans may use it with confidence and pride. Having preserved the historic Episcopate at the Reformation as a gift of God for which Anglicans are thankful, Anglicans gladly commend the traditional and biblically rooted orders of Deacon, Presbyter, and Bishop in historic succession to all churches that bear the marks of a visible church as stated in Article 19.

3. All who have been or shall be ordained or consecrated through the Anglican Ordinal are rightly and lawfully ordained.

Explanation

This declaration in Teaching Point 3 follows logically from the previous two teaching points. Since the Ordinal, in all of its editions from its appearance under Edward VI to the present, has contained the essentials for valid ordinations in the Church Catholic, and since nothing superstitious or ungodly is found therein, therefore all who have been and will be ordained and consecrated using this Ordinal are truly and validly ordained or consecrated in the Church Catholic and should be recognized as such throughout the Church.

False Teaching Denied/Objections Answered

With Rome finding reasons to question the validity of Anglican ordinations, with groups of the radical Reformation and some Puritans also raising objections, and because some minor changes were made in the Ordinal along the way, it was important for the Anglican Church to declare its mind on all of the ordinations subsequent to its break with Rome. This they did with clarity in this Article which was approved by the Sovereign, by Parliament, by the Archbishops of Canterbury and York, and by their Provincial Chapters.

Implications

The Anglican Ordinal passes the biblical test and, in fact, is more biblical than the ordinal or manner of ordination of those who bring objections against it. Therefore, Anglicans have every confidence that their clergy are rightly and truly ordained as Deacons, Priests, or Presbyters and consecrated as Bishops in Christ's One, Holy, Catholic, and Apostolic Church. It follows that Anglican clergy should be recognized as such throughout the entire Church Catholic.

Conclusion

The Anglican Ordinal is fully sufficient and contains nothing that is not in accord with Scripture. Those who have been ordained by the Lord through the church using it are truly and validly ordained. Their ordination should be recognized throughout the One, Holy, Catholic, and Apostolic Church.

The 1662 Anglican Ordinal is an outstanding liturgical set of rites for the ordaining and consecrating of ministers of the Gospel. It sets forth the nature and responsibilities of the ordained ministries of the Church with great power and biblical profundity. Those ordained by the Lord as well as the laity of the Church will find that a frequent meditation upon these rites is a helpful means for understanding and encouraging the godly exercise of these ministries.

Section Five

Civic Rights and Duties (Articles 37 – 39)

In this final and shortest section of the Thirty-Nine Articles, we touch upon several matters concerning the dual citizenship of Christians. We Christians are citizens of Heaven, members of the Church, a colony of Heaven. And we are also citizens of the State and the society in which we live. This dual citizenship or membership has given rise to views and practices in the relationship of Church and State of which some are biblical and some unbiblical.

What is needed is a statement of the relationship between Church and State in which each serves the other, while each retains its own integrity and limits as ordained by God. The Articles seek to do this by addressing three topics.

Article 37 addresses the place of the political and legal or judicial authority of the State in relation to the Church and to Christians. There are two forms of the 37th Article because not all Anglicans are in the Church of England and live under different arrangements with the State. Article 38 speaks of the place of private property in society and in relation to Christians. Article 39 treats of the place of legal oaths or promises in society and in relation to Christians.

All of these matters were issues of some dispute at the time the Thirty-Nine Articles were being written. Christians differ on these matters today. Since we Christians all live in relation to both Church and State, have possessions, and take vows and make promises, knowing basic biblical principles regarding these relationships is important.

THE ORIGINAL ARTICLE 37

Of the Civil Magistrates

The Queen's Majesty hath the chief power in this realm of <u>England</u> and other her dominions, unto whom the chief government of all estates of this realm, whether they be ecclesiastical or civil, in all causes doth appertain, and is not nor ought to be subject to any foreign jurisdiction.

Where we attribute to the Queen's Majesty the chief government, by which titles we understand the minds of some slanderous folks to be offended, we give not to our princes the ministering either of God's word or of sacraments, the which thing the Injunctions also lately set forth by <u>Elizabeth</u> our Queen doth most plainly testify: but only that prerogative which we see to have been given always to all godly princes in Holy Scriptures by God himself, that is, that they should rule all estates and degrees committed to their charge by God, whether they be temporal, and restrain with the civil sword the stubborn and evildoers.

The Bishop of <u>Rome</u> hath no jurisdiction in this realm of <u>England</u>.

The Laws of the Realm may punish Christian men with death for heinous and grievous offences.

It is lawful for Christian men at the commandment of the Magistrate to wear weapons and serve in the wars.

THE REVISED ARTICLE 37

Of the Power of the Civil Magistrates

The Power of the Civil Magistrate extendeth to all men, as well Clergy as Laity, in all things temporal; but hath no authority in things purely spiritual. And we hold it to be the duty of all men who are professors of the Gospel, to pay respectful obedience to the Civil Authority, regularly and legitimately constituted.

Introduction

This Article addresses the legal and judicial relationship of Church and State. It will be helpful for us, by way of introduction, to consider briefly the purpose of the State and the Church, according to the Scriptures.

We consider the Church first. According to Scripture, the Church is the New Covenant expression of God's chosen people. As such, it is a community called into being by God in Christ and the Holy Spirit and united to Him spiritually as a head is to a body or a branch is to the vine. It is sustained by the faithful preaching of God's Word, the proper administration of the Sacraments of the Gospel according to Christ's institution, and by godly oversight and discipline being exercised to ensure that such faithful preaching and sacramental administration is being done. Essential to the Church's purpose, to its nature, life and calling are: 1) the worship of God, according to God's Word and in the power of His Spirit, 2) the fellowship, care, and mutual up-building of the Saints, and 3) the exercise of the evangelistic mission to take the Gospel to all nations and to exercise such social influence and action as to show Christ's love to the neighbor.

The Church is a spiritual entity, and while it exists in this world, and in and among the several nations of the world, it is not of the world. It does not extend its mission by political means or force. It claims the whole person and speaks of a new heart and a new Creation. In Christ, motive counts as much as action. It looks for a final home only in a New Heaven and a New Earth.

The Church does, however, see all things heavenly and earthly in the light of Christ, including moral principles which are rooted in God's nature, embodied in Creation, and are therefore binding on all those created in His image. These moral principles are written into the conscience of everyone, though the knowledge of them is dimmed and somewhat distorted by the Fall. They are republished in Holy Scripture and modeled supremely by Christ. The Church therefore may and must speak of these moral principles to itself and to any and every society in which it is set. Its means of influence, however, is only that of preaching and by living an infectious witness. What use the Holy Spirit may choose to make of this Word and witness in the nations, lies entirely in the sovereign hand and decision of God.

The State is not always happy to hear such preaching or accept such a witness. At times, the State sees the Church's primary loyalty and surrender to the Lordship of Christ to be a profound threat to its claims for obedience. Repression and persecution of the Church by the State can arise at any time. The potential for such is ever present as long as the Church believes and states that Jesus is Lord and lives faithfully to Him.

(The visible Church has been considered more fully in Article 19; the reader is referred to that Article for additional material.)

The State is God's creation, also, and is answerable to Him. God created us to live in community or societies. Societies must have order and organization. In a fallen world, this entails police force and military protection. We read in Scripture that God has given to the State, or to the magistrate, the power of the sword, that is, the power to use force, even unto death, to restrain and punish evil.

We also read in Scripture that those leaders who are placed in authority in the State are placed there by God in His providential rule. Christians are to pray for, respect, and obey duly constituted authority. The leaders of the State are charged with the responsibility to restrain and punish evil, to reward good, and to give such general organization to society as the society needs. These leaders will answer to God for the exercise of their governance. Also according to the Scriptures, a great deal is left in the hands of the family and individuals, and the responsibilities of the State are rather limited.

One of the issues of the relationship between the Church and State that was important at the time of the Reformation concerned a controversy about who had the authority to judge and discipline clergy who break the laws of the State. Do Christian clergy have immunity from the jurisdiction and legal sanctions of the State? Can they appeal to Papal jurisdiction, analogous to the diplomatic immunity of foreign diplomats?

There were and are other issues. What of those laity and clergy whose consciences, having been shaped by their reading of Holy Scripture, feel compelled to disobey some specific law of the State? Can they plead a higher right to obey God rather than man and hence be excused from the normal judgment and discipline of the State?

On the other hand, does the State have the right to dictate to the Church in theological and moral (i.e., spiritual) matters? What if the State perceives the teaching of the Church to be seditious, or immoral in the light of the current, prevailing mores of the society? Or what if the State wants the Church to officially promote an unquestioning approval of the State's policies no matter what the State says or does, no matter how it relates to innate moral principles that are addressed to all and advocated by the Church?

Article 37 gives a general answer to the relation of Church and State and provides a framework to address specific issues that arise in that relationship.

We will discuss the revised form of Article 37, which is of more general application, and briefly comment on the original form of the Article that is addressed specifically to "the realm of England."

The Teaching of Article 37
Here are the teaching points for this Article:

1. The power of the civil magistrate, or the State, extends to all citizens and therefore all of the members of the Church are to respect the authority of the State in matters temporal.

2. The State has no authority over the Church in matters purely spiritual.

1. The power of the civil magistrate, or the State, extends to all citizens and therefore all of the members of the Church are to respect the authority of the State in matters temporal.

Explanation

As stated above, Christians have dual citizenship. Christians are citizens of the Kingdom of God, over which Christ has been given all power and authority and Who rules in grace over His Body the Church.

Christians are also citizens of a specific State or nation with its authority structures and magistrates, to which they are to be obedient and for which they are to pray. The State and its leaders are answerable to God. As citizens of both we cannot help but ask how the Church and State are to relate to each other under God.

The least biblical arrangement is one of domination. That is an arrangement in which one kingdom utterly dominates or even seeks to exclude the other. This has been tried by both State and Church.

On the one hand, some earthly States have simply denied any place to the Church and sought to eliminate the Church. One thinks of ancient Rome that could not accept the Christian claim that "Jesus is Lord"; it sounded subversive to them. It did, as well, to the former Communist USSR and does to the present North Korea. Other States have sought not to eliminate the Church but to utterly dominate and domesticate it by dictating what the Church should and may teach. This was the case in Nazi Germany when the government of the Third Reich infiltrated the official State Church and demanded that the Church espouse the anti-biblical teaching of the superiority of the "Aryan Race." The Church was to approve or at least ignore the ungodly cleansing of the German Race by forbidding "interracial marriage" and the horrendous extermination of the Jewish people during the Holocaust.

On the other hand, some Christian groups go to the opposite extreme and deny that they have any accountability to, duty to, or citizenship in, the State in which they geographically dwell. One thinks of certain Anabaptist groups at the time of the Reformation and various cults today. They believe that they owe allegiance to God alone and reject any dealings with, or compromise with earthly authority.

In these extreme oversimplifications, the State overreaches itself and the Church acts as if it had already been exalted to heaven and is no longer on earth. It is a relationship in which neither kingdom is true to its own God-intended nature, as indicated in Holy Scripture.

The alternative to these radical views is some form of the two-kingdom relationship, stated in the shorter, rewritten form of this Article. Therefore, we want to set forth some general principles of the two-kingdom relationship and mention several issues that arise in this relationship.

First, the two-kingdom relationship grants civil authority to the State but not spiritual authority. That is, the State, drawing upon conscience and natural law, has the authority and obligation to pass just and moral laws regulating the behavior of its citizens, and to discipline law breakers, but it may not legally determine what the Church is to preach and teach or meddle in the internal affairs of the governance of the Church.

Second, the Church may and must teach, preach, worship, and evangelize as it understands its responsibilities in Christ. However, the Church has no civic authority.

A special case involving the State's civil authority is the Christian understanding of civil disobedience. If the Church, in obedience to Christ based on Scripture, influences its individual members' conscience so that they disobey a specific law of the State which is seen to be unjust or immoral, then as the citizens of the State those Christians must suffer the civil punishment that the State determines. Christians suffer this in the hope and faith that such non-compliance and legal suffering on the part of the Christians will lead the State to take notice of the immorality and injustice of the specific legislation which is being disobeyed. At the same time, the willingness to suffer on the part of the Christians, witnesses to the State's rightful authority and calling under God to provide and enforce just laws, to punish the wicked and to encourage and protect the righteous.

Third, there is a more complex form of the two-kingdom relationship. We find it described in the original form of Article 37. This more complex form of the two-State arrangement is found and illustrated in England. The original and longer version of this Article has in view an officially Christian nation and an established national Church. This arrangement grants to the State, the King or Queen and Parliament, some degree of authority over the Church as well as full authority over the civil realm.

This is referred to as an Erastian arrangement, named after a 16th-century Swiss theologian, Thomas Erastus, who held that the State, not the Church, had final jurisdiction in all matters.

This arrangement grants the Church a privileged status in the nation in which the State assures that the Church has the liberty to carry out its life and mission in the realm. However, at the same time, this arrangement opens the Church to possible inordinate interference by the State in the inner life and teaching of the Church. When, in actual practice, the interference inhibits the faithful practice of the Church's life and mission, the question of the disestablishment of the Church arises in those nations where this arrangement prevails.

The Orthodox Churches of the East and the Church of England are usually referred to as Erastian Churches. Few other Anglican Churches are in Erastian arrangements with the States in which they are located.

The Church also exists in nations that are hostile to Christianity and that limit the Church's life severely. In Muslim countries where Islam is the dominant center of the culture, the State views the Church as comprised of infidels who, as people of the Book, teach some truth and much error. Therefore, the Church, while permitted to exist in Islamic societies, is radically limited and public evangelism is denied. Christians and Jews are generally afforded second-class citizenship, accompanied at times by severe persecution. The experience is often similar in Hindu-dominated nations and, to a lesser degree, in Buddhist countries.

Fourth, the original Article also spells out several aspects of the Christian's civic duty that were disputed by some at the time of the Reformation.

This includes an explicit statement of the lawful duty of Christians to bear arms when called to do so by the State. They do this as citizens of an earthly kingdom that must defend itself against unjust armed attack from beyond, and that must use police force to restrain violent criminals and lawless rebellion within.

In so stating the Christian's civic duty, this Article repudiates pacifism as a universal Christian obligation. Turning the other cheek is a divine obligation in personal relationships, but things are different in social and civic responsibility. The use of force is legitimate as determined by the magistrates, to whom God has given the authority and exercise of the sword. It is to be exercised with justice and mercy.

The Christian's submission to the State includes suffering the death penalty if the behavior of Christians merits it under the laws of the land. Some Christians have misunderstood the Commandment, "Thou shalt not kill," or more accurately, "Do no murder." They believe the Commandment forbids the death penalty. Actually, it forbids murder which is the killing of innocent life and the taking of life by private parties. It is not intended to take the sword from the magistrate's hands (see the discussion below on pacifism).

Fifth, a comment is in order concerning the role of the Church and the individual Christian in politics in a democratic State. On the one hand, the individual Christian is a citizen of the State and has the responsibility to choose a candidate and to vote and to seek to influence the State, whether as a member of a political party or as an independent. In this, he or she acts in accord with the general moral norms God addresses to all individuals and societies. This is part of the cultural mandate and is a responsibility of all human beings. As a citizen of the State in a democratic society with a vote, the Christian is in a real sense "Caesar" (i.e., a member of the leadership of the State). The duties of the State fall upon each citizen.

On the other hand, while the Church as a corporate body can and should stand for the application of Christian moral values and principles in society and encourage its members to do so, it cannot engage directly in political campaigns or endorse candidates or determine political strategy. It cannot do this, for: 1) it is in but not of the world; that is, it is not a political society such as the State and must not act as if it were, and 2) the Church as a corporate body cannot become politically active in campaigns and strategies because there is a difference between a value or goal that all Christians would embrace and the strategy to achieve that goal through political measures in a given society. Individual Christians who are members of the Church can share the same Christian principles, values, and even the same social goals but differ greatly in the priorities they assign to the several goals and in the specific political strategies that they believe will best serve to achieve those goals. For such reasons, all Christians do not join the same political parties.

In sum, the chief concern of this first teaching point is to assert that Christians are fully under the authority of the State in matters of civil law and duty. Christians cannot claim "diplomatic immunity" by appealing either to the Pope in Rome or to Heaven. We are to be responsible citizens for the sake of the society and the other citizens. Such is our God-given and Christian responsibility as citizens of the State. We are to do this while being faithful to Christ in all things.

Biblical Foundations

Whoever sheds the blood of man, by man shall his blood be shed, for God made man in his own image. Genesis 9:6

He said to them, "Then render to Caesar the things that are Caesar's, and to God the things that are God's." Luke 20:25

But Peter and the apostles answered, "We must obey God rather than men." Acts 5:29

Let every person be subject to the governing authorities. For there is no authority except from God, and those that exist have been instituted by God. Therefore whoever resists the authorities resists what God has appointed, and those who resist will incur judgment. For rulers are not a terror to good conduct, but to bad. Would you have no fear of the one who is in authority? Then do what is good, and you will receive his approval, for he is God's servant for your good. But if you do wrong, be afraid, for he does not bear the sword in vain. For he is the servant of God, an avenger who carries out God's wrath on the wrongdoer. Romans 13:1-4

Be subject for the Lord's sake to every human institution, whether it be to the emperor as supreme, or to governors as sent by him to punish those who do evil and to praise those who do good. For this is the will of God, that by doing good you should put to silence the ignorance of foolish people. Live as people who are free, not using your freedom as a cover-up for evil, but living as servants of God. Honor everyone. Love the brotherhood. Fear God. Honor the emperor. 1 Peter 2:13-17

First of all, then, I urge that supplications, prayers, intercessions, and thanksgivings be made for all people, for kings and all who are in high positions, that we may lead a peaceful and quiet life, godly and dignified in every way. 1 Timothy 2:1-2

False Teaching Denied/Objections Answered

1. As mentioned above, in the West at the time of the Reformation, when a clergyman broke a law of the State, Rome claimed that the secular courts did not have jurisdiction over the clergy but rather the papal courts did. The clergy should make their case there and the matter should be decided by the ecclesiastical courts.

This Papal claim to universal jurisdiction over all clergy rests upon four things. First, it assumes a particular interpretation of Matthew 16:18, "You are Peter, and upon this rock I will build my church and the gates of hell shall not prevail against it." Rome interprets this as referring to Peter himself. The "rock," however, seems most likely not to refer to Peter alone, but to the truth of the Apostolic confession of Jesus as the Messiah, the Son of God, with Peter as the leader and chief spokesman of the Apostles. After all, Christ, immediately after Peter's godly confession, referred to Peter as thinking like a fallen man; nor did Peter show himself as the most consistent of the Apostles. The Fathers of the Church did not interpret the "rock" to refer to Peter only. The Eastern Church has never done so. The Churches of the Reformation, including Anglicans, do not do so.

Second, the claim to Papal jurisdiction also rests upon Peter's being a frequent spokesman for the Apostles and his possible leadership among the Twelve. This claim for Peter's leadership may or may not be accurate, but even if granted, such "leadership" is not the same thing as an office. There is no indication in Scripture or history that Peter's leadership of the Apostles had the nature of an office with the right to pass the office on to a successor. Nor did Peter issue orders to the Twelve or to St. Paul. In fact, the Apostle Paul rebuked Peter publicly in Antioch, a rebuke that Peter accepted (Galatians 2:11). The Apostle Paul also explicitly stated that he was in no way inferior to those who were Apostles before him (2 Corinthians 12:11). James, not Peter, presided over the first Council of the Church in Jerusalem.

In addition, while there is some evidence that Peter died in Rome, there is none that he was the Bishop of Rome.

Third, the claim to Papal jurisdiction was based on the growing prominence of Rome in the life of the Church, particularly in the West after the division in the Church between East and West in the 11th century. Such prominence, however, is no proper basis for asserting a divine claim to be Christ's Vicar over all the churches on earth.

Fourth, this claim rested upon the claim that the Kingdom of Christ takes precedence over the kingdoms of this world. Where there is a clash, the authority of the Pope, who speaks for Christ, has superior authority to the authority of earthly kings or States. This, however, fails to see that the Church and State each have their own God-given place and authority and that the Church is not to intrude upon the authority of the State as if it were a political entity in the same sense as the State.

For these reasons, clergy of the Church of England could not appeal for immunity from the local courts by claiming they were under the jurisdiction of the Pope. As citizens of England, they were under the laws and authority of England.

Along with the Churches of the East and the other Churches of the Reformation, Anglicans do not recognize a universal jurisdiction of the Bishop of Rome. While respecting his primatial authority over Roman Catholic congregations, Anglicans affirm their right of jurisdiction over the clergy in the Anglican Church and the State's rights over all of the citizens of the State, including the clergy, with regard to their obligations as citizens.

2. Some Christians reject the State's right to use force. They believe that all people should renounce the use of force in all circumstances. Quakers, Anabaptists, Amish, Mennonites, and other "peace" churches have at times espoused pacifism, and many continue to do so today.

A commitment to pacifism has a value; it is a dramatic warning about the tendency of fallen human beings and nations to misuse force in their own interests and in unjust ways.

The belief in total pacifism is often based on: 1) the fact that we are all made in the image of God, 2) that God loves the world, 3) on Jesus teaching to forgive seventy times seven, 4) on His exhortation to turn the other cheek, 5) on His own example with the woman caught in adultery, 6) on His statement that His followers would not fight, and 7) on His willingness to die on the Cross rather than call on angelic hosts.

Pacifism is strengthened by observing the examples of abuse of physical power, including the misuse of the death penalty and of aggressive war to conquer nations and territory, seen in countless examples in human history.

However, there are very compelling reasons against adopting total pacifism. They are: 1) the fact that the 6th Commandment "Thou shalt not kill" really means "Do no murder," 2) that John the Baptist's instruction to soldiers about how they were to act did not tell them to resign, 3) on Jesus' teaching to render unto Caesar, Caesar's due, 4) on Paul's clear statement that God has given the sword to the magistrate, 5) on the case of Cornelius, the believing Centurion, who was not told to leave the military, and 6) on the pervasive affirmation of the death penalty throughout the Scripture, especially when intentional murder was involved. These all illustrate and point to a rightful place for the use of force in police action and defensive war.

Therefore, given the biblical teaching and the human impulse to use force when needed in order to protect the innocent and weak, pacifism has never been the dominant view in the Church. Whether Christians could serve in the military was a disputed issue for some time. However, by the time of St. Augustine in the fifth century, Christian participation in the military and in war was generally affirmed, assuming that the war was just.

The Roman Catholic Church takes an unusual position. In its canons, it holds that clergy are not to be involved as warriors in the shedding of blood, although they may and do serve as chaplains in the military and serve in the combat areas in times of war.

St. Thomas Aquinas spelled out the conditions of a "Just War" in the 13th century. The conditions for a just war that he set forth have never really been improved upon. Four conditions are outlined by Aquinas:

1. War is justifiable only in defense, never as an act of aggression.

2. War is only to be done as a last resort, all else having failed.

3. It must be restricted in scope, so as to do as little damage as possible to non-combatants.

4. It must be winnable.

Anglicans generally believe that a closer reading of all of the Scriptures pertinent to the issue of the use of force affirms the just war theory. Anglicans have stood and stand with the majority in the Church down through the centuries in affirming that it is permissible for Christians to serve in the military and the police, to bear arms, and that it is right for the State to use force both in war and in police action when necessary and just and as a last resort.

Implications

Christians are called to support the State by praying for those in authority, by paying taxes, by fulfilling all civic responsibilities, and by seeking to do good to their neighbors. In democratic societies, they are to exercise their franchise by informed voting. Christians are to obey the State in all things lawful. When the conscience, duly informed by Scripture, requires it, a Christian may and must participate in civil disobedience and also be willing to pay the price of suffering the punishment required under the law. This is to be done in the hope and faith that God will use such suffering to reform the State, and, at the same time, to make a clear statement that affirms the State's God-given right to use force in the cause of safety and justice. Christians thereby bear witness to the moral claim of God upon all nations and states.

It is also true that God uses such suffering, even unto death, to commend the Gospel. "The blood of the Martyrs is the seed bed of the Church." In God's providence, no sacrifice is ever wasted.

2. The State has no authority over the Church in matters purely spiritual.

Explanation

While Christians are to be obedient to the State in civil responsibilities, they are also to be obedient to Christ in all things. "Jesus is Lord" is the earliest confession of the Church. Christ and Christ alone is Lord, and Lord of the Church: Lord of its teaching, its worship, its life, and its mission and Lord of each individual Christian. The Spirit of Christ indwells the Church. He glorifies Christ as He takes the things of Christ from the Scriptures and guides and empowers the Church in its life and mission. The Church bows to no other Lord but to the Father in the Son by the Spirit. This being the case, there is no place for the State to exercise any doctrinal authority over the spiritual life and mission of the Church.

It is true that the State may not recognize this limit, but the Church should have no confusion about Whom it serves. The Church is called to resist any intrusion on the part of the State that hinders its faithful obedience to God. Civil disobedience can become and often has become a Christian obligation.

Biblical Foundations

You call me Teacher and Lord, and you are right, for so I am. If I then, your Lord and Teacher, have washed your feet, you also ought to wash one another's feet. For I have given you an example, that you also should do just as I have done to you. Truly, truly, I say to you, a servant is not greater than his master, nor is a messenger greater than the one who sent him. John 13:13-16

And what is the immeasurable greatness of his power toward us who believe, according to the working of his great might that he worked in Christ when he raised him from the dead and seated him at his right hand in the heavenly places, far above all rule and authority and power and dominion, and above every name that is named, not only in this age but also in the one to come. And he put all things under his feet and gave him as head over all things to the church, which is his body, the fullness of him who fills all in all. Ephesians 1:19-23

Now as the church submits to Christ, so also wives should submit in everything to their husbands. Ephesians 5:24

For Jesus has been counted worthy of more glory than Moses—as much more glory as the builder of a house has more honor than the house itself. (For every house is built by someone, but the builder of all things is God.) Now Moses was faithful in all God's house as a servant, to testify to the things that were to be spoken later, but Christ is faithful over God's house as a son. And we are his house if indeed we hold fast our confidence and our boasting in our hope. Hebrews 3:3-6

False Teachings Denied/Objections Answered

1. The domination of the Church by State or Culture is a constant threat to the Church. As mentioned earlier, a tragic example took place in the 1930s in Germany. The Nazi Government of the Third Reich infiltrated and dominated the State Church in Germany. Godly Christians led by Pastor Martin Niemuller formed an underground confessing Church. They rejected the claims of "blood and land," *Blut und Boden,* which was a mixture of German nationalism and Christian faith, and the claim that Hitler was God's new Messiah, and to be obeyed.

A group of pastors led by Professor Karl Barth affirmed the Barmen Declaration (1934) that said in its first Article: "Jesus Christ as He is testified to us in Holy Scripture, is the one word of God whom we are to hear, whom we are to trust and obey in life and in death."

Both groups were confessing that there was no room for another "Messiah" who was to be worshiped and obeyed.

It was hearing and affirming the supreme authority of God speaking through the Scriptural revelation that allowed these faithful Christians to see, when others could not see, that the claims of Aryan racial purity and the horrendous persecution of the Jews was an evil abomination to be resisted at the cost of death.

2. A less obvious but real cultural domination of the Church can take place when, in attempting to preach and teach the faith in a manner that will gain the interest of the un-churched, the preacher changes the biblical message to a message more acceptable to the convictions and tastes of the culture and the age.

The Church is well served by keeping in mind the wise statement of Bishop Leslie Newbigen to the effect that Jesus is the Word of God Who fits into no worldview except the one of which He is the primary revelation. It is not that Jesus must fit in with our contemporary worldview, but that our contemporary worldview must be measured against and corrected by the worldview of which Jesus is the chief revelation.

Implications

Whether we as Christians are concerned about the political domination of the Church by the State or the more informal impact of culture capturing the Church, we are to resist and stand faithful to the Word of God revealed to us in Jesus Christ and the Scriptures read in His light. Cost what it may.

Conclusion

God has made us citizens of His Heavenly Kingdom and of an earthly State. He has a purpose for both as set forth in Scripture. We are to fulfill our Christian duty and witness in each kingdom. In both we are to serve Christ. In one, by being good citizens of the State as it carries out its God-given mandate to protect and encourage the righteous and to restrain and punish the unrighteous, and in the Kingdom of Grace by faithful membership in the Church in obedience to the Lord Jesus as revealed to us in Scripture as we are empowered by His Holy Spirit. Should the State ask us to do what in Christian conscience we cannot do, we are called to "obey God rather than man," but to honor the State at the same time by willingly accepting, in hope, the punishment which the State determines is appropriate. God will use the witness and our reward will be granted in Heaven.

ARTICLE 38

Of Christian Men's Goods, Which Are Not Common

The riches and goods of Christians are not common, as touching the right, title, and possession of the same, as certain Anabaptists do falsely boast; notwithstanding every man ought of such things as he possesseth liberally to give alms to the poor, according to his ability.

Introduction

The words of the Lord, "You cannot serve God and mammon," ring in our ears. But what do they imply about our money and possessions? Wealth is unequally distributed. What are we to think about that as Christians? Questions concerning wealth abound.

During the 16th century Reformation, certain Anabaptist groups arose that believed that Christians should hold all goods in common. Were they right? If not, what are we to make of the example of the early Christians in Jerusalem at Pentecost cited in Acts 4?

Larger issues arise for Christians. What economic social pattern best agrees with biblical teaching about wealth? Is socialism the best economic arrangement? It seems so generous and fair. What about communism? Perhaps that is better, since fallen people don't seem to have the wisdom to make the right choices with wealth or to control their greed. What about capitalism? It does seem to be the most productive of wealth and takes work and industriousness into account. But it can lead to the unequal distribution of wealth and severe poverty. Is any one of these economic arrangements more biblical that the others?

Assuming that Christians are to own private wealth, what is to be their attitude toward this wealth and the right use of it? What is the calling of Christians toward those in need?

These questions deserve a principled answer. This Article provides some of the crucial principles that address these questions.

The Teaching of Article 38
Here are the teaching points for this Article:
1. Christians may own private property.

2. Christians are to give compassionately to those in need.

1. Christians may own private property.
Explanation

How could anyone come to the thought that owning private property is wrong? Some extreme Anabaptist groups held that Christians should hold all things in common, and denied the right of Christians to hold private or personal property. Their teaching was based on the belief that all persons are made in the image of God and all Christians are redeemed by the blood of Christ. So the Church is a community of equals as constituted in Christ. That equality in community, they believed, should be given expression in common ownership and the abdication of private property. In addition, owning things was a temptation to the sins of idolatry and pride. Their view was strengthened by an inference that they drew from the example of the Jewish Messianic believers who came to faith on Pentecost in Jerusalem in A.D. 30. These Jewish Christians decided to share their resources and to hold all things in common, under the leadership of the Apostles.

"Now the full number of those who believed were of one heart and soul, and no one said that any of the things that belonged to him was his own, but they had everything in common" (Acts 4:32).

The radical Anabaptists assumed that this action of the early Church taken in their specific circumstances was a general rule for all Christians in all circumstances. While it is surely legitimate for a congregation of Christians to hold all things in common if they believe that God is calling them to do that, the assumption that the decision of those early Christians is a rule for all Christians was and is an error.

It is an error for several reasons:

First, the owning of private property is practiced, assumed, and viewed positively throughout all of Scripture, in both the Old and New Testaments. Therefore the teaching that Christians cannot own private property contradicts Scripture. Here are but a few scriptural examples: without private property, the 10th Commandment on coveting that which belongs to your neighbor makes no sense. In Deuteronomy, we read "Remember the Lord your God, for it is He that gives you power to get wealth" (Deuteronomy 8:8). Jesus in His parables assumes private ownership of property. One thinks of the owner of the vineyard to whom rent was due, or those to whom the owner of a field agreed to pay specific wages or the pearl of great price for which one was to sell all that he had to purchase it. St. Paul admonishes Christians to work in quietness and eat their own bread (2 Thessalonians 3:12).

Second, to reject private ownership of property rests on an inaccurate understanding of the decision of the early Church at Pentecost. The example of the early Christians in Jerusalem was voluntary. Theirs was a voluntary sharing by individuals of what they owned. It was not a requirement laid on any, much less on all.

Third, the circumstances were unusual. These pilgrims were from out of town, having come to celebrate the Passover. After their conversion to Jesus as the promised Messiah, they chose to stay in Jerusalem because they believed that Jesus would shortly return to Jerusalem in glory. Over time, when Jesus did not return and days, months, and even years passed, the Christians of the Gentile congregations founded by St. Paul had to send financial help to the Christians in Jerusalem, the Mother Church, who had used up their shared resources.

There is another reason why the call to common ownership arises. It is that some Christians seem to have an undue bias against wealth, or at least an uneasy conscience about it. They seem to think that being wealthy is, in and of itself, an expression of greediness. Such an attitude or bias is understandable because of the way many people relate to wealth. As fallen sinners, we tend to ignore the dangers of wealth and the warnings of Scripture about the worship of wealth, and are inclined to look to wealth as a matter of status and a source of security.

However, whether disliking the wealthy or being offended by wealth, or idolizing the poor or idolizing wealth, these are all attitudes that are contrary to the basic teaching of Scripture concerning wealth.

Here are several key points in a biblical view of wealth:

1. The doctrine of Creation is fundamental to a biblical view of wealth. It sets Christians apart from all religions and philosophies that denigrate matter and physical property. We read in Scripture that "the earth is the Lord's and the fullness thereof" (Psalm 24:1). The whole of creation, including its physical and its spiritual aspects, is essentially good in and of itself. This view is contrary to the Gnostic doctrine that views matter as bad and spirit as good. Christians reply, "Matter is not always bad and what is spiritual is not always good."

2. God as the Creator is the ultimate owner of all creation. We human beings are His stewards and will render to Him an account of our stewardship of His creation. In this stewardship, God gives ownership to individuals, groups, and governments. We, into whose hands God has given this stewardship, are to carry it out by working to domesticate the creation while taking care of it, and by shaping society in accordance with God's purpose for humanity.

3. Work is part of God's plan for human beings. It was so from the beginning. Work remains our calling, though it has been rendered painful to a serious degree by the Fall. Using our gifts wisely and industriously in this stewardship generally leads to God's blessing and wealth. In Scripture, wealth is seen as a gift and a blessing from God Who makes our efforts possible and causes them to bear fruit. Wealth, therefore, is not something of which to be ashamed, but rather that for which we are to give thanks and which we are to use responsibly.

4. Wealth brings with it obligations and particularly obligations to those who are needy. We will treat this under the second teaching point of this Article.

5. According to Scripture, there are dangers that come with wealth. Among others, these are: a) failing to attribute wealth to the gift and providence of God, b) trusting in riches and not in God, c) greediness or loving riches inordinately, "For the love of money is a root of all kinds of evils" (I Timothy 6:10), d) viewing wealth as the measure of personal value or dignity, and e) the abuse of wealth by dishonesty, stealing, and by using it to oppress others. These dangers, temptations, and abuses are not to be taken lightly, and need to be overcome by the strength of God's grace and with the support of the Body of Christ. We are reminded of the Lord's admonition that "It is more difficult for a rich man to enter the Kingdom of Heaven than for a camel to go through the eye of a needle" (Matthew 19:24).

To summarize: Wealth in the Scripture is seen as God's gift and blessing visited on faithful and industrious believers. Wealth is connected to calls for human faithfulness, industry, and wise stewardship, that are enabled by the grace of God which is in Christ Jesus.

In a fallen world, God's righteous pattern is often not followed. There are the lazy rich and the hard-working poor, just as there are the lazy poor and hard-working rich. If wealth is not to be a matter of self-congratulatory pride, so poverty is not, in and of itself, to be a matter of shame, though it can be so severe as to be a matter of genuine need (as we discuss further in the next teaching point).

The main point of this first teaching point is simply that owning private property is not the problem; the problem arises with our false attitudes toward wealth and our use of it, which arise when we fail to see that we are stewards of God, to Whom we will render an account of our stewardship of wealth in all its forms.

In summary, the voluntary communal ownership of all property has never been a universal rule for all Christians and to require it is contrary to Scripture and generally proves to be or becomes impractical.

Biblical Foundations
Thus says God, the Lord, who created the heavens and stretched them out, who spread out the earth and what comes from it, who gives breath to the people on it and spirit to those who walk in it. Isaiah 42:5

The Lord God took the man and put him in the garden of Eden to work it and keep it. Genesis 2:15

The Lord commanded, *"You shall not steal. "You shall not bear false witness against your neighbor. "You shall not covet your neighbor's house; you shall not covet your neighbor's wife, or his male servant, or his female servant, or his ox, or his donkey, or anything that is your neighbor's."* Exodus 20:15-17

This book of the law shall not depart from your mouth, but you shall meditate on it day and night, so that you may be careful to do according to all that is written in it. For then you will make your way prosperous, and then you will have good success. Joshua 1:8

Blessed is the man who walks not in the counsel of the wicked, nor stands in the way of sinners, nor sits in the seat of scoffers; but his delight is in the law of the Lord, and on his law he meditates day and night. He is like a tree planted by streams of water that yields its fruit in its season, and its leaf does not wither. In all that he does, he prospers. Psalm 1:1-3

In the day of prosperity be joyful, and in the day of adversity consider: God has made the one as well as the other, so that man may not find out anything that will be after him. Ecclesiastes 7:14

No one can serve two masters, for either he will hate the one and love the other, or he will be devoted to the one and despise the other. You cannot serve God and money. Matthew 6:24

The kingdom of heaven is like treasure hidden in a field, which a man found and covered up. Then in his joy he goes and sells all that he has and buys that field. Matthew 13:44

For it will be like a man going on a journey, who called his servants and entrusted to them his property. To one he gave five talents, to another two, to another one, to each according to his ability. Then he went away. Matthew 25:14-15

And all who believed were together and had all things in common. And they were selling their possessions and belongings and distributing the proceeds to all, as any had need. Acts 2:44-45

But now I am writing to you not to associate with anyone who bears the name of brother if he is guilty of sexual immorality or greed, or is an idolater, reviler, drunkard, or swindler—not even to eat with such a one. 1 Corinthians 5:11

Now such persons we command and encourage in the Lord Jesus Christ to do their work quietly and to earn their own living. 2 Thessalonians 3:12

But sexual immorality and all impurity or covetousness must not even be named among you, as is proper among saints. Ephesians 5:3

My brothers, show no partiality as you hold the faith in our Lord Jesus Christ, the Lord of glory. For if a man wearing a gold ring and fine clothing comes into your assembly, and a poor man in shabby clothing also comes in, and if you pay attention to the one who wears the fine clothing and say, "You sit here in a good place," while you say to the poor man, "You stand over there," or, "Sit down at my feet," have you not then made distinctions among yourselves and become judges with evil thoughts? Listen, my beloved brothers, has not God chosen those who are poor in the world to be rich in faith and heirs of the kingdom, which he has promised to those who love him? But you have dishonored the poor man. Are not the rich the ones who oppress you, and the ones who drag you into court? Are they not the ones who blaspheme the honorable name by which you were called? James 2:1-7

False Teaching Denied/Objections Answered
    1. An error is committed by those who equate the communal sharing of the early Christians in Jerusalem with communism. Aside from the metaphysical, religious philosophy that undergirds much communism, communism in history has various forms, but at its heart, that which distinguishes communism from Christian communal sharing is communism's forced or involuntary character. Ananias and Sapphira were not condemned because they did not share all they had, for the choice whether to share and what to share was entirely theirs to make. They were condemned for lying, specifically for lying to the Holy Spirit, seeking thereby to deceive the Apostles and the Christian community.
    2. It is also unbiblical and an error to consider the monastic communal way of life with its vows of poverty, obedience, and chastity to be superior to the common Christian life of ownership of private property, whether as single or as married, with or without children. To own wealth or to own none voluntarily, these are distinct vocations from the Lord and each is honorable and of value

in His eyes. Each has its challenges, difficulties, and sacrifices. One is not better than the other.

3. The view that the possession of wealth is a sign of God's approval of the wealthy person was widely held in biblical times and is a view that is still held by many today. This explains the shock that the disciples felt when Jesus said to them that it was nearly impossible for a wealthy man to enter the kingdom of Heaven. His exchange with the rich young ruler and His parable of Dives and Lazarus make the same point. Wealth is not an unambiguous sign that a person is in God's good graces. Wealth is a blessing that brings a responsibility and ministry to the faithful believer. It will prove a curse to those who idolize it, selfishly misuse it, and tyrannize over others by it.

Implications

Owning wealth or private property is God's gift and calling for most people, Christians included. Wealth generally is a blessing from the Lord, for which we are to be thankful and of which we are to be responsible stewards. However we must not put our trust in anything but God Himself and serve His eternal purposes with all of our gifts including our wealth, including our private property.

2. Christians are to give compassionately to those in need
Explanation

What are the responsibilities toward the neighbor for Christians who have ownership of time, of talent and of material or monetary wealth?

This is an unavoidable question for Christians. When Christ was asked, "What is the greatest commandment of the Law?" Jesus replied, "You shall love the Lord your

God with all your heart and with all your soul and with all your mind. This is the great and first commandment. And a second is like it: You shall love your neighbor as yourself. On these two commandments depend all the Law and the Prophets" (Matthew 22:37-40). Jesus also told the unforgettable parable of the Good Samaritan who cared for the Jewish neighbor in need. Above all, Jesus embodied this love for the neighbor Himself, in His coming, His deeds of healing, His teaching, His relations with all sorts of people, and especially in His dying. Jesus, Who was rich, became poor for our sakes, in order that we who were poor might become rich toward God. And, many of our neighbors are poor.

When it is genuine, Christian alms-giving or compassion for the needy has a remarkable and uniquely generous character. Here are a few of its unique characteristics:

1. Perhaps most fundamentally is the cause of this Christian giving. Its cause is unique. Christian giving is described as the only appropriate response to Christ's laying down His life for us. We are told in Scripture that as He laid down His life for us, so ought we to lay our lives down for others. This awareness of our deliverance at the extreme cost of His Self-giving gives a grateful, overflowing generosity to Christian giving. At times this will lead to sacrificial giving, such as that of the widow who gave only a little but that little was all she had; she gave from her substance and not from her surplus.

2. St. Paul speaks of giving from the heart with joyfulness, or with hilarity, as a characteristic of genuine Christian giving. Christian giving is a privilege. It is not to be done in a grudging manner. "The Lord loves a hilarious giver."

3. This giving is humble and unselfconscious; it seeks no reward or notoriety. As Jesus warned, we are not to give to be seen by people, but out of a desire to help.

4. Christian giving of our possessions is responsive to what possessions we have received. It is not one size fits all. St. Paul tells us that we are to give proportionately according to how God has prospered us and to give according to our ability.

5. There is also a sense of justice in Christian giving. Huge inequalities are disturbing. St. Paul also states that we are to give that there might be an element of fairness in the Church and the world. Are we not all made in the image of God?

Genuine Christian giving affects societies. In most societies, giving is very limited and usually restricted to one's own family or group or special friends. By contrast, in societies that have been deeply influenced by the Gospel, we find a tradition of generosity that ranges widely, wherever there is need. It embraces strangers and even enemies. Such generosity is otherwise largely unknown. This quality of giving remains, though to a lesser degree, even after those societies are no longer as rooted in the Gospel as they once were. It is unlikely that such generosity will last over the long haul in increasingly secular societies.

This Article specifically states that Christians have an obligation to share wealth with the needy neighbor. The neighbor appears in various forms. The Christian has a particular obligation toward his or her family, toward the Church, and the society in which he or she lives and even toward himself or herself. But the obligation and concern does not end there; it has world-wide boundaries.

Since neighbors exist not simply as isolated individuals but in social settings, the Christian has an obligation to give time, energy, and wealth to help the society in which he or she and the neighbors dwell to be a just society that allows its members to have life with dignity, to earn a living, to have food and shelter and be cared for during conditions of physical weakness and need, such as illness and old age.

As the Article specifically points out, the neighbor is present as one who is poor or as a group of those who are poor. Due to the Fall and to a variety of secondary reasons, the distribution of wealth will always be unequal in every society. There are the rich and the poor even in societies where the existence of poverty is denied. In fact, there is throughout Scripture a special concern for the poor. Perhaps this is true because the poor are so often vulnerable, lacking in political power and looked upon with distain by those better off.

Poverty is a complex reality and we need to be careful not to fall victim to the over simplifications that abound concerning the poor and let our attitudes be shaped by them. In considering poverty, it is important to realize that there are a variety of reasons why people can be poor. It is not always a matter of laziness or lack of effort, as some seem to think.

Here are a few causes of poverty that might escape notice: 1) Some societies oppress particular groups due to religious prejudices or for other unjustifiable reasons, barring them from education and well paying jobs. 2) Some countries have not developed their natural resources, resulting in wide-spread poverty. 3) Other nations have developed a two-class society, a wealthy land-owning class and a poor working class with practically no middle class, and those well-off are happy to maintain that arrangement. 4) Individuals may be poor because they are physically or mentally limited, or due to lack of training or educational opportunities. 5) Work may be unavailable. 6) One could have had an emotionally crippling family life growing up or have been raised with a lack of any solid social support. The reasons are too numerous to list all of them.

What, then, are Christians to do about this situation of unequal distribution that so often develops to the point of extreme poverty? The Article speaks of "liberality" or of giving generously to those in need. Christian love asks what sort of help really helps, and takes into consideration the specific causes and circumstances. The aim is to help the needy person or persons to become contributing, productive, and generous members of society. "Let him labor, doing honest work with his own hands, so that he may have something to share with anyone in need" (Ephesians 4:28).

Lest we become sentimental about the poor, it is important that we take note of the realism of Scripture. There are those who will not be helped and are unwilling to shoulder their part of the burden of life. As a result, they are the primary cause of their own poverty and dependency. St. Paul speaks of this when he says, "We would give you this command: If anyone is not willing to work, let him not eat" (2 Thessalonians 3:10). However, Christian love of the neighbor gives help until it becomes clear that here is one who will not be helped. And even then, it does not give up easily.

The attraction of communism and socialism lies in the need for helping people who are poor and disadvantaged in life. Serious poverty involving a large percentage of a population is difficult for a caring Christian to see and bear. Therefore, it seems wise to include a few brief remarks about communism, socialism, and capitalism as economic systems and their relation to the Christian concern for the poor.

Communism may be defined in several ways. At its heart, it is an economic system in which the State alone owns and controls the means of production and the distribution and consumption of wealth. It has the extreme disadvantage of its enforced character and a tendency to tyranny within. Corruption haunts those who wield the power in the State. "Power corrupts and total power corrupts totally." In addition, the system lacks incentive for productivity. "From each according to his ability, to each according to his need" does not happen naturally in a fallen world. If you drop the profit motive, you can't make up for its lack by the fear of the State. Something more is needed.

The result is that extreme poverty is addressed but that most live in a low standard of life economically and with little personal freedom, while the leadership tends to live in hidden luxury.

Socialism, aside from the metaphysical, religious philosophy that often underlies it, is generally found in democratic societies where personal freedoms are allowed and private businesses are allowed in a number of areas, but with some limits and regulation. As an economic system, socialism is an arrangement in which the key means of production are owned by the State or heavily subsidized by it, and distribution is also largely managed by the State. The economy is a planned economy, planned by the government. In democratic socialist societies, however, the leadership of the State is accountable to the people in regular elections which helps with, but does not remove the problem of corruption. Socialism, like communism, lacks sufficient incentive for productivity and for the same reasons as listed for communism. The result tends to produce a very sluggish economy, high taxes, and large government programs to provide for all the members of the society. Extreme poverty is addressed but, again, the general level of the society has a lower standard of living than in more productive societies where personal freedoms are less curtailed.

Capitalism is based on the profit motive, on competition in a free market and on industriousness. It is an economic arrangement in which the production and distribution of wealth, goods, and services are generally privately owned and managed. In capitalism, profit or personal wealth provides a strong incentive for hard work and productivity. To him who works hard and wisely come the rewards of wealth. While this honors the value of hard work and makes for a dynamic economy, it does not deal well with the those who, for whatever reason, cannot work or are disadvantaged in the earning of wealth. Despite the leveling influence of competition, there is a tendency in capitalism for wealth to become concentrated in the hands of the few, while some people fall into deep poverty. Usually, some sort of general tax, as well as government programs, are used to redistribute the wealth in order to moderate the inequalities that arise and to provide for those who cannot help themselves. In democratic societies, these matters come up for review when elections take place. Again, democracy can help with economic problems and corruption but cannot exclude them.

The question the Christian has to ask is this: Is it better to try to improve the productivity of socialism through some incentives that honor hard work (which, to date, seems extremely difficult) or is it better through: a) private charity, and b) a graduated income tax or a flat tax or some tax mechanism to spread the wealth generated in the highly productive economy of capitalism? Christians are to be found holding either view.

To answer that question the Christian should consider these questions: A) What was practiced among God's people in biblical times? B) Which system accords best with fallen human nature? C) Which system best supports human responsibility and freedom? D) Which system best accords with the biblical view of the role of the State? E) Which system gives the widest place for charitable giving? F) Which system best serves economic justice for society as a whole and the individual in particular?

The Christian is concerned that extreme poverty be addressed without creating family traditions or cycles of dependency and concerned that hard work be valued and rewarded. It should be added that the presence of Christians in any economic system is a blessing, because the industriousness, the love and regard for family, and hence desire to save and provide for family and those in need, which serious Christians exhibit, act like leaven in the society.

Biblical Foundations

And the King will answer them, "Truly, I say to you, as you did it to one of the least of these my brothers, you did it to me." Matthew 25:40

So the disciples determined, everyone according to his ability, to send relief to the brothers living in Judea. Acts 11:29

Contribute to the needs of the saints and seek to show hospitality. Romans 12:13

On the first day of every week, each of you is to put something aside and store it up, as he may prosper, so that there will be no collecting when I come. 1 Corinthians 16:2

I do not mean that others should be eased and you burdened, but that as a matter of fairness your abundance at the present time should supply their need, so that their abundance may supply your need, that there may be fairness. 2 Corinthians 8:13-14

Each one must give as he has made up his mind, not reluctantly or under compulsion, for God loves a cheerful giver. 2 Corinthians 9:7

You will be enriched in every way for all your generosity, which through us will produce thanksgiving to God. 2 Corinthians 9:11

Let the thief no longer steal, but rather let him labor, doing honest work with his own hands, so that he may have something to share with anyone in need. Ephesians 4:28

But if anyone does not provide for his relatives, and especially for members of his household, he has denied the faith and is worse than an unbeliever. 1 Timothy 5:8

As for the rich in this present age, charge them not to be haughty, nor to set their hopes on the uncertainty of riches, but on God, who richly provides us with everything to enjoy. They are to do good, to be rich in good works, to be generous and ready to share. 1 Timothy 6:17-18

But if anyone has the world's goods and sees his brother in need, yet closes his heart against him, how does

God's love abide in him? Little children, let us not love in word or talk but in deed and in truth. 1 John 3:17-18

Do not neglect to do good and to share what you have, for such sacrifices are pleasing to God. Hebrews 13:16

If anyone says, "I love God," and hates his brother, he is a liar; for he who does not love his brother whom he has seen cannot love God whom he has not seen. And this commandment we have from him: whoever loves God must also love his brother. 1 John 4:20-21

False Teaching Denied/Objections Answered

1. What degree of giving should be expected of Christians? Tithing to the Church is often taught as the Christian standard of giving. This comes from adopting the teaching on tithing in the Old Testament. In the Old Testament to tithe is to set aside the first ten percent of grain, or the harvest of a crop, or a flock or herd for the support of the Levites who served in the worship of Israel. They had no land and hence no other income of their own. There were other obligations for tithing as well. In short, the first tenth belonged to the Lord.

Given our fallen tendency to give only out of our surplus to the Lord's work, it is wise to have a specific guideline, such as the tithe, as a kind of minimum below which we will not fall. It is important, however, to note that the tithe is not just any ten percent; it is the first ten percent.

But to call the tithe the standard for Christian giving is an error. A tithe falls far short of the more searching guidelines found in the New Testament; consider the discussion of the character of genuine Christian giving discussed above.

Actually, the tithes were required in the Old Testament and charitable giving began after the tithe was paid. Christians are to give abundantly and in proportion to what the Lord has provided to us and over which He has made us stewards. Presumably our giving to the Lord's work and human need will be well beyond the initial ten percent of our disposable wealth.

In one sense, all that we have – our time, talent and treasure – all belong to the Lord, and we are but stewards of it all. One day we will render an account to Him concerning how we have invested it or given it and ourselves away in our lifetime.

2. Congregations often err concerning the priorities of their giving. Churches have a calling to be active in supporting missions and supporting work done outside the congregation. It is an error when the vestry or board of governors says, "We will take care of our needs first and what is left over we can divide up between missions and other important causes."

3. Christians also err when they believe that all generous, sustained giving is good and wise. Giving should be giving that actually helps and does not make matters worse by creating sustained dependency and passivity on the part of the recipients. This principle is the basis for the old adage, "It is better to teach a man to fish than to give him a fish." One of the most important and difficult decisions in giving is deciding how to give in such a way as to actually help the recipients become able and willing to do what they can rightly be expected to do. In missionary giving, for example, the aim of the help given is to produce congregations that will become self-sustaining, self-governing, and self-propagating.

Implications

Giving is a far greater part of the Christian life than many have discovered. It is a joyful privilege and a rightful response to the sacrificial and abundant giving of God to us. One should note that giving also requires receiving. Being willing to admit our need and to accept help is also a Christian virtue, without which no giving on the part of others could be possible.

Conclusion

For the Christian, wealth is a blessing and responsibility, and poverty is no shame but a call to trust God and to look forward to better days in this world and the next. Sharing our wealth and giving to the needy generously and happily is a mark of genuine faith and a thankful heart.

ARTICLE 39

Of a Christian Man's Oath

As we confess that vain and rash swearing is forbidden Christian men by our Lord Jesus Christ, so we judge that Christian religion doth not prohibit but that a man may swear when the magistrate requireth in a cause of faith and charity, so it be done according to the Prophet's teaching in justice, judgement, and truth.

Introduction

A Christian man or woman should keep his or her word. But what about oaths and vows? Do we really need them? Has Jesus forbidden us to take a vow or make an oath? In court, in some countries, Christians are asked to raise their right hand, place their left hand on the Bible, and swear in the name of God that what they shall say will be "the truth, the whole truth, and nothing but the truth, so help me God!" Can a Christian do that in good conscience? What is the place of oaths? What exactly do we mean by making a vow?

As mentioned before, at the time of the Reformation some Anabaptist groups held that the Church was to have as little as possible to do with the State. This combined with Jesus' teaching on the taking of oaths as found in Matthew 5:34 *("But I say to you, Do not take an oath at all")* led these groups, as well as other Christians, to believe that it was wrong to take oaths in court as required by the State.

In this Article, Anglicans affirm that Christians can and should take oaths when required by duly constituted authority, provided that in doing so they are being truthful and serving the cause of justice.

The Teaching of Article 39
Here are the teaching points for this Article:
1. Christians may not take oaths rashly or insincerely.

2. Christians may take oaths when required by the State in a cause of faith and charity, so long as it is done according to justice, judgment and truth.

1. Christians may not take oaths rashly or insincerely.
Explanation

"But I say to you, Do not take an oath at all". The context for understanding the injunction of our Lord's words and the prohibition of this Article lies in the biblical view of truth, of oaths and of vows.

"Truth" is a major theme in the Holy Scriptures. Both the Third Commandment, *"You shall not take the name of the Lord your God in vain, for the Lord will not hold him guiltless who takes his name in vain"* (Exodus 20:7), and the Ninth Commandment, *"You shall not bear false witness against your neighbor"* (Exodus 20:16), affirm a fundamental obligation to speak truthfully and with particular solemnity when one is invoking the Name of the Lord.

Truth as it is used in Scripture has two aspects. These aspects are intertwined and cannot be separated. The first aspect refers to truth as the agreement of what is said with the reality of that which is spoken about. The assertion spoken is true when it corresponds to the facts of the case or to the reality described. St. Paul states that if Christ is not raised, we Christians are fools and most to be pitied and have been lying about God, for we have preached that God raised Jesus from the dead. He then goes on to say, "But Christ is risen." Preaching the Resurrection of Christ is true because Christ is actually risen. This concern for factual truth is, at times, extended in Scripture usage to refer to the nature of the object that is being discussed. For example, God is referred to as "the true God" as over against idols which are no gods at all. They are counterfeit "gods." Here, "true" means something like "genuine" or "real."

The second basic connotation or aspect of "truth" in Scripture builds on the first and is about the speaker. It emphasizes honesty in character and thus honesty in speech. It refers to trustworthiness. To be truthful is to be one who does not lie, whose word is good and reliable, to be one who keeps his or her promises or threats. A truthful person has integrity. God is truthful and reliable in all of His words and deeds, in His promises and His warnings. He speaks and acts as He does because in Himself, in His nature, He is truthful. His truthfulness is an expression of His holiness and moral purity. And His people are called to be righteous and truthful as well.

As we keep this biblical concern for truth in mind, we will understand the biblical use and appreciation of oaths and vows which are a particular form of truth speaking.

An oath is an assertion of loyalty, or the making of a promise, or the truthful assertion about a state of affairs that calls upon God to witness to the truthfulness of the oath. It includes calling on the name of God in some form. Sometimes the oath will spell out the dire consequences that will occur if the one making the oath does not fulfill the oath or was lying in the oath. This warning is always implied, however, by the very invocation of the Name of the Lord, for He will surely judge those who take His name in vain.

Oaths are solemn, for they are not only addressed to men but they are also acts of worship in that they call upon the Lord. As such, they also assume our accountability to God, recognized in all of His biblical attributes.

Since oaths are taken before the Lord, they are binding as long as they affirm what is acceptable to God. It is unlawful to make an oath affirming that which is contrary to God's character or His revealed will. Such false oaths should be repented of and are not binding.

Vows in Scripture are similar to oaths but simpler. They are not addressed to fellow human beings but directly to God. They are promises to God. Like oaths, they cannot rightly promise that which is unacceptable to God and they must promise only that which we have the capacity or power to keep. Like oaths, they are solemn acts of worship, freely made and are not to be made thoughtlessly or about trivial matters.

Given the nature of oaths and vows in Scripture, it is clear that, as the Article states, they are not to be done rashly – that is, without due consideration of what is being said or without an awareness of the solemnity of invoking God. Nor are they to be undertaken in vain. A vain oath or vow is one made in an empty or superficial or insincere manner. Such oaths or vows contradict their very nature.

In Jesus' day, such rash and vain taking of oaths and making of vows had become popular. People called upon the Name of the Lord easily and often in daily conversation. In these oaths, they, being Jews, often referred to God indirectly. They did this because they were fearful of speaking God's Name directly. It also appears that they believed that if one swore by some sacred or weighty object that was associated with, but was less than, the Name of the Lord, the oath or vow was not as earnest and as binding. So, they vowed or swore in reference to Heaven or the altar in the Temple and other such ways.

Jesus forbade such rash and vain swearing:
Again you have heard that it was said to those of old, 'You shall not swear falsely, but shall perform to the Lord what you have sworn.' But I say to you, Do not take an oath at all, either by heaven, for it is the throne of God, or by the earth, for it is his footstool, or by Jerusalem, for it is the city of the great King. And do not take an oath by your head, for you cannot make one hair white or black. Let what you say be simply 'Yes' or 'No'; anything more than this comes from evil
(Matthew 5:33-37).

In these words, Jesus was making one point that involves two assumptions. The first assumption is that an oath or vow is not weakened by using indirect references to God. The second assumption is that an oath is a solemn matter and involves the heartfelt intent to keep it to the fullest. It is a matter of faithfulness and integrity.

His singular point is that daily conversation among His followers in the Kingdom of God should not include any oaths, for one should be so truthful and have such a reputation for truthfulness that an oath would be entirely unnecessary and inappropriate. It is noteworthy that in this fallen world, it is often those who have difficulty telling the truth who are the ones who use oaths most often.

The words of Jesus cited above and these words of the Apostle James, *"But above all, my brothers, do not swear, either by heaven or by earth or by any other oath, but let your 'yes' be yes and your 'no' be no, so that you may not fall under condemnation"* (James 5:12), clearly forbid frequent and superficial swearing.

Biblical Foundations

You shall not swear by my name falsely, and so profane the name of your God: I am the Lord. Leviticus 19:12

"Do not devise evil in your hearts against one another, and love no false oath, for all these things I hate," declares the Lord. Zechariah 8:17

He who has clean hands and a pure heart, who does not lift up his soul to what is false and does not swear deceitfully. He will receive blessing from the Lord and righteousness from the God of his salvation. Psalm 24:4-5

[Jesus said,] "Again you have heard that it was said to those of old, 'You shall not swear falsely, but shall perform to the Lord what you have sworn.' But I say to you, Do not take an oath at all, either by heaven, for it is the throne of God, or by the earth, for it is his footstool, or by Jerusalem, for it is the city of the great King. And do not take an oath

by your head, for you cannot make one hair white or black. Let what you say be simply 'Yes' or 'No'; anything more than this comes from evil." Matthew 5:33-37

But above all, my brothers, do not swear, either by heaven or by earth or by any other oath, but let your "yes" be yes and your "no" be no, so that you may not fall under condemnation. James 5:12

False Teaching Denied/Objections Answered

1. There are those who seem to believe that truth is not of primary importance. Being pleasant and making people feel good is of more importance. Some cultures so stress honoring the guest, the prominent, and the elderly that truth is sacrificed to hospitality and cultural honor. Even in cultures that have been deeply influenced by the biblical witness, those in positions of high office, of responsibility and power, often find themselves surrounded by "yes" men and women, who tell them what they want to hear, in order to curry their favor. This is contrary to the teaching of Jesus and the Scriptures. Truth is of central and primary significance in Scripture.

2. It is obvious that a liar believes that he or she can lie and fool everyone, including God. That belief is ill founded; it is not true. The omniscience of God, Who looks upon the heart, ensures that there is always one Person that a lie does not fool. Even the atheist will one day discover that to be true.

In addition, it is impossible to lie consistently. The day will come when the lie and the many false additions that are needed to sustain and justify the original lie will be exposed.

3. Some religions teach that it is acceptable to lie to unbelievers or infidels. That, too, is contrary to the teaching of Scripture. Everyone is to be given the respect of

receiving our best effort to speak the truth in love to them and with them.

4. There are difficult situations. What are we to do in the dire circumstances when someone's life is dependent upon our telling a lie? Here we are faced with two values: to protect life and to tell the truth. In this case, we cannot satisfy both at the same time. If we speak the truth, some innocent person will die at the hands of a violent person. If we do not speak the truth to save the person's life, we lie and truth is sacrificed. A third possibility would be to refuse to speak at all and then die at the hands of the violent person.

In this scenario, since the violent person has no right to murder, the decision can be made more easily. We choose the better of two bad options. We lie to protect innocent life. Many times, the situation is not so clear.

In the clear cases and in the ambiguous cases involving a conflict of obligations, we do the best we can and ask for forgiveness for not having been able to satisfy all of the obligations that we believe are good and godly. Truth always matters even in those rare life and death situations when we believe the better thing to do is to lie.

Implications

Oaths and vows are very solemn and serious matters. They are rightly reserved for very important occasions. We are called to be so truthful in all we say and do that there should be no need for oaths in the normal conversation of our lives. We are never justified in making rash or vain oaths.

Speaking the Lord's Name casually in conversation as an expression of emphasis or of surprise is an improper use of the Lord's Name and should be avoided and rebuked.

2. Christians may take oaths when required by the State in a cause of faith and charity, so long as it is done according to justice, judgment and truth.

Explanation

Given the strong language of Jesus about not swearing at all, the question arises: Are we never to take an oath or make a vow? Or, are there moments and situations in which taking an oath or making a vow is appropriate?

This Article addresses one situation in which swearing an oath is seen to be appropriate. When the magistrate requires an oath, we are to take the oath with a good conscience, provided that we take it honestly after due consideration and in the cause of justice. The Article, we note, does not deny that there are other appropriate occasions for taking an oath or making a vow.

The reason why the Article can take the position that Christians may take an oath when required to do so by the magistrate is found 1) in the New Testament's teaching on the place and authority of the magistrate and 2) in the practice of taking oaths and making vows found in both the Old and New Testament Scriptures. There we find that the saints of the Old Testament, the prophets and kings as well as common people take oaths. God Himself does so. Jesus took an oath without objection. The Apostles made vows and took oaths, even after having heard Jesus' teaching on oaths. This being the case, it cannot be that Jesus meant that oaths and vows were never to be made. The early Church did not so understand Him. In a fallen world and in the intersection of the Kingdom of God and the kingdom of this world, making a vow and taking an oath will be, at times, an appropriate act.

When, then, might they be appropriate? It would appear, from their use in the Old and New Testaments, that taking an oath or making a vow is appropriate 1) on particularly solemn moments, or 2) when the speaker wants to commit himself publicly to a particular promise or warning with great emphasis because of the importance of the matter, or 3) if for some reason the hearers are prone to doubt what is being said and the speaker wishes to leave no reason for such doubt to continue. A goodly number of examples are cited under Biblical Foundations so the reader can examine a cross section of biblical oaths and vows.

Biblical Foundations

And the angel of the Lord called to Abraham a second time from heaven and said, "By myself I have sworn, declares the Lord, because you have done this and have not withheld your son, your only son, I will surely bless you, and I will surely multiply your offspring as the stars of heaven and as the sand that is on the seashore. And your offspring shall possess the gate of his enemies, and in your offspring shall all the nations of the earth be blessed, because you have obeyed my voice." Genesis 22:15-18

And Abraham said to his servant, the oldest of his household, who had charge of all that he had, "Put your hand under my thigh, that I may make you swear by the Lord, the God of heaven and God of the earth, that you will not take a wife for my son from the daughters of the Canaanites, among whom I dwell, but will go to my country and to my kindred, and take a wife for my son Isaac." Genesis 24:2-4

And if the Lord your God enlarges your territory, as he has sworn to your fathers, and gives you all the land that he promised to give to your fathers. Deuteronomy 19:8

And as soon as he saw her, he tore his clothes and said, "Alas, my daughter! You have brought me very low, and you have become the cause of great trouble to me. For I have opened my mouth to the Lord, and I cannot take back my vow." Judges 11:35

And the men of Israel had been hard pressed that day, so Saul had laid an oath on the people, saying, "Cursed be the man who eats food until it is evening and I am avenged on my enemies." So none of the people had tasted food." 1 Samuel 14:24

That I may confirm the oath that I swore to your fathers, to give them a land flowing with milk and honey, as at this day." Then I answered, "So be it, Lord." Jeremiah 11:5

If you return, O Israel, declares the Lord, to me you should return. If you remove your detestable things from my presence, and do not waver, and if you swear, 'As the Lord lives,' in truth, in justice, and in righteousness, then nations shall bless themselves in him, and in him shall they glory." Jeremiah 4:1-2

And all the trees of the field shall know that I am the Lord; I bring low the high tree, and make high the low tree, dry up the green tree, and make the dry tree flourish. I am the Lord; I have spoken, and I will do it. Ezekiel 17:24

But Jesus remained silent. And the high priest said to him, "I adjure you by the living God, tell us if you are the Christ, the Son of God." Jesus said to him, "You have said so. But I tell you, from now on you will see the Son of Man seated at the right hand of Power and coming on the clouds of heaven. Matthew 26:63-64

The oath that he swore to our father Abraham, to grant us. Luke 1:73

Being therefore a prophet, and knowing that God had sworn with an oath to him that he would set one of his descendants on his throne. Acts 2:30

For God is my witness, whom I serve with my spirit in the gospel of his Son, that without ceasing I mention you always in my prayers, asking that somehow by God's will I may now at last succeed in coming to you. Romans 1:9-10

But I call God to witness against me—it was to spare you that I refrained from coming again to Corinth. 2 Corinthians 1:23

(In what I am writing to you, before God, I do not lie!) Galatians 1:20

For God is my witness, how I yearn for you all with the affection of Christ Jesus. Philippians 1:8

And to whom did he swear that they would not enter his rest, but to those who were disobedient? Hebrews 3:18

For when God made a promise to Abraham, since he had no one greater by whom to swear, he swore by himself, saying, "Surely I will bless you and multiply you." And thus Abraham, having patiently waited, obtained the promise. For people swear by something greater than themselves, and in all their disputes an oath is final for confirmation. So when God desired to show more convincingly to the heirs of the promise the unchangeable character of his purpose, he guaranteed it with an oath, so that by two unchangeable things, in which it is impossible for God to lie, we who have fled for refuge might have strong encouragement to hold fast to the hope set before us. We have this as a sure and steadfast anchor of the soul, a hope that enters into the inner place behind the curtain. Hebrews 6:13-19

False Teachings Denied/Objections Answered

As mentioned in the introduction, the position of some of the Anabaptist groups was and is that Christians may never take an oath. This is contrary to the practice of God and His people as recorded in the Scriptures. In particular, when the State or Courts require us that we take an oath that we are telling the truth, we may do so out of respect for the solemnity of the occasion, a concern for truth and justice, and respect for the legitimate requirements of the government.

Implications

On one hand, in the Kingdom of God our lives should be of such integrity and faithfulness that there is no reason to ever doubt our words. On the other hand, we are citizens of two kingdoms; there are hypocrites in the Church and even genuine Christians are not yet perfectly sanctified. Therefore it is not inappropriate for the State to ask all of its citizens to take an oath, including Christians.

In addition, there are occasions in life and in the Church where an oath in the name of the Lord or a vow to the Lord is appropriate. One thinks of the baptismal vows, of marriage vows, or of ordination vows as important examples.

Conclusion

Speaking truth is fundamental to all relationships. It is rooted in the very nature of God and underlies all knowledge and conversation. Christians who are made in the image of God, are redeemed by Christ, and are being sanctified by His Spirit, are to be forthright and honest and to speak the truth in love.

To call upon the Name of the Lord is a high privilege and profound responsibility. The making of vows to God and the taking of oaths, calling upon His name, will be rare in our conversation and are not to be done lightly or in trivial matters. They should be done seriously and only when the occasion warrants it.

To lie to God while invoking the Name of the Lord is foolish and will lead to God's discipline, for He is never fooled.

Concluding Remarks

Having worked your way through this book, several things will have become clear.

First, you will have noted that this book has gone beyond a bare discussion of the teaching of the Thirty-Nine Articles. It has sought to indicate the Articles' biblical authority and to answer some of the objections and questions that Christian doctrine always raises. A measure of apologetics thereby weaves its way through the book. In addition, the book seeks, if only very briefly, to touch upon all the areas of Christian theology or systematic theology. Personal spirituality and churchly mission also come to expression often.

Second, you will have seen that there is a coherence to Christian doctrine when it is faithful to Scripture, and interpreted in the light of Jesus Christ as its center. Coherence roots in the fact that there is one God, the triune God of biblical revelation. That coherence is also rooted in the unity of Scripture, which is the inspired Word of the one, triune God. One can see this most clearly in the Articles' teaching on sin and the objective and subjective aspects of salvation, and the sovereign grace of God.

This does not mean there are no mysteries in revelation and hence in Scripture and churchly doctrine. However, mystery and incomprehensibility are far different from being a contradiction. We may never fully comprehend how the persons of the Trinity indwell one another or exist in and through one another, so that the threefoldness in God is comprehended within His unity and singularity. Nor can we fully comprehend how the inner work of the Holy Spirit, by which He sovereignly gives us a new heart and sets our will free for Christ and the Gospel, does not violate but empowers our will and responsibility. But, only by affirming these biblical truths does the full coherence of

Christian doctrine, the comfort of the Gospel and the living of life in Christ become clear.

Awareness of this coherence that arises from faithfulness to the facts and truths of God's revelation in Christ is much to be prized. Coherence and consistency satisfy something deep in us because we are made in the image of God. It is the reward of faith seeking understanding.

The third thing that will have come clear is that these Articles are remarkable, in that they are "Catholic and Reformed." Anglicanism stands alongside the other Catholic Churches, the Orthodox Churches of the East and the Roman Catholic Church of the West, in keeping all the wisdom into which the Holy Spirit had led the Church prior to the great Reformation of the 16th Century. There are no strange innovations, no errant subtractions, and no unnecessary or odd additions, just a due appreciation of the Fathers, the Ecumenical Creeds and the Ecumenical Councils of the undivided Church, except where they contradicted Scripture or required things not required by sound exegesis of Scripture. We find the retention and continuity of the historic order of Bishops, Presbyters and Deacons. At the same time, Anglicanism also stands alongside the Churches of the Reformation, fully embracing the doctrines of grace and the ministry of the laity including their place in the governance of the Church. In addition, while retaining the order of Bishops, Presbyters and Deacons in historic succession, Anglicans do not "unchurch" the theologically orthodox Reformation or Protestant Churches that, for a variety of reasons, did not retain the ancient order. There is an open heartedness as well as a remarkable blend of the ancient and the modern in the Anglican way, which bodes well for the future of faithful Anglicanism. Anglicanism is reformed Catholicism.

Lastly, this book has been written to serve as a resource for teaching in congregations, in families, as well as in seminaries. It is written to become a reference book, quite as much as to serve as an initial orientation to the richness of the Thirty-Nine Articles in particular and to Christian doctrine and theology in the reformed Catholic tradition.

Growing in theological maturity and confidence is essential to a growing life in Christ and to the vigorous exercise of ministry and mission, both on the part of the individual, and of a congregation.

Follow the pattern of the sound words that you have heard from me, in the faith and love that are in Christ Jesus. (2 Timothy 1:13)

Select Bibliography

Allison, C. F. *The Cruelty of Heresy*. Harrisburg, PA: Morehouse Publishing, 1994.

Barry, A. *The Teacher's Prayer Book*. London: Eyre & Spottiswoode., n.d.

Bicknell, E.J. *A Theological Introduction to the Thirty-Nine Articles of the Church of England,* Third Edition revised by E.J. Carpenter. London: Longmans, Green, & Co., 1955.

Bridge, G.R. (ed.) *The Thirty-Nine Articles*. Charlottetown: St. Peter Publications Inc., n.d.

Boultbee, T.P. *A Commentary on the Thirty-Nine Articles.* London: Longmans, Green, & Co., 1880. Reprinted by Wipf & Stock Publishers, September 2005.

Browne, E.H. *An Exposition of the Thirty-Nine Articles*. London: Longman, Green, Longman, Roberts, & Green, 1864. (Available from Classical Anglican Press with the Reformed Episcopal Church.)

Burnet, G. *An Exposition of the Thirty-Nine Articles of the Church of England*, revised by J.R. Page. London: Scott, Webster, and Geary, 1841. Reprinted by Wipf & Stock Publishers, October 2005.

Clarkson, J.F. S.J. et. al. *The Church Teaches, Documents of the Church in English Translation*. St. Louis: B. Herder Book Co., 1995.

Cloquet, R.L. *An Exposition of the Thirty-Nine Articles of the Church of England.* London: James Nisbet & Co., 1885.

Cranmer, T. & Jewel, J. *The Homilies,* Focus Christian Ministries Trust edition. London: Prayer-Book and Homily Society, 1986.

Gibson, E.C.S. *The Thirty-Nine Articles of the Church of England, Explained with An Introduction.* London: Methuen & Co., 1896 (Vol 1); 1897 (Vol 2). Both volumes have been combined in a one volume reprint by Wipf & Stock Publishers, May 2005.

Green, E.T. *The Thirty-nine Articles and the Age of the Reformation.* London: Wells, Gardner, Darton & Co., 1896.

Hardwick, C. *A History of the Articles of Religion.* Philadelphia: Herman Hooker, 1852.

Hughes, P.E. *The Thirty-Nine Articles: A Re-statement.* Cape Town: Church of England in South Africa, 1988.

Kidd, B.J. *The Thirty-nine Articles,* in two volumes. New York; Edwin S. Gorham, 1903. Both volumes are available in a one volume reprint, Wipf & Stock Publishers, May 2005.

Knox, D.B. *Thirty-Nine Articles, The Historic Basis of Anglican Faith. London*: Hodder and Stoughton, 1967.

Maclear, G.F. & Williams, W.W. *An Introduction to the Articles of the Church of England.* London: Macmillan and Co., Ltd., 1896.

Matthews, W.R. *The Thirty-Nine Articles, A Plea For A New Statement Of The Christian Faith As Understood By The Church Of England.* London: Hodder and Stoughton, 1961.

Moss, C.B. *The Thirty-Nine Articles Revised.* London: A. R. Mobray & Co. Limited, 1961.

O'Donovan, Oliver, *On the Thirty Nine Articles: A Conversation with Tudor Christianity.* Exeter: The Paternoster Press, 1986.

Packer, J.I. *The Thirty-Nine Articles.* London: Church Pastoral-Aid Society, 1961.

Pascoe, S. *The Thirty-Nine Articles: Buried Alive?* Dallas: Latimer Press, 1998.

Ratzinger, Joseph Cardinal (Imprimi Potest). *Catechism of the Catholic Church.* Liguori, MO: Liguori Publications, 1994.

Rogers, T. *The Catholic Doctrine of the Church of England, An Exposition of the Thirty-Nine Articles,* Parker Society edition. Cambridge: University Press, 1854.

Ross, K.N. *The Thirty-Nine Articles.* London: A.R. Mowbray & Co. LTD., 1960.

Ryle C.R. *Knots Untied,* Duffield edition. London: James Clarke & Co. LTD., 1964.

Satge, J.C. *de,* et al. *The Articles of the Church of England.* London: A.R. Mobray & Co. LTD., 1964.

Temple, W. (ed.) *Doctrine in the Church of England, The 1938 Report,* edition with introduction by G.W.H. Lampe. London: SPCK, 1982.

Thomas, W.H.G. *The Principles of Theology, An Introduction to the Thirty-Nine Articles,* edition with Intro. by J.I. Packer. London: Vine Books LTD., 1978. Reprinted by Classical Anglican Press of the Reformed Episcopal Church.

Wilson, W.G. & Templeton, J.H. *Anglican Teaching, An Exposition of the Thirty-Nine Articles.* Dublin: Association for Promoting Christian Knowledge, 1962.

Appendix A

Reflections on the Arguments for the Existence of God

There are many good books on the Arguments. These brief remarks are included for general orientation and to suggest a line of interpretation.

I. Why these arguments do not convince everyone

1. These are syllogistic arguments. The conclusions follow logically from the premises. If one does not accept either or both of the premises the conclusion may follow logically, but will not be convincing as truth.

2. These arguments rest upon an intellectual awareness of the surrounding world, and upon inner self-awareness. Both of these sorts of awareness vary between individuals and cultures. This being the case, different arguments will seem to be more convincing to different persons.

3. These arguments function not so much as proofs as they do as evidence. In that case they have the strongest impact when viewed together; they have a cumulative effect.

4. As sinners who do not wish to be accountable to God, people "suppress the truth in unrighteousness", as St. Paul tells us. (Romans 1: 18) Today we call this "denial" and/or "rationalization." Some do not believe because they do not want to believe.

5. There is also an eschatological reason. This is the time of the Lord's patience, the time He has provided for missions and evangelism. At present God does not generally make His reality so undeniable that people must acknowledge Him even when they do not wish to honor him as Savior and Lord. When the 'Last Day" comes the time for

repenting and believing will be over. All rational creatures will see and acknowledge Him, some with joy and some with the gnashing of teeth.

II. The Arguments stated in brief syllogistic form
To sense the full effect of these arguments, they need to be illustrated from reality as we experience it.

A. The Cosmological Argument
This argument may be in stated a number of forms. Here are two:
1. All contingent beings are dependent for their existence upon external causation and continual support.
2. The world as we know it is composed of dependent beings. That which is composed of dependent entities is itself dependent.
3. Therefore the world is caused by and depends for its continued existence upon that power which is itself uncaused, whose nature is to be, and which has the power to cause and sustain the world. This power is that which Christians call God.

Or:
1. Nothing can come from nothing.
2. There is something (the world and all therein, which has come into being, which is finite, caused and dependent).
3. Therefore there is that uncaused, eternal Being whose nature is to be, and from which all dependent things come into being and on which they depend. This uncaused eternal Being is that which Christians call God.

B. The Teleological Argument
1. Where there is intelligent design and purpose there must be an intelligent designer.
2. The universe bears pervasive evidence of intelligent design and purpose.

3. Therefore there must be One who is the purposeful, intelligent designer of the Universe. This designer is the One which Christians call God.

C. The Ontological Argument.
1. God exists as the greatest reality that we can think. He is the greatest in every respect.
2. That which exits in reality apart from the mind is greater than that which exists only in the mind.
3. Therefore God exists as the greatest in the mind and as the greatest in reality outside of the mind.

D. The Moral Argument
1. People have a conscience, which unavoidably affirms the reality and crucial significance of morality and justice.
2. Morality and Justice require that right and wrong are real and that humans are accountable to do the right and avoid the wrong. Moreover they require that people will one day be judged according to their conformity in motive and action to the norms of right and wrong.
3. Therefore there is one who is both the source of moral norms and the Judge who will one day dispense justice. This is the one the Christians call God.

E. The Argument from Love
1. Human needs which are universal and essential always have resources to meet those needs. (food, shelter, friendship).
2. All finite human persons have a need to be loved with an unconditional, eternal love that will not end.
3. Therefore there is One who loves people with an unconditional and eternal love. This is the one that Christians call God.

F. The Argument from Religion
1. What is universal among persons and societies reflects reality.
2. Religion is universal in every society.
3. Therefore the God of which true religion speaks is real. This is the one that Christians call God.

III. What these Arguments affirm about God

1. That God alone is the one whose nature is to be and is the uncaused cause of the Universe.
2. That God is the wise, intelligent One who designed and purposed the Universe.
3. That God is the righteous Judge whose character and creative act defines right and wrong and who will insure that justice is satisfied in the end.
4. That God is the unconditional, eternal lover of humanity. (*Nota bene*, to love is not the same as to be reconciled; reconciliation is an aspect of Redemptive Revelation not General Revelation).
5. That God is the One whom all religions seek to honor.
6. That God is not just a reality in our minds but exists in reality apart from our minds.

Conclusion
These arguments seek to express and state in logical form the innate and inner awareness that every person has of God. (See Romans 1: 19-20, 25; Romans 2: 15)

Appendix B

The Thirty-Nine Articles and Anglican Hermeneutics

In these brief remarks, we have listed the basic guidelines pertaining to the interpretation of Scripture, that are faithful to the Anglican formularies.

A. Scripture as the Church's Book: The Rule of Faith (Art. 8)

It is foreign to the nature of the Scripture and a right understanding of it to interpret it as if it were not first addressed to, kept by, treasured and interpreted by the Church. In one sense the Bible is the Church's book. Interpretation of Scripture is not essentially an individualistic act but a communal act done in, by and for the Church. That being the case, we affirm that the Rule of Faith held and confessed by the Church initially guides biblical interpretation.

Keeping this ecclesiastical character of interpretation in mind, we note that there are certain assumptions one brings to the act of interpretation:

1. We assume that the Christian Faith is unique for it rests on God's redemptive, revealing work in Christ, given to a particular chosen people in and through historical events, including events that are sometimes miraculous.

2. We assume that the Scriptures are "the Word of God written," that is, they are the inspired, faithful, authoritative Canonical writings given by God to the Church.

3. We assume that the Church's Rule of Faith, found in its formularies, is a faithful interpretation of Scripture and our interpretation is initially guided by the Rule of Faith.

4. These assumptions will be tested in the very act of reflecting upon, and interpreting the texts of Scripture.

B. Scripture as God's Word written: The Authority of Scripture (Art. 20)

Since Holy Scripture is God's Word written, it bears His authority, and we read it to hear Him in order to know, trust and obey Him. Proper interpretation of Holy Scripture is a sacred responsibility. Scripture's authority (or God speaking through Scripture) in the Church is supreme and norms all lesser norms or formularies that have subordinate authority in the Church. This is the Anglican meaning of *Sola Scriptura*. Scripture is alone on its level, but it is not isolated from lesser authorities. This relatedness to lesser explanatory norms is the meaning of *Sola Suprema* with reference to Holy Scripture.

C. All Scripture is God-breathed: Canonical Interpretation (Arts. 2, 7, 20)

"All of Scripture is inspired and profitable for teaching..." (2 Tim.3: 16-17) There is a central message in Scripture concerning God's salvation of sinful man to the glory of God. Seen in that context, all of Scripture has its part to play. Canonical interpretation consists in letting all of the pertinent passages in the Canon speak to any given issue. While there is variety in terminology and development in Scripture, there is no theological contradiction; instead there is an underlying harmony. This is because Scripture, unlike any other writing, has dual authorship. While being written by and in the words of men who have been chosen and inspired by God, it is at the same time the very Word of the One God. His mind, speaking through the many human authors, forms and assures us of its unity and coherence. It is therefore "not lawful to so expound one part of Scripture as to be repugnant to another."

D. Scripture is full and clear in essential matters: The sufficiency and clarity of Scripture (Art. 6)

Sufficiency: nothing may be required of anyone for salvation that is not required in Scripture or that may not be logically deduced from its clear statements.

Clarity: in matters of doctrine the clear texts will be used to cast light on the less clear texts that pertain to the topic under consideration. In general, later statements will interpret earlier ones. Descriptive or narrative sections will need interpretation from texts asserting a clear command, statement of doctrine or principle. It may also be the case that a text may be clear as to its central point but may contain references that are not entirely clear. In such cases proper caution is to be used in interpreting those less clear portions and due humility toward one another concerning any differing interpretations in these secondary matters is appropriate.

E. The humanity of Scripture: the historical-grammatical aspect of interpretation

Scripture is the Word of God written in the words of men who were chosen from among the people of God in differing times and places. Since these human authors wrote at specific times and in specific situations to specific recipients, we must consider and take into account word usage, grammatical form, literary types, literary context as well as cultural, historical contexts and situations as far as we can determine them. In so doing we approach the sacred writings as we would other human writings when seeking to understand them. By taking such care we seek to let the texts bear their message in their original sense to us. It is through that original sense as part of the entire Canonical harmony of Scripture that we hear the Lord's address to us.

F. The Application of Scripture: Interpretation as Obedience

We properly understand God's Word only when we stand under His Word, when we see how it is to be heard and obeyed in our situation. Sometimes this will be easy to understand even if not easy to do. In one sense human nature has not changed much down through the ages. Generally understanding an appropriate application or applications comes easily.

But in some places, Scripture may prove more difficult to apply due to changes in situation and culture. We do not want to universalize and bind on the Church today merely cultural practices of a by-gone period and culture. Therefore we will need, at times, to distinguish the doctrine or principle that God is speaking to us from its application at the time of the original reception of that Word in order to be able to relate the point or principle to our situation in another cultural setting.

This raises the question as to how we will be able to discern those applications in Scripture that are limited to a past culture. We cannot assume that everything in Scripture that contradicts our culture is culture-bound and now irrelevant. To do so could mute the Word that the Lord is speaking to us. We might err by treating as relative a principle that God intends to be absolute and universal in every culture and therefore to be obeyed by us in our setting. How then do we make this judgment?

Here are some of the questions that we can ask to determine when a principle or application is universal or trans-cultural: We should treat any declaration or command of Scripture as universally binding:

1. When the text itself does not indicate it is limited in application.
2. When it is grounded in the unchanging character of God.
3. When it is grounded in the nature of creation, the *ordo creationis*.

APPENDIX B

We can conclude the application found in Scripture is not trans-cultural or not directly applicable to our cultural situation when:

1. It is clearly stated to be limited.
2. It has been expressly fulfilled and ended by Christ.
3. It is unable to be implemented in our situation, showing that it is incapable of universal application.

Caution is needed on this last point for "unable to be implemented" is quite different from being counter-cultural. We will often be called to be counter-cultural in a fallen society.

The reader may have additional suggestions concerning this point; this is an important and delicate matter. Missiologists wrestle with this much of the time, as do Bible translators and preachers, as must every Christian when reading his or her Bible.

However, most of the Bible is very clear and clearly applicable. We recall what Mark Twain once said, "It is not what I do not understand in the Bible that troubles me; it is what I do understand."

Appendix C

Contemporary Anglican Views of the Ordained Ministry

I. Common Convictions

Despite the differences among Anglicans regarding the ordained ministry, in our Anglican Practice, in the Ordinal, and in the Thirty Nine Articles of Religion we find a number of convictions that Anglicans all hold in common:

A. That the Anglican Practice of the Christian Faith is a constituent part of the one, holy catholic and apostolic Church founded by Jesus Christ. Article VIII establishes the Nicene, the Apostles and the Athanasian Creeds as elements of our faith. In these Creeds, and in the baptismal covenant, we declare our participation to be in this one visible body.

B. That God has instituted in His Church an Office of Word and Sacrament *jure divino* in and through the Apostles and by means of which Christ by the Spirit continues to minister to and through His Church. The example of Jesus and the Apostles, as well as the synagogue, provided the basic pattern for the oversight, preaching and teaching in the New Testament period. Paul went about in all of the congregations setting apart Elders. In this conviction, we disagree with those Christian Bodies such as the Quakers and some of the Brethren that have no ordained ministry or those bodies that see the authority of the ordained ministry arising solely or primarily from the congregation.

C. That there have been in the Church since the beginning the orders of Bishop, Presbyters/Priests and Deacons. It is true that the words "Presbyteros and Episcopos" referred to the same group initially, but soon the expansion of the Church led to a division of those common responsibilities into separate orders and offices. In fact, we can see in Timothy and Titus who are under an Apostle and placed over a region of congregations together with their elders, an early emergence of the beginning of a distinct Episcopate.

Most scholars hold that by 180 AD, the Church was almost universally ordered under the pattern of the threefold ministry. Anglicans have always seen this to be a godly development in accord with Scripture, expressing what was implicit in the beginning. Anglicans have not all held this developed form of the ministry of Word and Sacrament to be essential to the Church or even to be of the fullness of the Church, but we have all consistently maintained and treasured it. Anglicans have regularly commended it to the wider ecumenical Church wherever it has been lacking in other bodies as desirable and as containing nothing superstitious as it is set forth in our ordinal.

A. According to our Formularies (I refer to 1662 Ordinal and the Articles) the following may be affirmed about each of these offices:

1. *Of a Priest*
   (a) He must be of godly character, converted and given to reading the Scriptures and prayer.
   (b) He must be truly called by those in the body appointed to do the same.
   (c) He must believe that the Holy Scriptures are the Word of God written and be of sound learning.
   (d) He must preach and teach the Word of God and drive out from the Church all false and erroneous doctrine contrary to the Word of God.
   (e) He must administer the Sacraments rightly in accordance with the Word of God expressed in the rites of the Church. (i.e., he must not seek to offer

Christ bloodlessly for merit at the Lord's Supper nor withhold the cup from the laity (Arts. 30 & 31). *This is the chief ground of Rome's not recognizing Anglican orders.*

(f) With reference to the ministry of Word and Sacrament, the Priest does share with the Bishop in the ordination of fellow Priests who will exercise the ministry of Word and Sacrament with and under the Bishop's oversight.

(g) He must exercise the discipline of the Church duly.

(h) He must seek Christ's sheep that are presently lost and bring them home.

(i) He must obey his Bishop and those rightly in authority over him.

(j) He must be the husband of one wife.

2. *Of a Bishop*

(a) All of the above affirmations also apply to the Bishop.

(b) In addition, the Bishop confirms, consecrates other Bishops, and ordains Priests and Deacons.

(c) The Bishop's ministry of Word and Sacrament and his exercise of the discipline of the Church are over a wider sphere of responsibility.

(d) The Bishop serves as a link with the wider Church in time and space through collegiality in conference, convention and council.

(e) He is accountable to the authorities and instrumentalities set over him in the Church.

3. *Of a Deacon*

(a) The deacon must share in the same character and marks of piety that characterize the Priest and Bishop and also must be duly called and ordained by those appointed in the Church to do the same.

(b) The Deacon is charged to read the Scripture to the congregation assembled.

(c) The Deacon is to assist the Priest in the administration of the Holy Communion.
(d) The Deacon is to instruct the youth of the Parish (Parish here involves both Church and region) in the catechism.
(e) The Deacon is to seek out the sick, poor and needy in the Parish (again both in the congregation and civic community) and to help the Church see to their needs.
(f) The Deacon, when the Priest is absent, is to Baptize and Preach when licensed by the Bishop.
(g) The Deacon is to obey the Bishop and those under whose authority the Deacon serves.

In addition to the above commonalties, we are aware that the Ministry of Word and Sacrament has until recently been exercised only by men. The ordination of women to any of these orders and offices is very recent and has not yet been permitted by the great majority of Christians or even the majority of Anglicans. Especially, it has not been permitted by most of those Churches ordered in the historic three-fold ministry. Where it has been permitted among Anglicans, it is regarded as in the process of reception or evaluation by the Church.

II. Differences: The Three Traditions

In addition to all that we hold and practice in common, there are the specific emphases of the three orthodox traditions found in Anglicanism: Catholic, Evangelical and Charismatic. These will color an approach to the issue of the ordination of women, so it is important to state some of the leading characteristics of each. This outline is in no sense exhaustive.

<u>1. The Catholic Tradition</u>
Priesthood is viewed in the context of the Apostolic Succession of the Church. The Apostolic Succession of the

Church involves more than the succession of Bishops in the historic Episcopate. It includes the Canonical Scriptures, the Ecumenical or Catholic Creeds, the Chief Sacraments of the Gospel in faithful liturgical forms, and the faithful Ministry of Word and Sacrament and Oversight as well as the continuity of the witness of all of the faithful. These are all expressions of continuity with the life and witness of the Apostles and serve the continuation of the *"Apostles' teaching, fellowship, breaking of bread, prayers and mission"* in and through the Church. Bishops in historic succession are a symbol and servant of this wider apostolic succession.

In ordained ministerial succession, the central figure is the Bishop who, according to historic succession, is the link to the common ministry of the wider Church. He has the authority to give pastoral care and oversight to the Church under his care as well as to consecrate Bishops and ordain Priests, who will, by his delegation and appointment, share in his ministry. As the successor to the Apostles, the Bishop ministers in the authority given to him through them in the name of Christ. The exercise of his authority is in the Church and is exercised in conjunction with the whole Church but is not primarily derived from the Church but from the Lord.

The Bishop in historic succession from the early Church is therefore both an expression of and also a servant of the unity of the Church Catholic. There is little or no chance that any other form of ministry would gain the recognition of (and be the bearer and servant of) the unity of the whole Church, particularly when one thinks of the Roman and Orthodox Communions.

The "catholic" perspective is that ordained ministries arising at the Reformation that are not in historic succession may be blessed and used by God but are not part of the historic ministry of the Church. They are, therefore, of a temporary nature. It is important to realize that the Catholic tradition always has a strong concern for the ecumenical unity of the Church and has both the Roman and Orthodox Communions ever in view.

Ordination by the Bishop conveys entrance into the given Order (of Bishops, Priests or Deacons), that gives the ones ordained the authority to act when installed in a given cure. Concomitant with (accompanying) the authority of ordination is the grace given to exercise those virtues necessary to the faithful exercise of the office to which one is called and ordained.

The Priestly Order and office centers in the celebration of the Eucharist. In this, the Priest offers the sacrifice of the Eucharist, that is, the sacrifice of Praise and Thanksgiving, recalling the completed sacrifice of Christ. He leads the congregation in offering itself, soul and body as a living sacrifice to the Lord in response to the Lord's completed gift of Himself for us and His present gift of Himself to us. The Holy Eucharist is not to be celebrated privately nor without preaching.

At the Altar during the Eucharist, the Priest represents both the congregation to the Lord and the Lord to the Church; he is therefore a mediator, an icon of Christ in that setting. This iconic character which has wider symbolic implications along with the example of Christ's appointing only men to the Apostolate, as well as various biblical texts in the Apostolic writings, lead most Anglo-Catholics as well as Rome and the Orthodox to believe the Church has no authority to ordain women to the Priesthood/Presbyterate and Episcopate. The Catholic Tradition is not as clear about the Diaconate and people hold views both pro and con with regard to the ordination of women in the Diaconate.

Along with the above, the Bishop and the Priest only are authorized and commissioned on behalf of the Church to absolve sinners in the Name of the Lord, and pronounce the Lord's Blessing. As "Pater Familias," they exercise discipline and pastoral care for the welfare of the congregation committed by the Lord through the Bishop to their care.

2. The Evangelical Tradition

The Evangelical view of the Presbyterate/Priesthood has as its starting point less the developed views of the ordained ministry, which took shape in the early centuries of the undivided Church, but more in the biblical teaching and practice of the ministry of Elders. This is understandable when one thinks that at the Reformation the "Ecclesia Anglicana" was in the process of testing and reforming the traditions of the Western Church by the standard of Scripture. It was repeatedly stated that no one ought to be required to hold any doctrine as necessary for salvation that could not be proved by or clearly deduced from Scripture.

This being the case, appeals to the tradition of the early Fathers were primarily to show that the Fathers were scriptural and that the Evangelical Tradition stood with them within the historic Rule of Faith in accord with the great Ecumenical, Catholic Creeds. Appeals to later traditions that did not contradict Scripture or to traditions that could not be seen to derive from Scripture, while often held to be important, have less authority in the Evangelical stream than they do in the Catholic stream of the Church.

Being aware that *"faith cometh by hearing and hearing cometh by the preaching of the Word of God,"* the Evangelical tradition places the preaching and teaching of the Word at the center of the calling, authority and work of the Presbyter. It is by such means that the congregation is built up in faith, that justification and sanctification occur and that the mission of the Church flourishes. It is also by such means that false doctrine contrary to the Word of God is driven from the Church. False teaching can never be undone by discipline alone, for falsehood must be countered by truth. Both true teaching and ecclesiastical discipline are needed.

The Sacraments of the Gospel, particularly Baptism and the Lord's Supper, are held in high regard and with St. Augustine are seen as *verba visibilis*. They are the visible, enacted Word in and through which Christ Himself by the Spirit ministers to the faithful. The Presbyter/Priest sees himself not so much an icon of Christ as he is the servant of the Risen Lord Who Himself is present as the Host at the Table, and as the One who baptizes. It is all done in "His Name." The focus is not on the Presbyter representing the Lord but on the Lord as present in the sacrament and in the Word.

Since both of the Gospel sacraments center in the Cross and since the Cross is the once for all, fully sufficient and completed or finished work of Christ, the Evangelical is leery of sacerdotal language about the Presbyteral Order as if somehow the Presbyter were thought to be offering Christ anew (Art. 31). One notes that not once in the New Testament is *hierus* (Gk.) or *sacerdos* (Lat.) used of those referred to as *presbyteroi /episcopoi* or for that matter of any ministry in the Church except that of Christ Himself or of the ministry of the whole Church viewed collectively. The Evangelical Presbyter does not so much "offer the Eucharist" as preside over the Congregation's celebration of the Eucharist.

Along with a central emphasis on the Worship of the Congregation and preaching the Word, leadership in evangelism, mission and edification by Bible Study in small groups has been a strong part of the Presbyter/Priest's exercise of headship in the Congregation.

A concern for the proper exercise of headship in authoritative preaching, in ordained leadership and the exercise of discipline and the emergence of the question of the ordination of women has led to a renewed concern for understanding and protecting the biblical teaching of "male headship" in family and Church. This too has been seen as having wider symbolic significance, connected as it is with the names of the Father and the Son in the self-revelation of God.

These concerns have led many Evangelical people to wonder if the ordination of women to the Presbyterate and Episcopate is contrary to Scripture. This, along with the example of Christ in not appointing women to the Apostolate and various texts of Scripture, has raised "an amber if not red flag" for a number in the Evangelical tradition. The biblical teaching on "male headship" and its practical application requires careful examination and clarification .

The Ordained Ministry of Word and Sacrament is seen as a part of equipping the saints for the work of ministry. At the Reformation, the focus of the ministry of the Priesthood of all Believers was affirmed with an eye toward the service of Christ in the various secular vocations in which the saints of the congregation lived and worked. Some of this emphasis has been lost in recent years. The Church has come more and more into a counter-cultural stance and the spiritual gifts that are to be used within the Body have been recovered and emphasized by the Evangelical, Charismatic and Catholic streams.

The unity of the Church is seen in the Evangelical perspective to lie fundamentally in faithful agreement with the teaching of the Apostles. To put it more accurately, both Right Doctrine and Right Order are seen as expressions of and servants of the unity of the Church; but a priority is given to the Truth. As one Evangelical put it, "There is a succession of Judas as well."

This emphasis on the Word and Sacraments of the Gospel as the foundation of the Church is reflected in the practice of the Lambeth Fathers. Lambeth Conferences have always referred to those Churches that do not have the historic Episcopate as Churches, thereby considering them to be Churches if they have affirmed the Faith and have the Scriptures and the Gospel Sacraments while at the same time commending the historic Episcopate to them.

3. The Charismatic Tradition

The recent recovery of the "charismata" in the life of the Church has taken place in the context of an Anglican Communion where strong Catholic and Evangelical traditions concerning the Priesthood/Presbyterate were already present. It is therefore no surprise that in the Charismatic stream one can find either Evangelical or Catholic viewpoints or a combination of both along with the Charismatic emphases.

The Charismatic tradition adds to the other traditions a new openness to the exercise of the "spiritual gifts" in the leading, life and ministry of the Congregation and in the corporate worship of the Church. The Priest/Presbyter is called to teach about these gifts and see that they are exercised in a biblical and orderly manner. Since we live in a secular age which is anti-supernatural on the one hand but open to all sorts of "spiritual phenomena" on the other, the role of the Priest both in leadership and in discernment is key.

Without teaching and leadership, the "charismata" will not be understood or permitted in the life of the congregation. Without discernment and discipline, permission will be given to that which is not biblical, and the extremists will take over and drive out the cautious and tender. One Bishop in the Episcopal Church has said, "The three greatest congregations in my diocese have been renewal congregations and the three most problematic congregations were also."

The recovery of spiritual gifts has led to a new awareness that the ministry of the Body includes all of the members, for each has been given a gift or gifts to use for the up-building of the Body and the exercise of its mission. In this respect, the Priest is to equip the saints and to orchestrate and oversee the discernment and use of gifts in ministry by the whole Body. All of the saints are to be involved in the Gospel ministry, not just the ordained saints. As noted above, this understanding of the Priesthood of all Believers is somewhat different from the emphasis at the Reformation and is more body-oriented. Both views of the Priesthood of all Believers are needed and both are biblical.

There is a new sense of the unity of the Church found in the manifestation of the gifts in ministry, a rediscovery that cuts across denominations and traditions. The "sense of kinship in Christ" this gives is a fresh contribution of the Renewal Movement. We do well to appreciate it along with the Catholic and Evangelical contributions concerning the unity of the Church and the work of the Priesthood/Presbyterate. Unfortunately at times, this leads people to a sort of warm-heartedness that undervalues the significance of true doctrine and godly order.

General Index

1662 Book of Common Prayer, 388, 511, 587
1662 Catechism, 515
1662 Ordinal, 388
Abelard, Peter, 107
abiding grace. *See* grace, accompanying
Abraham, 182, 245
Abrahamic Covenant, 245, 497
ad inferos, 110
Adam, 218, 249, 294
adiaphora, 583
adiaphorous, 585
adoption, 82, 340
Adoration of the Blessed Sacrament, 472, 531
Age to Come, 133
aging. *See* human beings, aging
agnostics, 13
All Saints' Day, 429
allylos, 148
Alpha, 455
Ambrose, 457
Amillennialism, 138
Anabaptists, 4, 318, 392, 393, 479, 594, 595, 603
  objection to Anglican Ordinal, 615
  private property, views of, 646
  state, view of, 631
Ananias, 120, 146, 652
Anglican Church of North America (ACNA), 5
Anglican Communion
  doctrines of, 388
  rites and ceremonies, 387
Anglican Ordinal, 609
Anglican tradition, 170
Anglo-Catholic Movement, 388
anointing of priest's hands, 614
Anselm, 106
anthropomorphism, 27–28
antinomianism, 105, 193, 283, 284
Apocrypha, 167, 176–78
Apollinarianism, 72
Apollinarius, 72, 92
apostasy, 326–27, 343, 494
apostles, 66, 435, 562
Apostles' Creed, 110, 198, 204–5, 388
Apostles' Creed, 109
Apostolic Benediction, 147
apostolic succession of the church, 619
Aquinas, Thomas, 523, 533, 639
Archbishop of Canterbury, 594
Arians, 213
Aristotle, 21
Arius, 86, 91, 200, 389
Arminianism, 235, 241, 248, 336
Arminius, Jacobus, 235, 236, 336
ascension, 134–37
assurance of salvation, 270, 338
Athanasian Creed, 109, 110, 198, 200–203, 213, 388
Athanasius, 200, 389
atheism, 18
atonement, 69, 94–107, 134, 310–13, 549
Augsburg Confession, 4

authority, response to, 605
Baha'i religion, 173, 356
baptism, 285, 463, 484–505
   as adoption, 488
   as being grafted into Church, 488
   as dying to sin, 488
   as effective sign, 492
   as faith confirmed, 488
   as forgivenessof sin, 488
   as grace increased, 488
   as public profession, 485–88
   as regeneration, 488
   conversion unto, 501
   grafting into church, 492–97
   in Holy Spirit, 490
   in State Churches, 487
   instruction for those being baptized, 492
   mark of the New Covenant, 498
   mode of application of water, 496
   of Jesus, 147
   private, 486, 495
   promise of forgiveness, 489
   water, 490
baptism unto conversion, 501
Barmen Declaration, 642
Barnabas, 175
Barth, Karl, 29, 153, 267, 406, 642
believers, genuine, 368
Berengarius, 523
Bible. *See* Holy Scriptures
big bang theory, 34
birth sin. *See* sin,original
Bishop as intermediary, 435
Bishop of Rome, 409
Bishop of the Diocese, 443
   role in excommunication, 568
bishops, 435
   consecration of, 607–24
   necessity of, 446
   objection to the authority of, 616
blood of Jesus, 98
bondage of the will, 234, 237–45, 258, 390
Bondage of the Will, 236
bondage, external, 237
Book of Common Prayer, 2, 4, 377, 387, 390, 429, 468, 472, 599, 607
Brunner, Emil, 14
Buddha, 81
Buddhist countries, 633
Bultmann, Rudolph, 71
Bunyan, John, 347
Calvin, John, 111
capitalism, 658
Catechism, 2, 377
Catechism, 1662 Book of Common Prayer, 458
celibacy, 562, 563
ceremonial laws, 103
chance, 41
Chantry Masses, 510, 546
character, holiness of, 425
Charismatic churches, 146
charismatic renewal movement, 490
charitable giving, 653–63
charity, to those holding different views, 113
Charles I, 3
choice, human, 42
Christian freedom. *See* freedom, Christian
Christian living, 137
Christianity Explained, 455
Christus Victor, 106
church
   apostolic, 370
   authority of, 386–407
   catholic, 369
   creedal marks of, 369–70
   denominations, 375
   essential activities, 370

GENERAL INDEX

holy, 369
invisible, 367–69
keeper of Holy Scriptures, 404
mission of, 19
one, 369
purpose of, 627–28
relationship to state, 395
rise of, 116
to decide controversies of faith, 390
visible, 367–85
witness of Holy Scriptures, 404
church and state, relationship of, 630–44
church discipline, 567
Church in Rome, 374
circumcision, 497
civil disobedience, 632, 641
civil law, 243
civil laws (Israel), 188
claritas Scripturae, 585
clergy
  as godly examples, 477, 482
  marriage of, 561–65
  role in excommunication, 568
  role in sacraments, 475–83
  sinful, 476
  unworthiness, 475–83
comfort (Christian), 269–71
comfort from Gospel, 254
commandment, fourth, 117
common grace, 164, 289
common language. *See* language, common
common order, respect of, 589
common property, objections to, 647
communion. *See* Lord's Supper
Communion of Evangelical Episcopal Churches, 5
Communion of the Saints, 429, 431

communism, 652, 657
concomitance, 544, 545
concupiscence, 232, 233
Confession of Wuertemburg, 4
confidence, Christian, 136
confirmation, 401, 467, 499
Congregationalism, 445
conscience, troubled, 276
Constantine, 395
Continuing Churches, 5
cor incurvatus in se, 222, 238
corporate worship, 370
Corpus Christi, 530
Council of Chalcedon, 90, 92, 199
Council of Constance, 544
Council of Constantinople, 72, 92, 151, 199
Council of Dort, 236, 336
Council of Ephesus, 90, 92
Council of Nicea, 86, 91, 151, 198, 389
Council of Nicea, Second, 425
Council of Trent, 4, 231, 233, 236, 255, 399, 414, 417, 453, 469, 473, 480, 520, 524, 533, 538, 544, 594
  sacrifice of the Mass, 554
Covenant of Grace, 182, 497
Cranmer, Thomas, 2, 3, 30, 110, 393, 516, 524, 528, 599, 600, 610, 613
creation, 30–32, 182, 400
creation, 33
creed, baptismal form, 120
creedal marks of church. *See* church, creedal marks of
Creeds, 2, 196–214, 585
  place in worship, 207
cross, 262
  as pattern of life, 106
  substitutionary, 104
  sufficiency of, 105, 265
  theological meaning, 97
crucifixion, 95

Cry of Dereliction, 111
cults, contemporary, 213
Cur Deus Homo?, 106
Cyprian, 435, 479
Daily Office, 377
damnation clauses, 213
Day of Atonement, 310, 558
Day of Judgment, 79, 228
deacons (New Testament), 435, 562
dead, communicating with, 428
death, 227
  Christian view of, 125
  victory over, 132
death penalty, 634
deism, 40, 355–56
desires of the flesh, 231
determinism, 241
Didache, 175
dietary laws, 188
disciples, 78
Disciples (original), 116
diversity, permissable, 583
Divine Society, 161
docetism, 71, 92
doctrinal development, 399, 417
doctrine, individual discernment of, 392
Donatism, 318, 479
donum superadditum, 294
dualism, 18, 19, 30
Eastern Church
  theology of the Holy Spirit, 154–62
Eastern Fathers, 111
Eastern mystic religions, 92, 154
Eastern Orthodox Churches, 586
Eastern Orthodox tradition, 399
Eastern Orthodoxy
  communicating infants, 521

ecclesiastical discipline, 328, 378, 481, 482
Ecclesiastical Polity, 596
economic social patterns, 645
Ecumenical Councils, 399, 585
ecumenical discussion, 255, 295, 300, 442
Ecumenical Gathering in Lund, Sweden, 375
Ecumenical Movement, 375, 410, 622
Edward VI, 610, 623
effetctual calling, 339
elders, 435
elders (New Testament), 435, 445
elect, 553
election, 216, 236, 331–50
  assurance of, 344–45
  mystery of, 503
Elizabeth I, 526
Elwell, Walter A., 9
English Standard Version (ESV), 9
Enlightenment, 388, 406
Episcopal Church, USA, 4, 5
episcopate, historic, 619
episcopate, three historic views, 621
Erasmus, Desiderius, 236
Erastianism, 395, 409, 633
Erastus, Thomas, 395, 633
eschatology, 137–40
ethics, 38–39, 73
ethics, Christian, 72
Eucharist. *See* Lord's Supper
Eutyches, 90, 92
evangelism, 143, 348, 360, 454
Eve, 218
ex cathedra, 413, 546, 586, 594
ex nihilo, 31
ex opera operato, in Lord's Supper, 521
ex opere operato, 461

excommunication, 566–79
  avenues of appeal, 579
  corporate aspects of, 575–79
  greater, 567
  lesser, 567
  limits of, 571
  misuse of, 574
  of false teachers, 363
  purpose of, 571–73
  two forms, 567
  versus shunning, 578
exhortation, 245
Exile (Old Testament), 434
exorcisms, 322
expiation, 101, 102
extreme unction, 468
faith, 265–69
  as gift, 268
  invisibility of, 368
  related to good works, 281–86
  role of mind in, 450
  saving, 343
  superficial, 343
Faith seeking understanding, 451
Fall, 182
fatalism, 41
fellowship, 370
Fellowship of Confessing Anglicans, 5
Filioque clause, 156, 154–62, 199, 201
Final Events. *See* eschatology
final judgment, 104, 140, 214, 224, 254, 256
first chance (teaching), 114
Ford, Henry, 136
forgiveness, 319, 577
Forsyth, Peter Taylor, 431
free will, 234–53, 344
freedom, Christian, 190, 195
freedom, true, 243
fruit of the Spirit, 282
Garden of Eden, 294

Gehenna, 110, 111
general calling, 339
General Councils
  authority of, 408–18
  calling of, 409–12
  fallibility, 412
general revelation, 15, 17, 227, 361
Gethsemane, 95
giving, congregational, 662
Global Anglican Future Conference (2008), 5
glorification, 169, 215, 358, 488
Gnosticism, 95, 150, 176, 309, 648
God
  as judge, 97, 104, 228, 256
  attributes, 20–23
  awe of, 29
  being of, 16, 17–20
  character of, 16
  chief actor in sacraments, 458
  creator, 30–32
  delight in human beings, 281
  dependence upon, 31
  election of, 344
  eternal, 22, 24
  everlasting, 24
  faith in, 13
  foundation of reality, 15
  glory of, 23
  grace. *See also* grace
  grace of. *See* grace
  holiness of, 23, 24, 97, 228, 259
  immanence, 21
  immaterial, 24
  indivisible, 21
  is love, 59
  judgment of, 98
  living, 20
  love for, 222

708   ESSENTIAL TRUTHS FOR CHRISTIANS

love for human beings, 97, 360
love of, 23
majesty of, 29
moral wrath of, 101
mystery of, 350
not arbitrary, 337
omnipotent, 25
omnipresent, 21
omniscient, 25, 336, 669
providential ruler, 39–43
relational, 60
reliance on, 30
response to, 23
saving movement in history, 182–85
self-revelation, 15, 16
simplicity of, 18
singularity of, 17, 19
sovereignty of, 106, 338
transcendence, 21, 24
work of, 16
wrath of, 223
godliness, 253
good works. *See* also sanctification
good works
  by unbelievers, 287–98
  imperfection of, 276–79
  pleasing to God, 279–81
  related to faith, 281–86
Gospel authors, 66
Gospel, benefits of, 228
Gospels
  as witness, 121
  popular history, 71
grace, 23, 82, 96, 235, 236, 244, 259, 294, 302
  accompanying, 250–53, *See* also sanctification
  prevenient, 245–50
grace of congruity, 293
Great Commission, 147, 370, 376, 499
great exchange, 262

Hades, 111, 112
heaven, 141, 293, 302
Heidegren, John, 207
Heine, Heinrich, 258
hell, 112, 141, 142, 143, 224, 293, 302
  definition of, 110
  predestination to, 337
Hellenistic culture, 393
heteros, 148
hieirus, 613
Holiness Churches, 318
Holiness tradition, 278
Holocaust, 154
Holy Communion, 253
holy living, 349
Holy Orders, 468
Holy Scriptures, 167–78, 285, 388, 390
  additions to, 172
  attributes of, 402
  authority of, 403, 417
  canon, 174–76, 176–78
  Christ-centered, 181–87
  church as keeper of, 404
  church as witness of, 404
  clarity of, 404
  coherence of, 400
  efficacy of, 404
  inspired by Holy Spirit, 174
  interpretation of, 349
  limits of Canon, 582
  necessity of, 404
  original wording of, 405
  sufficiency for salvation, 174
  sufficiency of, 404, 415, 417
  translation of, 450
  translations, 453
Holy Spirit, 68, 76, 145–64, 184, 221, 237, 308, 400, 585
  active, 145
  as God, 146–54
  as personal, 153
  at Pentecost, 163

attributes of, 151, 152
baptism in, 490
common grace, 164
conception of Christ, 163
divinity of, 150
Filioque, 154–62
fruit of, 264
fully personal, 148
Holy Scriptures, 400
in Scripture, 162
link to human hearts, 153
neglected, 146
procession of, 154–62
role in Holy Scriptures, 174
sanctifying work of, 482
sending of, 155
spiritual gifts, 163
supernatural gifts, 163
unforgivable sin against, 319–25
work of, 245, 258
works of, 148
Homilies, Book of, 377, 388, 587, 598–606
homily
definition of, 600
Homily for Whitsunday, 378
homoiousios, 198
homoousios, 149, 198
homosexuality, 400
honor, feudal concept of, 106
Hooker, Richard, 394, 515, 596
hope, Christian, 125
hubris, 222
human beings
accountable to God, 256
aging, 143
bound & free, 242
bound & responsible, 242
dependence on God, 253
dignity of, 310
enslaved by sin, 225
fallen nature, 219
fallen nature of, 309
final state in Christ, 143
free will. *See* free will
God's love for, 360
guilt, 221
inability to turn to God, 248
legal standing with God, 256
made in the image of God, 60
mind, role in faith, 450
motives, 233
personal preferences, 396, 588–90
rebellion against God, 238
relationship to God, 16
reliance on self, 251
responsibility of, 249
responsibility re. sin, 221
sinful condition, 220
subjectivity of, 267
universal sin of, 20
value of, 73, 105
humility, 43, 279, 338
hypocrisy, 224, 362
icons, 414, 425–28
idolatry, 224
Imitatio Christi, 73
imputation, 263
incarnation, 64–91
Incarnation, 21
indefectibility of the Church, 382
indeterminacy, 242
indulgences, 422
infant baptism, 485, 487, 497–504
infant dedication, 500, 504
influences, negative, 220
institutional authoritarianism, 160
intellectual mission, of Christians, 126
intentional effort, 283
intercession, 134
intercession, 431
Intervarsity Fellowship, 5

Islam, 95, 449, 633
Israel, 16
James (New Testament), 617
Jarius' daughter, 132
Jerusalem Declaration, 5
Jesus. *See* Son of God, *See* Son of God
Jewel, John, 4, 558, 601
John the Baptist, 323
Joseph of Arimathea, 95, 124
Judaism, 451
judgment, 98
Just War theory, 639
justification, 103, 169, 184, 191, 193, 215, 254–71, 273, 339, 358, 488
   human role in, 259, 260
   isolation from sanctification, 275
   legal implications, 256
   related to sanctification, 264, 273–76
   universal, 267
Kant, Immanuel, 220, 242
King, Martin Luther, 244, 320
Koran, 172
Lambeth Conferences, 375
Lamentations (book of), 174
language, common, in worship, 448–55
Larger Catechism, 599
Last Supper, 117
latreia, 426
Law (Mt. Sinai), 182
law, civil, 243
law, moral, 244
Laws of Ecclesiastical Polity, 394
Lazarus, 132
leadership, authoritarian, 393
legal fiction, 259
legalism, 244, 275
Levites, 434
Lewis, C. S., 79
liberalism, 104

limbo, 502
Liturgy, 2
liturgy, translations of, 453
logikein, 448
Lord's Supper
   completed sacrifice of Christ, 548–60
   exhortations before, 472
Lord's Day. *See* Sunday
Lord's Prayer, 77
Lord's return, timing of, 143
Lord's Supper, 76, 103, 117, 184, 187, 285, 377, 463, 471, 506–34
   as love among Christians, 508–11
   as presence of the Lord, 514
   as remembrance, 512–13
   as sacrifice, 513–14
   as spiritual, 530
   believer participation, 511
   community meal, 508–11
   corporate sacrament, 510
   exhortations, 511
   for partaking, 530–33
   instrumental view, 515
   judgment from unworthy participation, 539
   Lutheran view, 517, 529
   Lutheran views, 538
   more than human response, 510
   nature of, 511
   observation vs. participation, 530
   observation vs.participation, 449
   partaking rightly, 518
   physical presence, 529
   real presence of Christ, 522
   receive in repentant faith, 560
   reconciliation, 541
   Reformed view, 517
   reservation of, 531

GENERAL INDEX

transubstantiation, 516
unworthy reception of, 535–42
views of Presence of the Lord, 515–18
wine to be received, 543–47
withholding of cup, 473
Zwinglian view, 517
Lund Principle, 375
Luther, Martin, 111, 236, 238, 254, 262, 488, 525, 599
Lutheran church, 236
Lutheran Church, 4, 201, 236, 436
Lutherans, 111
Macbeth, 136
magisterium, 585
Marcion, 33, 176, 180, 186
marriage, 468
Martyr, Justin, 531
martyrdom, 299, 486
martyrs, 81, 425, 616
Mass, sacrifice of, 435
material possessions, 645–63
meditation (upon predestitnation), 345–48
medium of Endor, 428
merit of congruity, 297
merit, transfer of, 300
meritum de congruo, 293
Messiah, 75
Messianic Jews, 187
metanoia, 126
Millenium, 138–39
miracles, 35, 37, 78
mission, 126, 137, 454
monastic vocation, 300
monastic way of life, 652
monism, 18, 30
Montanism, 479
Montanists, 317
Moral Influence (theory), 107
moral law, 190–95, 244, 355, 628
moral values, Christian, 634

moralism, 244
Mormonism, 27
Mosaic Covenant, 245
Mosaic Law, 186
Moses, 76, 245, 434
multiplicity (witness), 122
mysterion, 457
name
  importance of, 493
  in biblical use, 357–58
  of Jesus, 357–63
natural evils, 36
natural world
  redemption of, 131
Nazi Germany, 631, 642
Nazism, 154
neighbor, 655
Neo-Pentecostal churches. *See* Charismatic churches
Neo-Platonism, 151
Nestorius, 90, 92
New Testament canon, 174–76
New Understanding of Paul (movement), 102
Newbigen, Leslie, 643
Newman, John Henry, 557
Nicene Creed, 109, 155, 156, 198–200, 388, 389
Nicene Fathers, 389
Niebuhr, Reinhold, 276
Niemuller, Martin, 642
Nietzsche, Friedrich, 72
Noah, 112
norma normans, 403
North Korea, 631
Novatians, 479
oaths, 664–75
offering of Christ, 550
Offices of Instruction, 377
Old Covenant, 310
Old Testament, 179–95
  canon, 176–78
  listing of books, 167
  moral law, 190–95

not contrary to New, 181, 185
prophecies fulfilled, 184
relation to New Testament, 125
rites, 187–90
types, 184
Old Testament believers, 181, 361
Open Communion, 510
ordained ministry, 370
   Anabaptist perspective, 437
   Anglican guidelines for, 437–39
   Anglican perspective, 436
   authority to call to, 443
   authority to send, 443
   being sent, 439
   call to, 438
   external call to, 439, 442
   historical background, 434–36
   inner call to, 438, 442
   Lutheran perspective, 436
   Presbyterian perspective, 437
   Quaker perspectives, 437
   Reformed perspective, 437
   three-fold nature, 435
ordinal, 607
ordinances. *See* sacraments
ordination, 607–24
   of clergy, 433–47
   rites, elements of, 610
   rites, Roman Catholic objections to, 612–14
   validity of, 607
ordination of clergy. *See* also clergy
Original sin. *See* sin,original
Orthodox Church in Russia, 395
Orthodox Churches of the East, 382, 395, 409
pacifism, 634, 638

Packer, J.I., 5
pagan religion, 81, 101
pantheism, 18
Papal jurisdiction, 636
Parable of the Soils, 343
parables, 68, 79
Parker, Matthew, 4
Passion Week, 95
Passover, 184, 187, 513
pastoral care, 441
pastoral oversight, 441
patience, 43
Paul III, 4
peace, 43
Pelagius, 218, 220, 235, 248, 389
penal substitution, 106, 262
penance, 468, *See* also reconciliation
Pentecostal churches, 146
perfection
   Christian, 307
   doctrine of, 277, 315, 316, 318
   of sinners, 216
perfection, doctrine of, 318
perfectionism, doctrine of, 278
Perseverance of the Saints, 343
personal witness, 118
pessimism, 252
Pharisees, 244, 322
Phillips, J. B., 29
philosophy, 353
physical matter, 309
Pilgrim's Progress, 347
polytheism, 18, 19
Pontius Pilate, 65, 68, 95
Postmilleniallism, 139
poverty, 656, 659
prayer, 285
prayer, intercessory, 136
preaching, 2, 377, 600
predestination, 216, 331–50
   basis of choice, 334
   benefits of, 339–45

definition, 333–35
meditation upon, 345–48
to hell, 337
Premillenialism, 139
Presbuteros, 613
presbyters, 435
  as priests, 435
  New Testament, 562
prevenient grace. *See* grace, prevenient
priesthood, nature of, 521
priests (Old Testament), 434, 561
priests as intermediaries, 435
private property, 646–53
progress, 173
prophets (Old Testament), 353
propitiation, 101–2, 555, 558
providence, 39–43, 135, 136
proximity (witness), 118
punishment, degrees of, 293
punishment, degrees of, 302
purgatory, 300, 432
  definition of, 421
  lack of biblical warrant, 420
Puritans, 393, 394, 590, 594, 602
Quakers, 380, 437, 441, 595
Quakers, 466
Radbert, Paschasius, 523
Radical Reformation, 392, 393
rebaptism, 496
reception, 401
reconciliation, 126, 577
  between God and humanity, 98, 99
  between Jew and Gentile, 102–3
Reformation, 2
Reformed Churches, 4
Reformed Episcopal Church, 5
regenerate, 229
regeneration, 229, 246
relationships troubled, 325
relationships, broken, 326

relativism, 353, 394
reliability (witness), 122
religions, other, 352–57
repentance
  for sins after baptism, 325–29
repristination, 393
reservation (Lord's Supper), 531
restoration, 37
resurrection, 115–44
  bodily, 115–44
  hermeneutical implcations, 125
  historical evidence, 116–26
  nature of, 115–44
  objective, 115–44
  of human beings, 131
  of the dead, 140
Resurrection of Jesus, 115–44
  cosmic implications, 131
  to glory, 131–33
  women, witness of, 129
revisionist theologians, 213
reward in heaven, degrees of, 302
rewards in heaven, degrees of, 293
Ridley, Nicholas, 3, 601
Rogers, Thomas, 110, 603
Roman Catholic Church, 2, 4, 201, 236, 299, 307, 312, 374, 382, 399, 411, 413, 417, 419, 442, 469, 502
Roman Ordinal, 613
Romantic Movement, 388
rosary, 448
rule of faith, 197, 207
Ryle, J. C., 252, 282
sacramental acts, 467
sacraments, 377, 456–74
  administred in Christ's name, 480
  as corporate events, 457
  as effective signs, 462, 463

714   ESSENTIAL TRUTHS FOR CHRISTIANS

as means of grace, 459
as tokens of profession of
    faith, 462
block to, 473
characteristics of, 460–66
definition of, 466
definiton of, 456–59
ordained by Christ, 460
right use of, 470–74
using physical elements, 463
worthy reception of, 472
sacramentum, 457
sacrifice, 262
Sacrifice of the Mass, 555, 558
sacrificial lamb, 98
Saducees, 244
saints, 427
    invocation of, 428–32
salvation, 181, 358, 351–64
    by grace, 186, 422
    corporate aspect, 216
    in Christ alone, 216
    need for, 215
    only in Jesus, 358
    personal responses to, 500
    theme of Holy Scriptures,
        169
Salvation Army, 381, 466
salvation, conditions for, 173
sanctification, 169, 193, 215,
    221, 250, 256, 272–86, 318,
    340, 358, 488, 490
    isolation from justification,
        275
    means of, 285
    related to justification, 264,
        273–76
Sapphira, 652
sarcedotal perspective, 435
Saul, King, 428
saving revelation, 17
scholarship, 173
science, modern natural, 33–
    36, 41
Scripture, 2

authoritative over tradition,
    399
authority over Church, 396
coherence of, 396
faithfulness to, 6
inspiration of, 397
sufficiency of, 397
second change (teaching), 114
Second Coming, 323
secular relativism, 389
secularists, 13
security, 43
self love, 238
self-examination, 252, 285
self-reliance, 251
self-salvation, 352
semi-Pelagianism, 235, 241,
    248, 297
separation of Church and State,
    409
Septuagint, 452
service, 94
sessio, 134
Shakespeare, William, 136
Sheen, J. Fulton, 30
Sheol, 110, 111, 112
Shepherd of Hermes, 175
Shi'ite Islam, 356
Simeon, Charles, 349
simul justus et peccator, 258
sin, 278, 295–98
    absolution of, 326
    after baptism, 315–30
    after baptism, forgiveness
        for, 325–29
    Christian struggles against,
        319
    confession of, 326
    deadly nature of, 320
    doctrine of, 105
    enslaving power of, 235,
        237
    indwelling nature of, 318
    inevitability of, 329
    intentional, 318

original, 217–33
  struggle against, 344
  unforgiveable, 319–25
sin, original
  as rebellion against God, 223
  definition, 218–29
  in believers, 232
sin, original
  as self-worship, 222
sin, original
  social implications of, 224
Sinai Covenant, 182
skepticism, historical, 67
social works, 293
socialism, 658, 659
Socians, 213
Socinians, 87
Sola Scriptura, 403
Son of God, 62–108
  as Davidic King, 76
  as intercession for believers, 431
  as intercessor for believers, 429
  as judge, 137–44
  as Judge, 79
  as judical substitute, 104
  as judicial substitute, 98
  as King, 134
  as mediator, 76
  as prophet, 75
  as sacrificial lamb, 98
  as suffering servant, 76
  as Word of God, 78
  ascension, 134–37
  atonement, 94–107, 134
  atoning work, 313
  attitude toward children, 498
  baptism, 77
  character, 66
  descent into hell, 114
  direct claim as, 77
  divine authority, 78–79
  divinity, 91, 198, 389
  exorcisms, 322
  First coming, 139
  forgiver of sins, 78
  fulfillment of the Old Testament, 190
  full experience of death, 113
  full humanity, 306
  fully divine, 73–88
  fully human, 67–73, 92
  heavenly priestly ministry, 558
  historic person, 64–67
  historical evidence, 116
  historical fact, 96
  Holy Spirit's witness to, 81
  incarnation, 64–91
  intercession, 134
  life on earth, 80
  love for human beings, 105
  Old Testament preparation for, 75
  purpose, 66
  resurrection, 80
  resurrection of, 115–44
  sacraments instituted by, 466
  salvation in, 351–64
  salvation in name of, 357–63
  saving work, 94
  second coming, 139
  sinlessness, 216, 306–14
  sufficiency of, 276
  teaching, 78
  transfiguration, 77
  victory, 106
  witnesses to, 81
  worship of, 81, 117
spiritual gifts, 163
St. Athanasius, 87
St. Augustine, 158, 201, 219, 222, 232, 235, 243, 307, 318, 368, 389, 479, 527
St. Chrysostom, 479
St. James, 121

St. Paul, 20, 121, 134, 147, 261, 285, 368, 374, 396, 397, 446
St. Paul, 445
St. Peter, 121, 146, 397
St. Stephen, 120, 121
St. Thomas, 117
St. Thomas of Aquinas, 422
Standard Sermons, 599
state
   purpose of, 628–30
   relationship to church, 395
Stott, John R. W., 5
submission (within the Godhead), 160
substitutionary sacrifice, 312
suffering of believers, 228
Sunday worship, 117
supererogation, works of, 287, 299–305, 422
swearing, 670
Symbolum Quincunque, 200
synagogue, development of, 434
syncretism, 172
Synoptic Gospels, 65
Tacitus, 65, 96
Temple (Jerusalem), 77, 147, 184
Temple, William, 261
Ten Commandments, 190, 195, 245
Tertullian, 318, 479
textual criticism, 405, 407
The Jesus Seminar, 71
theocracy, 188
theonomy, 194
theophany, 69
Thirty-Nine Articles, scope of, 6
Timothy (New Testament), 445, 617
tithing, 661
Titus (New Testament), 445, 617

Topical Analysis of the Bible, 9
Toplady, Augustus Montague, 221
Torah, 186
Toynbee, Arnold, 351
traditions, 170
   changing of, 591–93, 597
   definition of, 581–84
   not higher than Scripture, 399
   of the church, 580–97
transubstantiation, 449, 471, 507, 523–26, 530, 538, 545
Treasury of Merit, 300, 422, 555
Trinity, 32, 154–62, 493
Trinity, 43–61
Trinity formulae, 147
truth, 125, 665–66, 669
types, 184
tyranny, individualistic, 154
unbelievers, 287–98
unchurched, ministry to, 454
understanding worsip, importance of, 451
Undogmatishes Christentum,, 450
universalism, 227, 334, 361
USSR, 631
Vatican II, 374
vestments, liturgical, 614
Virgin Mary, 68, 96, 307
visible church. *See* church, visible
vocation, 301, 302
vows
   definition of, 667
wealth, biblical view of, 648
Wesley, John, 336, 599
Western authority problem, 61
Western Church
   theology of the Holy Spirit, 154–62
Western Fathers, 111

Westminster Shorter Catechism, 30
Whitefield, George, 336
widow of Nain's son, 132
Windows into Heaven (icons), 426
women, witness of, 129
work, value of, 657
works of supererogation. *See* supererogation, works of
World Council of Churches, 410, 587
worldview, 13–15, 125
worship
  centrality of, 448
  in common language, 448–55
  in the early church, 452
  in the New Testament, 452
  in the Old Testament, 452
worship, corporate, 2, 326
Württemberg Confession, 255
Yom Kippur, 310
Your God is Too Small, 29
Zwingli, Ulrich, 465, 510
Zwinglianism, 465, 510, 517, 520, 526

Scripture Index

Genesis
1:1-2, 49
1:2, 150
1:26, 46
2:15, 650
2:15-17, 225
3:6, 225
6:3, 324, 325
6:5, 225, 294, 296
8:21, 240
9:6, 635
13:4, 430
15:6, 266
16:7-13, 47
17:9-14, 497, 501
18:25, 97, 257
22:15-18, 672
24:2-4, 672
50:19-20, 40

Exodus
3:5-6, 50
3:13-14, 50
12:19, 568, 573
15:11, 24
20:4-5, 426
20:7, 665
20:15-17, 650
20:16, 665
28:1, 440

Leviticus
2:1-3, 562
7:20, 568
19:12, 668

Numbers
3:5-7, 440

Deuteronomy
4:35, 48
4:39, 24
5:7, 17
6:4, 47
8:8, 647
11:18, 347
18:9-14, 428, 430
18:15, 82
19:8, 672
32:39, 48

Joshua
1:8, 650

Judges
11:35, 672

1 Samuel
3:13, 563
4:24, 673
16:7, 528, 536
28:7ff, 428
28:7-9, 430

2 Samuel
7:22, 18, 208

1 Kings
8:5, 373

2 Chronicles
5:13b, 26

Ezra
10:8, 568

Nehemiah
8:7-8, 453
9:6, 32
9:31, 26

Job
12:13, 26

Psalms
1:1-3, 651
1:2, 347
5:4, 26
9:4, 257
14:1-3, 226, 295, 296
16:10, 111, 112
19:8, 192
24:1, 648
24:4-5, 668
33:6, 47
36:6, 208
48:9, 347
50:15, 430
51:5, 292
68:26, 385
89:14, 26
90:1-2, 25
119:9, 405
119:11, 405
119:15-16, 406
119:29, 192
119:103-104, 192
119:103-105, 406
119:148, 347
135:5-6, 25
139:7, 49

Ecclesiastes
7:14, 651

Isaiah
6:5, 206
7:14, 51, 82
9:6-7, 47, 83
11:2, 152
42:5, 650

42:8, 48
52.1, 184
53, 184
53:1-6, 100
53:3-5, 551

Jeremiah
4:1-2, 673
10:10, 24
10:14-15, 427
11:5, 673
17:9, 226, 240, 295, 296
17:9-10, 292
17:10, 50
31:31, 83
31:41, 497
51:15, 33

Ezekiel
17:24, 673

Daniel
2:19-23, 26
7, 323
7:13-14, 47, 82

Habakkuk
1:13, 92
Zechariah
8:17, 668
9:9, 83, 184

Malachi
3:6, 25

Matthew
1:18-25, 51, 70
1:23, 48
3:11, 464, 494
3:13-17, 147
3:16-17, 52, 58
4:4, 398
4:18-19, 83
5:17-18, 185

5:18-19, 398, 584
5:33-37, 667, 669
5:34, 664
5:43-44, 83
6:6, 347, 430
6:9-13, 280, 431
6:9-15, 317
6:24, 651
7:28-29, 51
8:14, 563
10:5, 440
10:40, 440
11:20-24, 292
11:27, 83, 359
11:27-28, 49
12:22-32, 321
12:32, 49
12:33-35, 282
13:3-9, 342
13:44, 651
15:3-9, 172, 416
16:18, 414, 636
18, 572
18:6, 363
18:15-17, 379, 569, 573, 576, 578
18:20, 519
19:13-15, 498
19:24, 649
19:26, 208
21:28-31, 605
22:11-12, 539
22:14, 340
22:29, 405
22:36-40, 192
22:37-40, 654
23:2-3, 590
23:25, 189
24:22, 335
24:24, 335
24:31, 335
25:14-15, 651
25:20-21, 280
25:40, 660

25:46, 142
26:26-29, 464, 519, 523
26:27, 545
26:28, 497
26:63-64, 673
28:18ff, 499
28:18-19, 135
28:18-20, 359, 373, 469, 502
28:19, 45, 52, 147, 153, 212, 469, 493
28:19-20, 464, 519

Mark
1:32-34, 84
1:35, 70
2:10-12, 84
2:5-7, 84
3:28-30, 321
4:37-39, 70
5:22, 430
6:38-44, 85
7:6, 459
7:7-9, 413
7:13, 413
7:15-23, 527, 528, 537,
7:18-19, 189
10:14-16, 498, 501
14:22-25, 519
14:23, 545
15:24-25, 96
16:1-2, 128
16:4-7, 128
16:15-16, 340

Luke
1:5, 563
1:35, 308
1:37, 25
1:73, 673

2:1-12, 209
2:6-7, 70
3:22, 611
4:8, 427
5:21, 78
6:12-13, 611
7:44-48, 84
10:16, 478
11:13, 317
11:20, 49
11:46, 584
12:10, 321
14:25-26, 84
16:22-23, 424
17:7-10, 277, 303, 423
18:9-14, 472
18:10-14, 277, 303, 423
18:15-17, 498
20:25, 635
22: 13-20, 519
23:43, 424
24:25-27, 398
24:27, 83, 185
24:39, 24
24:44-45, 185
24:46-47, 327

John
1:1, 49, 208
1:1,14, 78, 89
1:1-3, 33, 453
1:12, 266, 341
1:14, 48, 49, 51, 208
1:18, 48, 51, 453
3:3, 226, 230, 240
3:3-8, 247
3:5, 226, 230, 240
3:8, 150
3:16, 266
3:16-18, 359
3:36, 226, 295, 297, 327
4:24, 24
5:26, 25
5:28-29, 142
5:39-40, 185
5:44, 48
6:27, 48
6:35, 359
6:37, 335
6:43-44, 247
6:44, 85, 240
6:50-57, 537
6:63, 211
6:64-65, 247
7:46, 78
8:12, 359
8:29, 308
8:46, 308
8:58, 359
9:20-23, 569
10:27-30, 360
10:28-29, 341
11:25-26, 360
13:13-16, 641
13:34-35, 509
14:1-3, 425
14:6, 360
14:16, 148, 150
14:16-17, 50, 52
14:26, 211
15:1-2, 482
15:4-5, 251
15:5, 280
15:26, 52, 162, 212
16:14, 148
17:17-18, 440
19:30-42, 210
20: 1-8, 211
20:21-23, 618
20:22-23, 390
20:28, 49
20:28-29, 85

Acts
1:9, 211
1:10-11, 211
1:16, 185
2:14-17, 391
2:23, 96, 185
2:25, 112
2:25ff, 111
2:27, 113
2:29-31, 129
2:30, 673
2:31-32, 113
2:32-33, 53
2:37-39, 266
2:38, 327, 465, 472, 489
2:38-41, 498
2:38-42, 379, 487
2:42, 373, 379
2:44-45, 651
3:12, 478
3:19, 327
4:12, 360
4:27-28, 40
4:32, 646
5:3-4, 50, 146, 149
5:29, 635
6, 610
6:1-6, 612
7:48-50, 24
10:2, 431
10:15, 584
10:19-20, 52
10:28, 189
10:43, 327
10:44-48, 487
11:29, 660
13:2, 150
13:38-39, 327
13:48, 335
14:23, 440, 441, 612
15, 445, 586
15:2, 391, 410

SCRIPTURE INDEX

15:4-6, 391, 410
15:6-11, 399
15:10, 584
15:13-22, 618
15:22-29, 411, 593
15:28-29, 391
16:13-15, 473
16:14-15, 86, 340
16:15, 33, 498, 562
16:25, 434
16:31, 267
16:33, 502
17:11, 405
20:28, 557
22:16, 465, 495

Romans
1:9-10, 673
1:16, 267
1:18-32, 354
2:13, 257
2:16, 50
2:28-29, 368
3:19-20, 193
3:21-26, 100, 257, 263, 267
3:23, 20, 226, 260, 292, 295, 296, 309
3:23-26, 311
3:25-26, 26
4, 245
4:3, 185
4:5, 341
4:23-25, 263
5:5, 152
5:6, 552
5:8, 100
5:12, 226, 295, 296
6:1-4, 495
6:3-4, 465, 489
6:9-11, 132

6:10, 552
6:17-18, 193
6:20-23, 274
7, 252
7:14-15, 226, 295, 297
7:15, 232
7:18-25, 278, 304, 424
7:21-24, 231
8, 131, 227. 252
8:1, 232
8:3-4, 282
8:5-9, 275
8:11, 152
8:14, 162
8:19-23, 131
8:26, 52
8:28-29, 368
8:29-30, 335, 342
8:33-34, 135
9:22-23, 335
10:14, 601
12:1, 448
12:1-2, 453
12:4-5, 373
12:13, 660
13:1-4, 636
14:14, 590
14:19, 593
15:16, 53
16:17, 391, 573, 590

1 Corinthians
1:2, 373
1:7-14, 498
1:10-17, 491
1:16, 498, 502
1:20, 354
2:9-11, 150
2:10-11, 50
2:14, 86, 247, 413
2:14-16, 354

3:5-7, 478
5:5-6, 573
5:7-8, 189
5:9-11, 380
5:11, 569, 574, 577, 651
5:13, 569
6:11, 424
6:19-20, 552
7:2, 563
8:4-6, 18
9:1, 120
9:5, 563
9:16, 602
10:3-5, 473
10:7, 427, 584
10:14, 427
10:16-17, 509, 520, 525, 532
10:21, 539
10:31-11:1, 70
11:17-34, 472
11:20-21, 541
11:23-25, 465, 469
11:23-26, 392
11:23-27, 526, 532
11:23-28, 379
11:23-29, 512, 519
11:23-30, 379
11:27-28, 473
11:27-30, 540
11:27-33, 509
11:29, 520
12-14, 452
12:4-6, 53, 147
12:11, 52, 150
12:13, 373, 491, 495
14:19, 453
14:26, 590, 593
14:40, 590
15, 119, 121, 129

15:1-11, 118-122
15:3-7, 120, 127
15:3-11, 123
15:10, 251
15:12-18, 212
15:20, 71, 123
15:42-44, 132
16:2, 660

2 Corinthians
1:23, 673
2:7-8, 578
3:17-18, 317, 341
3:18, 275, 278, 304
4:5-7, 478
4:6, 24
5:9-10, 143
5:20-21, 100
5:21, 263, 308, 311, 552
7:10, 328
8:13-14, 660
9:7, 660
9:11, 660
12:11, 637
13:5, 520
13:14, 53, 58, 147, 149, 212

Galatians
1:6-9, 172, 384, 416
1:8-9, 363
1:20, 673
2:3, 584
2:11, 637
2:20, 251
2:20-21, 193
3:13, 100, 263, 552
3:26, 465
3:26-27, 495
4:4-6, 53, 280
4:6, 162

5:17, 232
6:1, 578

Ephesians
1:3-6, 336
1:7, 489
1:11, 40, 336
1:17-18, 247
1:19-23, 642
1:20, 211
1:22-23, 135
2:1, 3-5, 240
2:1-3, 260, 292
2:1-6, 231
2:1-10, 247
2:7, 26
2:8, 341
2:8-10, 86, 260, 275, 423
2:14, 585
4:1-6, 383
4:4-6, 212, 489
4:5, 490
4:18, 226, 295, 297
4:28, 657, 600
4:30, 150
5:3, 651
5:18, 491
5:24, 642

Philippians
1:1, 424, 440
1:2, 85
1:6, 251
1:8, 674
1:21-23, 424
2:5-7, 49
2:5-8, 90
2:12-13, 251, 280

Colossians
1:15, 90, 208
1:16, 208
1:19, 86, 90

2:9, 49, 89
2:11, 499, 502
2:13-15, 489
2:16, 585
3:16-17, 379

1 Thessalonians
1:1, 373
2:13, 602
4:16-17, 142
5:9, 336
5:19, 52

2 Thessalonians
3:6, 590
3:10, 657
3:12, 647, 651
3:13-14, 569

1 Timothy
1:1-5, 619
1: 13-14, 171, 205
1:17, 48
1:20, 569, 574
2:1-2, 636
3:13, 612
4:1-5, 563
5:8, 660
5:17, 612
5:19-20, 482
5:20, 569, 574, 590
5:21-22, 619
5:22, 482
6:3-5, 391
6:10, 649
6:17-18, 660

2 Timothy
1:6, 612
1:13, 593, 678
2:1-2, 440, 619
2:2, 602

3:14-15, 171, 206, 416
3:14-17, 398
3:15, 405
4:3, 390
4:18, 341

Titus
1:4-9, 619
3:5, 409
3:10, 574

Hebrews
1:1-2, 85
2:14, 51
3:3-6, 642
3:18, 674
4:15, 70, 308
4:16, 348, 558
5:5, 611
6:4-6, 322, 328, 342
6:13-19, 673
7:23-25, 556
7:26-27, 552, 556
7:26-28, 311
8:1, 556
8:10, 250
9:11-12, 552, 556
9:13-14, 495
9:14, 53
9:24-26, 557
9:26-28, 552
10:1-4, 312
10:10-14, 553
10:12, 135
10:12-14, 312
10:19-22, 529, 538
10:24-25, 462
10:26-29, 322, 328, 342
11:3, 208
13:4-5, 563
13:16, 661

James
1:14, 232
1:17, 25
2:1-7, 652
2:10, 320
2:17-18, 282
2:17-19, 283
5:12, 605, 668, 669

1 Peter
1:2, 48, 52, 58
1:3, 123
1:18-19, 101, 553
1:19, 312
1:23, 341, 416
2:11, 232
2:13-17, 636
2:22, 303
2:24, 263
3-4, 112
3:18, 553
3:18-20, 112, 113, 210
3:21, 489, 499, 502
4:6, 112, 113

2 Peter
1:10, 341
1:11, 85
1:21, 150

3:15-16, 413

1 John
1:7, 424
1:8-10, 231, 317
1:9, 328
2:2, 100, 553
2:19, 342
3:4-6, 283
3:5, 308
3:6, 318
3:17-18, 661
4:7-10, 26
4:19-21, 283
4:20-21, 661
5:16, 322
5:20-21, 354
5:21, 354
5:21, 427

2 John
9-10, 569

Jude
20-21, 53
24, 85

Revelation
1:8, 25
22:18-19, 172, 416